Lecture Notes in Computer Science 5829

Commenced Publication in 1973
Founding and Former Series Editors:
Gerhard Goos, Juris Hartmanis, and Jan van Leeuwen

Alberto H. F. Laender Silvana Castano
Umeshwar Dayal Fabio Casati
José Palazzo M. de Oliveira (Eds.)

Conceptual Modeling - ER 2009

28th International Conference on Conceptual Modeling
Gramado, Brazil, November 9-12, 2009
Proceedings

Springer

Volume Editors

Alberto H. F. Laender
Federal University of Minas Gerais
31270-901 Belo Horizonte, MG, Brazil
E-mail: laender@dcc.ufmg.br

Silvana Castano
Università degli Studi di Milano
20135 Milano, Italy
E-mail: castano@dico.unimi.it

Umeshwar Dayal
Hewlett-Packard Laboratories
Palo Alto, CA 94304, USA
E-mail: umeshwar.dayal@hp.com

Fabio Casati
University of Trento
38050 Povo (Trento), Italy
E-mail: casati@disi.unitn.it

José Palazzo M. de Oliveira
Universidade Federal do Rio Grande do Sul (UFRGS)
91.501-970 Porto Alegre, RS, Brasil
E-mail: palazzo@inf.ufrgs.br

Library of Congress Control Number: 2009935563

CR Subject Classification (1998): D.2, I.6, C.0, D.4.8, I.2.6, I.2.11, D.3

LNCS Sublibrary: SL 3 – Information Systems and Application, incl. Internet/Web and HCI

ISSN 0302-9743
ISBN-10 3-642-04839-0 Springer Berlin Heidelberg New York
ISBN-13 978-3-642-04839-5 Springer Berlin Heidelberg New York

springer.com

Printed in Germany

Typesetting: Camera-ready by author, data conversion by Scientific Publishing Services, Chennai, India
Printed on acid-free paper SPIN: 12772087 06/3180 5 4 3 2 1 0

Foreword

Conceptual modeling has long been recognized as the primary means to enable software development in information systems and data engineering. Conceptual modeling provides languages, methods and tools to understand and represent the application domain; to elicit, conceptualize and formalize system requirements and user needs; to communicate systems designs to all stakeholders; and to formally verify and validate systems design on high levels of abstraction. Recently, ontologies added an important tool to conceptualize and formalize system specification.

The International Conference on Conceptual Modeling – ER – provides the premiere forum for presenting and discussing current research and applications in which the major emphasis is centered on conceptual modeling. Topics of interest span the entire spectrum of conceptual modeling, including research and practice in areas such as theories of concepts and ontologies underlying conceptual modeling, methods and tools for developing and communicating conceptual models, and techniques for transforming conceptual models into effective implementations.

The scientific program of ER 2009 features several activities running in parallel. The core activity is the presentation of the 31 papers published in this volume. Such papers were selected out of 162 submissions (an acceptance rate of 19%) by a large Program Committee co-chaired by Alberto Laender, Silvana Castano, and Umeshwar Dayal. We thank the PC co-chairs, the PC members, and the additional reviewers for their hard work, often within a short time. Thanks are also due to Antonio L. Furtado from the Pontifical Catholic University of Rio de Janeiro (Brazil), John Mylopoulos from the University of Trento (Italy), Laura Haas from IBM Almaden Research Center (USA), and Divesh Srivastava from AT&T Labs Research (USA), for accepting our invitation to present keynotes. Thirteen sessions of the conference are dedicated to the seven ER workshops selected by the Workshops Co-chairs, Carlos Heuser and Günther Pernul. We express our sincere appreciation to the co-chairs and to the organizers of those workshops for their work. The proceedings of these workshops have been published in a separate volume, and both volumes were edited with the help of Daniela Musa, the Proceedings Chair. Three sessions are dedicated to the PhD Workshop, organized by Stefano Spaccapietra and Giancarlo Guizzardi, whose efforts are highly appreciated. Fabio Casati organized the industrial presentations, and Renata Matos Galante took on the hard task of being the Financial Chair, to both our reconnaissance. Thanks also to the Tutorial Co-chairs, Daniel Schwabe and Stephen W. Liddle, and to the Panel Chair, David W. Embley, for their work in selecting and organizing the tutorials and the panel, respectively. Special thanks to Arne Sølvberg, the ER Steering Committee Liaison officer, for the advice and help he gave to us whenever we needed it. We also thank Mirella M. Moro for taking good care of the ER publicity, and for advertising the conference and its workshops in different venues. Finally, the Demonstrations and Posters Track was conducted by Altigran S. da Silva and Juan-Carlos Trujillo Mondéjar. To everyone involved in the ER 2009 technical organization, many congratulations on their great, thriving work.

Likewise, we acknowledge the engagement and enthusiasm of the local organization team, chaired by José Valdeni de Lima. The members of the team were Ana Paula Terra Bacelo, Carina Friedrich Dorneles, Leonardo Crauss Daronco, Lourdes Tassinari, Luís Otávio Soares, Mariano Nicolao, and Viviane Moreira Orengo.

August 2009 José Palazzo Moreira de Oliveira

Program Chairs' Message

Welcome to the 28th International Conference on Conceptual Modeling – ER 2009! We are very pleased to present you with an exciting technical program in celebration of the 30th anniversary of the ER conference. Since its first edition held in Los Angeles in 1979, the ER conference has become the ultimate forum for presentation and discussion of current research and applications related to all aspects of conceptual modeling. This year we received 162 submissions and accepted 31 papers for publication and presentation (an acceptance rate of 19%). The authors of these submissions span more than 30 countries from all continents, a clear sign of the ER prestige among researchers all around the world.

The assembled program includes nine technical sessions covering all aspects of conceptual modeling and related topics, such as requirements engineering, schema matching and integration, ontologies, process and service modeling, spatial and temporal modeling, and query approaches. The program also includes three keynotes by prominent researchers, Antonio L. Furtado, from the Pontifical Catholic University of Rio de Janeiro, Brazil, John Mylopoulos, from the University of Trento, Italy, and Laura Haas, from IBM Almaden Research Center, USA, which address fundamental aspects of conceptual and logical modeling as well as of information integration. This year's program also emphasizes the industrial and application view of conceptual modeling by including an industrial session, with two regular accepted papers and an invited one, and an industrial keynote by Divesh Srivastava, from AT&T Labs Research, USA.

This proceedings volume also includes a paper by Peter P. Chen in celebration of the 30th anniversary of the ER conference. In his paper, Prof. Chen reviews the major milestones and achievements of the conference in the past 30 years, and suggests several directions for the organizers of its future editions. We believe that all those interested in any aspect of conceptual modeling will enjoy reading this paper and knowing a bit more about the conference history.

Many people helped to put together the technical program. First of all, we would like to thank José Palazzo M. de Oliveira, ER 2009 General Conference Chair, for inviting us to co-chair the program committee and for his constant support and encouragement. Our special thanks go to the members of the program committee, who worked many long hours reviewing and, later, discussing the submissions. The high standard of their reviews not only provided authors with outstanding feedback but also substantially contributed to the quality of this technical program. It was a great pleasure to work with such a prominent and dedicated group of researchers. We would also like to thank the many external reviewers who helped with their assessments and Daniela Musa, the Proceedings Chair, for helping us organize this volume of the conference proceedings. All aspects of the paper submission and reviewing processes were handled using the EasyChair Conference Management System. We thus thank the EasyChair developing team for making this outstanding system freely available to the scientific community.

Finally, we would like to thank the authors of all submitted papers, whether accepted or not, for their outstanding contributions. We count on their continual support for keeping the high quality of the ER conference.

August 2009

Alberto H. F. Laender
Silvana Castano
Umeshwar Dayal
Fabio Casati

ER 2009 Conference Organization

Honorary Conference Chair

Peter P. Chen	Louisiana State University, USA

General Conference Chair

José Palazzo M. de Oliveira	Universidade Federal do Rio Grande do Sul, Brazil

Program Committee Co-chairs

Alberto H. F. Laender	Universidade Federal de Minas Gerais, Brazil
Silvana Castano	Università degli Studi di Milano, Italy
Umeshwar Dayal	HP Labs, USA

Industrial Chair

Fabio Casati	Università degli Studi di Trento

Workshops Co-chairs

Carlos A. Heuser	Universidade Federal do Rio Grande do Sul, Brazil
Günther Pernul	Universität Regensburg, Germany

PhD Colloquium Co-chairs

Giancarlo Guizzardi	Universidade Federal do Espírito Santo, Brazil
Stefano Spaccapietra	Ecole Polytechnique Fédérale de Lausanne, Switzerland

Demos and Posters Co-chairs

Altigran S. da Silva	Universidade Federal do Amazonas, Brazil
Juan Trujillo	Universidad de Alicante, Spain

Tutorials Co-chairs

Daniel Schwabe	Pontifícia Universidade Católica do Rio de Janeiro, Brazil
Stephen W. Liddle	Brigham Young University, USA

Panel Chair

David W. Embley	Brigham Young University, USA

Proceedings Chair

Daniela Musa	Universidade Federal de São Paulo, Brazil

Publicity Chair

Mirella M. Moro	Universidade Federal de Minas Gerais, Brazil

Financial and Registration Chair

Renata Galante	Universidade Federal do Rio Grande do Sul, Brazil

Steering Committee Liaison

Arne Sølvberg	NTNU, Norway

Local Organization Committee

José Valdeni de Lima (Chair)	Universidade Federal do Rio Grande do Sul
Ana Paula Terra Bacelo	Pontifícia Universidade Católica do Rio Grande do Sul
Carina Friedrich Dorneles	Universidade de Passo Fundo
Lourdes Tassinari	Universidade Federal do Rio Grande do Sul
Luís Otávio Soares	Universidade Federal do Rio Grande do Sul
Mariano Nicolao	Universidade Luterana do Brasil
Viviane Moreira Orengo	Universidade Federal do Rio Grande do Sul

Webmaster

Leonardo Crauss Daronco	Universidade Federal do Rio Grande do Sul

Program Committee

Marcelo Arenas	Pontificia Universidad Catolica de Chile, Chile
Zohra Bellahsene	Université de Montpellier II, France
Boualem Benatallah	University of New South Wales, Australia
Sonia Bergamaschi	Università di Modena e Reggio Emilia, Italy
Alex Borgida	Rutgers University, USA
Mokrane Bouzeghoub	Université de Versailles, France
Marco A. Casanova	Pontfícia Universidade Católica do Rio de Janeiro, Brazil
Fabio Casati	Università degli Studi di Trento, Italy
Malu Castellanos	HP Labs, USA
Tiziana Catarci	Università di Roma "La Sapienza", Italy
Sharma Chakravarthy	University of Texas-Arlington, USA
Roger Chiang	University of Cincinnati, USA
Isabel Cruz	University of Illinois-Chicago, USA
Philippe Cudre-Mauroux	MIT, USA
Alfredo Cuzzocrea	Università della Calabria, Italy
Valeria De Antonellis	Università degli Studi di Brescia, Italy
Johann Eder	Universität Wien, Austria
David W. Embley	Brigham Young University, USA
Alfio Ferrara	Università degli Studi di Milano, Italy
Piero Fraternali	Politecnico di Milano, Italy
Helena Galhardas	Instituto Superior Técnico, Portugal
Paulo Goes	University of Arizona, USA
Jaap Gordijn	Vrije Universiteit Amsterdam, Netherlands
Giancarlo Guizzardi	Universidade Federal do Espírito Santo, Brazil
Peter Haase	Universität Karlsruhe, Germany
Jean-Luc Hainaut	University of Namur, Belgium
Terry Halpin	LogicBlox, USA
Sven Hartmann	Technische Universität Clausthal, Germany
Carlos A. Heuser	Universidade Federal do Rio Grande do Sul, Brazil
Howard Ho	IBM Almaden Research Center, USA
Manfred Jeusfeld	Tilburg University, Netherlands
Paul Johannesson	Stockholm University & the Royal Institute of Technology, Sweden
Gerti Kappel	Technische Universität Wien, Austria
Vipul Kashyap	CIGNA Healthcare, USA
Wolfgang Lehner	Technische Universität Dresden, Germany
Ee-Peng Lim	Singapore Management University, Singapore
Tok-Wang Ling	National University of Singapore, Singapore
Peri Loucopoulos	The University of Manchester, UK
Heinrich C. Mayr	Universität Klagenfurt, Austria
Michele Missikoff	IASI-CNR, Italy
Takao Miura	Hosei University, Japan
Mirella M. Moro	Universidade Federal de Minas Gerais, Brazil
John Mylopoulos	Università degli Studi di Trento, Italy
Moira Norrie	ETH Zurich, Switzerland

Antoni Olivé	Universitat Politècnica de Catalunya, Spain
Sylvia Osborn	University of Western Ontario, Canada
Christine Parent	Université de Lausanne, Switzerland
Jeffrey Parsons	Memorial University of Newfoundland, Canada
Oscar Pastor	Universidad Politécnica de Valencia, Spain
Zhiyong Peng	Wuhan University, China
Barbara Pernici	Politecnico di Milano, Italy
Alain Pirote	Université Catholique de Louvain, Belgium
Dimitris Plexousakis	University of Crete, Greece
Rachel Pottinger	University of British Columbia, Canada
Sudha Ram	University of Arizona, USA
Colette Rolland	Université Paris 1, France
Gustavo Rossi	Universidad de La Plata, Argentina
Motoshi Saeki	Tokyo Institute of Technology, Japan
Klaus-Dieter Schewe	Information Science Research Centre, New Zealand
Amit Sheth	Wayne State University, USA
Peretz Shoval	Ben-Gurion University, Israel
Altigran S. da Silva	Universidade Federal do Amazonas, Brazil
Mário Silva	Universidade de Lisboa, Portugal
Il-Yeol Song	Drexel University, USA
Stefano Spaccapietra	Ecole Polytechnique Fédérale de Lausanne, Switzerland
Veda Storey	Georgia State University, USA
Rudi Studer	Universität Karlsruhe, Germany
Ernest Teniente	Universitat Politècnica de Catalunya, Spain
Bernhard Thalheim	Christian-Albrechts-Universität zu Kiel, Germany
Riccardo Torlone	Università Roma Tre, Italy
Juan Trujillo	Universidad de Alicante, Spain
Vassilis Tsotras	University of California-Riverside, USA
Aparna Varde	Montclair State University, USA
Vânia Vidal	Universidade Federal do Ceará, Brazil
Kyu-Young Whang	Korea Advanced Inst. of Science and Technology, Korea
Kevin Wilkinson	HP Labs, USA
Carson Woo	University of British Columbia, Canada
Yanchun Zhang	Victoria University, Australia

External Reviewers

Sofiane Abbar
Sudhir Agarwal
Ghazi Al-Naymat
Toshiyuki Amagasa
Sofia Athenikos
Petko Bakalov
Pablo Barceló
Ilaria Bartolini
Domenico Beneventano
Devis Bianchini
Sebastian Blohm
Matthias Boehm
Eduardo Borges
Loreto Bravo
Paula Carvalho
Marcirio Chaves
Tibermacine Chouki
Dulce Domingos
Carina F. Dorneles
Jianfeng Du
André Falcão
Eyal Felstaine
Ahmed Gater
Karthik Gomadam
Stephan Grimm
Adnane Guabtni
Francesco Guerra

Yanan Hao
Hans-Jörg Happel
Mountaz Hascoet
Jing He
Cory Henson
Guangyan Huang
Christian Huemer
Shah Rukh Humayoun
Felipe Hummel
Prateek Jain
Dustin Jiang
Tetsuro Kakeshita
Kyoji Kawagoe
Stephen Kimani
Henning Koehler
Haris Kondylakis
Wai Lam
Ki Jung Lee
Xin Li
Thérèse Libourel
Philipp Liegl
Marjorie Locke
Deryle Lonsdale
Francisco J. Lopez-Pellicer
Hsinmin Lu
Tania Di Mascio
Hui Ma
José Macedo
Javam Machado
Bruno Martins
Jose-Norberto Mazon
Sergio L.S. Mergen
Isabelle Mirbel
Mauricio Moraes
Antonio De Nicola
Mirko Orsini
Paolo Papotti
Horst Pichler
Laura Po
Antonella Poggi
Maurizio Proietti
Anna Queralt
Ruth Raventos
Satya Sahoo
Sherif Sakr
Giuseppe Santucci
Martina Seidl
Isamu Shioya
Alberto Silva
Sase Singh
Fabrizio Smith
Philipp Sorg
Serena Sorrentino
Christian Soutou
Laura Spinsanti
Umberto Straccia
Arnon Sturm
Amirreza Tahamtan
Adi Telang
Thanh Tran
Thu Trinh
Zografoula Vagena
Marcos Vieira
Maurizio Vincini
Denny Vrandecic
Hung Vu
Jing Wang
Qing Wang
Xin Wang
Emanuel Warhaftig
Jian Wen
Manuel Wimmer
Guandong Xu
Mathieu d'Aquin

Organized by

Instituto de Informática, Universidade Federal do Rio Grande do Sul, Brazil

Sponsored by

The ER Institute
Sociedade Brasileira de Computação (Brazilian Computer Society)

In Cooperation with

ACM SIGMIS
ACM SIGMOD

Table of Contents

ER 30th Anniversary Paper

Keynotes

Conceptual Modeling

Requirements Engineering

Foundational Aspects

Query Approaches

Space and Time Modeling

Schema Matching and Integration

Ontology-Based Approaches

Application Contexts

Process and Service Modeling

Industrial Session

Thirty Years of ER Conferences: Milestones, Achievements, and Future Directions

Peter P. Chen*

Computer Science Department, Louisiana State University
Baton Rouge, LA 70803, U.S.A.
pchen@lsu.edu

Abstract. This paper describes the milestones/achievements in the past 30 years and the future directions for the Entity-Relationship (ER) Conferences or the Conceptual Modeling Conferences. The first ER Conference was held in 1979 in Los Angeles. The major milestones and achievements of the ER Conferences are stated. Several interesting points about the ER Conferences are pointed out including: (1) it is one of the few longest running IT conference series, (2) It is not a conference sponsored directly by a major IT professional societies such as ACM or IEEE, (3) It does not depend on the financial support of a major IT professional society or a commercial company, (4) It maintains very high quality standards for papers and presentations. The reasons for the successes of the ER Conferences are analyzed. Suggestions for its continued successes are presented.

Keywords: Conceptual Modeling, Entity-Relationship model, ER Model, Entity-Relationship (ER) Conferences, Conceptual Modeling Conferences.

1 Introduction

This year (2009) is the 30th anniversary of the Entity-Relationship (ER) Conferences (or the Conceptual Modeling Conferences). The Information Technology (IT) field changes very fast. New ideas popped up every day. It is not easy for a series of conferences to survive and to continue its successes in the IT field for 30 years. Why can it succeed and others fail? Is it because of its major theme? Is it because of its organizers? Is it because of its locations for the meetings? Is it because of its quality of the presentations and papers?

In this article, we will first review the major milestones and achievements of the ER Conference series. Then, we will try to analyze the reasons of its survival and successes. Finally, we will suggest several directions for the organizers of the future ER Conferences to consider.

* This research was supported in part by U.S. National Science Foundation (NSF) grant: ITR-IIS-0326387 and a Louisiana Board of Regents Grant. The opinions here are the opinions of the author and do not represent the opinions of the sponsors of the research grants.

A.H.F. Laender et al. (Eds.): ER 2009, LNCS 5829, pp. 1–8, 2009.

2 Major Milestones of the ER Conferences in the First 30 Years

There are many important milestones in the first 30 years of the ER Conferences [1]. In the following, we will state some of the important ones.

2.1 The Beginning – The First ER Conference in 1979 in Los Angeles

The Entity-Relationship Model ideas were first presented in the First Very Large Database Conference in Framingham, MA, USA in 1975, and the paper on the "Entity-Relationship Model: Toward a Unified View of Data," was published in the first issue of the *ACM Transaction on Database Systems* [2]. At that time, the database community was heavily into the debates between the Network Data Model camp led by Charles Bachman and the Relational Data Model camp led by E. F. Codd. The Entity-Relationship (ER) model got some attentions of the community. It also attracted some criticisms, partially because most people were already having their hands full with the pros and cons of two major existing data models and were reluctant to spend time to understand a new model, which was even claimed to be a "unified" model. So, the receptions for the ER model were mixed in the beginning.

In 1978, I moved from MIT Sloan School of Management to UCLA Graduate Management School (GSM). Things started to change in the IT industry and the academic community. More and more people began getting interested in the ER approach and its applications. Just like other major business schools in the U.S., UCLA GSM offered special 1-to-5 day short seminars to professionals for fees. With increasing interest in the community and the strong support of two senior Information System (IS) faculty members at UCLA, Eph McLean and R. Clay Sprowls, and two senior UCLA Computer Science faculty members, Wesley Chu and Alfonso Cardenas, I was encouraged to organize an enlarged short seminar and to make it a mini-conference. That was the birth of the First Entity-Relationship (ER) Conference, which was held at UCLA in 1979. Most short seminars attracted only about 20 attendees in average, but, to the surprise of the UCLA's seminar organizers, the number of registrants for the 1st ER Conference kept on increasing. So, the meeting rooms had to be changed several times to larger rooms to accommodate more attendees. In the morning of the first day of the conference, more tables and chairs were added to the meeting room to accommodate additional on-site registrants. In short, the level of interest on the subject greatly exceeded everyone's expectations.

2.2 The 2nd to the 4th ER Conferences (ER'81, ER'83, ER'85) – Held in Different Cities of the U.S.

With the success of the first ER Conference, the 2nd ER Conference, emphasizing ER applications to Information Modeling and Analysis, was held two years later (1981) in Washington, D.C. This Conference was the first time I presented the linkages between the ER Diagram and the English sentence structure. These ideas were published in a paper [3], which was adopted by some large consulting companies as a part of their standard methodologies in systems analysis and design (particularly, in translating the requirements specifications in English into ER diagrams). The proceedings of the 1st and 2nd ER Conference Proceedings were published in the book form by North-Holland (Elsevier).

The 3rd ER Conference was held in Chicago two years later (1983), and the Conference administration was shifted from me to Jane Liu (then, with the University of Illinois, Urbana-Champaign). The proceedings of the 3rd ER Conference were published by the IEEE Computer Society. The 4th ER Conference, emphasizing the ER applications to software engineering, was held in the Disney Hotel in Anaheim, California in 1985 and was organized primarily by Peter Ng, Raymond Yeh, and Sushil Jajodia. North-Holland (Elsever) was the publisher for the 4th ER Conference proceedings and for several more years until Springer became the publisher.

2.3 The 5th ER Conferences (ER'86 Conference) – First ER Conference Outside of the U.S.

The 5th ER Conference was held in Dijon, France in 1986 – the first time that an ER Conference was held outside of the U.S. Furthermore, the 5th Conference was one year after the 4th Conference. Thus, the series of ER Conferences became an annual event. The 5th ER conference was primarily organized by Stefano Spaccapietra. Besides a strong technical program, the attendees had the opportunities to visit a winery and to have the conference banquet in a Chateau.

2.4 The 6th ER Conferences (ER'87 Conference) – The World Trade Center Will Stay in Our Memory Forever

The 6th ER Conference was held in New York City one year later (1987), and the administration was handled mostly by Sal March (then, with the University of Minnesota). John Zachman was one of the keynote speakers in the 6th ER Conference. A memorable event was that the conference banquet was held in the "Windows on the World" restaurant on the top floor of one of the twin towers of the World Trade Center. So, in 2001, when the World Trade Center was under attacks from terrorists, those who attended the 6th ER Conference banquet, including me, felt very painful to watch the human tragedy playing live on the TV screens.

2.5 The ER'88 to ER'92 Conferences – Conference Locations Were Rotated between Two Continents and the ER Steering Committee Was Formed

From 1988 to 1992, the ER conferences became more established, and the ER Steering Committee was formed for planning the major activities of the future ER Conferences. I served as the first ER Steering Committee Chair, and then passed the torch to Stefano Spaccapietra after a few years. At this time, the ER Conferences established a pattern of rotating the conference locations between two continents (Europe and the North America), which have the largest number of active researchers and practitioners.

ER'88 (Rome, Italy) was organized primarily by Carlo Batini of University of Rome. ER'89 (Toronto, Canada) was administered primarily by Fred Lochovsky (then with University of Toronto). ER'90 (Lausanne, Switzerland) was organized primarily by Hannu Kangassalo and Stefano Spaccapietra. Regrettably, it was the only ER Conference in the past thirty years that I missed due to sickness. ER'91 (San Mateo, California) was organized primarily by Toby Teorey. It was the first time the ER Conference organized in a large scale together with Data Administration Management Association (DAMA). The San Francisco Bay area Chapter of the DAMA was actively involved. It was a showcase of close cooperation between the academic people and the practitioners. The next year, ER'92 was held in Karlsruhe, Germany and was organized primarily by Günther Pernul and A. Min Tjoa.

2.6 The ER'93 to ER'96 Conferences – Survival, Searching for New Directions, and Re-bounding

The ER'93 (Arlington, TX) was the lowest point in the history of the ER Conferences with the lowest level of attendance. There was a discussion then on whether the ER Conference series should be discontinued or should change directions significantly. The ER'93 Conference was organized primarily by Ramez Elmasri. In the following year, ER'94 Conference was held in Manchester, the United Kingdom and was administrated primarily by Pericles Loucopoulos. Things were getting better, and the attendance was up. OOER'95 Conference (Gold Coast, Australia) was organized primarily by Mike P. Papazoglou. It was the first time the ER Conference was held outside of Europe and North America. Furthermore, the name of the conference was changed to OOER to reflect the high-interest of Object Oriented methodologies at that time. After the conference name change experiment for one year (in 1995), the next conference went back to the original name (ER). Due to the excellent effort of Bernhard Thalheim, ER'96 Conference (Cottbus, Germany) was a success both in terms of quality of papers/presentations and the level of attendance, rebounding fully from the lowest point of attendance several years prior. ER'96 was also the first time that the ER Conference was held in the so-called "Eastern Europe", a few years after the unification of Germany.

2.7 The ER'97 to ER2004 Conferences – Steady Growth, Back to the Origin, and Going to Asia

The ER'97 Conference (Los Angeles, California) was the 18th anniversary of the first ER Conference, and the ER Conference went back to the place it originated – Los Angeles – eighteen years before. Significantly, the ER'97 Conference was primarily organized by Wesley Chu, Robert Goldstein, and David Embley. Wesley Chu was instrumental in getting the first ER Conference at UCLA taking off.

The ER'98 Conference was primarily organized by Tok Wang Ling and was held in Singapore. Yahiko Kambayashi was a major organizer of the workshops in this conference. Unfortunately, he passed away a few years after the conference. ER'98 Conference was the first time that an ER Conference was held in Asia. The ER'99 Conference (Paris, France) was administrated primarily by Jacky Akoka, who participated in the first ER Conference in 1979, exactly 20 years ago. The ER2000 was organized in Salt Lake City, primarily by David Embley, Stephen Liddle, Alberto Laender, and Veda Storey. The large repository of ancestry data in Salt Lake City was of great interest to the conference attendees. Hideko S. Kunii, Arne Sølvberg, and several first ER Conference participants including Hiroshi Arisawa and Hirotaka Sakai were the active organizers of the ER2001 Conference, which was held in Yokohama, Japan. At this time, the ER Conferences had established a pattern to rotate the locations among three major geographical areas: Europe, North America, and Asia/Oceania. ER2002 Conference (Tampere, Finland), which was the first time an ER Conference was held in Scandinavian Countries, was organized primarily by Hanu Kangassalo. ER2003 Conference (Chicago) was administrated primarily by Peter Scheuermann, who presented a paper in the first ER Conference. Il-Yeol Song and Stephen Liddle were also key organizers. ER2004 Conference was held in Shanghai, China, which gave the practitioners and researchers in China and surrounding countries an opportunity to exchange ideas with active researchers in conceptual modeling. The Conference was organized primarily by Shuigeng Zhou, Paolo Atzeni, and others.

2.8 The ER2005 to ER2007 Conferences – Rekindling the Connections with the Information System (IS) Community

The ER2005 Conference (Klagenfurt, Austria) was organized primarily by Heinrich Mayr, and the conference program was handled primarily by John Mylopoulos, Lois Delcambre, and Oscar Pastor. With Heinrich's connections to the Information System (IS) and practitioner community, the ER Conferences reconnected with the IS community. Furthermore, Heinrich developed a comprehensive history for the ER approach, and this history was posted in the ER website [1]. This Conference also marked the first time that a formal meeting of the Editorial Board of the Data & Knowledge Engineering Journal was co-located with an ER Conference even though informal editorial board meetings were conducted before.

The ER2006 Conference (Tucson, Arizona) continued this direction of re-connecting with the IS community. This re-connection was made easier and naturally because Sudha Ram, the major organizer of ER2006 Conference, was a senior faculty member in the business school of University of Arizona and a well known figure in the IS community. This conference marked another major milestone in the ER Conference history – it was the 25th ER Conference. The ER2007 Conference was organized primarily by Klaus-Dieter Schewe and Christine Parent and was held in Auckland, New Zealand. This marked the return of the ER Conference to another major country in the Oceania after the Conference was held in Australia in 1995.

2.9 The ER2008 Conference – Establishing the Peter Chen Award and the Ph.D. Workshop

The ER2008 Conference was held in Barcelona, Spain, and was organized by Antoni Olive, Oscar Pastor, Eric Yu, and others. Elsevier was one of the co-sponsors of the Conference. It co-sponsored a dinner for the conference participants, an editorial board meeting of the Data & Knowledge Engineering Journal. More importantly, it supported financially the first Peter Chen Award, which was presented by the award organizer, Reind van de Riet, to the recipient, Bernhard Thalheim. The Peter Chen Award was set up to give one individual each year for his/her outstanding contributions to the conceptual modeling field. Reind van de Riet was the key person who made this series of awards a reality. Unfortunately, he passed away in the end of 2008. We all felt the loss of a great scientist, a dear friend, and a strong supporter of the conceptual modeling community. The ER2008 Conference also marked the first time that a formal Ph.D. workshop was conducted. The main objective of the workshop was to accelerate the introduction of new blood into the conceptual modeling community. It accomplished this objective successfully in the first Ph.D. Workshop.

2.10 The ER2009 Conference – 30th Anniversary Conference, the First ER Conference Held in South America, and Establishing the ER Fellow Awards

The ER2009 Conference (Gramado, Brazil) is the first ER Conference held in the South America – a major milestone. The year 2009 is the 30th anniversary of the ER Conference series – another major milestone. The Conference is organized by José Palazzo Moreira de Oliveira, Alberto Laender, Silvana Castano, Umeshwar Dayal, and others. Their efforts make the 30th anniversary of the ER Conference memorable. Besides continuing the Peter Chen Award and the Ph.D. Workshop as the ER2008 Conference, this conference also starts a new series of awards – the ER Fellow Awards, which will be given to a small number of individuals to recognize their contributions to the conceptual modeling field.

3 Major Achievements of the ER Conferences in the First 30 Years

There are several major achievements of the ER Conference series including the following:

- Longevity: It is one of the longest running conference series in the IT field. Because the IT field changes very fast, it is not easy to keep a professional conference with a fixed theme going for a long time. Reaching the 30th anniversary is a major achievement of the ER Conference series.
- High Quality: The papers published in the ER conference proceedings are of very high quality. In the past 15 years or so, the conference proceedings have been published in the book form as Lecture Notes in Computer Science (LNCS), published by Springer. The published papers are indexed by SCI.
- Independence: Many conferences are directly sponsored by major Professional Societies such as ACM and IEEE. By being independent of the direct sponsorships of major professional societies, the ER Conferences are able to move faster to satisfy the needs of the community.
- Financially Sound: Most of the ER Conferences generate surpluses in the balance sheet. This is another major achievement of the ER Conference series because many conferences in the IT field cannot sustain for a very long time without the financial backing from a major professional society.

Why can the ER Conference series sustain for 30 years without the direct sponsorships and financial backings of a major professional society? There are many reasons including the following:

- Enthusiasm: The organizers and attendees of the ER Conferences are enthusiastic with the ER Concepts and Approach. The success of the ER Conferences is due to the efforts of a large group of people, not just a few individuals.
- Important Subject: The subject of conceptual modeling is very important in many domains. The concepts of entity and relationship are fundamental to the basic theories in many fields. Since the ER Conference series addresses a very important subject, it provides a good forum for exchanging ideas, research results, and experience for this important subject.
- Good Organization and Leadership: I have not been involved in the paper selections of the ER Conferences for 27 years. I also have not been the ER Steering Committee Chairman for 20 years or so. The leaders and members of the ER Steering Committee in the past 20 years and the organizers of the ER conferences in the past 27 years have built a very strong organization to run each individual conference successfully and to plan for the future.

4 Wish List for the ER Conferences in the Future

Even though the ER Conference Series has been successful for the past 30 years, we should not be content with the status quo and should think about how to build on top of its past successes [4]. In the following, we would like to suggest a wish list for the organizers of the future ER Conferences to consider:

- Building a stronger tie with the Information System (IS) Community and practitioners: The connections with IS community and practitioners are not consistent over time – sometimes, the connections are strong while in other times, the connections are weak. There is a strong need and necessity to get the IS community and practitioners heavily involved in future conferences.
- Including "Modeling and Simulation" as another underlying major core discipline: "Modeling and Simulation" uses the concepts of entity and relationship heavily. In addition to Computer Science (CS) and IS as the two major underlying core disciplines, it is important and useful to add "Modeling and Simulation" as the third major underlying core disciplines so that we can learn from each other.
- Expanding into other application domains: There are many fields such as biology which utilize conceptual modeling heavily. The ER Conference can expand its scope to include more papers and presentations in conceptual modeling applications in different domains.
- Exploring new technical directions: In addition to the new application domains, we would recommend that new technical directions be explored. In recent years, each ER Conference has organized workshops to explore new directions. Most of these workshop proceedings are also published as LNCS books, and we recommend the interested readers take a look at those

conference proceedings for possible new areas to explore. More details of these workshops can be found at the Springer website or the ER Website [1]. In my talk at the ER2006 Conference, I pointed out a new research direction on "Active Conceptual Modeling". Papers on this subject can be found in the workshop proceedings on this subject published in 2007 [5]. Another workshop on this subject is co-located with the ER2009 Conference. This is just one example of new technical directions. We would recommend that the readers explore new technical areas pointed out by many other workshops associated with the ER Conferences.

5 Summary and Conclusion

In the past thirty years, the series of ER Conferences has established as a well respected and well organized series of conferences. ER2009 is the 30th anniversary of the first ER Conference in Los Angeles. There have been many milestones and achievements in the past thirty years. The ER conferences have been held in different parts of the world. ER2009 Conference is the first ER conference held in South America. The ER Conference series is one of the few longest running conference series in the IT fields without the direct sponsorship and financial backing from a major IT professional society. Its success should be credited to a large number of people involving in the planning and execution of the conferences and associated matters. For future ER Conferences, it is recommended to build a stronger tie with the IS community and practitioners, to include the "modeling and simulation" as another underlying core disciplines, to expand the conceptual modeling applications to non-traditional domains, and to explore new technical directions. Finally, we wish the ER Conferences can be even more successful in the next thirty years than in the past thirty years.

References

1. ER Steering Committee, ER Website, `http://www.conceptualmodeling.org`
2. Chen, P.P.: The Entity-Relationship Model: Toward a Unified View of Data. ACM Transactions on Database Systems 1(1), 9–36 (1976)
3. Chen, P.P.: English Sentence Structures and Entity-Relationship Diagrams. Information Sciences 29(2-3), 127–149 (1983)
4. Chen, P.P.: Entity-Relationship Modeling: Historical Events, Future Trends, and Lessons Learned. In: Broy, M., Denert, E. (eds.) Software Pioneers: Contributions to Software Engineering, pp. 296–339. Springer, Heidelberg (2002) (with 4 DVD's)
5. Chen, P.P., Wong, L.Y. (eds.): ACM-L 2006. LNCS, vol. 4512. Springer, Heidelberg (2007)

A Frame Manipulation Algebra for ER Logical Stage Modelling

Antonio L. Furtado, Marco A. Casanova, Karin K. Breitman, and Simone D.J. Barbosa

Departamento de Informática. Pontifícia Universidade Católica do Rio de Janeiro
Rua Marquês de S. Vicente, 225, Rio de Janeiro, RJ. Brasil - CEP 22451-900
{furtado,casanova,karin,simone}@inf.puc-rio.br

Abstract. The ER model is arguably today's most widely accepted basis for the conceptual specification of information systems. A further common practice is to use the Relational Model at an intermediate logical stage, in order to adequately prepare for physical implementation. Although the Relational Model still works well in contexts relying on standard databases, it imposes certain restrictions, not inherent in ER specifications, which make it less suitable in Web environments. This paper proposes frames as an alternative to move from ER specifications to logical stage modelling, and treats frames as an abstract data type equipped with a Frame Manipulation Algebra (FMA). It is argued that frames, with a long tradition in AI applications, are able to accommodate the irregularities of semi-structured data, and that frame-sets generalize relational tables, allowing to drop the strict homogeneity requirement. A prototype logic-programming tool has been developed to experiment with FMA. Examples are included to help describe the use of the operators.

Keywords: Frames, semi-structured data, abstract data types, algebra.

1 Introduction

It is widely recognized [29] that database design comprises three successive stages:

a. conceptual,
b. logical,
c. physical.

The Entity-Relationship (ER) model has gained ample acceptance for stage (a), while the Relational Model is still the most popular for (b) [29]. Stage (c) has to do with implementation using some DBMS compatible with the model chosen at stage (b).

Design should normally proceed top-down, from (a) to (b) and then to (c). Curiously the two models mentioned above were conceived, so to speak, in a bottom-up fashion. The central notion of the Relational Model – the relation or table – corresponds to an abstraction of conventional file structures. On the other hand, the originally declared purpose of the ER model was to subsume, and thereby conciliate, the Relational Model and its competitors: the Hierarchic and the Codasyl models [9].

A.H.F. Laender et al. (Eds.): ER 2009, LNCS 5829, pp. 9–24, 2009.

Fortunately, the database research community did not take much time to detect the radical distinction between the ER model and the other models, realizing that only the former addresses *conceptual modelling*, whereas the others play their part at the stage of *logical modelling*, as an intermediate step along the often worksome passage from world concepts to machine implementation. To that end, they resort to different data structures (respectively: tables, trees, networks). Tables in particular, once equipped with a formal language for their manipulation – namely Relational Algebra or Relational Calculus [12] – constitute a full-fledged *abstract data type*.

Despite certain criticisms, such as the claim that different structures might lead to a better performance for certain modern business applications [28], the Relational Model still underlies the architecture of most DBMSs currently working on conventional databases, some of which with an extended object-relational data model to respond to the demand for object-oriented features [3,29]. However, in the context of Web environments, information may come from a variety of sources, in different formats, with little or no structure, and is often incomplete or conflicting. Moreover the traditional notion of classification as conformity to postulated lists of properties has been questioned [21], suggesting that similarity to typical representatives might provide a better criterion, as we investigated [1] employing a three-factor measure.

We suggest that *frames*, with a long tradition in Artificial Intelligence applications [4,22], provide an adequate degree of flexibility. The main contribution of the present paper is to propose a Frame Manipulation Algebra (FMA) to fully characterize frames and frame-sets as an abstract data type, powerful enough to help moving from the ER specifications to the logical design stage.

The paper is organized as follows. Section 2 recalls how facts are characterized in the ER model, and describes the clausal notation adopted for their representation. In section 3, four kinds of relations between facts are examined, as providing a guiding criterion to choose a (in a practical sense) *complete* repertoire of operators for manipulating information-bearing structures, such as frames. Section 4, which is the thrust of the paper, discusses frames, frame-sets and the FMA operators, together with extensions that enhance their application. Section 5 contains concluding remarks.

2 Facts in Terms of the ER Model

A database *state* consists of all *facts* that hold in the mini-world underlying an information system at a certain moment of time. For the sake of the present discussion, we assume that all incoming information is first broken down into basic facts, represented in a standard unit clause format, in full conformity with the ER model. We also assume that, besides facts, meta-level conceptual schema information is represented, also in clausal format.

Following the ER model, facts refer to the existence of entity *instances* and to their *properties*. These include their attributes and respective values and their participation in binary relationships, whose instances may in turn have attributes. Schema information serves to characterize the allowed *classes* of entity and relationship instances. Entity classes may be connected by is_a and part_of links. A notation in a logic programming style is used, as shown below (note that the identifying attribute of an entity class is indicated as a second parameter in the `entity` clause itself):

```
Schema
entity(<entity name>,<identifying attribute>)
attribute(<entity name>,<attribute name>)
domain(<entity name>,<attribute name>,<value domain specification>)
relationship(<relationship name>,[<entity name>,<entity name>])
attribute(<relationship name>,<attribute name>)
is_a(<entity name>,<entity name>)
part_of(<entity name>,<entity name>)

Instances
<entity name>(<identifier value>)
<attribute name>(<identifier value>,<attribute value>)
<relationship name>([<identifier value>,<identifier value>])
<relationship attribute>([<identifier value>,<identifier value>],
<attribute value>)
```

For entities that are *part-of* others, `<identifier value>` is a list of identifiers at successive levels, in descending order. For instance, if companies are downward structured in departments, sections, etc., an instance of a `quality control` section might be designated as `section(['Acme', product, quality_control])`.

A common practice is to *reify* n-ary relationships, for n > 2, i.e. to represent their occurrence by instances of appropriately named entity classes. For example, a `ships` ternary relationship, between entity classes `company`, `product` and `client`, would lead to an entity class `shipment`, connected to the respective participating entities by different binary relationships, such as `ships_agent`, `ships_object`, `ships_recipient` to use a case grammar nomenclature [16]. To avoid cluttering the presentation with details, such extensions and other notational features will not be covered here, with two exceptions to be illustrated in examples 3 and 8 (section 4.3). Also not covered are non-conventional value domains, e.g. for multimedia applications, which may require an extensible data type feature [27].

The clausal notation is also compatible with the notation of the RDF (*Resource Description Framewok*) language. A correspondence may be established between our clauses and RDF statements, which are triples of the form `(<subject>, <property or predicate>, <object>)`[6], if we replace `<subject>` by `<identifier value>`. It is worth noting that RDF has been declared to be "a member of the Entity-Relationship modelling family" in *The Cambridge Communiqué*, a W3C document[1].

3 Relations between Facts

Facts should be articulated in a *coherent* way to form a meaningful utterance. Starting from semiotic studies [5,7,8,24], we have detected four types of relations between facts – *syntagmatic*, *paradigmatic*, *antithetic*, and *meronymic* – referring, respectively, to *coherence* inside an utterance, to *alternatives* around some common paradigm, to negative *restrictions*, and to successive *levels of detail*.

Such relations serve to define the dimensions and limits of the information space, wherein facts are articulated to compose meaningful utterances, which we represent at the logical stage as frames, either standing alone or assembled in frame-sets. In turn, as will be shown in section 4.2, the characterization of the relations offers a criterion to configure an adequate repertoire of operators to handle frames and frame-sets.

[1] www.w3.org/TR/schema-arch

3.1 Syntagmatic Relations

Adapting a notion taken from linguistic studies [24], we say that a *syntagmatic relation* holds between facts F1 and F2 if they express properties of the same entity instance Ei. Since properties include relationships in which the entity instance participates, the syntagmatic relation applies transitively to facts pertaining to other entity instances connected to Ei via some relationship. The syntagmatic relation acts therefore as a fundamental reason to chain different facts in a single *cohesive* utterance. For example, it would be meaningful to expand John's frame by joining it to the `headquarters` property belonging to the frame of the `company` he works for.

On the other hand, if an entity instance has properties from more than one class, an utterance may either encompass all properties or be restricted to those of a chosen class. For example, if John is both a student and an employee, one might be interested to focus on properties of John as a `student`, in which case his `salary` and `works` properties would have a weaker justification for inclusion.

3.2 Paradigmatic Relations

Still adapting [24], a *paradigmatic relation* holds between facts F1 and F2 if they constitute *alternatives* according to some criterion (paradigm). The presence of this relation is what leads to the formation of frame-sets. To begin with, all facts involving the same property are so related, such as John's salary and Mary's salary. Indeed, since they are both `employees`, possibly sharing additional properties, a frame-set including their frames would make sense, recalling that the most obvious reason to create conventional files is to gather all data pertaining to instances of an entity class.

Property similarity is still another reason for a paradigmatic relation. For example, `salary` and `scholarship` are similar in that they are alternative forms of income, which would justify assembling `employees` and `students` in one frame-set with the purpose of examining the financial status of a population group.

Even more heterogeneous frame-sets may arise if the unifying paradigm serves an occasional pragmatic objective, such as to provide all kinds of information of interest to a trip, including flight, hotel and restaurant information. A common property, e.g. `city`, would then serve to select whatever refers to the place currently being visited.

3.3 Antithetic Relations

Taken together, the syntagmatic and paradigmatic relations allow configuring two dimensions in the information space. They can be described as orthogonal, if, on the one hand, we visualize the "horizontal" syntagmatic axis as the one along which frames are created by aligning properties and by the concatenation with other frames or subsequences thereof, and, on the other hand, the "vertical" paradigmatic axis as the one down which frames offering alternatives within some common paradigm are assembled to compose frame-sets.

And yet orthogonality, in the specific sense of independence of the two dimensions, sometimes breaks down due to the existence of antithetic relations. An *antithetic relation* holds between two facts if they are *incompatible* with each other. Full orthogonality would imply that a fact F1 should be able to coexist in a frame with any alternative facts $F2_1$, ..., $F2_n$ characterized by the same paradigm, but this is not so. Suppose we are told that Mary is seven years old; then she can have `scholarship` as income, but not `salary`, if the legislation duly restricts the `age` for employment.

Thus antithetic relations do not introduce a new dimension, serving instead to delimit the information space. Suggested by semiotic research on binary oppositions and irony [5,7], they are the result of *negative prescriptions* from various origins, such as natural impossibilities, laws and regulations, business rules, integrity constraints, and any sort of decisions, justifiable or arbitrary. They may motivate the absence of some property from a frame, or the exclusion of one or more frames from a frame-set. For example, one may want to exclude the recent graduates from a students frame-set. Ironically, such restrictions, even when necessary for legal or administrative reasons, may fail to occur in practice, which would then constitute cases of violation or, sometimes, of admissible exceptions.

3.4 Meronymic Relations

Meronymy is a word of Greek origin, used in linguistics to refer to the decomposition of a whole into its constituent parts. Forming an adjective from this noun, we shall call *meronymic relations* those that hold between a fact F1 and a lower-level set of facts $F2_1$, $F2_2$, ..., $F2_n$, with whose help it is possible to achieve more *detailed* descriptions. The number of levels may of course be greater than two.

The correspondence between a fact, say F1, with a lower-level set of facts $F2_1$, $F2_2$, ..., $F2_n$ requires, in general, some sort of mapping rule. Here we shall concentrate on the simplest cases of decomposition, where the mapping connections can be expressed by *part-of* semantic links of the component/ integral-object type (cf. [31]). A `company` may be subdivided into `departments`, which may in turn have `sections` and so on and so forth. A `country` may have `states`, `townships`, etc. Outside our present scope is, for instance, the case of `artifacts` whose `parts` are interconnected in ways that could only be described through maps with the descriptive power of a blueprint.

Meronymic relations add a third dimension to the information space. If discrete levels of detail are specified, we can visualize successive two-dimensional planes disposed along the meronymic axis, each plane determined by its syntagmatic and paradigmatic axes.

Traversing the meronymic axis is like zooming in or out. After looking at a `company` frame, one may want to come closer in order to examine the frames of its constituent `departments`, and further down towards the smallest organizational units, the same applying in turn to each frame in a frame-set describing several `companies`. And while the *is-a* links imply top-down property inheritance, *part-of* links induce a bottom-up aggregation of values. For example, if there is a `budget` attribute for each `department` of a `company`, summing up their values would yield a corporate total.

4 Towards an Abstract Data Type for ER Logical-Stage Modelling

4.1 Frames and Frame-Sets

Frames are sets of P:V (i.e. `<property>:<value>`) pairs. A frame-set can either be the empty set [] or consist of one or more frames.

The most elementary frames are those collecting P:V information about a single entity or binary relationship instance, or a single class. In a frame displaying information on a given entity instance E, each property may refer to an attribute or to a relationship. In the latter case, the P component takes the form R/1 or R/2 to indicate whether E is the first or the second entity participating in relationship R, whereas the V component is the identifier (or list of identifiers) of the entity instance (or instances) related to E by R. In a frame displaying information about a relationship instance, only attributes are allowed as properties. For frames concerning entity or relationship classes, the V component positions can be filled up with variables.

We require that a property cannot figure more than once in a frame, a restriction that has an important consequence when frames are compared during the execution of an operation: by first sorting each frame, i.e. by putting the P:V pairs in lexicographic order (an `n×log(n)` process), we ensure that the comparisons proper take linear time.

A few examples of elementary frames follow. The notation "_" indicates an anonymous variable. Typically not all properties specified for a class will have known values for all instances of the class. If, among other properties, Mary's `age` is unknown at the moment, this information is simply not present in her frame. The last line below illustrates a frame-set, whose constituent frames provide information about two employees of company Acme.

Class employee: `[name:_, age:_, salary:_, works/1:_]`
Class works: `[name:_,cname:_,status:_}`
Mary: `[name:'Mary', salary:150, works/1:'Acme']`
John: `[name: 'John', age: 46, salary: 100, scholarship: 50, works/1: 'Acme']`
Acme: `[cname:'Acme', headquarters:'Carfax', works/2:['John','Mary']]`
Acme employees: `[ [name:'Mary', salary:150, works/1:'Acme'], [name:'John', age: 46, salary: 100, scholarship: 50, works/1: 'Acme'] ]`

Both Acme's frame and Mary's frame contain, respectively, properties of a single class or instance. However, if we want that frames should constitute a realistic model for human utterances, more complex frames are needed. In particular, the addition of properties of related identifiers should be allowed, as in:

```
[name: 'Mary', salary: 150, works/1: 'Acme', headquarters: 'Carfax',
 status: temporary, 'John'\salary: 100]
```

where the third property belongs to the company for which Mary works, and the fifth is a relationship attribute concerning her job at the company. The inclusion of the sixth property, which belongs to her co-worker John, would violate the syntactic requirement that property names be unique inside a frame; the problem is solved by prefixing the other employee's salary property with his identifier. Further generalizing this practice, for the sake of clarity, one may choose to fully prefix in this way all properties attached to identifiers other than Mary:

```
[name:'Mary', salary:150, works/1:'Acme',
 'Acme'\headquarters:'Carfax', ['Mary','Acme']\status: temporary,
 'John'\salary: 100]
```

Recalling that every instance is distinguished by its `<identifier value>`, we may establish a correspondence between an instance frame and a labelled RDF-graph whose edges represent triples sharing the same `<subject>` root node [6].

4.2 Overview of the Algebra

Both frames and frame-sets can figure in FMA expressions as operands. To denote the evaluation of an expression, and the assignment of the resulting frame or frame-set to a variable `F`, one can write:

```
F := <algebraic expression>.
```

or optionally:

```
F#r := <algebraic expression>.
```

in which case, as a side-effect, the expression itself will be stored for future use, the indicated `r` constant serving thereafter as an identifier. Storing the result rather than the expression requires two consecutive steps:

```
F1 := <algebraic expression>
F2#r := F1.
```

A stored expression works like a database *view*, since every time the expression is evaluated, the result will vary according to the current state, whereas storing a given result corresponds to a *snapshot*.

The simplest expressions consist of a single frame, which may be represented explicitly or by an instance identifier (or `r` constant) or class name, in which case the FMA engine will retrieve the respective properties to compose the result frame. Note that the first and the second evaluations below should yield the same result, whereas the third yields a frame limited to the properties specified in the *search-frame* placed after the ^ symbol (example 11 shows a useful application of this feature). If the "\" symbol is used instead of "^", the full-prefix notation will be applied. Note, in addition, that lists of identifiers or of class names yield frame-sets.

```
Fm1 := [name:'Mary', salary:150, works/1:'Acme']
Fm2 := 'Mary'.
Fms1 := 'Mary' ^ [salary:S, works/1:C].
Fmsp := 'Mary' \ [salary:S, works/1:C].
Fmsr#msw := 'Mary' \ [salary:S, works/1:C].
Fms2 := msw.
Fmj1 := [[name:'Mary', salary:150, works/1:'Acme'], [name:'John', age:46,
        salary:100, scholarship:50, works/1:'Acme']]
Fmj2 := ['Mary','John'].
Fc := student.
```

Instances and classes can be treated together in a particularly convenient way. If John is both a student and an employee, his properties can be collected in separate frames, by indicating the name of each class, whose frame will then serve as search-frame:

```
Fjs := 'John' ^ student.
Fje := 'John' ^ employee.
```

Over these simple terms, the *algebraic operators* can be used to build more complex expressions. To build the operator set of FMA, the five basic operators of Relational Algebra were redefined to handle both frames and frame-sets. Two more operators had to be added in order to take into due account all the four relations between facts indicated in section 3.

An intuitive understanding of the role played by the first four operators is suggested when they are grouped into pairs, the first operator providing a *constructor* and the second a *selector*. This is reminiscent of the LISP primitives, where `cons` works as constructor and `car` and `cdr` as selectors, noting that `eq`, the primitive on which value comparisons ultimately depend, induces yet another selector mechanism. For FMA the two pairs are:

- *product* and *projection*, along the syntagmatic axis;
- *union* and *selection*, along the paradigmatic axis.

Apart from constructors and selectors, a negation operator is needed, as demanded by antithetic restrictions. To this end, FMA has the *difference* operator and enables the selection operator to evaluate logical expressions involving the *not* Boolean operator. LISP includes *not* as a primitive, and Relational Algebra has difference. Negation is also essential for expressing universal in terms of existential quantification. Recall for example that a `supplier` who `supplies` all `products` is anyone such that there is *not* some `product` that it does *not* `supply`. Also, difference being provided, an intersection operator is no longer needed as a primitive, since $A \cap B = A - (A - B)$.

To traverse the meronymic dimension, zooming in and out along part-of links, FMA includes the *factoring* and the *combination* operators. One must recall at this point that the Relational Model originally required that tables be in first-normal form (1NF), which determined the choice of the Relational Algebra operators and their definition, allowing only such tables as operands. However, more complex types of data, describing for example assembled products or geographical units, characterized conceptually via a semantic *part-of* hierarchy [26], led to the use of the so-called NF^2 (non first normal form) or nested tables at the logical level of design. To handle NF^2 tables, an extended relational algebra was needed, including operators such as "partitioning" and "de-partitioning" [18], or "nest" and "unnest" [19] to convert from 1NF into NF^2 tables and vice-versa.

We claim that, with the seven operators indicated here, FMA is complete in the specific sense that it covers frame (and frame-set) manipulation in the information space spanned by the syntagmatic, paradigmatic, antithetic and meronymic relations holding between facts.

It has been demonstrated that Relational Algebra is *complete*, in that its five operators are enough, as long as only 1NF tables are permitted, to make it equivalent in expressive power to Relational Calculus, a formalism based on first-order calculus. Another aspect of completeness is *computational completeness* [14,30], usually measured through a comparison with a Turing machine. To increase the computational power of relational DBMSs, the SQL-99 standard includes provision for recursive queries.

Pursuing along this trend, we decided to embed our running FMA prototype in a logic programming language, which not only made it easier to define virtual attributes and relationships, a rather flexible selection operator and an iteration extension, but also to take advantage of Prolog's pattern-matching facilities to deal simultaneously with instance frames and (non-ground) frame patterns and class frames.

4.3 The Basic Algebraic Operators

Out of the seven FMA operators, three are binary and the others are unary. All operators admit both frames and frame-sets as operands. For union, selection and difference, if frames are given as operands, the prototype tool transforms them into frames-sets as a preliminary step; conversely, the result will be converted into frame format whenever it is a frame-set containing just one frame.

Apart from this, the main differences between the way that FMA and the Relational Algebra treat the five operators that they have in common are due to the relaxation of the homogeneity and first-normal form requirements. In Relational Algebra, union and difference can only be performed on union-compatible tables. Since union-compatibility is not prescribed in FMA, the frames belonging to a frame-set need not be constituted of exactly the same properties, which in turn affects the functioning of the projection and selection operators. Both operators search for a number of properties in the operand, but no error is signaled if some property is missing in one or more frames: such frames simply do not contribute to the result. FMA also differs from Relational Algebra by permitting arbitrary logical expressions to be tested as an optional part of the execution of the selection operator. Moreover the several uses of variables, enabled by logic programming, open a number of possibilities, some of which are illustrated in the examples.

The empty list "[]" (nil) is used to ambiguously denote the empty frame and the empty frame-set. As such, [] works as the neutral element for both product and union and, in addition, is returned as the result when the execution of an operator fails, for example when no frame in a frame-set satisfies a selection test.

The FMA requirement that a property can occur at most once in a frame raises a conflict if, when a product is executed, the same property figures in both operands. The conflict may be solved by default if the attached values are the same, or may require a decision, which may be fixed beforehand through the inclusion of appropriate tags. Handling conflicts through the use of tags is a convenient expedient that serves various purposes, such as to replace a value, or form sets or bags (recalling that multiple values are permitted), or call for aggregate numerical computations, etc. If no tag is supplied, our prototype tool offers a menu to the user's choice.

The two operators without counterpart in Relational Algebra, namely factoring and combination, act on frame-structured identifiers associated with *part-of* links, and also on attributes with frame-structured value domains. When working on a list of identifiers, the result of factoring is a frame-set composed of the frames obtained from each identifier in the operand list. When working on properties with frame-structured value domains, factoring has a flattening effect, breaking the property into separate constituents so as to bring to the front the internal structure.

When examining the examples, recall that, although the operands of every FMA operation are always frames or frame-sets, identifiers or lists of identifiers may figure in their place, being converted into the corresponding frames or frame-sets as a preliminary step in the execution of the operation. Both in the description of the operators and in the examples, we shall employ a notation that is unavoidably a transliteration imposed by the Prolog character set limitations and syntax restrictions. For instance, "+" denotes union. Also, since blank spaces are not allowed as separators, the operand of a projection or selection is introduced by an "@" symbol.

Product. The product of two frames F1 and F2, denoted F1 * F2, returns a frame F containing all F1 and F2 properties. If one or both operands are (non-empty) frame-sets, the result is a frame-set containing the product of each frame taken from the first operand with each frame from the second, according to the standard Cartesian product conventions. If one of the operands is the empty frame, denoted by [], the result of the product operation is the other operand, and thus [] behaves as the neutral element for product. The case of an empty frame-set, rather than an empty frame, demanded an implementation decision; by analogy with the zero element in the algebra of numbers, it would be justifiable to determine that a failure should result whenever one or both operands are an empty frame-set. However we preferred, here again, to return the other operand as result, so as to regard the two cases (i.e. product by empty frame or by empty frame-set) as frustrated attempts to extend frames, rather than errors.

When two operand frames have one or more properties in common, a conflict arises, since, being a frame, the result could have no more than one P:V pair for each property P. Except if V is the same in both operands, the criterion to solve the conflict must be indicated explicitly through a P:τ(V) notation, where, depending on the choice of the tag τ, the values V1 and V2 coming from the two operands can be handled as follows to obtain the resulting V, noting that one or both can be value lists:

- τ ∈ {`set`,`bag`} – V is a set or bag (which keeps duplicates and preserves the order), containing the value or values of property P taken from V1 and V2;
- τ = `del` – V is the set difference V1 - V2, containing therefore the value or values in V1 not also present in V2;
- τ = `rep` – V is V2, where V2 is either given explicitly, or results from an expression indicating the replacement of V1 by V2 (cf. example 1);
- τ ∈ {`sum`,`min`,`max`,`count`,`avg`} – V is an aggregate value (cf. section 4.4, example 9).

A more radical effect is the removal of property P, so that no pair P:V will appear in the result, which happens if one operand has P:`nil`.

Notice, finally, that the conflict may be avoided altogether by adding a suitable prefix to the occurrence in one or both operands, as in S1\P:V1 and/or S2\P:V2, in which case the two occurrences will appear as distinct properties in the result.

Example 1: Suppose that one wishes to modify the values of the salary attribute of a group of employees, say John and Mary, figuring in a frame-set, by granting a 5% raise. This can be done by specifying a frame containing a replacement tag and then performing the product of this frame against the given frame-set. In the replacement tag shown in the first line, X refers to the current salary and Y to the new salary, to be obtained by multiplying X by 1.05 (note that "`:-`" is the prompt for Prolog evaluation):

```
:- F := [salary:rep(X/(Y:(Y is X * 1.05)))] *
        [[name:'John',salary:130], [name:'Mary',salary:150]].
```

result: `F = [[name:John, salary:136.50], [name:Mary, salary:157.50]]`

Projection. The projection of a frame F', denoted proj [T] @ F', returns a frame F that only contains the properties of F' specified in the projection-template T, ordered according to their position in T. The projection-template T is a sequence of property names P or, optionally, of P:V pairs, where V is a value in the domain of property P or is a variable. In addition to (or instead of) retrieving the desired properties, projection can be used to display them in an arbitrary order. Note that, for efficiency, all operations preliminarily sort their operands and, as a consequence – with the sole exception of projection, as just mentioned – yield their result in lexicographic order.

If the operand is a frame-set, the result is a frame-set containing the projection of the frames of the operand. Note however that, being sets, they cannot contain duplicates, which may arise as the consequence of a projection that suppresses all the property-value pairs that distinguish two or more frames – and such duplicates are accordingly eliminated from the result. If the projection fails for some reason, e.g. because the projection-template T referred to a P or P:V term that did not figure in F', the result will be [] rather than an error.

Example 2: Product is used to concatenate information belonging to Mary's frame with information about the company she works for, and with an attribute pertaining to her work relationship. Projection is used to display the result in a chosen order.

```
:- F1 := 'Mary' ^ [name:N,works/1:C] *
        C ^ [headquarters:H] *
     works(['Mary',C]) ^ [status:S],
   F2 := proj [name,status,works/1,headquarters] @ F1.
```

result: `F = [name:Mary, status:temporary, works/1:Acme,headquarters:Carfax]`

Example 3: Given a list of identifiers, their frames are obtained and the resulting frame-set assigned to F1. Projection on `name` and `revenue` fails for Dupin. Notice that `revenue` has been defined as a virtual attribute, a sum of `salary` and `scholarship`.

```
revenue(A, D) :-
        bagof(B, (salary(A, B);scholarship(A, B)), C),
        sum(C, D).

:- F1 := ['Mina','Dupin','Hercule'],
   F2 := proj [name,revenue] @ F1.
```

result: `F = [[name:Mina, revenue:50], [name:Hercule, revenue:130]]`

Union. The union of two frames F1 and F2, denoted by F1 + F2, returns a frame-set containing both F1 and F2. If one or both operands are frame-sets, the result is a frame-set containing all frames in each operand, with duplicates eliminated. One or both operands can be the empty frame-set, ambiguously denoted as said before by [], functioning as the neutral element for union; so, if one of the operands is [], the union operator returns the other operand as result. In all cases, resulting frame-sets consisting of just one frame are converted into single frame format.

Example 4: The common paradigm, leading to put together hotel and airport-transfer frames, is the practical need to assemble any information relevant to a trip. The resulting frame-set is assigned to F and also stored under the `my_trip` identifier.

```
:- F#my_trip := [[hotel: 'Bavária',city: 'Gramado'],
                 [hotel: 'Everest',city: 'Rio']] +
                [transfer_type: executive,airport:'Salgado Filho',
                 to: 'Gramado', departure: '10 AM'].
```

result:
```
F = [[hotel: 'Bavária',city: 'Gramado'],
     [hotel: 'Everest',city: 'Rio'],
     [transfer_type: executive,airport:'Salgado Filho',
      to: 'Gramado', departure: '10 AM']]
```

Selection. The selection of a frame F', denoted sel [T]/E @ F', returns the frame F' itself if the selection-template T matches F', and the subsequent evaluation of the selection-condition E (also involving information taken from F') succeeds. The presence of E is optional, except if T is empty. If the test fails, the result to be assigned to F is the empty frame []. If the operand is a frame-set, its result will be a frame-set containing all frames that satisfy the test, or the empty frame-set [] if none does. Resulting frame-sets consisting of just one frame are converted into frame format. In order to select one plot at a time from a resulting frame-set S containing two or more frames, the form sel [T]/E @ one(S) must be employed.

Example 5: Since `my_trip` denotes a previously computed and stored frame-set (cf. example 4), it is now possible to select from `my_trip` all the information concerning Gramado, no matter which property may have as value the name of this city (notice the use of an anonymous variable in the selection-template). The result is stored, under the `er_venue` identifier.

```
:- F#er_venue := sel [_: 'Gramado'] @ my_trip.
```

result:
```
F = [[airport: Salgado Filho, time: 10 AM, to: Gramado,
      transfer_type: executive],
     [city: Gramado, hotel: Bavária]]
```

Difference. The difference of two frames F1 and F2, denoted F1 – F2, returns [] if F1 is equal to F2, or F1 otherwise. If one or both operands are frame-sets, the result is a frame-set containing all frames in the first operand that are not equal to any frame in the second. Resulting frame-sets with just one frame are converted into frame format.

Example 6: Assume, in continuation to examples 4 and 5, that one is about to leave Gramado. Difference is then used to retrieve information for the rest of the trip.

```
:- F := my_trip - er_venue.
```

result:
```
F = [hotel: 'Everest', city: 'Rio']
```

Factoring. The factoring of a frame-structured identifier I' of an entity instance, denoted by fac I', is a frame-set I containing the frame-structured identifiers I1,I2,...,In of all entity instances to which I' is directly connected by a *part-of* link.

Factoring can also be applied to frames that include attributes with frame-structured values. If F' is one such frame, its factoring F := fac F' is the result of expanding F', i.e. all terms A:[A1:V1,A:2:V2,...,An:Vn] will be replaced by the sequence A_A1:V1, A_A2:V2,..., A_An:Vn.

In both cases, if the operand is a frame-set, the result is a frame-set containing the result obtained by factoring each constituent of the operand.

Example 7: Given a list of company identifiers, the frame-structured identifiers of their constituent departments are obtained through factoring.

```
:- F := fac ['Acme', 'Casa_Soft'].
```

result:
```
F = [[1:VL, 2:personnel], [1:VL, 2:product], [1:VL, 2:sales],
     [1:BK, 2:audit], [1:BK, 2:product]]
```

Combination. The combination of a frame-structured identifier I' of an entity instance, denoted by comb I', is the frame-structured identifier I of the entity instance such that I' is *part-of* I. If the operand is a frame-set composed of frame-structured identifiers (or frame-sets thereof, as those obtained by factoring in example 7), the result is a frame-set containing the combinations of each constituent frame. Since duplicates are eliminated, all frame-structured identifiers Ij1',Ij2',...,Ijn' in I' that are *part-of* the same entity instance Ij will be replaced by a single occurrence of Ij in the resulting frame-set I.

Combination can also be applied to a frame F' containing expanded terms. Then F := comb F' will revert all such terms to their frame-structured value representation.

The operand can be a frame-set, in which case the resulting frame-set will contain the result of applying combination to each constituent of the operand.

Example 8: Applying combination to frame F1, containing Carrie Fisher's data in flat format, yields frame F2, where `address` and `birth_date` are shown as properties with frame-structured values. This only works, however, if the two attributes have been explicitly defined, with the appropriate syntax, over frame-structured domains.

```
attribute(person,address).
domain(star,address,[street,city]).

attribute(person,birth_date).
domain(person,birth_date,[day,month,year]).

:- F := comb [name: 'Carrie Fisher', address_city: 'Hollywood',
              address_street: '123 Maple St.', birth_date_day: 21,
              birth_date_month:10,birth_date_year: 56,
              starred_in/1:'Star Wars'].
```

<u>**result:**</u>
```
F =  [name:Carrie Fisher,starred_in/1:Star Wars,
      address:[street:123 Maple St., city:Hollywood],
      birth_date:[day:21, month:10, year:56]
```

4.4 Extensions

As a convenient enhancement to its computational power, FMA allows to *iterate* over the two basic constructors, product and union.

Given a frame F', the iterated product of F', expressed by F := prod E @ F', where E is a logical expression sharing at least one variable with F', is evaluated as follows:

- first, the iterator-template T is obtained, as the set of all current instantiations of E, and then:
- if T is the empty set, F = []
- else, if T = {t1, t2, ..., tn}, $F = F'_{t1} * F'_{\{t2, ..., tn\}}$

where F'_{ti} is the same as F' with its variables instantiated consistently with those figuring in ti, and letting the subscript in $F'_{\{ti+1, ..., tn\}}$ refer to the remaining instantiations of T to be used recursively at the next stages. As happens with (binary) product, this feature applies to single frames and to frame-sets.

Similarly, given a frame F', the iterated union of F', expressed by F := uni E @ F', where E is a logical expression sharing at least one variable with F', is thus evaluated:

- first, the iterator-template T is obtained, as the set of all current instantiations of E, and then:
- if T is the empty set, F = []
- else, if T = {t1, t2, ..., tn}, $F = F'_{t1} + F'_{\{t2, ..., tn\}}$

where F'_{ti} is the same as F' with its variables instantiated consistently with those figuring in ti, and letting the subscript in $F'_{\{ti+1, ..., tn\}}$ refer to the remaining instantiations of T to be used recursively at the next stages. Once again, as happens with (binary) union, this feature applies to single frames and to frame-sets.

Example 9: If departments have a `budget` attribute, we may wish to compute a total value for each company by adding the `budget` values of their constituent departments. Two nested iteration schemes are involved, with `uni` finding each company C, and `prod` iterating over the set SD of departments of C, obtained by applying the factoring operator to C. For all departments D which are members of SD, the corresponding `budget` values are retrieved and added-up, as determined by the sum tag in the selection-template, yielding the corporate budget values. Notice the use of C\ at the beginning of the second line, in order to prefix each value with the respective company name.

```
:- F := uni (company(C)) @
        C\(prod (SD := fac C, member(D,SD)) @
              (sel [budget:sum(B)] @ D ^ [budget:B])).
```

result: `F = [[Acme\budget:60], [Casa_Soft\budget:20]]`

Example 10: The same constant can be used an arbitrary number of times to serve as an artificial identifier, which may provide a device with an effect similar to that of "tagging", in the sense that this word is used in the context of folksonomies [13]. Looking back at Example 4, suppose we have, along a period of time, collected a number of frames pertinent to the planned trip, and marked each of them with the same my_trip constant (cf. the notation F#r at the beginning of section 4.2). Later, when needed, the desired frame-set can be assembled by applying iterated union. Notice in this example the double use of variable T, first as iterator-template and then as operand. As iterator-template, T is obtained through the repeated evaluation of the expression T := my_trip, which assigns to T the set of all instances of my_trip frames, whose union then results in the desired frame-set F.

```
:- F#my_trip := [hotel: 'Bavária',city: 'Gramado'] ...
:- F#my_trip := [hotel: 'Everest',city: 'Rio'] ...
:- F#my_trip := [transfer_type: executive,airport:'Salgado Filho',
                 to: 'Gramado', departure: '10 AM'] ...
.......
:- G := uni (T := my_trip) @ T.
```

result:
```
G = [[hotel: 'Bavária',city: 'Gramado'],
     [hotel: 'Everest',city: 'Rio'],
     [transfer_type: executive,airport:'Salgado Filho',
      to: 'Gramado', departure: '10 AM']]
```

Another extension has to do with the obtention of *patterns*, in special for handling class frames and instance frames simultaneously, and for similarity [15] rather than mere equality comparisons. Given a frame F, the pattern of F, denoted by patt F, is obtained from F by substituting variables for the values of the various properties.

Example 11: The objective is to find which employees are somehow similar to Hercule. Both in F1 and F2, the union iterator-template is obtained by evaluating all instances of the expression employee(E), not E == 'Hercule', Fe := E, which retrieves each currently existing employee name E, different from Hercule, and then obtains the frame Fe having E as identifier. The operand of both union operations is a product, whose second term is the more important. In F1, it is determined by the sub-expression 'Hercule' ^ Fe, which looks for properties of Hercule using Fe as search-frame (see section 4.2). In F2, a weaker similarity requirement is used; the sub-expression 'Hercule' ^ (patt Fe) produces the properties shared by the frames of Hercule and E with equal or different values, which are all displayed as variables thanks to a second application of patt. Finally, product is used to introduce same_prop_val or same_prop as new properties, in order to indicate who has been found similar to Hercule.

```
:- F1 := uni (employee(E), not E == 'Hercule', Fe := E) @
             ([same_prop_val:E] * 'Hercule' ^ Fe).
```

result:
```
F1 = [[same_prop_val: Jonathan, salary: 100, works/1: Acme],
      [same_prop_val: Mina, works/1:Acme]]
```

```
:- F2 := uni (employee(E), not E == 'Hercule', Fe := E) @
             ([same_prop:E] * (patt ('Hercule' ^ (patt Fe)))).
```

result:
```
F2 = [[same_prop: Jonathan, salary:_, works/1:_],
      [same_prop: Mina, salary:_, works/1:_],
      [same_prop: Hugo, salary:_, scholarship:_, works/1:_]]
```

5 Concluding Remarks

We have submitted in the present paper that frames are a convenient abstract data type for representing heterogeneous incomplete information. We have also argued that, with its seven operators, our Frame Manipulation Algebra (FMA) is complete in the specific sense that it covers frame (and frame-set) manipulation in the information space induced by the syntagmatic, paradigmatic, antithetic and meronymic relations holding between facts. These relations, besides characterizing some basic aspects of frame handling, can be associated in turn, as we argued in [11], with the four major tropes (metonymy, metaphor, irony, and synecdoche) of semiotic research [5,8].

Frames aim at partial *descriptions* of the mini-world underlying an information system. In a separate paper [17], we showed how to use other frame-like structures, denominated *plots*, to register how the mini-world has evolved (cf. [10]), i.e. what *narratives* were observed to happen. Moreover we have been associating the notion of plots with plan-recognition and plan-generation, as a powerful mechanism to achieve *executable specifications* and, after actual implementation, *intelligent systems* that make ample use of online available meta-data originating from the conceptual modelling stage (comprising *static*, *dynamic* and *behavioural* schemas).

To business information systems we have added literary genres as domains of application of such methods. In fact, the *plot manipulation algebra* (PMA), which we developed in parallel with FMA in order to also characterize plots as abstract data types, proved to be applicable in the context of digital entertainment [20].

Another example of the pervasive use of frame or frame-like structures, in the area of Artificial Intelligence, is the seminal work on *stereotypes* [23] to represent personality traits. In the continuation of our project, we intend to pursue this line of research so as to enhance our behavioural characterization of *agents* (or *personages*, in literary genres), encompassing both cognitive and emotional factors [2].

References

1. Barbosa, S.D.J., Breitman, K.K., Furtado, A.L.: Similarity and Analogy over Application Domains. In: Proc. XXII Simpósio Brasileiro de Banco de Dados, João Pessoa, Brasil, SBC, Casanova (2007)
2. Barsalou, L., Breazeal, C., Smith, L.: Cognition as coordinated non-cognition. Cognitive Processing 8(2), 79–91 (2007)
3. Beech, D.: A foundation for evolution from relational to object databases. In: Schmidt, J.W., Ceri, S., Missikoff, M. (eds.) Extending Database Technology, pp. 251–270. Springer, New York (1988)
4. Bobrow, D.G., Winograd, T.: An overview of KRL-0, a knowledge representation language. Cognitive Science 1(1), 3–46 (1977)
5. Booth, W.: A Rhetoric of Irony. U. of Chicago Press (1974)
6. Breitman, K., Casanova, M.A., Truszkowski, W.: Semantic Web: Concepts, Technologies and Applications. Springer, London (2007)

7. Burke, K.: A Grammar of Motives. U. of California Press (1969)
8. Chandler, D.: Semiotics: The Basics. Rout¬ledge (2007)
9. Chen, P.P.: The entity-relationship model: toward a unified view of data. ACM Trans. on Database Systems 1(1), 9–36 (1976)
10. Chen, P.P.: Suggested Research Directions for a New Frontier – Active Conceptual Modeling. In: Embley, D.W., Olivé, A., Ram, S. (eds.) ER 2006. LNCS, vol. 4215, pp. 1–4. Springer, Heidelberg (2006)
11. Ciarlini, A.E.M., Barbosa, S.D.J., Casanova, M.A., Furtado, A.L.: Event Relations in Plan-Based Plot Composition. ACM Computers in Entertainment (to appear 2009)
12. Codd, E.F.: Relational completeness of data base sublanguages. In: Rustin, R. (ed.) Database Systems, pp. 65–98. Prentice-Hall, Englewood Cliffs (1972)
13. Damme, C.V., Heppe, M., Siorpaes, K.: FolksOntology: An Integrated Approach for Turning Folksonomies into Ontologies. In: Proc. ESWC Workshop - Bridging the Gap between Semantic Web and Web 2.0, SemNet, pp. 57–70 (2007)
14. Date, C.J.: An Introduction to Database Systems. Addison-Wesley, Reading (2003)
15. Fauconnier, G., Turner, M.: The Way We Think. Basic Books, New York (2002)
16. Fillmore, C.: The case for case. In: Bach, E., Harms, R.T. (eds.) Universals in Linguist Theory, Bach, E, pp. 1–88. Holt, New York (1968)
17. Furtado, A.L., Casanova, M.A., Barbosa, S.D.J., Breitman, K.K.: Analysis and Reuse of Plots using Simi¬larity and Analogy. In: Li, Q., Spaccapietra, S., Yu, E., Olivé, A. (eds.) ER 2008. LNCS, vol. 5231, pp. 355–368. Springer, Heidelberg (2008)
18. Furtado, A.L., Kerschberg, L.: An algebra of quotient relations. In: Proc. ACM SIGMOD International Conference on Management of Data, pp. 1–8 (1977)
19. Jaeschke, G., Scheck, H.J.: Remarks on the algebra of non first normal form relations. In: Proc. 1st ACM SIGACT-SIGMOD symposium on principles of database systems, pp. 124–138 (1982)
20. Karlsson, B.F., Furtado, A.L., Barbosa, S.D.J., Casanova, M.A.: PMA: A Plot Manipulation Algebra to Support Digital Storytelling. In: Proc. 8th International Conference on Entertainment Computing (to appear 2009)
21. Lakoff, G.: Women, Fire, and Dangerous Things. The University of Chicago Press (1987)
22. Minsky, M.: A Framework for Representing Knowledge. In: Winston, P.H. (ed.) The Psychology of Computer Vision, pp. 211–277. McGraw-Hill, New York (1975)
23. Rich, E.: Users are individuals – individualizing user models. International Journal on Man-Machine Studies 18, 199–214 (1983)
24. Saussure, F., Bally, C., et al.: Cours de Linguistique Générale. Payot (1916)
25. Schank, R.C., Colby, K., Freeman, W.H.: Computer Models of Thought and Language (1973)
26. Smith, J.M., Smith, D.C.P.: Data abstraction: aggregation and generalization. ACM Transactions on Database Systems 2(2), 105–133 (1977)
27. Stonebraker, M.: Inclusion of New Types in Relational Data Base Systems. In: Proc. Second International Conference on Data Engineering, pp. 262–269 (1986)
28. Stonebraker, M., Madden, S., Abadi, D.J., Harizopoulos, S., Hachen, N., Helland, P.: The end of an architectural era. In: Proc. VLDB 2007, pp. 1150–1160 (2007)
29. Ullman, J.D., Widom, J.: A first Course on Database Systems. Prentice-Hall, Englewood Cliffs (2008)
30. Varvel, D.A., Shapiro, L.: The Computational completeness of extended database query languages. IEEE Transactions on Software Engineering 15.5, 632–638 (1989)
31. Winston, M.E., Chaffin, R., Herrmann, D.: A taxonomy of part-whole relations. Cognitive Science 11, 4 (1987)

Conceptual Modeling in the Time of the Revolution: Part II

John Mylopoulos

Department of Information Engineering and Computer Science
University of Trento, Italy
jm@disi.unitn.it

Abstract. Conceptual Modeling was a marginal research topic at the very fringes of Computer Science in the 60s and 70s, when the discipline was dominated by topics focusing on programs, systems and hardware architectures. Over the years, however, the field has moved to centre stage and has come to claim a central role both in Computer Science research and practice in diverse areas, such as Software Engineering, Databases, Information Systems, the Semantic Web, Business Process Management, Service-Oriented Computing, Multi-Agent Systems, Knowledge Management, and more. The transformation was greatly aided by the adoption of standards in modeling languages (e.g., UML), and model-based methodologies (e.g., Model-Driven Architectures) by the Object Management Group (OMG) and other standards organizations. We briefly review the history of the field over the past 40 years, focusing on the evolution of key ideas. We then note some open challenges and report on-going research, covering topics such as the representation of variability in conceptual models, capturing model intentions, and models of laws.

Notes: A keynote with a similar title was given 12 years ago at CAiSE'97, hence the "part II". The research presented in the talk was conducted jointly with colleagues at the Universities of Toronto (Canada) and Trento (Italy).

A.H.F. Laender et al. (Eds.): ER 2009, LNCS 5829, p. 25, 2009.

Data Auditor: Analyzing Data Quality Using Pattern Tableaux

Divesh Srivastava

AT&T Labs-Research, Florham Park, NJ, USA
divesh@research.att.com

Abstract. Monitoring databases maintain configuration and measurement tables about computer systems, such as networks and computing clusters, and serve important business functions, such as troubleshooting customer problems, analyzing equipment failures, planning system upgrades, etc. These databases are prone to many data quality issues: configuration tables may be incorrect due to data entry errors, while measurement tables may be affected by incorrect, missing, duplicate and delayed polls. We describe Data Auditor, a tool for analyzing data quality and exploring data semantics of monitoring databases. Given a user-supplied constraint, such as a boolean predicate expected to be satisfied by every tuple, a functional dependency, or an inclusion dependency, Data Auditor computes "pattern tableaux", which are concise summaries of subsets of the data that satisfy or fail the constraint. We discuss the architecture of Data Auditor, including the supported types of constraints and the tableau generation mechanism. We also show the utility of our approach on an operational network monitoring database.

Note: This is a joint work with Lukasz Golab, Howard Karloff and Flip Korn.

A.H.F. Laender et al. (Eds.): ER 2009, LNCS 5829, p. 26, 2009.

Schema AND Data: A Holistic Approach to Mapping, Resolution and Fusion in Information Integration

Laura M. Haas[1], Martin Hentschel[2], Donald Kossmann[2], and Renée J. Miller[3]

[1] IBM Almaden Research Center, San Jose, CA 95120, USA
[2] Systems Group, ETH Zurich, Switzerland
[3] Department of Computer Science, University of Toronto, Canada
laura@almaden.ibm.com, martin.hentschel@inf.ethz.ch,
donald.kossmann@inf.ethz.ch, miller@cs.toronto.edu

Abstract. To integrate information, data in different formats, from different, potentially overlapping sources, must be related and transformed to meet the users' needs. Ten years ago, Clio introduced nonprocedural *schema mappings* to describe the relationship between data in heterogeneous schemas. This enabled powerful tools for mapping discovery and integration code generation, greatly simplifying the integration process. However, further progress is needed. We see an opportunity to raise the level of abstraction further, to encompass both data- and schema-centric integration tasks and to isolate applications from the details of how the integration is accomplished. *Holistic information integration* supports iteration across the various integration tasks, leveraging information about both schema and data to improve the integrated result. *Integration independence* allows applications to be independent of how, when, and where information integration takes place, making materialization and the timing of transformations an optimization decision that is transparent to applications. In this paper, we define these two important goals, and propose leveraging *data mappings* to create a framework that supports both data- and schema-level integration tasks.

1 Introduction

Information integration is a challenging task. Many or even most applications today require data from several sources. There are many sources to choose from, each with their own data formats, full of overlapping, incomplete, and often even inconsistent data. To further complicate matters, there are many information integration problems. Some applications require sub-second response to data requests, with perfect accuracy. Others can tolerate some delays, if the data is complete, or may need guaranteed access to data. Depending on the application's needs, different integration methods may be appropriate, but application requirements evolve over time. And to meet the demands of our fast-paced world there is increased desire for rapid, flexible information integration. Many tools

A.H.F. Laender et al. (Eds.): ER 2009, LNCS 5829, pp. 27–40, 2009.

have been created to address particular scenarios, each covering some subset of goals, and some portion of the integration task.

Integration is best thought of not as a single act, but as a process [Haa07]. Since typically the individuals doing the integration are not experts in all of the data, they must first understand what data is available, how good it is, and whether it matches the application needs. Then they must determine how to represent the data in the application, and decide how to standardize data across the data sources. A plan for integrating the data must be prepared, and only then can they move from design to execution, and actually integrate the data. Once the integration takes place, users often discover problems – expected results may be missing, strange results appear – or the needs may change, and they have to crawl through the whole process again to revise it. There are different tools for different (overlapping) parts of the process, as well as for different needs. Figure 1a illustrates the current situation. Information integration is too time-consuming, too brittle, and too complicated. We need to go beyond the status quo, towards a radically simplified process for information integration.

Ten years ago, a new tool for information integration introduced the idea of *schema mappings* [MHH00]. Clio was a major leap forward in three respects. First, it raised the level of abstraction for the person doing the integration, from writing code or queries to creating mappings, from which Clio could generate the code. This higher level of abstraction enabled Clio to support many execution engines from a common user interface [PVM+02]. Second, Clio let users decompose their integration task into smaller pieces, building up complex mappings from simpler ones. Finally, it allowed for iteration through the integration design process, thus supporting an incremental approach to integration. The user could focus first on what they knew, see what mappings were produced, add or adjust, and so on, constantly refining the integration design [FHH+09].

Clio simplified the schema mapping part of the integration process and made it more adaptive. But we need to do more. There is room for improvement in two respects: we need to extend the benefits of a higher level of abstraction to cover both data-centric and schema-centric integration tasks, and we need to make the design phases (and the applications) independent of the actual integration method. We call the first of these *holistic information integration*, and the second *integration independence*.

Holistic information integration. Clio only deals with schema-level relationships between a data source and a target (though Clio does data transformation at run-time based on these relationships). Today, other tools are needed to handle data-level integration tasks. Such tasks include entity resolution, which identifies entities in a data source that may represent the same real-world object, and data fusion, which creates a consistent, cleansed view of data from potentially multiple conflicting representations. There is little support for iteration between schema-level and data-level tasks in the integration process. This is unfortunate, because there is no perfect ordering of the tasks. Sometimes, mapping can help with understanding the data and hence with entity resolution and data fusion. But those tasks can also provide valuable information to a mapping process. By handling both schema and data-level tasks in a common framework, holistically, we hope to enable easier iteration among these phases, and hence, a smoother integration process.

Integration Independence. There are two radically different integration methods: virtualization and materialization. Virtualization (aka, *data integration*) leaves the data where it is, as it is, and dynamically retrieves, merges and transforms it on request. Materialization (*data exchange*) does the integration up front, creating a new data set for requests to run against. Each has its strengths. Virtualization always gets the freshest data, and does no unnecessary work, since the data is integrated only if needed (a lazy form of integration). Materialization often provides better performance, but may process data that will never be requested (an eager approach). Often, the best solution will require a combination of these two approaches. In fact, virtualization cannot solve the whole integration problem today, as we simply do not understand how to do much of integration, including data fusion and entity resolution, virtually. The materialization process handles these data-specific tasks, but it is too heavy duty for some use cases, and a materialization often takes too long to design and build. The decision of which approach to use, and when, must be made early in the integration design process, and, as different integration tools must then be used for the different pieces, is difficult to change. Ideally, applications should be independent of how, when, and where information integration takes place.

Integration independence is analogous to the well-understood concept of data independence. Clio took a large step towards integration independence, by providing a declarative representation of how schemas differ. As a result, applications can be written in a way that is independent of the structural representation of the data. Furthermore, since Clio mappings can be used with either the virtual, data integration, approach or the materialized, data exchange, approach, schema differences may be reconciled either eagerly or lazily. However, current integration engines force the user to choose between the two approaches. For full integration independence, the timing of when structural heterogeneity is reconciled should be an optimization decision that is transparent to applications.

While progress may be made on holistic information integration and integration independence separately, together they hold the potential for truly radical simplification. It would clearly be a leap forward to have a single engine that could move seamlessly between virtualization and materialization, with no changes to the application program [Haa07], and we are currently working towards that goal. However, as long as we continue to need different tools at the design level to handle the schema- and data-specific portions of the integration task, there will always be confusion, overlap, and complexity. If we can, in fact, tackle both schema and data-related integration issues within the same framework, we can use all available information to improve and refine the integration without changing the application. We will be able to move easily among such tasks as understanding, mapping, fusion, and entity resolution, and even to execution and back. It will enable us to handle the ever-changing dynamics of application needs for performance, completeness, and accuracy, and to react

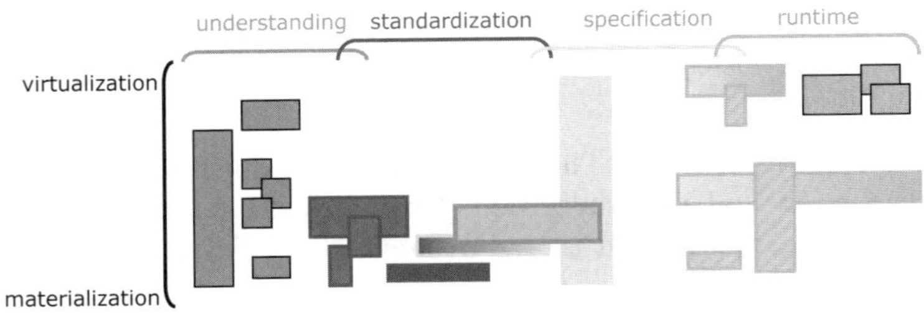

(a) Today's Tool Space

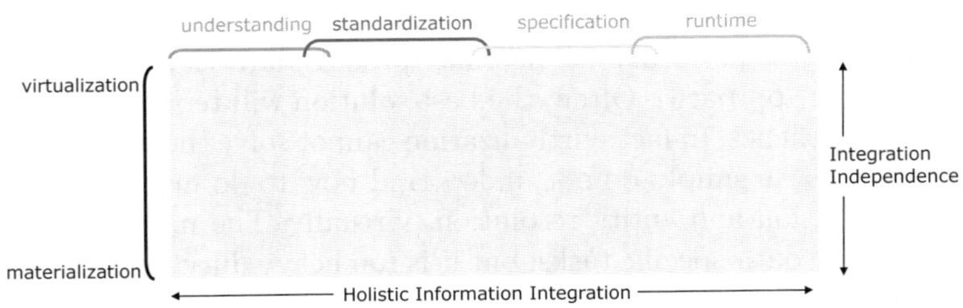

(b) Tomorrow's?

Fig. 1. Effect of Holistic Information Integration and Integration Independence

quickly to data and schema evolution. Rapid prototyping and what-if scenarios will be more effectively supported. We expect that a unified framework will also reduce the knowledge needed by the integrator – of different tools, schemas and the data itself. Holistic information integration and integration independence together can lead to the simplicity of Figure 1b.

This paper is organized as follows. In the next section we describe some foundational work. Section 3 proposes leveraging data mappings to extend the benefits of nonprocedural mappings to the data level. We illustrate the benefits and the challenges through a detailed example. Finally, we conclude with some thoughts on next steps and our current work in Section 4.

2 Foundations: Schema and Data Mapping

Up until ten years ago, most metadata management research focused on the schema matching problem, where the goal was to discover the existence of possible relationships between schema elements. The output of matching was typically modeled as a relation over the set of elements in two schemas (most often as a set of attribute pairs) [RB01]. Often such work was agnostic as to the semantics of the discovered relationships. At best, a matching had very limited transformational power (for example, a match might only allow copying of data, but no joins or complex queries). Indeed this feature was viewed as a virtue as it enabled the development of generic matchers that were independent of a specific data model.

However, the last decade has shown how important the semantics of these relationships are. During this period, we have made remarkable progress, due to the development and wide-spread adoption of a powerful declarative schema mapping formalism with a precise semantics. Clio [HMH01] led the way in both developing this formalism and in providing solutions for (semi)-automatically discovering, using and managing mappings. The benefits of considering semantics are clear. First, having a common agreement on a robust and powerful transformation semantics enables the exploitation of schema mappings for both virtual and materialized integration. Second, schema mapping understanding and debugging tools rely on this semantics to help elicit nuanced details in mappings for applications requiring precise notions of data correctness. Third, having a widely adopted semantics has enabled a large and growing body of research on how to manage schema mappings, including how to compose, invert, evolve, and maintain mappings. Indeed, schema mappings have caused a fundamental change in the research landscape, and in the available tools.

2.1 Schema Mappings

Informally, schema mappings are a relationship between a query over one schema and a query over another. A query can be as simple as an expression defining a single concept (for example, the set of all clients) and the relationship may be an *is-a* or containment relationship stating that each member of one concept *is-a* member of another. We will use the arrow $\rightarrow$ to denote an *is-a* relationship, e.g., `Client -> Guest`. Since queries can express powerful data transformations, complex queries can be used to relate two concepts that may be represented completely differently in different data sources.

To precisely define the semantics of a schema mapping, Clio adapted the notion of *tuple-generating dependencies* or referential constraints from relational database theory [BV84]. A schema mapping is then a *source-to-target tuple-generating dependency* from one schema to another (or in the case of schemas containing nesting, a nested referential constraint) [PVM^{+}02]. Such constraints (which express an *is-a* or containment relationship) were shown to have rich enough transformational power to map data between complex independently-created schemas. Furthermore, this semantics was useful in not only (virtual) data integration [YP04], but it also fueled the development of a new theory of data exchange [FKMP05]. This theory provides a foundation for materialized information integration and is today one of the fastest growing areas in integration research.

Because Clio mappings have the form $Q(S) \rightarrow Q(T)$, they are declarative and independent of a specific execution environment. Early in its development, Clio provided algorithms for transforming mappings into executable data exchange programs for multiple back-end integration engines [PVM^{+}02]. Specifically, Clio mappings can be transformed into executable queries (in SQL or Xquery), XSLT scripts, ETL scripts, etc. This is one of the key aspects to Clio's success as it freed application writers from having to write special-purpose code for navigating and transforming their information for different execution environments.

In addition, this clean semantics forms the foundation for a new generation of user front-ends that support users developing applications for which the correctness of the data (and hence, of the integration) is critical. Tools such as data-driven mapping GUIs [YMHF01, ACMT08] help users understand, and possibly modify, what a mapping will do by showing carefully chosen examples from the data. Likewise, tools for debugging mappings [CT06, BMP+08] help a user discover how mappings have created a particular (presumably incorrect) dataset. Visual interfaces like Clip [RBC$^+$08] permit users to develop mappings using a visual language. There has also been a proliferation of industry mapping tools from companies including Altova, IBM, Microsoft and BEA. The existence of a common mapping semantics has enabled the development of the first mapping benchmark, STBenchmark [ATV08], which compares the usability and expressibility of such systems.

2.2 Data Mappings

Schema mappings permit data under one schema to be transformed into the form of another. However, it may be the case that two schemas store some of the same information. Consider a simple schema mapping that might connect two hotel schemas:

```
M:  Client -> Guest
```

Given a Client tuple c, this mapping states that c is also a Guest tuple. However, we may want to assert something stronger. We may know that c actually represents the same real world person as the Guest tuple g. (For example, entity resolution techniques can be used to discover this type of relationship.) Ideally, we'd like to be able to make the assertion: c `same-as` g, as an ontology language such as OWL would permit.

This is a common problem, so much so that it has been studied not only in ontologies, but also in relational systems where the data model does not provide primitives for making `same-as` assertions and where there is a value-based notion of identity. Kementsietsidis et al. [KAM03, KA04] explored in depth the semantics of data mappings such as this. They use the notion of *mapping tables* to store and reason about sets of data mappings. Mapping tables permit the specification of two kinds of data mappings, `same-as` and `is-a`. If c `same-as` g, then any query requesting information about client c will get back data for guest g as well, and vice versa. However, for the latter, if c `is-a` g, then for queries requesting information about g the system will return c's data as well, but queries requesting c will not return values from g. A given mapping table can be declared to have a closed-world semantics meaning that *only* the mappings specified in the table are permitted. This is a limited form of negation which we will discuss further in the next section.

2.3 Mapping Discovery

Clio pioneered a new paradigm in which schema mapping creation is viewed as a process of query discovery [MHH00]. Given a matching (a set of correspondences) between attributes in two schemas, Clio exploits the schemas and their constraints to generate a set of alternative mappings. Detailed examples are given in Fagin et al. [FHH+09] . In brief, Clio uses logical inference over schemas and their constraints to generate all possible associations between source elements (and all possible associations between target elements) [PVM+02]. Intuitively, Clio is leveraging the semantics that is embedded in the schemas and their constraints to determine a set of mappings that are consistent with this semantics.

Since Clio laid the foundation for mapping discovery, there have been several important advances. First, An et al. [ABMM07] showed how to exploit a conceptual schema or ontology to improve mapping discovery. Their approach requires that the relationship of the conceptual schema to the schemas being mapped is known. They show how the conceptual schema can then be used to make better mapping decisions.

An interesting new idea is to use data mappings (specifically *same-as* relationships) to help in the discovery of schema mappings. Suppose we apply an entity-resolution procedure to tuples (entities) stored under two schemas to be mapped. We then also apply a schema mapping algorithm that postulates a set of possible mappings. For a given schema mapping $m : A \rightarrow B$, suppose further that mapping m implies that two entities (say e_1 from A and e_2 from B) must be the same entity (this may happen if e_1 and e_2 share a key value). If the similarity of e_1 and e_2 is high, then the entity-resolution procedure will likely come to the same conclusion, agreeing with the schema mapping algorithm. This should increase the confidence that mapping m is correct. If however, e_1 and e_2 are dissimilar, then this should decrease confidence in the mapping m. This is the basic idea behind Iliads [UGM07]. Evidence produced by entity-resolution is combined with evidence produced by schema mapping using a concept called *inference similarity*. This work showed that combining the statistical learning that underlies entity-resolution algorithms with the logical inference underlying schema mapping discovery can improve the quality of mapping discovery.

Iliads is a step towards our vision for holistic information integration. As we explore in the next section, there is much more that can be done.

3 A Holistic Approach to Information Integration

We would like to bring to the overall information integration process the benefits of a higher level of abstraction and a unified framework. We envision a holistic approach, in which all integration tasks can be completed within a single environment, moving seamlessly back and forth between them as we refine the integration. A key element in achieving this vision will be *data mappings*. In this section, we define this concept, and illustrate via an example how data mappings enable holistic information integration.

3.1 Our Building Blocks

By analogy to schema mappings, a data mapping defines a relationship between two data elements. It takes the form of a rule, but rather than identifying the

Table 1. Las Vegas schema for Guest and sample data

(ID)	Name	Home	Income	TotalSpent	Comps
@GuestRM	Renée Miller	Toronto	1.3M	250K	Champagne
@GuestLA	Laurence Amien	Toulouse	350K	75K	None
@GuestDK	Donald Kossmann	Munich	575K	183K	Truffles
@GuestLH	Laura Haas	San Jose	402K	72K	None

Table 2. French schema for Client and sample data

(ID)	Prénom	Nom	Ville	Logements	Casino	RV	Cadeau
@ClientRM	René	Miller	Toronto	300	10K	100K	rien
@ClientLA	Laurence	Amiens	Toulouse	5K	250K	350K	chocolate
@ClientDK	Donald	Kossmann	Munich	15K	223K	575K	truffles
@ClientMH	Martin	Hentschel	Zurich	10K	95K	250K	bicycle
@ClientLH	Laura	Haas	San Jose	1K	50K	402K	rien

data it refers to by that data's logical properties (as would a schema mapping), it uses object identifiers to refer directly to the data objects being discussed. A data mapping, therefore, relates together two objects. The simplest relationship we can imagine might be *same-as*, e.g., *Object34 same-as ObjectZ18* (where Object34 and ObjectZ18 are object identifiers in some universe). Data mappings could be used for specifying the results of entity resolution, or as part of data fusion.

It is not enough to add such rules; we also need an integration engine that can work with both data mappings and schema mappings, and allow us to move seamlessly from integration design to integration execution and back again. We are currently building such an engine, exploiting a new technique that interprets schema mappings at integration runtime [HKF$^+$09]. Conceptually, as the engine sees data objects in the course of a query, it applies any relevant rules (schema or data mappings) to determine whether the objects should be returned as part of the data result. Enhancements to improve performance via caching, indexing, pre-compiling, etc., can be made, so that the engine provides integration independence as well. This in turn enables a single design environment. In this paper, we assume the existence of such an engine, without further elaboration.

3.2 Holistic Information Integration: An Example

Suppose a casino in Las Vegas has just acquired a small casino in France. The management in Las Vegas would like to send a letter to all the "high rollers" (players who spend large amounts of money) of both casinos, telling them the news, and inviting them to visit. They do not want to wait a year while the two customer records management systems are integrated. Fortunately, they have available our new integration engine. Jean is charged with doing the integration.

Table 1 and Table 2 show the existing (highly simplified) schemas, and a subset of data, for the Las Vegas and French customer management systems, respectively. Jean's first step is to define "high roller". To this end, she creates the following rules:

```
Client [Logements+Casino > 100K] -> HighRoller Guest [TotalSpent >
100K] -> HighRoller
```

The above syntax is used for illustration only. The first rule says that when we see a Client object, where the lodging plus the casino fields total more than 100K, then that Client is a high roller – it should be returned whenever HighRoller's are requested. Likewise, the second says that Guests whose TotalSpent is over 100K are also HighRollers. Such rules can be easily expressed in most schema mapping rule languages. With these two rules, it is possible to enter a query such as "Find HighRollers" (this might be spelled `//HighRoller` in XQuery, for example), with the following results:

Guest: [Renée Miller, Toronto, 1.3M, 250K, Champagne]
Guest: [Donald Kossmann, Munich, 575K, 183K, Truffles]
Client: [Laurence, Amiens, Toulouse, 5K, 250K, 350K, chocolats]
Client: [Donald, Kossmann, Munich, 15K, 223K, 575K, truffles]
Client: [Martin, Hentschel, Zurich, 10K, 95K, 250K, bicycle]

Note that a mixture of Guests and Clients are returned, since there has been no specification of an output format. We believe that this type of tolerance of heterogeneity is important for a holistic integration system, as it preserves information and allows for later refinement of schema and data mappings.

Jean notices that there are two entries for Donald Kossmann, one a "Guest", from the Las Vegas database, and the other a "Client" from the French one. She decides they are the same (they come from the same town, receive the same gift, etc). She only wants to send Donald one letter, so she'd like to ensure that only one entry comes back for him. Ideally, she would just specify a rule saying that the guest and client Donald Kossmann are the same.

We enable Jean to do this by the following rule (again, syntax is for illustration only):

```
@GuestDK <- @ClientDK
```

where the two sides represent the "addresses" or unique ids of the two objects she wants to equate. This rule says that the guest Donald Kossmann is really the same as the client, and that the merge of the two nodes should be returned, with the Client fields being added to the Guest. In other words, the Client object is merged into the Guest object, creating an asymmetric *merge into* semantics. Other semantics are definitely possible. For example, the objects could be merged into a new object (symmetric *merge* semantics), or not merged at all, but treated as one during query processing (*equivalence* semantics) so that only one is returned. From an implementation perspective, *merge into* is simpler to model, and seems to offer sufficient power for the scenarios we have worked with so far, but more investigation is clearly needed. With this new rule, Jean gets the following query result:

Guest: [Renée Miller, Toronto, 1.3M, 250K, Champagne]
Guest: [Donald Kossmann, Munich, 575K, 183K, Truffles, Donald, Kossmann, Munich, 15K, 223K, 575K, truffles]
Client: [Laurence, Amiens, Toulouse, 5K, 250K, 350K, chocolats]
Client: [Martin, Hentschel, Zurich, 10K, 95K, 250K, bicycle]

Note that Donald is only returned once, as a `Guest`, but with all the fields of both guests and clients, preserving all the information associated with the object.

With a simple query and just a few schema and data mapping rules, Jean has found the high rollers and all the available information about each. Or has she? Seeing Donald in both lists reminds her that there could be customers who have visited both casinos, not spending enough in either to qualify as high rollers, but in total spending across the two casinos clearly qualifying. She would like to add these folks, if any, to the list. This requires entity resolution to detect when two entities (here casino visitors) are the same. Many algorithms for entity resolution exist; most do some form of clustering of records, often with user input on which fields are important, or how to measure similarity. Jean runs such an algorithm, and accepts the results when they are shown to her, creating the following additional rules.

```
@GuestLA <- @ClientLA @GuestLH <- @ClientLH @GuestRM <- @ClientRM
```

She then can add her new schema mapping rule, to wit:

```
Guest [TotalSpent+Logements+Casino > 100K] -> HighRoller
```

`Find HighRollers` now returns:

Guest: [Renée Miller, Toronto, 1.3M, 250K, Champagne, René, Miller, Toronto, 300, 10K, 100K, rien]
Guest: [Donald Kossmann, Munich, 575K, 183K, Truffles, Donald, Kossmann, Munich, 15K, 223K, 575K, truffles]
Guest: [Laura Haas, SJ, 402K, 72K, None, Laura, Haas, SJ, 1K, 50K, 402K, rien]
Guest: [Laurence Amien, Toulouse, 350K, 75K, None, Laurence, Amiens, Toulouse, 5K, 250K, 350K, chocolats]
Client: [Martin, Hentschel, Zurich, 10K, 95K, 250K, bicycle]

Jean is happy with this result; now she wants to transform it into a simple form for the two casinos to use. At this point, she is more familiar with the data, so she can create an output schema and map the Guest and Client schemas to that. She does this by replacing our earlier, simple mapping rules by the refined versions in Figure 2. This pair of rules not only specify that Clients and Guests that spend a certain amount are HighRollers, but tells how to construct a High Roller instance from a Client or Guest instance. Note that the Guest rule, in concert with the earlier data mappings, completes data fusion, by telling how the various fields from the merged objects should be reconciled. For example,

```
Client [Logements+Casino > 100K] as $c -> <HighRoller>
                  <FullName>$c.Prenom ||$c.Nom </FullName>
                  <City>$c.Ville </City>
                  <Spent>$c.Logements + $c.Casino </Spent>
                  <Gift>$c.Cadeau </Gift>
               </HighRoller>

Guest [TotalSpent+Logements+Casino > 100K] as $g ->   <HighRoller>
                  <FullName>$g.Name </FullName>
                  <City>$g.Home </City>
                  <Spent>$g.TotalSpent + $g.Logements + $g.Casino </Spent>
                  <Gift>$g.Comps || $g.Cadeau</Gift>
               </HighRoller>
```

Fig. 2. Mapping Rules

the `Spent` field of HighRoller is defined to be the sum of all the fields that have anything to do with spending in Guest (+ the merged Client) objects. The `Gift` field is defined as the concatenation of the `Comps` and `Cadeau` fields for simplicity; Jean could, of course, have used a fancier rule to resolve the Gift values, for example, preferring a value other than "Rien" or "None", or choosing one gift based on its monetary value.

Now if Jean runs the query again, with these new rules, her result would be:

HighRoller: [Renée Miller, Toronto, 260.3K, Champagne rien]
HighRoller: [Donald Kossmann, Munich, 421K, Truffles truffles]
HighRoller: [Laurence Amien, Toulouse, 330K, None chocolats]
HighRoller: [Laura Haas, SJ, 123K, None rien]
HighRoller: [Martin Hentschel, Zurich, 105K, bicycle]

The integration is now ready to use. These results could be saved in a warehouse for reference, or the query could be given to the two casinos to run as needed, getting the latest, greatest information. This in itself is a major advance over the state of the art, where totally different design tools and runtime engines would be used depending on whether the goal was to materialize or federate (provide access to the virtual integration). Further, Jean was able to do this with minimal knowledge of the French schema, leveraging the mapping rules, the data, and the flexibility to iterate. The two types of rules work well together. Schema mapping rules gather the data; they can be used to transform it when ready. Data mapping rules record decisions on which entities are the same, and ensure that the query results contain all available information about each entity.

Another benefit of this holistic integration approach is that data-level and schema-level operations can be interwoven. In our example, defining some simple schema-level mappings between Guest and Client (e.g., `Client/(Prénom || Nom) -> Guest/Name` might make it easier to do comparisons for entity resolution. However, if we've done entity resolution and can observe that for each pair that we've found, the Client RV field is the same as the Guest Income field, we may be able to guess that RV (for *revenu*) should be mapped to Income if we wanted that value.

Of course, life is not this simple, and we need to explore what cases our holistic framework should handle. Continuing our example, let's suppose that René Miller visits the French casino again, and an alert clerk notes that René is a guy, while Renée is a woman's name. Not wishing to waste champagne on the wrong person, he investigates, and discovers that this is, indeed, a different person, although both are from Toronto. Thus the rule

```
@GuestRM <- @ClientRM
```

is wrong, and must be removed. However, without changes to the entity resolution logic, it is quite possible that such a rule would be re-produced sometime in the future, and no one would notice. In addition to the champagne issue, it could be dangerous financially to extend to Mr. Miller the type of credit that Ms. Miller legitimately enjoys. Hence, it would be useful to be able to have negative data mapping rules, i.e.,

```
@GuestRM !<-! @ClientRM
```

Where `!<-!` means "under no circumstances merge these entities", here the client entity René Miller with the guest entity Renée Miller. Such rules seem quite useful, but adding negation into rule languages has typically proven to add complexity to query processing. We need to understand whether this very specific form of negation causes similar problems.

3.3 Further Opportunities

While the above example shows the immediate value that could be provided by data mappings, we believe that the concept will enable new tools that can provide further value. An obvious place to start is with discovering various types of data mappings. Entity resolution essentially discovers *same-as* relationships today, and data mappings allow us to harness that power and include it within our holistic framework. But other types of relationships between entities are possible, and can be useful for the integration process. For example, understanding *part-of* relationships can help with schema mapping. The linked open data community is providing typed links between objects, where the types may come from a data model or an ontology, specifying any type of relationship. Specialized discovery tools for certain domains and relationships could be valuable, as semantics of those constructs could be leveraged [HXK+09]. For example, the *same-as* relationship between genes is quite different than *same-as* between people.

Along similar lines, we may consider generalizing the notion of schema mappings, which today focus on *contained-in* relationships. There may be other types of schema-level relationships we may be able to discover that could aid the integration process. Meanwhile, the principles of open linked data include not only using URIs, but also providing useful information when someone looks up a URI or dereferences an HTTP URI. Clearly mappings, data and schema, can be a key to providing semantically relevant information.

4 Conclusions

In this paper, we have argued that *holistic information integration* and *integration independence* are important, inter-related goals for research in information integration. Ten years ago we took a big step towards integration independence by enriching our modeling capabilities with schema-level mappings. That gave us a nonprocedural expression of the differences between schemas, allowing us to produce code to reconcile those differences automatically, for different integration engines, whether a data integration engine using virtualization, or an engine for data exchange that uses materialization. However, the engines remained distinct, with differing capabilities. Further, the schema and data worlds have for the most part been considered independently, forcing separate tools to be developed for each, and fragmenting the integration design process. Hence, applications have continued to be impacted by the choice of integration methods, and users have been baffled by the variety of tools.

This paper proposed a step towards holistic information integration. By adding *data mappings*, we enable both schema and data issues to be addressed within a single integration framework, opening the door to new tools, and a more iterative approach to integration. Still, much work remains to be done. It is not trivial to build an integration engine that can move easily between virtualization and materialization of integrated data, especially one that can also deal with the implications of data mappings. Algorithms to handle typical data-level tasks such as data fusion and entity resolution must be made efficient and effective during data integration, when the end result will not be materialized. Research is also needed on the semantics, limits and types of data mappings, and on tools that leverage these mappings to make the integration task easier. These are doubtless just a few of the challenges ahead, on our path to integration independence and holistic information integration.

References

[ABMM07] An, Y., Borgida, A., Miller, R.J., Mylopoulos, J.: A Semantic Approach to Discovering Schema Mapping Expressions. In: IEEE ICDE Conf., pp. 206–215 (2007)

[ACMT08] Alexe, B., Chiticariu, L., Miller, R.J., Tan, W.-C.: Muse: Mapping Understanding and deSign by Example. In: IEEE ICDE Conf., pp. 10–19 (2008)

[ATV08] Alexe, B., Tan, W.-C., Velegrakis, Y.: STBenchmark: towards a benchmark for mapping systems. In: Proceedings of the VLDB Endowment, vol. 1, pp. 230–244 (2008)

[BMP+08] Bonifati, A., Mecca, G., Pappalardo, A., Raunich, S., Summa, G.: Schema Mapping Verification: The Spicy Way. In: EDBT Conf., pp. 85–96 (2008)

[BV84] Beeri, C., Vardi, M.Y.: A Proof Procedure for Data Dependencies. Journal of the ACM 31(4), 718–741 (1984)

[CT06] Chiticariu, L., Tan, W.-C.: Debugging Schema Mappings with Routes. In: VLDB Conf., pp. 79–90 (2006)

[FHH+09] Fagin, R., Haas, L.M., Hernández, M., Miller, R.J., Popa, L., Velegrakis, Y.: Clio: Schema Mapping Creation and Data Exchange. In: Borgida, A.T., Chaudhri, V.K., Giorgini, P., Yu, E.S. (eds.) Conceptual Modeling: Foundations and Applications, Essays in Honor of John Mylopoulos. LNCS, vol. 5600. Springer, Heidelberg (2009)

[FKMP05] Fagin, R., Kolaitis, P.G., Miller, R.J., Popa, L.: Data Exchange: Semantics and Query Answering. In: Calvanese, D., Lenzerini, M., Motwani, R. (eds.) ICDT 2003. LNCS, vol. 2572, pp. 207–224. Springer, Heidelberg (2002); Extended version of ICDT 2003

[Haa07] Haas, L.M.: Beauty and the Beast: The Theory and Practice of Information Integration. In: Schwentick, T., Suciu, D. (eds.) ICDT 2007. LNCS, vol. 4353, pp. 28–43. Springer, Heidelberg (2006)

[HKF+09] Hentschel, M., Kossmann, D., Florescu, D., Haas, L., Kraska, T., Miller, R.J.: Scalable Data Integration by Mapping Data to Queries. Technical Report 633, ETH Zurich, Systems Group, Dept. of Computer Science (2009)

[HMH01] Hernández, M.A., Miller, R.J., Haas, L.M.: Clio: A Semi-Automatic Tool For Schema Mapping. In: ACM SIGMOD Conf., p. 607 (2001); System Demonstration

[HXK+09] Hassanzadeh, O., Xin, R., Kementsietsidis, A., Lim, L., Miller, R.J., Wang, M.: Linkage Query Writer. In: VLDB Conf. (2009); System Demonstration

[KA04] Kementsietsidis, A., Arenas, M.: Data Sharing Through Query Translation in Autonomous Sources. In: VLDB Conf., pp. 468–479 (2004)

[KAM03] Kementsietsidis, A., Arenas, M., Miller, R.J.: Mapping Data in Peer-to-Peer Systems: Semantics and Algorithmic Issues. In: ACM SIGMOD Conf., vol. 32(2), pp. 325–336 (2003)

[MHH00] Miller, R.J., Haas, L.M., Hernández, M.: Schema Mapping as Query Discovery. In: VLDB Conf., pp. 77–88 (2000)

[PVM+02] Popa, L., Velegrakis, Y., Miller, R.J., Hernández, M.A., Fagin, R.: Translating Web Data. In: VLDB Conf., pp. 598–609 (2002)

[RB01] Rahm, E., Bernstein, P.A.: A Survey of Approaches to Automatic Schema Matching. The VLDB Journal 10, 334–350 (2001)

[RBC+08] Raffio, A., Braga, D., Ceri, S., Papotti, P., Hernández, M.A.: Clip: a Visual Language for Explicit Schema Mappings. In: IEEE ICDE Conf., pp. 30–39 (2008)

[UGM07] Udrea, O., Getoor, L., Miller, R.J.: Leveraging Data and Structure in Ontology Integration. In: ACM SIGMOD Conf., pp. 449–460 (2007)

[YMHF01] Yan, L.L., Miller, R.J., Haas, L., Fagin, R.: Data-Driven Understanding and Refinement of Schema Mappings. In: ACM SIGMOD Conf., vol. 30(2), pp. 485–496 (2001)

[YP04] Yu, C., Popa, L.: Constraint-Based XML Query Rewriting For Data Integration. In: ACM SIGMOD Conf., vol. 33(2), pp. 371–382 (2004)

A Generic Set Theory-Based Pattern Matching Approach for the Analysis of Conceptual Models

Jörg Becker, Patrick Delfmann, Sebastian Herwig, and Łukasz Lis

University of Münster, European Research Center for Information Systems (ERCIS), Leonardo-Campus 3, 48149 Münster, Germany
{becker,delfmann,herwig,lis}@ercis.uni-muenster.de

Abstract. Recognizing patterns in conceptual models is useful for a number of purposes, like revealing syntactical errors, model comparison, and identification of business process improvement potentials. In this contribution, we introduce an approach for the specification and matching of structural patterns in conceptual models. Unlike existing approaches, we do not focus on a certain application problem or a specific modeling language. Instead, our approach is generic making it applicable for any pattern matching purpose and any conceptual modeling language. In order to build sets representing structural model patterns, we define operations based on set theory, which can be applied to arbitrary sets of model elements and relationships. Besides a conceptual specification of our approach, we present a prototypical modeling tool that shows its applicability.

Keywords: Conceptual Modeling, Pattern Matching, Set Theory.

1 Introduction

The structural analysis of conceptual models has multiple applications. For example, single conceptual models are analyzed in order to check for syntactical errors [1]. In the domain of Business Process Management (BPM), process model analysis helps identifying process improvement potentials [2]. Whenever modeling is conducted in a distributed way, model integration is necessary to obtain a coherent view on the modeling domain. Multiple models are compared with each other to find corresponding fragments and to evaluate integration opportunities [3].

Structural model patterns can be applied in these scenarios to support modelers in their analyses. In the BPM domain, for example, model patterns can help identifying media disruptions, lack of parallelism, or redundancies. Model patterns have already been subject of research in the fields of database schema integration and workflow management, to give some examples. However, our literature review shows that existing approaches are limited to a specific domain or restricted to a single modeling language (cf. Section 2). We argue that the modeling community would benefit from a more generic approach, which is not limited to particular modeling languages or application scenarios.

In this paper, we present a set theory-based model pattern matching approach, which is generic and thus not restricted regarding its application domain or modeling language. We base this approach on set theory as any model can be regarded as a set of objects

A.H.F. Laender et al. (Eds.): ER 2009, LNCS 5829, pp. 41–54, 2009.

and relationships – regardless of the model's language or application domain. Set operations are used to construct any structural model pattern for any purpose. Therefore, we propose a collection of functions acting on sets of model elements and define set operators to combine the resulting sets of the functions (cf. Section 3). This way, we are able to specify structural model patterns in form of expressions built up of the proposed functions and operators. These pattern descriptions can be matched against conceptual models resulting in sets of model elements, which represent particular pattern occurrences. As a specification basis, we use a generic meta-meta model being able to instantiate any modeling language. To illustrate the application of the approach, we provide an application example for Event-driven Process Chains (EPCs) [4] (cf. Section 4) and present a prototypical modeling tool implementation (cf. Section 5). Finally, we conclude our paper and outline the further need for research (cf. Section 6).

2 Related Work

Fundamental work is done in the field of graph theory addressing the problem of graph pattern matching [3, 6, 7]. Based on a given graph, these approaches discuss the identification of structurally equivalent (homomorphism) or synonymous (isomorphism) parts of the given graph in other graphs. To identify such parts, several pattern matching algorithms are proposed, which compute walks through the graphs in order to analyze the nodes and the structure of the graphs. As a result, they recognize patterns representing corresponding parts of the compared graphs. Thus, a pattern is based on a particular labeled graph section and is not predefined independently. Some approaches are limited to specific types of graphs (e.g., the approaches of [5, 6] are restricted to labeled directed graphs).

In systems analysis and design, so-called *Design Patterns* are used to describe best-practice solutions for common recurring problems. Common design situations are identified, which can be modeled in various ways. The most desirable solution is identified as a pattern and recommended for further usage. The general idea originates from [7], who identified and described patterns in the field of architecture. [8] and [9] popularized this idea in the domain of object-oriented systems design. Workflow Patterns is another dynamically developing research domain regarding patterns [10]. However, the authors of these approaches do not consider pattern matching. Instead, the modeler is expected to manually adopt the patterns as best-practice and to apply them intuitively whenever a common problem situation is met. An implementable pattern matching support is not addressed.

In the domain of database engineering, various approaches have been presented, which address the problem of schema matching. Two input schemas (i.e., descriptions of database structures) are taken and mappings between semantically corresponding elements are produced [11]. These approaches operate on single elements only [12] or assume that the schemas have a tree-like structure [13]. Recently, the methods developed in the context of database schema matching have been applied in the field of ontology matching as well [14]. Additionally, approaches explicitly dedicated to matching ontologies have been presented. They usually utilize additional context information (e.g., a corresponding a collection of documents [15]), which is not given in standard conceptual modeling settings. Moreover, as schema matching approaches operate on approximation basis, only similar structures – and not exact pattern occurrences – are addressed [16]. Consequently, these approaches lack the opportunity of including explicit structure descriptions (e.g., paths of a given length or loops not containing given elements) in the patterns.

Patterns are also proposed as an indicator for possible conflicts typically occurring during the modeling and model integration process. [17] proposes a collection of general patterns for Entity-Relationship Models (ERMs [18]). On the one hand, these patterns depict possible structural errors. For such error patterns corresponding patterns are proposed, which provide correct structures. On the other hand, a number of model patterns is discussed, which possibly lead to conflicts while integrating such models into a total model. Similar work in the field of process modeling is done by [1]. Based on the analysis of EPCs, he detects a collection of general patterns, which depict syntactical errors in EPCs.

In the context of process modeling, so-called behavioral approaches have been proposed [19, 20, 21]. Two process models are considered equivalent if they behave identically during simulation. This implies that the respective modeling languages possess formal execution semantics. Therefore, the authors focus on Petri Nets and related languages [22]. Moreover, due to the requirement of model simulation these approaches generally consider process models as a whole. Patterns as model subsets are only comparable if they are also executable.

Summarizing, applying the analyzed approaches to pattern matching in conceptual models in the contexts outlined in Section 1 leads to a set of restrictions outlined in Table 1.

Table 1. Restrictions of Existing Pattern Approaches

Category	Restriction, Approach
Special preconditions	• Only directed graphs [5, 6] • Only acyclic models [13] • Additional text mining is required [15] • Only suitable for executable models [19, 20, 21, 22]
Similarity-based matching	• Similarity check rather than exact matching [12, 13, 14, 15] • Only patterns with defined number of elements (no paths of arbitrary length etc.) [12, 13, 14, 15] • No element type match, only particular element match [12, 13, 14, 15]
No matching support	• Patterns for reuse [8, 9, 10] • Syntax error patterns [1, 17]

In contrast, we aim at supporting pattern matching in conceptual models of any modeling language and for any type of patterns (i.e., patterns with a predefined or unlimited number of elements). In particular, these are patterns like "activity precedes activity" as well as "path starts and ends with activity". Furthermore, a pattern matching process should return every model section (e.g., *activity 1* precedes *activity 2*) representing an exact match of the pattern (e.g., *activity* precedes *activity*).

3 Specification of Structural Model Patterns

3.1 Sets as a Basis for Pattern Matching

The idea of our approach is to regard a conceptual model as a set of model elements and relationships. Starting from this set, pattern matches are searched by performing set operations on this basic set. By combining different set operations, the pattern is built up successively. Every match found is put into an own set. The following example demonstrates our approach in general.

A pattern definition consists of three objects of different types that are interrelated with each other by relationships. An according pattern match within a model is represented as a set containing three different objects and three relationships that connect them. To distinguish multiple pattern matches, each match is represented as an own set of elements. Thus, the result of a pattern matching process is represented by a set of pattern matches (i.e., a set of sets, cf. Fig. 1).

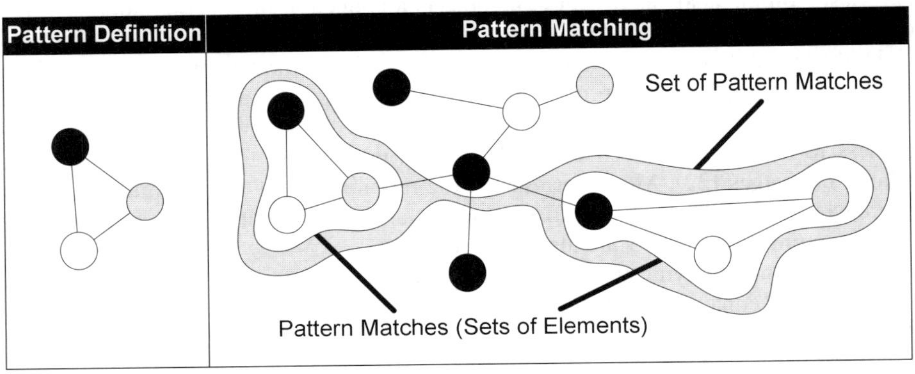

Fig. 1. Representation of Pattern Matches through Sets of Elements

3.2 Definition of Basic Sets

As a basis for the specification of structural model patterns, we use a generic meta-meta model for conceptual modeling languages (cf. Fig. 2), which is closely related to the Meta Object Facility (MOF) specification [23]. Here, we only use a subset, which is represented in the Entity-Relationship notation with (min,max)-cardinalities [24].

Modeling languages typically consist of modeling objects that are interrelated through relationships (e.g., vertices and edges). In some languages, relationships can be interrelated in turn (e.g., association classes in UML Class Diagrams [25]).

Hence, modeling languages consist of *element types*, which are specialized as *object types* (e.g., nodes) and their *relationship types* (e.g., edges and links). In order to allow relationships between relationships, the relationship type is defined as a specialization of the element type. Each relationship type has a *source* element type, from which it originates, and a *target* element type, to which it leads. Relationship types are either *directed* or *undirected*. Whenever the attribute *directed* is FALSE, the direction of the relationship type is ignored. The instantiation of modeling languages leads to models, which consist of particular *elements*. These are *instantiated* from their distinct element type. Elements are specialized into *objects* and *relationships*. Each of the latter leads from a *source* element to a *target* element. Objects can have *values*, which are part of a distinct *domain*. For example, the value of an object "name" contains the

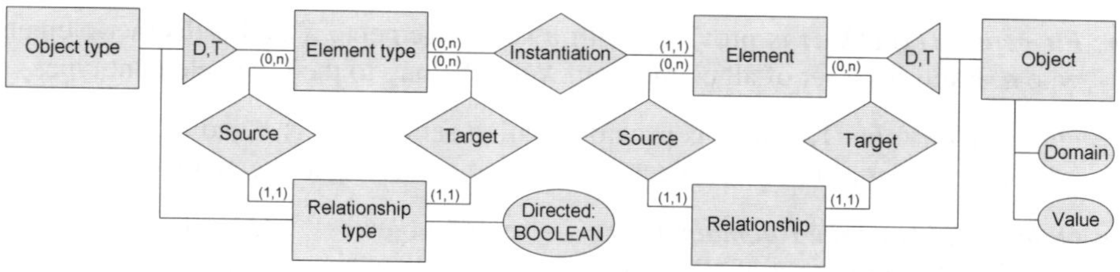

Fig. 2. Generic Specification Environment for Conceptual Modeling Languages and Models

string of the name (e.g., "product"). As a consequence, the domain of the object "name" has to be "string". Thus, attributes are considered as objects.

For the specification of structural model patterns, we define the following sets and elements originating from the specification environment:

- E: finite set of all elements; $e \in E$ is a particular element.
- O: finite set of all objects with $O \subseteq E$; $o \in O$ is a particular object.
- R: finite set of all relationships with $R \subseteq E$; $r \in R$ is a particular relationship.
- A: finite set of all element types; $a \in A$ is a particular element type.
- B: finite set of all object types with $B \subseteq A$; $b \in B$ is a particular object type.
- C: finite set of all relationship types with $C \subseteq A$; $c \in C$ is a particular relationship type.

In addition, we introduce the following notations, which are needed for the specification of set-modifying functions (cf. Section 3.3):

- X: set of elements with $x \in X \subseteq E$.
- X_k: sets of elements with $X_k \subseteq E$ and $k \in \boldsymbol{N_0}$
- Y: set of objects with $y \in Y \subseteq O$.
- Z: set of relationships with $z \in Z \subseteq R$.
- n_X: positive natural number $n_X \in \boldsymbol{N_1}$

3.3 Definition of Set-Modifying Functions

Building up structural model patterns successively requires performing set operations on the basic sets. In the following, we introduce predefined functions on these sets in order to provide a convenient specification environment dedicated to conceptual models. However, in order to make the approach reusable for multiple purposes, the formal specification of these functions is based on *predicate logic*. For clarity reasons, we will not present the detailed formal specifications here. We rather present the functions as black boxes and exclusively focus on their input and output sets.

Each function has a defined number of input sets and returns a resulting set. First, since a goal of the approach is to specify any structural pattern, we must be able to reveal specific properties of model elements (e.g., type, value, or value domain):

- *ElementsOfType(X,a)* is provided with a set of elements X and a distinct element type a. It returns a set of all elements of X that belong to the given element type.
- *ObjectsWithValue(Y,value*$_Y$*)* is provided with a set of objects Y and a distinct value $value_Y$. It returns a set of all objects of Y whose values equal the given one.
- *ObjectsWithDomain(Y,domain*$_Y$*)* takes a set of objects Y and a distinct domain $domain_Y$. It returns a set of all objects of Y whose domains equal the given one.

Second, relations between elements have to be revealed in order to assemble complex pattern structures successively. Functions are required that combine elements and their relationships and elements that are related respectively.

- *ElementsWithRelations(X,Z)* is provided with a set of elements X and a set of relationships Z. It returns a set of sets containing all elements of X and all undirected relationships of Z, which are connected. Each occurrence is represented by an inner set.
- *ElementsWithOutRelations(X,Z)* is provided with a set of elements X and a set of relationships Z. It returns a set of sets containing all elements of X that are connected to directed, outgoing relationships of Z, including these relationships. Each occurrence is represented by an inner set.
- *ElementsWithInRelations(X,Z)* is defined analogously to *ElementsWithOutRelations*. In contrast, it only returns incoming relationships.
- *ElementsDirectlyRelatedInclRelations*(X_1,X_2) is provided with two sets of elements X_1 and X_2. It returns a set of sets containing all elements of X_1 and X_2 that are connected directly via relationships of R, including these relationships. The directions of the relationships given by their "Source" or "Target" assignment are ignored. Furthermore, the attribute "directed" of the according relationship types has to be FALSE. Each occurrence is represented by an inner set.
- *DirectSuccessorsInclRelations*(X_1,X_2) is defined analogously to *ElementsDirectlyRelatedInclRelations.* In contrast, it only returns relationships that are directed, whereas the source elements are part of X_1 and the target elements are part of X_2.

Third, to construct model patterns representing recursive structures (e.g. a path of an arbitrary length consisting of alternating elements and relationships) the following functions are defined:

- *Paths*(X_1,X_n) takes two sets of elements as input and returns a set of sets containing all sequences, which lead from any element of X_1 to any element of X_n. The directions of the relationships, which are part of the paths, given by their "Source" or "Target" assignment, are ignored. Furthermore, the attribute "directed" of the according relationship types has to be FALSE. The elements that are part of the paths do not necessarily have to be elements of X_1 or X_n, but can also be of $E\backslash X_1\backslash X_n$. Each path found is represented by an inner set.
- *DirectedPaths*(X_1,X_n) is defined analogously to *Paths.* In contrast, it only returns directed paths leading from X_1 to X_n.

- *Loops(X)* takes a set of elements as input and returns a set of sets containing all sequences, which lead from any element of X to itself. The directions of the relationships, which are part of the loops, given by their "Source" or "Target" assignment, are ignored. Furthermore, the attribute "directed" of the according relationship types has to be FALSE. The elements that are part of the loops do not necessarily have to be elements of X, but can also be of $E\backslash X$. Each loop found is represented by an inner set.
- *DirectedLoops(X)* is defined analogously to *Loops*. In contrast, it only returns loops, the relationships of which have the same direction.

To avoid infinite sets, only finite paths and loops are returned. As soon as there exists a complete sub-loop on a loop or a path, and this sub-loop is passed the second time, the search aborts. The path or loop that was searched for is excluded from the result set. To provide a convenient specification environment for structural model patterns, we define some additional functions that are derived from those already introduced:

- *ElementsWithRelationsOfType(X,Z,c)* is provided with a set of elements X, a set of relationships Z and a distinct relationship type c. It returns a set of sets containing all elements of X and relationships of Z of the type c, which are connected. Each occurrence is represented by an inner set.
- *ElementsWithOutRelationsOfType(X,Z,c)* is provided with a set of elements X, a set of relationships Z and a relationship type c. It returns a set of sets containing all elements of X that are connected to outgoing relationships of Z of the type c, including these relationships. Each occurrence is represented by an inner set.
- *ElementsWithInRelationsOfType(X,Z,c)* is defined analogously to *ElementsWithOutRelationsOfType*.
- *ElementsWithNumberOfRelations(X,n_X)* is provided with a set of elements X and a distinct number n_X. It returns a set of sets containing all elements of X, which are connected to the given number of relationships of R, including these relationships. Each occurrence is represented by an inner set.
- *ElementsWithNumberOfOutRelations(X,n_X)* is provided with a set of elements X and a distinct number n_X. It returns a set of sets containing all elements of X, which are connected to the given number of outgoing relationships of R, including these relationships. Each occurrence is represented by an inner set.
- *ElementsWithNumberOfInRelations(X,n_X)* is defined analogously to *ElementsWithNumberOfOutRelations*.
- *ElementsWithNumberOfRelationsOfType(X,c,n_X)* is provided with a set of elements X, a distinct relationship type c and a distinct number n_X. It returns a set of sets containing all elements of X, which are connected to the given number of relationships of R of the type c, including these relationships. Each occurrence is represented by an inner set.
- *ElementsWithNumberOfOutRelationsOfType(X,c,n_X)* is provided with a set of elements X, a distinct relationship type c and a distinct number n_X. It returns a set of

sets containing all elements of X, which are connected to the given number of outgoing relationships of R of the type c, including these relationships. Each occurrence is represented by an inner set.

- *ElementsWithNumberOfInRelationsOfType(X,c,n_X)* is defined analogously to *ElementsWithNumberOfOutRelationsOfType*.
- *PathsContainingElements(X_1,X_n,X_c)* is provided with three sets of elements X_1,X_n, and X_c. It returns a set of sets containing elements that represent all paths from elements of X_1 to elements of X_n, which each contain at least one element of X_c. The elements that are part of the paths do not necessarily have to be elements of X_1 or X_n, but can also be of $E \backslash X_1 \backslash X_n$. The directions of the relationships, which are part of the paths, given by their "Source" or "Target" assignment, are ignored. Furthermore, the attribute "directed" of the according relationship types has to be FALSE. Each such path found is represented by an inner set.
- *DirectedPathsContainingElements(X_1,X_n,X_c)* is defined analogously to *PathsContainingElements*. In contrast, it only returns directed paths containing at least one element of X_c and leading from X_1 to X_n.
- *PathsNotContainingElements(X_1,X_n,X_c)* is defined analogously to *PathsContainingElements*. It returns only paths that contain no elements of X_c.
- *DirectedPathsNotContainingElements(X_1,X_n,X_c)* is defined analogously to *DirectedPathsContainingElements*. It returns only paths that contain no elements of X_c.
- *LoopsContainingElements(X,X_c)* is defined analogously to *PathsContainingElements*.
- *DirectedLoopsContainingElements(X,X_c)* is defined analogously to *LoopsContainingElements*. In contrast, it only returns directed loops containing at least one element of X_c.
- *LoopsNotContainingElements(X,X_c)* is defined analogously to *LoopsContainingElements*. It returns only those loops that contain no elements of X_c.
- *DirectedLoopsNotContainingElements(X,X_c)* is defined analogously to *DirectedLoopsContainingElements*. It returns only loops that contain no elements of X_c.

3.4 Definition of Set Operators for Sets of Sets

By nesting the functions introduced above, it is possible to build up structural model patterns successively. The results the functions can be reused adopting them as an input for other functions. In order to combine different results, the basic set operators UNION ($\cup$), INTERSECTION ($\cap$), and COMPLEMENT ($\backslash$) can be used in general. Since it should be possible to combine not only sets of pattern matches (i.e., sets of sets) but also the pattern matches themselves (i.e., the inner sets), we define additional set operators. These operate on the inner sets of two sets of sets respectively.

The UNION operator combines the elements of a set. Applied to sets of sets, it simply puts the inner sets of two sets into a resulting set (cf. Fig. 3).

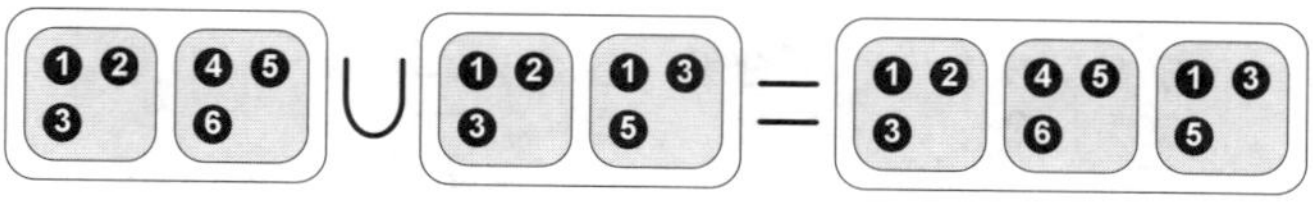

Fig. 3. UNION Operator

The JOIN operator performs a UNION operation on each inner set of the first set with each inner set of the second set. Since we regard patterns as cohesive, only inner sets that have at least one element in common are considered (cf. Fig. 4).

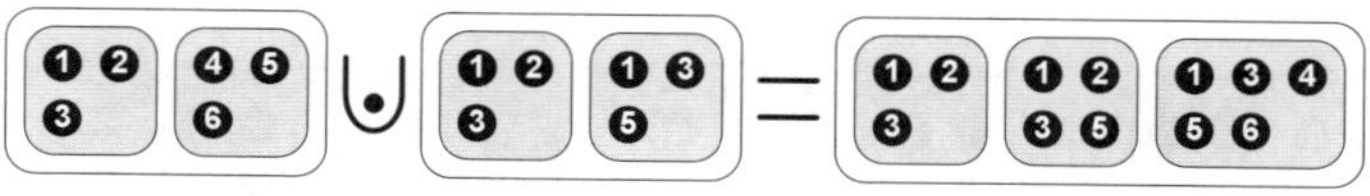

Fig. 4. JOIN Operator

The INTERSECTION operator compares the elements of two sets. Only elements that occur in both sets are put into the resulting set. Applied to sets of sets, it puts the inner sets of two sets containing exactly the same elements into a resulting set (cf. Fig. 5).

Fig. 5. INTERSECTION Operator

The INNER_INTERSECTION operator INTERSECTs each inner set of the first set with each inner set of the second set (cf. Fig. 6).

Fig. 6. INNER_INTERSECTION Operator

Applying the COMPLEMENT operator, elements occurring in the first set are removed if they occur in the second set as well. Applied to sets of sets, inner sets of the first outer set are removed, if they occur in the second outer set as well (cf. Fig. 7).

Fig. 7. COMPLEMENT Operator

The INNER_COMPLEMENT operator applies a COMPLEMENT operation to each inner set of the first outer set with each inner set of the second outer set. Only inner sets that have at least one element in common are considered (cf. Fig. 8)

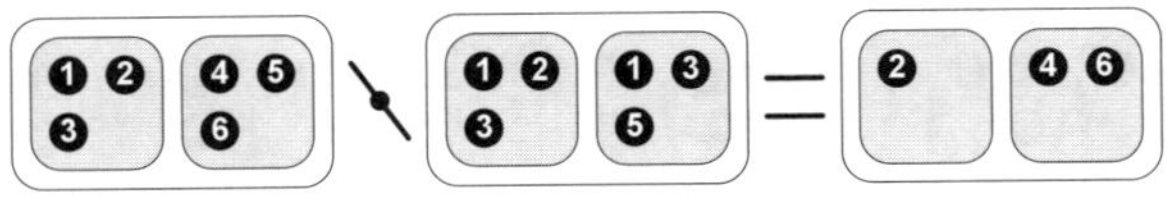

Fig. 8. INNER_COMPLEMENT Operator

Since most of the functions introduced in Section 3.3 expect simple sets of elements as inputs, we introduce further operators that turn sets of sets into simple sets. The SELF_UNION operator merges all inner sets of one set of sets into a single set performing a UNION operation to all inner sets (cf. Fig. 9).

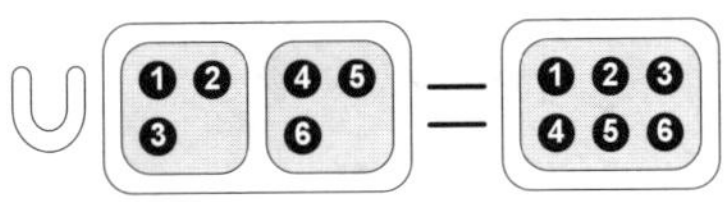

Fig. 9. SELF_UNION Operator

Fig. 10. SELF_INTERSECTION Operator

The SELF_INTERSECTION operator is defined analogously. It performs an INTERSECTION operation to all inner sets of a set of sets successively. The result is a set containing elements that each occur in all inner sets of the original set (cf. Fig. 10).

4 Application of Structural Model Patterns

To illustrate the usage of the set functions, we apply our pattern matching approach to syntax verification in EPCs. Therefore, we regard a simplified modeling language of EPCs. Models of this language consist of the object types *function*, *event*, *AND connector*, *OR connector*, and *XOR connector* (i.e., *B={function, event, AND, OR, XOR}*). Furthermore, EPCs consist of different relationship types that lead from any object type to any other object type, except from *function* to *function* and from *event* to *event*. All these relationship types are directed (i.e., *c.directed=TRUE* $\forall c \in C$).

A common error in EPCs is that decision splits are modeled successively to an event. Since events are passive element types of an EPC, they are not able to make a decision [4]. Hence, any directed path in an EPC that reaches from an event to a function and contains no further events or functions but a XOR or OR split is a syntax error. In order to reveal such errors, we specify the following structural model pattern:

DirectedPathsNotContainingElements (*ElementsOfType (O, 'Event'),* *ElementsOfType (O, 'Function'),* *(ElementsOfType (O, 'Event') UNION ElementsOfType (O, 'Function')))*	1
INTERSECTION	
DirectedPathsContainingElements (*ElementsOfType (O, 'Event'),* *ElementsOfType (O, 'Function'),*	2
((ElementsOfType (O, 'OR') UNION ElementsOfType(O, 'XOR'))	3

COMPLEMENT
(O INNER_INTERSECTION (ElementsWithNumberOfOutRelations (
(ElementsOfType (O, 'XOR') UNION ElementsOfType (O, 'OR')), 1)
UNION ElementsWithNumberOfOutRelations (4
(ElementsOfType (O, 'XOR') UNION ElementsOfType (O, 'OR')), 0)
))))

The first expression (cf. 1st block) determines all paths that start with an *event* and end with a *function* and do not contain any further *functions* or *events*. The result is intersected with all paths starting with an *event* and ending with a *function* (cf. 2nd block) that contain *OR* and/or *XOR* connectors (cf. 3rd block), but only those that are connected to two or more outgoing relationships. Thus, these *XORs* and *ORs* are subtracted by *XORs* and *ORs* that are only connected to one or less relationship(s) (cf. 4th block). Summarizing, all paths are returned that lead from an *event* to a *function* not containing any further *events* and *functions*, and that contain splitting *XOR* and/or *OR* connectors (cf. Section 5 for implementation issues and exemplary results). This way, any syntax error pattern can be specified and applied to any model base.

5 Tool Support

In order to show the feasibility of the approach, we have implemented a plug-in for a meta modeling tool that was available from a former research project [26]. The tool consists of a meta modeling environment that is based on the generic specification approach for modeling languages shown in Fig. 2.

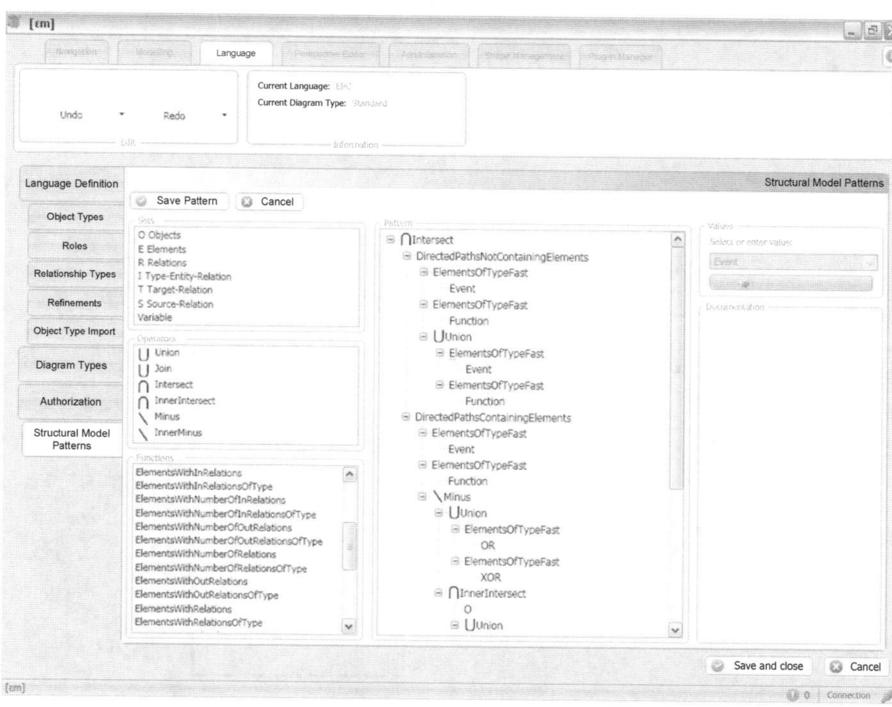

Fig. 11. Specification of the Pattern "Decision Split after Event" to Detect Errors in EPCs

The plug-in provides a specification environment for structural model patterns, which is integrated into the meta modeling environment of the tool, since the patterns are dependent on the respective modeling language. All basic sets, functions, and set operators introduced in Section 3 are provided and can be used to build up structural model patterns successively. In order to gain a better overview over the patterns, they are displayed and edited in a tree structure (cf. Fig. 11; here, the pattern example of Section 4 is shown).

The tree structure is built up through drag-and-drop of the basic sets, functions, and set operators. Whenever special characteristics of an according modeling language (e.g., *function*, *event*, *ET-RIRT*), numeric values, or names are used for the specification, this is expressed by using the "variable" element from the "sets" menu. The variable element, in turn, is instantiated by selecting a language-specific characteristic from the "values" menu or by entering a particular value (such as "2").

The patterns specified can be applied to any model that is available within the model base and that was developed with the according modeling language. Fig. 12 shows an exemplary model that was developed with the modeling language of EPCs and that contains a syntax error consisting of a decision split following an event. The structural model pattern matching process is started by selecting the appropriate pattern to search for. Every match found is displayed by marking the according model section. The user can switch between different matches. In our example, two matches are found, as the decision split following the event leads to two different paths (the second match is shown in the lower right corner of Fig. 12).

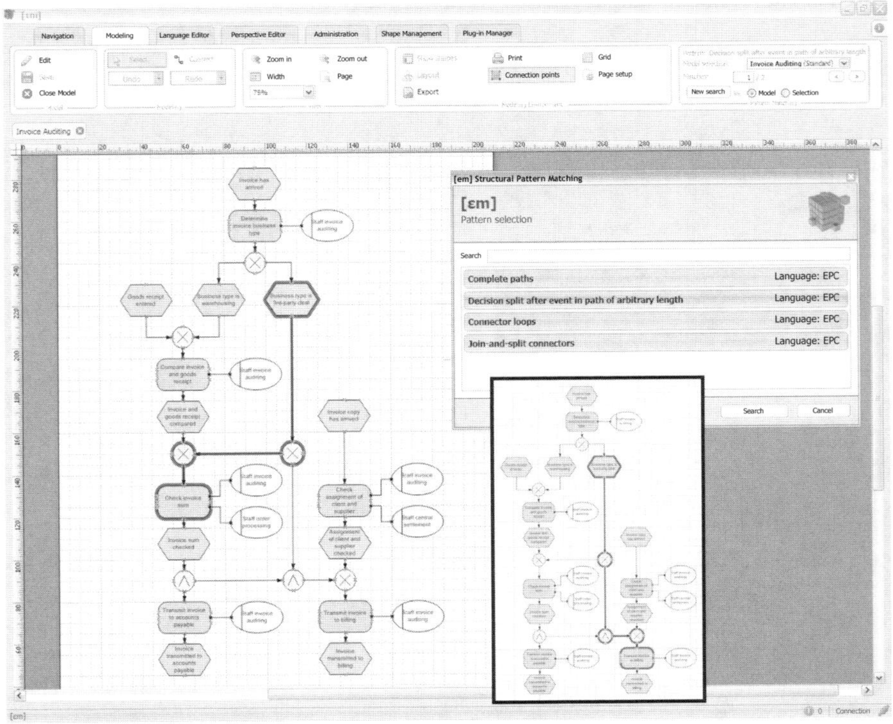

Fig. 12. Result of the Pattern Matching Process of "Decision Split after Event"

6 Conclusion and Outlook

Supporting model analysis by a generic pattern matching approach is promising, since it is not restricted to a particular problem area or modeling language. A first rudimentary evaluation through implementation and exemplary application of the approach has shown its general feasibility. Nevertheless, there still remains need for further research.

Hence, in the short term, we will focus on completing the evaluation of the presented approach. Although our current prototypical implementation already shows its general feasibility, further evaluation of our approach is necessary. We will conduct a series of with-without experiments in real-world scenarios. They will show if the presented function set is complete, if the ease of use is satisfactory for users not involved in the development of the approach, and if the application of the approach actually leads to an improved model analysis support. Although we strongly believe that our tool-implemented approach will inevitably support modelers in the task of model analysis, this needs to be objectively proven.

Medium-term research will address further applications for the structural model pattern matching approach presented here. For instance, we will question if modeling conventions on the basis of structural model patterns that are provided prior to modeling are able to increase the comparability of conceptual models.

References

1. Mendling, J.: Detection and Prediction of Errors in EPC Business Process Models. Doctoral Thesis, Vienna University of Economics and Business Administration (2007)
2. Vergidis, K., Tiwari, A., Majeed, B.: Business process analysis and optimization: beyond reengineering. IEEE Transactions on Systems, Man, and Cybernetics 38(1), 69–82 (2008)
3. Gori, M., Maggini, M., Sarti, L.: The RW2 algorithm for exact graph matching. In: Singh, S., Singh, M., Apté, C., Perner, P. (eds.) Proceedings of the 4th International Conference on Advances in Pattern Recognition, Bath, pp. 81–88 (2005)
4. Scheer, A.-W.: ARIS – Business Process Modelling, 3rd edn., Berlin (2000)
5. Fu, J.: Pattern matching in directed graphs. In: Galil, Z., Ukkonen, E. (eds.) Proceedings of the 6th Annual Symposium on Combinatorial Pattern Matching, pp. 64–77. Espoo (1995)
6. Varró, G., Varró, D., Schürr, A.: Incremental Graph Pattern Matching: Data Structure and Initial Experiments. In: Margaria, T., Padberg, J., Taentzer, G. (eds.) Proceedings of the 2nd International Workshop on Graph and Model Transformation, Brighton (2006)
7. Alexander, C., Ishikawa, S., Silverstein, M. A.: Pattern Language. New York (1977)
8. Gamma, E., Helm, R., Johnson, R., Vlissides, J.: Design Patterns: Elements of Reusable Object-Oriented Software. New York (1995)
9. Fowler, M.: Patterns of Enterprise Application Architecture. Reading (2002)
10. van der Aalst, W.M.P., ter Hofstede, A.H.M., Kiepuszewski, B., Barros, A.P.: Workflow Patterns. Distributed and Parallel Databases 14(3), 5–51 (2003)
11. Rahm, E., Bernstein, P.A.: A survey of approaches to automatic schema matching. The VLDB Journal – The International Journal on Very Large Data Bases 10(4), 334–350 (2001)
12. Li, W., Clifton, C.: SemInt: a tool for identifying attribute correspondences in heterogeneous databases using neural network. Data & Knowledge Engineering 33(1), 49–84 (2000)

13. Madhavan, J., Bernstein, P.A., Rahm, E.: Generic schema matching with Cupid. In: Apers, P.M.G., Atzeni, P., Ceri, S., Paraboschi, S., Ramamohanarao, K., Snodgrass, R.T. (eds.) Proceedings of the 27th International Conference on Very Large Data Bases, Roma, pp. 49–58 (2001)
14. Aumueller, D., Do, H.-H., Massmann, S., Rahm, E.: Schema and ontology matching with COMA++. In: Proceedings of the 2005 ACM SIGMOD international Conference on Management of Data (SIGMOD 2005), New York, pp. 906–908 (2005)
15. Stumme, G., Mädche, A.: FCA-Merge: Bottom-up merging of ontologies. In: Nebel, B. (ed.) Proceedings of the 17thInternational Joint Conference on Artificial Intelligence, IJCAI 2001, August 4-10, 2001, pp. 225–230 (2001)
16. Shvaiko, P., Euzenat, J.: A Survey of Schema-Based Matching Approaches. In: Spaccapietra, S. (ed.) Journal on Data Semantics IV. LNCS, vol. 3730, pp. 146–171. Springer, Heidelberg (2005)
17. Hars, A.: Reference Data Models: Foundations of Efficient Data Modeling. In: German: Referenzdatenmodelle. Grundlagen effizienter Datenmodellierung, Wiesbaden (1994)
18. Chen, P.P.-S.: The Entity-Relationship Model: Toward a Unified View of Data. ACM Transactions on Database Systems 1(1), 9–36 (1976)
19. Hirschfeld, Y.: Petri nets and the equivalence problem. In: Börger, E., Gurevich, Y., Meinke, K. (eds.) Proceedings of the 7th Workshop on Computer Science Logic, Swansea, pp. 165–174 (1993)
20. de Medeiros, A.K.A., van der Aalst, W.M.P., Weijters, A.J.M.M.: Quantifying process equivalence based on observed behavior. Data & Knowledge Engineering 64(1), 55–74 (2008)
21. Hidders, J., Dumas, M., van der Aalst, W.M.P., ter Hofstede, A.H.M., Verelst, J.: When are two workflows the same? In: Atkinson, M., Dehne, F. (eds.) Proceedings of the 11th Australasian Symposium on Theory of Computing, pp. 3–11. Newcastle (2005)
22. van Dongen, B.F., Dijkman, R., Mendling, J.: Measuring similarity between business process models. In: Bellahsene, Z., Léonard, M. (eds.) Proceedings of the 20th International Conference on Advanced Information Systems Engineering, Montpellier, pp. 450–464 (2008)
23. Object Management Group (OMG): Meta Object Facility (MOF) Core Specification. Version 2.0 (2009), `http://www.omg.org/spec/MOF/2.0/PDF`
24. ISO: Concepts and Terminology for the conceptual Schema and the Information Base. Technical report ISO/TC97/SC5/WG3 (1982)
25. Object Management Group (OMG): Unified Modeling Language (OMG UML), Infrastructure, V2.1.2 (2009), `http://www.omg.org/docs/formal/07-11-04.pdf`
26. Delfmann, P., Knackstedt, R.: Towards Tool Support for Information Model Variant Management – A Design Science Approach. In: Österle, H., Schelp, J., Winter, R. (eds.) Proceedings of the 15th European Conference on Information Systems (ECIS 2007), St. Gallen, pp. 2098–2109 (2007)

An Empirical Study of Enterprise Conceptual Modeling

Ateret Anaby-Tavor[1], David Amid[1], Amit Fisher[1], Harold Ossher[2], Rachel Bellamy[2], Matthew Callery[2], Michael Desmond[2], Sophia Krasikov[2], Tova Roth[2], Ian Simmonds[2], and Jacqueline de Vries[2]

[1] Haifa and [2] IBM T.J. Watson Research Centers
{atereta,davida,amitf}@il.ibm.com, {ossher,rachel,mcallery, mdesmond,kras,tova,simmonds,devries}@us.ibm.com

Abstract. Business analysts, business architects, and solution consultants use a variety of practices and methods in their quest to understand business. The resulting work products could end up being transitioned into the formal world of software requirement definitions or as recommendations for all kinds of business activities. We describe an empirical study about the nature of these methods, diagrams, and home-grown conceptual models as reflected in real practice at IBM. We identify the models as artifacts of "enterprise conceptual modeling". We study important features of these models, suggest practical classifications, and discuss their usage. Our survey shows that the "enterprise conceptual modeling" arena presents a variety of descriptive models, each used by a relatively small group of colleagues. Together they form a "long tail" that extends from "drawings" on one end to "standards" on the other.

Keywords: Conceptual modeling, Business analysis, Modeling techniques.

1 Introduction

Conceptual modeling is defined as the process of formally documenting a problem domain for the purpose of understanding and communicating among stakeholders [19]. Most of the published research in the conceptual modeling space is theoretical, conceptual, and/or analytical, with a limited share of empirical papers [15]. Hence, the research presented in this paper is an empirical study into the nature of the conceptual models used in practice. Traditionally, it is acknowledged that "in practice, almost all conceptual models are used to develop, acquire, or modify information systems" (Moody et al. [15]). However, recent studies [3][16] observed that "conceptual modeling" has gained popularity for purposes beyond traditional systems analysis and design. This paper aims to corroborate this contemporary approach by providing insight into business stakeholders' usage of conceptual modeling and the nature of the artifacts they create. Throughout this paper we use the term *enterprise conceptual models* to refer to conceptual models that focus on the business\enterprise domain rather than the traditional information systems domain.

The significance of this research lies in its theoretical, empirical, and practical levels. This study contributes to the extant body of research by contributing to the understanding of the special characteristics of enterprise conceptual modeling,

A.H.F. Laender et al. (Eds.): ER 2009, LNCS 5829, pp. 55–69, 2009.

thereby recognizing it as a sub-discipline of conceptual modeling. Empirically, we focus on two aspects: the nature of enterprise conceptual models and the nature of business stakeholders' practice. Specifically we try to answer the following questions:

- For what tasks do practitioners use conceptual models?
- What types of conceptual models do practitioners use while undertaking each task?
- What types of methods/guidance do practitioners use to support their conceptual models?
- How can business stakeholders distinguish drawings from conceptual models?

Practically, we aim to provide guidelines to practitioners, tool vendors, and researchers that will help increase the quality and usefulness of enterprise conceptual modeling.

The rest of the paper is organized as follows: Section 2 describes related work. Section 3 specifies our research method and Sections 4 describes the empirical results on the nature of enterprise conceptual models and the nature of business stakeholders' practice. We conclude in Section 5.

2 Related Work

Kaindal et al. [12] examined why, for many years, research results in requirements engineering (RE) have been developed without much interaction with, or impact on, industrial practice. Conceptual modeling as a sub-discipline of requirements engineering suffers from the lack of empirical studies as well. Though the need for such studies is well recognized, very little research exists [14]. Most of the published research in the conceptual modeling space is theoretical, conceptual, and/or analytical, with a limited share of empirical papers [15]. Davis et al. [7] noted the lack of empirical investigation of modeling in practice. Their work, however, was limited in that it was a survey based only on web textual interviews and focused on conceptual modeling in the software engineering space. They described the principal tools and techniques, and the purposes for which conceptual modeling is performed. In particular, they described differences due to the size of the organization and years of experience. Others [17] [4] interviewed experienced consultants to explore the advantages and disadvantages of process modeling, which covers 30% of the conceptual modeling space [7]. Of the few empirical studies, most concentrated on process modeling, a sub discipline of enterprise conceptual modeling [4][9][17]. Davis et al. provide further background on other empirical studies, which are either dated (done in the late 1980s), focused on system development, or limited to interviews [7].

Amber [1] claims that the vast majority of modeling teams are sketching and not using CASE or CAD tools. Although Amber mainly refers to software teams, his finding counters approaches like that of H. Kilov et al [10] that suggest the RM-ODP standard for semantic interoperability between the different business stakeholders. Our experience shows that in reality, business analysts prefer using their own plurality of methods with different guidelines, patterns, syntaxes, and notations. Corroborating that, a recent survey [16] concluded that enterprise modeling activities require a modeling expert. In fact, most modeling experts look for tools that provide as much freedom as possible.

3 Background and Research Method

The genesis of this research was a three-day workshop in June 2007 for 12 IBM business architects. The workshop focused on attendees' life in the field. A central finding of that workshop was that business analysts use a holistic approach, including ideas from business and, to a lesser extent, IT. They gather information relevant to a business or pre-identified business problem, and then organize and make sense of it to identify business issues and potential solutions. A presentation is created that is used to communicate to a client proposed solutions and their value to the client's business. Thus business analysts help their clients frame business problems and explore a variety of feasible solutions. Their role is one of envisioning that often results in business transformation. The final outcome of their work is a presentation or report, containing a variety of tables, business process diagrams, organizational diagrams, as-is system diagrams, etc.

Template reuse is a common working style. This is particularly true for consultants who apply their accumulated experience and expertise to address similar issues for a series of clients. Templates help organize findings into pre-defined categories and representations that have been found helpful in past engagements. Often the template will be adapted to fit the needs of a particular engagement. A common adaptation is to change the style and vocabulary to fit the storyline, taste, and culture of the client.

To further understand the nature of their day-to-day work and the artifacts they produce, we sent an appeal to the broad community of business analyst thought leadership in IBM. The goal was to understand how conceptual models are used in day-to-day practice by collecting a large number of "home grown" conceptual models that have an underlying structure and are likely to be reused in many engagements. We got around 60 actual requests to take part in the experiment, with approximately 70 artifacts such as slide decks and reports. Sixty percent of the participants were business architects or business consultants from various industries and divisions, such as finance, the public sector, sales, marketing, and business development. They included solution consultants, strategy consultants, portfolio architects, application architects, and more. The rest of the participants came from other divisions of the company. The survey in this paper is based on a sample of 186 different diagrams that were elicited from the above collection, each serving as a representative of a distinct conceptual model or drawing. Accordingly, the figures of conceptual models and diagrams in this paper are real artifacts, in which meaningful text has been obfuscated for the sake of confidentiality.

Our sample shows that artifacts can be grouped according to the following formality levels:

- Unstructured diagrams – drawings
- Semi-structured diagrams – "home grown" conceptual models
- Fully structured diagrams – standards or "known methods" that have established norms and vast agreement on their syntax and structural constraints like ERD

Although semi-structured diagrams represent more "fuzzy" models than the fully structured diagrams, they still obey specific syntactic rules (as opposed to drawings). Such semi-structured artifacts are likely to be built within client projects, and gain more structure over time. In our collection, 108 diagrams were identified as semi-structured diagrams; this was the majority (58%) of diagrams in our sample, 73 (39%) of the artifacts were drawings and 5 (3%) work products were based on standards. The significant number of semi-structured artifacts probably stems from the fact that we deliberately asked for "home grown" conceptual models that are likely to be reused across engagements. In this paper we focus on the characteristics of the "home grown" conceptual models, comparing them to drawings and standards. We chose to focus on graphic models, although some of the participants sent us text documents and MS-Excel files.

In the next section, we provide our analysis of the results and conclusions. All the qualitative analysis was done in the form of dual coding. When the artifact analysis was not clear or was subjective, we returned to the practitioner who sent the artifact and consulted them on the appropriate analysis. Throughout this paper, we measure the strength of relationships between different factors (such as method, repeated instances, associated task context, etc.) associated with the diagrams. We use two statistical coefficients both are adequate for nominal data:

A. The Goodman and Kruskal Lambda coefficient [8] is used for its asymmetric flavor when we want to measure predictive associations between two factors. It introduces the proportional reduction in error (PRE) measure, which means that its value reflects the percentage reduction in errors in predicting the dependent variable given knowledge of the independent variable. This coefficient takes values on the unit interval, while a value of unity indicates a perfect predictive association. We designate a dependency of factor A on factor B by: $\lambda_{A|B}$. For example, a lambda of .35 means that there was a 35% reduction in error in predicting the dependent variable when the independent variable was taken into account.

B. Cramer's *V* [18] is used to measure the symmetric association between two attributes. It compares the observed joint distribution of the two variables and the expected one (if there was no correlation). The square of the result indicates how much shared variance is taken into account by the relationship. As in the Lambda coefficient, the closer the result is to unity, the stronger the relationship. We designate Cramer's *V* correlation by: V_c.

It's worth noting that 9% of the diagrams (16 diagrams) were obtained within an eclectic deck. To keep the sample unbiased, these diagrams were used only where the values of examined attributes were known. Therefore these diagrams were used in the analysis that appears till Section 4.3.

4 The Nature and Practice of Enterprise Conceptual Modeling

In this section, we describe useful classifications and characteristics of the artifacts in our sample. Such artifacts gain structure incrementally over time. Consequently, elements of the conceptual model become repeatable constructs, with certain relationships between them, when practitioners must utilize the same way of thinking in different environments, e.g., in a different engagement. This is the point in time where sketching transforms into a semi-structured artifact. We further discuss the elements in the research framework on conceptual modeling as defined by Wand and Weber [20]. We examine the context in which conceptual models are created and evaluate the types of methods that accompany them. We believe these insights illuminate important aspects in the nature and practice of the enterprise conceptual modeling world.

4.1 What Tasks Do Practitioners Use Conceptual Models for?

Wand et al. [20] assert that the creation and use of conceptual models are undertaken within a particular context termed the task contextual factor. Moreover, Wyssusek et al. [22] claim that conceptual modeling is not an end in itself; the conceptual models eventually created are not a terminal but an intermediate goal since those models—once created—serve as means for further ends. Specifically, Kung et al. [13] identify the following uses for conceptual models: Helping analysts to reason about domains; Communication between analysts and users; Communication between analysts and designers; Documenting system requirements for future reference. Following we describe the tasks for which the conceptual models in our sample were meant.

Table 1. Context usages

Context topic	Description	# models	Percentage
Organizational structure	Organizational structural forms, sub-units, hierarchies, entity interaction	26	24%
IT architecture	Technology components/layers	18	17%
Service centers	Organizational competencies and components	13	12%
Business context	Relationships between business systems/entities, business concepts interaction	9	8%
Corporate culture	Social relationships, vision, values, focus	9	8%
Value chain management	Value creation, Value capturing, Value networks	7	6%
Competition landscape	Competitive performance, competitive advantage, players in business environment	6	6%
Business operations architecture	Process models, hierarchies and decompositions	4	4%
Solution offering/application portfolio	To-be view of application portfolio, architectural building blocks-systems, sub-systems	4	4%
Organize/generate ideas/concepts	Change management, decision making, mappings	4	4%
Documentation	As-is models, manuals, proposals	3	3%
Information entities interaction	Concepts of information and their relationships/associations	2	2%
Requirements analysis	Use cases and flows	2	2%
Financial analysis	Cost vs. revenue	1	1%

Table 1 presents a list of context topics, the themes each topic encompasses, and the usage frequency of each theme as found in our sample. The table clearly demonstrates that *organizational structure, IT architecture, and service centers are the three prominent topics accounting for more than 50% of the artifacts.* We are aware that the second and third themes may be related to the specific audience of participants, as both are typical of the work of IBM consultants. These three context topics also lead to the corollary that *the prevailing task of the practitioners in our sample is the alignment of IT with business aspects*. The next discussion examines the relations between these tasks and the types of conceptual models used for each.

4.2 What Type of Conceptual Models Do Practitioners Use While Undertaking Each Task?

We classified the conceptual models into families according to common properties and underlying structures. Such a categorization may reveal that some families are more typically used for certain tasks than others, hence guiding practitioners and tool vendors to choose the relevant type of diagram for the task at hand. The following is the list of families extracted from our sample with our interpretation of each family:
A. Nodes and edges (graphs) – all the members of this group comprise edges that connect pairs of nodes. Some may have directed edges (in the form of arrows), while others may have unconnected nodes.
B. Tables – the underlying model of the members of this group is composed of a composite object that has part-whole hierarchies with column objects, which in turn have part-whole hierarchies with row objects. Rows can further contain components or free text.
C. Trees - models in this family have an underlying connected acyclic graph with hierarchical structure. It is worth noting that some of the diagrams included aberrations from the original underlying structure. For example, Fig. 2 shows a "mind map" hierarchy with relations between leaves.
D. Cartesian coordinate systems – family members have static axes where points / shapes are placed in a plane.
E. Layer diagrams - elements in these diagrams are placed above one another and may be semi-detached. Some of these models may demonstrate hierarchal relationships between elements (by using hierarchical numbering of these elements).
F. Circle/Onion maps – diagrams are in the form of concentric circles sometimes with the addition of slices. Fig. 1 shows an example of such diagram.

The above categories are not necessarily mutually exclusive nor are they exhaustive. For example, the trees group can certainly be viewed as a subset of the graphs family. In the same way, "stars" (which are very significant to social network analysis) can be viewed as another distinct group of graphs. Four-square models (which are commonly used in strategy and market analysis) can also be viewed as a distinct group within the coordinate system family.

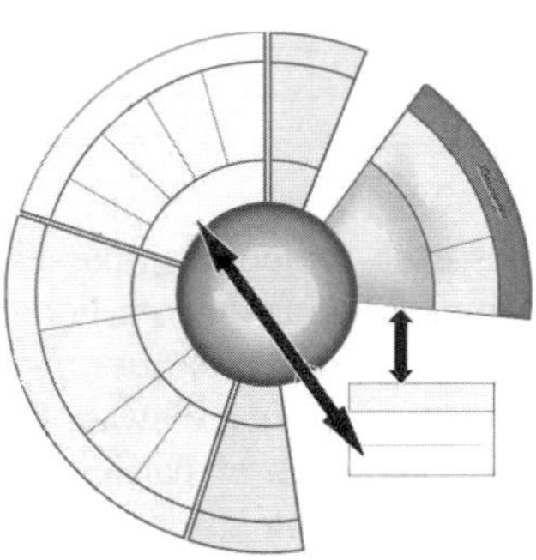

Fig. 1. An Onion Map

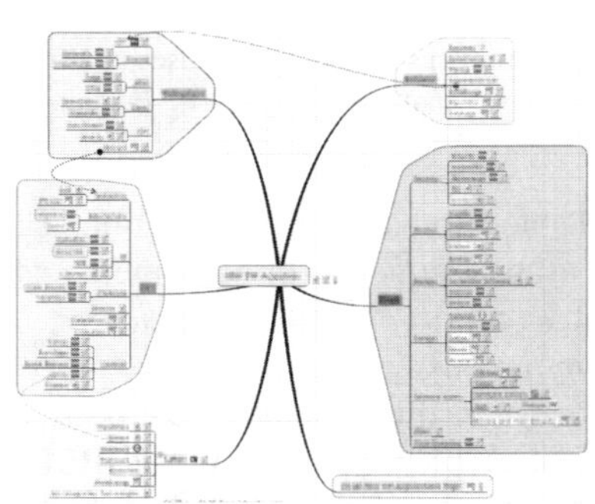

Fig. 2. A mind map hierarchy

Fig. 3 shows the distribution of our sample according to families. According to our sample, the graph family is the largest, with 49% of the diagrams. Together with trees, they form 60% of the sample. It is interesting to note that 37% of the graphs' artifacts were flow charts (which form 13% of the whole sample). Next we examine if there is a correlation between the task at hand and the type of conceptual model selected to undertake it.

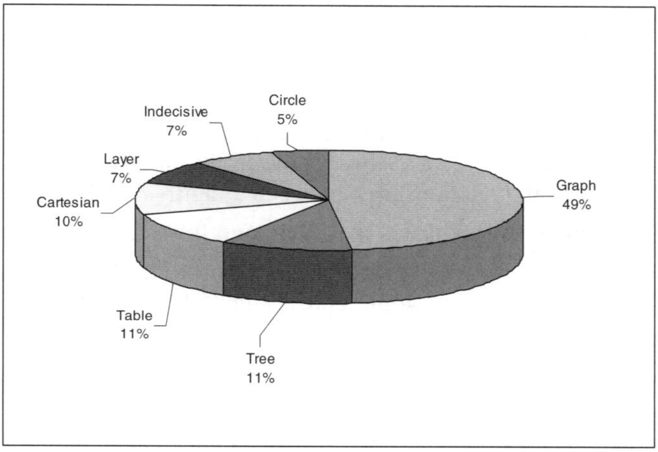

Fig. 3. Semi-structured models' distribution according to families

Table 2. Frequencies of context topics for each family

	Graph	Tree	Flow Chart	Circle	Layer	Table	Cartesian	Unknown
Organizational structure	11%	**75%**	21%		25%	8%	9%	75%
Service centers			7%		25%	**75%**	9%	
Information entities interaction	5%							
Business operations architecture	3%	8%	7%		13%			
Solution offering/application portfolio	5%	8%					9%	
Corporate culture	5%			20%		8%	**45%**	
Competition landscape	8%				13%		18%	
IT architecture	26%	8%		40%	25%	8%	9%	13%
Value chain management	5%		**29%**					13%
Organize/generate ideas/concepts	11%							
Business context	18%			40%				
Financial analysis	3%							
Documentation			21%					
Requirements analysis			14%					

Table 2 presents the data frequencies of context topics for each family. Percentages were computed longitudinally for each family category, and results of 0% were removed for the sake of legibility. Indeed *it is apparent that some families are more typically used for certain tasks than others.* Comparing the frequencies of context topics across the families reveals that the IT architecture and the Organizational structure topics are quite dominant and appear in almost every family. In addition, some topics are very dominant in a specific family although they also appear in others – for example, 75% of the diagrams in the tree family relate to the organizational structure context topic. In the same way, 75% of the diagrams in the table family relate to the service centers context topic, and corporate culture/social relationships form 45% of the Cartesian coordinates family. This analysis leads us to the hypothesis that there is a correlation between the family of a diagram and its context. The general relationship between family and context resulted in: $V_c = 0.512$. This result indicates that such a correlation exists, thus supporting our hypothesis. Next we used the Lambda coefficient to try to obtain a measure of the dependency between context topic and the underlying family of the diagram. The result for family dependency on context is $\lambda_{Family|Context} = 0.343$. This mild correlation can be validated by looking at Table 2. Consider, for example, the topics of financial analysis, organize/generate ideas, information entities interaction, service centers, and business context. Each of these topics has only one suitable family. This is less prominent in the opposite direction, i.e., the degree to which a family indicates the appropriate context. For example, the graph family has several appropriate context topics. Therefore, a smaller coefficient was obtained, and $\lambda_{Contex|Family} = 0.256$. These findings imply *that some families are more typically used for certain tasks than others, hence practitioners and CASE tools may suggest a layout for a conceptual model based on the required context.*

Table 3 presents the data frequencies of context topics according to drawing\conceptual model characteristics. Percentages were computed for each topic across characteristics. Our hypothesis is that *certain context topics increase the likelihood of a diagram being a conceptual model and other contexts increase the likelihood of a diagram being merely a drawing.* Such a correlation may help in providing the right kind of diagram for specific communication needs. The data demonstrate a pronounced relationship between the context of a diagram and its characteristic resulting in $V_c = 0.625$. Further examination of the dependency between the two variables yields $\lambda_{Characteristics|Context} = 0.493$. It is worth noting that the opposite question, i.e., whether we could predict context from characteristics yields $\lambda_{Context|Characteristics} = 0.0533$, which prompts that characteristics is dependant on context. In other words, for a specific task, practitioners may prefer a conceptual model rather than merely a drawing. These results *may help in directing practitioners to decide whether to use a drawing or a conceptual model for a given task.* In addition, *it may guide tool developers in their quest for the right editors for the business analysts' community by answering questions like: What tasks will probably be done when using syntax aware editors* [5][6].

Table 3. Frequencies of context topics vs. diagram characteristics

	CM	Drawings	Total
Organizational structure	26 (84%)	5 (16%)	31
Service centers	13 (81%)	3 (19%)	16
Information entities interaction	2 (100%)	0	2
Business operations arch	4 (57%)	3 (43%)	7
solution offering/application portfolio	4 (27%)	11 (73%)	15
Knowledge management	0	2 (100%)	2
Corporate culture/social relationships	9 (90%)	1 (10%)	10
Competition landscape/competitive performance/competitive advantage/players in business environment	6 (100%)	0	6
IT architecture	18 (78%)	5 (22%)	23
Value chain management/value creation/value capturing	7 (78%)	2 (22%)	9
Organize/generate ideas/concepts	4 (67%)	2 (33%)	6
Business context	9 (41%)	13 (59%)	22
Financial analysis/cost vs. revenue	1 (11%)	8 (89%)	9
Documentation	3 (100%)	0	3
Requirements analysis	2 (33%)	4 (67%)	6
Misc. - business models	0	13 (100%)	13
Plans, e.g., steps over time	0	1 (100%)	1
Total	108	73	181

4.3 What Types of Methods/Guidance Do Practitioners Use to Support Their Conceptual Models?

Several scholars have addressed the topic of conceptual modeling methods. According to Wyssusek et al. [22], modeling methods are tools that help accomplish a task—the creation and representation of conceptual models. Thus, modeling methods are technologies, i.e., a means to an end. Accordingly, Wand et al. [20] describe conceptual modeling methods as aids to the creation of faithful representations using conceptual models that conform to an associated grammar that defines the syntax of the conceptual model. They claim that grammars are often well formalized, but their creators provide neither a detailed nor unambiguous way of using them. Lastly, Davies et al. [7] show that inexperienced practitioners make strong use of techniques and methods. As experience is gained, however, usage decreases significantly. We next present our findings and conclusions in connection with the existence of method for grammar (i.e. method for describing how to use the constructs defined in the grammar) in our sample. Often grammars are well formalized but their creators provide neither a detailed nor unambiguous way of using them [20]. We conclude the discussion on method existence with an analysis on the usage of method for phenomena, i.e., the kind of guidelines that enable stakeholders to identify the phenomena to be modeled.

Our sample shows that methods for grammar are either full or partial. When a diagram was accompanied with a comprehensive explanation of its building blocks and constructs, we clustered it under the "full method" classification. An example for a “full method” is a comprehensive description of the constructs done in the Process Modeling Notation (BPMN) standard specification [21]. The opposite was true for the "no method" classification. When only a partial explanation was provided – e.g., for only some of the constructs — the "partial method" classification was selected. An

Table 4. Source of artifact vs. degree of method for grammar

	Total		No method		Partial method		Full method	
	#	%	#	%	#	%	#	%
Dedicated	44	48%	32	35%	7	8%	5	5%
Engagement	48	52%	42	45%	6	7%	0	0%
Totals	92[1]	100%	74	80%	13	15%	5	5%

example for "partial method" is when the accompanied description includes a legend which associates a name for each symbol.

Table 4 presents the relationships between method levels and the source of each artifact within the conceptual models group in our sample.

Artifact sources were designated as either dedicated or engagement artifact. A dedicated artifact is created for the purpose of documenting, educating, and describing the conceptual models it holds. An engagement artifact is a work product that resulted from a client engagement. The table shows that a significant proportion (80%) of the conceptual models in our sample were obtained with no methods associated with their grammars and that only a marginal proportion (5%) had full methods. More than half (52%) of the artifacts in our corpus were work products that resulted from engagements; within these, no "full method" description was found. One might have expected the conceptual models identified as "dedicated" artifacts to be accompanied by explanations of the grammars; however, even within this group (48% of the conceptual models), only 11% were obtained with full methods.

In summary, it appears that our sample adheres to the claims noted above about the scarcity of method explaining the conceptual models' grammars. Our practical corollary for tool vendors is that they should *provide a means for model authors to generate methods for using the grammars that define the syntax of new conceptual models.*

Next we look into the extent of phenomena identification provided by the methods in our sample. For each of the conceptual models we examined the phenomena method for single/multiple grammar [20] which designates whether the conceptual model method provided guidance as to what real-world phenomena the conceptual model is intended to model and how to map those phenomena to the model constructs.

Table 5. Phenomena identification for single grammar

# Conceptual models	# Conceptual models with phenomena method for single grammar	%
92	69	75%

Table 6. Phenomena identification for multi-grammar

# Multi grammar conceptual models	# Conceptual models with phenomena method for multi grammar	%
67	63	94%

[1] From now onward we exclude the artifacts that were obtained within the eclectic deck.

The distinction between single and multiple grammars was important. We noticed that some practitioners provided deliberate guidance regarding the stages in the method and the place of each conceptual model in the complex, and these methods were different from the guidance provided for the mapping of a single conceptual model to the right business circumstances. Table 5 indicates that a high proportion (75%) of the conceptual models was accompanied by a method for determining the right phenomena to be modeled. Table 6 clearly indicates that most of the multi-grammar conceptual models were obtained with such phenomena methods. We assert that this is a fundamental result of our survey, and that *the complexity of multi-grammar conceptual models brought about the necessity to provide guidance for the right phenomena identification when applying them.* We also think this result, combined with the scarcity of methods explaining grammars, might indicate that *practitioners rely on methods for phenomena to compensate for the lack of detailed grammar construct specification and mapping.* Another explanation may be that the practitioners' work is more focused on the business problem at hand than on the methods' constructs and correct grammar.

4.4 How Can Business Stakeholders Distinguish Drawings from Conceptual Models?

Being able to decide what conceptual model each artifact contains is vital for the organization for reuse of intellectual capital captured in conceptual models. Capturing intellectual capital in a reusable form is key to enabling knowledge transfer within an organization. Currently, many organizations suffer from a knowledge transfer problem. The organization seeks to organize, create, capture, or distribute knowledge and ensure its availability for future users [16]. Knowledge transfer is considered to be more than just a communication problem. If it were merely that, then a memorandum, e-mail, or meeting would accomplish the knowledge transfer [10]. The complexity of knowledge transfer stems from the following reasons: A. Knowledge resides in organizational members, tools, tasks, and their subnet works [2]. B. Much knowledge in organizations is tacit or hard to articulate [14]. Hence, in facing an artifact created by a business stakeholder it is important for the organization to understand whether the artifact contains conceptual models that are reusable or merely drawings. This is especially true in the light of template reuse across engagements that was found so prominent in the aforementioned workshop. Automating the cleansing of artifacts, and extracting from them the conceptual models for further use can enable organizations to manage this knowledge transfer problem.

For various business stakeholders, drawings serve to convey thoughts. These diagrams are created to communicate a "one-shot" thought and are not intended to be reproduced in similar contexts. They are missing two major parts relative to conceptual models: grammar and method [20]. As noted, we identified 73 of 186 diagrams as merely drawings – an illustrative explanation that replaces a textual one. We combined our understanding of the artifacts with occasional help from the authors to understand whether a diagram in an artifact is a drawing or a conceptual model (or part of it). As a result of this process we devised a method to distinguish a conceptual model from a drawing. We identified four factors that can influence whether a diagram is defined as a conceptual model or not:

A. Method existence – if the business stakeholder provides within the artifact a detailed and unambiguous description of the constructs of the diagram, and a way of using them in the business circumstances, then they suggest that the diagram is a conceptual model.
B. Multiple interwoven diagrams – if the artifacts contain diagrams that relate to each other then it implies the diagrams are part of a multi-grammar conceptual model.
C. Standard manipulation – if the diagram is a manipulation of a standard, it implies the diagram reflects a conceptual model created by a variation of the standard's conceptual model.
D. Repetitiveness –Diagrams can be repeated with slight modifications and different data/text in the same artifact. If a diagram is repeated it implies the author has found this method of conveying a thought useful enough to be repeated in similar context.

Ideally cleansing an artifact produced in a client engagement yields a template in which consultants can apply their accumulated experience to address similar issues for a series of clients. We assert that these factors can *help experts to accelerate their ability to identify potential for template reuse.* Furthermore, *tool vendors can automate the cleansing procedure by identifying the existence of most if not all of these factors.*

Table 7. Number of diagrams per factor

Characteristic	Total	Manipulation	Method existence	Multiple interwoven diagrams	Repetitiveness
Drawings	29	0 (0%)	8 (28%)	13 (45%)	1 (3%)
Conceptual models	48	7 (15%)	40 (83%)	34 (71%)	17 (35%)

We chose to focus on diagrams in engagement artifacts since the need to cleanse engagement artifacts may be much prominent than the need to cleanse dedicated artifacts. Accordingly, Table 7 presents the frequencies of factors by characteristic in the artifacts that stem from engagements. The parentheses show the ratio between diagrams associated with the appropriate factor and the total diagrams in each characteristic category. The table shows that the two most prominent factors for predicting whether a diagram is a conceptual model or not are method existence (83%) and multiple interwoven diagrams (71%).

The analysis showed that all the conceptual models containing multiple interleaved diagrams were also received with an accompanying method. This evidence led us to conclude that *conceptual models that are multi-grammar are naturally more complex and hence less intuitive—and require method guidance.* Accordingly, a high correlation was found: $V_c = 0.698$ which was evident in both directions: $\lambda_{Multiple \backslash Method} = 0.633$ and $\lambda_{Method \backslash Multiple} = 0.621$.

Our hypothesis is that *the existence of a combination of the aforementioned factors in a diagram will increase the likelihood of it being a conceptual model rather than merely a drawing.* Therefore we checked if the data indicates a relationship between the characteristic of a diagram as a conceptual model\drawing and the number of factors it associated with it. We examined the existence of the following factors: Method existence, Repetitiveness, and Standard manipulation. Out of the two dependent factors "Multiple interwoven diagrams" and "Method existence", we selected "Method existence" due to its prominence. A slight relationship between "Repetitiveness" and "Method existence" was found by the Cramer coefficient ($V_c = 0.239$), nevertheless this finding was neither verified by the Lambda coefficient ($\lambda_{Method|repetitiveness} = 0$, $\lambda_{repetitiveness|Method} = 0$) nor by running the Cramer coefficient over the whole sample (both dedicated and engagement artifacts), and therefore it was considered negligible. All Other factors were found independent of one another. The combined factor values are {0,1,2,3} corresponding to the number of factors that exist in the subject diagram.

Table 8. Characteristic vs. Number of factors

	Conceptual Model	Drawing	Total
0	2 (9%)	20 (91%)	22
1	29 (78%)	8 (22%)	37
2	16 (94%)	1 (6%)	17
3	1 (100%)	0 (0%)	1
Total	48	29	77

Table 8 presents the frequencies of number of factors by characteristic. The parentheses show the percentage of diagrams with each characteristic having the indicated number of factors. Inspection of the table clearly shows that the more factors a diagram has, the more likely it is to be a conceptual model. Accordingly the Cramer correlation coefficient yields a pronounced relationship between the characteristic of a diagram and the existence of the aforementioned factors: $V_c = 0.707$. Furthermore, $\lambda_{Characteristics|CombinedFactor} = 0.621$, so information about these three factors decreases the error in predicting the diagram's characteristic by 62.1%.

5 Conclusions and Future Work

In this paper, we have investigated some major aspects of enterprise conceptual modeling through an empirical analysis over real-world work products. We reported the results relating to two aspects: the nature of enterprise conceptual models and the nature of the business stakeholders practice.

We began by examining the context of the conceptual models in our sample which yielded the result that organizational structure, IT architecture, and service centers are the three prominent topics accounted for more than 50% of artifacts. This led to the corollary that the prevailing task of the practitioners in our sample is the alignment of IT with business aspects. We classified the conceptual models in our sample into six families and threw light on the correlation between the family of a diagram and its context, having some families more typically used for certain tasks than others. Moreover, a pronounced relationship was demonstrated between the context of a diagram and its identification as drawing or conceptual model.

A large proportion of the conceptual models were accompanied by methods for phenomena. We assert that the complexity of multi-grammar conceptual models resulted in the need to provide guidance for the right phenomena identification when applying them. The study corroborated the assertion about scarcity of methods that explain conceptual models' grammars. Our practical corollary to tool vendors is that they should provide a means for conceptual model builders to generate methods for the conceptual model grammar.

Finally, we introduced four factors that positively affect the likelihood of identifying a diagram as a conceptual model rather than merely a drawing. We assert that these factors can help experts to accelerate their ability to identify potential for template reuse, and tool vendors to automate the cleansing procedure by identifying the existence of most, if not all, of these factors.

As future work, we intend to report on additional findings we have revealed in this study and were not reported in this paper such as: the characteristics of the grammar of conceptual models during their early inception phase, and the business stakeholders use of standards. We also plan to extend the empirical study to a wider audience in more industries and disciplines. Consequently, we envision a study into approaches and tools, in which we will develop and support methods and practices that reflect the reality presented here. The outcome of that study would be thorough research into the tooling aspects of the enterprise conceptual modeling arena. This research will aim at combining the benefits of drawing tools with the benefits of modeling tools, and is likely to aid the understanding of the needs of the marketplace in terms of desired features and main pain points.

Acknowledgments. Our thanks go to Dave Bartek for the insights from his world of practice and the examples that appear in this paper.

References

1. Ambler, S.W.: Agilists Write Documentation! Dr. Dobb's (2008), modeling and documentation survey, `http://www.ddj.com/architect/211201940`
2. Argote, L., Ingram, P.: Knowledge transfer A Basis for Competitive Advantage in Firms. Organizational Behavior and Human Decision Processes 82(1), 150–169
3. Bandara, W., Tan, H.W., Recker, J., Indulska, M., Rosemann, M.: Bibliography of process modeling: An Emerging research field. (2007), `http://eprints.qut.edu.au/8754/`
4. Chang, S., Kesari, M., Seddon, P.: A content-analytic study of the advantages and disadvantages of process modeling. In: Burn, J., Standing, C., Love, P. (eds.) ACIS 2003 (2003)
5. Chock, S., Marriot, K.: Automatic generation of intelligent diagram editors. ACM Trans. Comput.-Hum. Interact. 10(3), 244–276 (2003)
6. Costagliola, G., Deufemia, V., Polese, G.: A framework for modeling and implementing visual notations with applications to software engineering. ACM Trans. Softw. Eng. Methodol. 13(4), 431–487 (2004)
7. Davies, I., Green, P., Rosemann, M., Indulska, M., Gallo, S.: How do practitioners use conceptual modeling in practice? Data & Knowledge Engineering 58, 358–380 (2006)
8. Goodman, L.A., Kruskal, W.H.: Measures of association for cross classifications. Part I. J. Amer. Statist. Assoc. 49, 732–764 (1954)

9. Gorla, N., Pu, H.-C., Rom, W.: Evaluation of process tools in systems analysis. Information and Software Technology 37(2), 119–126 (1995)
10. http://en.wikipedia.org/wiki/Knowledge_transfer
11. Kilov, H.: Using RM-ODP to bridge communication gaps between stakeholders Workshop on ODP for Enterprise Computing in the proceedings of WODPEC 2004 (2004), http://www.lcc.uma.es/~av/wodpec2004/
12. Kaindl, H., Brinkkemper, S., Bubenko, J.A., Farbey, B., Greenspan, S.J., Heitmeyer, C.L., Leite, J.C.S.P., Myopolous, M.N.R.J., Siddiqui, J.: Requirements engineering and technology transfer: obstacles, incentives and improvement agenda. Requirements Engineering 7, 113–123 (2002)
13. Kung, C.H., Solvberg, A.: Activity modelling and behaviour modelling. In: Olle, T.W., Sol, H.G., Verrijn-Stuart, A.A. (eds.) Information Systems Design Methodologies: Improving the Practice, IFIP, Amsterdam, North-Holland, pp. 145–171 (1986)
14. Nonaka, I., Takeuchi, H.: The knowledge-creating company. Oxford University Press, New York
15. Moody, D.L.: Theoretical and practical issues in evaluating the quality of conceptual models: current state and future directions. Data & Knowledge Engineering 55, 243–276 (2005)
16. Persson, A., Stirna, J.: Why Enterprise Modelling? An Explorative Study into Current Practice. In: Dittrich, K.R., Geppert, A., Norrie, M.C. (eds.) CAiSE 2001. LNCS, vol. 2068, pp. 465–468. Springer, Heidelberg (2001)
17. Sedera, W., Gable, G., Rosemann, M., Smyth, R.: A success model for business process modeling: findings from a multiple case study. In: Liang, T.P., Zheng, Z. (eds.) 8th Pacific Asia Conference on Information Systems (PACIS 2004), Shanghai (2004)
18. Sheskin, D.J.: Handbook of parametric and nonparametric statistical procedures, 2nd edn. Chapman&Hall/CRC, Boca Raton ISBN 1-58488-133-X
19. Siau, K.: Informational and computational equivalence in comparing information modelling methods. Journal Of Database Management 15(1), 73–86 (2004)
20. Wand, Y., Weber, R.A.: Research commentary: information systems and conceptual modeling—a research agenda. Information Systems Research 13(4), 363–376 (2002)
21. White, S.A.: Business Process Modeling Notation (BPMN) Version 1.0. Business Process Management Initiative, BPMI.org (May 2004)
22. Wyssusek, B., Zaha, J.M.: Towards a pragmatic perspective on requirements for conceptual modeling methods. In: EMMSAD 2007, held in conjunction with the 19th Conference on Advanced Information Systems (CAiSE 2007), Trondheim, Norway, pp. 17–26 (2007)

Formalizing Linguistic Conventions for Conceptual Models

Jörg Becker, Patrick Delfmann, Sebastian Herwig, Łukasz Lis, and Armin Stein

University of Münster, European Research Center for Information Systems (ERCIS), Leonardo-Campus 3, 48149 Münster, Germany
{becker,delfmann,herwig,lis,stein}@ercis.uni-muenster.de

Abstract. A precondition for the appropriate analysis of conceptual models is not only their syntactic correctness but also their semantic comparability. Assuring comparability is challenging especially when models are developed by different persons. Empirical studies show that such models can vary heavily, especially in model element naming, even if they express the same issue. In contrast to most ontology-driven approaches proposing the resolution of these differences ex-post, we introduce an approach that avoids naming differences in conceptual models already during modeling. Therefore we formalize naming conventions combining domain thesauri and phrase structures based on a linguistic grammar. This allows for guiding modelers automatically during the modeling process using standardized labels for model elements. Our approach is generic, making it applicable for any modeling language.

Keywords: Conceptual Modeling, Naming Conventions, Linguistics.

1 Introduction

Empirical studies show that especially those conceptual models which are being developed in a timely and regionally distributed way can vary heavily concerning terms and structure. Thus, so-called *naming conflicts* and *structural conflicts* [1, 2] may occur, even if the same issue is addressed [3]. Moreover, even models of the same issue developed by the same persons at different times may show intense variations. Consequently, the analysis of conceptual models – for example for integration or benchmarking purposes – may be extremely laborious. Information that is expressed in different ways has to be "standardized" in some way in order to make the models comparable. Usually, an according standardization process requires discussions including all involved modelers in order to reach a consensus. Sometimes, even external consultants are involved additionally [4, 5].

In order to solve this problem, approaches are required that are able to assure model comparability. In the literature, there exist many contributions that propose approaches for resolving modeling conflicts in conceptual models subsequent to modeling (cf. Section 2). Unlike these approaches, the goal of this article is to introduce an approach that ensures the comparability of conceptual models by avoiding potential conflicts already *during* modeling. This way, we prevent problems that result

A.H.F. Laender et al. (Eds.): ER 2009, LNCS 5829, pp. 70–83, 2009.

from the ex-post resolution of conflicts and make the standardization process described above dispensable. This article focuses on *naming conflicts*. We define naming conventions for elements of modeling languages and ensure their compliance by an *automated, methodical guiding* during modeling. The conventions are set up using *domain terms* and *phrase structures* that are defined as valid in the regarded modeling context. As a formal specification basis, we use thesauri that provide term conventions not only for nouns but also for verbs and adjectives, including descriptions of their meanings. In order to provide conventions for phrase structures, we make use of a linguistic specification approach. During modeling, model element names are validated simultaneously against both the term and phrase structure conventions. Our approach is generic so that it can be applied to any conceptual modeling language. The approach is suitable for modeling situations, where it is possible to provide all involved stakeholders with the necessary information about the modeling conventions, meaning modeling projects that are determined regarding organization and/or business domain. These modeling situations usually occur in companies, corporate groups, or modeling communities.

This paper is structured as follows. First, we analyze related work on naming conflict resolution in Section 2 and discuss the research gap that led to the development of the approach presented in this paper. Since process model elements are usually named with complex phrases rather than with single terms, they are extra prone to naming conflicts. An explorative analysis of naming practice in process models shows the potential of our approach in the case of process modeling. Furthermore, we outline our research methodology. In Section 3, we introduce a conceptual framework for the specification and enforcement of naming conventions. The feasibility of our approach is shown exemplarily with a demonstrator software in Section 4. We conclude the paper in Section 5 and motivate further research.

2 Foundations

2.1 Related Work

Early approaches of the 1980s and 1990s discussing the resolution of naming conflicts address the integration of company databases and use the underlying *schemas* as a starting point [1, 2, 6, 7]. Hence, these approaches focus on data modeling languages, mostly dialects of the Entity-Relationship Model (ERM) [8]. Names of schema elements are compared, and this way, similarities are revealed. The authors state that such a semantic comparison can exclusively happen manually. Moreover, only single nouns are considered as names. In contrast, in common conceptual modeling languages (especially process modeling languages), names are used that consist of sentence fragments containing terms of any word class. Thus, these early approaches are only suitable for data modeling languages as a specific class of conceptual modeling languages.

Other approaches make use of *ontologies* [9, 10] in order to address the problem of semantic comparison of names. Those approaches can be distinguished into two different kinds. On the one hand, authors act under the assumption that there exists a "generally accepted" ontology describing a certain modeling domain. It is assumed that all considered models of this domain comply with its ontology, meaning that modelers had a thorough knowledge of the ontology *before* the modeling took place. On the other hand, approaches suggest deriving an ontology from the models that have to be analyzed, which has to be performed *after* the modeling took place.

There are a few examples for the former approach. For example, [11] propose adopting terms from existing ontologies for process models manually. But due to manual adoption, correctness cannot be assured. [12] propose semi-automated adoption of model element names. However, they restrict their approach to BPMN models [13]. Furthermore, only the fact that two modelers act in the same business domain does not guarantee that they share the same or an equivalent understanding of business terms. If a "generally accepted" ontology is available, it is suitable for model comparison if and only if it is explicated and can be accessed by all involved modelers already *during* the modeling process. Additionally, in order to ensure comparability of the models, modelers have to comply strictly with the ontology. Most approaches make the implicit assumption that these preconditions are already given rather than addressing a methodical support.

For the latter approach, [14] connects domain ontologies to the terms that are used as names in conceptual models. This way, he establishes relationships between elements of different models that are to be analyzed. In addition to ontologies, [15] define combined similarity measures that consist of syntactic and semantic parts. These serve as a basis for the decision whether the model elements compared are equivalent or not. Consequently, it is argued that if identical terms – or those that are defined as synonymous within the ontology – are used in different models and by different modelers, these can be considered as semantically identical as well [16, 17]. It has to be questioned whether the advantage of the subsequent connection of the models via the ontology warrants the efforts in comparison to a conventional manual analysis.

Only a few approaches, mainly originating from the German speaking area, suggest standardized phrases for model element names in order to increase the clarity of process models. For example, [18] and [19] propose particular phrase structure guidelines for names of process activities (e.g., *<verb, imperative>* *<noun, singular>*; in particular "check invoice"). Moreover, the authors propose so-called *Technical Term Models* [20] that have to be created previously to process modeling and that specify the terms to be used within the phrases. However, the scope of Technical Term Models is restricted to nouns. Similar approaches provided by [16] and [17] propose the provision of generally accepted vocabularies. Further approaches recommend connecting names of model elements to online dictionaries (e.g., [21]) in order to establish semantic relationships of terms [22, 23]. These online dictionaries consist of extensive collections of English nouns, verbs, and adjectives as well as their semantic relationships. Actually, the proposed approaches are promising regarding increased comparability of conceptual models since all of them aim at standardizing names for model elements *prior to modeling*. However, up to now, a methodical realization is missing.

To sum up, we identify the following need for development towards avoiding naming conflicts in conceptual models: Up to now, methodical support for (1) the formal specification of naming conventions for all word classes and (2) the formal specification of phrase structure conventions is missing. Furthermore, there exists no methodical support for (3) guiding modelers in order to *comply* with the conventions.

To realize such a methodical support, we propose an approach that consists of (1) a formalism to specify thesauri covering nouns, verbs, and adjectives, (2) a grammar to specify phrase structures that can hold terms specified as valid within the thesauri, and (3) a procedure model to guide modelers automatically in complying with the conventions.

2.2 Naming Practice in Process Models

Naming practices in process models provide evidence concerning the danger of naming conflicts as well as requirements to approaches that aim at resolving or even avoiding them. Therefore, we conducted an exploratory empirical analysis of two modeling projects consisting of overall 257 Event-driven Process Chain (EPC [24]) models containing in turn overall 3918 elements (1827 functions and 2091 events). Within these modeling projects, modeling conventions were available in terms of glossaries and phrase structures. However, these conventions solely existed as textual recommendations rather than methodical support. All model element names were parsed with *TreeTagger* [25] and revised manually. We found out that, first, most elements were named with complex phrases rather than with single terms (cf. Fig. 1).

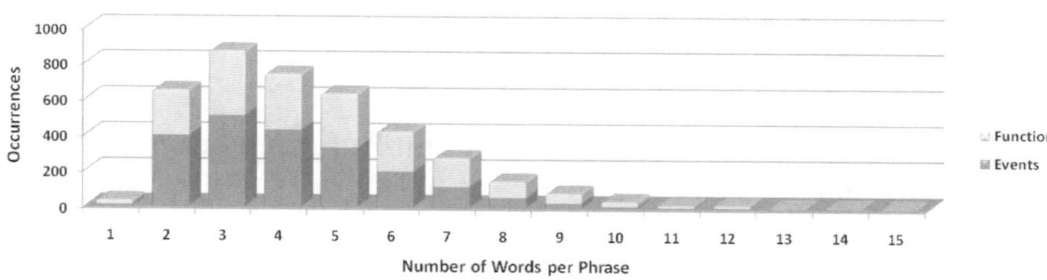

Fig. 1. Average Number of Words Used in Process Model Element Names

Second, element names containing a certain number of terms consisted of many different phrase structures (e.g., *<verb, imperative><noun, singular>*, in particular "audit invoice" or *<noun, singular><verb, gerund>*, "invoice auditing"; cf. Table 1). The results show that process models are extra prone to naming conflicts, since process model elements are usually named with sentence fragments rather than with single terms. Approaches towards resolving or avoiding naming conflicts therefore have to consider not only the terms but also the phrase structures used in model element names.

Table 1. Phrase Structures in Process Model Element Names

# of Terms	1	2	3	4	5	6	7	8	9	10	11	12	13	14	15
# of Events	10	396	509	429	331	197	114	55	27	10	4	4	2	2	1
# of Different Phrase Structures (Event)	6	37	136	221	248	175	102	54	26	10	4	4	2	2	1
# of Functions	21	252	358	310	301	225	160	90	52	26	12	13	2	3	2
# of Different Phrase Structures (Function)	3	29	85	157	204	193	141	87	52	25	12	13	2	3	2

2.3 Research Methodology

The research methodology followed here complies with the Design Science approach [26] that deals with the construction of scientific artifacts like methods, languages, models, and implementations. Following the Design Science approach, it is necessary to assure that the research addresses a *relevant problem*. This relevance has to be proven. Furthermore, the artifacts to be constructed have to represent an *innovative contribution* to the existing knowledge base within the actual research discipline. Similar or identical solutions must not be already available. Subsequent to the *construction* of the *artifacts*, these have to be *evaluated* in order to prove their fulfillment of the research goals.

In this contribution the *scientific artifact* is the modeling approach outlined in Section 1. This artifact aims at solving the *relevant problem* of the lacking comparability of conceptual models (cf. Section 1). Related work does not provide satisfactory solutions up to now (cf. Section 2). Hence, the approach presented here (cf. Section 3) makes an *innovative contribution* to the existing knowledge base. In order to *evaluate* the approach, we have implemented a demonstrator software that shows the general applicability of the approach (cf. Section 4). Further evaluations concerning acceptance as well as efficiency and increase of comparability will be the subject of empirical studies to be performed in the short term (cf. Section 5).

3 A Framework for the Specification and Enforcement of Naming Conventions

3.1 Procedure Model

In order to provide a framework for naming conventions, we propose the usage of a specific language that is used for naming model elements in a certain modeling context (i.e., a specific modeling domain, project, or company). This domain language is a subset of the respective natural language (here: English) used in the modeling context. The domain language consists of a set of valid domain terms that are allowed to be used in model element names exclusively. That is, the set of domain terms is a subset of all terms available in the respective natural language. Furthermore, every natural language has a certain syntax that determines the set of grammatically correct phrases. In our framework, we restrict the syntax of the respective natural language as well. This means that the possibilities to construct sentences for model element names are limited. In summary, we restrict the *grammar of a natural language* in order to provide a formal basis for naming model elements (cf. Fig. 2).

Natural language grammars are usually defined by a formalism that consists of a *lexicon* and a *syntax specification* [27]. Such a grammar is complemented with naming conventions, which again consist of term and phrase structure conventions. Term conventions are specified by a *thesaurus* containing domain terms with a precise

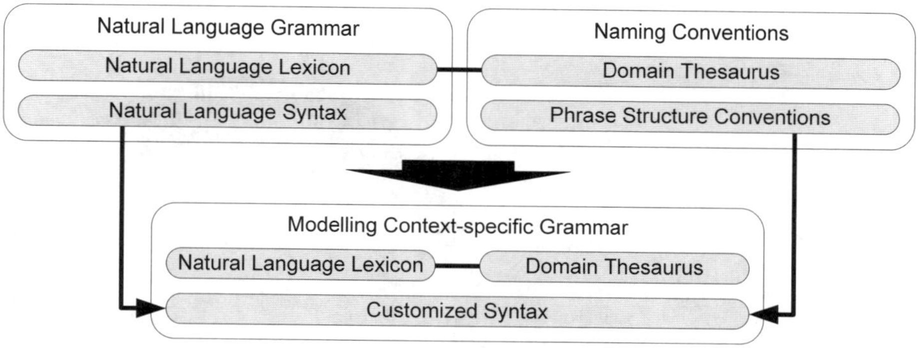

Fig. 2. Customizing the Natural Language Grammar with Naming Conventions

specification of their synonym, homonym, and word formation relationships as well as a textual description of their meaning. The thesaurus is then connected to the natural language's lexicon. Moreover, valid phrase structures are specified by *phrase structure conventions*. Hence, the natural language is customized for the needs of a specific modeling context. This allows for subsequent validation of the model element names and the enforcement of naming conventions. A conceptual overview of the naming conventions' specification is given in Section 3.2.

The thesaurus can be created from scratch, or by reusing possibly existing thesauri or glossaries. It includes single nouns, verbs, and adjectives that are interrelated. Other word classes are generally domain independent. Thus, as they are already included in the general lexicon, they do not need to be explicitly specified in the thesaurus. The terms in the thesaurus are linked to their synonyms, homonyms, and linguistic derivation(s) in the general lexicon. This additional term related information can be obtained from linguistic services, which already exist for different natural languages. For example, *WordNet* is such a lexicon service for the English language providing an online interface [21]. Therefore, in case of a later violation of the naming conventions by the modeler, synonymous or derived valid terms can be automatically identified and recommended. The terms specified are provided with short textual semantic descriptions, allowing modelers to look up the exact meaning of a term. The thesaurus should not be changed during a modeling project in order not to violate the consistency of application.

The naming conventions have to be specified once for every modeling context, whereas already existing conventions can be reused (in the following, cf. Fig. 3). Naming conventions are modeling language-specific. For example, functions in EPCs are labeled with activities (e.g., *<verb, imperative><noun, singular>*; in particular "check invoice") and events are labeled with states (for example *<noun, singular><verb, past participle>*; in particular "invoice checked") [24]. For each model element type at least one phrase structure convention has to be defined. For the sake of applicability, the conventions should be specified in a manner, which is compatible with the formalism of the natural language grammar.

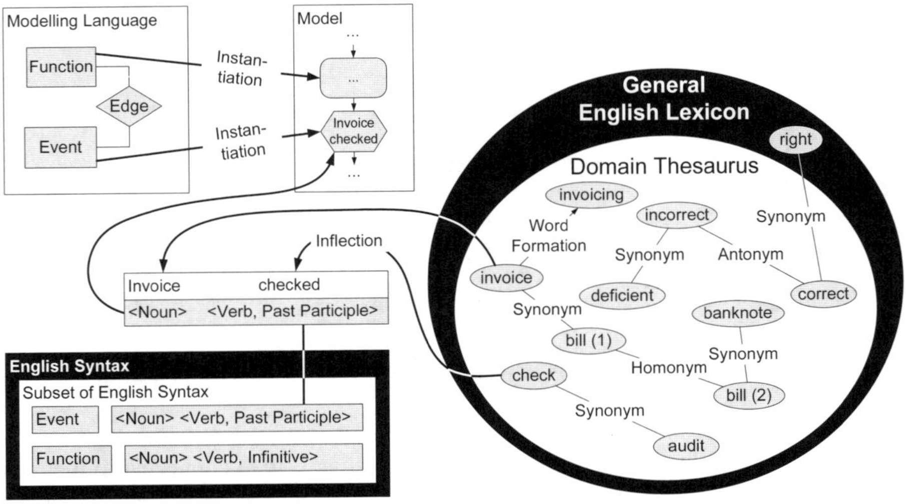

Fig. 3. Using Formalized Naming Conventions

The conventions should be defined by a project team consisting of domain experts and modeling experts. This means that the stakeholders responsible for the conventions should have thorough knowledge of the actual modeling context in order to reach a consensus. Most commonly, the thesaurus part of the conventions already exists in terms of corporate or domain-specific glossaries (e.g., [28, 29, 30]), which should be reused and adapted depending on the modeling situation (cf. Section 2.1).

During modeling, the entered model element names are verified simultaneously against the specified context-specific grammar. On the one hand, the structure of an entered model element name is validated against the customized syntax specification. On the other hand, it is checked whether the used terms are allowed. Nouns, verbs, and adjectives, meaning word classes covered by the thesaurus, are validated against it. Other word classes are validated against the natural language lexicon.

In case of a positive validation, the entered model element name is declared as valid against the modeling context-specific grammar. In case of a violation of one or both criteria, alternative valid phrase structures, terms or both are suggested based on the user input. The modelers themselves have to decide, which of the recommendations fits their particular needs. By looking up the semantic descriptions of the terms, modelers can choose the appropriate one. Alternatively, they can choose a valid structure as a pattern and fill in the gaps with valid terms on their own. However, it should be possible for the modeler to propose a new term with a short textual semantic description. In order not to distract the modeler from his current modeling session, the proposed term is accepted temporarily. In a next step, it is up to the modeling project expert team whether they accept the term or not. If the term is accepted, it is added to the thesaurus. Otherwise, the modeler is informed to revise the model element. Hereby, we ensure that equal model element names represent equal semantics, which is a precondition for comparability of conceptual models.

3.2 Conceptual Specification

In the following, we provide a conceptual framework for the specification and the enforcement of naming conventions using Entity-Relationship Models in (min,max)-notation [31] (cf. Fig. 4). *Phrase structure conventions (PSC)* are defined depending on distinct *element types* of conceptual modeling languages (e.g., *activities* in process models are named differently from *events*).

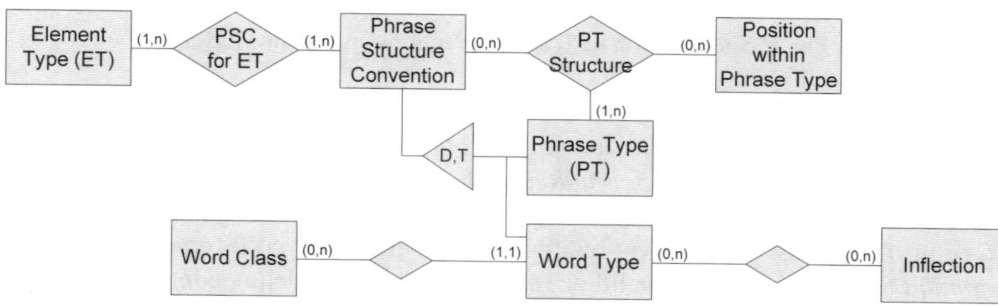

Fig. 4. Specification of Phrase Structure Conventions on Type Layer

Phrase structure conventions consist of *phrase types* or *word types*. A phrase type specifies the structure of a phrase, which can be used as a model element name. Therefore, we compose a phrase type recursively using further phrase types or word types. Representing atomic elements of a phrase type, word types are acting as placeholders for particular words. An example of a word type is *<noun, singular>*, an example of a phrase type is *<noun, singular><verb, infinitive>*. The composition of phrase types is specified by the *phrase type structure*. Here, we define the allocation of sub phrase types or word types to a phrase type and their *position* in the superordinate phrase type.

A word type consists of a distinct *word class* (noun, verb, adjective, adverb, article, pronoun, preposition, conjunction, or numeral) – and its *inflection*. Inflections can be specialized as case, number, tense, gender, mood, person, and comparative and these are usually combined. For example, a particular combined inflection is *<3rd person, singular>*. In respect to specific word classes, not every inflection is applicable. Based on the recursive composition of phrase types, it is possible to specify arbitrary phrase structure conventions.

Phrase structure conventions restrict the underlying English syntax and thus limit modelers in their freedom of naming model elements. In order to facilitate the synchronization between the syntax of the natural language and the applied phrase structure conventions, compatible formalisms for both syntax specifications are necessary. Hence, it should be possible to verify phrase structure conventions against the underlying natural language and to signalize potential conflicts directly during the specification process. For this purpose, we establish the connection to linguistic parsing approaches in Section 3.3.

Independently from their corresponding word class, particular uninflected words are called *lexemes* (e.g., the verb "check"). Inflected words are called *word forms* (e.g., past participle "checked" of the lexeme "check"). Word forms are assigned to the corresponding word types (i.e., their word classes and inflections) Thus, word forms represent lexemes of a particular word type (cf. Fig. 5).

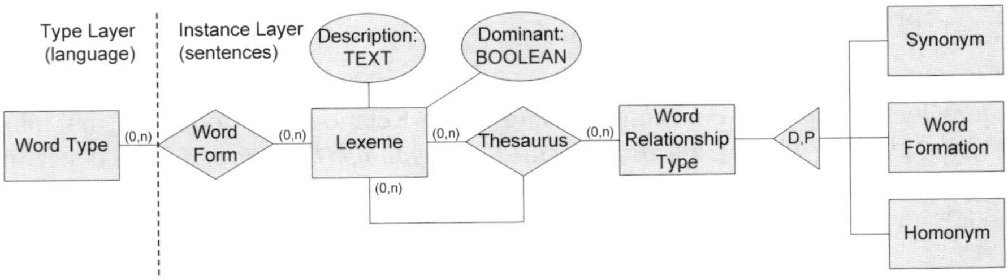

Fig. 5. Specification of Term Conventions on Instance Layer

In order to specify the domain *thesaurus*, we store the allowed words in the form of lexemes that are related by different *word relationship types*. They are specialized as *homonym*, *synonym*, and *word formation* relations. *Word formation* means that a lexeme originates from (an)other one(s) (e.g., the noun "control" originates from the verb "to control"). In case of synonym relations, one of the involved lexemes is marked as *dominant* to state that it is the valid one in the particular modeling context. Homonym relations are necessary in order to distinguish lexemes that consist of the same string but have a different meaning and to prevent errors during modeling. We use word formation relations to search for appropriate alternatives when a modeler has used invalid terms and phrase structures. For example, if the phrase "order clearance" violates the conventions, the alternative phrase "clear order" can be found via the word formation relation of "to clear" and "clearance". Based on the word relationship types, we connect the domain thesaurus to lexical services (cf. Section 3.1). To specify what is actually meant by a lexeme, a semantic *description* is added at least to each dominant lexeme. This way, modelers are enabled to check if the lexeme they have used actually fits the modeling issue.

3.3 Specification of Linguistic Restrictions

To assure the correctness of both specified phrase structure conventions and the structure and words of model element names, we make use of linguistic syntax parsing. According parsing methods detect the syntax of a given sentence based on so-called *universal grammar frameworks*. For example, an according parsing method analyzes the phrase "invoice checked" and returns the phrase type *<noun, singular><verb, past participle>* as well as the lexemes "invoice" and "check". For reasons of clarity, we do not introduce these methods in detail (cf. [27] for an overview). Given a phrase structure convention, according parsing methods are able to determine whether the convention complies with the syntax of a natural language. Furthermore, given a model element name, they determine whether the syntax of the name complies with the phrase structure conventions. This way we check the convention-related correctness of model element names concurrently.

In our approach, we parse sentences against the domain thesaurus and the restricted English syntax. If the terms used within model element names do not comply with the conventions, alternative but valid lexemes are searched in the domain thesaurus via the defined word relationships or in the general language lexicon and are proposed in the appropriate inflection form for proper use (cf. Fig. 6).

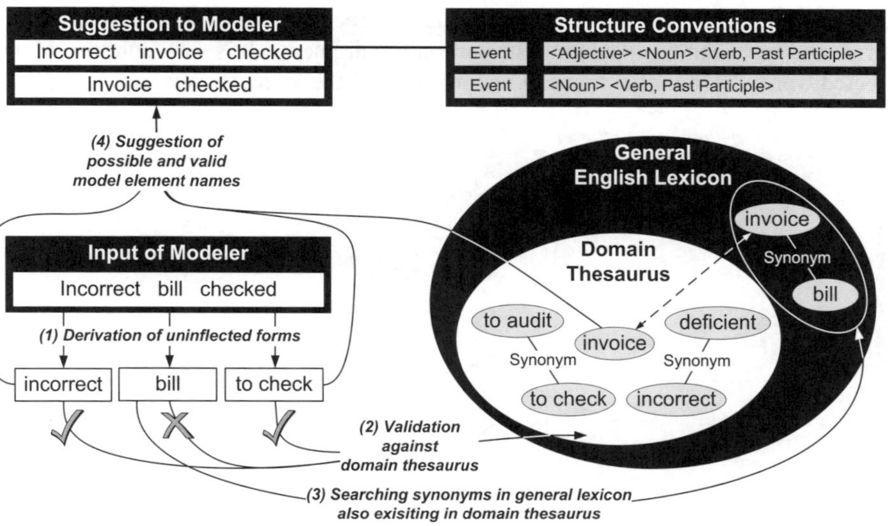

Fig. 6. Validation and Suggestion of Model Element Names

In particular, we decompose a model element name into single terms and derive their uninflected forms (1). In a next step, we validate the lexemes against the domain thesaurus (2). Lexemes contained in the domain thesaurus are denoted as valid. For those lexemes that do not exist in the domain thesaurus, we search synonyms in the general lexicon and match them against the domain thesaurus (3). If no such synonyms are available or a lexeme is not contained in the general lexicon, we exclude them from further validation steps. Based on the defined structure conventions, we suggest possible model element names to the modelers that contain the valid lexemes in the appropriate inflection form (4). If a phrase structure is violated in turn, alternative but valid phrase structures are proposed that contain the valid terms.

4 Modeling Tool Support

To validate the general applicability of our approach, we developed a modeling prototype. The way of navigating through the software and its handling is tightly connected to the procedure model motivated in Section 3.

As described above, the connection of our approach with modeling languages requires the adoption of the respective meta model. For the tool support, this indicates the necessity of meta modeling abilities, which is supported by our research prototype. Hence, virtually any modeling language that can be created or exists inside the prototype can be extended with naming conventions. The software follows a fat client/thin server three tier architecture, thus enabling distributed modeling. As the presentation layer is abstract, we chose the widespread drawing engine *Microsoft Visio*, accessing it with the *Microsoft .NET Framework*.

As a preliminary step, the person responsible for specifying the modeling conventions has to define the terms, which are allowed for the modeling context. Subsequently, the phrase structure conventions have to be specified. If the actual modeling context represents a domain which has been processed before, the existing set of terms and rules can be adapted to the current requirements. It is sufficient to add uninflected words, as the inflection can be looked up in the lexical services.

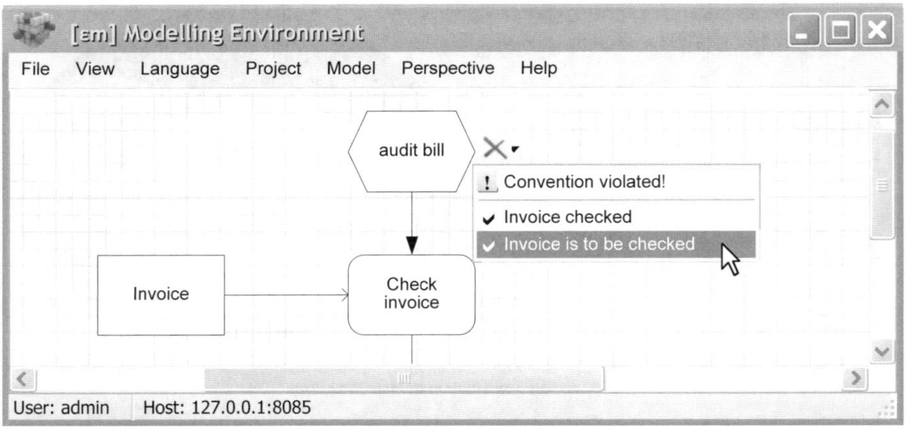

Fig. 7. Automatic Guidance in Order to Comply with Naming Conventions

In the next step, the user defines phrase structure conventions and connects them to those language elements for which they are valid. For example, it is necessary to create different phrase structure conventions for EPC events (i.e., separate conventions for *trigger events* and *result events*). Trigger events start functions and result events conclude them. Different phrase structures can be attached to each of them in regard to their different semantics. An example of a trigger event is "invoice is to be checked", hence an appropriate phrase structure convention called "Trigger" is *<noun, singular><verb, passive infinitive>*. With this phrase structure, a set of trigger events can be named.

However, different aspects might require additional phrase structures to be defined. For resulting events, an adequate phrase structure is *<noun, singular><verb, past participle>*, allowing phrases like "invoice checked". Once generated, the phrase structure conventions in combination with the domain thesaurus are used during modeling. Modelers get hints as soon as they violate a convention (cf. Fig. 7).

First, the modeler might have chosen invalid terms (e.g., *bill* instead of *invoice* or *audit* instead of *check*). As soon as (s)he has entered a phrase, it is parsed to determine its compliance with the conventions. The tool transforms every term into its uninflected form and compares it with the domain thesaurus. If the term is not found, synonymous valid terms are searched in the lexicon. If according alternatives are found, they are proposed to the modeler. Otherwise, (s)he has to rename the respective element – optionally by choosing a valid term from the domain thesaurus. Second, violations of phrase structure conventions are signaled and alternative valid structures are proposed.

Summarizing this example, the name *audit bill* is suggested to be changed to *invoice is to be checked*. Phrases corresponding with both the domain thesaurus and the phrase structure conventions are accepted without any feedback.

5 Conclusion and Outlook

Integrating naming conventions into conceptual modeling languages is promising for increasing the comparability of conceptual models. Two characteristics are significant to avoid common problems:

- Defining and providing naming conventions *previously to modeling* is the basis for *avoiding* naming conflicts rather than resolving them. Therefore, time-consuming alignment of namings becomes dispensable.
- *Guiding the modeler automatically during modeling* is of substantial importance, since only this way the compliance with the modeling conventions can be assured.

Certainly, specifying naming conventions in the proposed way is time-consuming. Our approach is therefore mainly suited for large-scaled regionally distributed modeling projects. Nevertheless, for every project, business domain, or company, the conventions have to be specified only once and are reusable. Moreover, term models, thesauri and/or glossaries that may already exist in companies or business domains can be reused. Furthermore, our approach is restricted to models that are developed from scratch. It is not suitable for existing models that are to be made comparable, as it can be seen by the ontology-based approaches presented in Section 2.

Future research will focus on further evaluating the proposed approach. In the short-term, we will instantiate the approach for different modeling languages, different natural languages and different application scenarios. In particular, we will evaluate the capability of our approach to increase the efficiency of distributed conceptual modeling and its acceptance. To assure the applicability of the approach, we will enhance the demonstrator software in order to make it usable in practice.

Moreover, as linguistic grammar approaches and according parsers usually vary in terms of linguistic coverage, it has to be empirically evaluated which ones provide the best coverage for certain natural languages and application scenarios. In addition to conducting this in batch using artificially prepared test samples, we will implement a set of different parsers in our tool and conduct empirical evaluations of these in real-life modeling settings. In the course of evaluation, we will also investigate whether ambiguities play a role in model element names. For example, the sentence "They hit the man with a cane" is ambiguous, even if the meanings of all of the used words are considered definite. Thus, we will perform further studies on existing conceptual models and determine if phrase structures promoting ambiguities are common in conceptual modeling. A result of this analysis could be a recommendation to restrict phrase structure conventions to phrases that do not lead to ambiguities.

References

1. Batini, C., Lenzerini, M., Navathe, S.B.: A Comparative Analysis of Methodologies for Database Schema Integration. ACM Computing Surveys 18(4), 323–364 (1986)
2. Lawrence, R., Barker, K.: Integrating Relational Database Schemas using a Standardized Dictionary. In: Proceedings of the 2001 ACM symposium on Applied computing (SAC), Las Vegas (2001)

3. Hadar, I., Soffer, P.: Variations in conceptual modeling: classification and ontological analysis. Journal of the AIS 7(8), 568–592 (2006)
4. Phalp, K., Shepperd, M.: Quantitative analysis of static models of processes. Journal of Systems and Software 52(2-3), 105–112 (2000)
5. Vergidis, K., Tiwari, A., Majeed, B.: Business process analysis and optimization: beyond reengineering. IEEE Transactions on Systems, Man, and Cybernetics 38(1), 69–82 (2008)
6. Batini, C., Lenzerini, M.: A Methodology for Data Schema Integration in the Entity Relationship Model. IEEE Transactions on Software Engineering 10(6), 650–663 (1984)
7. Bhargava, H.K., Kimbrough, S.O., Krishnan, R.: Unique Name Violations, a Problem for Model Integration or You Say Tomato, I Say Tomahto. ORSA Journal on Computing 3(2), 107–120 (1991)
8. Chen, P.P.-S.: The Entity-Relationship Model: Toward a Unified View of Data. ACM Transactions on Database Systems 1(1), 9–36 (1976)
9. Gruber, T.R.: A Translation Approach to Portable Ontology Specifications. Knowledge Acquisition 5(2), 199–220 (1993)
10. Guarino, N.: Formal Ontology and Information Systems. In: Guarino, N. (ed.) Proceedings of the 1st International Conference on Formal Ontologies in Information Systems, Trento, pp. 3–15 (1998)
11. Greco, G., Guzzo, A., Pontieri, L., Saccá, D.: An ontology-driven process modeling framework. In: Galindo, F., Takizawa, M., Traunmüller, R. (eds.) DEXA 2004. LNCS, vol. 3180, pp. 13–23. Springer, Heidelberg (2004)
12. Born, M., Dörr, F., Weber, I.: User-friendly semantic annotation in business process modeling. In: Weske, M., Hacid, M.-S., Godart, C. (eds.) Proceedings of the International Workshop on Human-Friendly Service Description, Discovery and Matchmaking (Hf-SDDM 2007). 8th International Conference on Web Information Systems Engineering (WISE 2007), Nancy, pp. 260–271 (2007)
13. White, S.A., Miers, D.: BPMN Modeling and Reference Guide. Understanding and Using BPMN. Lighthouse Point (2008)
14. Höfferer, P.: Achieving business process model interoperability using metamodels and ontologies. In: Österle, H., Schelp, J., Winter, R. (eds.) Proceedings of the 15th European Conference on Information Systems (ECIS 2007), St. Gallen, pp. 1620–1631 (2007)
15. Ehrig, M., Koschmider, A., Oberweis, A.: Measuring Similarity between Semantic Business Process Models. In: Proceedings of the 4th Asia-Pacific Conference on Conceptual Modelling (APCCM) 2007, Ballarat (2007)
16. Koschmider, A., Oberweis, A.: Ontology Based Business Process Description. In: Enterprise Modelling and Ontologies for Interoperability, Proceedings of the Open Interop Workshop on Enterprise Modelling and Ontologies for Interoperability, Co-located with CAiSE 2005 Conference, Porto (2005)
17. Sabetzadeh, M., Nejati, S., Easterbrook, S., Chechik, M.: A Relationship-Driven Framework for Model Merging. In: Proceedings of the Workshop on Modeling in Software Engineering. 29th International Conference on Software Engineering, Minneapolis (2007)
18. Rosemann, M.: Complexity Management in Process Models. Language-specific Modelling Guidelines. Komplexitätsmanagement in Prozeßmodellen. Methodenspezifische Gestaltungsempfehlungen für die Informationsmodellierung (in German). Wiesbaden (1996)
19. Kugeler, M.: Organisational Design with Conceptual Models. Modelling Conventions and Reference Process Model for Business Process Reengineering Informa-tionsmodellbasierte Organisationsgestaltung. Modellierungskonventionen und Referenzvorgehensmodell zur prozessorientierten Reorganisation (in German). Berlin (2000)

20. Rosemann, M.: Preparation of Process Modeling. In: Becker, J., Kugeler, M., Rosemann, M. (eds.) Process Management – A Guide for the Design of Business Processes, Berlin, pp. 41–78 (2003)
21. Fellbaum, C. (ed.): WordNet: An Electronic Lexical Database. Cambridge (1998)
22. Rizopoulos, N., Mçbrien, P.: A General Approach to the Generation of Conceptual Model Transformations. In: Pastor, Ó., Falcão e Cunha, J. (eds.) CAiSE 2005. LNCS, vol. 3520, pp. 326–341. Springer, Heidelberg (2005)
23. Bögl, A., Kobler, M., Schrefl, M.: Knowledge Acquisition from EPC Models for Extraction of Process Patterns in Engineering Domains. In: Proceedings of the Multi-Conference on Information Systems Multikonferenz Wirtschaftsinformatik 2008 (MKWI 2008)(in German), Munich (2008)
24. Scheer, A.-W.: ARIS – Business Process Modelling, 3rd edn., Berlin (2000)
25. Schmid, H.: Probabilistic Part-of-Speech Tagging Using Decision Trees. In: Proceedings of the First International Conference on New Methods in Natural Language Processing, Manchester, pp. 44–49 (1994)
26. Hevner, A.R., March, S.T., Park, J., Ram, S.: Design Science in Information Systems Research. MIS Quarterly 28(1), 75–105 (2004)
27. Kaplan, R.M.: Syntax. In: Mitkov, R. (ed.) The Oxford handbook of computational linguistics, Oxford, pp. 70–90 (2003)
28. Automotive Thesaurus, `http://automotivethesaurus.com`
29. Tradeport – Reference Library for Global Trade, `http://tradeport.org/library`
30. WWW Virtual Library: Logistics, `http://logisticsworld.com/logistics/glossary.htm`
31. ISO: ISO/TC97/SC5/WG3: Concepts and Terminology for the Conceptual Schema and the Information Base (1982)

Monitoring and Diagnosing Malicious Attacks with Autonomic Software*

Vítor E. Silva Souza and John Mylopoulos

Department of Information Engineering and Computer Science,
University of Trento, Italy
{vitorsouza,jm}@disi.unitn.it

Abstract. Monitoring and diagnosing (M&D) software based on requirement models is a problem that has recently received a lot of attention in field of Requirement Engineering. In this context, Wang et al. [1] propose a M&D framework that uses goal models to diagnose failures in software at different levels of granularity. In this paper we extend Wang's framework to monitor and diagnose malicious attacks. Our extensions include the addition of anti-goals to model attacker intentions, as well as context-based modeling of the domain within which our system operates. The extended framework has been implemented and evaluated through a series of experiments intended to test its scalability.

1 Introduction

Monitoring requirements for a software system during runtime and diagnosing failures is an old problem in Requirements Engineering (e.g., [2]). The problem has received considerable attention recently because of the importance that Industry and Academia are placing on adaptive/autonomic software systems. Such systems monitor their environment, diagnose problems (such as failures, sub-optimal behaviour, malicious attacks) and resolve them through some sort of a compensation mechanism. Our work addresses problems in this general area.

Wang et al. have proposed a general monitoring framework, paired with a SAT-based diagnostic reasoner adapted from Artificial Intelligence (AI) theories of action and diagnosis [1]. In this framework, software requirements are represented as goal models [3], and they determine what data to monitor for. At run-time, log data along with system requirements are coded into a propositional formula that is fed into a SAT solver. If the formula is unsatisfiable, then log data are consistent with the requirements model. If not, every possible interpretation that satisfies the formula represents a possible diagnosis of system failure(s). The proposed framework is able to diagnose failures at different levels of granularity. For instance, the diagnosis may be simply that the root-level goal failed, or it may detail which lower-level goal actually failed. Unfortunately,

* We are grateful to Yiqiao Wang for providing us with the implementation of her system and helping us understand it while designing its extensions.

A.H.F. Laender et al. (Eds.): ER 2009, LNCS 5829, pp. 84–98, 2009.

Wang's framework is limited to monitoring and diagnosing system requirements-related failures, such as system function failures. This means that the framework does not diagnose failures caused by unanticipated changes in the environment (for example, a system that was built to handle up to 10 users and fails when 20+ users log in concurrently). Nor can the system deal with malicious attacks, or failures caused by discrepancies between design models and the system's operations.

The main objective of this work is to extend Wang's framework with the purpose of monitoring and diagnosing malicious attacks. To this end, we have added support for a richer goal model that can represent not only stakeholder needs (goals), but also attacker intentions (anti-goals). Since the relationship between anti-goals and attacks (the plans by which an attacker attempts to fulfill his intentions) is notoriously context-dependent, we have also extended Wang's framework to represent and reason with contextual variability.

Anti-goals were proposed by van Lamsweerde et al. [4] to model security concerns during requirements elicitation. They are goals that belong to external malicious agents, whose purpose is to prevent the system from working by targeting one or more of its goals or tasks. By proposing this extension to Wang's framework and integrating it with the diagnostic reasoning, we cover the case in which all system components are working properly, but an external agent is preventing the system from functioning correctly.

Contextual variability in goal models was proposed by Lapouchnian [5] as a way to explicitly specify in the modeling notation how domain variability affects requirements. In this work we integrate this idea in the diagnostic framework, allowing for it to verify which goals and tasks of the model have an active context at any given time. This mechanism fits well in the architecture of systems that have a monitoring capability, and offers additional requirements for the monitoring component of such systems.

The rest of the paper is divided into the following sections: section 2 presents an overview of Wang's framework proposed in [1]; section 3 describes our extensions to Wang's framework. Section 4 details the implementation of these extensions, while section 5 presents the results of the evaluation experiments for the extended framework. Section 6 compares our proposal with related work. Finally, section 7 concludes and sketches ideas for future work.

2 The Diagnostic Framework

Wang et al. propose a framework to monitor the satisfaction of software requirements and diagnose what goes wrong in its execution in case of failure [1]. Figure 1 shows an overview of the framework's architecture.

The framework receives as input a goal model representing system requirements, a common use for goal models in the past decade [3]. Goal models represent requirements in a tree-like structure that starts at the main goal of the system and is decomposed (using AND or OR decomposition) in subgoals and tasks, which are the monitorable leaves of the tree. Functional and non-functional

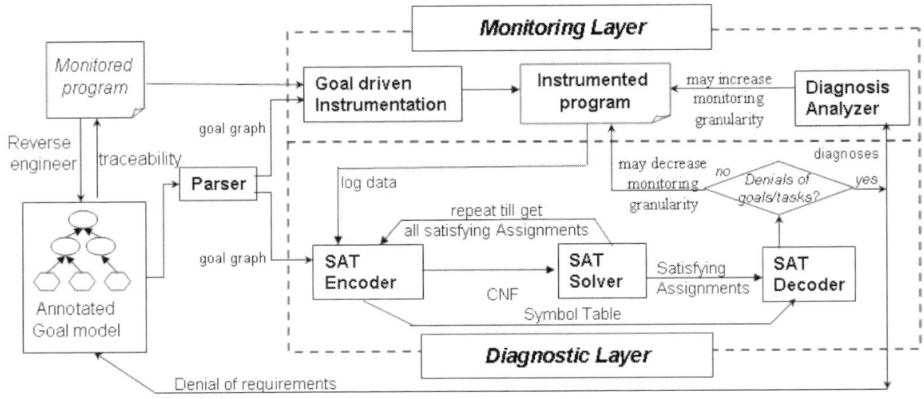

Fig. 1. Overview of the monitoring and diagnostic framework [1]

requirements are modeled as hard and soft goals respectively. Tasks and goals can also affect one another through contribution links: graph-like edges that indicate how the satisfiability or deniability of an element can affect another element.

Figure 2 shows the decomposition of one of the goals of the webmail system SquirrelMail [6]. To send an e-mail, one must fulfill all the sub-goals and tasks of goal $g1$'s AND-decomposition, namely, load the login form, process the send mail request and send the message. To process the send mail request, on the other hand, it's enough to accomplish one of the OR-decomposed children of goal $g1.2$: either you get the compose page or you report an IMAP error. The latter contributes positively to the non-functional requirement of usability. Possible contributions are helps (+), hurts (−), makes (++) and breaks (−−) [3].

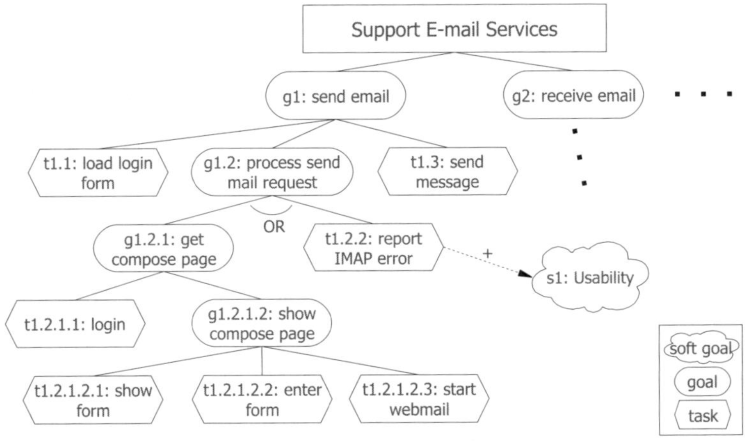

Fig. 2. Goal model of SquirrelMail [6] adapted from [7]

Each goal and task is given a precondition, an effect and a monitor status. Preconditions and effects are propositional formulas representing conditions that must be true before and after, respectively, a goal is satisfied or a task is executed [1]. The monitor status indicates if a task or goal should be monitored or not, making it possible to control the desired granularity level of diagnostics. Preconditions and effects for the SquirrelMail example can be seen in [1].

The monitoring layer instruments the source code of the program in order to provide the diagnostic layer a log, i.e., a set of truth values for an observed literal (preconditions and effects) or the occurrence of a task at a specific time-step [1]. The diagnostic layer can then produce axioms for three main purposes:

- **Deniability axioms**: if, according to the log, a task or goal occurred but either its precondition or its effect were not true before or after its occurrence, respectively, it's deemed denied, meaning there has been a problem with it;
- **Label propagation axioms**: propagate satisfiability and deniability between tasks and subgoals towards their parent goals, respecting the type of boolean decomposition (*and* or *or*) of the ancestors;
- **Contribution axioms**: calculate the effect that contribution links have on their targets based on the satisfiability or deniability of the source goal/task.

Together with the information from the log, the framework encodes all axioms in CNF and passes them to the SAT solver. The satisfying assignments are given to the SAT decoder, which translates them into diagnoses, i.e., information on task/goal satisfiability/deniability. Complete formalism on the axioms produced and algorithms used by the framework can be found in [1].

We have extended this framework in order to support contextual variability on goals and tasks and to take into account possible anti-goals that could be successfully preventing the system from working properly. These extensions and the changes in the goal meta-model that were necessary to accommodate them are presented in the following section.

3 The Proposed Extensions

In this work we propose two extensions to the framework described in section 2:

- **Anti-goals**: by supporting the inclusion of anti-goals in the requirements model, the framework can correctly diagnose the case in which none of the software components are faulty, but an external agent is preventing the system from working properly;
- **Contextual variability**: by supporting contextual variability in goal models, we allow for much richer requirement models "that will in turn lead to software systems that will deliver functionality closely matching customer expectations under many different circumstances" [5].

These extensions not only change the implementation of the framework, but also the format of the goal model input files, meaning they affect the goal meta-model, which describes how goal models are built. The goal meta-model for the

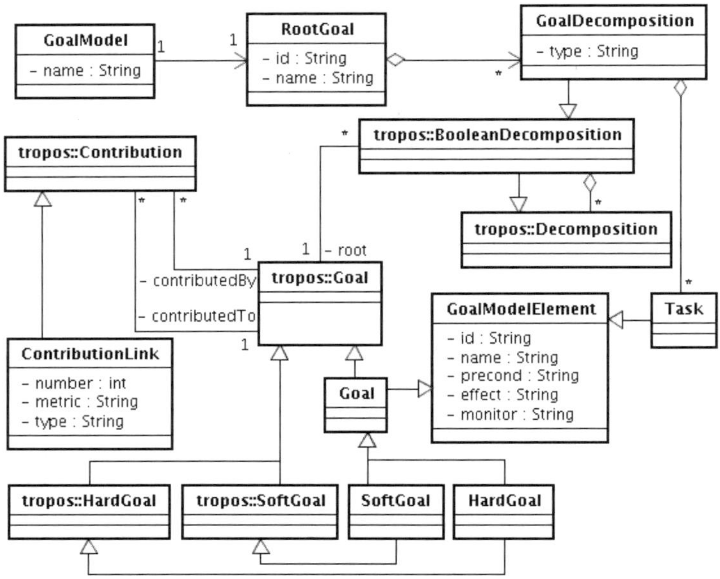

Fig. 3. The goal meta-model and its relationship with the Tropos meta-model in [8]

diagnostic framework extends the Tropos meta-model [8]. Figure 3 shows the goal meta-model and its relationship with the Tropos meta-model of [8].

Starting from the `GoalModel` class, we can see that a goal model has a root goal, which represents the objective of the system as a whole (in figure 2, "Support E-mail Services"). The root goal has a set of goal decompositions – *and* or *or*, depending on the `type` attribute –, which allows us to define complex goals in terms of sub-goals and tasks. Goals and tasks receive ID, name, precondition, effect and monitor status, which can be either *on* or *off*. Goals can contribute to other goals, specifying the metric – *helps*, *hurts*, *makes*, *breaks* – and the type: *s* (propagate satisfiability), *d* (propagate deniability) or *dual* (propagate both).

Next, we detail the changes in this meta-model and in the diagnostic framework for the inclusion of support for anti-goals and contextual variability.

3.1 Support for Anti-goals

Van Lamsweerde et al. propose a methodology for anti-goal analysis and their inclusion in requirement models in order to ensure the system satisfies critical properties such as safety, security, fault-tolerance and survivability [4]. Assuming the use of this methodology for the elicitation of anti-goals, we'd like to support them in the diagnostic framework.

The first step is the inclusion of the `AntiGoal` class and the `antiGoalTrees` association in the meta-model, as shown in figure 4 (affected classes are shaded). This allows for the inclusion of anti-goals in our goal models.

Next, we change the framework to consider the success of an anti-goal as a diagnosis. We assume the monitoring framework is capable of instrumenting the

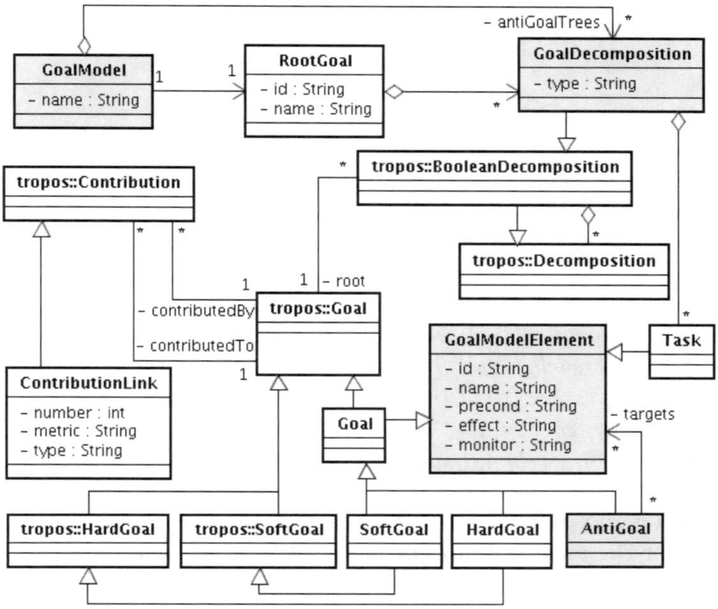

Fig. 4. New goal meta-model with support for anti-goals

source code of the system in a way it can detect when the tasks of the anti-goal tree successfully occur, as it already does with the tasks below the root goal. The current diagnostic framework is then capable of telling if an anti-goal occurred. To produce a SAT-based diagnosis we include axiom 1 in the encoded axioms.

AXIOM 1. **(Anti-goal satisfiability axioms)** *Given an anti-goal a, with starting and ending time-steps t_s and t_e and a set of target elements (goals or tasks) $\{e_1, e_2, \ldots, e_n\}$, the following axiom is produced*:

$$\forall e \in \{e_1, e_2, \ldots, e_n\} : occ(a, t_s, t_e) \wedge fd(e, s) \rightarrow fs(a, s) \qquad (1)$$

Intuitively, if a goal or task e is one of the targets of anti-goal a and we know that a has been attempted and that e has been denied, we can propose as a diagnose that a has been satisfied, meaning that there is a probability that e is not faulty[1], but a successfully prevented it from working properly. In other words, if it weren't for the anti-goal's success, e would also have been successful. As we cannot be sure the target goal/task hasn't failed by itself, both *fd(e, s)* and *fs(a, s)* diagnoses are proposed.

Figure 5 shows an example of an anti-goal for the SquirrelMail example of figure 2. The anti-goal *ag1* targets the goal *g1* and task *t1.3*.

The example below shows the log for an execution of the system under a Denial of Service (DoS) attack. Preconditions and effects for the anti-goal and its tasks can be inferred from the log:

[1] We use fault in the sense proposed by ISO/CD 10303-226: an abnormal condition or defect at the component, equipment, or sub-system level which may lead to a failure.

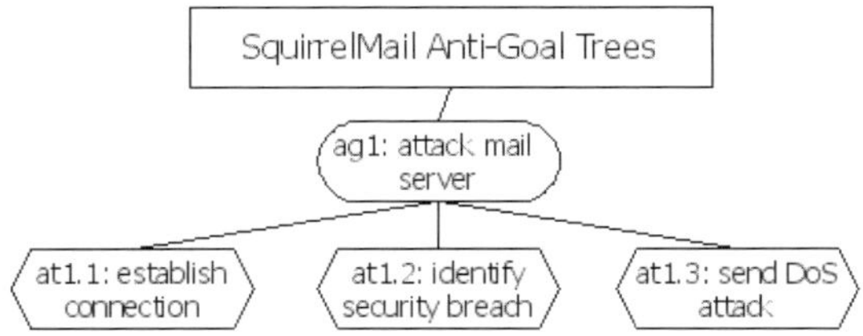

Fig. 5. Example anti-goal for the SquirrelMail goal model

connection_available(1); occ(at1.1, 2); connection_established(3); occ(at1.2, 4); breach_found(5); occ(at1.3, 6); dos_attack_performed(7); url_entered(8); occ(t1.1, 9); correct_form(10); ∼ wrong_imap(11); occ(t1.2.1.1, 12); correct_key(13); occ(t1.2.1.2.1, 14); occ(t1.2.1.2.2, 15); occ(t1.2.1.2.3, 16); webmail_started(17); occ(t1.3, 18); ∼ email_sent(19);

The proposed diagnoses for the example are *fd(t1.3, s); fs(ag1, s)*, i.e., either task *t1.3* is faulty or the anti-goal *ag1* prevented it from working.

3.2 Support for Contextual Variability

Lapouchnian believes that taking domain variability into consideration during requirements modeling will lead to software systems that match more closely customer expectations under many different circumstances. High-variability goal models attempt to capture many different ways goals can be met in order to facilitate in designing flexible, adaptive or customizable software [5].

Take, for instance, the example of figure 6. In this example, we extended the SquirrelMail example of figure 2 to capture the possibility of serving Web Services requests and performing auto-login in case the user has been authenticated before. New elements added to the goal model are shaded and, for reasons of space, only the subtree of goal *g1.2* is shown.

This causes a problem in our diagnostic framework: for goal *g1.2.1* to occur, since it's AND-decomposed, both *login* and *auto-login* tasks must occur, which is redundant. With support for contexts, all we have to say is that these tasks occur in different contexts. Furthermore, contexts can help decide which route to take to fulfill a goal in case of an OR-decomposition, such as goal *g1.2*: when a Web Services request is detected, follow goal *g1.2.3*, otherwise try goal *g1.2.1*.

To define contexts and annotate goal model elements with them, changes in the goal meta-model are necessary. Figure 7 shows the new classes added to the meta-model (shaded) and their relationship with the existing ones.

Goal models can now define context dimensions and organize them in hierarchies: a context dimension is either defined by sub-dimensions or by a formula in propositional logic. Then, goals, tasks and links can be annotated with context to indicate it only makes sense for them to occur if the context is active.

Figure 8 presents the context hierarchies for the new SquirrelMail example shown in figure 6. The formulas that define each leaf-level context dimension are

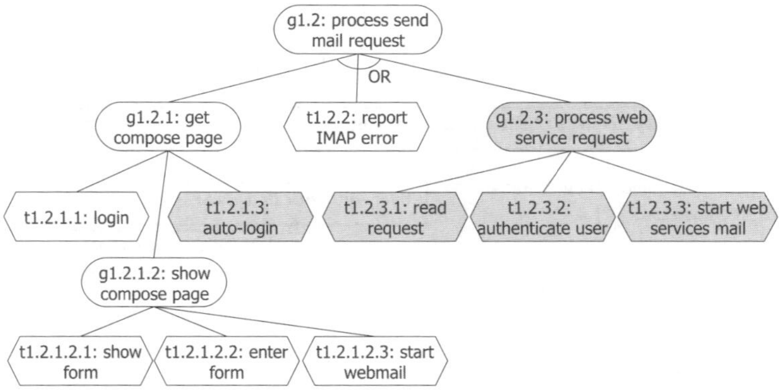

Fig. 6. Example of a contextual goal-model based on the SquirrelMail example

shown in the diagram. Tasks *t1.2.1.1* and *t1.2.1.3* are annotated with dimensions *User Not Authenticated* and *User Authenticated*, respectively, while goals *g1.2.1* and *g1.2.3* are annotated with *Web Client* and *Web Services Client* respectively.

Contexts are deemed inactive at time-step 0 and considered active in a given time-step if any of their sub-contexts are active or, in the case of leaf-level dimensions, if the formula is true at that time-step, considering the latest information on the log. This means that the program code instrumented by the monitoring framework must be capable of logging information related to these formulas.

Moreover, we'd also like to know when a goal or task has occurred outside its context. This could mean the instrumented program code isn't able to detect context change or that the software is not following the specifications. For this purpose, we also encode axioms so the result is provided as a diagnosis:

AXIOMS 2 AND 3. **(Invalid occurrence axioms)** *Given a goal g, with starting and ending time-steps t_s and t_e or a task a, with occurring time-step t_{occ}. Suppose the function $context\_formula(e,t)$ that calculates the truth value of the conjunction of all the context formulas of the annotations of element e in a given time-step t. The following axioms are produced:*

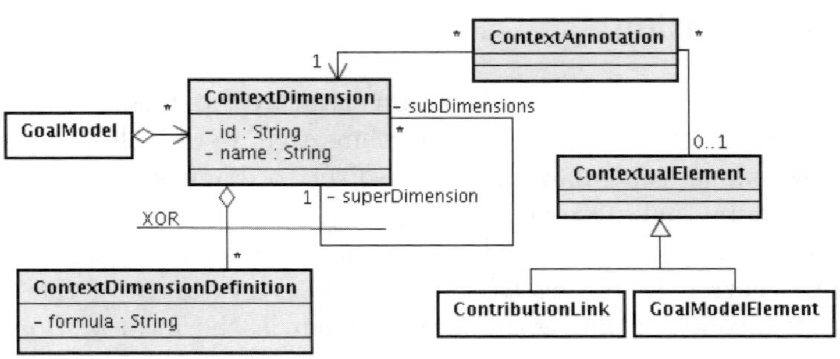

Fig. 7. Additions to the goal meta-model to deal with contextual variability

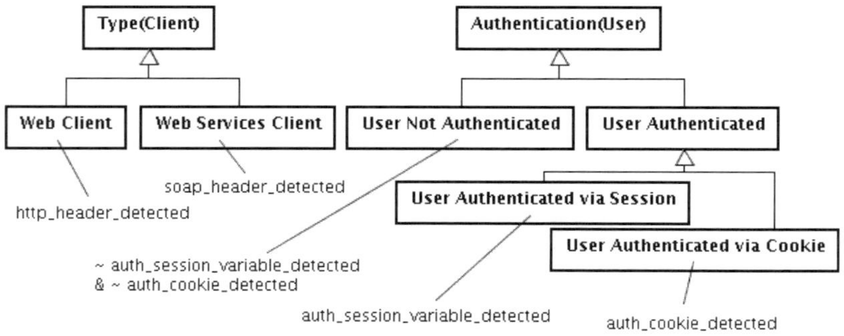

Fig. 8. Contexts for the new SquirrelMail example of figure 6

$$occ(g, t_s, t_e) \wedge \neg context\_formula(g, t_s) \rightarrow iocc(g, s) \tag{2}$$

$$occ(a, t_{occ}) \wedge \neg context\_formula(a, t_{occ}) \rightarrow iocc(a, s) \tag{3}$$

Intuitively, a goal or task has an active context at a given time-step t if all of its annotated context dimensions are active at that moment. A dimension is active if its context formula is true. If non-leaf, its context formula is the disjunction of the context formulas of its sub-dimensions (a non-leaf dimension is active if any of its sub-dimensions is). Thus, axioms 2 and 3 state that if any of the contexts annotated in the goal or task isn't active but the goal or task occurred anyhow, an invalid occurrence (*iocc()*) diagnosis should be produced.

The example below shows an execution log for the case where the *auto-login* task has occurred because a cookie was detected in the user's computer. No diagnoses are produced, as no errors occurred.

url_entered(1); http_header_detected(2); auth_cookie_detected(3); ∼ wrong_imap(4); occ(t1.2.1.3, 5); correct_key(6); occ(t1.2.1.2.1, 7); occ(t1.2.1.2.2, 8); occ(t1.2.1.2.3, 9); webmail_started(10); occ(t1.3, 11); email_sent(12);

4 Implementation

Wang et al. [1] describe the main algorithms used by the diagnostic framework. In this section, we present the new algorithms that were included in order to produce new axioms that allow the SAT solver to diagnose malicious attacks and consider contextual information.

The *encode_anti_goal_axioms* algorithm analyzes all anti-goals in the goal model that occurred according to the log. For every target of the occurring anti-goals, it encodes an anti-goal success axiom in the form $occ(ag, t_s, t_e) \wedge fd(e, s) \rightarrow fs(ag, s)$.

$encode\_anti\_goal\_axioms(goal\,model,\ log)\ \{$
  $for\ each\ occurring\ anti\ goal\ ag$

```
        if (precond(ag) ≠ null) ∨ (effect(ag) ≠ null)
            for each element e in targets(ag)
                Φ ← Φ ∧ encodeAntiGoalSuccessAxiom(ag, e)
    return Φ
}
```

To produce invalid occurrence axioms such as $occ(g, t_s, t_e) \wedge \neg context\_formula(g, t_s) \rightarrow iocc(g, s)$ (for goals) and $occ(a, t_{occ}) \wedge \neg context\_formula(a, t_{occ}) \rightarrow iocc(a, s)$ (for tasks), the algorithm *encode_invalid_occurrence_axioms* was implemented. This algorithm analyzes every goal and task that has occurred and is annotated with contextual information. For each context dimension annotated in the element, it builds the contexts formula and encodes the invalid occurrence axiom.

```
encode_invalid_occurrence_axioms(goal model, log) {
    for each occurring goal and task e
        if (context_annotations(e) ≠ null)
            for each context dimension c in annotations(e)
                Δ ← Δ ∧ build_context_formula(c, log)
                Φ ← Φ ∧ encodeInvalidOccurrenceAxiom(e, Δ)
    return Φ
}
```

Each context dimension's formula is built with algorithm *build_context_formula*, which recursively navigates the context hierarchy depth-first, joining the leaf-dimensions' formulas in a disjunction.

```
build_context_formula(c, log) {
    if (hasSubDimension(c))
        for each context sub dimension sc of c
            δ ← δ ∨ build_context_formula(sc, log)
        return δ
    else
        return formula(c)
}
```

Last, but not least, changes on how the framework decides if a goal has or hasn't occurred were made due to the new contexts support. After defining any goal with a descendant occurring task as having occurred, *confirm_goal_occurrence* navigates each goal sub-tree from bottom-up, canceling the goal occurrence if any non-occurring sub-goal or task is found with an active context.

```
confirm_goal_occurrence(goal model, log, g) {
    for each sub goal sg
        confirm_goal_occurrence(goal model, log, sg)
    if (decompositionType(g) = AND)
        for each sub goal and task e of g
```

$$if\ (hasNotOccurred(e) \wedge isContextActive(e))$$
$$return\ false$$
$$return\ true$$
}

A prototype of the diagnosing framework was developed in Java.

5 Evaluation of the Proposed Extensions

As done previously in [1], we used the SquirrelMail example to illustrate the characteristics of the framework and evaluated its scalability using the Automated Teller Machine (ATM) simulation example [9]. The experiments were run in a computer with an Intel Core 2 Duo P8400 2.26GHz with 3Mb L2 1066MHz cache and 2GB DDRII 800MHz RAM.

5.1 The SquirrelMail Example

The SquirrelMail example used in [1] has been adapted to demonstrate throughout the paper the new features of the framework.

The log data in section 3.1 shows an error in task *t1.3* (and, consequently, on goal *g1*), since the task has occurred but its effect (*email_sent*) wasn't true in the subsequent time-step. This would usually mean task *t1.3* is faulty. However, with new support for malicious attacks diagnosis, the system also monitors for the successful occurrence of tasks *at1.1*, *at1.2* and *at1.3*, shown in figure 5, meaning anti-goal *ag1* might have been successful in stopping task *t1.3* from working. Therefore, $fs(ag1, s)$ is included as diagnosis alongside $fd(t1.3, s)$.

Another log is shown in section 3.2, referring to the extended SquirrelMail example of figure 8. The log shows the case in which task *t1.2.1.3* occurs instead of *t1.2.1.1*, as the former has an active context (cookie detected on time-step 3) and the latter doesn't. The result is no diagnosis produced and the goal *g1.2.1* occurs normally even though it's AND-decomposed and *t1.2.1.1* doesn't occur, as that child has an inactive context. The exact same log without $auth\_cookie\_detected(3)$ produces $iocc(t1.2.1.3, s)$ as diagnosis, as a task (or goal) should not occur with an inactive context.

5.2 Performance Evaluation with the ATM Example

Tests with the ATM case study were based in the goal model obtained in [1] by reverse-engineering its OO design [9] and were also adapted to include malicious attacks and contextual information.

The base test set is composed of 20 goal models and their respective logs. The first model contains 50 goal model elements extracted from the ATM simulation requirements. The other models repeat these elements to produce goal models of sizes varying from 100 to 1000. Two new test sets were generated, one with anti-goals and another with contextual information.

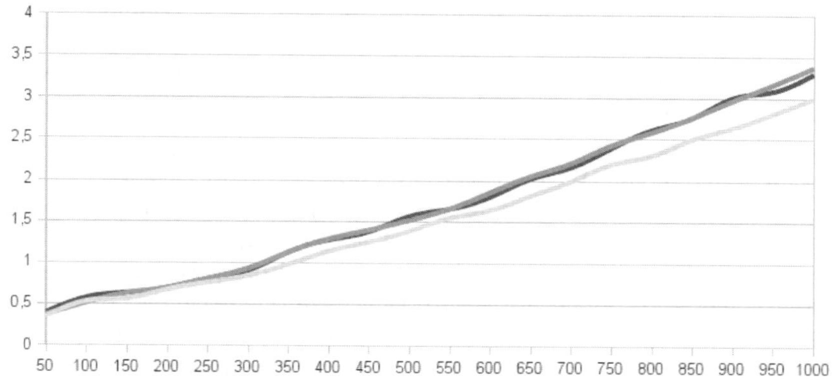

Fig. 9. Performance evaluation of the ATM Simulation case study

Figure 9 shows the time in seconds (y-axis) taken to execute the diagnose in each test set (x-axis). The lines are very close together, which shows the inclusion of anti-goals and contextual information hasn't changed the performance of the diagnosing framework. The base test set starts with 0,39s in the 50-elements goal model and goes up to 3,30s in the 1000-elements model. The test cases for anti-goals and contextual information have times that vary from 0,36s to 3,37s and from 0,34s to 3,00s, respectively. When contextual information is taken into account, processing is faster because only parts of the goal model are considered for each active context.

6 Related Work

As related work to her proposal, Wang et al. [1] cite the ReqMon framework [10] and the works by Fickas & Feather [2] and Winbladh et al. [11]. However, none of these deal specifically with malicious attacks or contextual information.

There are many proposals for security requirement engineering. Haley et al. [12] define security requirements as constraints to functions of the system and propose a framework that explicitly includes context and determines satisfaction of the security requirements. Elahi & Yu [13] incorporate security trade-off analysis into requirements engineering and develop an i*-based, goal-oriented framework for modeling and analyzing them, accompanied by a knowledge base of security trade-offs. Sindre & Opdahl propose ReqSec [14], a methodology that builds on misuse cases to integrate elicitation, specification and analysis of security requirements with the development of functional requirements of the system. Rodriguez et al. [15] propose M-BPSec, a UML 2.0 profile over the Activity Diagram which allows for the capturing of security requirements and creating of secure business processes. Mellado et al. [16] have extended the Security Requirements Engineering Process for Software Product Lines (SREPPLine) for the management of security requirements variability. These proposals focus on security requirements from analysis to validation, but not on runtime. Our work focuses on monitoring software at runtime, for purposes of diagnosing attacks and the system components they might affect.

Some proposals include a monitoring component, but without an associated diagnostic engine. Giorgini et al. [17] extend the i*/Tropos modeling framework to define Secure Tropos, which includes the concepts of trust, ownership and delegation of permission. Within this framework, they model certain types of security requirements (for example, access control policies) and can apply formal reasoning techniques to determine whether a system specification violates any security requirements. This proposal does use monitoring (by actors, who can be system, human, or organizational) to legitimize the delegation of services to untrusted actors. Graves & Zulkernine [18] have modified an existing Intrusion Detection System (Snort) in order to use rules with context information translated from attack scenarios written in a software specification language (AsmL). Snort monitors the runtime operation of a system and alerts when a security requirement has been violated.

On the context variability side, many works on context-aware systems focus on the requirements phase. For instance, Hong et al. [19] focus on context-awareness for product families and use problem frames for representing variability in the problem space, rather than the solution space. For ubiquitous computing, Salifu et al. [20] extends the notion of context as basis of the proposed methodology for requirement elicitation. Semmak et al. [21] extends the Kaos meta-model with variability concepts (along similar lines to our own work) in order to specify a requirements family model, which then derives different specifications depending on stakeholders needs. The key difference in our approach is purpose: we model contextual variability to be able to monitor applications that have richer goal models, such as for autonomic systems.

Ali et al. [22] propose an extension to the Tropos framework for developing location-based software. Our proposal shares a lot of similarity with theirs (namely, context/location-based or-decomposition, and-decomposition and contribution to softgoals), but focuses on monitoring and diagnosing instead of modeling and analysis. Both works can be considered complimentary, as our framework could be used to monitor and diagnose location-based software developed with location-based Tropos.

7 Conclusion

By supporting anti-goals and contextual variability in the monitoring & diagnosis framework, we have extended the domain of applicability of Wang's M&D framework, notably to support monitoring and diagnosis for failures provoked by malicious attacks. The extensions have been evaluated for feasibility and scalability up to medium-sized goal models.

Future work includes the study of possible compensation mechanisms. Once our system has determined that an attack is in progress, it needs to select a compensation that will hopefully prevent the attack from succeeding. In addition, our diagnostic reasoner needs to be complemented with probabilistic reasoning techniques that looks for probable attacks, their chances of success and the chances of particular compensation mechanisms thwarting such attacks.

References

1. Wang, Y., McIlraith, S.A., Yu, Y., Mylopoulos, J.: Monitoring and diagnosing software requirements. Automated Software Engineering 16, 3–35 (2009)
2. Fickas, S., Feather, M.: Requirements monitoring in dynamic environments. In: Proceedings of the Second IEEE International Symposium on Requirements Engineering, vol. 1995, pp. 140–147 (1995)
3. Giorgini, P., Mylopoulos, J., Nicchiarelli, E., Sebastiani, R.: Reasoning with goal models. In: Spaccapietra, S., March, S.T., Kambayashi, Y. (eds.) ER 2002. LNCS, vol. 2503, pp. 167–181. Springer, Heidelberg (2002)
4. van Lamsweerde, A., Brohez, S., De Landtsheer, R., Janssens, D.: From system goals to intruder anti-goals: Attack generation and resolution for security requirements engineering. In: Workshop on Requirements for High Assurance Systems (RHAS 2003), pre-workshop of the 11th International IEEE Conference on Requirements Engineering, Software Engineering Institute Report, September 2003, pp. 49–56 (2003)
5. Lapouchnian, A., Mylopoulos, J.: Modeling domain variability in requirements engineering with contexts. In: Laender, A.H.F., et al. (eds.) ER 2009. LNCS, vol. 5829, pp. 115–130. Springer, Heidelberg (2009)
6. Castello, R.: Squirrelmail (2009), `http://www.squirrelmail.org`
7. Yu, Y., Wang, Y., Mylopoulos, J., Liaskos, S., Lapouchnian, A., do Prado Leite, J.: Reverse engineering goal models from legacy code. In: Proceedings of the 13th IEEE International Conference on Requirements Engineering, 2005, August -2 September 2005, pp. 363–372 (2005)
8. Susi, A., Perini, A., Mylopoulos, J., Giorgini, P.: The tropos metamodel and its use. Informatica 29, 401–408 (2005)
9. Bjork, R.C.: Atm simulation (2009), `http://www.cs.gordon.edu/courses/cs211/ATMExample/`
10. Robinson, W.N.: Implementing rule-based monitors within a framework for continuous requirements monitoring. In: HICSS 2005: Proceedings of the 38th Annual Hawaii International Conference on System Sciences - Track 7, p. 188a. IEEE Computer Society, Los Alamitos (2005)
11. Winbladh, K., Alspaugh, T.A., Ziv, H., Richardson, D.J.: An automated approach for goal-driven, specification-based testing. In: ASE 2006: Proceedings of the 21st IEEE/ACM International Conference on Automated Software Engineering, Washington, DC, USA, pp. 289–292. IEEE Computer Society, Los Alamitos (2006)
12. Haley, C.B., Moffett, J.D., Laney, R., Nuseibeh, B.: A framework for security requirements engineering. In: SESS 2006: Proceedings of the 2006 international workshop on Software engineering for secure systems, pp. 35–42. ACM, New York (2006)
13. Elahi, G., Yu, E.: A goal oriented approach for modeling and analyzing security trade-offs. In: Parent, C., Schewe, K.-D., Storey, V.C., Thalheim, B. (eds.) ER 2007. LNCS, vol. 4801, pp. 375–390. Springer, Heidelberg (2007)
14. Sindre, G., Opdahl, A.L.: Reqsec - requirements for secure information systems, project proposal for fritek (2007), `http://www.idi.ntnu.no/~guttors/reqsec/plan.pdf`

15. Rodríguez, A., Fernández-Medina, E., Piattini, M.: M-bPSec: A method for security requirement elicitation from a UML 2.0 business process specification. In: Hainaut, J.-L., Rundensteiner, E.A., Kirchberg, M., Bertolotto, M., Brochhausen, M., Chen, Y.-P.P., Cherfi, S.S.-S., Doerr, M., Han, H., Hartmann, S., Parsons, J., Poels, G., Rolland, C., Trujillo, J., Yu, E., Zimányie, E. (eds.) ER Workshops 2007. LNCS, vol. 4802, pp. 106–115. Springer, Heidelberg (2007)
16. Mellado, D., Fernandez-Medina, E., Piattini, M.: Security requirements variability for software product lines, pp. 1413–1420 (March 2008)
17. Giorgini, P., Massacci, F., Mylopoulos, J., Zannone, N.: Modeling security requirements through ownership, permission and delegation. In: RE 2005: Proceedings of the 13th IEEE International Conference on Requirements Engineering, Washington, DC, USA, pp. 167–176. IEEE Computer Society, Los Alamitos (2005)
18. Graves, M., Zulkernine, M.: Bridging the gap: software specification meets intrusion detector. In: PST 2006: Proceedings of the 2006 International Conference on Privacy, Security and Trust, pp. 1–8. ACM, New York (2006)
19. Hong, D., Chiu, D.K.W., Shen, V.Y.: Requirements elicitation for the design of context-aware applications in a ubiquitous environment. In: ICEC 2005: Proceedings of the 7th international conference on Electronic commerce, pp. 590–596. ACM, New York (2005)
20. Salifu, M., Nuseibeh, B., Rapanotti, L., Tun, T.T.: Using problem descriptions to represent variability for context-aware applications. In: First International Workshop on Variability Modelling of Software-intensive Systems (2007)
21. Semmak, F., Gnaho, C., Laleau, R.: Extended kaos to support variability for goal oriented requirements reuse. In: Proceedings of the International Workshop on Model Driven Information Systems Engineering: Enterprise, User and System Models (MoDISE-EUS 2008, in conjunction with CAiSE), pp. 22–33 (2008)
22. Ali, R., Dalpiaz, F., Giorgini, P.: Location-based software modeling and analysis: Tropos-based approach. In: Li, Q., Spaccapietra, S., Yu, E., Olivé, A. (eds.) ER 2008. LNCS, vol. 5231, pp. 169–182. Springer, Heidelberg (2008)

A Modeling Ontology for Integrating Vulnerabilities into Security Requirements Conceptual Foundations*

Golnaz Elahi[1], Eric Yu[2], and Nicola Zannone[3]

[1] Department of Computer Science, University of Toronto
gelahi@cs.toronto.edu
[2] Faculty of Information, University of Toronto
yu@ischool.utoronto.ca
[3] Eindhoven University of Technology
n.zannone@tue.nl

Abstract. Vulnerabilities are weaknesses in the requirements, design, and implementation, which attackers exploit to compromise the system. This paper proposes a vulnerability-centric modeling ontology, which aims to integrate empirical knowledge of vulnerabilities into the system development process. In particular, we identify the basic concepts for modeling and analyzing vulnerabilities and their effects on the system. These concepts drive the definition of criteria that make it possible to compare and evaluate security frameworks based on vulnerabilities. We show how the proposed modeling ontology can be adopted in various conceptual modeling frameworks through examples.

1 Introduction

Security needs are responses to being or feeling vulnerable. Vulnerable actors take measures to mitigate perceived risks, by using locks on the doors, surveillance cameras, etc. Existing security requirements engineering frameworks focus on various aspects for eliciting security requirements, such as attacker behavior [29,31] and attacker goals [32], design of secure components [15], social aspects [18,11], and events that can cause system failure [1]. However, attacks and consequent security failures often take place because of the exploitation of weaknesses or backdoors within the system. These weaknesses of the system or its environment that in conjunction with an internal or external threat can lead to a security failure are known as *vulnerabilities* [28] in security engineering. Vulnerabilities such as buffer overflow or weak passwords may result from misspecifications in the requirements, neglecting required pre- and post-conditions checks, faulty design and architecture, and programming errors.

In recent years, software companies and government agencies have become particularly aware of the security risks that vulnerabilities impose on system security and have started analyzing and reporting detected vulnerabilities of products and services [5,6,23,27]. This empirical knowledge of vulnerabilities is used for monitoring and maintaining system security and updating patches. However, vulnerability analysis has

* Financial support from Natural Science and Engineering Research Council of Canada and Bell University Labs is gratefully acknowledged.

A.H.F. Laender et al. (Eds.): ER 2009, LNCS 5829, pp. 99–114, 2009.

not played a significant role in the elicitation of security requirements. There is evidence that knowing how systems have failed can help analysts build systems resistant to failures [24]. For this purpose, analysts should answer three basic questions [17]: (1) how a vulnerability enters into the system; (2) when it enters into the system; (3) where it is manifested in the system.

Vulnerabilities are introduced into the system by performing some activities or employing some assets. By identifying vulnerabilities and explicitly linking them to the activities and assets that introduce them into the system, analysts can recognize the vulnerable components of the system, study how vulnerabilities spread within the system, trace security failures back to the source vulnerability, and relate vulnerabilities to the stakeholders that ultimately are hurt. This information helps analysts understand how threats compromise the system, assess the risks of vulnerabilities, and decide on countermeasures to protect the system [9]. Some contributions [2,17] collect and organize vulnerabilities and security flaws for providing analysts with more precise security knowledge. However, they do not provide a conceptual framework that allows analysts to elicit security requirements according to the identified vulnerabilities. To define a systematic way for linking empirical security knowledge, we need to identify the basic concepts that come into play when facing security issues. Those concepts influences the security analysis that analysts can perform.

This paper proposes a modeling ontology for integrating vulnerabilities into the security requirements conceptual foundations. We refer to the structure of conceptual modeling elements and their relationships as the conceptual foundation of a modeling framework. The proposed ontology, which is independent of the existing conceptual modeling foundations, aims to detect the missing security constructs in security requirements modeling frameworks and facilitates their enhancement. The ontology can be used as a unified way for comparing different conceptual foundations and their reasoning power as well as extending their ability for modeling and analyzing vulnerabilities. We propose the modeling ontology by means of a general meta-model. The meta-model helps integrate vulnerabilities into the conceptual foundation of a target framework, and the extended framework can be used for modeling and analyzing security requirements. To make the discussion more concrete, the proposed meta-model is adopted in three target conceptual frameworks, and the benefits and limitations of such adoptions are discussed.

The paper is organized as follows. Section 2 discusses the conceptual foundation for security analysis with a particular focus on vulnerabilities. Section 3 discusses and compares existing security frameworks centered on vulnerabilities. Section 4 introduces a vulnerability modeling ontology. Section 5 discusses how the modeling ontology can be realized in different target frameworks. Section 6 gives examples of integrating the ontology into three security requirements engineering frameworks. Finally, Section 7 draws conclusions and discusses future work.

2 The Conceptual Foundation for Vulnerability Analysis

This section reviews the security literature with the aim of defining a conceptual foundation for security requirements engineering centered on vulnerabilities. We discuss the basic security conceptual constructs together with the analysis facilities they offer.

A basic concept that comes into play when eliciting security requirements is the concept of *asset*. In security engineering, an asset is *"anything that has value to the organization"* [13]. Assets can be people, information, software, and hardware [7].

Assets and services can be the target of *attackers* (or *malicious actor*), and consequently, they need to be protected. Attackers can be internal or external entities of the system. They perform *malicious actions* which attempt to break the security of a system or a component of a system. An *attack* is a set of intentional unwarranted (malicious) actions designed to compromise confidentiality, integrity, availability or any other desired feature of an IT system [30]. By analyzing the possible ways in which a system can be attacked, analysts can study attackers' behavior, estimate the cost of attacks, and determine their impact on system security.

Malicious actors often exploit *vulnerabilities* within the system to attack it. A vulnerability is a weakness or a backdoor which allows an attacker to compromise its correct behavior [28]. In the physical world, vulnerabilities are usually tangible and measurable. A crack in the wall is a concrete example of physical weakness. In the context of computer security, vulnerabilities are less tangible and visualizable. Vulnerabilities are *brought* to the system by adopting a software product or executing a service. By identifying the source of the vulnerability (e.g., software product, service, or data), analysts can identify what are the vulnerable components of the system, propagate the vulnerabilities in the model of the system, evaluate the benefits and risks of (vulnerable) entities, and decide on cost-effective countermeasures accordingly.

Risk has been proposed as a measure to evaluate the impact of an attack on the system. Risk involves the probability (*likelihood*) of a successful attack and its *severity* on the system [12]. Risk assessment is a type of analysis one can perform using security conceptual models. Therefore, risk is not a primitive concept and we do not include it into the meta-model for security requirements frameworks (Section 4).

Analyzing attacks and vulnerabilities allows analysts to understand how attackers can compromise the system. However, to assess the risk of an attack, analysts also need to consider the motivations (*malicious goals*) of attackers. Understanding why the attackers may attack the system helps identify the target of the attack and estimate the efforts (e.g., time, cost, resources, etc.) that attackers are willing to spend to compromise the system. Schneier [29] argues that understanding who are the attackers along with their motivations, goals, and targets, aids designers in adopting proper countermeasures to mitigate threats.

When the risk of an attack is higher than the risk tolerance of some stakeholder, analysts need to take the adequate measure to mitigate such risks [1]. A *countermeasure* is a protection mechanism employed to secure the system [30]. Countermeasures can be actions, processes, devices, solutions, or systems, such as firewalls, authentication protocols, digital signature, etc. Knowledge about attackers' behavior and vulnerabilities helps analysts in the identification of appropriate countermeasures to protect the system. Countermeasures intend to prevent attacks or vulnerability exploitations from compromising the system. For instance, they are used to patch vulnerabilities or prevent their exploitation. Modeling and analyzing the countermeasures is important for evaluating their efficacy and consequently the ultimate security of the system.

Several conceptual modeling frameworks for security analysis take advantage of *temporally-ordered* models for analyzing attacks [21,25]. Incorporating the concept of time into the attack modeling helps understand the sequence of actions and vulnerability exploitations which lead to a successful attack. The resulting model is useful for analyzing attacks as well as designing and evaluating countermeasures that prevents the attacks at the right step. On the other hand, temporally-ordered models of the system and stakeholders' interactions increase the complexity of requirements models which may not be suitable for the early stages of the development.

3 Vulnerability Modeling and Analysis Approaches

This section surveys and compares different approaches proposed in the literature for modeling, organizing, and analyzing vulnerabilities. We also discuss the types of reasoning that the existing conceptual frameworks support.

3.1 Vulnerability Catalogs

The most primitive way for modeling and organizing vulnerabilities is grouping detected and reported flaws and weaknesses into catalogs. Although catalogs are not conceptual models, they are not entirely structure-less. Various web-based software vulnerability knowledge bases provide searchable lists of vulnerabilities. Catalogs of vulnerabilities contain different types of information with different information granularity which are useful for specific stages of the development and types of analysis. These web portals aim to increase the level of awareness about vulnerable products and severity of vulnerabilities. For example, the National Vulnerability Database [27], SANS top-20 annual security risks [27], and Common Weakness Enumeration (CWE) [6] provide updated lists of vulnerabilities and weaknesses. CVE contains vendor-, platform- and product-specific vulnerabilities. SANS list and CWE catalog include more abstract weaknesses, errors, and vulnerabilities. Some entries in these lists are technology and platform independent, while some of the vulnerabilities are described for specific product, platform, and programming language.

3.2 Vulnerability Analysis for Computer Network Security

Modeling and analyzing vulnerabilities within computer networks is common, because vulnerabilities in such systems can be easily associated to physical nodes of the network. Several attack modeling and analysis approaches [25,19,10,14] take advantage of Attack Graphs and Bayesian Networks for vulnerabilities assessment at the network level. Phillips et al. [25] introduce Attack Graphs to analyze vulnerabilities in computer networks. Attack graphs provide a method for modeling attacks and relating them to the machines in a network and to attackers. Liu and Man [19] use Bayesian Networks to model all potential atomic attack steps in a network. Causal relationships between vulnerabilities encoded in an attack graph are used to model the overall security of a network in [10]. Jajodia [14] proposes a mechanism to quantify the security of the network by calculating the combined effect of all the vulnerabilities present in the network.

Table 1. Comparison of modeling notations. N indicates that the concept or relation is not considered, and Y indicates the relation is considered explicitly in the notation. P means the relation is implicitly considered or its semantics is not well defined.

Method	Web-based vulnerabilities knowledge sources	Network security analysis methods	CORAS Framework [3]	Secure Tropos by Matulevicius et al. [20]	Risk-Based Security Framework by Mayer et al. [22]	Extensions to misuse case diagram [26]	Security extension on i* framework by Elahi et al. [8, 9]
Conceptual Foundation	Structured and searchable catalogs	Network configuration models, AG, BN	CORAS UML-profile based models	Secure Tropos	i* framework	Misuse case models	i* framework
Vulnerability graphical representation	None	None		 Belief		 Vulnerability	
Relation of vulnerabilities to vulnerable elements	N	Y	N	N	N	P	Y
Relation of vulnerabilities to other vulnerabilities	Y	Y	P	N	N	N	N
Propagation of vulnerabilities to other system elements	N	Y	N	N	N	N	Y
Effects of vulnerabilities	Y	Y	Y	Y	P	N	Y
Severity of vulnerabilities	Y	Y	N	N	N	N	Y
Relation of vulnerabilities and attacks (exploitation)	P	Y	P	P	Y	Y	Y
Countermeasures' impacts on vulnerabilities	N	P	P	N	N	Y	Y
Steps of vulnerability exploitation (sequence)	N	Y	N	N	N	N	N

3.3 Modeling Vulnerabilities for Security Requirements Engineering

In secure software engineering frameworks, vulnerabilities usually refer to the general openness to attacks and risks. For example, Liu et al. [18] propose a vulnerability analysis method for eliciting security requirements, where vulnerabilities are the weak dependencies that may jeopardize the goals of depender actors in the network of social and organizational dependencies.

Only a few software engineering approaches consider analyzing vulnerabilities, as weaknesses of the system, during the elicitation of security requirements. Matulevicius et al. [20] treat vulnerabilities as beliefs in the knowledge base of attackers which may contribute to the success of an attack. In [22], the i* framework is extended to represent vulnerabilities and their relation with threats and other elements of the i* models.

The CORAS project [7] proposes a modeling framework for model-based risk assessment in the form of a UML profile. The profile defines UML stereotypes and rules to express assets, risks that target the assets, vulnerabilities, accidental and deliberate threats, and the security solutions. CORAS provides a way for expressing how a vulnerability leads to another vulnerability and how a vulnerability or combination of vulnerabilities lead to a threat. CORAS also provides the means to relate treatments to threats and vulnerabilities.

Rostad [26] suggests extending the misuse case notation for including vulnerabilities into requirements models. Vulnerabilities are defined as a weakness that may be exploited by misuse cases. Vulnerabilities are expressed as a type of use case, with an *exploit* relationship from the misuse case to the vulnerability and an *include* relation with the use case that introduces the vulnerability.

3.4 Comparison of the Conceptual Modeling Frameworks

Table 1 compares capabilities of the reviewed conceptual structures based on the conceptual foundation discussed in Section 2. The conceptual modeling frameworks that focus on security requirements engineering, model vulnerabilities in various ways. Among them, CORAS [7] does not investigate which design choices, requirements, or processes have brought the vulnerabilities to the system, and the semantics of relationships among vulnerabilities, and between vulnerabilities and threats are not defined. Similar to CORAS, the resulting models in [20,22] do not specify how, by what actions and actors the vulnerability is brought to the system. These models do not capture the impact of countermeasures on the vulnerabilities and attacks. In [22], threats are not related to the attacker that poses them, and the semantics of the relation between threats and vulnerabilities is not well defined.

In summary, the missing point in the surveyed approaches is lack of modeling constructs that express how vulnerabilities enter into the system and how they spread out within the system. The link between attacks and vulnerabilities are implicitly (and explicitly) modeled in all of the surveyed approaches. However, among the modeling notations that provide explicit constructs for modeling vulnerability, only a few frameworks such as CORAS [7], i* security extensions [9,8], and extensions of misuse case models [26] relate the countermeasures to vulnerabilities. The semantics of the countermeasure impact in [7,26] is not well defined, and the model cannot be used to evaluate the impact of countermeasures on the overall system security. Although modeling and analyzing the order of actions to accomplish an attack may affect the countermeasure selection and development, the existing frameworks for security requirements engineering do not consider the concept of sequence (temporal order) in their meta-model.

4 A Modeling Ontology for Vulnerabilities

This section presents a vulnerabilities modeling ontology which aims to incorporate vulnerabilities into requirements models for expressing how vulnerabilities are brought to the system and propagated, how the vulnerabilities get exploited by attackers and affect different actors, and how countermeasures mitigate the vulnerabilities. The ontology is described by an abstract meta-model in Fig. 1, which defines and relates the conceptual constructs gathered in Section 2. The conceptual modeling framework that one may integrate with ontology elements is called the *target* framework. The target framework can be any conceptual modeling foundation, such as business process modeling frameworks, UML static and dynamic diagrams, agent- and goal-oriented modeling frameworks, etc.

Vulnerability Definition in the Ontology. A *concrete element* is a tangible entity, which epending on the target framework, can be an activity, task, function, class, use case, etc. Concrete elements may introduce vulnerabilities into the system, which are then called *vulnerable elements*. In the meta-model the relationship between a vulnerability and a concrete element is captured by the *bring* relation. Exploitation of vulnerabilities can have *effects* on other elements These elements are called *affected elements*. The *effect* relation is presented as a class and is characterized by the attribute *severity* that specifies the criticality of vulnerabilities effects. Concrete elements have two attributes, *duraion* and *sequence*, to support the concept of time in the target framework.

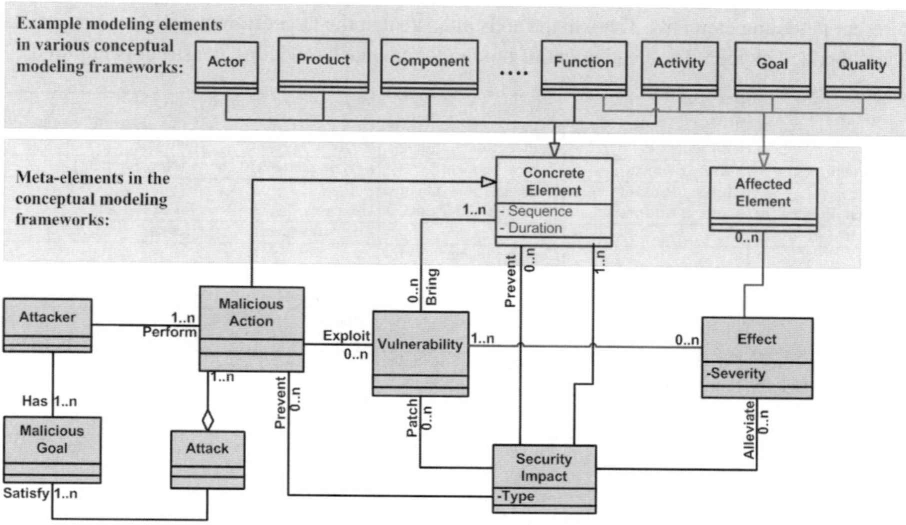

Fig. 1. The vulnerability-centric modeling ontology for security concepts

Attack and Attacker Definition in the Ontology. An *attack* involves the execution of (a *sequence* of) *malicious actions* that one or more actors perform to satisfy some *malicious goal*. Linking attackers to malicious actions allows modeling attacks that require the collaboration of different attackers. A *malicious action* can *exploit* a number of vulnerabilities, which has (negative) effects on the *affected elements*. This negative effect is captured as a relation which links vulnerabilities to the affected elements. This relation is modeled as a class in the meta-model, which enables defining the severity of the effect as an attribute of the class.

Countermeasure Definition in the Ontology. A concrete element may have a *security impact* on attacks. Such an element can be interpreted as a security countermeasure. The *security impact* is a relationships which is expressed as a class in the meta-model. Security countermeasures can be used to *patch* vulnerabilities, *alleviate* the effect of vulnerabilities, *prevent* the malicious actions that exploit vulnerabilities or can prevent (or remove) the concrete elements that bring the vulnerabilities. By patching a vulnerability, the countermeasure fixes the weakness in the system. Examples of such a countermeasure is a software update that the vendors provide. A countermeasure that alleviates vulnerability effects, does not address the source of the problem, but it intends to reduce the effects of the vulnerability exploitation. For example, a backup system alleviates the impact of security failures that cause data loss. Countermeasures can also prevent an attacker to perform some actions. For example, an authentication solution prevents unauthorized access to assets. Countermeasure may prevent performing vulnerable actions or using vulnerable assets, which results in removing the vulnerable elements that have brought vulnerabilities to the system. For example, disabling JavaScript option in the browser prevents the browser to run a malware.

Table 2. The mapping of the elements in the vulnerability modeling ontology to elements of different modeling elements. The x in the cells indicate that the target framework does not provide any embedded element for the element of ontology and a new modeling construct is required.

	Static models (UML Class diagram)	Dynamic models (UML Sequence diagram)	Requirements models (UML use case diagram)	Goal modes (i* agent- and goal-oriented model)
Vulnerability	x (New Element)	x (New Element)	x (New Element)	x (New Element)
Concrete Element	Classes, Packages, Operations, Attributes	Messages, Guards, Combined Fragments	Use cases	Tasks, Resources
Attacker	x	Roles	Actors (misuser)	Actors
Malicious Action	x	Concrete elements for modeling behavior	Misuse Cases	Tasks
Malicious Goals	x	x	x	Goals
Effect	x	x	Adding new Stereotypes	Contribution Links
Affected Element	Classes, Packages, Operations, Attributes	Messages, Guards, Combined Fragments	Use Cases	Goals, Tasks, Resources
Security Impact	x	x	Adding new Stereotypes	Using and extending Contribution Links

5 Adoption of the Modeling Ontology

In the previous section, we defined the modeling ontology that can be used to integrate vulnerabilities into existing conceptual modeling frameworks. This section discusses the adoption and realization of the proposed modeling ontology in various types of conceptual modeling frameworks. Table 2 provides a mapping between the modeling constructs in four example conceptual modeling frameworks and the elements of the vulnerability-centric modeling ontology. The mapping illustrates which modeling constructs in the frameworks can be used (or inverted) for expressing the ontology's elements, and which elements of the ontology need to be incorporated in the target conceptual framework by adding a new construct. In this table, UML class and sequences diagrams are examples of static and dynamic modeling approaches, respectively. Use case and i* models are examples of requirements models. The comparison can be generalized to other similar conceptual frameworks (e.g., the properties for sequence diagrams can be generalized to other dynamic modeling approaches).

Realization of Vulnerabilities in the Target Framework. To incorporate *vulnerabilities* into a target framework, a new modeling construct (with a graphical representation) need to be added to the target framework. Vulnerabilities need to be (graphically) linked to the vulnerable element, which expresses the *bring* relationship. The vulnerability effect and its severity need to be defined in each specific conceptual modeling framework according to the semantics of relationships in that conceptual framework. For example, in the UML use case diagram, one may define a new stereotype to specify the effect of vulnerabilities exploitation (and its severity), and in a goal-oriented modeling framework like i*, contribution links can be used to represent the effect of vulnerabilities and their severity. Existing relationship in static and dynamic modeling approaches do not provide the required semantics to model the vulnerability effects.

Modeling vulnerabilities (and related concepts) in different conceptual modeling frameworks facilitate different types of analysis and reasoning. Adding vulnerabilities to static models such as deployment diagrams allows one to propagate vulnerabilities from the elements that bring the vulnerabilities to other system components, by analyzing the function that vulnerable components play in the system. By integrating vulnerabilities into dynamic models, one can detect the sequence of vulnerability propagation in a period of time. Integration of vulnerabilities into requirements and goal models help detect the functionalities that introduce risks to the system (by bringing vulnerabilities). In addition, vulnerabilities can be propagated into the network of functions, goals, and actors. Examples of vulnerabilities propagation can be found in [9].

Realization of Attacks and Attackers in the Target Framework. The definition of attacks is fundamentally a matter of perspective: the nature and semantics of *malicious actions* are similar to the nature of conceptual elements that model the normal behavior of the system. Therefore, distinguishing the malicious and non-malicious behavior does not affect the analysis one can perform on the models. However, Sindre and Opdahl [16] show that graphical models become much clearer if the distinction between malicious and non-malicious elements is made explicit and the malicious actions are visually distinguished from the legitimate ones. They show that the use of inverted elements strongly draws the attention to dependability aspects early on for those who discuss the models. Therefore, in the target frameworks, the (inverted) concrete elements that model normal actions and interactions within the system is semantically sufficient to model *malicious actions*. For example, in a sequence diagram, by using the existing sequence modeling constructs, the sequences of messages to mount an attack can also be modeled.

Several conceptual modeling frameworks, such as sequence diagrams and state charts, provide the required foundations for modeling sequence of actions in a temporally-ordered fashion. On the other hand, the modeling approaches that provide a static view to the system, such as UML class, deployment, package, and component diagrams do not support modeling actions and dynamic behavior of the system. Such frameworks are not expressive enough for modeling (malicious) actions. Some conceptual frameworks provide means to model the system and actors' actions in a static way (e.g., use case diagrams and i* agent- and goal-oriented models). Such modeling approaches provide a static view of the malicious actions and vulnerability exploitations, and cannot model the temporally-ordered sequence of actions or messages, vulnerability exploitations, and pre-conditions that lead to an attack.

Attackers can be modeled using the (inverted) actor element in the target framework. For example, an attacker can be a role with a lifeline in UML sequence diagrams or an actor that triggers misuse cases in use case diagrams. However, some conceptual modeling frameworks, such as UML class or deployment diagrams do not provide constructs for expressing actors, which limits the security analysis that they can perform.

Several conceptual modeling frameworks focus on "what" and "how" in the system. Such frameworks, such as UML static and dynamic diagrams, do not allow modeling the intentions and motivations of the interacting parties in the system. Goal-oriented conceptual modeling frameworks such as i*, Tropos, and KAOS provide required means to model goals; therefore, the attackers' malicious goals can be modeled by using (inverted) conceptual constructs that these frameworks provide for modeling goals of interacting parties.

Realization of Countermeasures in the Target Framework. We do not distinguish security elements from non-security elements in the meta-model, because the nature of elements which specify the system behavior is not different from the elements that model the security mechanisms of the system, and the distinction does not affect the security requirements analysis. Similar to the vulnerabilities' effects, the semantics of countermeasures' impact need to be defined in each specific conceptual modeling framework according to the semantics of relationships in the target framework.

6 Examples of Adopting the Proposed Ontology

In this section, the proposed ontology is adopted in three conceptual foundations to illustrate the realization of the ontology and its benefits. These examples aim to illustrate how the elements of the meta-model are realized in different conceptual frameworks for (security) requirements and risk analysis. We integrate the concept of vulnerability into misuse case models, as an example of a static requirements modeling approach. We revise CORAS, as an example of risk analysis frameworks which is able to express vulnerabilities. In this example, we analyze how the adoption of the ontology can enhance reasoning and analysis power based on CORAS models. Finally, we show how vulnerabilities and related security concepts can be added to the i* framework, as an example of goal-oriented requirements modeling frameworks. All the enhancements are illustrated with the meta-model and concrete examples based on a browser and web application scenario.

6.1 Integrating Vulnerability Modeling in (Mis)Use Case Diagrams

Misuse case analysis is known as a useful technique for eliciting and modeling security requirements and threats [31]. In misuse case models, attacks and attackers are expressed using inverted use cases and actors, where misuse cases threaten other use cases and security use cases mitigate the attacks. However, misuse case models do not capture the vulnerabilities that attackers may exploit to compromise the system. In addition, models are not expressive enough to fully capture the impact of security uses case on other (mis)use cases. For instance, one can only model countermeasures that prevent misuse cases, whereas countermeasures for patching vulnerabilities and alleviating their exploitation impacts cannot be represented.

Fig. 2 shows the revised meta-model of misuse case models by adopting the proposed modeling ontology to fill the discussed gaps. In the enhanced meta-model, highlighted classes and dashed relationships represent the element and relationships added from the ontology respectively. The concrete elements in the use case models is the "use case" element which may *bring* vulnerabilities to the system. An attack (misuse case) exploits a vulnerability, and the effect of the exploitation is a *threaten* relation to other use cases. New relationships such as *exploits* and *effects* of security use cases are modeled by new stereotypes. Fig. 3 depicts adoption of the ontology elements into an example misuse case diagram. The left hand side of the figure shows the misuse case model [31] for a web application scenario where a cross site scripting attack occurs, and the right hand side of the model shows our proposal for modeling vulnerabilities and linking them to (mis)use cases.

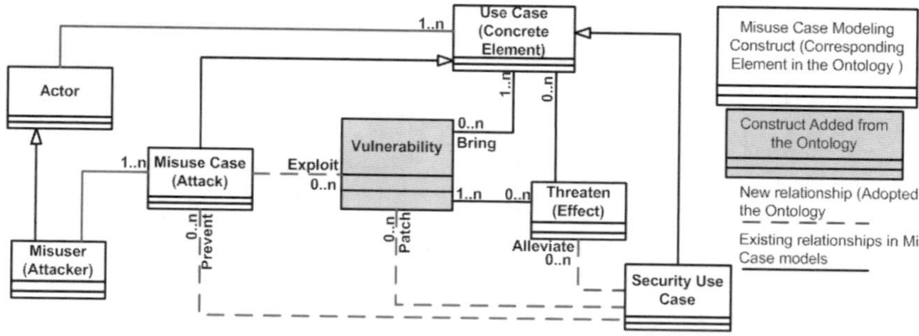

Fig. 2. Revising the misuse case modeling notation by adopting the modeling ontology

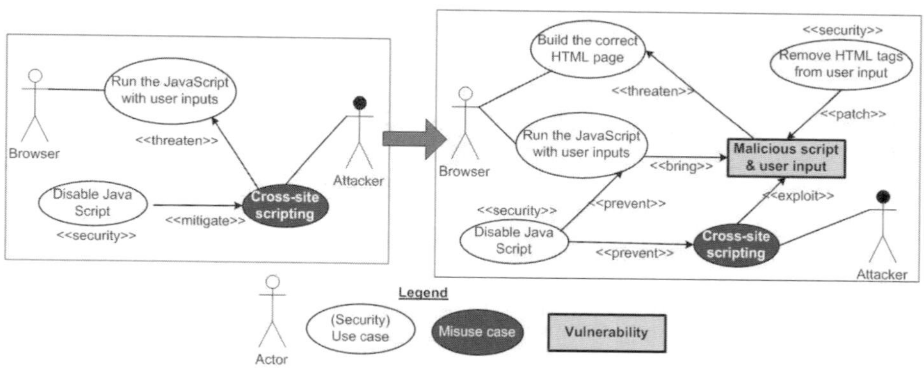

Fig. 3. Integrating vulnerabilities into the misuse case diagrams, example of a web application and brower scenario

6.2 Revising Vulnerability Modeling in the CORAS Approach

CORAS [7] provides modeling constructs to express threats, vulnerabilities, threat scenarios, unwanted incidents, risks, assets, and treatment scenarios. CORAS models show the causal relationships from the vulnerabilities to threat scenarios; however, CORAS models do not show what actions or scenario in the system introduce the vulnerabilities. In the CORAS models, the *exploit* relationship is not explicitly expressed, and effects of vulnerabilities' exploitation cannot be expressed explicitly. Besides, treatment scenarios are only connected to vulnerabilities and the semantics of this relationship is not well defined in CORAS.

Fig. 4 shows the revised meta-model of CORAS by adoption of the proposed vulnerability modeling ontology. In the enhanced meta-model, the elements and relationships that are adopted from the ontology are represented as highlighted classes and dashed relationships, respectively. The right hand side of Fig. 5 gives an example of adopting the proposed ontology in the graphical CORAS modeling language for the browser and web application case study. The left hand side of the Fig. 5 shows the CORAS model of the scenario without the ontology enhancements.

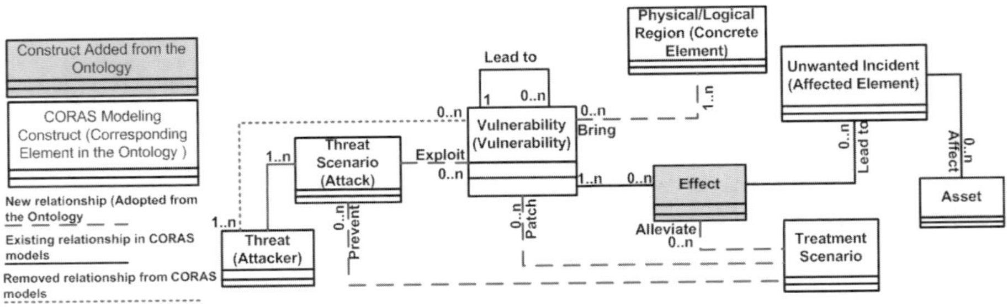

Fig. 4. Revising the CORAS risk modeling language by adopting the modeling ontology

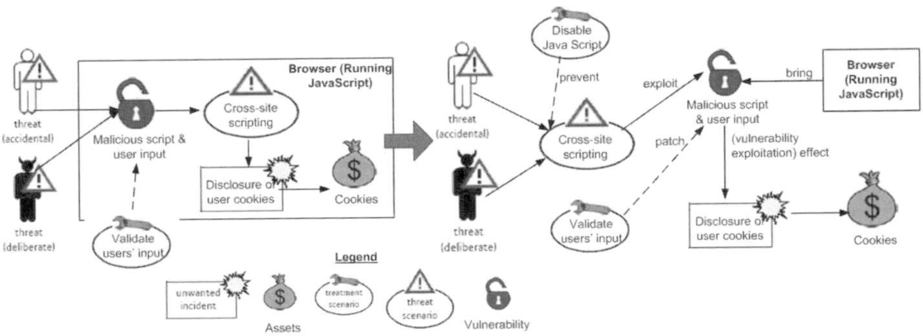

Fig. 5. Revising vulnerability modeling in the CORAS risk modeling approach, example of a web application and brower scenario

In the enhanced model, the logical or physical region boxes are used as concrete elements; for example, the *browser* brings the vulnerability of *malicious script and user input*. Threatening actors and threat scenarios (*Cross-site scripting*) are directly connected, and the relationship between threat scenario and vulnerabilities is reversed. The exploitation effects and countermeasures impacts are modeled using the existing CORAS relationships with additional tags. Treatments (*validate users' input* and *disable JavaScript*) patch the vulnerabilities, prevent threat scenarios or alleviate the effect of vulnerabilities.

6.3 Integrating Vulnerabilities into the i* Framework

The ability of the i* framework [33] to model agents, goals, and their dependencies makes it suitable for understanding security issues that arise among multiple malicious or non-malicious social agents with competing goals. i* provides the basic elements for incorporating vulnerabilities into security requirements models and representing their propagation within the system and agents.

Fig. 6 presents a fragment of the i* meta-model integrated with the vulnerability ontology and extended with malicious elements. The concrete elements in the i* framework that may bring vulnerabilities are tasks and resources. The effect of vulnerabilities and its severity in the i* framework are defined as Hurt (−), Break (−−), and Unknown (?) contribution links. Malicious tasks, goals, softgoals, and attackers are specialization

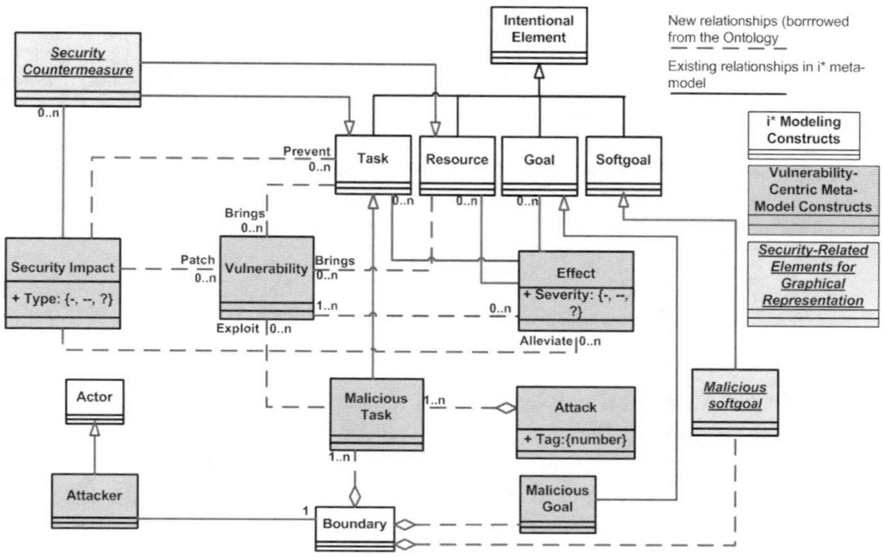

Fig. 6. The fragment of the i* meta-model extended by adopting the modeling ontology [9]

of i* tasks, goals, softgoals, actors. Some tasks and resources may function as security countermeasures.

Fig. 7 shows how vulnerabilities and related security constructs are graphically integrated into i* models in the browser and web application example. The i* notation is enriched with a "black circle" to graphically represent vulnerabilities (*Malicious script*). The proposed notation graphically distinguishes malicious and non-malicious elements using a black shadow in the background of malicious elements as originally proposed in [18,8]. The exploitation of a vulnerability by an attacker is represented by a link labeled *exploit* from the malicious task to the vulnerability. The exploitation of a vulnerability or a combination of vulnerabilities may affect goals, tasks, and availability of resources. Countermeasures are modeled using ordinary task elements[1], and their impacts as contribution links with *alleviate*, *prevent*, or *patch* tags. Detailed models and the goal model evaluation reasoning on the browser and web application case study can be found in [9].

6.4 Lessons Learned

The adoption of the proposed vulnerability modeling ontology in different conceptual foundations helps understanding the limitations of the conceptual foundations and facilitates their enhancement. The enhanced misuse case models provide additional information about vulnerabilities that enables a finer-grained security analysis for deciding on proper security use cases. The revised CORAS models explicitly express which threat scenario exploits the vulnerabilities and what are the effects of each exploitation, while

[1] The different color of countermeasure tasks in Fig. 7 does not indicate an additional semantics and the color is used for the sake of clarity and distinction.

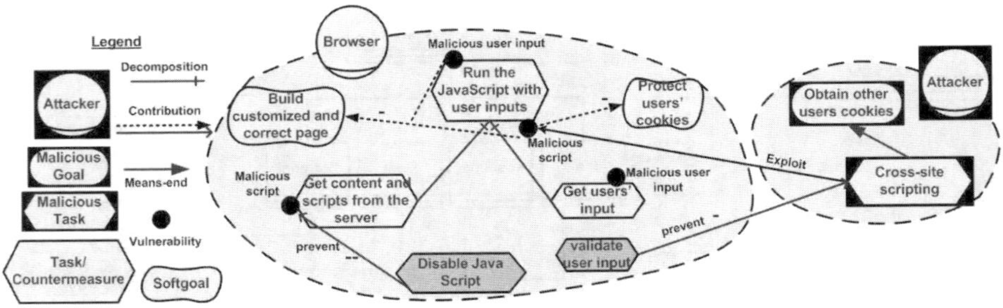

Fig. 7. Graphical representation of vulnerabilities in i* models

the original CORAS models only express the impacts of the whole scenario. The additional tags for expressing the exploitation effects and countermeasures impacts make the semantics of CORAS relationships explicit. Analyzing the effects of vulnerabilities in the i* models allows one to assess the risks of attacks, analyze the efficacy of countermeasures, and decide on patching or disregarding the vulnerabilities by taking advantage of goal model evaluation techniques [4]. In particular, analysts can verify whether stakeholders' goals are satisfied with the risks of vulnerabilities and attacks, and assess the efficacy of security countermeasures against such risks. In addition, the resulting security goal models and goal model evaluation can provide a basis for trade-off analysis among security and other quality requirements [8].

However, conceptual foundations may not be suitable or expressive enough to model all the ontology elements. Each conceptual foundation has been proposed for a specific purpose and is suitable for a certain type of modeling and analysis. For instance, misuse cases and CORAS do not provide constructs to represent delegations of assets and dependencies between actors. Therefore, they cannot model and analyze the propagation of vulnerabilities to system components. In addition, misuse cases and CORAS models cannot express why a misuser attacks the system and link the misuser's actions to his/her goals. Another limitation of i*, misuse case, and CORAS models is lack of constructs to model temporally-ordered actions and vulnerabilities exploitations that lead to an attack. Enhancing these conceptual foundations to address above limitations require a deep restructuring of their conceptual foundation, which imposes a trade-off between complexity of models and their reasoning power. Therefore, analysts need to identify the objectives of their analysis and select the target framework accordingly. For instance, it may be more appropriate to extend a dynamic modeling approach such as sequence diagrams rather than adding temporal constructs to misuse case diagrams.

7 Conclusions and Future Work

This paper proposes a modeling ontology for integrating vulnerabilities into conceptual modeling frameworks. We reviewed the security engineering and security requirements engineering literature to identify the set of core concepts needed for security requirements elicitation. The ontology is defined as an abstract meta-model which relates the elements of any conceptual framework to vulnerabilities and related security concepts.

We also discussed how the ontology can be adopted and realized in different conceptual modeling frameworks through some examples. These examples show that different frameworks have different conceptual structure and capabilities; therefore, by adopting the ontology elements into each conceptual framework, different types of analysis can be done based on the resulting models. We found that since some conceptual modeling frameworks do not provide the required structures, they are not able to express concepts such as malicious goal, vulnerable element of the system, temporal order, etc.

We adopted the ontology in the misuse case diagrams, i* models, and CORAS risk models. In addition to those examples, in future work, the proposed ontology needs to be adopted into a wider variety of modeling frameworks to provide stronger empirical evidences for usefulness, expressiveness, and comprehensiveness of the ontology. In order to evaluate the proposed ontology, we are performing empirical studies including case studies with human subjects that use the extended conceptual modeling frameworks. The aim of such case studies is to discover the security related concepts or types of analysis that the elements of the ontology cannot express or human subjects have difficulties to express. We aim to interview the subjects and critically analyze the models to draw conclusions about the expressiveness of the proposed conceptual elements.

An issue not explored in this paper is the scalability concerns that come with graphical visualization of complex models. The resulting models extended with security concepts, may become complex and hard to understand. In order to manage the complexity, defining views of the system and filtering some views would be necessary.

References

1. Asnar, Y., Moretti, R., Sebastianis, M., Zannone, N.: Risk as Dependability Metrics for the Evaluation of Business Solutions: A Model-driven Approach. In: Proc. of DAWAM 2008, pp. 1240–1248. IEEE Press, Los Alamitos (2008)
2. Avizienis, A., Laprie, J.-C., Randell, B., Landwehr, C.E.: Basic Concepts and Taxonomy of Dependable and Secure Computing. TDSC 1(1), 11–33 (2004)
3. Braber, F., Hogganvik, I., Lund, M.S., Stolen, K., Vraalsen, F.: Model-based security analysis in seven steps — a guided tour to the coras method. BT Technology Journal 25(1), 101–117 (2007)
4. Chung, L., Nixon, B.A., Yu, E., Mylopoulos, J. (eds.): Non-Functional Requirements in Software Engineering. Kluwer Academic Publishing, Dordrecht (2000)
5. Common Vulnerability Scoring System, `http://www.first.org/cvss/`
6. Common Weakness Enumeration, `http://cwe.mitre.org/`
7. den Braber, F., Dimitrakos, T., Gran, B.A., Lund, M.S., Stolen, K., Aagedal, J.O.: The CORAS methodology: model-based risk assessment using UML and UP. In: UML and the unified process, pp. 332–357. IGI Publishing (2003)
8. Elahi, G., Yu, E.: A goal oriented approach for modeling and analyzing security trade-offs. In: Parent, C., Schewe, K.-D., Storey, V.C., Thalheim, B. (eds.) ER 2007. LNCS, vol. 4801, pp. 375–390. Springer, Heidelberg (2007)
9. Elahi, G., Yu, E., Zannone, N.: A vulnerability-centric requirements engineering framework: Analyzing security attacks, countermeasures, and requirements based on vulnerabilities. Manuscript submitted to Req. Eng. Journal (2009)
10. Frigault, M., Wang, L., Singhal, A., Jajodia, S.: Measuring network security using dynamic bayesian network. In: Proc of QoP 2008, pp. 23–30. ACM Press, New York (2008)

11. Giorgini, P., Massacci, F., Mylopoulos, J., Zannone, N.: Modeling security requirements through ownership, permission and delegation. In: Proc. of RE 2005, pp. 167–176. IEEE Press, Los Alamitos (2005)
12. ISO/IEC. Risk management-vocabulary-guidelines for use in standards. ISO/IEC Guide 73 (2002)
13. ISO/IEC. Management of Information and Communication Technology Security – Part 1: Concepts and Models for Information and Communication Technology Security Management. ISO/IEC 13335 (2004)
14. Jajodia, S.: Topological analysis of network attack vulnerability. In: Proc. of ASIACCS 2007, p. 2. ACM, New York (2007)
15. Jürjens, J.: Secure Systems Development with UML. Springer, Heidelberg (2004)
16. Krogstie, J., Opdahl, A.L., Brinkkemper, S.: Capturing dependability threats in conceptual modelling. Conceptual Modelling in Information Systems Engineering, 247–260 (2007)
17. Landwehr, C.E., Bull, A.R., McDermott, J.P., Choi, W.S.: A taxonomy of computer program security flaws. CSUR 26(3), 211–254 (1994)
18. Liu, L., Yu, E., Mylopoulos, J.: Security and privacy requirements analysis within a social setting. In: Proc. of RE 2003, p. 151. IEEE Press, Los Alamitos (2003)
19. Liu, Y., Man, H.: Network vulnerability assessment using bayesian networks. In: Data mining, intrusion detection, information assurance, and data networks security. Society of Photo-Optical Instrumentation Engineers, pp. 61–71 (2005)
20. Matulevičius, R., Mayer, N., Mouratidis, H., Dubois, E., Heymans, P., Genon, N.: Adapting Secure Tropos for Security Risk Management in the Early Phases of Information Systems Development. In: Bellahsène, Z., Léonard, M. (eds.) CAiSE 2008. LNCS, vol. 5074, pp. 541–555. Springer, Heidelberg (2008)
21. McDermott, J.P.: Attack net penetration testing. In: Proc. of NSPW 2000, pp. 15–21. ACM, New York (2000)
22. Meyer, N., Rifaut, A., Dubois, E.: Towards a Risk-Based Security Requirements Engineering Framework. In: Proc. of REFSQ 2005 (2005)
23. National Vulnerability Database, `http://nvd.nist.gov/`
24. Petroski, H.: To Engineer is Human: The Role of Failure in Successful Design. St. Martin's Press, New York (1985)
25. Cynthia, P., Painton, S.L.: A graph-based system for network-vulnerability analysis. In: Proc. of NSPW 1998, pp. 71–79. ACM, New York (1998)
26. Rostad, L.: An extended misuse case notation: Including vulnerabilities and the insider threat. In: Proc. of REFSQ 2006 (2006)
27. SANS, `http://www.sans.org/`
28. Schneider, F.B. (ed.): Trust in Cyberspace. National Academy Press (1998)
29. Schneier, B.: Attack trees. Dr. Dobb's Journal 24(12), 21–29 (1999)
30. Schneier, B.: Beyond Fear. Springer, Heidelberg (2003)
31. Sindre, G., Opdahl, L.: Eliciting security requirements with misuse cases. Requir. Eng. 10(1), 34–44 (2005)
32. van Lamsweerde, A.: Elaborating security requirements by construction of intentional anti-models. In: Proc. of ICSE 2004, pp. 148–157. IEEE Press, Los Alamitos (2004)
33. Yu, E.: Modeling Strategic Relationships for Process Reengineering. PhD thesis, University of Toronto (1995)

Modeling Domain Variability in Requirements Engineering with Contexts

Alexei Lapouchnian and John Mylopoulos

Department of Computer Science, University of Toronto,
Toronto, ON M5S 3G4, Canada
{alexei,jm}@cs.toronto.edu

Abstract. Various characteristics of the problem domain define the context in which the system is to operate and thus impact heavily on its requirements. However, most requirements specifications do not consider contextual properties and few modeling notations explicitly specify how domain variability affects the requirements. In this paper, we propose an approach for using contexts to model domain variability in goal models. We discuss the modeling of contexts, the specification of their effects on system goals, and the analysis of goal models with contextual variability. The approach is illustrated with a case study.

1 Introduction

Domain models constitute an important aspect of requirements engineering (RE) for they constrain the space of possible solutions to a given set of requirements and even impact on the very definition of these requirements. In spite of that, domain models and requirements models have generally been treated in isolation by requirements engineering approaches (e.g., [7]). As software systems are being used in ever more diverse and dynamic environments where they have to routinely and efficiently adapt to changing environmental conditions, their designs must support *high variability* in the behaviours they prescribe.

Not surprisingly, high variability in requirements and design have been recognized as cornerstones in meeting the demands for software systems of the future [14,11,16]. However, the variability of domain models, which captures the changing, dynamic nature of operational environments for software systems, and its impact on software requirements, has not received equal attention in the literature. The problem is that traditional goal models assume that the environment of the system-to-be is mostly uniform and attempt to elicit and refine system goals in a way that would make the goal model adequate for most instances of a problem (e.g., selling goods, scheduling meetings, etc.) in a particular domain. In other words, traditional techniques ignore the impact of domain variability on the requirements to be fulfilled for a system-to-be. Thus, *these approaches are missing an important source of requirements variability.*

A recent proposal [17] did identify the importance of domain variability on requirements. However, it assumes that requirements are given, and concentrates on making sure that they are met in every context. Thus, the approach does not explore

A.H.F. Laender et al. (Eds.): ER 2009, LNCS 5829, pp. 115–130, 2009.

the effects of domain variability on intentional variability – the variability in stakeholder goals and their refinements. Also, in pervasive and mobile computing, where contexts have long been an important research topic, a lot of effort has been directed at modeling various contexts (e.g., [9]), but little research is available on linking those models with software requirements [10].

In a recent paper [14], we concentrate on capturing *intentional* variability in early requirements using goal models. There, the main focus was on identifying all the ways stakeholder goals can be attained. We pointed out that non-intentional variability (that is, time, location, characteristics of stakeholders, entities in the environment, etc.) is an important factor in goal modeling as it constrains intentional variability in a significant way. However, we stopped short of systematically characterizing such domain variability and its effects on requirements. To that end, in this paper, we propose a coherent process for exploring domain/contextual variability and for modeling and analyzing its effects on requirements goal models. We propose a fine-grained model of context that represents the domain state and where each context contains partial requirements model representing the effects of that context on the model. Unlike, e.g., the method of [17], our approach results in *high-variability context-enriched goal models* that capture and refine stakeholder goals in *all* relevant contexts. Moreover, context refinement hierarchies and context inheritance allow incremental definition of the effects of contexts on goal models specified relative to higher-level contexts. These goal models can then be formally analyzed.

As a motivation for this research, let us look at system for supplying customers with goods. At a first glance, it seems that gathering requirements for such a system is rather straightforward: we have the domain consisting of the distributor, the customers, the goods, the orders, the shipping companies, etc. Following a goal-oriented RE approach, we can identify the functional goals that the system needs to achieve (e.g., Supply Customer, see Fig. 1) and the relevant softgoals/quality constraints (the cloudy shapes) like Minimize Risk and then refine them into subgoals until they are simple enough to be achieved by software components and/or humans. The produced requirements specification assumes that the domain is uniform – i.e., the specification and thus the system will work for *all* customers, *all* orders, etc. However, it is easy to see that this view is overly simplistic as it ignores the variations in the domain that have important effects on system requirements. E.g., international orders need to have

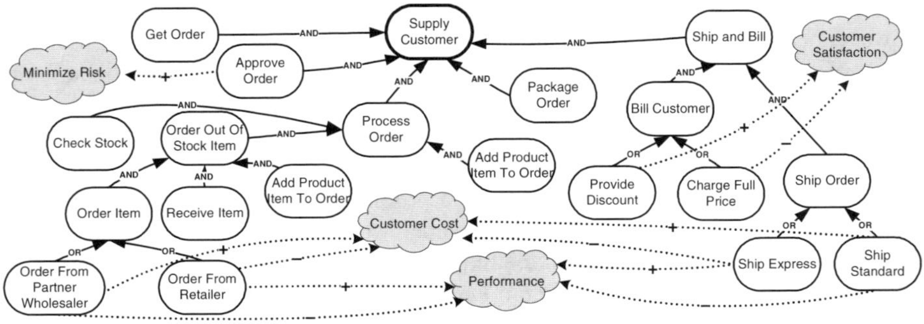

Fig. 1. A high-level goal model for the Distributor

customs paperwork filled out, while domestic orders do not. Large orders are good for business, so they may be encouraged by discounts or free shipping. And the list goes on. So, our aim in this paper is to introduce an approach that allows us to model these and other effects of domain non-uniformity and variability on software requirements.

The rest of the paper is structured as follows. Section 2 is the research baseline for this work, covering context, goal modeling and related work. Section 3 presents our formal framework. Section 4 talks about context-dependent goal models. Discussion and future work are presented in Section 5, while Section 6 concludes the paper.

2 Background and Related Work

There exist a lot of definitions of context in Computer Science. E.g., [4] defines context as "any information that can be used to characterize persons, places or objects that are considered relevant to the interactions between a user and an application, including users and applications themselves". Brezillon [2], says that "context is what constrains problem solving without intervening in it explicitly". McCarthy states that "context is a generalization of a collection of assumptions" [15]. This definition fits well with our treatment of context as properties of entities in the environment and of the environment itself that influence stakeholder goals and means of achieving them. Thus, we define a context as an abstraction over a set of environment assumptions.

In various areas of computing, the notion of context has long been recognized as important. For example, in the case of context-aware computing the problem is to adapt to changing computational capabilities as well as to user behaviour and preferences [4]. In pervasive computing, context is used to model environment and user characteristics as well as to proactively infer new knowledge about users.

There have been quite a few recent efforts directed at context modeling. While some approaches adapt existing modeling techniques, others propose new or significantly modified notations. Henricksen and Indulska present their Context Modeling Language (CML) notation [9]. Their graphical modeling notation allows for capturing of fact types (e.g., *Located At*, *Engaged In*) that relate object types (e.g., location, person, and device). The model can distinguish between static and dynamic facts. Moreover, it classifies dynamic facts into profiled facts (supplied by users), sensed facts (provided by sensors), and derived facts (derived from other facts through logical formulas). Dependencies among facts can also be specified. A special temporal fact type can be used to capture time-varying facts. Additional features of the approach include, for example, support for ambiguous context as well as for context quality (e.g., certainty).

Standard modeling approaches like UML and ER have been used for context modeling. However, they are not well suited for capturing certain special characteristics of contextual information [9]. For example, in [6], UML class diagrams are used to model user, personalization, and context metadata subschemas together in one model. Ontologies have are also used for context modeling. They provide extensibility, flexibility and composability for contexts. In [4], a generic top ontology, which can be augmented with domain-dependent ones, is proposed. These approaches do not focus on the use of context in applications.

Much research has also been dedicated to the formal handling of contexts in the area of Artificial Intelligence and Knowledge Representation and Reasoning [1].

Goal models. Goal models [5,7] are a way to capture and refine stakeholder intentions to generate functional and non-functional requirements. The main concept there is the *goal*, such as Supply Customer for a distributor company (Fig. 1). Goals may be AND/OR decomposed. For example, Supply Customer is AND-decomposed into subgoals for getting customer orders, then processing and shipping them. All of these subgoals need to be achieved for the parent goal to be achieved. On the other hand, one or more subgoals in an OR decomposition need to be achieved for the parent goal to be attained (e.g., achieving either Ship Standard or Ship Express will satisfy Ship Order). OR decompositions thus introduce variability into the model. *Softgoals* are qualitative goals (e.g., [Maximize] Customer Satisfaction). Softgoals do not have a clear-cut criterion for their fulfillment, and may be *satisficed* – met to an acceptable degree. In addition, goals/softgoals can be related to softgoals through help (+), hurt (–), make (++), or break (--) relationships (represented with the dotted line arrows in Fig. 1). These *contribution links* allow us to *qualitatively* specify that there is evidence that certain goals/softgoals contribute positively or negatively to the satisficing of softgoals. Then, a softgoal is satisficed if there is sufficient positive and little negative evidence for this claim. This simple language is sufficient for modeling and analyzing goals during early requirements, covering both functional and quality requirements, which in this framework are treated as first-class citizens.

High-variability goal models attempt to capture many different ways goals can be met in order to facilitate in designing flexible, adaptive, or customizable software [11,12,14]. In [14], an approach for systematic development of high-variability goal models is presented. The approach, however, does not cover domain variability and its affect on requirements.

Related Work. Our view of contexts is somewhat similar to the CYC common sense knowledge base [13]. CYC has 12 context dimensions along which contexts vary. Each region in this 12-dimensional space implicitly defines an overall context for CYC assertions. We, however, propose more fine-grained handling of context with possibly many more domain-specific dimensions.

Brezillon et al. [3] propose an approach for modeling the effects of context on decision making using contextual graphs. Contextual graphs are based on decision trees with event nodes becoming context ones. They are used to capture various context-dependent ways of executing procedures. Whenever some context plays a role in the procedure, it splits it up into branches according to the value of the context. Branches may recombine later. This work is close to our approach in the sense that it attempts to capture all the effects of contextual variability in one model. However, we are doing this at the intentional level, while contextual graphs is a process-level notation. Moreover, quality attributes are not considered there. We have looked at generating process-level specifications from goal models [12] and we believe that contextual graphs can be generated from the context-enriched goal models as well.

Salifu et al. [17] suggest a Problem Frames-based approach for the modeling of domain variability and for the specification of monitoring and switching requirements. They identify domain variability (modeled by a set of domain variables) using variant problem frames and try to assess its impact on requirements. For each context that causes the requirements to fail, a variant frame is created and analyzed in order to ensure the satisfaction of requirements. This approach differs from ours in that it assumes that the requirements specification is given, while we are concentrating on activities that precede its formulation. Another substantial difference is that we propose the use of a single high-variability requirements goal model for capturing all of the domain's variability.

3 The Formal Framework

In this section, we present a formal framework for managing models through the use of contexts. While we are mainly interested in the graphical models such as requirements goal models, our approach equally applies to any type of model, e.g., formal theories. We view instances of models (e.g., the Supply Customer goal model) as collections of model element instances (e.g., Ship Order). There may be other important structural properties of models that need capturing, but we are chiefly concerned with the *ability to model under which circumstances certain model elements are present (i.e., visible) in the model* and with the ability to display a version of the model for the particular set of circumstances. Thus, we are concerned with capturing *model variability* due to a wide variety of *external factors*. These factors can include viewpoints, model versions, domain assumptions, etc. This formal framework can be instantiated for any model to help with managing this kind of variability. In section 4.3, we present an algorithm that generates this formal framework given an instance of a requirements goal model.

We assume that there are different types of elements in a modeling notation. For example, in graphical models, we have various types of nodes and links among them. Let **M** be the set of model element instances in a model. Let **T** be the set of various model element types available in a modeling notation (e.g., goals, softgoals, etc.). The function *L* maps each element of **M** into an element of **T**, thus associating a type with every model element instance. Only certain types of elements in a modeling notation may be affected by contexts and thus belong to a variable part of a model. We define $\mathbf{T^C}$ as the subset of **T** containing such *context-dependent* model element types. If a model element type is not in $\mathbf{T^C}$, it is excluded from our formalization. The contents of the $\mathbf{T^C}$ set are notation- and model-dependent. Let $\boldsymbol{M^C} \overset{\text{def}}{=} \{n |\ n \in \boldsymbol{M} \wedge L(n) \in \boldsymbol{T^C}\}$ be the set of modeling elements of the types that can be affected by contexts.

We next define the set **C** of *contextual tags*. These are labels that are assigned to model elements to capture the conditions that those elements require to be visible in the model. To properly define what contextual tags model, we assign each tag a Boolean expression that specifies when the tag is *active*. Since the tags represent domain properties, assumptions, etc., the associated expressions precisely define when the contextual tags affect the model and when they are not (we define **P** to be the set of Boolean expressions): $active\colon \boldsymbol{C} \rightarrow \boldsymbol{P}$. For example, the tag *largeOrder* describes a real world entity and may be defined as an order with the sum being over $10K. So, when some order *is* over $10K, the tag becomes active and thus can affect the model. The approach can also be used to capture viewpoints, model versions, etc. In those cases, the definition of tags can be simple: they can be turned on and off depending on what the modeler is interested in (e.g., *versionOne* = *true*). We also allow negated tags to be used in the approach: $(\forall t \in \boldsymbol{C})\ active(\neg t) \stackrel{\text{def}}{=} \neg active(t)$.

We define a special *default* tag that is always active and if assigned to an element of a model signifies that the element does not require any assumptions to hold to be present in the model. To associate tags with model elements we create a special unit called *taggedElement* ($\wp$ is a powerset): $taggedElement \subseteq \boldsymbol{M}^c \times \wp(\wp(\boldsymbol{C}))$.

To each element of $\mathbf{M}^{\mathrm{C}}$ we assign possibly many tag combinations (sets of tags). E.g., the set *{{a,b},{c,d}}* assigned to an element *n* specifies that *n* appears in the model in two cases: when both *a* and *b* are active or when both *c* and *d* are active. The outer set is the set of alternative tag assignments, either of which is enough for the element to be visible. In fact, the above set can be interpreted as $(a \wedge b) \vee (c \wedge d)$, so our set of set of tags can be viewed as a propositional DNF formula.

The function *newTaggedElement* creates a new tagged element entity given a model element and a set of tags. It can be called from within algorithms that process input models for which we want to use the formal framework. Given a model element, the function *tags* returns the set of contextual tags of a *taggedElement.* In order to eliminate possible inconsistent sets of tags (i.e., having both a tag and its negation) from the set returned by *tags(n)*, we define the following set for each model ment: $context(n) = \{K | K \in tags(n) \wedge \neg inconsistent(K)\}$.

Inheritance of contextual tags. Contextual tags can *inherit* from other tags (no circular inheritance is allowed). This is to make specifying the effects of external factors on models easier. E.g., we have a tag *substantialOrder* applied to certain elements of a business process (BP) model. Now, we define a tag *largeOrder* inheriting from *substantialOrder*. Then, since *largeOrder is-a substantialOrder*, the derived tag can be substituted everywhere for the parent tag. Thus, the elements that are tagged with *substantialOrder* are effectively tagged with *largeOrder* as well. Of course, the converse is not true. Apart from being automatically applied to all the elements already tagged by *substantialOrder*, we can explicitly apply *largeOrder* to new nodes to specify, for example, that the goal Apply Discount requires large orders. The benefits of contextual tag inheritance include the ability to reuse already defined and applied tags and thus to develop context-dependent models incrementally. We state that one tag inherits from another by using the predicate *parent(parentTag,childTag). Multiple inheritance* is allowed, so a tag can inherit from more than one parent tags. In this case, the derived tag can be used in place of all of its parent tags, thus inheriting the elements tagged by them. *parent* is extensionally defined based on the contextual tag inheritance hierarchy associated with the source model. *ancestor(anc,dec)* is defined trough *parent* to indicate that the tag *anc* is an ancestor of *dec*.

We also support a simple version of *non-monotonic inheritance* where certain elements tagged by an ancestor tag may not be inherited by the derived tag. Suppose the goal Apply Shipping Discount is tagged with *substantialOrder*, i.e., applies to substantial (large and medium) orders only. However, we might not want this goal to apply to large orders (as it would with regular inheritance) since we want them to ship for free. So, we declare this model element *abnormal* w.r.t. the inheritance of *largeOrder* from *substantialOrder* and that particular activity, which means that the *largeOrder* tag will not apply to it. We can do this by using the following: *ab(dec,anc,n)*, where *dec*, *anc* $\in \mathbf{C}$ and *n* $\in \mathbf{M}^{\mathrm{C}}$. This states that for the element *n* the descendent contextual tag (*dec*) cannot be substituted for the ancestor tag (*anc*). In fact, given tag combinations applied to *n*, we can determine if it is abnormal w.r.t. some inheritance hierarchy if there is a tag combination with an ancestor tag and a negation of a descendent tag:

$$ab(dec, anc, n) \stackrel{\text{def}}{=} (\exists K \in context(n))\; ancestor(anc, dec) \wedge \\ anc \in K \wedge \neg dec \in K$$

Once a context *dec* is found to be abnormal w.r.t. one of its ancestors *anc* and a node *n*, all of *dec*'s descendents are automatically declared abnormal as well:

$$(\forall c, dec, anc \in \boldsymbol{C})(\forall n \in \boldsymbol{M^C}) ab(dec, anc, n) \wedge ancestor(dec, c) \rightarrow ab(c, anc, n)$$

Visibility of modeling elements. Given the sets of contextual tags applied to context-dependent model elements and the formulas defining when those tags are active, we can determine for each such element whether it is visible in the model. We define the following function:

$$visible: \boldsymbol{M^C} \rightarrow \{true, false\}$$
$$visible(n) \stackrel{\text{def}}{=} (\exists K \in context(n))(\forall e_i \in K)$$
$$\bigwedge\nolimits_{1 \le i \le |K|} active(e_i) \vee (ancestor(e_i, d) \wedge \neg ab(d, e_i, n) \wedge active(d))$$

Thus, we define a context-dependent model element to be visible in a model if there exists a contextual tag assignment *K* for that element where each tag is either active itself or there exists its active non-abnormal descendent tag. Now we can produce the definition of the subset of visible context-dependent elements of a model: $\boldsymbol{V} \stackrel{\text{def}}{=} \{n | n \in \boldsymbol{M^C} \wedge visible(n)\}$. Note that for most modeling notations we also need other (e.g., structural) information in addition to the set **V** to produce a valid submodel corresponding to the current context. Since that information is notation-dependent, it is not part of our generic framework. Also note that since the definitions of contextual tags likely refer to real world phenomena, if the approach is used at runtime, the visibility of model elements can dynamically change from situation to situation.

4 Contextual Variability in Goal Modeling

In this section, we introduce our approach for modeling and analysing the effects of context on requirements goal models. We use the Distributor case study (see Fig. 1), which is a variation of the one presented in [12]. Due to space limitations, we are unable to present the complete goal model for the case study, although, we will be illustrating the approach with portions of it. The complete case study featured over 60 goals and six context refinement hierarchies.

Our method involves a number of activities. Some of these activities are discussed in the subsequent sections, while here we outline the approach:

1. Identify the main purpose of the system (its high-level goals) and the domain where the system is to operate.
2. *Iterative step*. Refine the goals into lower-level subgoals.
3. *Iterative step*. Identify the entities in the domain and their characteristics that can affect the newly identified goals. Capture those effects using *contextual tags*. Update the context model.

4. Generate the formal model for managing context-dependent variability.
5. Analyze context-enriched goal models
   a. Given currently active context(s), produce the corresponding goal model.
   b. Analyze whether top-level system goals can be attained given currently active context(s). The standard goal reasoning techniques can be applied since *the contextual variability has been removed.*

4.1 Context Identification and Modeling

Our goal in this approach is to systematically identify domain variability and its effect on stakeholder goals and goal refinements. Unlike intentional variability discussed in [14], domain variability is external to the requirements model, but influences intentional variability and thus requirements. We represent domain models in terms of *contexts* – properties or characteristics of the domain that have effect on requirements – and thus variability in the domain is reflected in the contextual variability.

Note that there may be certain aspects of the domain that do not affect requirements and these are not important to us. *Context entities*, such as actors, devices, resources, data items, etc., are things in the domain that influence the requirements (e.g., an *Order* is a context entity). They are the *sources of domain variability*. We define a context entity called *env* for specifying ambient properties of the environment. A *context variability dimension* is an aspect of a domain along which that domain changes. It may be related to one or more context entities (e.g., *size(Order)* and *relativeLocation(Warehouse,Customer)*). A dimension can be thought of as defining a range or a set of values. A *context* is a particular value for a dimension (e.g., *size(Order,$5000)*, *relativeLocation(Warehouse,Customer,local)*).

Fig. 2B shows the metamodel that we use for capturing the basic properties of domain variability (such as context entities and variability dimensions) in our approach. Additional models can also be useful. As mentioned in Section 2, there are a number of notations that can be employed for context modeling. Fig. 2A presents a UML class diagram variation showing the context entities in our case study (their corresponding context dimensions are modeled as attributes). In addition to UML or ER diagrams for context modeling, specialized notations like the CML are able to specify advanced properties of contexts (e.g., derived contexts).

Unlike the simpler notion of context in CML and in some other approaches, we are proposing the use of *context refinement hierarchies* for the appropriate context dimensions. Their purpose is twofold: first, they can be used to map the too-low-level contexts into higher-level ones that are more appropriate for some particular application (e.g., GPS coordinates can be mapped into cities and towns). This is commonly

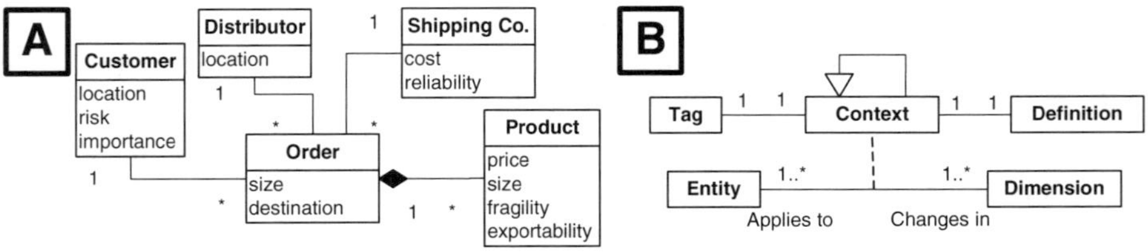

Fig. 2. UML context model for the case study (A) and our context metamodel (B)

done in existing context-aware applications in the fields such as mobile and pervasive computing. Second, abstract context hierarchies may be useful in terms of splitting contexts into meaningful, appropriately named high-level ranges. For example, an order size (in terms of the dollar amount) is a number. So, one can specify the effects of orders of over $5,000 on the achievement of the subgoal Approve Order, then orders over $10,000, etc. However, very frequently, and *especially during requirements elicitation and analysis*, it is more convenient to specify what effect certain *ranges* of context have on goal models. For example, instead of thinking in terms of the dollar amounts in the example above, it might be more convenient to reason in qualitative terms like *Large Order* or *Medium Order* (see Fig. 3A, where *Size* is the context dimension of the *Order* context entity, while the arrows represent IS-A relationships among contexts and the boxes capture the possible contexts in the hierarchy). The high-level contexts will need to be refined into lower-level ones and eventually defined using the actual order amounts. We call such defined contexts *base contexts* (note the "B" label on the leaf-level contexts in Fig. 3).

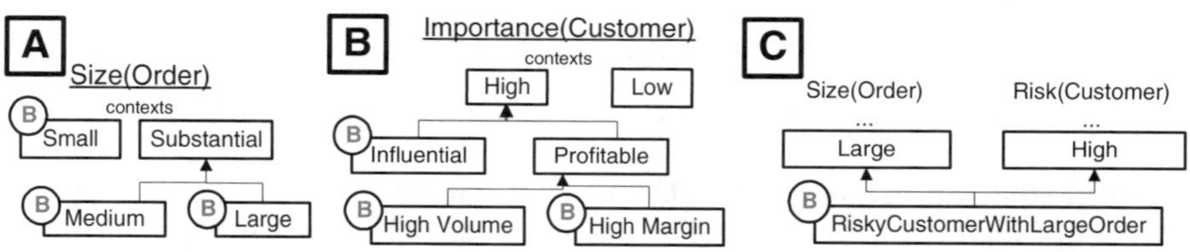

Fig. 3. Order size (A) and Customer importance (B) context hierarchies and multiple inheritance (C)

A context must be defined through a *definition*, a Boolean formula, which is specified using the expression of the type *Dimension(Entity(-ies),Context)* $\stackrel{\text{def}}{=}$ *definition*. If it holds (i.e., the domain is currently in the state defined by the context), we call that context *active*. For example, large orders may be defined as the ones over $1000. Thus, formally: $\forall Order\ size(Order, large) \stackrel{\text{def}}{=} \exists n\ size(Order, n) \wedge n \geq \$1000$. As mentioned before, contexts may have concrete definitions or may be defined through their descendant contexts: $\forall Order\ size(Order, substantial) \stackrel{\text{def}}{=} size(Order, large) \vee size(Order, medium)$. There should be no cycles in context dependencies.

Contexts may be derived from several direct ancestors, thus inheriting their effects on the goal model. In Fig. 3C, we create a new context by deriving it from the contexts *size(Order,large)* and *risk(Customer,high)*. This produces a new context dimension with both context entities becoming its parameters. We also need to provide the definition for the new context, i.e., to specify when it is active: $sizeRisk(Customer, Order, riskyCustomerWithLargeOrder) \stackrel{\text{def}}{=} size(Order, large) \wedge risk(Customer, high)$. Thus, it is active precisely when the customer is risky and the order is large.

While context refinement hierarchies provide more flexibility for handling contexts, their design should not be arbitrary. When developing context hierarchies in our approach, care must be taken to ensure that they are not unnecessarily complicated, i.e., that the contexts are actually used in goal models.

4.2 Modeling the Effects of Contextual Variability on Goal Models

In Section 4.1, we discussed the modeling of domain characteristics using contexts. Here, we show how the effects of domain variability on requirements goal models can be captured. The idea is to be able to model the effects of all relevant contexts (i.e., the domain variability) conveniently in a single model instance and to selectively display the model corresponding to particular contexts. We use *contextual tags* (as in Section 3) attached to model elements to visually specify the effects of domain variability on goal models. While context definitions and inheritance hierarchies make up the domain model, we need to specify how contexts affect the graphical models, i.e., which elements of the models are *visible* in which contexts.

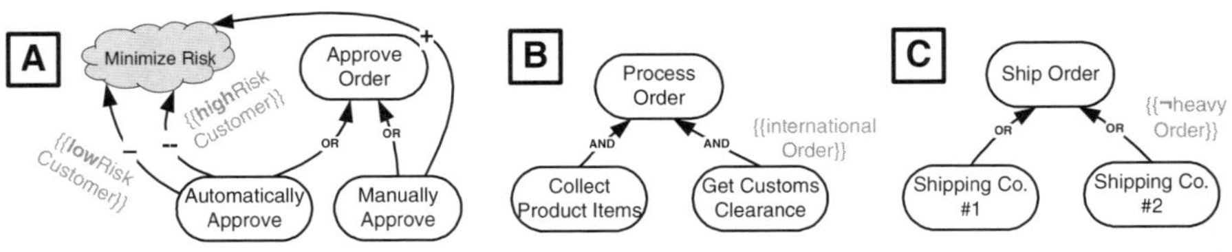

Fig. 4. Specifying effects of domain variability using contextual tags

Effects of contexts on goal models. Domain variability can influence a goal model in a number of ways. Note from the following that it can only affect (soft)goal nodes and contribution links. Domain variability affects:

- *The requirements themselves.* (Soft)goals may appear/disappear in the model depending on the context. For instance, if a customer is willing to share personal details/preferences with the seller, the vendor might acquire the goal Up-sell Customer to try and sell more relevant products to that customer.
- *The OR decomposition of goals.* New alternative(s) may be added and previously identified alternative(s) or may be removed in certain contexts. For example, there may be fewer options to ship heavy orders to customers (Fig. 4C).
- *Goal refinement.* For example, the goal of processing an international order is not attained unless the customs paperwork is completed (Fig. 4B). This, of course, does not apply to domestic orders.
- *The assessment of various choices in the goal model.* E.g., automatic approval of orders from low-risk customers may hurt ("–") the Minimize Risk softgoal, while doing the same for very risky ones will have a significantly worse ("--") effect on it (Fig. 4A).

Effects identification. The activities of developing contextual models and the identification of the effects of contexts on goal models need to proceed iteratively. While it is possible to attempt to identify all the relevant context entities and their dimensions upfront, it is very likely that certain important dimensions will be overlooked. For example, after the modeler refines the goal Package Order enough (see Fig. 1), he/she will elicit the goal Package Product. Only after analyzing which properties of a product can affect its packaging, will the modeler be able to identify the dimension *Fragility* as relevant for the context entity *Product*. Therefore, to gain the maximum benefit from the approach, the activities of context modeling need to be interleaved with the development of context-enriched goal models. Thus, the context model will be gradually expanded as the goal model is being created.

In our approach, when refining a goal, we need to identify the relevant context entities and their context dimensions that may influence the ways the goal is refined. There are a number of ways such relevant context entities can be identified. For example, in some versions of the goal modeling notation, goals have parameters (e.g., Process Order(Customer,Order), as in [12]), which are clearly context entities since their properties influence the way goals can be attained. Alternatively, a variability frame of a goal [14] can be a powerful tool for identifying relevant context entities and dimensions for a goal. We can use a table to document *potentially* relevant context entities (columns) and their dimensions (rows) for goals. While certain entities and/or dimensions currently may have no effect on the refinement of the goal, it is still prudent to capture them for traceability and future maintenance. For instance, below is the table where we identified order size and destination as well as customer importance as dimensions affecting the goal Apply Discount.

Apply Discount	Entity: Order	Entity: Customer
Dimensions	Size, Destination	Importance

Specifying the effects of contexts on goal models. Tags are mnemonic names corresponding to contexts. For example, *largeOrder* may be the tag for the context *size(Order,large)*. Contextual tags are applied to model elements to specify the effects of domain variability on goal models – i.e., to indicate that certain contexts are required to be active for those elements to be visible in the model. As in Section 3, we have sets of alternative tag assignments and all the tags within any such assignment must be active for the model element to be visible. E.g., the set of tags *{{largeOrder},{importantCustomer,mediumOrder}}* attached to the goal Apply Discount indicates that ether the order has to be large or there must be an important customer with a medium-sized order to apply a discount. *Not* (¬) can be used with tags to indicate that the corresponding context cannot be active if the node is to be visible (see Fig. 4C).

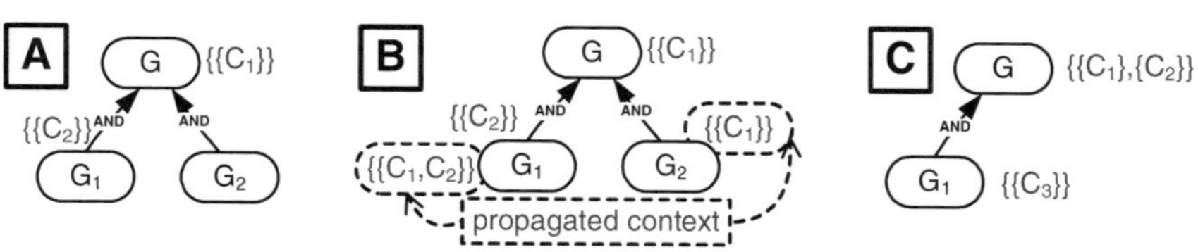

Fig. 5. Contextual tag assignment examples

By default, model elements are said to be contained in the *default context*, which is always active (*{{default}}*). To specify that a goal G must only be achieved when the context C_1 is active, we apply the tag *{{C_1}}* to G (Fig. 5A). If we want a goal to be achieved when either of contexts is active, several sets of tag assignments must be used. E.g., the tag *{{C_1},{C_2}}* applied to G (Fig. 5C) indicates that C_1 C_2. When a set of tags is applied to a goal node G, it is also applied (implicitly propagated, see Fig. 5B) to the whole subtree rooted at that goal. The hierarchical nature of goal models allows us to drastically reduce the number of contextual tags used in the model.

Tag sets are combined when used in the same goal model subtree. E.g., if a tag set *{{C₂}}* is applied to the node G₁ in the subtree of G (Fig. 5B), then G₁ (and thus the subtree rooted at it) is to be attained only when *both* contexts corresponding to C_1 and C_2 are active, which is indicated by the tag $\{\{C_1,C_2\}\}$ (i.e., C_1 C_2). The tags applied to G and G₁ (Fig. 5C) when combined produce $\{\{C_1,C_3\},\{C_2,C_3\}\}$ since $(C_1$ $C_2)$ $C_3=$ $(C_1$ C_3 $(C_2$ $C_3)$. The above also applies to softgoals.

4.3 Analyzing Context-Dependent Goal Models

In Section 3, we presented a generic formal framework for handling context-dependent models. It provides the basis for managing model variability due to external factors such as domain assumptions, etc. Here, we show how the formal framework can be used together with requirements goal models to analyze domain variability in requirements engineering. In order to use the framework with goal models, we need a procedure that processes these models together with context inheritance hierarchies and generates the required sets and facts for the formal framework to operate on.

There are several steps in the process of generating the formal framework for goal models. First, we create the *parent* facts that model the tag inheritance hierarchy based on the context hierarchies described in Section 4.1. Similarly, definitions of the contexts will be assigned to the corresponding contextual tags and will be returned by the *active(context)* function for evaluation to determine if these tags are active.

We then state which elements of goal models we consider context-dependent. In general, the set $\mathbf{T}^C$ = {G (goals), S (softgoals), R (contribution links)}. Below is the algorithm that completes the creation of the formal framework: it traverses the goal model and generates *taggedElement* instances corresponding to the context-dependent elements of the model along with the sets of tags assigned to these elements.

Algorithm 1. *Formal model generation*
Input: a set O of root (soft)goals of a goal model
Output: a formal model in the notation described in Section 3

```
procedure generateFormalModel(O)
  for each e ∈ O do
    processNode(e, {{default}})
  endFor
endProcedure
```

Algorithm 2. *Traverse goal model*
Input: element e and its parent context pC
Output: *taggedElement* entities in the formal model

```
procedure processNode(e, pC )
  newContext ← ∅
  if context annotation A exists for e then
    if pC = {{default}} then
      newContext ← A
    elseIf //parent context is not default
      for each K1 ∈ pC do
        for each K2 ∈ A do
          newContext ← newContext ∪
                                  {K1 ∪ K2}
        endFor
      endFor
    endIf //default context
  elseIf
    newContext ← pC
  endIf //annotation
  newTaggedElement(e, newContext)
  for each child contribution link l of e do
    processLink(l, newContext)
  endFor
  for each child (soft)goal node c of e do
    processNode(c, newContext)
  endFor
endProcedure
```

The procedure *generateContextModel* takes the set of root (soft)goals as the input and calls the procedure *processNode* on the (potentially) many (soft)goal trees that comprise the goal model. *processNode* has two parameters: the node *e* being processed and the set of tag assignments from the parent node, *pC* (parent context). Since we start from the root goals, initially *pC* has the value *{{default}}*. Within the *processNode* procedure we first check if the node *e* has a set of context tags *A* attached. If it does, it means that we must combine the parent context *pC* with *A* to produce the complete set of tags for *e*. If *pC* is the default context, it will simply be replaced by the tag set *A*. Otherwise, both *pC* and *A* are combined (as described in Section 4.2) to produce the new set of tags for *e* (see lines 7-11). We create the *taggedElement* unit for *n* with the newly produced context in line 16. The softgoal contribution links emanating from *n* are processed by the *processLink* function that computes the tag assignment for the link in the same way we have done it for *n*. Note that *newContext* is provided to *processLink* as it becomes its parent context. Then we recursively process all the child nodes of *n* providing *newContext* as their parent context.

After *generateFormalModel* and other mapping procedures have been executed, we have a formal context framework that can be used to produce the set of elements visible in the model in the current context. Below we show the analysis that can be done on context-enriched goal models with the aid of our approach. Fig. 6A shows a fragment of the process Supply Customer for calculating shipping charges. Influential customers are not charged for shipping, so the context *{{¬F}}* (see the legend in Fig. 6 for abbreviations) is applied to it. We apply discounts only for important customers or for substantial orders, so Apply Discount is tagged with *{{I},{S}}*. [Provide] Large Discount is tagged with *{{I},{L}}*: it applies to large orders or to important customers. Finally, Medium Discount applies to international orders only. Fig. 6B shows a fragment of the formal model generated by the algorithm presented earlier (the inheritance hierarchies are based on those in Fig. 3). Note that the influential customer context tag (*F*) is found to be abnormal w.r.t. important customer (*I*) in the subtree Apply Discount. The sets of tags for each node are also calculated (Fig. 6B). By using context definitions (not shown), we can determine which contextual tags are active and thus affect the model. Suppose that we are in the context of a large international order (Fig. 6C). ¬*F* is active, so Charge for Shipping is visible. Apply Discount is too since a large order *is-a* substantial order and so both tags in *{¬F,S}* are active. Similar reasoning reveals that the remaining nodes are also visible. Note that we have *bound contextual variability* in the model by stating whether each context is active or not and by producing the corresponding version of the model. This process does not remove *non-contextual* variability from the model as shown in Fig. 6C where two choices for applying the shipping discount remain. The selection among them can be made using the conventional goal model analysis techniques (e.g., [18]).

Fig. 6D shows the model in the context of a medium order. Here, Charge for Shipping is visible again as is Apply Discount since medium orders are substantial orders. However, there are no combinations of active tags (see Fig. 6B) that make the other two goals visible. The analysis reveals a problem with the resulting model since no refinement of a *non-leaf* goal Apply Discount is available and thus any goal depending on it will not be achieved. One solution is to tag Medium Discount with *{{N},{M}}* instead of *{{N}}*. Finally, Fig. 6E shows the model resulting from the context *highVolumeCustomer* being active. Since these customers are important customers, they are given large discounts.

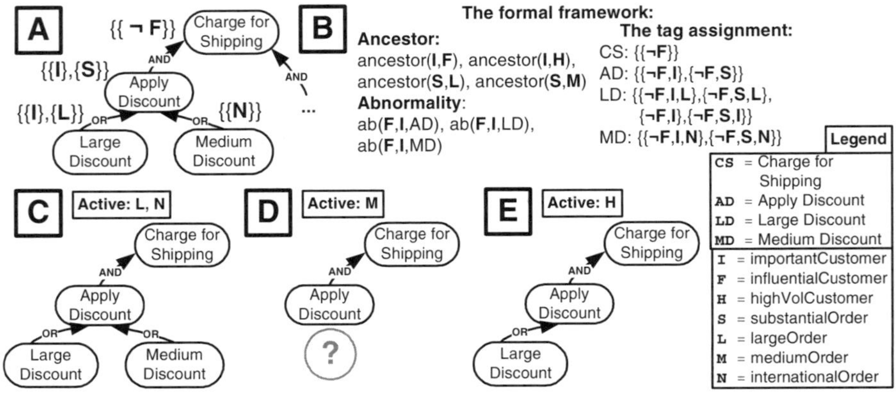

Fig. 6. Analyzing the effects of domain variability on goal models

5 Discussion and Future Work

Our formal framework presented in Section 3 only deals with the visibility of context-dependent model elements. It does not guarantee that the resulting model is well-formed (e.g., as in Fig. 6D). So, we need additional formalization for each modeling notation to construct and verify model variants given the sets of elements visible in specific contexts. Thus, our framework represents the generic component for reasoning about contextual variability upon which complete solutions can be built. An example of such a solution is our approach to context-enriched goal models, where, unlike in most goal-based RE methods, we always do goal refinement *in context*.

The hierarchical nature of goal models helped us to reduce the number of tags and to simplify the creation of context-enriched models. Other modeling notations can also benefit from the same idea. We have dealt with limited non-monotonic inheritance and are also exploring ways of modeling richer notion of context inheritance.

We do not capture relationships among contexts other than inheritance. In future work, we would like to be able to recognize which contexts are compatible and which are in conflict, to handle different contexts with different priorities and in general to be able to choose whether and under what circumstances to recognize the effects of contexts on requirements. We are looking into developing or adopting richer context modeling notations to help in analyzing and documenting domain variability in RE.

Recently, context-based approaches for designing adaptive software have been growing in popularity (e.g., [17]). While high-variability goal models have been proposed as a vehicle for designing autonomic software [11], that approach did not consider the effects of domain variability on requirements and on the adaptive systems design. Thus, we are augmenting the approach of [11] with the context framework presented here to support both intentional and domain variability. We are exploring ideas like [17] for introducing context-based adaptation into the approach. Also, for adaptive systems design, we need to consider advanced context issues such as context volatility, scope, monitoring, etc., some of which were identified in [9]. We plan to further assess the approach using case studies in the area of BP modeling. While the complexity is the inherent property of many domains, the emphasis in the future work will be on improving the methodology to help reduce the complexity of context-enriched goal models by guiding the development of context hierarchies and by focusing only on relevant domain properties as well as on fully automating the generation of goal model variants for specific contexts. We are applying our framework to the problem of BP design and reconfiguration, further extending the method of [12].

6 Conclusion

We have shown a method for representing and reasoning about the effects of domain variability on requirements goal models as well as the underlying generic framework for reasoning about visibility of context-dependent model elements. We use a well-understood goal modeling notation enriched with contexts to capture and explore *all* the effects of domain variability on requirements in a *single* model. Given a particular domain state, a goal model variation can be generated presenting the requirements for that particular domain variation. We propose the use of context refinement hierarchies, which help in structuring the domain, in decoupling context definitions from their effects, and in incremental development of context-enriched goal models.

Taking domain variability into consideration allows us, in conjunction with the approach of [14], to increase the precision and usefulness of requirements goal models, by explicitly capturing domain assumptions and their effects on software requirements.

References

1. Bouquet, P., Ghidini, C., Giunchiglia, F., Blanzieri, E.: Theories and uses of context in knowledge representation and reasoning. Journal of Pragmatics 35(3), 455–484 (2003)
2. Brezillon, P.: Context in Problem Solving: A Survey. The Knowledge Engineering Review 14(1), 1–34 (1999)
3. Brezillon, P., Pasquier, L., Pomerol, J.-C.: Reasoning with Contextual Graphs. European Journal of Operational Research 136(2), 290–298 (2002)
4. Cappiello, C., Comuzzi, M., Mussi, E., Pernici, B.: Context Management for Adaptive Information Systems. Electronic Notes in Theoretical Comp. Sci. 146(1), 69–84 (2006)
5. Castro, J., Kolp, M., Mylopoulos, J.: Towards Requirements-Driven Information Systems Engineering: The Tropos Project. Information Systems 27(6), 365–389 (2002)
6. Ceri, S., Daniel, F., Facca, F., Matera, M.: Model-Driven Engineering of Active Context-awareness. World Wide Web 10(4), 387–413 (2007)
7. Dardenne, A., van Lamsweerde, A., Fickas, S.: Goal-Directed Requirements Acquisition. Science of Computer Programming 20(1-2), 3–50 (1993)
8. Giorgini, P., Mylopoulos, J., Nicchiarelli, E., Sebastiani, R.: Reasoning with Goal Models. In: Spaccapietra, S., March, S.T., Kambayashi, Y. (eds.) ER 2002. LNCS, vol. 2503, p. 167. Springer, Heidelberg (2002)
9. Henricksen, K., Indulska, J.: A Software Engineering Framework for Context-Aware Pervasive Computing. In: Proc. PERCOM 2004, Orlando, FL (March 2004)
10. Hong, D., Chiu, D., Shen, V.: Requirements Elicitation for the Design of Context-aware Applications in a Ubiquitous Environment. In: Proc. ICEC 2005, Xian, China, August 15-17 (2005)

11. Lapouchnian, A., Yu, Y., Liaskos, S., Mylopoulos, J.: Requirements-Driven Design of Au-to-nomic Application Software. In: Proc. CASCON 2006, Toronto, Canada, Oct. 16-19 (2006)
12. Lapouchnian, A., Yu, Y., Mylopoulos, J.: Requirements-driven design and configuration management of business processes. In: Alonso, G., Dadam, P., Rosemann, M. (eds.) BPM 2007. LNCS, vol. 4714, pp. 246–261. Springer, Heidelberg (2007)
13. Lenat, D.: The Dimensions of Context-Space. Technical Report, CYC Corp., http://www.cyc.com/doc/context-space.pdf
14. Liaskos, S., Lapouchnian, A., Yu, Y., Yu, E., Mylopoulos, J.: On Goal-based Variability Acquisition and Analysis. In: Proc. RE 2006, Minneapolis, USA, September 11-15 (2006)
15. McCarthy, J., Buvac, S.: Formalizing Context (Expanded Notes). In: Aliseda, A., et al. (eds.) Computing Natural Language, pp. 13–50. CSLI Publications, Stanford
16. Prieto-Diaz, R.: Domain Analysis: an Introduction. SIGSOFT Software Engineering Notes 15(2), 47–54 (1990)
17. Salifu, M., Yu, Y., Nuseibeh, B.: Specifying Monitoring and Switching Problems in Context. In: Proc. RE 2007, New Delhi, India, October 15-19 (2007)
18. Sebastiani, R., Giorgini, P., Mylopoulos, J.: Simple and Minimum-Cost Satisfiability for Goal Models. In: Persson, A., Stirna, J. (eds.) CAiSE 2004. LNCS, vol. 3084, pp. 20–35. Springer, Heidelberg (2004)

Information Networking Model

Mengchi Liu[1] and Jie Hu[2]

[1] School of Computer Science, Carleton University, Canada
[2] School of Computer, Wuhan University, China

Abstract. Real world objects are essentially networked through various natural and complex relationships with each other. Existing data models such as semantic data models, object-oriented data models, and role models oversimplify and ignore such relationships and mainly focus on the roles that objects play, and properties they have with these roles independent of their relationships. As a result, they fail to naturally and directly model various kinds of relationships between objects, between objects and relationships, and between relationships, and support context-dependent representation and access to object properties. In this paper, we propose a novel data model called Information Networking Model that can overcome these limitations.

Keywords: information modeling, semantic data model, complex relationships, context-dependent representation.

1 Introduction

Since the late 1970s, various semantic data models (SDMs) [1,2] and object-oriented data models (OMs) [3,4,5,6,7,8] have been proposed to model the real world objects and relationships by using high level concepts such as object identity, aggregation, classification, instantiation, generalization/specialization, class hierarchies, non-monotonic inheritance, etc. They are mainly concerned about the static aspects of the real world and normally require an object to be an instance of a most specific class. Thus they are not well suitable to model dynamic and evolutionary situations such as object migration. To solve this problem, some object-oriented data models allow multiple inheritance with intersection classes. However, multiple inheritance may lead to combinatorial explosion in the number of subclasses [9]. Some object-oriented data models support overlapping generalizations, which lead to multiple classification and avoid the combinatorial explosion of multiple inheritance [8]. However they don't support complex relationships and context-dependent accesses to object properties.

To capture evolutionary aspects of real-world objects, various role models (RMs) have been proposed [9,10,11,12,13,14,15]. The main characteristics of these role models is the separation of object classes and role classes so that an object can play several roles. Roles concern dynamic and many-faceted aspects of objects. Like object classes whose class hierarchy deal with the static classification of objects, role classes can also be organized hierarchically and can

A.H.F. Laender et al. (Eds.): ER 2009, LNCS 5829, pp. 131–144, 2009.

have property inheritance as well to deal with the dynamic classification of objects. Also, they support simple context-dependent access to object properties. The main problem with role models is that they just focus on roles of objects independently rather than the roles that objects play in the context of complex relationships with other objects.

In our view, real world objects are essentially networked through various natural and complex relationships with each other. Via these relationships, they play various roles that form their context, and then demonstrate the corresponding context-dependent properties. Existing data models such as semantic data models, object-oriented models, and role models oversimplify and ignore these relationships and mainly focus on the roles that objects play, and properties they have with these roles independent of their relationships. Thus, they fail to naturally and directly model various kinds of relationships between objects, between objects and relationships, and between relationships and support context-dependent representation and access to object properties. As a result, they can only provide a partial model of the real world and fail to provide one-to-one correspondence between the real world and the corresponding information model.

In this paper, we propose a novel data model called Information Networking Model (INM) that can overcome these limitations. It allows us to represent not only static but also dynamic context-dependent information regarding objects and various kinds of relationships between objects, between objects and relationships, and between relationships naturally and directly, and support context-dependent access to object properties.

This paper is organized as follows. Section 2 gives the motivation of our model. Section 3 introduces the core concepts including object classes, role relationships, context relationships, identification, normal attributes and relationships, context-based attributes and relationships, induced role relationship class and context-dependent information, and instance. Section 4 shows hierarchies and inheritance. In section 5, we conclude and comment on our future plans.

2 Motivation

Now let us consider university information modeling. A university involves several kinds of people such as vice presidents, faculty, and students. A vice president has length, office, and start year and is specialized into vice president research and vice president academic; inversely, a person can hold a position of a university's vice president, vice president research, or vice president academic if he or she plays the corresponding role. A faculty has start year and is specialized into associate professor, and professor and a professor may supervise graduate students; inversely, a person works at a university with occupation faculty and title associate professor or professor if he or she plays the corresponding role. A student has a student number and is specialized into graduate student and undergraduate. Also, a graduate student may be supervised by a professor and is further specialized into master's student and Ph.D student; inversely, a person studies at a university if he or she is a student with status undergraduate,

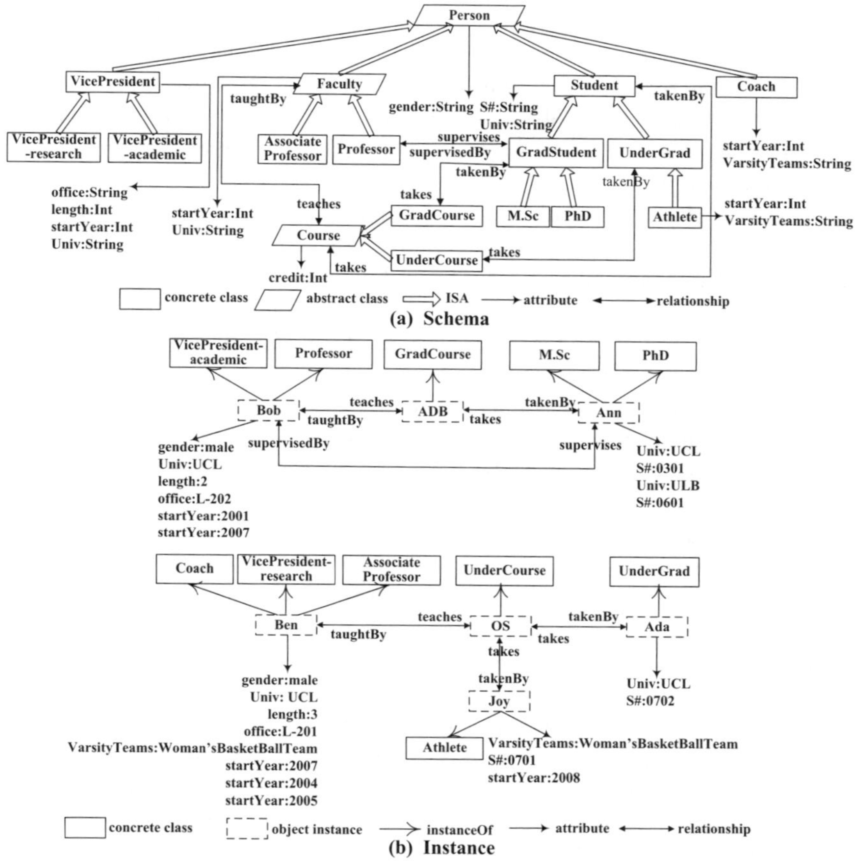

Fig. 1. Sample Example in Object-Oriented Models

master's student, or Ph.D student if he or she plays the corresponding role. A university may have various kinds of varsity teams that involve several kinds of people such as athletes and coaches. An athlete must be an undergraduate and has start year; inversely, a person may be a member of varsity teams with start year. A course has credit and is specialized into graduate course and undergraduate course and is taught by faculty and taken by students; inversely, faculty teach courses and students take courses. Moreover, an undergraduate course is taken by undergraduates but a graduate course is taken by graduate students; inversely, an undergraduate takes undergraduate courses while a graduate student takes graduate courses.

Object-oriented models mainly focus on object classification, complex objects, generalization/specialization, class hierarchy and inheritance. Most object-oriented models require an object to be an instance of a most specific class. Thus, class hierarchy requires careful planning and object cannot evolve and change classification. Some object-oriented data models allow multiple inheritance with intersection classes. However, multiple inheritance may lead to combinatorial explosion in the number of subclasses. Other object-oriented data models support overlapping generalizations, which lead to multiple classification and avoid the combinatorial explosion of multiple inheritance. However, they disallow context-dependent access to object properties. To model the above application in object-oriented data models, we can use Fig. 1 to represent the schema and instance respectively.

For example, if we want to represent that Ben is a VicePresident-research and also an AssociateProfessor at university UCL, and a Coach of varsity team Woman'sBasketBallTeam with the corresponding attributes and relationships, we might represent it using multiple classifications shown in Fig. 1-(b) where Ben has values for attributes gender, Univ, length, office, VarsityTeams, and relationship teaches with undergraduate course OS. Note that there are three distinct attributes with same name startYear that cannot be distinguished here. For Bob who is a VicePresident-academic and also a Professor at UCL, the case is similar. For another example, if we want to represent that Ann is both a M.Sc and a PhD student at universities UCL and ULB respectively with the corresponding attributes and relationships, we might represent this also shown in Fig. 1-(b). Again two attributes S# cannot be distinguished either as we cannot distinguish at which university Ann is as a M.Sc and a PhD respectively.

In role models, two kinds of classes are distinguished: static class and dynamic class that behave differently with respect to object migration. Instances of static subclasses will never migrate but instances of dynamic subclasses can migrate. For the above application, if GradCourse is a static subclass of Course, then a course that is not a graduate course will never migrate to GradCourse subclass. If Student is a dynamic subclass of Person, then a person that is not a student may migrate to Student subclass. In both cases, an instance of the subclass is also an instance of the superclass. That is, the instances of GradCourse and Student are also instances of their superclasses Course and Person respectively. Dynamic subclasses are modeled as role subclasses that can form role class hierarchies. Every role instance differs from every object instance, but an object instance can acquire one or more role instances as roles and all attributes defined on role classes are under corresponding role instances. Therefore, role models support simple context-dependent access to properties. For the above application, VicePresident, Faculty, and Student are modeled as direct role subclasses of Person. Also, role subclasses can form hierarchies such as VicePresident→{VicePresident-research, VicePresident-academic}, Faculty →{AssociateProfessor, Professor}, and Student →{GradStudent →{M.Sc, PhD}, UnderGrad}. A Person instance Ben can acquire five role instances CoachBen, VicePresidentBen, VicePresident-researchBen, FacultyBen, and AssociateProfessorBen as roles. Also, three distinct attributes with the same name startYear are under role instances CoachBen, VicePresident-researchBen, and AssociateProfessorBen respectively thus they can be distinguished. Fig. 2 shows the schema and instance respectively.

Note that role models just treat VicePresident, Faculty, Student, etc, as independent role subclasses of Person, the context such as Univ just as attribute rather than relationship. They thus just support simple context representation.

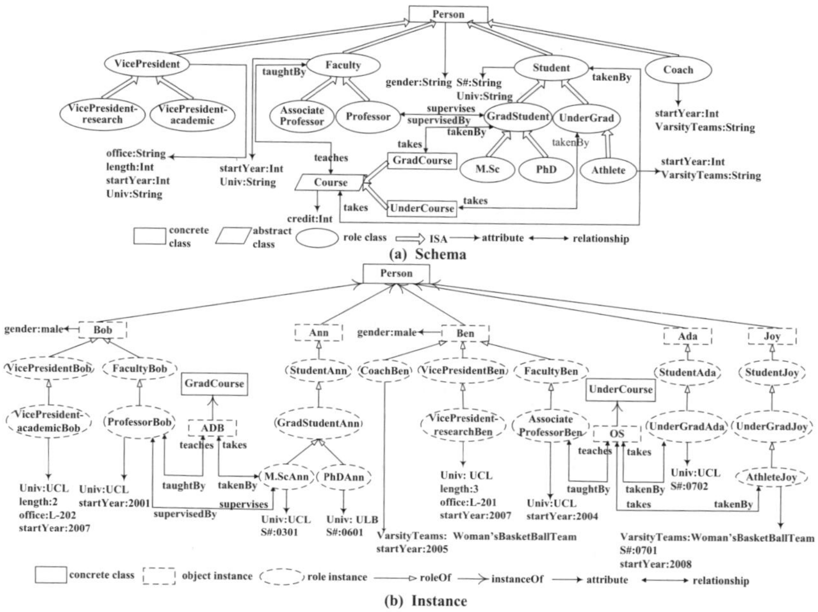

Fig. 2. Sample Example in Role Models

Also, role models can not naturally represent the inverse related to the role classes. Moreover, the information about a person is scattered in a hierarchy of objects such as one Person instance Bob and two role instances VicePresident-academicBob and ProfessorBob rather than using a single object.

In our model, we treat Univ and Person as object classes, VicePresident, Faculty, Student, and their subclasses as role relationship hierarchies from Univ to Person. Also, each role relationship in the hierarchy induces a corresponding role relationship class and generates context in terms of context relationship and identification specified on the role relationship. Moreover, context-dependent information of a role relationship class is composed of context, context-based attributes and relationships and can be naturally and directly represented. In the following section, we present the core concepts of our model.

3 Core Cocepts

3.1 Object Classes and Role Relationship

In our model, we classify two kinds of classes based on their functionality: object classes and role relationship classes.

An *object class* is used to describe the static aspects of the real world objects. Object classes can form static subclass hierarchies as in object-oriented data models and role models and support inheritance with overriding, see Section 4.

Fig. 3 shows the schema of the running example in our model where Univ, Course, UnderCourse, GradCourse, VarsityTeams, and Person denoted graphically

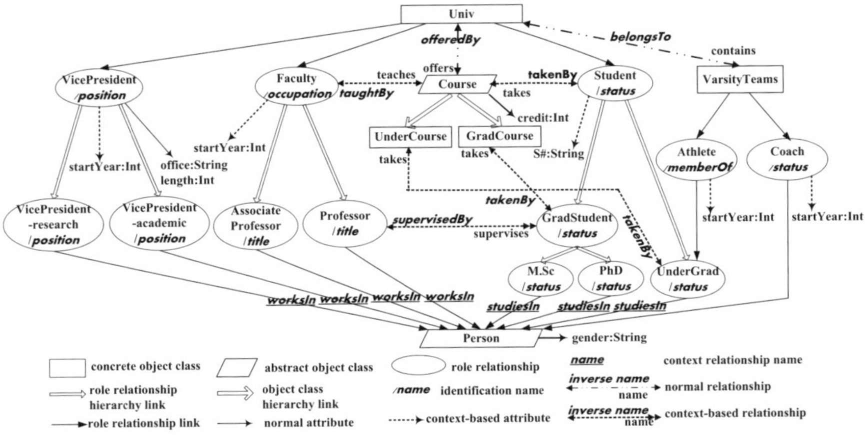

Fig. 3. Sample Example in our Model

with rectangles and parallelogram are object classes. GradCourse and UnderCourse are (static) subclasses of object class Course for a course that is not a grad course can never migrate to grad course. Therefore, Course, UnderCourse and GradCourse form an object class hierarchy.

The main novel feature of our model is the introduction of novel mechanisms to represent relationships and complex context-dependent information based on these relationships between objects and reflect the dynamic and many-faceted aspects of real world objects in a natural and direct way. Instead of just defining independent role subclasses of classes regardless of the complex context-dependent information between objects as in many role models, we introduce role relationships.

A *role relationship* r represents the relationship from an object class c to either an object class or a role relationship class c', where c and c' are called *source class* and *target class* of r respectively. A role relationship has two functions:

(1) as a relationship to connect objects in c to objects in c'.
(2) as a role that the objects in c' play in objects in c.

For example, VicePresident, VicePresident-reserach, VicePresident-academic, Faculty, AssociateProfessor, Professor, Student, GradStudent, M.Sc , PhD, and UnderGrad denoted graphically with ellipses in Fig. 3 are role relationships from source class Univ to target class Person. On one hand, we can consider them as relationships to connect objects in Univ to objects in Person. On the other hand, they can also be considered as roles the objects in Person play in the objects in Univ.

A role relationship between source class c and target class c' is directed and may have inverse relationship from c' to c as in ODMG [16]. We use *context relationship* to represent this kind of inverse relationship and *identification* to denote further context of r under corresponding context relationship. Also, role relationships can have attributes and other relationships, see Section 3.2. A role relationship can have role sub-relationships and thus it can form hierarchy that supports inheritance both at the class level and at the instance level, see Section 4.

For example, VicePresident→{VicePresident-research, VicePresident-academic} in Fig. 3 is a role relationship hierarchy from source class Univ to target class Person that specifies that Univ has a role relationship VicePresident with Person, VicePresident is further specialized into role sub-relationships VicePresident-research and VicePresident-academic. Inversely, Person has context relationship worksIn with Univ, and all the identification names of role relationships are position.

Like an object class that denotes a set of instances with common properties, a role relationship r induces a set of instances of its target class c' participating in the role relationship in the context of source class c. We thus overload r to represent the role relationship class that denotes this set that is a subclass of target class c' and automatically generates its *context-dependent information*, see Section 3.3. Also, the target class of a role relationship r can be a role relationship class that is induced by another role relationship. For example, Athlete in Fig. 3 is a role relationship from VarsityTeams to UnderGrad that is an induced role relationship class. Athlete itself also induces a set of instances of UnderGrad participating in the role relationship Athlete in the context of source class VarsityTeams. So we overload role relationship Athlete to represent the role relationship class that is the subclass of the role relationship class UnderGrad.

3.2 Other Relationships and Attributes

Besides role relationships and its inverse (context relationships), we need additional notions to deal with other kinds of relationships. First of all, the instances of an object class may have simple relationships with other instances of either an object class or a role relationship class and the relationships can have inverse, we use normal relationship to represent this kind of relationships.

A *normal relationship* r from an object class c to target class c' has two cases to consider: c' is an object class or c' is a role relationship class. For the first case, the inverse relationship of r is also a normal relationship. This case is same as in other models. For example, Univ has normal relationship offers with Course, inversely, Course has relationship offeredBy with Univ in Fig. 3. As the target class Course is an object class, inverse relationship offeredBy is thus also a normal relationship. For the second case, the inverse relationship of r is a context-based relationship which is nested in the context of c', see Section 3.3. For example, Course has a normal relationship taughtBy with Faculty, inversely, Faculty has relationship teaches with Course. As the target class Faculty is a role relationship class induced by role relationship Faculty, inverse relationship teaches is thus a context-based relationship.

The instances of a role relationship class may also have relationships with other instances of either an object class or a role relationship class. We introduce context-based relationship to account for this case. A *context-based relationship* r_c specified on a role relationship r is used to describe the association between the instances of two role relationship classes or from the instances of a role relationship class to the instances of an object class. Also, r_c will be generated in the context of the role relationship class induced by r, see Section 3.3.

For example, the role relationship Professor in Fig. 3 has context-based relationship supervises with GradStudent; inversely, GradStudent has relationship supervisedBy with Professor which indicates that if a person becomes a professor at a university, he or she may have a relationship supervises with graduate students; inversely, if a person becomes a graduate student at the same university, he or she may have a relationship supervisedBy with a professor. Note that context-based relationships supervises/supervisedBy are specified on role relationships Professor and GradStudent, but they are used to describe the associations between the instances of corresponding role relationship classes. That is, context-based relationships will be generated in role relationship class, see Section 3.3.

In our model, both object classes and role relationship classes can have attributes. With the introduction of role relationship, not all attributes should be dealt with in the same way. Consider the role relationship VicePresident under Univ in Fig. 3, it has attributes office, length and startYear. No matter who is the VicePresident, VicePresident-research, or VicePresident-academic, the office and length should stay the same while the startYear depends on the individual person who is appointed to this position. When a person resigns, finishes the term, or is fired from the position, the startYear should be deleted from person as well. Thus, we introduce two kinds of attributes.

- *normal attributes*: the attributes that describe the properties of either instances of object classes or role relationships.
- *context-based attributes*: the attributes that describe the properties of instances of role relationship classes. They are also specified on role relationship r but will be generated in the role relationship class induced by r.

For example, in Fig. 3, gender on Person is a normal attribute which is used to describe the property of instances of object classes Person. Attributes office and length on VicePresident under Univ are also normal attributes which are used to describe the role relationship VicePresident, whereas, S# on Student is a context-based attribute which is used to describe the properties of instance of the role relationship class Student.

3.3 Induced Role Relationship Class and Context-Dependent Information

The key feature of our model is the introduction of role relationships. A role relationship r can induce a corresponding role relationship class c_r with the same name as r and context-dependent information of c_r can be naturally and directly represented through specifying context relationship and identification of r. In this section, we discuss these issues.

A role relationship hierarchy h from source class c to target class c' can generate a corresponding same order role relationship class hierarchy h' that is a subclass hierarchy of target class c'. Now we discuss the generation of the context of a node during the traversal of the role relationship class hierarchy h' that is

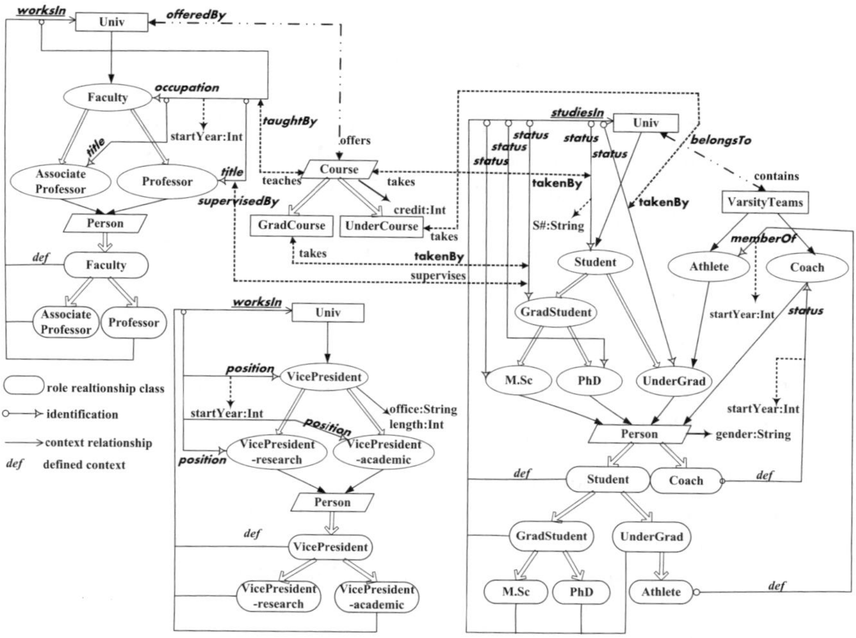

Fig. 4. Induced Role Relationship Class and Context-Dependent Information

used to generate context-dependent information. For each role relationship class node v in h', let Ç_v denote the context of v, r_v role relationship inducing v, h role relationship hierarchy inducing h', r_c context relationship name of h, i identification name of r_v, c source class name of h. We distinguish two cases: v is the root or all of its ancestors have empty context, and one of its ancestors has non-empty context. For the first case, if both r_c and i are not given, then Ç_v is empty; if only r_c is given, then Ç_v is a context relationship r_c from v to c; if only i is given, then Ç_v is an identification i from v to r_v under c; if both r_c and i are given, then Ç_v is a nested relationship composed of a context relationship r_c from v to c nesting identification i to r_v. For the second case, let Ç_p be the context of its nearest ancestor role relationship class node p that is non-empty, r_p role relationship inducing p. If r_v does not have an identification name i, then Ç_v is empty; if r_v has the same identification name as r_p, then Ç_v is obtained from Ç_p by replacing the identification target r_p with r_v; if r_v has a different identification name from r_p, then Ç_v is obtained from Ç_p by nesting identification i to r_v into Ç_p. Note that if v is the root of h', Ç_v is a *defined context*, otherwise, it is an *overriding context*.

For example, Fig. 4 is the schema with induced role relationship classes and context-dependent information corresponding to Fig. 3 where we duplicate object classes Univ and Person for presentation cleanness. Role relationship hierarchy h Student→{GradStudent →{M.Sc, PhD}, UnderGrad} from Univ to Person in Fig. 3 induces a corresponding role relationship class hierarchy h' Student→{GradStudent →{M.Sc, PhD}, UnderGrad} which is a subclass hierarchy of Person and denoted graphically with round rectangles in Fig.4. Student in

h' is the root and both r_c and i are given which are studiesIn and status respectively. Thus the context of Student is a defined context composed of a context relationship studiesIn from role relationship class Student to Univ nesting identification status to role relationship Student. For the node GradStudent in h' , as its parent Student has non-empty context and role relationship GradStudent has the same identification name status as Student. Thus the context of GradStudent is obtained from the context of Student by replacing the identification target Student with GradStudent. For the node M.Sc, PhD, and UnderGrad in h', the case is similar. Single role relationship h Athlete from VarsityTeams to role relationship UnderGrad in Fig. 3 also induces a corresponding role relationship class h' Athlete which is a subclass of role relationship class UnderGrad in Fig.4. Athlete in h' is the root and only i is given. Thus the context of Athlete is an identification memberOf from role relationship class Athlete to role relationship Athlete under VarsityTeams and is a defined context.

In our model, context-based attributes and relationships are specified on role relationships and are used to describe the properties of instances of role relationship classes. Therefore, they are nested in the context of role relationship class and form the context-dependent information. Our model provides this mechanism to naturally and directly support context-dependent representation and access to object properties.

For example, context-based attribute S# and relationship takes specified on role relationship Student in Fig. 3 are nested in the context of corresponding role relationship class Student in Fig. 4 to form the context-dependent information.

3.4 Instance

Based on the notions introduced above and the schema shown in Fig. 4, we demonstrate ten networked objects in the instance shown in Fig. 5 to model the application mentioned in Section 2 where UCL, ULB, Woman'sBasketBallTeam, ADB, OS, Ben, Bob, Ann, Ada and Joy are object identifiers, some of which are duplicated in the figure for presentation cleanness. For object classes, Univ has two instances identified by UCL and ULB, VarsityTeams has one instance identified by Woman'sBasketBallTeam, GradCourse has one instance identified by ADB, UnderCourse has one instance identified by OS. For role relationship classes, VicePresident-research and AssociateProfessor respectively have one instance identified by Ben, Coach has one instance identified by Ben, VicePresident-academic and Professor respectively have one instance identified by Bob, M.Sc and PhD respectively have one instance identified by Ann, UnderGrad has one instance identified by Ada, and Athlete has one instance identified by Joy.

In our model, all the information including complex context-dependent information regarding a real world object is grouped in one instance instead of scattering in a hierarchy of objects as in role models. Also, context-dependent representation and access to object properties can be supported naturally and directly. In Fig. 5, UCL has role relationship hierarchies VicePresident →{VicePresident-research, VicePresident-academic} with Ben and Bob, Student →{GradStudent → {M.Sc, PhD}, UnderGrad} with Ann, Ada, and Joy, Faculty →{AssociateProfessor,

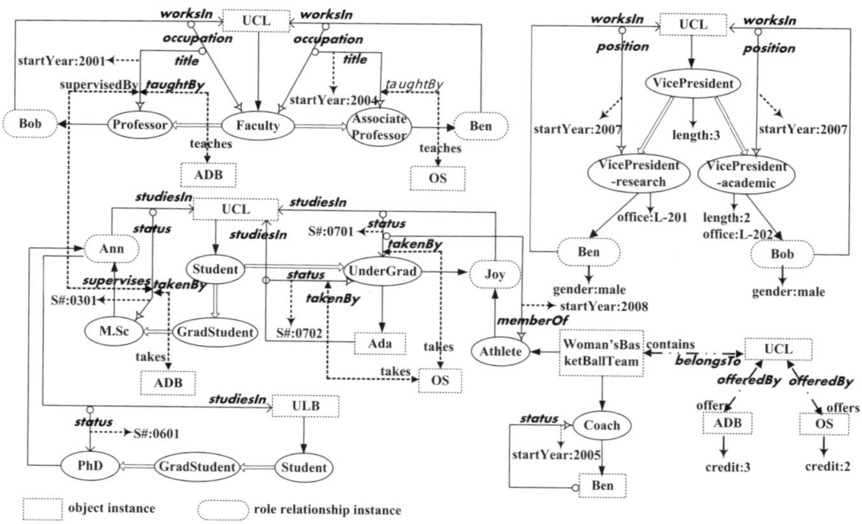

Fig. 5. Instance

Professor} with Ben and Bob. VicePresident of UCL has value 3 for attribute length, VicePresident-research of UCL has value L-201 for attribute office and VicePresident-academic of UCL has value 2 and L-202 for attributes length and office respectively which are independent of individual person Ben and Bob. Also, UCL offers ADB and OS and contains Woman'sBasketBallTeam. Inversely, ADB and OS are respectively offered by UCL and Woman'sBasketBallTeam belongs to UCL. ULB has role relationship hierarchy Student →GradStudent →PhD with Ann. Woman'sBasketBallTeam has role relationships Coach and Athlete with Ben and Joy respectively. For Ben, as a VicePresident-research, he works in UCL with position VicePresident-research, and in this context he has value 2007 for attribute startYear; as an AssociateProfessor, he also works in UCL with occupation Faculty and title AssociateProfessor, and in this context he has value 2003 for attribute startYear and teaches OS; as a Coach, his status is Woman'sBasketBall's coach, in this context he has value 2005 for attribute startYear. For Bob, as a VicePresident-academic, he works in UCL with position VicePresident-academic, and in this context he has value 2007 for attribute startYear; as a Professor, he also works in UCL with occupation Faculty and title Professor, and in this context he has value 2001 for attribute startYear, teaches ADB, and supervises Ann who is a M.Sc studying in UCL; For Ann, as a M.Sc, she studies in UCL with status M.Sc, and in this context she has value 0301 for attribute S#, takes ADB, and is supervised by Bob who is a Professor working in UCL; as a PhD, she studies in ULB with status PhD, and in this context she has value 0601 for attribute S#. For Ada, as a UnderGrad, she studies in UCL with status UnderGrad, and in this context she has value 0702 for attribute S# and takes OS. For Joy, as an Athlete, she studies in UCL with status UnderGrad, and in this context she has value 0701 for attribute S#, takes OS, and is a member of Woman'sBasketBallTeam's Athlete with value 2008 for attribute startYear.

4 Hierarchies and Inheritance

In our model, object classes, role relationships, and role relationship classes can form disjoint hierarchies. Now we first discuss object class inheritance. As mentioned in Section 2, object classes correspond to static classes and can have class hierarchies and inherit attributes and relationships from their superclasses as in object-oriented data models and role models. For example, object class Course in Fig. 4 is specialized into subclasses GradCourse and UnderCourse. Therefore, GradCourse and UnderCourse inherit credit, offeredBy, and taughtBy but override takenBy from their superclass Course .

A role relationship can be further specialized into role relationship hierarchies and supports inheritance both at the schema level and at the instance level. At the schema level, every role relationship in a role relationship hierarchy can have a set of attributes and relationships. Role sub-relationships inherit or override normal attributes from their role super-relationship. For example, VicePresident-research and VicePresident-academic in Fig. 4 are role sub-relationships of VicePresident. Therefore, they inherit normal attributes length and office from VicePresident. At the instance level, every role relationship only keeps the most relevant normal attribute values and inherits or overrides attribute values from its role super-relationship. For example, VicePresident of UCL in Fig. 5 has the most relevant value for attribute length. VicePresident-research inherits this value but VicePresident-academic overrides it.

Now we consider the inheritance between the target class and its role relationship subclasses, and the inheritance between role relationship classes. In our model, an object class does not have any context and context-based attributes and relationships. It thus does not have any context-dependent information. However, a role relationship class may have context and context-based attributes and relationships. It thus may have context-dependent information.

A role relationship class denotes a subset of instances of the target class participating in the corresponding role relationship in the context of source class. Therefore, the root of a role relationship class hierarchy inherits or overrides properties from its target class. When the target class is an object class, it just inherits or overrides normal attributes, normal relationships, and role relationships from the target class; when the target class is a role relationship class, it inherits or overrides not only normal attributes, normal relationships, role relationships but also context-dependent information from the target class, also the current context-dependent information of the root is nested into the context of its target class to form its final context-dependent information. Moreover, the role relationship class other than the root in a role relationship class hierarchy inherits or overrides all attributes and relationships and context from its superclass, and context-based attributes and relationships are nested into the context to form its context-dependent information.

For example, the role relationship class hierarchy Student $\rightarrow$\{GradStudent $\rightarrow$\{M.Sc, PhD\}, UnderGrad\} in Fig. 4 induced by the corresponding role relationship hierarchy is a subclass hierarchy of object class Person. Thus, the root Student inherits normal attribute gender from Person. UnderGrad inherits normal attribute gender, context-based attribute S# but overrides context-based relationship takes from Student. Context-based attribute and relationship S# and takes are nested into the context of UnderGrad to form its context-dependent information. For GradStudent, M.Sc, and PhD, the case is similar. The single role relationship class Athelte in Fig. 4, which is induced by role relationship Athelte, is a subclass of role relationship class UnderGrad. Thus, Athelte inherits normal attribute gender and context-dependent information from UnderGrad. Also, the current context-dependent information of Athlete such as identification memberOf from role relationship class Athlete to role relationship Athlete under VarsityTeams is nested into the context of UnderGrad to form final context-dependent information of Athlete.

5 Conclusion

In this paper, we have demonstrated the need to model various kind of complex relationships between objects, between objects and relationships, and between relationships and discussed the limitations of existing data models, such as semantic data models (SDMs), object-oriented models (OMs), and role models (RMs).

To overcome these limitations, we have proposed a novel data model called Information Networking Model. In this model, objects in the real world are uniquely represented with object identifiers that are networked through various relationships, which directly correspond to the real world. By modeling the real world based on its organizational structure directly, the data modeling process can be greatly simplified. Also, the information model created can evolve with the real world objects to reflect their evolutionary, dynamic and many-faceted aspects naturally. Moreover, it supports context-dependent information representation and context-dependent access to object properties.

Table 1 shows the comparison of our model with the other three kinds of models.

Based on the proposed Information Networking Model, we are currently working on a powerful query language that can explore the natural information network and extract meaningful results. Also we are systematically implementing a database management system and plan to use it for various applications. Furthermore, we would like to establish a firm foundation for this model.

Table 1. Comparison of different models

Criteria	SDMs	OMs	RMs	INM
relationship	simple	simple	simple	complex
object evolution	no	weak	strong	strong
many-faceted nature	no	no	weak	strong
context-dependent representation and access to properties	no	no	weak	strong

References

1. Hull, R., King, R.: Semantic database modeling: Survey, applications, and research issues. ACM Comput. Surv. 19(3), 201–260 (1987)
2. Peckham, J., Maryanski, F.J.: Semantic data models. ACM Comput. Surv. 20(3), 153–189 (1988)
3. Atkinson, M.P., Bancilhon, F., De Witt, D.J., Dittrich, K.R., Maier, D., Zdonik, S.B.: The object-oriented database system manifesto. In: Proceedings of SIGMOD, Atlantic City, NJ
4. Ghelli, A.A.G., Orsini, R.: A relationship mechanism for a strongly typed object-oriented database programming language. In: Proceedings of VLDB, Barcelona, Catalonia, Spain, September 1991, pp. 565–575 (1991)
5. Abiteboul, S., Bonner, A.: Objects and views. In: Proceedings of ACM SIGMOD, Denver, Colorado, May 1991, pp. 238–247 (1991)
6. Su, J.: Dynamic constraints and object migration. In: Proceedings of VLDB, Barcelona, Catalonia, Spain, September 1991, pp. 233–242 (1991)
7. Bancilhon, F., Delobel, C., Kanellakis, P.C. (eds.): Building an Object-Oriented Database System, The Story of O2. Morgan Kaufmann, San Francisco (1992)
8. Bertino, E., Guerrini, G.: Objects with multiple most specific classes. In: Olthoff, W. (ed.) ECOOP 1995. LNCS, vol. 952, pp. 102–126. Springer, Heidelberg (1995)
9. Wong, R.K., Chau, H.L., Lochovsky, F.H.: A data model and semantics of objects with dynamic roles. In: Proceedings of ICDE, Birmingham U.K., April 1997, pp. 402–411 (1997)
10. Richardson, J., Schwartz, I.: Aspects: Extending objects to support multiple, independent roles. In: Proceedings of SIGMOD, Denver, Colorado, May 1991, pp. 298–307 (1991)
11. Albano, A., Bergamini, R., Ghelli, G., Orsini, R.: An object data model with roles. In: Proceedings of VLDB, Dublin, Ireland, August 1993, pp. 39–51 (1993)
12. Gottlob, G., Schrefl, M., Röck, B.: Extending object-oriented systems with roles. ACM Transaction on Office Information Systems 14(3), 268–296 (1996)
13. Steimann, F.: On the representation of roles in object-oriented and conceptual modelling. Data Knowledge Engineering 35(1), 83–106 (2000)
14. Dahchour, M., Pirotte, A., Zimányi, E.: A Generic Role Model for Dynamic Objects. In: Pidduck, A.B., Mylopoulos, J., Woo, C.C., Ozsu, M.T. (eds.) CAiSE 2002. LNCS, vol. 2348, pp. 643–658. Springer, Heidelberg (2002)
15. Cabot, J., Raventós, R.: Roles as entity types: A conceptual modelling pattern. In: Proceedings of ER, Shanghai, China, November 2004, pp. 69–82 (2004)
16. Cattell, R.G.G., Barry, D., Berler, M., Eastman, J., dan, D.J., Russel, C., Schadow, O., Stanienda, T., Velez, F.: The Object Data Standard: ODMG 3.0. Morgan Kaufmann Publishers, San Francisco (2000)

Towards an Ontological Modeling with Dependent Types: Application to Part-Whole Relations

Richard Dapoigny and Patrick Barlatier

Université de Savoie, Laboratoire d'Informatique, Sytèmes, Traitement de l'Information et de la Connaissance
Po. Box 80439,
74944 Annecy-le-vieux cedex, France
Phone: +33 450 096529; Fax: +33 450 096559
richard.dapoigny@univ-savoie.fr

Abstract. Generally, mereological relations are modeled using fragments of first-order logic(FOL) and difficulties arise when meta-reasoning is done over their properties, leading to reason outside the logic. Alternatively, classical languages for conceptual modeling such as UML lack of formal foundations resulting in ambiguous interpretations of mereological relations. Moreover, they cannot prove that a given specification is correct from a logical perspective. In order to address all these problems, we suggest a formal framework using a dependent (higher-order) type theory such as those used in program checking and theorem provers (e.g., Coq). It is based on constructive logic and allows reasoning in different abstraction levels within the logic. Furthermore, it maximizes the expressiveness while preserving decidability of type checking and results in a coherent theory with a powerful sub-typing mechanism.

1 Motivations

In this paper we focus on the Ontological and Conceptual Correctness in Modeling. In the literature, there are many conceptual modelling and ontology languages like the Unified Modeling Language (UML), ORM, ER and Description Logics (DLs). Whereas adequately designed for conceptual modeling, UML is not suitable for capturing complex ontologies, since it is limited about some slot-related mechanisms (e.g., slot-value-restrictions cannot be defined by using the union/intersection of classes and there are no tools for the global management of slots). Furthermore, its semantics is not formally defined [11] [8], both leading to ambiguous interpretations of UML ontologies and preventing their automated analysis. A recent approach ([18]) proposes to extend conventional frame-based ontology modeling languages with modeling primitives, but this leads to complex models and doesn't solve the interpretation problem. Other languages such as Description Logics restrict their expressive power in order to avoid the kind of difficult reasoning problems. When Description Logics are used for conceptual modeling, it is normally used "in the background" and limited

A.H.F. Laender et al. (Eds.): ER 2009, LNCS 5829, pp. 145–158, 2009.

to $\mathcal{DLR}$ [5,9]. Let us mention also unresolved issues regarding differences between TBox and ABox reasoning with the parthood relation. In [6], the authors develop a theory of parthood, component hood, and containment relations in first order predicate logic and then discuss how description logics can be used to capture some aspects of the first order theory. They conclude that DL are not appropriate for formulating complex interrelations between relations.

Ontology languages should allow for deductive mechanisms that draw inferences from a body of statements. There is also a need for ontology validation, which checks the absence of errors (consistency) of an ontology. This aspect is crucial in ontology modeling and rarely solved with simple FOL-based languages (e.g., to prove the transitivity of relations). In a large ontology, maintaining consistency without automatic mechanisms is a considerable challenge. Moreover, the limited expressive power of FOL might result in reasoning problems that are known to be undecidable [2]. This paper provides a first attempt to address the above difficulties through a constructive type theory termed Dependent Type Framework (DTF) that provides a high expressive representation of ontological structures while maintaining tractability. This formal system is designed to act both as a proof system (constructive logic) and as a typed functional programming language (typed λ-calculus). We first summarize the type theoretical framework, then we explore a non-exhaustive list of classical problems relative to the part-whole relation in modeling and their definition in DTF.

2 The Language of DTF

Widely used for program verification (with very high reliability) and proof assistants [3], type theory, and more precisely dependent types has received little attention in knowledge representation. The core paradigm is that correct typing corresponds to provably correct models. Typing also provides typical software engineering principles such as modularization and data abstraction. The logical background uses a constructive type theory including a typing mechanism with polymorphism and functional dependency i.e., the Extended Calculus of Constructions (ECC) [15]. We have extended this theory to DTF with subtyping and constants that are useful for knowledge representation.

2.1 The DTF Core

ECC Type theory has explicit proof objects which are terms in an extension of the typed lambda-calculus while at the same time, provability corresponds to type inhabitation[1]. Proofs in a computational setting can be the result of a database lookup, the existence of a function performing a given action or the result of a theorem prover given assumption about entities, properties or constraints. Information states are formalized as sequences of judgments, built up according to a certain set of rules. Some types, that are always considered

[1] A proposition is true iff its set of proofs is inhabited.

well-formed, are introduced by means of axioms. These special types are usually called sorts. Three levels of stratification are available, a sort level, a type level and an object level (proofs). We will use two sorts here, *Type* and *Prop*, which denote respectively the sort of types and the sort of propositions.

Since types may contain terms, they can express arbitrarily complex properties. The building blocks of ECC are terms and the basic relation is the typing relation. The fundamental notion of typing judgment $a : T$ classifies an object a as being of type T. We call a an inhabitant of T, and we call T the type of a. The (logical) context Γ in a judgment $\Gamma \vdash a : T$ contains the prerequisites necessary for establishing the statement $a : T$. If Γ is a list of statements with variables such as $x_1 : T_1; \ldots ; x_n : T_n$ then, the term a has type T. ECC introduces two dependent types, the dependent product Π and the dependent sum Σ. Given two arbitrary types A and B, the dependent product of $B(x)$ noted $\Pi x : A.B(x)$, where x ranges over A, models functions whose output type may vary according to the input. Similarly, given the types A and B, the type forming operation for the dependent sum type (strong sum) of $B(x)$ is expressed as $\Sigma x : A.B(x)$, x ranging over A. The logical consistency[2] of ECC has been demonstrated and the decidability property has been deduced as a corollary [15].

Subtyping. According to the subtyping, a given term may have several types. However, it can be shown that whenever a term is typeable, it has a uniquely determined principal type. This principal type is the minimum type of the term with respect to the subtyping rule and relatively to a given context. There are two different perspectives in DTF about subtyping.

The first category of subtyping, is called *extensional subtyping*. This kind of subtyping considers that a type T' is a subtype of another type T if T' has a greater informational content than T. This definition reveals its extensional flavor, and corresponds to the subsumption mechanism in knowledge representation. The extensional subtyping is a partial order since it is reflexive and transitive. Then, hierarchies of types can be arranged, ranging from simple types to more complex ones. Complex types correspond to nested Σ-types. For the non-dependent sum-types, the type $\Sigma x : A.B$ is written as the Cartesian product $A \times B$ whenever x does not occur in B. In summary, in the extensional subtyping, forgetting information leads to a supertype.

The second category of subtyping will be referred to as *coercion*. The corresponding definition also illustrates the notion of polymorphism.

Definition 1 *(Coercive subtyping)*
A type A' is a subtype of another type A if there is a coercion $c : A' \to A$ that is expressed by: $\Gamma \vdash A' \leq_c A : Type$

if A' is a subtype of A via coercion c, then any object a of type A' can be regarded as an abbreviation of the object $c(a)$ of type A. Coercions between any two types must have the coherence property expressing that they are unique. Coercions are special functional operations that are declared by users.

[2] For a type theory, the logical consistency is identified with termination.

Constant values. The unit type, denoted by 1, is a type housing a single element $*$. Pre-defined values can be introduced with the *Intensional Manifest Fields* (IMF) and are usable through coercive subtyping (see [17]).

Definition 2. *An intensional manifest field (IMF) in a Σ-type is a field of the form: $x \sim a : A$ with $x : 1$, $A : Type$ and $a : A$.*

For example, with a maximum distance value d_m that is equal to 2, one can define a Σ-type comparing a distance value with the constant seen as a unit type through the definition:

$$\sigma = \Sigma d : distance\, .\Sigma d_m \sim 2 : distance\, .\, LowerThan(d, d_m)$$

which means that d_m is an IMF of the type *distance* and witnesses for a maximum value fixed at 2 miles.

2.2 Representing Knowledge with Dependent Types

***Π*-types.** Π-types such as $\Pi x : A.B(x)$ generalize function spaces, that is any proof of the input x of type A yields a proof of $B(x)$. For instance, to represent the fact that $MyNokia6125$ of type *Phone* is able to send calls, the following dependent product can be introduced:

$$\Pi x : Phone\, .\, sendCalls(x)$$

in which $sendCalls(x)$ is a predicate that depends on x (introduction rule). The elimination rule computes a term from the product-type. An instance (a proof) of the Π-type is given by the β-reduction: $\lambda x : A\, .\, sendCalls(x)(MyNokia6125)$, that is, $sendCalls(Nokia6125)$. In other words, $sendCalls$ is a predicate (i.e., a function from *phone* to *Prop*) which for each instance x (e.g., $MyNokia6125$) of the type *phone* yields a proof object (e.g., $sendCalls(MyNokia6125)$) for the proposition. Since it means that all phones send calls, Π-types also express the universal quantification $\forall$.

***Σ*-types.** For strong sums, the predicative universes are closed. When B is a predicate over A[3], it expresses the subset of all objects of type A satisfying the predicate B. Dependent sums Σ model pairs in which the second component depends on the first. Notice that we will use $< a, b >$ to denote pairs instead of $pair_A(a, b)$ when no confusion may occur. Let us consider the pair $\sigma_1 : \Sigma x : phone.mobile(x)$. A proof for this *Sigma*-type is given for example by the instance $< MyNokia6125, q_1 >$ indicating that for the individual $Nokia6125$, the proposition is proved (q_1 is a proof of $mobile(MyNokia6125)$). If we think of the set $\mathcal{B}$ of all phones, then the proved pairs express a subset of $\mathcal{B}$, the subset of mobile phones.

$$< MyNokia6125, q_1 >: \Sigma x : phone.mobile(x)$$

[3] A predicate over A is a propositional function $A \rightarrow Prop$.

A proof $s : \Sigma x : T.P$ in a sum is a pair $s =< \pi_1 s, \pi_2 s >$ that consists of an element $\pi_1 s : T$ of the domain type T together with a proof $\pi_2 s : P[\pi_1 s/x]$ stating that the proposition P is true for this element $\pi_1 s$. In other words, these two elimination rules extract the individual components of a pair. In the above example, with $s =< MyNokia6125, q_1 >$, we get $\pi_1 s = MyNokia6125$ and $\pi_2 s = mobile(MyNokia6125)$.

2.3 Representing Part-Whole Knowledge in DTF

Under the assumption that modeling languages should be founded on upper-level ontologies and that these ontologies must be themselves logically founded, we demonstrate in this section how DTF is able to do the job. For this purpose, assuming that there exists a mapping between an ontology and a Type Theory, a concept hierarchy (e.g., a subsumption hierarchy) corresponds to a hierarchy of types, that assigns each entity to a type. The type of an inhabitant constrains the types of other objects that we can combine with it and specifies the type of such a combination. Therefore, we can see a conceptualization as given by a set of types together with their constructors. Types and constructors belong to the ontology while proofs reside within the database. As underlined in [7], in a foundational ontology there should be no negative or disjunctive universals. Furthermore, a model for universals must be intensional [12]. These constraints are fully assumed in DTF.

Ontological components. The most basic conceptual modeling constructs include individuals and universals. Since types correspond to the result of a categorization procedure, they have a natural adequation with (ontological) universals. According to the Aristotelian conception of universals, types are justified in the sense that there are no uninstantiated universals just as there are no untyped objects.

Definition 3. *In DTF any universal of the domain under consideration is represented as a (non dependent) type. For any basic object (individual), there exists a universal such that this object is proof for it.*

For instance, the universal "house" in $x : house$ has the proof (is instancied by): $x = MyHouse$ while $house : Type$ asserts that "house" is a data-type.

Definition 4. *All mandatory properties of universals are captured by Π-types.*

Notice that we have an ontological equivalence between individuals in the General Ontological Language (GOL) and proofs in DTF.

Definition 5. *An association between universals is a n-ary relation Rel. It is formalized with a Σ-type having these universals as arguments and whose extension consists of all the proofs for that relation.*

$$Rel \triangleq \Sigma a_1 : Type \,.\, \Sigma a_2 : Type \,...\, \Sigma a_n : Type \,.\, R(a_1, a_2, ..., a_n) \quad (1)$$

in which R stands for the predicate $Type \rightarrow Type \rightarrow ... \rightarrow Prop$.

For example, the association $purchFrom$ introduced in [10] within the scope of the (GOL), relates three individuals, i.e., a person, an individual good and a shop. We get easily the corresponding DTF definition:

$$\Sigma x : Person \ . \ \Sigma y : Good \ . \ \Sigma z : Shop \ . \ purchaseFrom(x, y, z)$$

A proof for that ternary relation could be the tuple $< John, < PartsbySimons, < Amazon, p_1 >>>$ with $p_1 = purchaseFrom(John, PartsbySimons, Amazon)$ provided that this association exists in the database. Compare the DTF definition above with the following GOL expression:

$$[a1, a2, a3] :: R_{purchFrom}(Person, Good, Shop) \leftrightarrow John :: Person$$
$$PartsbySimons :: Good \wedge Amazon :: Shop \wedge \exists p(p :: Purchase \wedge$$
$$m(p, John) \wedge m(p, PartsbySimons) \wedge m(p, Amazon))$$

Representing Part-Whole Relations. Many formal taxonomies of part-whole relations have been proposed in the litterature to deal with part-whole relations in conceptual data models. We adopt a taxonomy [13] in which a first principal distinction is made between mereological and meronymic $part - of$ based on their transitivity property: the mereological $part - of$ relation is transitive while the meronymic is not necessarily. A general $part - of$ relation could be defined without any constraints over types (i.e., universals extracted from a foundational ontology) and using the coercion $part - of \leq R$. Any proof (instance) of that relation is a nested pair in which individuals appear.

In [14] the authors argue that for different types of part-whole relations, different categories of entity types have to be related. Extending that assumption, we claim that successive distinctions between the relations can be made according to i) the categories of the entity types participating in the relation and ii) the formal properties that the type of $part - of$ relation satisfies. Types are able to constrain the scope of individuals that appear within relations and to satisfy case (i), whereas case (ii) is addressed with specifications. For meronymic relations, we get the following definitions:

$$\Sigma x : Physical\_object \ . \ \Sigma y : Amount\_of\_matter \ . \ constituted\_of(x, y)$$
$$\Sigma x : Amount\_of\_matter \ . \ \Sigma y : Amount\_of\_matter \ . \ sub\_quantity\_of(x, y)$$
$$\Sigma x : Endurant \ . \ \Sigma y : Perdurant \ . \ participates\_in(x, y)$$
$$\Sigma x : Social\_object \ . \ \Sigma y : Social\_object \ . \ member\_of(x, y)$$

For mereological relations, the transitivity holds and the types of arguments are constrained. For example, $involved\_in$ does have its domain constrained to perdurants with the definition: $\Sigma x : Perdurant \ . \ \Sigma y : Perdurant \ . \ involved\_in(x, y)$. It means that only values of type $Perdurant$, or their sub-types in the hierarchy, are available. Such a subtype specification requires commitment to a foundatonial ontology to ensure unambiguous definitions. Compare this definition with:

$$\forall x, y(involved\_in(x, y) \triangleq part\_of(x, y) \wedge Perdurant(x) \wedge Perdurant(y))$$

It shows clearly that the $part - of$ relation must be defined with constraints operating on type.

The mereological continuism defended by [22], states that the part-whole relation should only be considered to hold among existents (ϵ), i.e., $\forall x, y\ (x \leq y) \rightarrow \epsilon(x) \wedge \epsilon(y)$. In DTF, the validity of this relation is dependent on the existence of proofs, then no additional axioms are required to satisfy this continuism. It means that, since part-whole relations are expressed through Σ-types, the intrinsic dependence classifies them as essential parts. Mandatory parts are expressed with Π-types. To state that all x are part of some y, one write:

$$\Pi x : Type\ .\ \Sigma y\ :\ Type\ .\ Part - of(x, y)$$

Some limitations of DL modeling in medical ontologies are underlined in [19]. They concern the re-usability of A-box assertions and the derived problem of unification that avoids drawing some quite reasonable conclusions. It is straightforward to see that these problems vanish in DTF due to the typing mechanism.

3 Representing Ontological (meta)Properties through Specifications

There is a need to define how important properties related to the part-whole relation such as transitivity and distributivity are expressed in DTF. When there are no typing mechanism inside the logic, other extra rules are needed to express properties of the relations. In [12], the author suggested a revised metamodel, in which he detailed the representation of meronymic associations, however, the logical foundations of such a metamodel are unclear. The existence of several types of part-whole relations, can be specified by a number of meta-properties that they can possess, i.e., the specifications. More precisely, each type of part-whole relation has to detail the (meta)knowledge structure together with the properties that the structure satisfies. With the specifications, meta-properties can be easily described and automatically checked within a single framework.

3.1 Working with Specifications

A major purpose of specifications is to provide a tool that can compute logical consistency of the modelling decisions taken by the modeller about the relations. In what follows, the notation $\sum[x_1 : T_1, x_2 : T_2, ..., x_n : T_n]$ will stand for $\Sigma x_1 : T_1.\Sigma x_2 : T_2. \ldots, .T_n$. Type theory allows for the so-called "meta" reasoning but without leaving the internal logic. For that purpose, a specification of some data structure is provided as the left member of a Σ-type, whereas the right member introduces the properties that the structure is supposed to fulfill.

Definition 6. *(Specification) A specification S in DTF consists of a pair whose objects are i) available proofs that realize the specification of a structure $Struct[S]$ and ii) a predicate $Pr[S]$ over $Struc[S]$ specifying the properties that the realization of the specification should satisfy:*

$$S \triangleq \sum[Struc : Type,\ \ Pr :\ Struc \rightarrow Prop]$$

In such a way, the computational contents (the structure type of the specification) is separated from the axiomatic requirements (correctness proofs). If the structure exists (if we get some proof of it) and if the properties are fulfilled for that structure, then that structure satisfies the constraints given in Pr. We shall use the definition (1) for any binary relation (i.e., with $n = 2$).

3.2 Transitivity

To support the specification of transitive relations, the following structure could be introduced:

$$Struc[Tr] \triangleq \sum \begin{bmatrix} Tr & : Rel \\ Transitive : Rel \rightarrow Prop \end{bmatrix}$$

and for any relation r of type $Struc[Tr]$ (where Tr abbreviates $Tr[r]$) :

$$Pr[Tr] \triangleq \begin{array}{l} \forall u, u' : Tr\ .\ (R_u = R_{u'} : Prop\ \&\ \pi_1\pi_2 u = \pi_1 u' : Type) \supset \\ (R_u(\pi_1 u, \pi_1\pi_2 u)\ \&\ R_{u'}(\pi_1 u', \pi_1\pi_2 u') \supset R_u(\pi_1 u, \pi_1\pi_2 u')) \end{array}$$

with $R_u \triangleq \pi_2\pi_2 u$ and $R_{u'} \triangleq \pi_2\pi_2 u'$. The axiom Pr states that if the propositions in Rel structures are identical ($R_u = R_{u'}$) and if the relation is applied twice with the second argument of the first relation being equal to the first argument of the second one, then the relation applies between the first argument of R_u and the second argument of $R_{u'}$. In other words, if we get a proof that there is a relation Tr and a proof that it is transitive (e.g., reading this information from a table), it yields a proof for the structure $Struc[Tr]$. Then, any relation of that type must satisfy the axioms of $Pr[Tr]$ in order for the specification to be fulfilled. A significant property of that mechanism is that a given specification can be extended and re-used in further specifications. This aspect is crucial for applying specifications to ontologies. The dependent type theory can express transitivity as a property that depends on values corresponding to the different ways in which parts contribute to the structure of the whole. A typical example could be given with the spatial (or temporal) part-of relation that is, for these versions, transitive. A proof of $Struc[Tr](part-of)$ is given by checking the pair $< part-of, q_1 >$ with q_1 a proof of $Transitive(part-of)$[4]. Since this $part-of$ relation is assumed to be transitive, let us consider that the terms u and u' from a knowledge base have the following contents:

$$u : \Sigma x : soldier.\Sigma y : section.\ Part-of(x, y)$$
$$u' : \Sigma x : section.\Sigma y : platoon.\ Part-of(x, y)$$

If we obtain from the database the respective proofs for the above relations: $< Paul, < sec35, p_1 >>$ and $< sec35, < P8, p_2 >>$ with p_1 and p_2 the respective proofs of $part-of(Paul, sec35)$ and $part-of(sec35, P8)$. From axiom $Pr[Tr](part-of)$, the premises are proved ($R_u = R_{u'} = part-of$ and

[4] This kind of knowledge is needed in order to exploit re-usability and (meta)-reasoning.

$\pi_1\pi_2 u = \pi_1 u' = sec35 : section$) then it yields a proof for $part - of(Paul, P8)$ since we have simultaneously $R_u(\pi_1 u, \pi_1\pi_2 u)$ (proof $part - of(Paul, sec35)$ and $R_{u'}(\pi_1 u', \pi_1\pi_2 u')$ (proof $part - of(sec35, P8)$). In summary, with dependent types, transitivity is expressed like a property that depends on a value related to the different ways in which the components contribute to the whole's structure.

3.3 Downward Distributivity over Part-Whole Relations

Another interesting case is that of the left- and right-downward-distributing properties of the $part - whole$ relations [1]. The downward distributivity within this context means that a relation may distribute its related predicate to the parts of a whole. For that aim, the relation has a structure such as $has\_ < property >$, where $< property >$ stands for any property (e.g., $has\_location$, $has\_objective$, ...). Let us consider for example, collections as aggregates of individuals called members of the collection. The distributivity operates on the $has - part$ relation[5]. If a relation is left-downward-distributive over a partonomic relation, then the relation which holds for the whole is also proved for the parts, i.e., more formally, the following structure holds provided that any relation DR left-propagates to the parts with respect to the relation DR' of type $invPW$ (inverse $part - whole$), a sub-relation of Rel (e.g., $has - part$):

$$Struc[DR, DR'] \triangleq \sum \begin{bmatrix} DR & : Rel \\ DR' & : invPW \\ L - DOWN - Propagate & : Rel \rightarrow invPW \rightarrow Prop \end{bmatrix}$$

and for any pair of relations r, r' of type $Struc[DR, DR']$ (with DR, DR' the abbreviation for $DR[r], DR'[r']$):

$$Pr[DR, DR'] \triangleq \begin{array}{l} \forall u : DR, \forall u' : DR' . \\ (\pi_2\pi_2 u = \pi_2\pi_2 u' \supset \perp \ \& \ \pi_1 u = \pi_1 u' : Type) \supset \\ (R_u(\pi_1 u, \pi_1\pi_2 u) \ \& \ R_{u'}(\pi_1 u', \pi_1\pi_2 u') \supset \\ R_u(\pi_1\pi_2 u', \pi_1\pi_2 u)) \end{array}$$

with $R_u \triangleq \pi_2\pi_2 u$ and $R_{u'} \triangleq \pi_2\pi_2 u'$. The axiom Pr says that provided that each of the propositions corresponding to the relations DR and DR' are distinct ($R_u = R_{u'} \supset \perp$) and that the first argument of the first relation is identical to the first argument of the second one, then the relation R_u is valid, having as respective arguments, the first argument of R_u and the second argument of $R_{u'}$. If we get a proof for the downward propagation of the relation DR with respect to DR', that is, a proof of $Struc[DR, DR']$, then any pair of relations of that type must satisfy the axioms in $Pr[DR, DR']$ in order to prove the specification. Predicates acting upon collections apply upon the articles that compose the collection. Let us show the expressive power of this property with some example. For instance, we may capture the fact, that the objectives of a group are the same as those of a member of the group.

[5] Also called has_item, $has\_participant$, $has\_element$, has_member, ...

A proof of $Struc[DR, DR']$ $(has\_objective, has\_member)$ is given according to the checking the nested pair $< has\_objective, < has\_member, q_1 >>$ with q_1 a proof of $L - DOWN - Propagate(has\_objective,\ has\_member)$. Provided that the relation *has_objective* is left-downward-distributive over *has_member*, if the knowledge base contains the terms u and u' such that:

$$u : \Sigma a : association.\Sigma b : topic.has\_objective(a, b)$$
$$u' : \Sigma x : association.\Sigma y : person.\ has\_member(x, y).$$

Then, assuming the respective proofs that state i) the difference between propositions ($has\_objective = has\_member$ is an absurd judgment) and ii) the identification of the head arguments (*association* is the common argument), the respective proofs of R_u and $R_{u'}$, e.g., $has\_objective(ACM - SIGART, AI)$ and $has\_member(ACM - SIGART, Patrick)$, yield a proof for $has\_objective$ $(Patrick,\ AI)$.

3.4 Upward Distributivity over Part-Whole Relations

A similar structure may represent the fact that a given property that operates on parts (e.g., *located_in*) left-upward-propagates to the whole within a $part - of$ relation. With the same notations as above, the specification is written:

$$Struc[DR, DR'] \triangleq \sum \begin{bmatrix} DR & : Rel \\ DR' & : PW \\ L - UP - Propagate & : Rel \rightarrow PW \rightarrow Prop \end{bmatrix}$$

where PW and $L - UP - Propagate$ denote respectively a part-whole relation and the assumption that DR propagates to the whole. Then the axioms become:

$$Pr[DR, DR'] \triangleq \begin{array}{l} \forall u : DR, \forall u' : DR'\ . \\ (\pi_2\pi_2 u = \pi_2\pi_2 u' \supset \bot\ \ \&\ \ \pi_1\pi_2 u = \pi_1 u' : Type) \supset \\ (R_u(\pi_1 u, \pi_1\pi_2 u)\ \ \&\ \ R_{u'}(\pi_1 u', \pi_1\pi_2 u') \supset \\ R_u(\pi_1 u, \pi_1\pi_2 u')) \end{array}$$

This specification avoids the introduction of extra-rules such as the *SpecializedBy* rule introduced in [20] for bio-medical ontologies. Let us consider an example given in [21] where one has to deduce that a fracture of the femoral shaft is also a fracture of femur. This problem can be easily expressed as a left-propagation problem. The relation *has_location* left-upward-propagates over $part - of$, with the terms u and u' such that:

$$u : \Sigma a : fracture.\Sigma b : shaftOfFemur.has\_location(a, b)$$
$$u' : \Sigma x : shaftOfFemur.\Sigma y : femur.\ Part - of(x, y)$$

The identification of the part arguments (the common argument $shaftOfFemur$) with the respective proofs of R_u and $R_{u'}$, e.g., $has\_location(fracture, shaftOf$ $Femur)$ and $Part - of(shaftOfFemur, femur)$, implies that $has\_location(frac$ $ture, femur)$. However, some problems can occur with particular relations. While the left propagation holds when applied to $has\_location(perforation, Appendix)$ and $Part{-}of(Appendix, Intestine)$ yielding the proof $has\_location(perforation, Intestine)$, it doesn't hold with $has\_location(inflammation, Appendix)$ [21]. The authors argue for a solution shifting the specification of constraints from the language designer to the ontology engineer. In DL, for example, complex role inclusion axioms imply that the relation $has\_location()$ is always propagated along hierarchies based on $Part - of()$. By contrast, the specification is a Σ-type and as such allows the predicate $has\_location(perforation, Intestine)$ to fail in some cases.

4 Extended Part-Whole Relations

4.1 Solving Part-Whole Ambiguities

The implementation of mereology in conceptual modeling requires some disambiguation. Let us consider a whole C as the mereological sum of parts D and E only. Conceptual models make C solely composed of at least one instance of D and at least one instance of E. However, this is expressed in a DL TBox with the statement: $C \sqsubseteq \exists has\_part.D \sqcap \exists has\_part.E$ resulting in a composite C not fully defined. Alternatively, in DTF the nested Σ-type can solve this problem:

$$\begin{aligned}\sigma_1 &\triangleq \Sigma C : Type \ . \ \Sigma D : Type \ . \ has\_part(C, D) \\ &\Sigma x : \sigma_1 \ . \ \Sigma E : Type \ . \ has\_part(\pi_1 x, E)\end{aligned}$$

The first sum states that a proof object for C has a single part, the proof object D whereas the second sum refers to the first sum and adds to the previous knowledge a new fact, i.e., the proof object C has the part witnessed by the proof object E (knowing that it has already the part D). Another semantic ambiguity arises in UML when we are considering a whole C and its parts D, E and F. Nothing prevents a user to create the diagram described in fig.1. Then any instance of C is made up of a set of instances of type D and/or a set of instances of type E and/or a set of instances of type F resulting in different aggregation types of parts. The same case expressed in DTF generates the sum-types:

$$\begin{aligned}\sigma_1 &\triangleq \Sigma C : Type \ . \ \Sigma D : Type \ . \ part - of(D, C) \\ \sigma_2 &\triangleq \Sigma x : \sigma_1 \ . \ \Sigma E : Type \ . \ part - of(E, \pi_1 x) \\ \sigma_3 &\triangleq \Sigma x : \sigma_2 \ . \ \Sigma F : Type \ . \ part - of(F, \pi_1 \pi_1 x)\end{aligned}$$

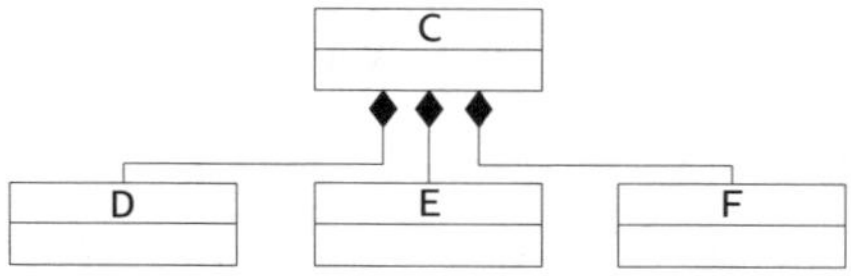

Fig. 1. Ambiguities in UML composite aggregation

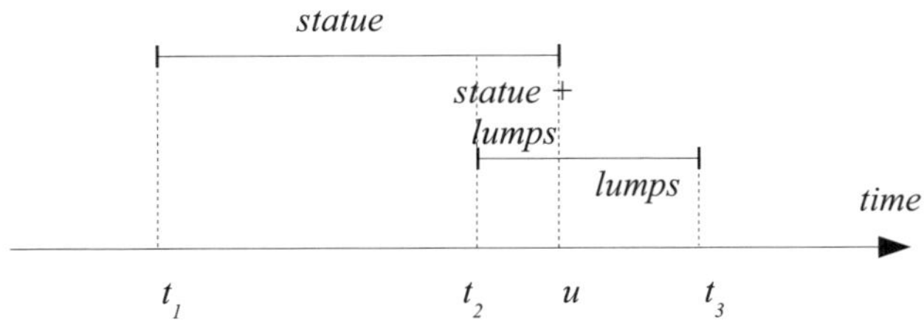

Fig. 2. The timeline for the demolition process

A proof for σ_3 could be $<<< c, < d, q_1 >>, < e, q_2 >>, < f, q_3 >>$ with q_1, q_2 and q_3, the respectives proofs for $part{-}of(d, c)$, $part{-}of(e, c)$ and $part{-}of(f, c)$. As a result, proof objects d, e and f together make up the the proof object for the whole entity c and provide a more precise semantics.

Sum-types also express partial knowledge. For example, the Σ-type:

$$\Sigma r : component\_of \ . \ transitive(r)$$

means that not all *component_of* relations are transitive since Σ-types express subsets (here, the subset of *component_of* relations that are transitive).

Finally, cardinality constraints are introduced by mean of specifications having a List structure collecting proofs. Then complex constraints can be assigned to that structure that can be embedded itself into, say a $part - of$ structure.

4.2 Temporal Part-Whole Relations

The following example already formalized in DOLCE and GFO corresponds to the schematic description "A statue of clay exists for a period of time going from t_1 to t_2. Between t_2 and t_3, the statue is crashed and so ceases to exist although the clay is still there". The statue denotes a persistant *st* of material objects and consists of an amount of clay *cl*. We assume that the following ordering holds between the time boundaries t_1, t_2 and t_3: $t_1 \leq t_2 \leq u \leq t_3$. The point in time u when the statue ceases to exist, reflects the fact that at this step of the process, there is a material structure (i.e., lumps of clay) that inherits from the statue. It turns out that during the time-interval $]t_2, u]$, the statue (altered) co-exists with some lumps that are parts of the entity statue. In other words, statue is a whole that exists until we cannot recognize it as a whole (time point u). Under these assumptions, the demolition process is divided into three sub-processes related to the time-intervals $t_1 - t_2$, $t_2 - u$ and $u - t_3$ (see fig.2). Each sub-process is related to some knowledge expressed through Σ-types and according to the value of variable t, only one of them can be proved:

$$\begin{aligned} \sigma_1 \triangleq \ & \Sigma t : time \ . \ \Sigma t' \frown u : time. \ leq(t, t') \times \\ & \Sigma x : statue \ . \ \Sigma y : substrate. \ constituted - of(x, y) \end{aligned}$$

$$\sigma_2 \triangleq \sigma_1 \times \Sigma t : time.\Sigma t' \backsim t_2 : time.\ gt(t, t') \times$$
$$\Sigma x : lump\ .\ \Sigma y : substrate.\ constituted - of(x, y) \times$$
$$\Sigma x : lump\ .\ \Sigma y : statue.\ part - of(x, y)$$
$$\sigma_3 \triangleq \Sigma t : time.\Sigma t' \backsim u : time.\ gt(t, t') \times$$
$$\Sigma x : lump\ .\ \Sigma y : substrate.\ constituted - of(x, y)$$

5 Conclusion

The approach proposed in this paper is independent of any environment and is therefore applicable to (or adaptable by) most ontologies with the objective of addressing important topics such as: (i) the general notion of types and their instances; (ii) the relation between subtyping and subsumption; (iii) distinctions among sorts of relational properties; (iv) Part-whole relations and v) evaluation of the ontological correctness of current conceptual representations produced using the language. Using dependent types leads to a more precise and concise modeling. The advantages to include different parthood relations are automated model verification, transitivity (derived relations), semi-automated abstraction operations, and enforcing good modeling practices. Incrementally adding further constraints like essential part, the whole-part relation, and inter-part relations, enable the conceptual modeler to gradually develop models that are closer to the real-world semantics and thereby improve quality of the software. Deriving implied relations, derived relations (e.g.,transitivity), and satisfiability can aid correcting large conceptual models. For that purpose, specifications formalized in DTF could enable reliable (automated type checking) and incremental (knowledge refinement) type structures.

This effort is a first attempt. A first implementation in knowledge representation requiring Σ-types and Π-types has been tested, highlighting both its expressiveness and a polynomial complexity [4]. A graphical user interface has yet to be implemented hiding as much as possible type theory from software engineers. Further refinement will be investigated, in particular for extending specifications to a wider scope. This work requires to formalize the syntax of an ontology within type theory. This can be done by defining the ontology as a (structured) type and defining rules of inference as inductive relations so as to give a computational understanding of the ontology.

References

1. Artale, A., Franconi, E., Guarino, N., Pazzi, L.: Part-whole relations in object-centered systems: An overview. Data & Knowledge Engineering 20, 347–383 (1996)
2. Baader, F., Calvanese, D., MCGuinness, D., Nardi, D., Patel-Schneider, P.: The Description Logic Handbook. Cambridge University Press, Cambridge (2003)
3. Barendregt, H., Geuvers, H.: Proof-Assistants Using Dependent Type Systems. In: Handbook of Automated Reasoning, pp. 1149–1238. Elsevier and MIT Press (2001)

4. Barlatier, P., Dapoigny, R.: A Theorem Prover with Dependent Types for Reasoning about Actions. In: Frontiers in Artificial Intelligence and Applications (Procs. of STAIRS 2008), vol. 179, pp. 12–23. IOS Press, Amsterdam (2008)
5. Berardi, D., Calvanese, D., De Giacomo, G.: Reasoning on UML class diagrams. Artificial Intelligence 168(1-2), 70–118 (2005)
6. Bittner, T., Donnelly, M.: Computational ontologies of parthood, componenthood, and containment. In: Procs. of the Nineteenth International Joint Conference on Artificial Intelligence, pp. 382–387 (2005)
7. Bunge, M.: Ontology I: The Furniture of the World. In: Treatise on Basic Philosophy, vol. 3. D. Reidel Publishing (1977)
8. Cranefield, S., Purvis, M.: UML as an ontology modeling language. In: Procs. of the 16th Workshop on Intelligent Information Integration (1999)
9. Franconi, E., Ng, G.: The iCom Tool for Intelligent Conceptual Modeling. In: 7th Intl. Workshop on Knowledge Representation meets Databases, KRDB 2000 (2000)
10. Guizzardi, G., Herre, H., Wagner, G.: On the General Ontological Foundations of Conceptual Modeling. In: Spaccapietra, S., March, S.T., Kambayashi, Y. (eds.) ER 2002. LNCS, vol. 2503, pp. 65–78. Springer, Heidelberg (2002)
11. Guizzardi, G., Wagner, G., Guarino, N., Van Sinderen, M.: An Ontologically Well-Founded Profile for UML Conceptual Models. In: Persson, A., Stirna, J. (eds.) CAiSE 2004. LNCS, vol. 3084, pp. 112–126. Springer, Heidelberg (2004)
12. Guizzardi, G.: Ontological Foundations for Structural Conceptual Models. PhD thesis, Enschede, The Netherlands (2005)
13. Keet, M.C.: Part-whole relations in Objects-Role-Models. In: OTM 2006 Workshops. LNCS, vol. 4278, pp. 1116–1127. Springer, Heidelberg (2006)
14. Keet, C.M., Artale, A.: Representing and reasoning over a taxonomy of part-whole relations. Applied Ontology 3(1-2), 91–110 (2008)
15. Luo, Z.: A Unifying Theory of Dependent Types: The Schematic Approach. In: Procs. of Logical Foundations of Computer Science, pp. 293–304 (1992)
16. Luo, Z.: Coercive subtyping. J. of Logic and Computation 9(1), 105–130 (1999)
17. Luo, Z.: Manifest fields and module mechanisms in intensional type theory. In: Berardi, S., Damiani, F., de'Liguoro, U. (eds.) TYPES 2008. LNCS, vol. 5497, pp. 237–255. Springer, Heidelberg (2009)
18. Meisel, H.: Ontology Representation and Reasoning: A Conceptual Level Approach. Phd thesis at the University of Aberdeen (2005)
19. Motik, B., Cuenca Grau, B., Sattler, U.: Structured Objects in OWL: Representation and Reasoning. In: Procs. of the Int. WWW Conference WWW 2008 (2008)
20. Rector, A.L., Bechhofer, S., Goble, C.A., Horrocks, I., Nowlan, W.A., Solomon, W.D.: The GRAIL concept modelling language for medical terminology. Artificial Intelligence in Medicine 9(2), 139–171 (1997)
21. Schulz, S., Hahn, U.: Part-whole representation and reasoning in formal biomedical ontologies. Artificial Intelligence in Medicine 34, 179–200 (2005)
22. Simons, P.: Parts: a study in Ontology. Clarendon Press, Oxford (1987)

Inducing Metaassociations and Induced Relationships*

Xavier Burgués[1], Xavier Franch[1], and Josep M. Ribó[2]

[1] Universitat Politècnica de Catalunya. J. Girona 1-3, Campus Nord. 08034 Barcelona, Spain
{diafebus,franch}@lsi.upc.edu
[2] Universitat de Lleida. Jaume II 69. 25001 Lleida, Spain
josepma@diei.udl.cat

Abstract. In the last years, UML has been tailored to be used as a domain-specific modelling notation in several contexts. Extending UML with this purpose entails several advantages: the integration of the domain in a standard framework; its potential usage by the software engineering community; and the existence of supporting tools. In previous work, we explored one particular issue of heavyweight extensions, namely, the definition of inducing meta-associations in metamodels as a way to induce the presence of specific relationships in their instances. Those relationships were intended by the metamodel specifier but not forced by the metamodel itself. However, our work was restricted to the case of induced associations. This paper proposes an extension to the general case in which inducing metaassociations may force the existence of arbitrary relationships at M1. To attain this goal, we provide a general definition of inducing metaassociation that covers all the possible cases. After revisiting induced associations, we show the inducement of the other relationship types defined in UML: association classes, generalization and dependencies.

Keywords: UML, MOF, Metamodels.

1 Introduction

In the last years, we may find several contexts in which UML [1, 2] has been tailored to be used as a domain-specific modeling notation. For instance, we may mention extensions to model data warehouses [3], software processes [4], real-time issues [5], etc. Extending the UML with this purpose entails several advantages: the integration of the domain in a standard framework; its potential usage by the software engineering community; and the existence of supporting tools.

Two different strategies may be adopted in order to extend UML:

- *Lightweight extensions*, which create a UML profile with the UML standard extension mechanisms provided in the profiles package (e.g., [6]).
- *Heavyweight extensions*, which enlarge the UML metamodel, creating a new metamodel specific for the target domain (e.g, [3, 4, 7]).

In this paper, we are interested in heavyweight extensions, that take place at the M2 level of the MetaObject Facility (MOF) Specification [8], where the UML metamodel

* This work has been partially supported by the Spanish project TIN2007-64753.

A.H.F. Laender et al. (Eds.): ER 2009, LNCS 5829, pp. 159–174, 2009.

is placed. Modifications to this M2 level impact on the form that UML models, located at the M1 MOF level, may take (and transitively on the possible model instances that conform to the M0 MOF level).

In [9], we explored one particular issue of heavyweight extensions, namely, the lack of expressive power that most metamodeling approaches have for building M2 metamodels that force a specific association in their model instances (at level M1). To overcome this limitation, we introduced the notions of *inducing metaassociations* and *induced associations*. In short, induced associations are those associations in a UML model whose existence is implied by a specific kind of metassociations (which are tagged as "inducing") that have been included in a UML metamodel extension. In that paper, we defined formally the notions of inducing metaassociation and induced association, we analyzed how several other UML constructs (like adornments and subsettings) were affected by these definitions, and we presented a method for introducing induced associations in a UML model based on tagging the appropriate metaassociations as inducing metaassociations. We explored the feasibility of the proposal in a complex case study for building a generic quality model as an extension of the UML metamodel (as proposed in [10]).

Once the concepts of induced associations and inducing metassociations were defined, the next natural step is to induce other kinds of UML relationships that are also needed in the process of UML metamodel extension. This need arose also in the heavyweight metamodel extensions that we have built. In this paper, we tackle the inducement of the other type of relationships defined in the UML metamodel [1, 2]: association classes, generalization relationships and dependencies. To avoid working in a case-by-case basis, we rephrase the notion of inducing metassociation in a way that it may induce all these relationship types, as well as induced associations as defined in [9], and eventually others that could arise in the future.

The rest of the paper is structured as follows. In Section 2, we revisit the problem of induced associations as explored in [9], which provides the necessary background to understand the rest of the paper. Then we present the general definition of inducing associations in Section 3 and explore its application in Section 4. Section 5 deals with the combination of induced elements and the presence of generalizations in models at M1. We finish the paper in Section 6 with the conclusions and future work.

2 Background

To illustrate the problem, let's consider the definition of a metamodel for quality aspects of software as presented in [10]. Such a *quality metamodel*, located at M2, is defined as a heavyweight extension of the UML metamodel and is responsible for defining the generic concepts that come up in the definition of a quality model and the relationships between these concepts. Each particular quality model will be defined as an instance in M1 of the quality metamodel. For example, the quality model ISO-9126 [11] could be defined as an instance of the quality metamodel.

This quality metamodel contains, among others, the metaclasses *Attribute* and *Metric*. *Attribute* represents the quality aspects that are to be measured by a specific model. *Metric* represents the element used to measure an attribute. A metaassociation *measures* between both metaclasses is defined in the metamodel. Also, we consider

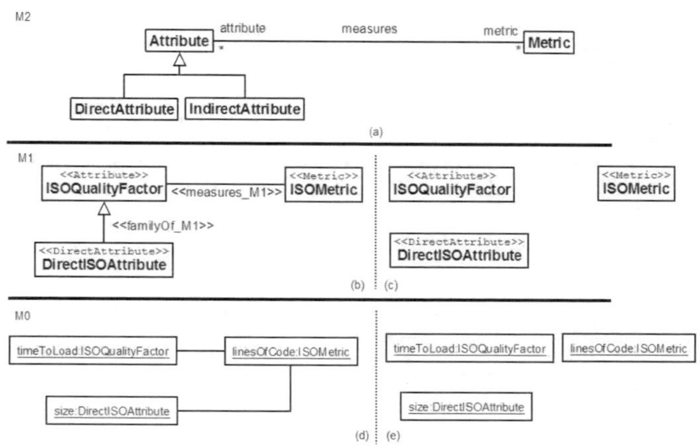

Fig. 1. The intention (b, d) and a possible non-intended result (c, e) of the instantiation of a metamodel for quality (a)

the existence of two types of attributes, direct attributes whose value is computed from direct observation of a software artefact, and indirect attributes, computed from other attributes' values. Fig. 1(a) presents this metamodel fragment.

Because of its semantics, the metaassociation *measures* is intended to be an inducing metaassociation: when a model instance of this quality metamodel is defined (thus, at level M1), for each pair of instances of *Metric* and *Attribute* that belong to the extension of *measures*, an association should come up at M1. Fig. 1(b) shows two instances of these two metaclasses for the ISO/IEC 9126 quality model, *ISOQualityFactor* and *ISOMetric*, that belong to *measures*' extension, and the association between them. As a consequence, classes and relationships among them (in particular, associations) defined in M1 are eventually instantiated by objects and links between them when that model is instantiated (level M0). In Fig. 1(d), we show how a specific instance of *ISOMetric*, named *linesOfCode*, can be used to measure a specific instance of *ISOQualityFactor*, named *timeToLoad*.

A similar reasoning applies to the specialization relationship that comes up in the metamodel. In particular, note in Fig. 1(d) that instances of *DirectISOAttribute* like *size* may be linked to *linesOfCode*, due to the M1 induced inheritance relationship.

However, a careful analysis reveals that the metamodeller intentions are, in fact, not really represented in the metamodel. The presence of the association at level M1 (which was meant by the metamodeller) is not implied by the semantics of the metamodel and, hence, is left to the modeller skills. As a result of this limitation, the M1 model may not convey all the information that was meant by the M2 metamodel which it is an instance of, leading to incompleteness and inaccuracies. This situation is shown in Fig. 1(c), and the effects on M0 are shown in Fig. 1(e), where no links between the instances appear. Furthermore, even if the association was correctly added, traceability is seriously damaged since no explicit link is established with the metaassociation at M2. This is what may happen if the issue is not taken into account or if, as is done in the Unified Process [12], stereotypes are attached to associations at layer M1 with no connection with the metamodel at M2.

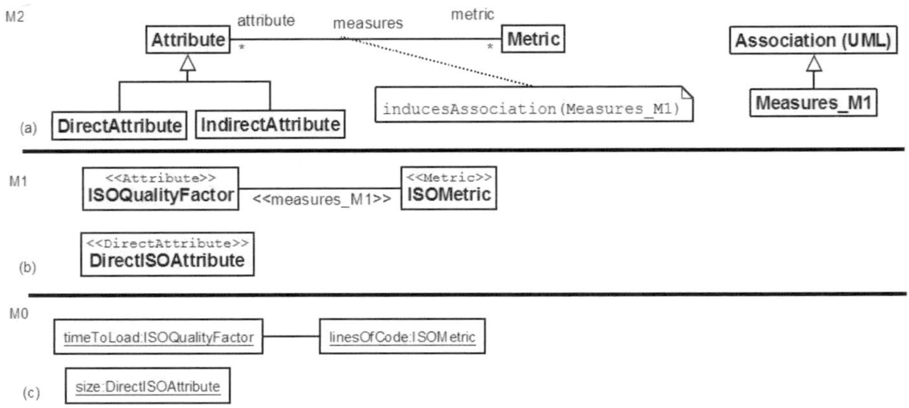

Fig. 2. Declaring inducing metaassociations at M2 and the consequences in the lower levels

In [9] we addressed this limitation by providing a technical solution for the case of inducing metaassociations. As shown in Fig. 2(a), metaassociations may be forced to be inducing by attaching an appropriate OCL constraint that connects it with a new class, declared as heir of the *Association* metaclass. As a consequence, now at M1 induced associations appear stereotyped with the metaclass name (Fig. 2(b)). Therefore, instances at M0 may be connected again as intended (Fig. 2(c)).

Whilst Fig. 2 shows our solution to the case of inducing metaassociations as given in [9], it also reveals the limitations of the approach: no other inducing metaelements have been considered. Therefore, the specialization declared at level M2 that is also intended to be inducing, is not covered by our solution, then it is not possible to force M1 models to contain those needed inheritance relationships, being thus the non-intended situation illustrated at Fig. 2(b) possible to occur. As a consequence, it may not be possible to link instances of *DirectISOAttribute* with instances of *ISOMetric* (i.e., to establish metrics for direct attributes) which of course was not intended by the metamodeller. The same would happen for any other type of metamodel element except metaassociations. The purpose of this paper is then to further refine the proposal given in [9] for avoiding situations like this in Fig. 2(b, c).

3 Relationship-Inducing Metaassociations

In this section, we generalize the idea of inducing metaassociation for induced associations presented in [9] to allow inducing metassociations to induce all type of relationships at M1. We call them *relationship-inducing metaassociations.*

Let *EM* be an extension of the UML metamodel (at layer M2) containing three metaclasses *MC1*, *MC2* and *MR* and a metaassociation *M2A* between *MC1* and *MC2*. In order to make the pair (*M2A*, *MR*) induce relationships (i.e., associations, association classes, generalizations or dependencies) at layer M1, the next procedure shall be followed (see Fig. 3):

a) Add to *EM* a generalization relationship from *MR* to one heir of the UML *Relationship* metaclass: *Association*, *AssociationClass*, *Generalization* or *Dependency*.

- The instances of *MR* will constitute *relationships induced* by (*M2A, MR*).
- If *MR* is a subclass of the *DirectedRelationship* UML metaclass (i.e., *MR* is *Generalization* or *Dependency*), *M2A* should be a unidirectional metaassociation and the *source* and *target* of the induced directed relationship are denoted by the navigability sense of *M2A*.
- (M2A, MR) constitutes a relationship-inducing metaassociation pair, where "relationship" refers to the specific relationship type induced. For short, M2A or MR can also be referred to as inducing metaassociation resp. relationship.

b) Add to *EM* a constraint attached to *MR* establishing that for all instances *C1* of *MC1* and *C2* of *MC2* s.t. <*C1, C2*> is in *M2A*'s extension, there is an instance of the relationship *MR* connecting *C1* and *C2* (and vice versa). The sense of the connection in the case of *DirectedRelationships* is given by the navigability sense of *M2A*.

c) Make *MR* subclass of *InducedRelationship*

In order to generate a more structured metamodel, we have introduced a new *InducedRelationship* metaclass that roots the hierarchy of M1-relationships that are induced by M2 metaassociations. Hence, each subclass of *InducedRelationship* is also an heir of the appropriate subclass of *Relationship*, according to its type. The following constraint holds: "for each subclass *MR* of *InducedRelationship* there is a metaassociation *M* such that all the *M1*-relationships which are instances of *MR* will be induced by *M*". This idea can be expressed by means of the OCL-helper *InducesRelationship(anyMA: Association)* which is defined in the context of *InducedRelationship* as shown in Fig. 4. It states the following:

(a) There will be an instance of the inducing relationship *self* binding each pair of classes that are linked by the extension of the metaassociation *anyMA*. This is stated by the part 1 in the case of directed relationships (the undirected case is similar to the directed and not included here for reasons of space).

(b) All instances of *self* are meant to be relationships induced by the extension of the metaassociation to which *self* is bound (*anyMA*). This is shown by the part 2 in the case of directed relationships.

Notice that, since all kinds of relationships are heirs of the *Relationship* class in the UML metamodel and the *inducesRelationship()* specification deals only with the

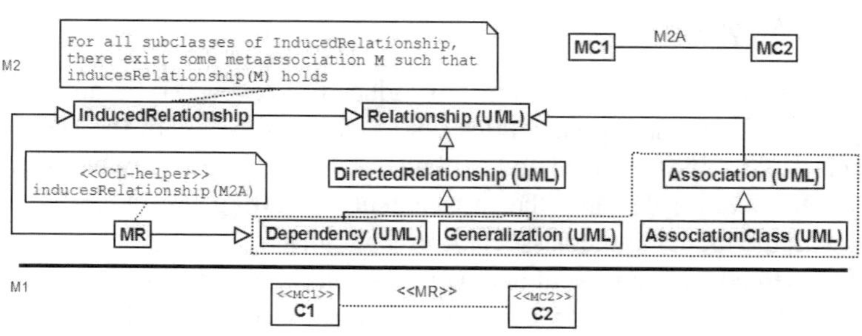

Fig. 3. Definition of relationship-inducing metaassociations

```
context InducedRelationship
def: inducesRelationship(anyMA: Association): Boolean =
      let MC1: Class = anyMA.memberEnd->at(1).class,
          MC2: Class = anyMA.memberEnd->at(2).class in
      self.oclIsKindOf(Relationship) and
              (MC1.allInstances()->forAll(c1 |
                    MC2.allInstances()->forAll(c2 | c2.mc1 = c1
                         implies if (anyMA.navigableOwnedEnd->size() = 2)
                                      inducesNonDirectedRelationship(anyMA)
                                 else inducesDirectedRelationship(anyMA) endif)))

context InducedRelationship
def: inducesDirectedRelationship(anyMA: Association): Boolean
      let TargetEnd: Class = anyMA.navigableOwnedEnd->at(1),
          SourceEnd: Class = if (anyMA.memberEnd->at(1) = TargetEnd)
                                  anyMA.memberEnd->at(2)
                             else anyMA.memberEnd->at(1) in
      self.oclIsKindOf(DirectedRelationship)
               and  -- PART 1
                  TargetEnd.allInstances()->forAll(c1 |
                  SourceEnd.allInstances()->forAll(c2 | c2.targetend = c1
                          implies self.allInstances()->exists(r |
                                     r.target = c1 and r.source = c2)))
               and -- PART 2
                  self.allInstances()->forAll(r |
                        r.source->size() = 1 and r.target->size() = 1 and
                        r.source->at(1).oclIsKindOf(SourceEnd) and
                        r.target->at(1).oclIsKindOf(TargetEnd) and
                        r.source->at(1).targetend = r.target->at(1))
```

Fig. 4. OCL representation of the *inducesRelationship* OCL-helper

features of (Directed)Relationship (in the UML metamodel), this operation covers the induction of any kind of such relationships (associations, association classes, generalizations and dependencies) from inducing metaassociations. If, in the future, some new relationship were added to the UML metamodel (or to a UML extension), this new type of relationship could be handled in the same way than the others.

4 Induced Relationships

In this section we define four types of M1 induced UML relationships.

4.1 Induced Associations

This is the case in which the relationship induced at level M1 by an M2-inducing metaassociation is an *association*. In this case, *MR* is a subclass of the UML *Association* metaclass. As opposed to [9] and explained in detail in the previous section, now the heir of *Association* declares the inducement by calling the *inducesRelationship* operation with the inducing metaassociation as parameter.

Sect. 1 presented an example of a situation requiring an inducing meta-association. Fig. 5 shows the modelling of that inducing metaassociation together with the corresponding induced associations following the definition proposed in Sect. 3.

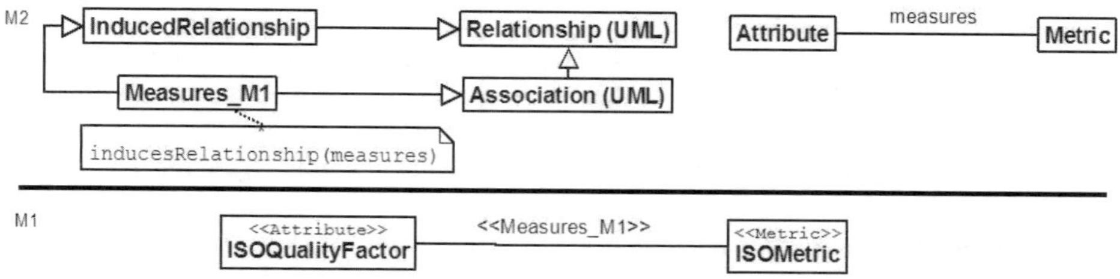

Fig. 5. Inducing metaassociations and induced associations

4.2 Induced Association Classes

Another particular case of relationship-inducing metaassociation takes place when the metaclass *MR* is, actually, a subclass of the UML *AssociationClass* metaclass (which, in turn, is a subclass of *Association*). In this case, the pair (*M2A, MR*) induces association classes at layer M1.

For induced association classes, the subclass *MR* of the UML metaclass *AssociationClass*, usually comes up as a metaclass that modelizes a (meta-)domain concept, while in the case of induced associations, *MR* usually models an association between (meta-)domain concepts.

Induced association classes constitute a common need in metamodeling situations. Consider, for instance, in the context of the quality metamodel, the metaclass *QualityModel* (which has been defined as a subclass of AssociationClass). The ontology proposed in [10] stated that quality models apply for a given software domain (e.g., the domain of business applications, or the software categories identified in a IT consulting company, …) and a given environment (e.g., public administration, SME, …). In that paper, this situation was modelled in M1 with an association class as shown in Fig. 6, where also some M0 instances are represented.

From the metamodelling perspective, this association class must be defined as induced, because it does not show up from scratch but from some metamodel concepts. Specifically, the quality metamodel includes the metaclasses *Domain* and *Environment*, and also

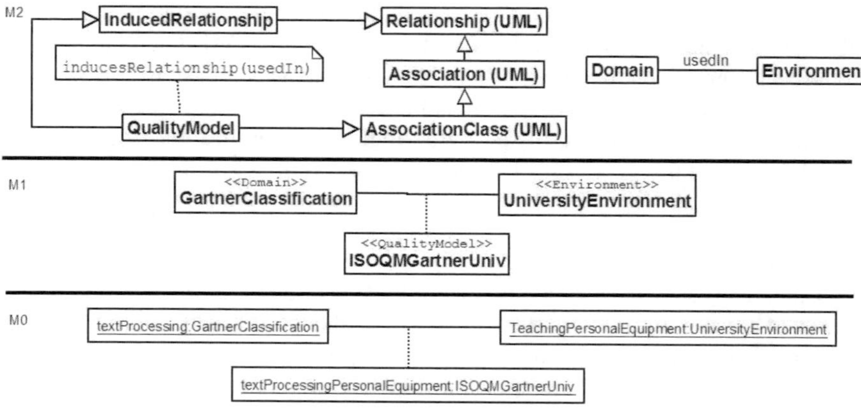

Fig. 6. Inducing metaassociations and induced association classes

a metaclass *QualityModel* for the association class itself. Finally, a metaassociation *usedIn* between *Domain* and *Environment* is introduced, and to make it association-class-inducing, *QualityModel* is declared as heir of *AssociationClass* with the usual constraint about inducement. As a result, the metamodeller has established that there is a different quality model associated to each specific (*Environment, Domain*) pair (see Fig. 6).

4.3 Induced Generalizations

This is the case in which the relationship induced at level M1 by an M2-inducing metaassociation is a generalization. In this case, *MR* is a subclass of the UML *Generalization* metaclass.

It is worth noting that *Generalization* is a subclass of the UML *DirectedRelationship*, which defines a non-symmetrical relationship from a source class to a target class. As it has been stated in the general definition, when a metaassociation induces a *DirectedRelationship,* it should be a unidirectional metaassociation directed from the metaclass whose instance acts as source (in generalizations, *subclass*) to the metaclass whose instance acts as target (in generalizations, *superclass*).

Although in our experience, induced generalizations are not as common as induced associations or induced association classes, there still exist situations in which it is interesting that the metamodel forces specific generalizations between the classes that are meant to instantiate it. One of those typical situations occurs if various groups of elements, each one belonging to a different family, are expected at M1. The metamodeller may want that the M1 instances of the metamodel make clear the separation between the different families and hence, force several (induced) generalizations.

Fig. 7 shows an example coming from the quality metamodel already outlined in Sect. 2. In this metamodel excerpt, three metaclasses come up which model the notions of *Attribute* (an element whose quality has to be measured), *DirectAttribute* (an attribute that can be measured directly) and *IndirectAttribute* (an attribute whose measure is obtained from that of other attributes). The inheritance relationships at M2 come from the fact that both direct and indirect attributes are themselves attributes and, hence, inherit its features. Obviously, this pair of generalization relationships does not imply any generalization relationship among their instances. With the generalization-inducing metaassociation *familyOf,* the metamodeller is stating that different families of attributes (instances of *Attribute*) may come up at M1. Each family will be composed of a group of specific attribute classes (instances either of *DirectAttribute* or *IndirectAttribute*). The classes that model direct and indirect attributes corresponding to the same family will be linked by an induced generalization to the class (instance of *Attribute*) that represents that family. Two families are shown in Fig. 7: The ISO-9126 family and the SEI family. Notice that the extension of the *familyOf* metaassociation determines which are the induced generalizations (i.e., the attribute classes belonging to the same family).

As usual, the metaclasses bound by the *familyOf* associations are themselves linked by means of a generalization relationship at M2. Although this is the normal case, it is not a compulsory requirement. In some occasions, the metamodeller is not interested in bringing up that generalization relationship (or one of the involved metaclasses) because either it requires to model an artificial element or it does not provide any relevant information to the metamodel.

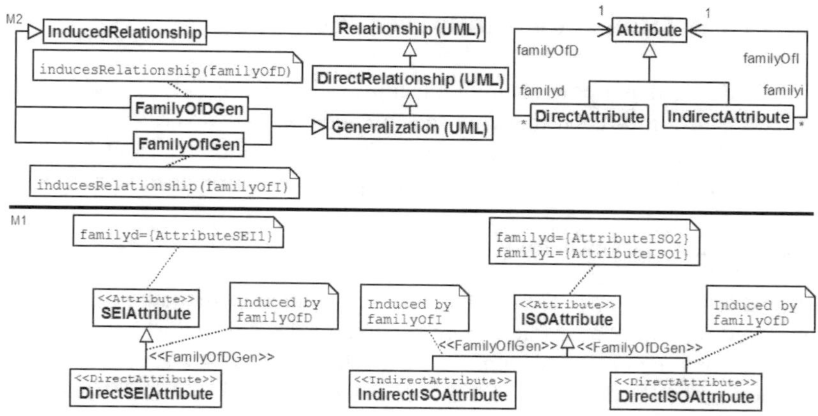

Fig. 7. Generalization-inducing metaassociations

4.4 Induced Dependencies

When the relationship induced at level M1 by an M2-inducing metaassociation is a UML dependency, *MR* is a subclass of the UML *Dependency* metaclass. Induced dependencies are, in our experience, not as frequent as the other kinds of induced relationships. In particular, no need for induced dependencies has been encountered in the quality metamodel that we are mentioning through this paper (although we needed them in other metamodeling experiences). However, the metamodeller could have eventually been interested in capturing the following situation: all the instances of a specific metaclass (e.g., *Metric*) should behave according to a specific M1 interface in every single model that is an instance of the quality metamodel, e.g., they should offer the operation *assessMetric(art:Artifact)*. This interface would be shared by all the models instance of the quality metamodel. This requirement can be modelled as shown in Fig. 8. In fact, *ImplementsMetric_M1* is a heir of *InterfaceRealization* which is an indirect heir of *Dependency*. We haven't depicted the entire path of the generalization hierarchy to avoid messing the figure up. Instances of *Realization* connect classes with *Interface* as the realizations depicted in the M1 level of Fig. 8 do.

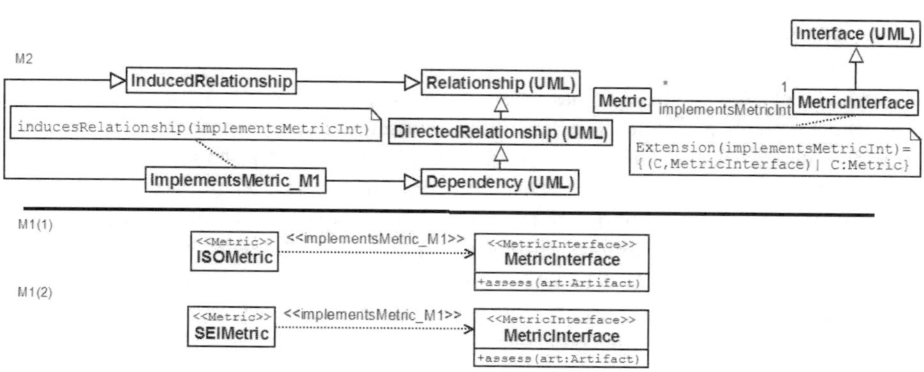

Fig. 8. Dependency-inducing metaassociation

5 Induced Relationships and Inheritance

We claimed above that a new M1-relationship would be induced for each pair of classes in the extension of each inducing metaassociation. However, when some of the classes in such extension are connected by inheritance relationships at M1, this may result in redefinitions in the induced relationships. This section deals with this issue.

5.1 Induced Associations with Inheritance

When some of the classes in the extension of an association-inducing metaassociation are connected by inheritance relationships, some of the induced M1-associations can be considered as *redefinitions* of other more general induced M1-associations.

UML does not consider the notion of *redefinition* applied to associations (i.e., they are not *RedefinableElements*). Next, we define a notion of association redefinition which is appropriate for the purposes of this article. Let *C1, C2, S1* and *S2* be classes such that *S1* conforms to *C1* and *S2* to *C2* (i.e., *S1* is *C1* or one of its descendants, and the same for *S2*). We say that an association *R* between classes *S1* and *S2* is a redefinition of another association *A* between *C1* and *C2* if:

a) *R* is derived from *A* by specialization [13] with the specialization condition: given a pair *(c1, c2)* of *A*'s extension, *c1* is an instance of *S1* and *c2* is an instance of *S2*.

b) Each association-end of *R* redefines its respective association end of *A*.

Intuitively, this idea corresponds to the fact that the association *R* is the same as *A* for the particular case in which instances of *S1* and *S2* are involved.

Notice in the definition above that neither b) implies a) nor the other way around. In particular, *R* could be derived from *A* by the specialization stated in a) but the extension of *A* could include a pair *(c1, c2)* where *c1* is an instance of *S1* and *c2* is not an instance of *S2* (thus, the *S2* end of *R* would not be a redefinition of the *C2* end of *A*). On the other hand, it could happen that each association end of *R* was a redefinition of the corresponding association end of *A* but certain attributes of *A* were not shared by *R*. For instance, *A* could have the metafeature *UML::Property::isReadOnly* corresponding to one of its ends defined as true, while *R* did not. In this case, *A* would not be a generalization of *R*.

As example, Fig. 9 presents a fragment of the ISO-9126 quality model, expressed as an instance of the quality metamodel (see Fig. 2 (a)). According to ISO-9126, this fragment splits the quality factors (the concept captured by the *Attribute* metaclass) into three categories: characteristics (*ISOCharacteristics*), subcharacteristics (*ISO-Subcharacteristics*) and attributes (*ISOAttribute*). On the other hand, the metamodel states that attributes can be direct (*DirectAttribute* metaclass, when they can be measured by observation) and indirect (*IndirectAttribute* metaclass, whose measure depends on that of other attributes). In the ISO framework, characteristics and subcharacteristics are indirect while attributes (*ISOAttributes*) may be of both kinds. Finally, we decide to classify our metrics into observation metrics (*ObservISOMetric*) and calculated metrics (*CalculatedISOMetric*). The following extension of the *measures* metaassociation makes the appropriate assignment of metrics to quality factors and induces M1-associations (as depicted in Fig. 9):

```
Ext(measures) = {(ISOQualityFactor, ISOMetric),
                 (ISOCharacteristic, CalculatedISOMetric),
                 (ISOSubcharacteristic, CalculatedISOMetric),
                 (ISOAttribute, ISOMetric),
                 (IndirectISOAttribute, CalculatedISOMetric),
                 (DirectISOAttribute, ObservISOMetric)}
```

Some of the associations of the above figure may be seen as *redefinitions* of others. For example, the association between *DirectISOAttribute* and *ObservedISOMetric* (named *measuresDirAttr* in Fig. 9) is a redefinition of the association between *ISOAttribute* and *ISOMetric* (named *measuresAttr* in the figure), which, in turn, is a redefinition of the association between *ISOQualityFactor* and *ISOMetric(measuresQF)*. The meaning of this redefinition is the following: when an instance of the class *DirectISOAttribute* is linked to some instance (say, *m*) of the class *ISOMetric*, *m* will be, actually, an *ObservedISOMetric* (and vice versa). In other words, the association *measuresDirAttr* is the same as the associations *measuresAttr* and *measuresQF* for the particular case in which instances of *DirectISOAttribute* or *ObservedISOMetric* are involved. Incidentally, notice that this forbids the existence of a link in the extension of the association *measuresAttr* between a *DirectISOAttribute* and a *CalculatedISOMetric*, among other similar cases.

In this way, all the associations in the above figure can be considered as redefinitions and just one of them is a non-redefining one: *measuresQF*. We think that this vision is the closest to the specifier's intention and, hence, we have adopted it. This kind of situation is repeated in many other modelling examples (e.g. [9]).

As a final remark, note that this redefinition notion applies whenever generalization relationships exist between classes connected by induced associations, not depending on the source of the generalizations, which may be induced by metaassociations (like those between quality factors in the example) or additionally stated by the modeller (like those between metrics in the example). In this last case, care should be taken not to introduce generalization relationships that are not compatible with induced ones leading to an incorrect instantiation of the metamodel. This would be the case if we pretend to state that an instance of *DirectAttribute* is a generalization of an instance of *Attribute*. This is left as future work (see Sect. 6).

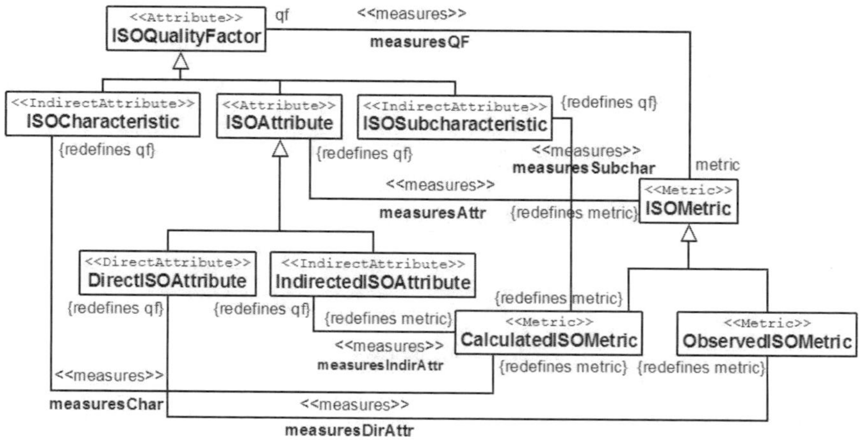

Fig. 9. An instantiation of the metamodel with redefined associations

5.2 Induced Association Classes with Inheritance

In a similar way as happened with induced associations, we may have an induced association class (*R*) whose ends are subclasses of the ends of some other induced association class (*A*). In this case, as before, *R* will be a redefinition of *A*.

In order to show an example, Fig. 10 presents an instantiation of a fragment of the quality metamodel (see Fig. 6, M2 level), together with the association classes that would be induced in the case that the extension of *usedIn* was the following:

Ext(*usedIn*) = {(*GartnerClassification, UniversityEnvironment*),
(*OfficeSuiteApp, AcademicEnvironment*)}

In the model we instantiate *Domain* with *GartnerClassification* because we want to structure the software domains according to this catalogue of domains. We also define a specialization, *OfficeSuiteApp*, to handle more specific software domains. In a similar way, we define two instances of *Environment.* Two quality models come up as induced association classes: *ISOQMGartnerUniv* (those quality models that result from applying the ISO-9126 to domains of the Gartner classification in University environments) and *ISOQMOfficeAcademic*, which applies the ISO-9126 principles to a specific subclass of domains (office suites) and to specific subclass of *university environment* (*academic environment*, as opposed to *administrative environment*, which is also a part of university environment but has different requirements).

The pair (*GartnerClassification, UniversityEnvironment*) induces the association class called *ISOQMGartnerUniv*, which is an instance of <<QualityModel>>. On the other hand, the pair (*OfficeSuiteApp*, *AcademicEnvironment*) induces the association class named *ISOQMOfficeAcademic*, also instance of <<QualityModel>>.

The association class *ISOQMOfficeAcademic* may be seen as a redefinition of *ISOQMGartnerUniv*. The meaning of this redefinition is the following: when an instance of the class *OfficeSuiteApp* is linked to some instance (say, *uenv*) of the class *UniversityEnvironment*, *uenv* will be, actually, an *AcademicEnvironment* (and vice versa). In other words, the association class *ISOQMOfficeAcademic* is the same as the association class *ISOQMGartnerUniv* for the particular case in which instances of *OfficeSuiteApp* and *AcademicEnv* are involved.

In order to make the formalization of this idea easier, we introduce, in next section, the notion of directed graph associated to the extension of a metaassociation.

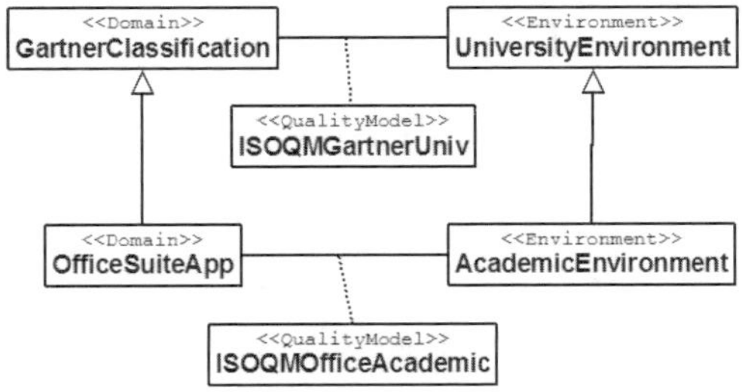

Fig. 10. An instantiation of the quality metamodel with redefined association-classes

5.3 Formal Definition

Let *M2A* be an association/association-class inducing metaassociation between the metaclasses *MC1* and *MC2*. Let *MA* be a heir of *Association*. Hence, (*M2A,MA*) is the pair that induces associations/association-classes at layer M1. Let *Ext(M2A)* be an extension of *M2A*. This extension is constituted by a set of pairs (*C1, C2*), where *C1* is an instance of *MC1* and *C2* is an instance of *MC2*. According to the declaration of *M2A* as inducing, each pair in *Ext(M2A)* will have an (induced) distinct instance of *MA* (i.e., an association/association class) connecting them.

We define the *directed graph associated to Ext(M2A,MA)* in a particular metamodel instantiation (denoted as *DGExt(M2A,MA)*) as a directed graph such that:

- The set of vertices of *DGExt(M2A,MA)* is the set of instances of *MA* that connect the pairs in *Ext(M2A,MA)*.
- Given two distinct vertices *A* and *A'* of *DGExt(M2A,MA)*, being *A*, *A'* associations or association-classes between *C1* and *C2*, and *C1'* and *C2'* respectively: there is an edge from *A* to *A'* iff *C1* conforms to *C1'* and *C2* conforms to *C2'*.

The idea conveyed by this graph is that an induced association/association class *A* between *C1* and *C2* is a redefinition (in the sense of the previous sections) of another induced association/association class *A'* between *C1'* and *C2'* if and only if there is a path from *A* to *A'*. For example, the directed graph *DGExt(measures, measures_M1)* corresponding to the example shown in Fig. 10 is shown in Fig. 11. Notice that the construction of this directed graph is straightforward from its definition.

Two issues can be easily drawn from the definition of *DGExt*:

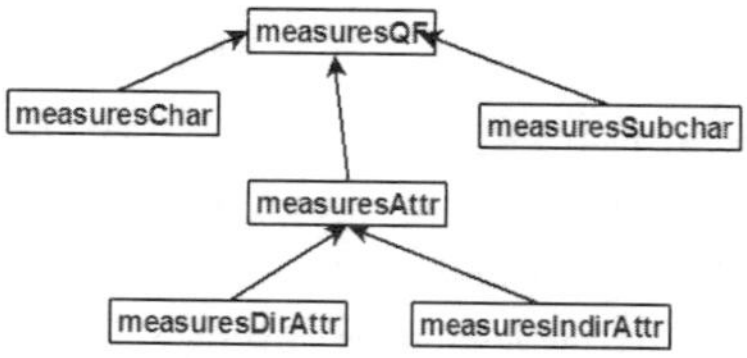

Fig. 11. *DGExt(measures,measures_M1)* corresponding to the model of Fig. 9

1) *DGExt(M2A,MA)* is acyclic as long as generalization hierarchies are also acyclic.

2) The relation (*V*, <) is a partial order, where:

- *V* is the set of vertices of *DGExt(M2A, MA)* and
- For any *A*, *A'* of *V*: *A* < *A'* iff *DGExt(M2A, MAC)* contains a path from *A* to *A'*.

The notion of directed graph associated to a metaassociation extension, together with the partial order that can be drawn from such definition, allows an easy formalisation of the idea presented in the previous sections concerning which induced M1-associations/association classes are, actually, redefinitions of which other. The idea is the following: given a metaassociation *M2A* and a metaclass *MA* (heir of *Association*) conceived as a pair that induces associations at level M1 and given also a specific model *mod*, an M1-association/association-class is induced in *mod* for each tuple in the *Ext(M2A,MA)*. In this context, the non-redefining M1-association/association classes are those corresponding to the maximal elements of (*V*, <), that is, the vertices of *DGExt(M2A,MA)* which have no successor (i.e., from which no edge is issued). In the case of the example, there is one of such vertices: *measuresQF*.

On the other hand, the redefining associations correspond to those vertices which are not maximal. In particular, a specific association/association-class represented by a vertex *v* of *DGExt(M2A,MAC)* redefines the associations/association classes that correspond to the vertices which are successors of *v*. For example, the association *measuresDirAttr* is a redefinition of *measuresQF*.

5.4 Inheritance in Other Relationships

Consider the situation in which an inducing metaassociation *MA* leads to an induced association *a1* between classes *A* and *B* and to another induced association *sa* between classes *SA* and *SB*, which are subclasses of *A* and *B* respectively. In such case, as it has been discussed above, the issue of redefined associations comes up in a natural way since: (a) both *a* and *sa* are induced from the same metaassociation, and (b) the extension of *sa* is constituted by pairs of instances of *SA* and *SB* and the extension of *a*, by pairs of instances of *A* and *B*. However, by definition of generalization, instances of *SA* (*SB*) are also instances of *A* (*B*). Hence, it makes sense that the pairs linked by *sa* are, in fact, a subset of those linked by *a* and, hence, the association *sa* can be seen as a redefinition of *a*. In the case of induced generalizations or dependencies, item (b) does not occur. Therefore, the notion of redefinition of either induced generalizations or dependencies has a less natural sense.

6 Conclusions and Future Work

We have presented a general notion of inducing metaassociation to be used in UML heavyweight extensions that extends our previous work in [9] by inducing not just associations but all type of UML relationships at M1. As a necessary complement to our work, we have also extended our analysis on how the presence of generaliza-tions in M1 models (either induced or directly defined) affects the induced elements.

We believe that our proposal supplies more expressiveness and accuracy in the definition of a heavyweight extension of the UML metamodel while keeping MOF-compliance and providing strict metamodelling. Remarkably, the ability to declare metaelements as inducing is a powerful conceptual tool for metamodelers since the intended semantics of the UML extension can be more accurately defined. The effort required is just to declare a new metaclass (heir of *Relationship* and the new *InducedRelationship* metaclass) for every inducing metaassociation, but even this declaration may be considered positive from the comprehensibility point of view, since the inducing nature of metaassociations is made explicit in the metamodel.

The induced relationships that have been presented in this article are binary relationships. In general, this is not a limitation since the vast majority of relationships that come up naturally in a model are (or can be decomposed into) binary relationships. However, the convenience of n-ary induced relationships cannot be excluded in the future. For this reason, it could be interesting to define inducing relationships for the case of n-ary relationships (specially, n-ary associations), which should be considered carefully due to the absence of ternary metaassociations.

As more future work, we are considering to complement our inducing mechanism providing the transformation of the heavyweight UML extension generated by our approach into an UML profile, following the ideas presented in [14]. To make our inducing mechanism even more useful and easy to apply we are also working on an accurate definition of correct instantiation of a metamodel. This definition should state which conditions must hold to guarantee the soundness of the models obtained as instantiations of a metamodel taking also into account the induced elements.

The problem faced in this article has also drawn the attention of other researchers, who have identified it as an important challenge [15, 16, 17]. We analyzed these approaches in [8] and found out that none of them was compliant with the MOF 2.0 architecture (thus being non-standard approaches) and some of them suffer from other drawbacks. A newest approach, [18], is based on the same principles than those cited above and, hence, suffers from the same difficulties.

It is worth mentioning that, if we look at metamodeling environments other than MOF/UML, we find that some of them induce relationships in a natural way because the instantiation of a relationship leads to another relationship in the next level, in the same way as the instantiation of an entity leads to another entity (metaclass to class in the MOF framework). This is the case of Telos [19], which defines individuals (to represent entities) and attributes (binary relationships between individuals) and a classification dimension (instantiation hierarchy) for both elements. Another metamodeling example with symmetrical treatment of entities and relationships is the MetaEdit+ Workbench tool [20]; it allows the user defining a relationship in a level and instantiating it in a lower level to obtain relationships in this last level. Induction of relationships proves to be a convenient option in those frameworks lacking this symmetry, as happens in the MOF-related metamodels. For instance, in [21] and other works around OWL [22], an ongoing research effort is adding metamodeling expressiveness taking into account the computational problems that may arise. Last but not least, we would like to remark that our proposal allows inducing not just associations but also association classes, generalizations and dependencies. These cases are not covered by the other approaches because the instantiation of the concept equivalent to that of association in UML cannot generate anything else than another association. Our future work includes a more detailed assessment of these facts.

References

1. UML 2.0 Infrastructure. OMG doc. formal/07-05-05, `http://www.omg.org/`
2. UML 2.0 Superstructure. OMG doc. formal/07-05-04, `http://www.omg.org/`
3. Common Warehouse Metamodel Specification. OMG doc. formal/2003-03-02, `http://www.omg.org`
4. Software Process Engineering Metamodel Specification (SPEM). OMG doc. formal/2005-01-06, `http://www.omg.org`
5. UML profile for CORBA. OMG doc. formal/02-04-01, `http://www.omg.org`
6. UML 2.0 testing profile. OMG doc. formal/05-07-07, `http://www.omg.org`
7. Knapp, A., Koch, N., Moser, F., Zhang, G.: ArgoUWE: A CASE Tool for Web Applications. In: Procs. EMSISE 2003 (2003)

8. MOF 2.0 Core Final Adopted Specification. OMG doc. formal/06-01-0, http://www.omg.org/spec/MOF/2.0/
9. Burgués, X., Franch, X., Ribó, J.M.: Improving the Accuracy of UML Metamodel Extensions by Introducing Induced Associations. In: SoSyM, vol. 7(1), Springer, Heidelberg (Febuary 2008)
10. Burgués, X., Franch, X., Ribó, J.M.: A MOF-Compliant Approach to Software Quality Modeling. In: Delcambre, L.M.L., Kop, C., Mayr, H.C., Mylopoulos, J., Pastor, Ó. (eds.) ER 2005. LNCS, vol. 3716, pp. 176–191. Springer, Heidelberg (2005)
11. ISO/IEC Standard 9126-1. Software Engineering – Product Quality – Part 1 (2001)
12. Kruchten, P.: The Rational Unified Process. An Introduction. Addison-Wesley, Reading (2000)
13. Olivé, A.: Conceptual Modeling of Information Systems. Springer, Heidelberg (2007)
14. Ribó, J.M.: PROMENADE: A UML-based Approach to Software Process Modelling. PhD. Thesis, UPC (2002)
15. Atkinson, C., Kühne, T.: Rearchitecting the UML Infrastructure. ACM TOMACS 12(4) (October 2002)
16. Álvarez, J., Evans, A., Sammut, P.: MML and the Metamodel Architecture. In: WTUML 2001 (2001)
17. Henderson-Sellers, B., Gonzalez-Perez, C.: The Rationale of Powertype-based Metamodelling to Underpin Software Development Methodologies. In: Procs. APCCM 2005 (2005)
18. Gutheil, M., Kennel, B., Atkinson, C.: A Systematic Approach to Connectors in a Multilevel Environment. In: Czarnecki, K., Ober, I., Bruel, J.-M., Uhl, A., Völter, M. (eds.) MODELS 2008. LNCS, vol. 5301, pp. 843–857. Springer, Heidelberg (2008)
19. Mylopoulos, J., Borgida, A., Jarke, M., Koubarakis, M.: Telos: Representing Knowledge about Information Systems. ACM TOIS 8(4) (October 1990)
20. The MetaEdit tool, http://www.metacase.com
21. Motik, B.: On the Properties of Metamodeling in OWL. In: JOLC, vol. 17(4), Oxford University Press, Oxford (August 2007)
22. OWL web page, http://www.w3.org/2007/OWL/wiki/OWL_Working_Group

Tractable Query Answering over Conceptual Schemata

Andrea Calì[2,1], Georg Gottlob[1,2], and Andreas Pieris[1]

[1] Computing Laboratory, University of Oxford
[2] Oxford-Man Institute of Quantitative Finance, University of Oxford
{andrea.cali,georg.gottlob,andreas.pieris}@comlab.ox.ac.uk

Abstract. We address the problem of answering conjunctive queries over extended Entity-Relationship schemata, which we call *EER (Extended ER)* schemata, with is-a among entities and relationships, and cardinality constraints. This is a common setting in conceptual data modelling, where reasoning over incomplete data with respect to a knowledge base is required. We adopt a semantics for EER schemata based on their relational representation. We identify a wide class of EER schemata for which query answering is tractable in data complexity; the crucial condition for tractability is the *separability* between maximum-cardinality constraints (represented as key constraints in relational form) and the other constraints. We provide, by means of a graph-based representation, a syntactic condition for separability: we show that our conditions is not only sufficient, but also necessary, thus precisely identifying the class of separable schemata. We present an algorithm, based on query rewriting, that is capable of dealing with such EER schemata, while achieving tractability. We show that further negative constraints can be added to the EER formalism, while still keeping query answering tractable. We show that our formalism is general enough to properly generalise the most widely adopted knowledge representation languages.

1 Introduction

Since Chen's original Entity-Relationship formalism [14], conceptual modelling has been playing a prominent role in database design. More recently, logic-based formalisms have been employed for conceptual data modelling, in particular *Description Logics* [13]. Such formalisms have relevant applications especially in data exchange, information integration, semantic web, and web information systems, where the data, coming from different, heterogeneous sources, are in general incomplete/inconsistent w.r.t. constraints imposed by a conceptual schema. In such a setting, answering queries posed on the schema requires reasoning under a knowledge base constituted by the conceptual schema [6]. A relevant issue in query answering is tractability; in particular, what is commonly considered relevant here is the *data complexity* of query answering, i.e., the complexity in the case both the schema (plus, possibly, additional constraints) and the query are fixed, and the complexity is calculated considering the data as the only input parameter; this is natural, since the data size is normally much larger than the size

A.H.F. Laender et al. (Eds.): ER 2009, LNCS 5829, pp. 175–190, 2009.

of the schema and of the query. An important class of languages that guarantees tractable data complexity is the *DL-Lite* family [7,22]. In particular, answering conjunctive queries (a.k.a. select-project-join queries) under DL-Lite knowledge bases is polynomial in data complexity; it is actually better than polynomial, more precisely, it is in AC_0 in data complexity, where AC_0 is the complexity of recognizing words in languages defined by constant-depth Boolean circuits with an (unlimited fan-in) AND and OR gates.

In this paper we consider an extended Entity-Relationship formalism, that we call EER[1], that comprises is-a among entities and relationships, mandatory and functional participation of entities to relationships, mandatory and functional attributes. The EER formalism is flexible and expressive, and at the same time well understood by database practitioners, differently from, for instance, Description Logics. We first illustrate, as in [6,3,4], a semantics of the EER formalism, by showing a translation of EER schemata into relational ones with a class of constraints (a.k.a. dependencies) called *conceptual dependencies (CDs)* [3]; in particular, CDs are *key dependencies (KDs)* and *tuple-generating dependencies (TGDs)* (more precisely, the TGDs in a set of CDs are *inclusion dependencies*). We then address the problem of answering conjunctive queries over EER schemata, that is, under CDs. Our contribution is the following. We identify a class of EER schemata, defined through a syntactic condition on the corresponding CDs, that guarantees *separation*, i.e., the absence of interaction between KDs and TGDs. We call such CDs *non-conflicting CDs (NCCDs)*. Answers to queries under NCCDs can be computed, if the data are consistent with the schema, considering TGDs only. We present an algorithm, inspired by the one in [11], that computes the answers to queries posed on an EER schema represented with NCCDs, given an instance for that schema. The algorithm is based on *query rewriting*, i.e., it produces a *rewriting* of the original query that, evaluated over the instance, returns the answers to the original query, provided that the data are consistent with the schema. The algorithm allows for tractable query answering, in particular, the computational complexity is AC_0 in data complexity (i.e., w.r.t. the data only). It is important to mention that here we present a version of our algorithm that is tailored for this particular, interesting case. The more general version [10] is capable of dealing with more expressive classes of constraints. We enrich the EER formalism by adding *negative constraints*, which serve to represent the fact that the data are inconsistent with respect to the schema, as well as further constraints enforcing, for example, (pairwise) disjointness between entities and relationships, and non-participation of an entity to a relationship. We show that adding negative constraints to CDs does not alter the computational complexity of conjunctive query answering.

The conceptual schemata for which we are able to compute query answering in a tractable way is general enough to comprise most practical cases, and it properly generalises well-known classes of languages for conceptual data modelling, in particular the DL-Lite family.

---

[1] While we use the same name adopted in [20], our formalism is not the same as the one in this paper.

2 Preliminaries

2.1 Relational Model and Constraints, Queries, and Chase

We define the following pairwise disjoint (infinite) sets of symbols: *(i)* a set Γ of *constants*; constitute the "normal" domain of a database, and *(ii)* a set Γ_f of *labeled nulls*, used as placeholders for unknown values, and that can be also seen as variables. A lexicographic order is defined on Γ and Γ_f, such that every value in Γ_f follows all those in Γ. A *relational schema* $\mathcal{R}$ (or simply *schema*) is a set of *relational symbols* or *predicates*, each with its associated arity. We write r/n to denote that the predicate r has arity n. A *position* $r[i]$ (in a schema $\mathcal{R}$) is identified by a predicate $r \in \mathcal{R}$ and its i-th argument (or attribute). A *term* t is a constant, null, or variable. An *atomic formula* (or simply *atom*) has the form $r(t_1, \ldots, t_n)$, where r/n is a relation, and $t_1, \ldots, t_n$ are terms. For an atom α, we denote as $dom(\alpha)$ the set of terms occurring in α; this notation naturally extends to sets and conjunctions of atoms. A *relational instance* (or simply *instance*) D for a schema $\mathcal{R}$ is a (possibly infinite) set of atoms of the form $r(t)$ (a.k.a. *facts*), where $r/n \in \mathcal{R}$ and $t \in (\Gamma \cup \Gamma_f)^n$. We denote as $r(D)$ the set $\{t \mid r(t) \in D\}$. We will sometimes use the term *database* for a finite instance.

A *substitution* is a function $h : S_1 \to S_2$ defined as follows: *(i)* $\varnothing$ is a substitution (empty substitution); *(ii)* if h is a substitution then $h \cup \{X \to Y\}$ is a substitution, where $X \in S_1$ and $Y \in S_2$, and h does not already contain some $X \to Z$ with $Y \neq Z$. If $X \to Y \in h$ we write $h(X) = Y$. A *homomorphism* from a set of atoms A_1 to a set of atoms A_2, both over the same schema $\mathcal{R}$, is a substitution $h : dom(A_1) \to dom(A_2)$ such that: *(i)* if $t \in \Gamma$ then $h(t) = t$, and *(ii)* if $r(t_1, \ldots, t_n)$ is in A_1 then $h(r(t_1, \ldots, t_n)) = r(h(t_1), \ldots, h(t_n))$ is in A_2. If there are homomorhisms from A_1 to A_2 and vice-versa, we say that A_1 and A_2 are *homomorphically equivalent*.

A *conjunctive query* (CQ) q of arity n over a schema $\mathcal{R}$, written as q/n, is a formula of the form $q(\mathbf{X}) \leftarrow \varphi(\mathbf{X}, \mathbf{Y})$, where $\varphi(\mathbf{X}, \mathbf{Y})$ is a conjunction of atoms over $\mathcal{R}$, where $\mathbf{X}$ and $\mathbf{Y}$ are sequences of variables or constants in Γ, and $|\mathbf{X}| = n$. The atom $q(\mathbf{X})$ is the *head* of q, denoted as *head*(q), and $\varphi(\mathbf{X}, \mathbf{Y})$ is the *body* of q, denoted as *body*(q). A *union of conjunctive queries* (UCQ) of arity n over $\mathcal{R}$ is a set Q of CQs over $\mathcal{R}$, written as Q/n, where each $q \in Q$ has the same arity n, and uses the same symbol in the head. The *answer* to a CQ q/n of the form $q(\mathbf{X}) \leftarrow \varphi(\mathbf{X}, \mathbf{Y})$ over a database D, denoted as $q(D)$, is the set of all n-tuples $t \in \Gamma^n$ for which there exists a homomorphism $h : \mathbf{X} \cup \mathbf{Y} \to \Gamma \cup \Gamma_f$ such that $h(\varphi(\mathbf{X}, \mathbf{Y})) \subseteq D$, and $h(\mathbf{X}) = t$. The *answer* to a UCQ Q over D, denoted as $Q(D)$, is defined as the set $\{t \mid \exists\, q \in Q \text{ such that } t \in q(D)\}$.

Given a schema $\mathcal{R}$, a *tuple-generating dependency (TGD)* σ over $\mathcal{R}$ is a first-order formula of the form $\forall \mathbf{X} \forall \mathbf{Y}\, \varphi(\mathbf{X}, \mathbf{Y}) \to \exists \mathbf{Z}\, \psi(\mathbf{X}, \mathbf{Z})$, where $\varphi(\mathbf{X}, \mathbf{Y})$ and $\psi(\mathbf{X}, \mathbf{Z})$ are conjunctions of atoms over $\mathcal{R}$, called the *body* and the *head* of σ, denoted as *body*(σ) and *head*(σ), respectively. Henceforth, to avoid notational clutter, we will omit the universal quantifiers in TGDs. A *key dependency (KD)* over $\mathcal{R}$ is an assertion of the form $key(r) = \mathbf{A}$, where $r \in \mathcal{R}$, and $\mathbf{A}$ is a set of attributes of r. A TGD of the form $\varphi(\mathbf{X}, \mathbf{Y}) \to \exists \mathbf{Z}\, \psi(\mathbf{X}, \mathbf{Z})$ is satisfied by a database D iff, whenever there exists a homomorphism h such that $h(\varphi(\mathbf{X}, \mathbf{Y})) \subseteq D$, there exists an extension h' of h (i.e., $h' \supseteq h$) such that $h'(\psi(\mathbf{X}, \mathbf{Z})) \subseteq D$. A KD of the form $key(r) = \mathbf{A}$ is satisfied by a database D iff, for each pair of distinct tuples $t_1, t_2 \in r(D)$, $t_1[\mathbf{A}] \neq t_2[\mathbf{A}]$, where $t[\mathbf{A}]$ is the projection of tuple t over $\mathbf{A}$.

We now define the notion of *query answering* under dependencies. Given a set Σ of dependencies over $\mathcal{R}$, and a database D for $\mathcal{R}$, the *models* of D w.r.t. Σ, denoted as $mods(D, \Sigma)$, is the set of all databases B such that B satisfies all the dependencies in Σ, and $B \supseteq D$. The *answer* to a CQ q w.r.t. Σ and D, denoted as $ans(q, \Sigma, D)$, is the set $\{t \mid t \in q(B) \text{ for each } B \in mods(D, \Sigma)\}$. The *decision problem* associated to query answering under dependencies is the following: given a set Σ of dependencies over $\mathcal{R}$, a database D for $\mathcal{R}$, a CQ q/n over $\mathcal{R}$, and an n-tuple $t \in \Gamma^n$, decide whether $t \in ans(q, \Sigma, D)$.

The *chase procedure* (or simply *chase*) is a fundamental algorithmic tool introduced for checking implication of dependencies [19], and later for checking query containment [17]. Informally, the chase is a process of repairing a database w.r.t. a set of dependencies so that the resulted database satisfies the dependencies. The chase works on an instance through the so-called TGD and KD *chase rules*. We shall use the term *chase* interchangeably for both the procedure and its result. The TGD chase rule comes in two different, equivalent fashions: *oblivious* and *restricted* [8], where the restricted one repairs TGDs only when they are not satisfied. In this paper we focus on the oblivious one for better technical clarity. The *chase* of a database D w.r.t. a set Σ_T of TGDs and a set Σ_K of KDs, denoted $chase(D, \Sigma)$, where $\Sigma = \Sigma_T \cup \Sigma_K$, is the (possibly infinite) instance constructed by iteratively applying *(i)* the TGD chase rule once, and *(ii)* the KD chase rule as long as it is applicable (i.e., until a fixpoint is reached). The chase rules follow.

TGD Chase Rule. Consider a database D for a schema $\mathcal{R}$, and a TGD $\sigma = \varphi(\mathbf{X}, \mathbf{Y}) \rightarrow \exists \mathbf{Z}\, \psi(\mathbf{X}, \mathbf{Z})$ over $\mathcal{R}$. If σ is *applicable* to D, i.e., there exists a homomorphism h such that $h(\varphi(\mathbf{X}, \mathbf{Y})) \subseteq D$ then: (i) define $h' \supseteq h$ such that $h'(Z_i) = z_i$ for each $Z_i \in \mathbf{Z}$, where $z_i \in \Gamma_f$ is a "fresh" labeled null not introduced before and following lexicographically all those introduced so far, and (ii) add to D the set of atoms in $h'(\psi(\mathbf{X}, \mathbf{Z}))$ if not already in D.

KD Chase Rule. Consider an instance D for a schema $\mathcal{R}$, and a KD η of the form $key(r) = \mathbf{A}$ over $\mathcal{R}$. If η is *applicable* to D, i.e., there are two (distinct) tuples $t_1, t_2 \in r(D)$ such that $t_1[\mathbf{A}] = t_2[\mathbf{A}]$, then for each attribute B of r s.t. $B \notin \mathbf{A}$: *(i)* if $t_1[B]$ and $t_2[B]$ are both constants of Γ, then there is a *hard violation* of η and the chase *fails*; in this case $mods(D, \Sigma) = \varnothing$ and we say that D is inconsistent with Σ; *(ii)* if $t_1[B]$ (resp., $t_2[B]$) is a constant of Γ and $t_2[B]$ (resp., $t_1[B]$) is a labeled null of Γ_f, then replace each occurrence of $t_2[B]$ (resp., $t_1[B]$) in D with $t_1[B]$ (resp., $t_2[B]$), and *(iii)* if $t_1[B]$ and $t_2[B]$ are both labeled nulls of Γ_f, then either replace each occurrence of $t_1[B]$ in D with $t_2[B]$ if the former follows lexicographically the latter, or vice-versa otherwise.

It is well-known that $chase(D, \Sigma)$ is a *universal instance* of D w.r.t. Σ, i.e., for each database $B \in mods(D, \Sigma)$, there exists a homomorphism from $chase(D, \Sigma)$

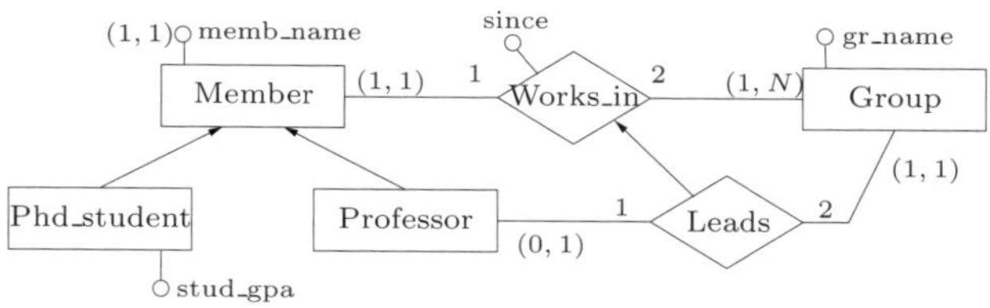

Fig. 1. EER Schema for Example 1

to B [16]. Using this fact, it can be shown that the answers $ans(q, \Sigma, D)$ to CQ q/n under a set Σ of TGDs and KDs, in the case where the chase does not fail, can be obtained by evaluating q over $chase(D, \Sigma)$ (which is possibly infinite) and discarding tuples containing at least one null [16]. In case the chase fails, $ans(q, \Sigma, D)$ contains all tuples in Γ^n.

We say that a set Σ of constraints (not necessarily TGDs and KDs) is *first-order rewritable (or FO-rewritable)* [9,22] iff, for every database D and for every CQ q, there exists a first-order query q_{FO} such that $q_{FO}(D) = ans(q, \Sigma, D)$.

2.2 The Conceptual Model

In this section we present the conceptual model we adopt in this paper, and we define it in terms of relational schemata with constraints. Our model incorporates the basic features of the ER model [14] and OO models, including subset (or is-a) constraints on both entities and relationships. We call our model *Extended Entity-Relationship (EER) model.* An *EER schema* consists of a collection of entity, relationship, and attribute definitions over an alphabet of symbols, partitioned into entity, relationship and attribute symbols. The model is similar as, e.g., the one in [3], and it can be summarised as follows: *(i)* entities and relationships can have attributes; an attribute can be mandatory (instances have at least one value for it), and functional (instances have at most one value for it); *(ii)* entities can participate in relationships; a participation of an entity E in a relationship R can be mandatory (instances of E participate at least once), and functional (instances of E participate at most once); *(iii)* is-a relations can hold between entities and between relationships. We refer the reader to [3] for further details.

Example 1. The schema in Figure 1, based on the usual ER graphic notation, describes members of a university department working in research groups. The is-a constraints specify that Ph.D. students and professors are members, and that each professor works in the same group that (s)he leads. The cardinality constraint $(1, N)$ on the participation of *Group* in *Works_in*, for instance, specifies that each group has at least 1 member and no maximum number of members (symbol N). The participating entities to each relationship are numbered (each number identifies a *component*). □

The semantics of an EER schema $\mathcal{C}$ is defined by associating a relational schema $\mathcal{R}_\mathcal{C}$ to it, and then specifying when a database for $\mathcal{R}_\mathcal{C}$ satisfies all the constraints

Table 1. Derivation of relation constraints from an EER schema

EER Construct	**Relational Constraint**
attribute A for an entity E	$a(X, Y) \rightarrow e(X)$
attribute A for a relationship R	$a(X_1, \ldots, X_n, Y) \rightarrow r(X_1, \ldots, X_n)$
rel. R with entity E as i-th component	$r(X_1, \ldots, X_n) \rightarrow e(X_i)$
mandatory attribute A of entity E	$e(X) \rightarrow \exists Y\, a(X, Y)$
mandatory attribute A of relationship R	$r(X_1, \ldots, X_n) \rightarrow \exists Y\, a(X_1, \ldots, X_n, Y)$
functional attribute A of an entity	$key(a) = \{1\}$ (a has arity 1)
functional attribute A of a relationship	$key(a) = \{1, \ldots, n\}$ (a has arity $n+1$)
is-a between entities E_1 and E_2	$e_1(X) \rightarrow e_2(X)$
is-a between relationships R_1 and R_2	$r_1(X_1, \ldots, X_n) \rightarrow r_2(X_1, \ldots, X_n)$
mandatory part. of E in R (i-th comp.)	$e(X) \rightarrow r(X_1, \ldots, X_{i-1}, X, X_{i+1}, \ldots, X_n)$
functional part. of E in R (i-th comp.)	$key(r) = \{i\}$

imposed by the constructs of $\mathcal{C}$. We first define the relational schema that represents the so-called *concepts*, i.e., entities, relationships and attributes, of an EER schema $\mathcal{C}$ as follows: *(i)* each entity E in $\mathcal{C}$ has an associated predicate $e/1$; *(ii)* each attribute A of an entity E in $\mathcal{C}$ has an associated predicate $a/2$; *(iii)* each relationship R of arity n in $\mathcal{C}$ has an associated predicate r/n, and *(iv)* each attribute A of a relationship R of arity n in $\mathcal{C}$ has an associated predicate $a/(n+1)$. Intuitively, $e(c)$ asserts that c is an instance of entity E. $a(c, d)$ asserts that d is the value of attribute A (of some entity E) associated to c, where c is an instance of E. $r(c_1, \ldots, c_n)$ asserts that $(c_1, \ldots, c_n)$ is an instance of relationship R (among entities $E_1, \ldots, E_n$), where $c_1, \ldots, c_n$ are instances of $E_1, \ldots, E_n$, respectively. Finally, $a(c_1, \ldots, c_n, d)$ asserts that d is the value of attribute A (of some relationship R of arity n) associated to the instance $(c_1, \ldots, c_n)$ of R.

Queries are formulated using the relations in the relational schema we obtain from the EER schema as described above.

Example 2. Consider again the EER schema shown in Figure 1. The schema $\mathcal{R}_\mathcal{C}$ associated to $\mathcal{C}$ consists of $member/1$, $phd\_student/1$, $professor/1$, $group/1$, $works\_in/2$, $leads/2$, $memb\_name/2$, $stud\_gpa/2$, $memb\_name/2$ and $since/3$. Suppose that we want to know the names of the students who work in the DB group since 2006. The corresponding CQ is

$$q(B) \leftarrow phd\_student(A), memb\_name(A, B), works\_in(A, C), since(A, C, 2006), memb\_name(C, db). \quad \square$$

We now define the semantics of the EER constructs. This is done by specifying, using the dependencies introduced in Section 2.1, what databases over $\mathcal{R}_\mathcal{C}$ satisfy the constraints imposed by the constructs of $\mathcal{C}$. We do that by making use of relational database dependencies, as shown in Table 1 (where we assume that the relationships are of arity n). Notice that, slightly differently from [3], we do not allow permutations of components in is-a between relationships; for example, we can never derive a TGD of the form $r_1(X_1, X_2, X_3) \rightarrow r_2(X_3, X_1, X_2)$. The dependencies we obtain are called *conceptual dependencies (CDs)* [3]. Observe that the constraints in a set of CDs are *key* and *inclusion dependencies* [1], where the latter are a special case of TGDs.

3 Separability

In this section we introduce a novel class of CDs, namely, the *non-conflicting CDs (NCCDs)*. In a set of NCCDs, the TGDs and the KDs do not interact, so that answers to queries over an EER schema can be computed by considering the TGDs only, and ignoring the KDs, once it is known that the initial data are consistent with respect to the schema, i.e., the chase does not fail. This semantic property, whose definition is given below, is usually known as *separability* [9,5]. Henceforth, when using the term TGD, we shall refer to TGDs that are part of a set of CDs (the results of this paper do not hold in case of general TGDs).

Definition 1. *Consider a set of CDs Σ over a schema $\mathcal{R}$, with $\Sigma = \Sigma_T \cup \Sigma_K$, where Σ_T are TGDs and Σ_K are KDs. Σ is said to be* separable *if for every instance D for $\mathcal{R}$, and for every CQ q/n, we have that either $chase(D, \Sigma)$ fails, or $ans(q, \Sigma, D) = ans(q, \Sigma_T, D)$.*

Before syntactically defining NCCDs, we need a preliminary notion, that is, the notion of *CD-graph*.

Definition 2. *Consider a set Σ of CDs over a schema $\mathcal{R}$. The CD-graph for $\mathcal{R}$ and Σ is defined as follows: (i) the set of nodes is the set of positions in $\mathcal{R}$; (ii) if there is a TGD σ in Σ such that the same variable appears in a position p_b in the body and in a position p_h in the head, then there is an arc from p_b to p_h.*

A node corresponding to a position derived from an entity (resp., a relationship) is called an e-node (resp., an r-node). Moreover, an r-node corresponding to a position which is a unary key in a relationship is called a k-node. We are now ready to give the notion of NCCDs.

Definition 3. *Consider a set Σ of CDs over a schema $\mathcal{R}$, and let G be the CD-graph for $\mathcal{R}$ and Σ. Σ is said to be* non-conflicting *if the following condition is satisfied: for each path $v_1 \frown v_2 \frown \ldots \frown v_m$ in G, where $m \geqslant 3$, such that: (i) v_1 is an e-node, (ii) $v_2, \ldots, v_{m-1}$ are r-nodes, and (iii) v_m is a k-node, there exists a path in G of only r-nodes from v_m to v_2.*

Example 3. Let us consider the schema in Example 1, ignoring the attributes for simplicity. The CD-graph for the CDs associated to the EER schema are depicted in Fig. 2. The k-nodes are *works_in*[1], *leads*[1], and *leads*[2]. It is immediate to see that the CDs are NCCDs. □

The following example shows that the KD chase rule can be applied during the chase procedure with respect to a set of NCCDs.

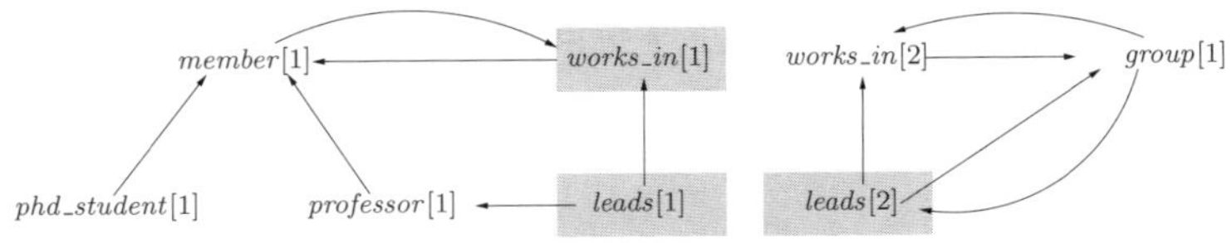

Fig. 2. CD-graph for Example 3. K-nodes are shaded.

Example 4. Let us consider the EER schema in Example 3, which we call $\mathcal{C}$. We omit for space reasons the CDs $\Sigma_{\mathcal{C}}$ associated to $\mathcal{C}$. Take $D = \{professor(p), leads(p, g)\}$. In the computation of $chase(D, \Sigma_{\mathcal{C}})$, we add the atoms $member(p)$, $works\_in(p, g)$ and $works\_in(p, z_1)$, where $z_1 \in \Gamma_f$. Since $\Sigma_{\mathcal{C}}$ contains the KD $key(works\_in) = \{1\}$, we apply the KD chase rule and replace all occurrences of z_1 with g. □

To prove that every set of NCCDs is separable, we now establish two results.

Lemma 1. *Consider a set of NCCDs Σ over a schema $\mathcal{R}$, with $\Sigma = \Sigma_T \cup \Sigma_K$, where Σ_T are TGDs and Σ_K are KDs, and let D be a database for $\mathcal{R}$. If $chase(D, \Sigma)$ does not fail, then there exists a homomorphism h such that $h(chase(D, \Sigma)) \subseteq chase(D, \Sigma_T)$.*

Proof (sketch). We give a very brief sketch of the rather long proof of this result, referring the reader to the full version of the paper [10] for further details. We proceed by induction on the number k of applications of the chase rule in the construction of $chase(D, \Sigma)$. We denote by $chase^k(D, \Sigma)$ the initial segment of $chase(D, \Sigma)$ starting from D and applying k times the chase rule. We need to prove that for each $k \geqslant 0$ there exists homomorphism h_k such that $h_k(chase^k(D, \Sigma)) \subseteq chase(D, \Sigma_T)$. The base step is trivial, since $chase^0(D, \Sigma) = D$. The induction step is proved by considering all possible cases of addition of an atom in the chase construction, when a KD is subsequently applied (if no KD is applied, the homomorphism is trivially determined). The nontrivial case is the one where the added atom is introduced by application of the TGD chase rule with respect to a TGD that represents an is-a among two relationships. In such a case, let μ be the substitution that corresponds to the application of the KD chase rule. The condition in the definition of NCCDs (in particular, the existence of the path from v_m to v_2; see Definition 3) guarantees that the atoms transformed by μ also appear in $chase(D, \Sigma_T)$. The difficulty here lies in the fact that such transformed atoms might have already generated other atoms in $h_k(chase^{k-1}(D, \Sigma))$ (which, by the induction hypothesis, can be mapped to $chase(D, \Sigma_T)$), and the application of μ might cause further applications of the KD chase rule. The homomorphism h_k is determined by a recursive algorithm applied on the atoms generated by the above affected atoms, making use of their representation in the so-called *chase graph* [9]. □

Lemma 2. *Consider a set of NCCDs Σ over a schema $\mathcal{R}$, and let D be a database for $\mathcal{R}$. If $chase(D, \Sigma)$ does not fail, then there exists a homomorphism h such that $h(chase(D, \Sigma_T)) \subseteq chase(D, \Sigma)$.*

Proof (sketch). If $chase(D, \Sigma)$ does not fail, then it satisfies all the constraints in Σ. Therefore, $chase(D, \Sigma) \in mods(D, \Sigma) \subseteq mods(D, \Sigma_T)$. Since $chase(D, \Sigma_T)$ is a universal instance of D w.r.t. Σ_T, the claim follows straightforwardly. □

By combining Lemma 1 and Lemma 2, it is straightforward to obtain the main result of this section.

Theorem 1. *Consider a set Σ of CDs over a schema $\mathcal{R}$. If Σ is non-conflicting, then it is separable.*

Proof. Let D be a database for $\mathcal{R}$ such that $chase(D, \Sigma)$ does not fail. By Lemmata 1 and 2 we get that $chase(D, \Sigma)$ and $chase(D, \Sigma_T)$ are homomorphically equivalent; therefore, for every CQ q we have $q(chase(D, \Sigma)) = q(chase(D, \Sigma_T))$. The claim follows straightforwardly. □

We now show that the property of being non-conflicting is not only sufficient for separability (as shown by the above theorem), but also necessary. This way, we precisely characterise the class of separable EER schemata by means of a syntactic condition.

Theorem 2. *Consider a set Σ of CDs over a schema $\mathcal{R}$. We have that if Σ is not non-conflicting, then it is not separable.*

Proof. We prove this result by exhibiting a database D and a Boolean[2] CQ q such that $chase(D, \Sigma)$ does not fail, and $\langle\rangle \in ans(q, \Sigma, D)$ but $\langle\rangle \notin ans(q, \Sigma_T, D)$. Since Σ is not non-conflicting, there exists a path $v_1 \frown v_2 \frown \ldots \frown v_m$ in the CD-graph for $\mathcal{R}$ and Σ, with $m \geqslant 3$, where v_1 is an e-node, $v_2, \ldots, v_m$ are r-nodes, and v_m is a k-node, but there is no path of only r-nodes from v_m to v_2. Let us assume, w.l.o.g., $v_1 = e_1[1]$ and $v_i = r_i[1]$, for all $i \in \{2, \ldots, m\}$. Consider the database $D = \{e_1(c), r_m(c, \ldots, c)\}$. The arc $e_1[1] \frown r_2[1]$ is necessarily associated to the TGD $e_1(X) \rightarrow r_2(X, X_2, \ldots, X_n)$ (n is the arity of $r_2, \ldots, r_m$). Therefore, the atoms $r_2(c, z_2, \ldots, z_n)$, $\ldots$, $r_m(c, z_2, \ldots, z_n)$ are generated during the construction of the chase. Since v_m is a k-node, we replace z_j with c for each $j \in \{2, \ldots, n\}$, thus getting (among others) the atom $r_2(c, \ldots, c)$. Instead, in $chase(D, \Sigma_T)$, the atom $r_2(c, z_2, \ldots, z_n)$ remains in place, and moreover there is no atom $r_2(c, \ldots, c)$ due to the absence of a path of only r-nodes from v_m to v_2. Now, let us define the CQ q as $q() \leftarrow r_2(c, \ldots, c)$. It is immediate to verify that $\langle\rangle \in ans(q, \Sigma, D)$ but $\langle\rangle \notin ans(q, \Sigma_T, D)$. Finally, since we have in $dom(D)$ a single constant in Γ, no failure is possible in $chase(D, \Sigma)$. □

It is important to mention that results analogous to Theorems 1 and 2 hold for EER schema with *binary* relationships only, and with is-a among relationships that allow for the *swapping* of the components (e.g., represented by a TGD of the form $r_1(X, Y) \rightarrow r_2(Y, X)$). The proofs, which we omit for space reasons, are analogous to those above. This result is important because with this variant of the EER formalism we are able to represent DL-Lite schemata.

[2] A Boolean CQ has no variables in the head, and has only the empty tuple $\langle\rangle$ as possible answer, in which case it is said that the query has *positive* answer.

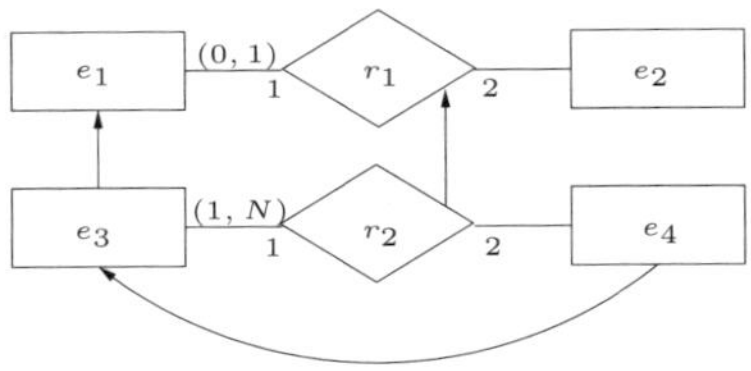

Fig. 3. EER Schema for the proof of Theorem 3

Before moving to the next section, where we show that NCCDs are FO-rewritable, we prove here that CDs are in general not FO-rewritable.

Theorem 3. *General CDs are not FO-rewritable.*

Proof (sketch). We give a counterexample schema and query such that no first-order rewriting exists for the query. Let $\mathcal{C}$ be the EER schema depicted in Figure 3, and $\Sigma_{\mathcal{C}}$ be the set of associated CDs, which we omit for space reasons. Let $D \supseteq \{e_4(c_1)\}$, and q be the (Boolean) CQ $q() \leftarrow e_4(c_n)$, with $n \geqslant 2$. It is not difficult to show that $\langle\rangle \in ans(q, \Sigma, D)$ iff D contains the atoms $r_1(c_1, c_2), r_1(c_2, c_3), \ldots, r_1(c_{n-1}, c_n)$. Verifying such condition for every database requires a query that computes of the transitive closure of $r_1(D)$, which is not possible with a first-order query. □

4 Query Answering by Rewriting

In this section we address the problem of query answering under NCCDs by adopting query rewriting techniques. From the previous section, given a set Σ of CDs, once we know that the chase does not fail, we can concentrate only on the set Σ_T of TGDs that are in Σ. We present a query rewriting algorithm that allow us to answer CQs under TGDs by reformulating a given CQ q into a UCQ Q_r, that encodes the information about the given TGDs, and then evaluate Q_r over a given database to obtain the correct answers to q.

Given a CQ q, we say that a variable V is *bound* in q if it occurs more than once in $body(q)$, otherwise is called *unbound*. A *bound term* in q is either a bound variable or a constant of Γ. Note that the variables that appear in the head are necessarily bound, since each one of them must occur also in the body.

Definition 4. *Given a CQ q, consider two atoms $\alpha_1 = r(X_1, \ldots, X_n) \in body(q)$ and $\alpha_2 = r(Y_1, \ldots, Y_n) \in body(q)$. We say that α_1 and α_2* unify *if, for each $i \in \{1, \ldots, n\}$, either $X_i = Y_i$ or X_i is unbound in q or Y_i is unbound in q. Moreover, if α_1 and α_2 unify we denote as $U(\alpha_1, \alpha_2)$ the atom $r(Z_1, \ldots, Z_n)$ where, for each $i \in \{1, \ldots, n\}$, if $X_i = Y_i$ or Y_i is unbound in q then $Z_i = X_i$, otherwise $Z_i = Y_i$. By $\sigma_{\alpha_1,\alpha_2}$ we refer to the substitution that maps both α_1 and α_2 to $U(\alpha_1, \alpha_2)$.*

Intuitively, two atoms unify if they can be made identical through a substitution of each unbound variable with other terms. We now introduce the important

Algorithm rewrite
Input: Relational schema $\mathcal{R}$, set Σ of TGDs over $\mathcal{R}$, CQ q over $\mathcal{R}$
Output: Rewritten query Q_r over $\mathcal{R}$

$Q_r := \{q\}$; $Q_r^{\mathsf{can}} := \varnothing$; $i := 0$;
repeat
  $Q' := Q_r$; $Q'' := Q_r^{\mathsf{can}}$;
  for each $q \in Q'$ do
  (a) for each $\alpha_1, \alpha_2 \in body(q)$ do
    if α_1, α_2 unify then
      $q' := \sigma_{\alpha_1,\alpha_2}(q)$
      $Q_r := Q_r \cup \{q'\}$
      $Q_r^{\mathsf{can}} := Q_r^{\mathsf{can}} \cup \{\tau(q')\}$;
  (b) for each $\alpha \in body(q)$ do
    for each $\sigma \in \Sigma$ do
      if σ is applicable to α then
        $i := i + 1$
        $q' := q[\alpha / rew_i(\alpha, \sigma)]$
        $Q_r := Q_r \cup \{q'\}$
        $Q_r^{\mathsf{can}} := Q_r^{\mathsf{can}} \cup \{\tau(q')\}$;
until $Q'' = Q_r^{\mathsf{can}}$;
return Q_r;

Fig. 4. The Algorithm rewrite

notion of *applicability* of a TGD to an atom. We assume w.l.o.g. that the set of variables that appear in TGDs and the set of variables that appear in queries are disjoint.

Definition 5. *Consider a TGD $\sigma = s(\mathbf{X}, \mathbf{Y}) \rightarrow \exists \mathbf{Z}\, r(\mathbf{X}, \mathbf{Z})$ over a schema $\mathcal{R}$, a CQ q over $\mathcal{R}$, and an atom $\alpha = r(W_1, \ldots, W_n) \in body(q)$. We say that σ is* applicable *to α if the homomorphism h such that $h(r(\mathbf{X}, \mathbf{Z})) = r(W_1, \ldots, W_n)$*[3] *satisfies the following condition: for each $i \in \{1, \ldots, n\}$, if W_i is a bound term in q then $h^{-1}(W_i) \in \mathbf{X}$. We denote as $rew_k(\alpha, \sigma)$, for $k \geqslant 1$, the atom $h'(s(\mathbf{X}, \mathbf{Y}))$, where h' is the extension of h such that $h'(Y_i) = Y_i^k$, for each $Y_i \in \mathbf{Y}$.*

Roughly, a TGD σ is applicable to an atom α if the relation associated to α is the same as the relation symbol in the head of σ, and if all the attributes at which bound terms occur in α are propagated by σ. The atom $rew_k(\alpha, \sigma)$ is the atom obtained from α by using σ as a rewriting rule whose direction is from right-to-left.

We are now ready to define the algorithm rewrite, shown in Figure 4. The rewriting of a CQ is computed by exhaustively applying two steps: *minimisation* and *rewriting*, corresponding to steps (a) and (b) of the algorithm, and informally described below.

Minimisation. If there exists a CQ $q \in Q_r$ such that $body(q)$ contains two atoms α_1 and α_2 that unify, then the algorithm computes the CQ q' by replacing α_1

[3] Recall that each variable in $r(\mathbf{X}, \mathbf{Z})$ occurs just once. Thus, h is a bijection that exists trivially.

and α_2 with $U(\alpha_1, \alpha_2)$, and then applying the substitution obtained during the computation of $U(\alpha_1, \alpha_2)$ to the whole query. The query q' is then added to Q_r. The CQ $\tau(q')$, obtained by replacing unbound variables with "$\star$", is then added to Q_r^{can}, the canonical form of Q_r.

Rewriting. During the i-th application of this step, if there exists a TGD σ and a CQ $q \in Q_r$ containing an atom α such that σ is applicable to α, then the algorithm computes the CQ $q' = q[\alpha/rew_i(\alpha, \sigma)]$, that is, the CQ obtained from q by replacing α with the atom $rew_i(\alpha, \sigma)$. In fact, this step adds new conjunctions obtained by applying TGDs as rewriting rules (from right-to-left). Then, $\tau(q')$ is added to Q_r^{can}.

Example 5. Consider the EER schema $\mathcal{C}$ defined in Example 1 (see Fig. 1). Let $\mathcal{R}_\mathcal{C}$ and $\Sigma_\mathcal{C}$ be the relational schema and the set of CDs, respectively, associated to $\mathcal{C}$. Let q_0 be the CQ $q(B) \leftarrow member(A), memb\_name(A, B), works\_in(A, C), gr\_name(C, db)$, asking for names of members who work in the db group. We describe a single step of the algorithm. The TGD $works\_in(X, Y) \rightarrow member(X)$ in $\Sigma_\mathcal{C}$ is applicable to the atom $member(A) \in body(q_0)$. Thus, at some application of the rewriting step, say the i-th, we get the CQ q_1 defined as $q(B) \leftarrow works\_in(A, Y^i), memb\_name(A, B), works\_in(A, C), gr\_name(C, db)$ (Y^i is a newly introduced variable; see Definition 5). The canonical form of q_1 is obtained by replacing the unbound variable Y^i with the symbol "$\star$". Observe now that the atoms $works\_in(A, Y^i)$ and $works\_in(A, C)$ in $body(q_1)$ unify. Hence, the minimisation step is (eventually) applied and we get the CQ q_2 defined as $q(B) \leftarrow works\_in(A, C), memb\_name(A, B), gr\_name(C, db)$. The canonical form of q_2 is the same as q_2, since q_2 has no unbound variables. □

The next result shows that the algorithm rewrite produces a so-called *perfect rewriting*, i.e., a rewritten query that produces the correct answers under TGDs when evaluated on a given database.

Theorem 4. *Let $\mathcal{R}$ be a relational schema. Consider a set Σ_T of TGDs over $\mathcal{R}$, a database D for $\mathcal{R}$, a CQ q/n over $\mathcal{R}$, and an n-tuple $t \in \Gamma^n$. Then, $t \in ans(q, \Sigma_T, D)$ iff $t \in Q_r(D)$, where $Q_r =$* rewrite$(\mathcal{R}, \Sigma_T, q)$.

Proof (sketch). Roughly, the depth $d \geqslant 0$ of a CQ $q' \in Q_r$ indicates that q' was obtained during the rewriting process starting from q, and applying at least d times either the rewriting step or the minimisation step. By induction on the depth of q', it is possible to prove that if $t \in q'(D)$ then $t \in q(chase(D, \Sigma_T))$; thus, if $t \in Q_r(D)$ then $t \in q(chase(D, \Sigma_T))$. By induction on the number of applications of the TGD chase rule, we can also prove that if $t \in q(chase(D, \Sigma_T))$ then $t \in Q_r(D)$. Consequently, $t \in Q_r(D)$ iff $t \in q(chase(D, \Sigma_T))$. The claim follows straightforwardly. □

We now establish the termination of the algorithm rewrite.

Theorem 5. *Let $\mathcal{R}$ be a relational schema. Consider a set Σ_T of TGDs over $\mathcal{R}$, and a CQ q over $\mathcal{R}$. The algorithm* rewrite *with input $\mathcal{R}$, Σ_T and q terminates.*

Proof. To prove the claim it suffices to show that the maximum number of CQs that can appear in the canonical form of the query $\mathsf{rewrite}(\mathcal{R}, \Sigma_T, q)$, denoted as Q_c, is finite. Since, for each $\sigma \in \Sigma_T$, each variable in $body(\sigma)$ occurs just once, it is easy to see that for each CQ $q' \in \mathsf{rewrite}(\mathcal{R}, \Sigma_T, q)$, if a "fresh" variable V (see Definition 5) generated during the rewriting process occurs in q' then V is unbound in q'. Therefore, by definition of τ, none of these variables can appear in Q_c since they are replaced by the symbol "$\star$". Consequently, the set of terms used to construct Q_c corresponds to the set of variables and constants occurring in the CQ q plus the symbol "$\star$"; thus, such set is finite. Moreover, only relations of $\mathcal{R}$ can appear in Q_c which is also finite. The claim follows since the number of atoms that can be written using a finite set of terms and a finite set of relations is finite. □

From the above results, and from those of Section 3, it is immediate to conclude that, if the chase does not fail given a certain instance, answering queries under NCCDs can be done in AC_0 in data complexity. This because the rewriting algorithm produces a UCQ, which is a first-order query. It remains to determine what is the complexity of checking whether the chase fails. This will be shown in the next section.

5 Negative Constraints

In this section we show how the EER model can be extended, in the same fashion as in [9], with negative constraints.

A *negative constraint* on a schema $\mathcal{R}$ is a first-order formula of the form $\forall \mathbf{X}\, \varphi(\mathbf{X}) \rightarrow \bot$, where $\varphi(\mathbf{X})$ is a conjunction of atoms over $\mathcal{R}$, and $\bot$ is the truth constant "false"; for conciseness of notation, we will omit the universal quantifiers. Such a constraint is satisfied by a database D iff there is no homomorphism h such that $h(\varphi(\mathbf{X})) \subseteq D$.

We first show how to express the failure of the chase with negative constraints. Given an instance D, we take all pairs c_1, c_2 of *distinct* constants of Γ in $dom(D)$, and for each pair we add to D the fact $neq(c_1, c_2)$, where neq is an auxiliary predicate. For every key constraint $key(r) = \{1, \ldots, m\}$ for a predicate r/n with $m < n$ (w.l.o.g., we assume the first m attributes to form the key; in particular, m can be only 1 or $n-1$), we add the following negative constraints, for all $j \in \{m+1, \ldots, n\}$:

$$r(X_1, \ldots, X_m, Y_{m+1}, \ldots, Y_n), r(X_1, \ldots, X_m, Z_{m+1}, \ldots, Z_n), neq(Y_j, Z_j) \rightarrow \bot.$$

As observed in [9], a constraint $\varphi(\mathbf{X}) \rightarrow \bot$ is satisfied by a database D iff the answer to the CQ $q() \leftarrow \varphi(\mathbf{X})$ over D is the empty set. Therefore, we can easily check the failure of the chase by answering such CQs, which has the same complexity as answering CQs under NCCDs. This straightforwardly implies FO-rewritability of NCCDs: we can answer a query q, given D and $\Sigma = \Sigma_T \cup \Sigma_K$, by evaluating over D the first-order query obtained by taking the logical disjunction of the CQs associated to the negative constraints $\Sigma_\bot$, expressive the chase failure as above, and of the output of rewrite($\mathcal{R}, \Sigma_T, q$) as in Section 4. We immediately get the following result.

Theorem 6. *Query answering on EER schemata represented by NCCDs is in* AC_0 *in data complexity.*

Negative constraints can be used to express several relevant constructs in EER schemata, for instance disjunction between entities and relationships, and non-participation of entities to relationships, but also more general ones.

Example 6. Consider an EER schema $\mathcal{C}$ obtained from the one in Example 1 (see Figure 1) by adding an entity *PensionScheme* and a relationship *Enrolled* between *PensionScheme* and *Member*, with no cardinality constraints; for space reasons, we do not show the new diagram. To express that students and professors are disjoint sets, we state $phd\_student(X), professor(X) \rightarrow \bot$ (entity disjunction). We can also express that a student cannot be enrolled in a pension scheme (i.e., it does not participate to *Enrolled*) with the negative constraint $phd\_student(X), enrolled(X, Y) \rightarrow \bot$ (non-participation). □

Consider a schema $\mathcal{R}$, a set of CDs Σ on $\mathcal{R}$, and a set of negative constraints $\Sigma_\bot$ on $\mathcal{R}$. The question remaining open so far is whether the fact that the CDs in Σ are NCCDs is necessary and sufficient to ensure separability of $\Sigma \cup \Sigma_\bot$. It is not difficult to show that for general negative constraints the property is not necessary; however, in particular cases, it is. For example, we claim that if we restrict to negative constraints expressing entity and relationship disjunction plus non-participation, and to *strongly consistent* EER schemata [2], having non-conflicting CDs is necessary and sufficient for separability. Results on negative constraints will be published elsewhere.

6 Discussion

Related work. The well-known Entity-Relationship model was introduced by the milestone paper of Chen [14]. A work giving a logic-based semantics is [15], which also provides an inference algorithm; [18] investigates cardinality constraints in the ER formalism. An investigation on reasoning tasks on different variants of ER schemata is found in [2]. Query answering is tightly related to query containment under constraints, a fundamental topic in database theory [12,17,3]. Data integration under ER schemata, strictly less expressive than EER schemata, is considered in [6]. [21] adopts a formalism which is more expressive than ours, thus not achieving similar tractability results. [12] considers query containment in a formalism similar to the EER model with less expressive negative constraints, focusing on decidability and combined complexity (i.e., the complexity w.r.t. the data, the schema and the query). No results on data complexity, nor a practical algorithm, are provided. A query rewriting algorithm for IDs and so-called *non-conflicting* KDs is presented in [11]. The works on DL-Lite [7,22] exhibit tractable query answering algorithm (in AC_0 in data complexity) for different languages in the DL-Lite family. Our EER formalism properly generalises languages DL-Lite$_{\mathcal{F}}$, DL-Lite$_{\mathcal{R}}$ and DL-Lite$_{\mathcal{A}}$ (this can be shown in a way similar to that of [9]), while providing a query answering algorithm with the same data complexity. Recent works [8,9] deal with expressive rules (TGDs) that consitute the languages of the *Datalog*$^{\pm}$ family, which are capable of capturing the EER formalism presented here, if we consider TGDs only. The languages in the *Datalog*$^{\pm}$ family are more expressive (and less tractable) than ours except for *Linear Datalog*$^{\pm}$, that allows for query answering in AC_0 in data complexity. However, the class of NCCDs is not expressible in Linear Datalog$^{\pm}$ (plus the class of KDs presented in [9]), and moreover the FO-rewriting algorithm in [9], unlike ours, is not very well-suited for practical implementations. Finally, the works [3,4] deal with general (not non-conflicting) CDs: PTIME data complexity of answering is obtained by paying a high price in combined complexity.

Conclusions and future work. In this paper we have identified, by means of a graph-based representation, a class of extended Entity-Relationship schemata for which query answering is tractable, and more precisely in AC_0 in data complexity. The tractability of answering in our setting hinges on the notion of separability, for which we have provided a precise characterisation in terms of a necessary and sufficient syntactic condition. We have presented an algorithm for answering queries on EER schemata, based on query rewriting. Such algorithm is an adapted version of a more general algorithm which can deal with much more expressive TGDs, and which we do not include in this paper for space reasons. We have also shown that negative constraints can be added to EER schemata, without increasing the data complexity of query answering. The class of EER schemata we deal with is general enough to include most conceptual modelling and knowledge representation formalisms; in particular, it is strictly more expressive than the languages in the DL-Lite family.

We plan to extend our results by studying the combined complexity of query answering problem under NCCDs, and employing variants of our general rewriting algorithm to deal with even more expressive constraints. It is also our intention to run experiments with the techniques presented here.

Acknowledgments. The authors acknowledge support by the EPSRC project "Schema Mappings and Automated Services for Data Integration and Exchange" (EP/E010865/1). Georg Gottlob's work was also supported by a Royal Society Wolfson Research Merit Award.

References

1. Abiteboul, S., Hull, R., Vianu, V.: Foundations of Databases. Addison-Wesley, Reading (1995)
2. Artale, A., Calvanese, D., Kontchakov, R., Ryzhikov, V., Zakharyaschev, M.: Reasoning over extended ER models. In: Parent, C., Schewe, K.-D., Storey, V.C., Thalheim, B. (eds.) ER 2007. LNCS, vol. 4801, pp. 277–292. Springer, Heidelberg (2007)
3. Calì, A.: Containment of conjunctive queries over conceptual schemata. In: Li Lee, M., Tan, K.-L., Wuwongse, V. (eds.) DASFAA 2006. LNCS, vol. 3882, pp. 628–643. Springer, Heidelberg (2006)

4. Calì, A.: Querying incomplete data with logic programs: ER strikes back. In: Parent, C., Schewe, K.-D., Storey, V.C., Thalheim, B. (eds.) ER 2007. LNCS, vol. 4801, pp. 245–260. Springer, Heidelberg (2007)
5. Calì, A., Lembo, D., Rosati, R.: On the decidability and complexity of query answering over incosistent and incomplete databases. In: Proc. of PODS 2003, pp. 260–271 (2003)
6. Calì, A., Calvanese, D., De Giacomo, G., Lenzerini, M.: Accessing data integration systems through conceptual schemas. In: Kunii, H.S., Jajodia, S., Sølvberg, A. (eds.) ER 2001. LNCS, vol. 2224, pp. 270–284. Springer, Heidelberg (2001)
7. Calvanese, D., De Giacomo, G., Lembo, D., Lenzerini, M., Rosati, R.: Tractable reasoning and efficient query answering in description logics: the DL-Lite family. J. Autom. Reasoning 39(3), 385–429 (2007)
8. Calì, A., Gottlob, G., Kifer, M.: Taming the infinite chase: query answering under expressive relational constraints. In: Proc. of KR 2008, pp. 70–80 (2008), `http://benner.dbai.tuwien.ac.at/staff/gottlob/CGK.pdf`
9. Calì, A., Gottlob, G., Lukasiewicz, T.: A general datalog-based framework for tractable query answering over ontologies. In: Proc. of PODS 2009, pp. 77–86 (2009)
10. Calì, A., Gottlob, G., Pieris, A.: Tractable query answering over conceptual schemata. Unpublished technical report, available from the authors (2009)
11. Calì, A., Lembo, D., Rosati, R.: Query rewriting and answering under constraints in data integration systems. In: Proc. of IJCAI 2003, pp. 16–21 (2003)
12. Calvanese, D., De Giacomo, G., Lenzerini, M.: On the decidability of query containment under constraints. In: Proc. PODS 1998, pp. 149–158 (1998)
13. Calvanese, D., Lenzerini, M., Nardi, D.: Description logics for conceptual data modeling. Logics for Databases and Information Systems, 229–263 (1998)
14. Chen, P.P.: The entity-relationship model: towards a unified view of data. ACM TODS 1(1), 124–131 (1995)
15. Di Battista, G., Lenzerini, M.: A deductive method for entity-relationship modeling. In: Proc. of VLDB 1989, pp. 13–21 (1989)
16. Fagin, R., Kolaitis, P.G., Miller, R.J., Popa, L.: Data exchange: semantics and query answering. TCS 336(1), 89–124 (2005)
17. Johnson, D.S., Klug, A.C.: Testing containment of conjunctive queries under functional and inclusion dependencies. JCSS 28(1), 167–189 (1984)
18. Lenzerini, M., Santucci, G.: Cardinality constraints in the entity-relationship model. In: Proc. of ER 1983, pp. 529–549 (1983)
19. Maier, D., Mendelzon, A.O., Sagiv, Y.: Testing implications of data dependencies. ACM TODS 4(4), 455–469 (1979)
20. Markowitz, V.M., Makowsky, J.A.: Identifying extended entity-relationship object structures in relational schemas. IEEE Trans. Software Eng. 16(8), 777–790 (1990)
21. Ortiz, M., Calvanese, D., Eiter, T.: Characterizing data complexity for conjunctive query answering in expressive description logics. In: Proc. of AAAI 2006, pp. 275–280. AAAI Press, Menlo Park (2006)
22. Poggi, A., Lembo, D., Calvanese, D., De Giacomo, G., Lenzerini, M., Rosati, R.: Linking data to ontologies. J. Data Semantics 10, 133–173 (2008)

Query-By-Keywords (QBK): Query Formulation Using Semantics and Feedback*

Aditya Telang, Sharma Chakravarthy, and Chengkai Li

Department of Computer Science & Engineering
The University of Texas at Arlington, Arlington, TX 76019
{aditya.telang,sharmac,cli}@uta.edu

Abstract. The staples of information retrieval have been *querying* and *search*, respectively, for structured and unstructured repositories. Processing queries over known, structured repositories (e.g., Databases) has been well-understood, and search has become ubiquitous when it comes to unstructured repositories (e.g., Web). Furthermore, searching structured repositories has been explored to a limited extent. However, there is not much work in querying unstructured sources. We argue that querying unstructured sources is the next step in performing focused retrievals. This paper proposed a new approach to generate queries from search-like inputs for unstructured repositories. Instead of burdening the user with schema details, we believe that pre-discovered semantic information in the form of taxonomies, relationship of keywords based on context, and attribute & operator compatibility can be used to generate query skeletons. Furthermore, progressive feedback from users can be used to improve the accuracy of query skeletons generated.

1 Motivation

Querying and search have served well, respectively, as mechanisms for retrieving desired information from structured and unstructured repositories. A query (e.g., SQL) is typically quite precise in expressing *what* information is desired and is usually formed with the prior knowledge of the data sources, the data model, and the operators of the data model. On the other hand, a search request (typically, in the form of keywords) is on text repositories (including HTML and XML) and does not assume the knowledge of sources or the structure of data. A search is likely to generate a large number of results (especially when the search corpus is large and the input, by definition, is imprecise with respect to the intent) and hence ranking or ordering the results to indicate their relevance or usefulness has received considerable attention. Queries, in contrast, generate more focused results and can also be ranked to generate top-k answers.

One of the significant differences between querying and search is that some forms of querying require training – in the query language, the data model on which the query is being expressed, and the syntax of the query language. It

* This work was supported, in part, by the NSF Grant IIS 0534611.

A.H.F. Laender et al. (Eds.): ER 2009, LNCS 5829, pp. 191–204, 2009.

also requires an understanding of the sources or schema. As a result, querying is the proclivity of those who are willing to spend time learning the intricacies of correct specification. In contrast, search is straightforward and easy, and as a result, has become extremely popular with the advent of the Web. The lack of a learning curve associated with search makes it useful to a large class of users. The proliferation of search and its popularity has lead researchers to apply it to structured corpus as well [1]; however, the main problem (from a users' viewpoint) being the post-processing effort needed to filter out irrelevant results.

Consider a user who wants to – "*Retrieve castles near London that can be reached in 2 hours by train*". Although all the information for answering the above request is available on the web, it is currently `not possible` to frame it as a *single query/search* and get meaningful results. Since this and similar queries (Section 3 provides examples of such queries) require combining information from multiple sources, search is not likely to be a preferred alternative. Although there are a number of systems [2], [3] that combine information from multiple sources belonging to the *same* domain (e.g., books, airlines etc.), they cannot answer the above class of queries.

The focus of this paper is to address the problems associated with querying unstructured data sources, especially the web. The *InfoMosaic* project [4] is investigating the integration of results from multiple heterogeneous Web sources to form meaningful answers to queries (such as the one shown above) that span multiple domains. As part of this project, we are investigating a mechanism for formulating a complete query from search-like keywords input (to avoid a learning curve) that can be processed over multiple unstructured domains to retrieve useful answers. Additionally, we are also investigating the generation and optimization of a query plan to answer the formulated structured query over the Web. More recently, this problem is also being addressed in the literature [5].

An intuitive approach to both search and querying would be to use natural language to express the query. This is certainly a preferred alternative as it frees the user from the data model and other considerations needed for expressing a structured query. We view structured queries being at one end of the spectrum and natural language queries being at the other end. Since the general capability to accept arbitrary natural language queries and convert them to structured queries is still not mature, our proposed approach (that lies somewhere in-between the two and even easier than a natural language) will provide a mechanism for querying unstructured repositories with intuitive inputs and minimal user interaction.

This paper advances the thesis that a query is essential to extract useful and relevant information from the web – especially when it involves integrating information that spans multiple domains and hence multiple disparate repositories. As most of the users are familiar and comfortable with search, we want to start with a search-like input and expand it to a complete query using different types of semantic information and minimal user feedback/interaction. For instance, in the case of the above query example, a user may provide his input as a set of the following keywords: *castle, train, London* in any order. For the same query, another user may input: *train, 2 hours, London, castle.* These list of words may mean several different things to different users. For example, the user may be looking for a castle in London or a book written by London in which Castle and Train appear in the title. The semantic information (that is assumed to be separately discovered and collected for this purpose) will assist in formulating the correct complete query with minimal interactions with the user.

As alluded to above, our proposed approach uses different types of semantic information: taxonomies (for context information such as travel or publishing in the above example), attributes associated with concept nodes in the taxonomy, their types, and whether they can participate in join, spatial or temporal conditions, alternative meanings of words as they appear in multiple taxonomies, compatibility of attributes across concept meanings, dictionary meaning and priority of word semantics from the dictionary to the extent possible, and finally user feedback on past interactions. The remainder of the paper will elaborate on the proposed Query-By-Keywords (QBK) approach that uses different types of semantics and workload statistics to disambiguate and generate a partial query to capture the intent of the user.

1.1 Contributions and Roadmap

One of the contributions of this paper is the novelty of the approach proposed to generate a structured query from an input that is characteristic of search. Other important contributions include: the identification of appropriate semantic information (e.g., taxonomies and other associated data) for the transformation of keywords, algorithms for generating alternative query skeletons and ranking them using compatibility and other metrics. Finally, the role and use of feedback for improving the ranking and generating the complete structured query.

We would like to clarify that the scope of this paper does not include the discovery (or automatic acquisition) of information used for the proposed approach. The thrust of this paper is to identify what information is needed, establish the effectiveness of this information, and an approach for transforming input keywords into a complete query. The discovery of this information, an independent problem in itself, is being addressed separately.

The rest of the paper is organized as follows. Section 2 contains related work. Section 3 provides an overview of the proposed approach with motivating examples of user intent, keyword input, and alternative queries that are generated by our approach. Section 4 discusses the details of steps for transforming input keywords into a complete query including keyword resolution, ranking, and query template generation. Conclusions and future work are in Section 5.

2 Related Work

The work closest to ours in formulating queries using templates/skeletons with multiple interactions from the user is the popular Query-By-Example (or QBE) paradigm [6]. In addition, template-based query formulation using multiple interactions with the user has been developed for database systems such as SQL

Server, Oracle and Microsoft Access. Similarly, the CLIDE framework[7] adopts a multiple-interaction visual framework for allowing users to formulate queries. The primary motivation of the CLIDE architecture is to determine which queries would yield results versus those which produce a null result-set. However, formulating queries using these mechanisms requires the user to have knowledge about the types of queries supported by the underlying schema as well as a minimal understanding of the query language of the data model. Deep-web portals such as Expedia (www.expedia.com) or Amazon (www.amazon.com) support the QBE paradigm; however, the queries to these systems are restricted to the schema of a single domain such as travel, shopping, etc. and thus, lack the flexibility to support complex queries that span multiple domains. To the best of our knowledge, the problem of formulating arbitrary queries that span multiple domains has not been addressed.

Search engines (e.g., Google) and meta-search engines (e.g., Vivisimo [8]) use the keyword query paradigm and its success forms the motivation for this work. However, they do not convert the keywords into queries as their aim is not query processing. Although some search engines (e.g., Ask.com) accept natural language input, we believe that they do not transform them into structured queries. Deep Web portals, on the other hand, support search through templates, faceted searches and natural language questions (e.g., START [9]). However, since the underlying schemas in these systems are well-defined and user queries are purely based on these schemas, the need to support arbitrary queries/intents with varying conditions on multiple types of operators does not arise.

Frameworks that support queries on multiple sources support either a keyword query paradigm [2] or mediated query interfaces [3][4] for accepting user intents. Similarly, commercial systems such as Google Base [10] advocate the usage of keyword queries. Faceted-search systems [11] support query formulation using keywords in multiple navigational steps till the user gets the desired results. However, the focus of these frameworks is to perform a simple text/Web-search to obtain different types of data in response to the keywords (e.g., blogs, web-links, videos, etc.) instead of formulating a query where every keyword corresponds to a distinct entity.

3 Overview of QBK Approach

User queries that span across multiple domains (such as Travel, Literature, Shopping, Entertainment etc.) and involve different join conditions across sources in these domains can be complex to specify. For example, consider some representative queries that users would like to pose on the web:

Q1: *Retrieve castles near London that are reachable by train in less than 2 hours*
Q2: *Retrieve lowest airfare for flights from Dallas to VLDB 2009 conference*
Q3: *Obtain a list of 3-bedroom houses in Houston within 2 miles of exemplary schools and within 5 miles of a highway and priced under 250,000$*

Although all the information for answering the above (and similar) intents is available on the Web, it is currently not possible to pose such queries. Ideally, it should be possible to accept minimal input that characterizes the above queries from the user, and refine it into a *complete* query (such as the one shown below in response to $Q1$) to reflect the user intent.

```
SELECT *
FROM
  SOURCES www.castles.org, www.national-rail.com
                  /* Using the travel domain */
  FOR ENTITIES castle, train
WHERE
   train.source = 'London' and
   train.destination = castle.location and
   train.start_date = 09/19/2008 and
   train.return_date = 09/19/2008 and
   train.duration < 02 hours /* temporal conditions */
```

The approach we are proposing is to generate the above complete query by accepting a set of keywords (can also be extracted using a natural language specification). It may be possible to derive the above query *completely* from the keywords given for $Q1$ by making some minimal default assumptions about the dates based on the context. However, if a set of keywords are input, the generation of a complete query may not always be possible. Hence, we have introduced the notion of a query skeleton in this paper.

Web users are comfortable expressing queries through keywords rather than a query language (as displayed by the popularity of search and meta-search engines). Furthermore, current language processing techniques do not posses the ability to process and translate any arbitrary natural language query into a structured query. Hence, it is preferable for the user to express a query using a set of representative words than in natural language. For instance, some of the possible keyword representations for $Q1$ could be:

$Q1_{K1}$: *castle, train, London*
$Q1_{K2}$: *train, from, London, to, castle*
...
$Q1_{Kn}$: *castle, reachable, train, from, London, 2 hours, or, less than*

The above can also be extended to specify phrases/conditions instead of only keywords. For example, "less than 2 hours" can be expressed together rather than separately. The phrase needs to be parsed with respect to a context. Irrespective of how the intent is mapped into keywords (e.g., alternatives $Q1_{K1}, Q1_{K2}, ..., Q1_{Kn}$ shown above), the final query formulated by the system in response to all these different inputs should correspond to $Q1$. Of course, this may not be possible without some interaction with the user once the domains and potential partial queries are identified and generated by the system. On the other hand, it is also possible that different user intents may result in the same set of keywords introducing ambiguity that needs to be identified and resolved systematically in order to arrive at the final query intended by the user. As an example, the following natural language queries can result in the *same* set of keywords from a user's perspective.

- *Retrieve Castles near London that are reachable by Train*
- *Retrieve Hotels near London that are Castles and can be reached by a Train*

Thus, for formulating query skeletons that converge to the actual user intent, it is necessary for the underlying system to intelligently correlate the specified keywords and generate alternative query skeletons based on the interpretation of the keywords in different domains. It is also possible that, within the same domain, multiple query skeletons can be generated by using alternative interpretations of keywords.

3.1 Specification, Precision, Usability, and Learning Tradeoffs

It is clear that there is a tradeoff between ease of query specification (or learning effort), its precision, and utility of results. Search is easy to specify but inherently vague and the result has to be sifted to obtain useful or meaningful answers (low utility). Although ranking helps quite a bit, as ranking is not always completely customized to an individual user, results need to be pruned by the user. On the other hand, a structured query is precise and the user does not have to interact with the system for obtaining meaningful answers (high utility). Of course, ranking can further help bring more meaningful answers to the top (or even avoid computing others).

Table 1. Specification Comparison Matrix

Specification	Learning Curve	Precision	Utility	Schema/Source Knowledge
SQL	High	High	Med-high	High
QBE	Low	High	Med-high	Medium
Templates	Low	High	Medium	Low
NL	Low-Med	Medium	Med-high	Low-Med
Search	Low	Low	Low	Low
QBK	**Low**	**High**	**High**	**Low**

Table 1 shows a back-of-the-envelope comparison of various search/query specifications across the dimensions of learning effort, precision, utility, and knowledge of schema/sources. The ultimate goal is to have a query specification mechanism that has low learning effort, precise, high utility, and does not require the knowledge of sources. QBK is an attempt in that direction as shown in the bottom row. The purpose of the table is to quickly understand a specification mechanism along a number of metrics and learn how it stacks up against other mechanisms. The table does not include specifications such as faceted search as it is navigational wit results refined at each step. The score of Medium-high utility for SQL and QBE is based on whether ranking is used or not. The Natural language (NL) row assumes ambiguities in the specification and hence the utility of results may not be high. This table can be used as a starting point to to compare different approaches used for search as well as for querying.

4 Details of the QBK Approach

Our approach to completing multi-domain queries is shown in Figure 1. In our approach, the user provides keywords deemed significant (e.g., $\{castle, train, London\}$ for *Q1*) instead of a query. The *Keyword Resolution* phase checks these keywords against the *Knowledge Base* for resolving each keyword to entities, attributes, values, or operators. For a keyword that occurs as a heteronym (i.e., same entity representing multiple meanings/contexts) in the *Knowledge Base*, all possible combinations for the different meanings of this keyword is generated. This occurs when the keyword occurs in different taxonomies corresponding to different domains/context. From these combinations, query skeletons and any other conditions (or attributes on which conditions are possible) are generated.

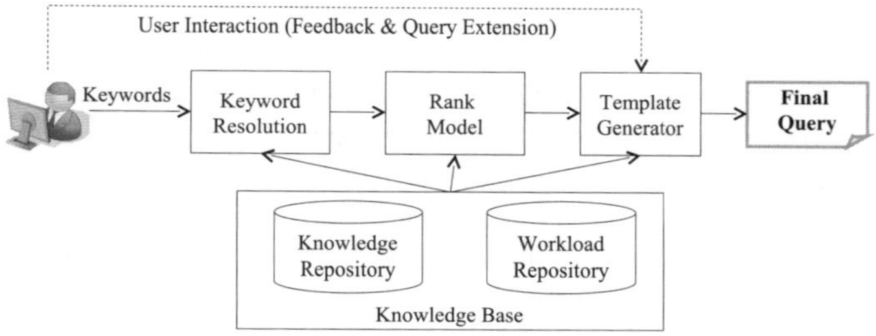

Fig. 1. Keywords to Query Formulation Steps

These query skeletons are ranked by the *Rank Model* in the order of relevancy (to the input and past usage) and shown to the user to choose one that corresponds to his/her intent. Both keyword resolution and ranking is based on the information in the *Knowledge Base*. Subsequently, a template is generated with all the details which can be further filled with additional conditions. The list of entities that are of interest, the domain and sources to which they map, and the possible list of simple conditions (e.g., $train.startTime < relationaloperator > value$) or attributes as well as join conditions (e.g., $castle.location < traditional/spatial/temporaloperator > train.startLocation$) is shown. Additionally, a list of attributes is displayed for the choice of result attributes. The user fills/modifies the template in a manner similar to filling a Web query interface so that an unambiguous and complete query can be generated for further processing.

4.1 Knowledge Base

The knowledge Base consists of a *Knowledge repository* that contains taxonomies organized by domains/context including meta-information about the entities, sources, operators, attributes and values. This is used in the keyword resolution phase and for constructing query skeletons. The knowledge base also consists of a *Workload repository* that organizes the past user of query skeleton for a set of input keywords as well as the conditions provided and output attributes selected. Workload repository, when available and statistically significant, is used for ranking.

Knowledge Repository: This repository contains pre-discovered *semantic* information in the form of a collection of taxonomies associated with domains and are populated with appropriate types of meta-data. For instance, the domain of *Travel* can be represented using taxonomies for – *transportation*, *travel lodging*, and *tourist attractions*. Similarly, the domain for *Literature* may contain taxonomies such as *journal*, *book*, etc.. These represent the roots of different taxonomies within the given domain. Nodes in each taxonomy represent entities (e.g., castle, museum, church, etc.) associated with the domain corresponding to a *is-a* relationship[1].

In addition to the *is-a* hierarchy, supplementary meta-data is associated with each node in a taxonomy. For instance, an entity *castle* in the *tourist attractions* domain may have several types of associated meta-data: i) *Web sources* (e.g., www.castles.org) from which attribute values relevant to this entity can be extracted, ii) common *attributes* (e.g., name, age, country_location) that are associated with the entity, and iii) *semantics* representing linguistic meaning and semantic popularity. Additionally, each attribute of the entity has a number of meta-data: i) data type of the attribute (e.g., string, numerics, etc.), ii) attribute category (spatial, temporal, generic), iii) possible attribute value range, and iv) synonyms. For leaf-level entities in a taxonomy, the *values* for certain categorical attributes are associated. This is needed to resolve keywords that are values themselves (e.g., London) and infer the entity for which it is a value (e.g., city). As this set can be arbitrarily large, a way to infer them (using something similar to a WordNet) instead of storing all the values is going to be important. The list of relevant Web sources corresponding to an entity can be obtained using search engines and the information associated with Web directories. The *entity-linguistic-score* based on its linguistic meaning can be captured using WordNet [12].

In addition to meta-data, the knowledge repository also contains information about the *compatibility* between entities. Two entities are said to be *compatible* if a meaningful *join* condition can be formulated between (one or more) attributes of the participating entities. For instance, the entities *castle* and *train* are compatible since their respective attributes *location* and *startLocation* can be compared. The join could result in traditional, spatial, or temporal conditions based on the attribute types and the operators associated with them. This compatibility across entities can be identified by matching the respective attribute data types. A compatibility matrix can be used as the number of operators is not that large. Compatibility information of successfully formulated past queries from the workload repository can also be used for this purpose. Another component of this repository is a list of operators that are applicable to attributes.

[1] In this paper, we assume the availability of such taxonomies. Simple taxonomies can be generated using a combination of Web directories (e.g., Yahoo Dictionary) and dictionaries (e.g., Webster).

We assume – simple relational operators (==, ! =, <, <=, >, >=), Boolean operators, temporal operators (derived from Allen's Algebra [13]), and a few spatial operators (such as near, within, etc. [14]).

It is evident that building this comprehensive knowledge repository is a separate problem in itself and is beyond the scope of this paper. Given such a repository, its completeness and algorithmic usage in formulating queries is of concern here.

Workload Repository: Past statistics based on user interaction can play an important role in the query formulation process as it indicates significance of user preferences. Hence, we maintain a repository that is a collection of statistics and feedback associated with past queries. Specifically, it comprises of the information associated with users' preference of the query skeletons from those generated by the *Rank Model*. Additionally, statistics of the attributes of entities used for specifying conditions or output are also collected. This information is used for choosing widely preferred attributes for an entity in the generation of skeletons and templates. This repository is constructed using the feedback collected as a by-product of the query formulation process. For every keyword, the following user preferences are collected: i) context of the individual keyword (e.g., *castle* belonging to the travel domain frequently chosen over others) and ii) frequency of the attributes used for specifying conditions or chosen for output.

4.2 Keyword Resolution

The purpose of this phase is to map specified keywords into the domains that are stored as part of the knowledge base. Coverage of keywords in each domain is important as it indicates the relevance of the domain to the input. This phase performs matching for each of the input keywords with – *entity* names in the taxonomies, *attribute* names associated with each node (entity) in the taxonomies, and *values* associated with leaf-level entity attributes.

Since a domain comprises multiple taxonomies, it is possible (as shown in Figure 3) that the same keyword (*castle*) will belong to multiple taxonomies (*tourist attractions* and *travel accommodations*) in a single domain (*Travel*). In such cases, determining which intent the user has in mind is not possible. Hence, the resolution phase checks for multiple instances of the same keyword in different taxonomies, each giving rise to a separate entity set (and hence, separate query intents) for each occurrence of the entity. Additionally, it is also possible for the same keyword to occur in taxonomies in multiple domains (*castle* occurs in the domains of *Travel* and *Literature* as shown in Figure 3). Hence, the resolution phase analyzes all the domains independently to get the list of entity sets within each domain.

It is possible that the keyword may not always match to an entity in the taxonomy i.e., it may match to an attribute of an entity or the value of an entity's attribute. In such cases, the immediate parent entity (to which the attribute/value belongs) is chosen to represent the input keyword. Further, the keywords not finding a match to any of these categories are compared against a

keyword	occurs as	taxonomy	domain	entity-attribute-value association
castle	entity	tourist attractions	travel	-
	entity	travel accommodation	travel	-
	value	literature	literature	book.title
train	entity	transport mode	travel	-
	value	literature	literature	book.title
	value	movie	entertainment	movie.title
london	value	city	geography	city.name
	value	literature	literature	book.author
	value	business	industry	company.name
	value	movie	entertainment	movie.title

Fig. 2. Keyword Resolution: $Q1_{K1}$

Entity Set	Domain	Taxonomies
castle, train, city	Travel	Tourist attractions, transport mode, city
castle, train, city	Travel	Travel accommodations, transport mode, city
book	Literature	Literature
movie	Entertainment	Movie

Fig. 3. Query Space: $Q1_{K1}$

set of operators to determine their occurrences as a spatial, temporal, or generic operators and an operator-list. These operator keywords do not occur in any entity set generated. The keywords that do not find any match are ignored.

Thus, for a given set of input keyword, the resolution process generates a list of entity sets belonging to the same or multiple domains where every set comprises of entities that belong to the same domain (but might map to multiple taxonomies within that domain). For instance, the outcome of the resolution process for intent $Q1_{K1}$ (for $Q1$) (based on the keyword matching results shown in Figure 2) is shown in Figure 3. As the figure indicates, it is possible that the given input may generate multiple combinations (of entities). This would make the task of separating the relevant intents from the irrelevant ones extremely hard. Hence, in order to establish an order amongst these combinations, the output generated by the *resolution* phase is fed to the *Rank Model.*

4.3 Rank Model

Since the set of entity combinations generated by the resolution process can be large, we propose a ranking technique to order these combinations based on the different characteristics of the entities in the an entity-set namely – i) linguistics, ii) statistics, and ii) join compatibility. In the rest of the section, we elaborate on each of these parameters, and explain their importance in ranking entity sets and discuss the mechanism to fuse them in a single ranking function.

Linguistics: It is a common observation [15] that *linguistic meaning* of a keyword plays an important role when users specify their input. For instance, as per WordNet [12], the keyword *castle* is considered to have the following linguistic meanings: i) a large and stately mansion, and ii) a piece in the game of chess. However, as established by WordNet, users generally use an established language model [16] to formulate their natural language queries as well as search queries. That is, they choose the meaning which is linguistically more popular than the rest of the meanings for the same keyword (in this case the former meaning of *castle* will be chosen over the latter in most cases). Thus, there is reason to believe that when users express their keyword input to formulate queries over multiple domains, they will use a similar language model of picking linguistically popular meanings for an entity.

Based on this observation, we assign a *entity-linguistic-score* to every entity in a taxonomy. The linguistic meanings for a given entity are obtained from WordNet, which gives the meanings for an entity in a ranked order such that the most popular linguistic meaning has a rank of 1. However, since we need to calculate a combined *linguistic score* for every entity set generated by the resolution process, we normalize WordNet's rank into a *entity-linguistic-score* (given by Equation 1). For an entity e_i whose WordNet rank is e_{rank}, and for which WordNet has a list of n distinct meanings:

$$entity\,linguistic\,score(e_i) = 1 - \frac{e_{rank} - 1}{n - 1} \tag{1}$$

Given an entity set $\{e_1, e_2, ..., e_n\}$, the ***linguistic-score*** for an entity set is calculated as a *product* of the individual *entity-linguistic-scores* using the independence assumption. That is, the entities in a set are not associated with each other in a linguistic context. For example, the *linguistic score* for the entity set $\{castle, train, andcity\}$ representing the input $Q1_{K1}$ is calculated as a product of the individual *entity-linguistic-scores* associated with *castle*, *train*, and *city*.

Statistics: Although linguistics can play an important role in ordering entity sets, it is based on a global language model which is static thus gives the same ordering for a given input. However, this order can be different as observed by the user behavior. Hence, in addition to linguistics, we also analyze the entity sets in terms of past user preferences i.e., we use the *usage statistics* associated with past user queries from the *workload repository* in our *Knowledge Base* as another component of the ranking model.

Based on the workload, an entity set that has been selected more number of times for the *same* input would rank higher. However, as is the case with ranking in general, it is not possible to have an exhaustive query workload which covers every possible query. In the absence of an exact query, we make the *independence assumption* i.e., we consider the statistics for individual entities of the combination and apply the product function to combine them. Hence, the statistics score for an entity set $\{e_1, e_2, ..., e_n\}$ is the product of the individual *entity-statistics-score*. For instance, the keywords input $Q1_{K1}$ may not exist in the query workload but entities *castle*, *train* and *London* may exist in different queries, either together with additional keywords or independently with other keywords. In this case, the *statistics score* for an entity set $\{castle, train, city\}$ representing the input $Q1_{K1}$ is calculated as outlined above.

Join Compatibility: Given an entity set $\{e_1, e_2, ..., e_n\}$, the user would most likely be interested in formulating query conditions that involve joining different entities based on the commonality of the attributes between the entities. Since, the exact query conditions at this stage cannot be determined, we believe that an entity set that allows the flexibility to join every entity to every other entity on some attribute is definitely desirable than a set that offers very less joins across entities. In addition, the flexibility to join any two entities on a larger

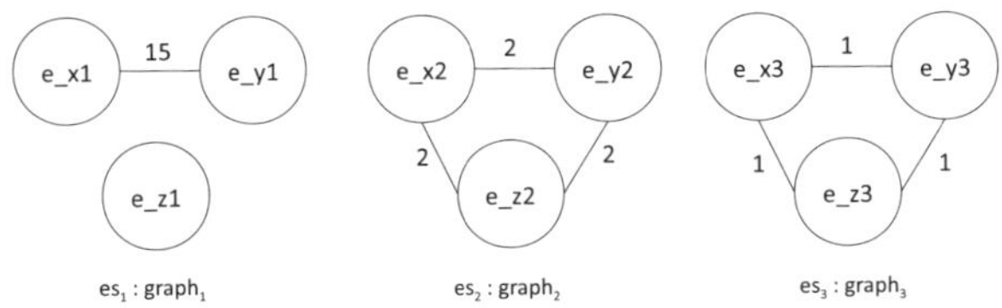

Fig. 4. Join compatibility for keyword combinations

number of attributes (instead of just one or two) is definitely desirable. Hence, for every entity-set, we define a ***join-compatibility-score***.

Consider the entity set $\{castle, train, city\}$ representing the input $Q1_{K1}$. It is possible to join the entities *castle* and *train* based on an attribute (e.g., location), the entities *train* and *city* based on an attribute (e.g., location) and the entities *castle* and *city* based on an attribute (e.g., name, location). On the other hand, an entity set $\{book, city\}$ representing the input $Q1_{K1}$ (considering the keywords 'castle' and 'train' refer to the name of a book i.e., its attribute value), will not allow any joins between the two entities and restrict a number of query conditions the user would like to formulate. Thus, it is clear that the first entity set should be ranked higher than the second.

Consider a list of entity sets $L = \{e_{s1}, e_{s2}, ..., e_{sm}\}$ where e_{si} represents a set of entities $\{e_1, e_2, ..., e_n\}$. We represent each entity set e_{si} by a graph G_i where the entities in the set represent the vertices of the graph. If any two entities in the set can be joined on an attribute, then an edge exists between the corresponding two vertices (representing the entities). The edge weight is represented by the total number of distinct attributes that can be used for the joining the two entities. For instance, consider the graphs representing the three entity sets shown in Figure 4. For the first graph, the vertices e_{x1}, e_{y1}, e_{z1} correspond to the entities in the entity set e_{s1}. The edge and the weight (15) between e_{x1} and e_{y1} indicates that the two entities can be joined on 15 different attributes.

Considering 'n' to be the maximum number vertices in a graph, the maximum number of edges is given as $m = n(n-1)/2$. We then sort the graphs (corresponding to the entity sets) based on the decreasing order of the number of edges. If two graphs have the same number of graphs, the tie is broken by running a maximum spanning tree (MST) that ranks the graphs based on the edge weights. From the above ordering of graphs, we achieve a final *join compatibility score* for every entity set in L by normalizing the rank of its graph (similar to method in Equation 1).

Putting it all Together: We have discussed three distinct components that play an important role in the ranking of entity sets. Since they are derived from linguistics, statistics, and join possibilities, we believe that when combined together, they form a comprehensive and suitable model to order the set of keyword combinations. We propose *logistic regression* to model our ranking function since it is a well-established and proven model used for predicting the outcome of an event when the parameters influencing the event are diverse and unrelated to each other (as is the case with our components). Initially, we set uniform regression parameters i.e., equal weight to every parameter (linguistics, statistics and join compatibility) to rank the entity sets. As more and more workload is collected, we believe it will act as a major component in generating a significant training data to learn the parameter weights.

4.4 Query Completion

Based on the previous phases, our approach generates a template with a partially-filled query. Each keyword in the input is accounted for. For an entity, the template is populated by its corresponding domain and the underlying Web source to which it belongs. For instance, for $Q1_{K1}$: $Intent01$ selected by the user where *castle* represents a *tourist attraction*, *train* represents the *transportation mode*, and *London* is identified as a *city*. For this intent, the domains (tourist attractions, transportation) and sources (www.castles.org) are populated.

For an attribute, if the attribute has not been listed in the query template in the first step, it is analyzed for its type (spatial, temporal, generic) and the entity associated with it is obtained to formulate query conditions of the type: *entity.attribute* {*operator*} {*value*}. If this attribute can be formulated as an integration condition, then the corresponding conditions are formulated. Similarly, if the attribute is a popular choice for the output, then the `SELECT` clause is populated with it. For a value (e.g., London), the corresponding attribute and its parent entity are derived and condition of the type *city.name* == *London* is formed. For operators, if they are not listed in the template in the above steps, the possible conditions between the entities for which the operators are applicable are analyzed and modified accordingly. For instance, if an *operator* "near" is specified for the above intent, then the integration condition can be modified as: *castle.location near* {*train.startLocation*, *train.endLocation*, *city.Location*}. As the last stage of user interaction, the template is filled/modified by the user based on his/her preferences and the complete query (similar to $Complete_Q$ *1*) is formulated that captures the exact user intent in terms of constraints and conditions across multiple domains.

5 Conclusion

In this paper, we have presented a novel approach to query specification it's usefulness for web users who are familiar with keyword search. This approach needs further attention. We have also demonstrated how this approach can be carried out with the help of a knowledge base consisting of a knowledge repository and a workload repository. We have detailed the steps involved in the generation of a query skeleton, its ranking, and how a complete query can be generated with meaningful user interaction. The project on information integration, InfoMosaic, currently underway is working on this as well as the subsequent phases of query transformation, optimization, and execution.

References

1. Hristidis, V., Papakonstantinou, Y.: DISCOVER: Keyword Search in Relational Databases. In: VLDB, pp. 670–681 (2002)
2. Nie, Z., Kambhampati, S., Hernandez, T.: BibFinder/StatMiner: Effectively Mining and Using Coverage and Overlap Statistics in Data Integration. In: VLDB, pp. 1097–1100 (2003)
3. Cohen, W.W.: A Demonstration of WHIRL. In: SIGIR (1999)
4. Telang, A., Chakravarthy, S., Huang, Y.: Information integration across heterogeneous sources: Where do we stand and how to proceed? In: International Conference on Management of Data (COMAD), pp. 186–197 (2008)
5. Braga, D., Ceri, S., Daniel, F., Martinenghi, D.: Optimization of multi-domain queries on the web. In: PVLDB, vol. 1(1), pp. 562–573 (2008)
6. Zloof, M.M.: Query-by-example: A data base language. IBM Systems Journal 16(4), 324–343 (1977)
7. Petropoulos, M., Deutsch, A., Papakonstantinou, Y.: Clide: Interactive query formulation for service oriented architectures. In: SIGMOD Conference, pp. 1119–1121 (2007)
8. zu Eissen, S.M., Stein, B.: Analysis of Clustering Algorithms for Web-Based Search. In: PAKM, pp. 168–178 (2002)
9. Katz, B., Lin, J.J., Quan, D.: Natural Language Annotations for the Semantic Web. In: CoopIS/DOA/ODBASE, pp. 1317–1331 (2002)
10. Madhavan, J., Cohen, S., Dong, X.L., Halevy, A.Y., Jeffery, S.R., Ko, D., Yu, C.: Web-Scale Data Integration: You can afford to Pay as You Go. In: CIDR, pp. 342–350 (2007)
11. Ley, M.: Faceted DBLP. dblp.l3s.de/ (2006)
12. Miller, G.A.: WordNet: A Lexical Database for English. Commun. ACM 38(11), 39–41 (1995)
13. Allen, J.F.: Maintaining knowledge about temporal intervals. ACM Communications 26(11), 832–843 (1983), http://dx.doi.org/10.1145/182.358434
14. Fonseca, F., Egenhofer, M., Agouris, P., Camara, G.: Using ontologies for integrated geographic information systems. Transactions in Geographic Information Systems 3 (2002)
15. Abadi, D.J., Marcus, A., Madden, S.R., Hollenbach, K.: Scalable Semantic Web Data Management Using Vertical Partitioning. In: International Conference on Very Large Databases (VLDB), pp. 411–422 (2007)
16. Waldinger, R., Appelt, D.E., Fry, J., Israel, D.J., Jarvis, P., Martin, D., Riehemann, S., Stickel, M.E., Tyson, M., Hobbs, J., Dungan, J.L.: Deductive question answering from multiple resources. In: New Directions in Question Answering. AAAI, Menlo Park (2004)

Cluster-Based Exploration for Effective Keyword Search over Semantic Datasets

Roberto De Virgilio[1], Paolo Cappellari[2], and Michele Miscione[1]

[1] Dipartimento di Informatica e Automazione
Universitá Roma Tre, Rome, Italy
{dvr,miscione}@dia.uniroma3.it
[2] Department of Computing Science
University of Alberta, Canada
cappellari@cs.ualberta.ca

Abstract. The amount of data available in the Web, in databases as well as other systems, is constantly increasing as increasing is the number of users that wish to access such data. Data is available in forms that may not be of easy access for not expert users. Keyword Search approaches are an effort to abstract from specific data representations, allowing users to retrieve information by providing a few terms of interest. Many solutions build on dedicated indexing techniques as well as search algorithms aiming at finding substructures that connect the data elements matching the keywords. In this paper, we present the development of Yaanii[1], a tool for effective Keyword Search over semantic datasets. Yaanii is based on a novel keyword search paradigm for graph-structured data, focusing in particular on the RDF data model. We provide a clustering technique that identifies and groups graph substructures based on template match. A scoring function, IR inspired, evaluates the relevance of the substructures and of the clusters, and supports the generation of Top-k solutions during its execution in the first k steps. Experiments demonstrate the effectiveness of our approach.

1 Introduction

Keyword search over graph-structured data is receiving a lot of attention from the database community because: (i) data available on the Web, XML documents and even relational database can be represented as a graph, (ii) keyword search does not require users to know the structure and the language to access data, and (iii) many graph structured data have no obvious schema (and query language). Current approaches rely on a combination of IR and tree or graph exploration techniques to overcome to the absence of an explicit schema, whose final goal is to rank results according to a relevance criterion. Keyword search on tree-structured data counts a good number of approaches already [2,3,5,6,8,12,15]. In this context many efforts focus on RDF data querying, given the great momentum of *Semantic Web* in which Web pages carry information that can be read and understood by machines in a systematic way. In many approaches, for instance [7,10], an exact matching between keywords and labels of data elements

[1] Yaanii, literally "path" in Sanskrit.

A.H.F. Laender et al. (Eds.): ER 2009, LNCS 5829, pp. 205–218, 2009.

is performed to obtain the keyword elements. For the exploration of the data graph, the so-called distinct root assumption is employed. Under this assumption, only substructures in the form of trees with distinct roots are computed and the root element is assumed to be the answer. Alternatively instead of computing answers directly, a more recent technique [19] first computes conjunctive queries from the keywords, allowing the user to choose the most appropriate, and finally, processes the selected query using a database engine [1,4]. In this case the answer is not a tree but a subgraph structure.

Simplifying, a generic approach first identifies the parts of the data structure matching the keywords of interest, possibly by using an indexing system or a database engine, then explores the data structure in order to discover a connection between such identified parts. Pruning techniques are implemented on the graph structure in order to overcome the intrinsic inefficiency of graph exploration paradigms. Candidate solutions, built on found connections, are first generated, then ranked through a scoring function. Top-k solutions are computed after all candidate ones have been generated.

In this paper we propose a novel approach to keyword search in the graph-structure data. We focus on RDF representation because it is a framework for (Web) resources description standardized by W3C and it explicitly builds on graphs. The approach aims to provide effective answers and computes the Top-k solutions in the first k steps. Although we make use of indexing techniques and we try to optimize computation in general, the focus of this paper is on effectiveness, so efficiency will not be discussed.

The main contributions of this paper are:

- A clustering technique that reduces the search space by avoiding the exploration of overlapping solutions. We analyze the paths, in the graph, matching the keywords and we extract their schemas. We refer to such extracted schemas as *templates*. Paths with the same template are grouped together in a cluster, each cluster being represented by a template. Solutions, answers to the input search, are built by composing paths in different templates, leveraging on the schema-instance paradigm. Excluding by algorithm the exploration of overlapping solutions, we gain in terms of computation cost.
- An algorithm that ranks solutions while it builds them. Unlike most of the approaches to keyword search that first identify all the solutions and then rank them, our approach leverages on the clusters to assembly a solution starting with the most relevant path in the most relevant cluster. As a result, the most relevant solution is the first to come out of the algorithm, then decreasing monotonically to the less relevant solutions. This allows users to explore the returned solutions, starting with the most relevant, while the elaboration of remaining solutions is undergoing.
- Scoring functions for both paths and clusters that balance the relevance of the keywords with their distribution in the structures. Intuitively, each path has a score that depends on the matched keywords and their relative positions in the path, while the score of a cluster is related to its most promising path. While scores of paths are constant with a given query, scores of clusters vary: when a path is composed in a solution it is removed from the cluster, whose score changes, as a consequence.

We implemented our approach into a tool, Yaanii, and we executed experiments on a real dataset to prove the effectiveness of results. The paper is organized as follows: Section 2 introduces the problem and a running example. Section 3 illustrates the data structures used. Section 4 describes query processing in detail, and Section 5 experimental results. Finally Section 6 discusses related works, and Section 7 sketches conclusions and future works.

2 Scenario of Reference

Problem Definition. Formally, the problem we are trying to solve may be defined as follows. Given a directed graph $G = (R, P)$, where each node (resource) r ∈ R and each edge (property) p ∈ P present a label (i.e. the URI of the resource, the name of the property), a query Q composed of a set of keywords, we find the answers $S_1, S_2, \ldots, S_k$ to Q where S_i is a set of paths in G where the final node r_f of each path satisfies one of the following:

- There exists some keyword $k \in Q$ that matches the label of node r_f either lexically or on semantic query expansion;
- There exists some keyword $k \in Q$ that matches the label of a property p, either lexically or on semantic query expansion, directly connected with r_f

In the graph G we call *roots* the nodes (resources) without incoming edges (properties).

An example of reference. Let's consider the example in Figure 1. It illustrates an ontology about Universities composed of Departments where a Staff works. The figure shows both the schema and a corresponding instance. We process a query composed of the keywords **University, CIV, Department, W1** that is *"all information about the Staff W1 working in a Department CIV into a University."*

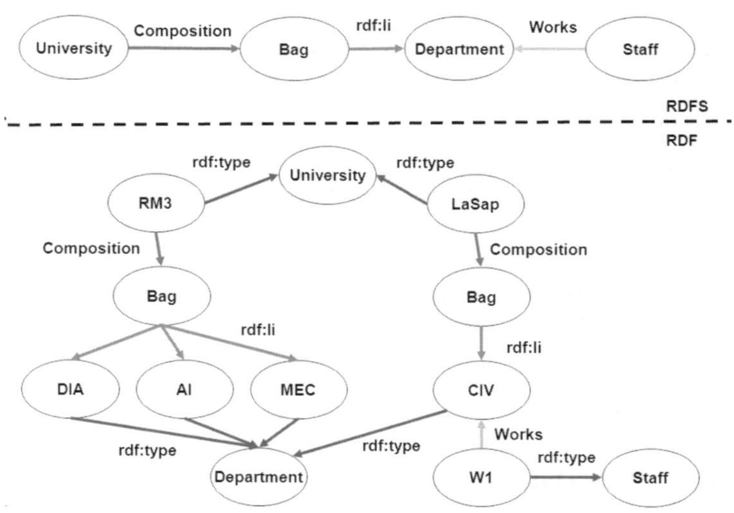

Fig. 1. An example of reference

3 Preliminaries

Before presenting our approach, let us introduce some definitions.

Definition 1 (Informative Path). *Given a directed graph graph G = (R,P) and a query Q, an informative path pt is in terms of* $r_1 - p_1 - r_2 - p_2 - ... - p_{n-1} - r_f$ *where each* r_i *is a resource* $\in R$*, each* p_i *is a property* $\in P$*, at least* r_f *matches a keyword* $k_i \in Q$ *(i.e. others* r_i *can match one or more keywords in case), and* r_1 *is a root. Moreover we say that each* r_i *(*p_i*) is a token in pt.*

For instance `W1-Works-CIV` is an informative path pt_k with tokens `W1`, `Works`, `CIV`. We use the notation $pos_{pt_k}(r_i)$ (or $pos_{pt_k}(p_j)$) to indicate the position of r_i (or p_j) in pt_k. For example $pos_{pt_k}(W1)$ returns 1. We compute the informative paths from root nodes because they allow to reach any node in the graph. In case a root node is not present, a fictitious one can be added. Having the information to navigate from the roots to nodes matching keywords is at the basis of our approach to build solutions. Given the informative paths, we extract their schemas: we refer to each schema as *template*.

Definition 2 (Template). *Given an informative path pt, we associate a template t to pt replacing each* $r_i \in pt$ *with the wild card #*

For instance the template t_{pt_k} associated to pt_k is `#-Works-#`. We say that pt_k *satisfies* t_{pt_k}, denoted by $pt_k \approx t_{pt_k}$. Then we introduce two basic notions as follows.

Definition 3 (Subsumption). *Given two informative paths* pt_1 *and* pt_2*, we say that* pt_1 *is subsumed by* pt_2*, denoted by* $pt_1 \lhd pt_2$*, if* $\forall r_i, p_j \in pt_1$ *then* $\exists r_m, p_n \in pt_2$ *such that* $r_i = r_m$ *and* $p_j = p_n$*, and* $pos_{pt_1}(r_i) = pos_{pt_2}(r_m)$ *and* $pos_{pt_1}(p_j) = pos_{pt_2}(p_n)$

Definition 4 (Graft). *Given two informative paths* pt_1 *and* pt_2*, there is a graft between* pt_1 *and* pt_2*, denoted by* $pt_1 \leftrightarrow pt_2$*, if* $\exists r_i \in pt_1$ *and* $\exists r_j \in pt_2$ *such that* $r_i = r_j$

Definition 5 (Cluster). *A Cluster Cl is a set of informative paths* $pt_1, pt_2, \ldots, pt_n$ *such that each* pt_i *matches the same template* t_{Cl} *(i.e.* $\forall pt_i \in Cl : pt_i \approx t_{Cl}$*)*

Informative paths are clustered according to their templates. In other words, a cluster Cl, represented by a template t_{Cl}, is a set of informative paths that share the same template t_{Cl}. Templates are the attempt of identifying and giving values to a structure in the information graph which is not explicitly provided with the query. We assume such a structure as the schema of the underlying data.

Finally a solution S is a directed graph built on a set of informative paths presenting pairwise grafts. The definition follows

Definition 6 (Solution). *A solution S is a set of informative paths* $pt_1, pt_2, \ldots, pt_n$ *where for each* pt_i *there exists* $pt_j \in S$ *such that* $pt_i \leftrightarrow pt_j$ *with* $i \neq j$*.*

4 Semantic Web Data Management

The approach is composed of two main phases: an *off-line indexing* where documents of interest are indexed in order to have immediate access to nodes, and the *keyword processing* (on-the-fly) where the query evaluation takes place.

4.1 Off-Line Indexing

This is the only off-line phase. During this phase, an index structure is built and incrementally updated while documents of interest are loaded or modified. While indexing, we augment the information in the graph by identifying the root nodes in the graph and by associating each node in the graph with the paths to reach such node from the roots. Each path (i.e. the shortest) is computed by implementing the breadth-first search (BFS) algorithm [13]. We remark BFS is exhaustive and does not use a heuristic. Moreover BFS is complete. This means that if there is a solution breadth-first search will find it regardless of the kind of graph. In particular, for unit-step cost, breadth-first search is optimal. Since the graph is not weighted, and therefore all step costs are equal, breadth-first search will find the nearest and the best solution. Moreover we enrich information associated to a node with the incoming properties and the set of synonyms (as for the node as for the incoming properties) to allow query expansion. In this phase, the indexing is supported by Lucene[2] and query expansion by WordNet [3].

For instance we store the following information for the node `University`

```
name: University

propIn: type

paths: [RM3-type-University], [LaSap-type-University]

nodeSynonyms: null

propSynonyms: case, character, eccentric, typecast, typewrite
```

The fields `nodeSynonyms, propSynonyms` represent the semantic expansion of `name, propIn` respectively.

Although this process could be expensive, let us remark that: (i) it is an incremental process, so its cost dramatically reduces once the system is loaded, and (ii) the index drastically speeds up the on-the-fly query evaluation. We do not have to navigate the graph at runtime and we have immediate access to the path root-matching node that is the basis for our clustering and solution construction.

4.2 Scoring of Data

Scoring function assesses the relevance of the computed queries. The database and information retrieval communities extensively discussed several scoring functions [7,17,18,19]. In this context common metrics proposed often consider both the graph structure and the label of graph elements. The former is evaluated by the path length, commonly used as a basic metric for ranking answer in recent approaches to keyword queries, the latter through specific implementation of TF/IDF (Term Frequency and Inverse Document Frequency) for scoring keyword elements.

In our approach, the scoring function aims to reflect both content and structural elements. Results to a query (i.e. solutions) are sub-graphs composed of informative paths. More in detail, the computation of queries meets three main *elements*, that are

[2] `http://lucene.apache.org/`

[3] `http://wordnet.princeton.edu`

informative paths, clusters and solutions. Each of them should be evaluated by a *score*. Then we define the score of an element with respect to a query $Q = k_1, k_2, \ldots, k_n$ as

$$R(e, Q) = \sum_{k \in Q} weight(k, Q) \cdot weight(k, e) \; ; weight(k, e) = \frac{weight_{ct}(k,e)}{weight_{str}(k,e)}$$

where $weight(k, Q)$ is the weight associated with each keyword k with respect to the query Q and $weight(k, e)$ is the weight associated with each keyword k with respect to the element e (i.e. a path, a cluster or a solution). Without loosing in generality, we assume that all the keywords in the input query have the same weight, i.e. from the user point of view all the keywords have the same relevance. However our approach is parametric with respect to $weight(k, Q)$, so a user can set the relevance of a keyword in a query based on different criteria (e.g distinguishing a property from a resource).

$weight(k, e)$ is the ratio between the *content* and the *structural* weights of k when considering e, where e changes with the stages of the query processing. Inspired by the pivoted normalization weighting method [17,18], one of the most used weighting methods in IR, $weight_{ct}$ aims to capture the *commonness* of a keyword k in the graph with respect to the element e, measured by the relative number of graph elements which it actually represents. The higher the commonness, the lower should its contribution be to the cost of e. $weight_{str}$ exploits the structural features of e, evaluating the *proximity* (distance) of a keyword k from the other keywords in e. The higher the structural weight, the lower should the proximity and its contribution be to the cost of e.

In details, we define the content and structural weights of an informative path pt with respect to a keyword k as follows

$$weight_{ct}(k, pt) = (1 + ln(1 + tf)) \cdot (1 + \frac{dl}{avg(dl)}) \cdot (1 + ln(\frac{N}{df+1}))$$

$$weight_{str}(k, pt) = \overline{d}_{pt}(k, Q) \cdot \frac{nt}{dl}; \; \overline{d}_{pt}(k, Q) = \frac{\sum_{k_i \in Q, k_i \neq k} d_{pt}(k, k_i)}{|Q|-1}$$

In $weight_{ct}(k, pt)$, pt is an informative path, tf is the number of times the keyword k occurs in pt, N is the number of paths containing at least one of the input keywords, df is the number of paths where k occurs, dl is the number of tokens in pt matching a keyword and $avg(dl)$ is the mean of all dl in all N paths. The logarithm function is used to smooth the values in presence of large numbers of terms and keywords. In $weight_{str}(k, pt)$, nt is the number of tokens in pt, dl has the same meaning as in $weight_{ct}(k, pt)$, $d_{pt}(k, k_i)$ is the distance between the tokens in pt matching the keywords k and k_i, that is the number of properties between the two tokens. Therefore $\overline{d}_{pt}(k, Q)$ is the mean distance between k and other k_i contained in pt. Let us consider that $\overline{d}_{pt}(k, Q)$ is 1 if k does not occur in pt or pt contains only k as keyword, and $d_{pt}(k, k_i)$ is 1 if $k_i \notin pt$ while $k \in pt$.

$weight_{ct}(k, pt)$ measures the commonness of a keyword k in terms of tf, df and dl. This weight is normalized with $weight_{str}(k, pt)$ that evaluates the structural correlation between the keywords matched (i.e. in terms of distance). $weight_{str}(k, pt)$ exploits the ratio between the length of pt and the number of *matching* tokens. In other words, it represents the percentage of matching tokens of pt and how they are correlated with respect the overall structure. By merging the contextual and the structural contributions, we have a score balanced between content and structural features.

A cluster Cl is evaluated with respect to its most representative path. Therefore the score of Cl is the highest score recurring in contained paths. Finally, the score of a solution is measured by the following function, similarly to how we measure the score of an informative path.

$$weight_{ct}(k,S) = (1 + ln(1 + ln(1 + tf))) \cdot (1 + \frac{\overline{dl}_S}{avg(dl)}) \cdot (1 + ln(\frac{N}{\frac{ln(df_S+1)}{ln(DF+1)}+1}))$$

$$weight_{str}(k,S) = \overline{d}_S(k,Q) \cdot \frac{NT}{DL};\ \overline{d}_S(k,Q) = \frac{\sum_{k_i \in Q, k_i \neq k} d_S(k,k_i)}{|Q|-1}$$

In $weight_{ct}(k, S)$, S is a solution, tf is the overall term frequency of k in S, $\overline{dl}_S$ is the mean number of keywords matched by the paths contained in S while $avg(dl)$ has the same meaning as described above. df_S is the number of paths in S where k occurs and DF is the number of overall paths where k occurs. Since DF could be much dominant over df_S, we use the logarithm to smooth the values. In $weight_{str}(k, S)$, NT is the number of tokens in S (i.e the total number of tokens from all paths in S) and DL the number of tokens in S matching a keyword. Finally $d_S(k, k_i)$ is the length of the shortest path between k and k_i in S calculated by using the Dijkstra algorithm, while $\overline{d}_S(k, Q)$ is the mean. As for an informative path, $\overline{d}_S(k, Q)$ is 1 if S does not contain a token matching k or if S contains tokens matching only k, and $d_S(k, k_i)$ is 1 if S does not contain a token matching k_i while a token in S matching k exists.

4.3 Computation of Queries

Given a keyword the index allows immediate access to the nodes with such a keyword. The index returns, also, all the informative paths from the roots to the nodes matching one of the specified keywords. We sort the list of informative paths by their length (i.e. number of tokens). Referring to our example we have:

```
(c) [score:  2,06] [RM3-Composition-Bag-rdf:li-DIA-type-Department]
(d) [score:  2,06] [RM3-Composition-Bag-rdf:li-AI-type-Department]
(e) [score:  2,06] [RM3-Composition-Bag-rdf:li-MEC-type-Department]
(f) [score: 11,85] [LaSap-Composition-Bag-rdf:li-CIV-type-Department]
(z) [score:  2,93] [LaSap-Composition-Bag-rdf:li-CIV]
(g) [score: 23,65] [W1-Works-CIV-type-Department]
(a) [score:  5,70] [RM3-type-University]
(b) [score:  5,70] [LaSap-type-University]
(y) [score: 22,10] [W1-Works-CIV]
```

We denote each path with a letter and we indicate the scores associated beside them. Path (y) is subsumed by (g) and there is a graft between the two in nodes $W1$ and CIV.

Clustering. Given the list PT of informative paths, we group the paths in clusters according to their template, and we return the set CL of all the clusters. We implement both a cluster and the set of clusters CL by using priority queues. In the former the priority is the score of an informative path (in descendant order), in the latter the priority is the score of a cluster (in descendant order). Therefore CL is computed as shown in Algorithm 1. In the algorithm the main step is to compare a path pt with CL. We

Algorithm 1. Clustering of Informative Paths

Input : An ordered List PT of informative paths, a query Q
Output: A Priority Queue CL of clusters

1 $\mathsf{CL}' \leftarrow$ `CreateSet();`
2 **while** PT *is not empty* **do**
3   PT- $\{pt\}$;
4   **if** $\exists Cl_i \in \mathsf{CL}' : pt \approx t_{Cl_i}$ **then**
5   **if** $\nexists pt' \in Cl_j : (Cl_j \in \mathsf{CL}'$ *and* $pt \lhd pt')$ **then**
6   `Enqueue(`*pt*, `Score(`*pt*,Q`)`, Cl_i`);`
7   `UpdateScore(`Cl_i`);`
8   **else**
9         $Cl_i \leftarrow$ `CreateCluster(`*pt*`);`
10   `Enqueue(`*pt*, `Score(`*pt*,Q`)`, Cl_i`);`
11         $\mathsf{CL}' \cup \{Cl_i\}$;
12 CL $\leftarrow$ `OrderClusters(`CL$'$`);`
13 **return** CL;

initialize a set CL'. If there exists a cluster Cl_i with a template t_{Cl_i} such that pt matches t_{Cl_i} (i.e. $pt \approx t_{Cl_i}$) and pt is not subsumed by another path pt' contained in a cluster Cl_j of CL' then we insert pt into Cl_i and update the score of Cl_i (lines 4 to 7). If pt is subsumed by pt' we skip the insertion and extract a new pt. If Cl_i does not exist then we create it, we insert pt into CL_i, we set the score of CL_i and insert it into CL' (lines 8 to 11). At the end, we generate the priority queue CL from CL'. The algorithm is supported by functions to execute different operations such as inserting a path pt into a cluster Cl_i in order (i.e. `Enqueue`) or updating the score of Cl_i (i.e. `UpdateScore`).

In the following we show the resulting CL computed over the reference example, indicating the score associated to each cluster.

```
Cl3: [score: 23,65] [#-Works-#-type-#] { (g) }
Cl2: [score: 11,85] [#-Composition-#-rdf:li-#-type-#] { (f) , (c,d,e) }
Cl1: [score:  5,70] [#-type-#] { (a,b) }
```

Building Top-n Solutions. The final step is combining the paths from different clusters to build a solution that answer the input query. A solution is a set of informative paths that present a graft in pairs. In Algorithm 2 we illustrate the generation of Top-n solutions. Paths in clusters are combined, when possible, starting from the most relevant paths in the most relevant cluster (lines 3 to 11). When including an informative path into a solution, we delete it from the cluster Cl', we update the score of Cl' and we insert it into the *visited* clusters set V. Then we combine the best candidate paths of each following cluster (i.e. in order of score value) to compose a single solution (lines 12 to 27). A path pt'' can be composed with a solution S_i with an initial score $R_{in}(S_i, Q)$, if $\exists pt \in S_i$ such that pt' presents a graft with pt and the final score $R_{fin}(S_i, Q)$ of S_i (i.e. including pt') satisfies a *tolerance threshold* τ (lines 15 to 18). We experimentally determined the threshold τ as $\frac{|V|}{|CL|+1}$, that is the ratio between the number of visited clusters $|V|$ and the number of current clusters in CL, increased with 1 ($|CL| + 1$).

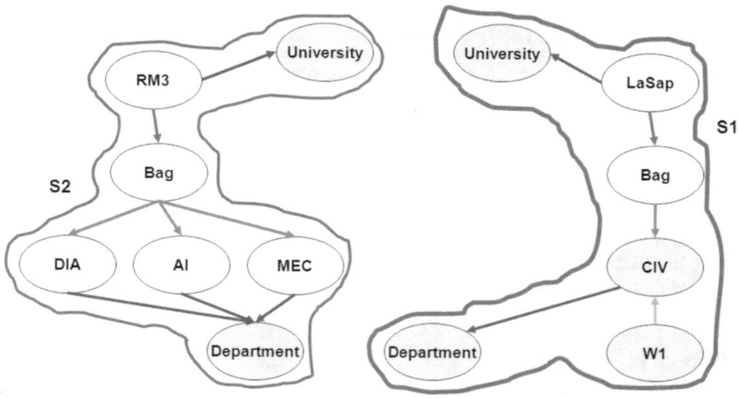

Fig. 2. Final Solutions

The satisfaction condition is $\frac{R_{fin}(S_i,Q)}{R_{in}(S_i,Q)} \geq \tau$. So the tolerance diminishes with the decreasing score of occurred paths. This is to guarantee the significance of the solution. When we generate a solution, we update the queue CL with the cluster in V (lines 26 to 30). Finally the solutions generation ends when we return n solutions or the set CL is empty. Because of the ranking on both clusters and paths in each cluster, solutions are returned starting with the most relevant one, descending to the least relevant.

Let us consider our running example. We want to generate the Top-10 answers with respect the query Q described in Section 2. We start from $Cl3$ and initialize the first solution $S1$ with the path (g). The current score $R_{in}(S1, Q)$ of $S1$ is $29, 17$. Then we consider the path (f) of $CL2$. We have to compare (f) with $S1$. If we include (f) into $S1$ we obtain a resulting score $R_{fin}(S1, Q)$ that is $14, 44$. Since the threshold τ is $\frac{1}{3+1} = 0, 25$ and $\frac{R_{fin}(S1,Q)}{R_{in}(S1,Q)}$ is $0, 49$, we can compose $S1$ with (f). Then we have to compare the updated solution $S1$ with (a, b). We can not compose (a) because it has not a graft with $S1$, while (b) presents a graft. We have $R_{fin}(S1, Q) = 7, 23$, $\tau = \frac{2}{3+1} = 0, 5$ and $\frac{R_{fin}(S1,Q)}{R_{in}(S1,Q)} = 0, 501 \geq \tau$. So we can compose (b) with $S1$. Following the process, at the end we result two solutions $S1$: [score: 7,23] {(g) , (f) , (b)} and $S2$: [score: 2,80] {(c,d,e) , (a)}, depicted in Figure 2. Together, the clustering and the path-combining techniques guarantee the generation of Top-n solutions in the first returning results. Moreover the combination of paths conforming to different schemas implicitly avoids the computation of overlapping solutions. Overlapping is undesired and time consuming.

5 Experimental Results

Experiments have been done to evaluate the effectiveness of our framework. In this section we relate on them.

RDF Benchmark. We used the public available DBLP monthly updated dataset, about computer science publications that has been commonly used for keyword search evaluation. It is a conversion of the DBLP dump into RDF and consists of roughly 26

Algorithm 2. Building of Top-n Solutions

```
Input  : A Priority Queue CL of clusters, a number n, a query Q
Output: An Ordered List S of solutions
V ← CreateSet();
for i ← 1 to n do
    S_i ← CreateSet(); Cl' ← Dequeue(CL ); PT' ← Dequeue(Cl');
    if Cl' is not empty then
        UpdateScore(Cl');
        V ∪ {Cl'};
    τ ← UpdateThreshold(V,CL);
    foreach pt' ∈ PT' do S_i ∪ { pt'};
    for j ← 1 to Size(CL) do
        Cl'' ← Dequeue(CL );
        PT'' ← Dequeue(Cl'');
        foreach pt'' ∈ PT'' do
            if Comparable(pt'', S_i, τ, Q) then
                PT'' - {pt''};
                S_i ∪ {pt''};
        if PT'' is not empty then
            foreach pt'' ∈ PT'' do Enqueue(pt'',Score(pt'',Q),Cl'');
        else
            if Cl'' is not empty then
                UpdateScore(Cl”);
                V ∪ {Cl''};
        τ ← UpdateThreshold(V,CL);
    InsertTail(S_i, S);
    while V is not empty do
        V- {Cl'''};
        Enqueue(Cl''',Score(Cl''',Q),CL);
return S;
```

million triples[4]. Therefore it provides a good (real) sample of the unstructured nature of Semantic Web data. The DBLP data structure is based on a custom ontology[5]. We implemented eight test queries as shown in Table 1. We query both resources and properties in the dataset. In particular we selected keywords matching a relevant amount of nodes. Let us consider properties `has-author`, `cites-publication-reference`, and `edited-by` occurring in 2.861.036 triples, 591.161 triples and 24.955 triples respectively. Our benchmarking system is a dual quad core 2.66GHz Intel Xeon, running Linux Gentoo, 8 GB of memory, 6 MB cache, and a 2-disk 1Tbyte striped RAID array.

[4] The dataset is split into smaller chunks. Each chunk corresponds to a specific *year* and it is available at `http://dblp.rkbexplorer.com/models/dblp-publications-$year$`

[5] Available at `http://www.aktors.org/ontology/portal` and `http://www.aktors.org/ontology/extension`

Table 1. Test Queries

Query	keywords
Q1	'paolo atzeni' '2008'
Q2	'paolo atzeni' 'edited-by'
Q3	'paolo atzeni' 'has-author'
Q4	'torlone' '2008' 'has-author'
Q5	'paolo atzeni' 'edited-by' 'has-author'
Q6	'torlone' 'cites-publication-reference' 'has-author'
Q7	'paolo atzeni' 'data' 'cites-publication-reference' 'has-author'
Q8	'torlone' 'paolo atzeni' 'data' 'cites-publication-reference'

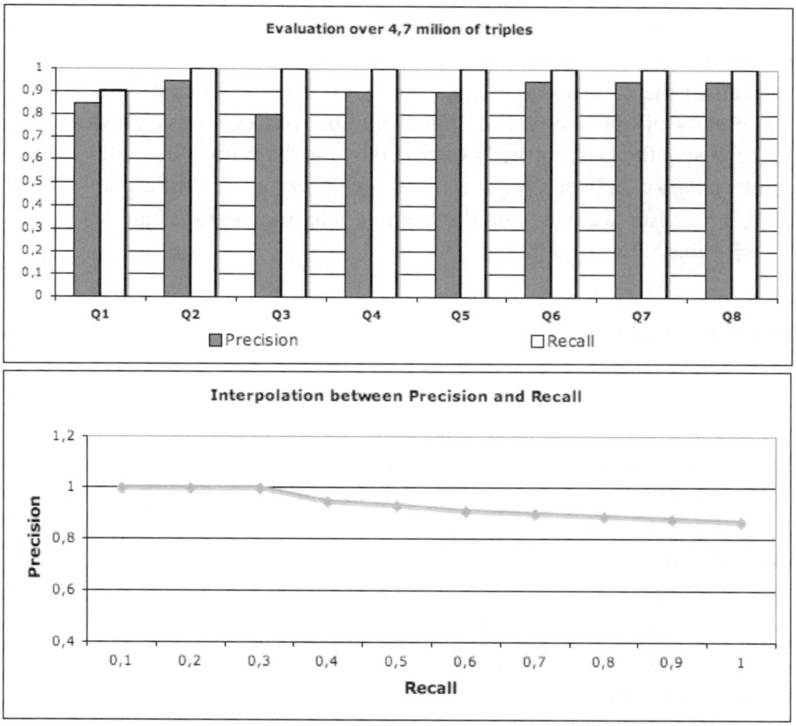

Fig. 3. Experimental Results over DBLP publications between 2007 and 2009

Effectiveness Evaluation. To guarantee the effectiveness of the approach, we have asked colleagues to submit keyword queries to the system and evaluate the results. In particular (ten) people of Database groups from the Roma Tre University (Italy) and from the University of Alberta (Canada) participated.

We evaluated the effectiveness of the generated answers in two ways. In a first experiment, we executed our queries over the entire DBLP dataset to obtain the Top-10 answers. We used a standard IR metric [16,20] called *Reciprocal Rank* (RR) defined as RR = 1/r, where r is the rank of the most relevant answer. Then we evaluated the average of the RR (MRR) scores obtained from the ten participants. We obtained the best MRR (i.e. the value 1) in all queries. The first resulting solution was always the most relevant. In a second experiment we used a subset of DBLP: all publications between years 2007 and 2009 (i.e. 4,7 millions of triples). This subset has been used to compute, manually, the most relevant solutions (MRS) for evaluating Precision and Recall. The former is the ratio between the number of relevant solutions returned (included in MRS) and the number of resulting solutions, the latter is the ratio between the number of relevant solutions returned, included in MRS, and the number of solutions in MRS. We computed all possible solutions. Figure 3 shows the results. This experiment demonstrates the completeness of the results: we have an overall best value of Recall. We obtained lower values of Precision, in particular in the first queries, due to many keywords that match several graph elements (e.g. `has-author` or `2008`). Consequently many substructures can be found, also substructures where the commonness of the keywords is high. This produces solutions quite general with respect the submitted query. Moreover the precision increases in Q6, Q7 and Q8 since it is supported by the higher specificity of query type (i.e. higher number of keywords). However irrelevant solutions represent the last returned as attested by the diagram in the bottom of Figure 3. It is the interpolation between precision and recall. For each standard level r_j of recall (i.e. 0.1, 0.2, ..., 1.0) we calculate the average max precision of queries in $[r_j, r_{j+1}]$, i.e. $P(r_j) = max_{r_j \leq r \leq r_{j+1}} P(r)$.

6 Related Works

There is a broad literature on information search. Graph based approaches are common because it is relatively easy to represent data by mean of a graph.

Early approaches addressed relational database systems. It's worth mentioning the following proposals: BANKS [3], DISCOVER [8], DBXplorer [2] and the work from Hristidis et al. [9]. In such works a database is represented as a graph where tuples are the nodes and foreign keys are the edges. Answers to query are so-called tuple trees, built from multiple tables. To rank answers, in [2,3,8] any IR technique is adopted: they associate a score with the number of joins in the tuple-tree. Hristidis et al. [9], on the other hand, incorporate an IR-like ranking function in a straightforward manner. However, generally, many factors critical to reach effectiveness are not investigated. Our work differs from above because we explicitly focus on effectiveness: our ranking and combining techniques are very effective. Keyword search over XML is another popular topic [5,6,11]. With respect to a graph data structure, search on XML data is a similar problem but with simplified pre-conditions. The tree structure guarantees each node to have a single incoming path: this allows the implementation of several ad-hoc optimizations. Unfortunately such optimization cannot be easily applied in general graphs. For instance in XRANK [6] an indexing solution is defined that allows the evaluation of a keyword query without requiring a tree traversal. Kaushik et al. [11] present an approach where they combine inverted indexes with structured indexes in order to improve the efficiency in keyword search in XML documents. XSearch [5] offers a free form query language however adopting a very simple

IR-like function to rank answers. With the exception of XSearch, XML works focus on efficiency above all. Although XSearch mentions effectiveness, the proposal limits its scope shedding some light on the task whereas we present deep experimental results. Approaches that specifically target query processing efficiency over graph-structured data are BLINKS [7] and SearchWebDB [19]. Both approaches address the Top-k most relevant answers to a keyword search. In BLINKS, however, although a scoring function is defined to find the Top-k most relevant solutions, a good part of the contribution relies on the novel indexing structure. Authors present a bi-level indexing structure that allows for early pruning that accelerates the search. In SearchWebDB authors propose an approach where the system, after a first computation on input keywords, returns a number of candidate queries in order to allow a user to refine its intended query. Computation of queries is based on the exploration of the Top-k matching subgraphs, exploiting an off-line built index structure and a variant of backward search where expansion (exploration) is driven by a cost function. The exploration is supported by optimizations of a database engine [1,4]. In [19] effectiveness studies evaluate the rank of the most relevant answer, resulting from the computation, but they do not analyze in depth the trend of results (e.g the number of irrelevant resulting answers).

Like in [7] and [19] our scoring function considers both the graph structure and its content. The main difference with respect to our approach is that we do not compute all the solutions first and rank them afterwards. We intrinsically assembly the solutions by starting with the most promising paths, where the ranking is a by-product of the process. Let us remark that our approach focus more on effectiveness rather than on efficiency. Although efficiency is relevant, we believe that effectiveness is more relevant. In our work effectiveness is achieved by the scoring functions. The goal is to assess the relevance of the matching paths and of the sub-graph in terms of both exhaustivity and specificity [14] using content and structural hint as in [21].

7 Conclusion and Future Works

We presented a full-text search index for RDF-graphs that provides matching capabilities based on semantic and morphological expansion of terms used for indexing the triples. Given a set of text matches, we proposed a method to construct the set of answer paths by a template based clustering technique. In this paper the paths retrieved by the system are ordered with respect to an effective scoring function that supports the process to present only the most relevant ones to users context. Future works concern efficiency issue and a set of sophisticated experimental results over (very) large datasets. `DBpedia`, `Yago` are recent efforts to generate semantic metadata by extracting structured information form the Web (`Wikipedia`). A keyword or natural language search interface to such knowledge bases would prove immensely useful as the end user need not be aware of the structure of the information. While this work is limited to handling keywords, it will be worthwhile to build a search interface that accepts queries in natural language.

References

1. Abadi, D.J., Madden, S., Hollenbach, K.J.: Scalable semantic Web data management using vertical partitioning. In: Int. Conf. on Very Large DataBase (VLDB 2007), Austria (2007)
2. Agrawal, S., Chaudhuri, S., Das, G.: Dbxplorer: enabling keyword search over relational databases. In: Int. Conf. on Management of Data (SIGMOD 2002), USA (2002)
3. Bhalotia, G., Hulgeri, A., Nakhe, C., Chakrabarti, S., Sudarshan, S.: Keyword searching and browsing in databases using banks. In: Int. Conf. on Data Engineering, ICDE 2002 (2002)
4. Chong, E.I., Das, S., Eadon, G., Srinivasan, J.: An efficient sql-based rdf querying scheme. In: Int. Conf. on Very Large DataBase (VLDB 2005), Norway (2005)
5. Cohen, S., Mamou, J., Kanza, Y., Sagiv, Y.: Xsearch: A semantic search engine for xml. In: Int. Conf. on Very Large DataBase (VLDB 2003), Germany (2003)
6. Guo, L., Shao, F., Botev, C., Shanmugasundaram, J.: Xrank: Ranked keyword search over xml documents. In: Int. Conf. on Management of Data (SIGMOD 2003), USA (2003)
7. He, H.: Wang, H., Yang, J., Yu, P.S. Blinks: ranked keyword searches on graphs. In: Int. Conf. on Management of Data (SIGMOD 2007), China (2007)
8. Hristidis, V., Papakonstantinou, Y.: Discover: Keyword search in relational databases. In: Int. Conf. on Very Large DataBase (VLDB 2002), China (2002)
9. Hristidis, V., Gravano, L., Papakonstantinou, Y.: Efficient ir-style keyword search over relational databases. In: Int. Conf. on Very Large DataBase (VLDB 2003), Germany (2003)
10. Kacholia, V., Pandit, S., Chakrabarti, S., Sudarshan, S., Desai, R., Desai, R., Karambelkar, H.: Bidirectional expansion for keyword search on graph databases. In: Int. Conf. on Very Large DataBase (VLDB 2005), Norway (2005)
11. Kaushik, R., Krishnamurthy, R., Naughton, J.F., Ramakrishnan, R.: On the integration of structure indexes and inverted lists. In: Int. Conf. on Management of Data (SIGMOD 2004), France (2004)
12. Kimelfeld, B., Sagiv, Y.: Finding and approximating Top-k answers in keyword proximity search. In: Int. Symposium on Principles of Database Systems (PODS 2006), USA (2006)
13. Knuth, D.E.: The Art Of Computer Programming, 3rd edn., vol. 1. Addison-Wesley, Reading (1997)
14. Lalmas, M., Tombros, A.: INEX 2002 - 2006: Understanding XML Retrieval Evaluation. In: Thanos, C., Borri, F., Candela, L. (eds.) DELOS 2007. LNCS, vol. 4877, pp. 187–196. Springer, Heidelberg (2007)
15. Liu, F., Yu, C.T., Meng, W., Chowdhury, A.: Effective keyword search in relational databases. In: Int. Conf. on Management of Data (SIGMOD 2006), USA (2006)
16. Radev, D.R., Qi, H., Wu, H., Fan, W.: Evaluating Web-based Question Answering Systems. In: Proc. of 3rd Int. Conf. on Language Resources and Evaluation (LREC 2002), Spain (2002)
17. Singhal, A., Buckley, M.C.: Mitra Pivoted Document Length Normalization. In: Int. Conf. on Information Retrieval (SIGIR), Switzerland (1996)
18. Singhal, A.: Modern Information Retrieval: A Brief Overview. In: IEEE Data Eng. Bull, Switzerland, pp. 35–43 (2001)
19. Tran, T., Wang, H., Rudolph, S., Cimiano, P.: Top-k exploration of query graph candidates for efficient keyword search on rdf. In: Int. Conf. on Data Engineering (ICDE 2009), China (2009)
20. Voorhees, E.M.: The TREC-8 Question Answering Track Report. In: Proc. of the 8th Text REtrieval Conference (TREC-8), Maryland (1999)
21. Yahia, S.A., Koudas, N., Marian, A., Srivastava, D., Toman, D.: Structure and Content Scoring for XML. In: Proc. of Int. Conf. on Very Large DataBase (VLDB 2005), Norway (2005)

Geometrically Enhanced Conceptual Modelling

Hui Ma[1], Klaus-Dieter Schewe[2], and Bernhard Thalheim[3]

[1] Victoria University of Wellington, School of Engineering and Computer Science, Wellington, New Zealand
hui.ma@ecs.vuw.ac.nz
[2] Information Science Research Centre, Palmerston North, New Zealand
kdschewe@acm.org
[3] Christian-Albrechts-University Kiel, Institute of Computer Science, Kiel, Germany
thalheim@is.informatik.uni-kiel.de

Abstract. Motivated among others by the need to support spatial modelling for the sustainable land use initiative we present a geometrically enhanced ER model (GERM), which preserves the key principles of ER modelling and at the same time introduces bulk constructions and types that support geometric objects. The model distinguishes between a syntactic level of types and an explicit internal level, in which types give rise to polyhedra that are defined by algebraic varieties. It further emphasises the stability of algebraic operations by means of a natural modelling algebra that extends the usual Boolean operations on point sets.

1 Introduction

The goal of our research is to provide a conceptual model supporting geometric modelling. One motivation is the need for spatial data modelling in the context of the sustainable land use initiative (SLUI), which addresses erosion problems in the hill country. At the core of SLUI whole farm plans (WFPs) are required, which capture farm boundaries, paddocks, etc. and provide information about land use capability (LUC) such as rock, soil, slope, erosion, vegetation, plants, poles, etc. This should then be used to get an overview of erosion and vegetation levels and water quality, and to use this information for sustainable land use change.

While there is a lot of sophisticated mathematics around to address geometric modelling in landcare, and this has a very long tradition as shown in [3], spatial and geometric modelling within conceptual modelling has mainly followed two lines of research – for an overview see [19]. The first one is based on modelling spatial relationships such as disjointness, touching, overlap, inside, boundary overlap, etc. and functions such as intersection, union, etc. that are used for spatial primitives such as points, lines, polygons, regions, etc. In [18] pictograms are added to the common ER model to highlight spatial objects and relationships. Price et al. [15] deal in particular with part-whole relationships, Ishikawa et al. apply constraint logic programming to deal with these predicates [10], McKenny et al. [12] handle problems with collections, and Chen et al. use the predicates in an extension of SQL [4].

A.H.F. Laender et al. (Eds.): ER 2009, LNCS 5829, pp. 219–233, 2009.

The work in [2,4] links to the second line of research expressing the spatial relationships by formulae defined on point sets applying basic Euclidean geometry or standard linear algebra, respectively. Likewise, point sets are used in [20] to express predicates on mesh of polygons in order to capture motion, and Frank classifies spatial algebra operation into local, focal and zonal ones based on whether only values of the same location, of a location and its immediate neighbourhood, or all of all locations in a zone, respectively, are combined [5].

We believe that more research has to be done to obtain adequate conceptual models supporting geometric modelling. For one, the spatial relationships and functions discussed in the literature are in fact derived from underlying representations of point sets, so we need representations on multiple levels as also proposed in [1]. Furthermore, when dealing with point sets it is not sufficient to define spatial relationships and functions in a logical way. We also have to ensure "good nature" in the numerical sense, i.e. the operations must be as accurate as possible when realised using floating point arithmetics. For instance, Liu et al. [11] discusses spatial conflicts such as determining the accurate spatial relationship for a winding road along a winding river as opposed to a road crossing a river several times, leading to a classification of line-line relationships. The accuracy problem has motivated a series of modifications to algebras on point sets that go way beyond the standard Boolean operators [8].

Our objective, however, is to go even further than geographic information systems, and to support other kinds of geometric modelling in the same manner. For instance, technical constructions such as rotary piston engines can be supported by trochoids, which are plan algebraic curves already known by the Greeks [3]. Bézier curves and patches [17] are also commonly applied in these applications. Together with hull operators [8] they can also be used for 3-D models of hill shapes in WFPs.

Paredaens et al. [13,14] compare five spatial data models: the raster model and the Peano model, which represent spatial data by finite point sets that are either uniformly or non-uniformly distributed over the plane, respectively, the Spaghetti model based on contours defined as polylines, the polynomial model based on formulae that involve equality and inequality of polynomials, and the PLA model, which only uses some kind of topological information without dealing with exact position and shape. While some models lack theoretical foundations, those that are grounded in theory do not bother about efficient implementations.

In this paper we introduce the geometrically enhanced ER model (GERM) as our approach to deal with the problems discussed. As the name suggests, our intent is to preserve the aggregation-based approach of the ER model [9] by means of (higher-order) relationship types [21], but we enhance roles in relationship types by supporting choice and bulk constructors (sets, lists, multisets). However, different from [7] the bulk constructors are not used to create first-class objects, neither is the choice constructor (defining so-called clusters in [21]).

Furthermore, we keep the fundamental distinction between data types such as points, polygons, Bézier curves, etc. and concepts. The former ones are used to define the domains of (nested) attributes, while the latter ones are represented by entity and relationship types, e.g. a concept such as a paddock is distinguished from the curve defining its boundary. In this way we also guarantee a smooth integration with non-geometric data such as farm ownership, processing and legal information, etc. that is also relevant for WFPs, but does not cause any novel modelling challenge.

As already said GERM supports modelling on multiple levels. On a syntactic level we provide an extendible collection of data types such as line sequences, polygons, sequences of Bézier curves, Bézier patches, etc. with easy surface representations. For instance, a polygon can be represented by a list of points, and a Bézier curve of order n can be represented by $n + 1$ points – the case $n = 2$ captures the most commonly known quadratic Bézier curves that are also supported in LaTeX. On an explicit internal level we use a representation by polyhedra [8] that are defined by algebraic varieties, i.e. sets of zeros of polynomials in n variables. All curves that have a rational parametric representation such as Bézier curves [17], can be brought into this "implicit" form, e.g. Gao and Chou describe a method for implicitisation based on Gröbner bases [6], and many classical curves that have proven their values in landcare for centuries can be represented in this way [3]. This kind of explicit representation bears some similarities to the polynomial model of spatial data introduced by Paredaens and Kuijpers [14].

The use of a good natured algebra on point sets defines in fact a third derived level. For the algebra we build on the research in [8] to guarantee stability by using a generalised natural modelling algebra, which supports much more than just Boolean operations. The leveling of GERM prescribes already the outline of the paper. In Section 2 we introduce the basic GERM model emphasizing the syntactic level. This remains more or less within the framework of the ER model in the general form defined in [21] with the differences discussed above. We continue in Section 3 with a discussion of the internal representation by means of algebraic varieties. In both sections we illustrate our approach by examples from WFP modelling. Finally, in Section 4 we introduce a natural modelling algebra, and discuss its merits with respect to expressiveness and accuracy.

2 Geometrically Enhanced ER Model (GERM)

In this section we start with the presentation of GERM focussing on the syntactic (or surface) level, which is what will be needed first for modelling geometrically enhanced applications. We will concentrate on the definition of entity and relationship types and their semantics, but we will dispense with discussing keys or other constraints. For attributes we will permit structuring.

2.1 Data Types and Nested Attributes

Definition 1. A *universe* is a countable set $\mathcal{U}$ of simple attributes together with a type assignment tp that assigns to each attribute $A \in \mathcal{U}$ a data type $tp(A)$.

In most case the associated type $tp(A)$ for $A \in \mathcal{U}$ will be a base type, but we do not enforce such a restriction. We do not further specify the collection of base types. These can be *INT*, *FLOAT*, *STRING*, *DATE*, *TIME*, etc. A base data type t is associated with a countable set of values $dom(t)$ called the domain of t. For the types listed the domain is the standard one. For an attribute $A \in \mathcal{U}$ we let $dom(A) = dom(tp(A))$, and also call $dom(A)$ the domain of A.

We use constructors to define complex data types. In particular we use $(\cdot)$ for record types, $\{\cdot\}$, $[\cdot]$ and $\langle\cdot\rangle$ for finite set, list and mutiset types, respectively, $\oplus$ for (disjoint) union types, and $\rightarrow$ for map types. Together with a trivial type $\mathbb{1}$ – its domain is a singleton set: $dom(\mathbb{1}) = \{\bot\}$ – we can define (complex types) t by abstract syntax (here b represents base types):

$$t = \mathbb{1} \mid b \mid (a_1 : t_1, \dots, a_n : t_n) \mid (a_1 : t_1) \oplus \dots \oplus (a_n : t_n) \mid \{t\} \mid [t] \mid \langle t \rangle \mid t_1 \rightarrow t_2$$

with pairwise different labels a_i in record and union types. Furthermore, we allow complex types to be named and used in type definitions in the same way as base types with the restriction that cycles are forbidden. Domains are then defined in the usual way.

Example 1. We can define named complex types that can be used for geometric modelling such as $Point = (x : FLOAT, y : FLOAT)$ for points in the two-dimensional plane, $Polygon = [Point]$, $PolyLine = [Point]$, $Bezier = [Point]$, and $PolyBezier = [Bezier]$. In particular, these constitute examples of types with equal surface representations, but different geometric semantics (as we will discuss in Section 3). A polyline is a curve that is defined piecewise linearly, while a polygon is a region that is defined by a polyline border. A sequence of n points defines a Bézier curve of order $n-1$, and a curve that is defined piecewise by Bézier curves is a Poly-Bézier curve.

The trivial type $\mathbb{1}$ can be used in combination with the union constructor to define enumerated types, i.e. types with finite domains such as $Bool = (\mathbf{T} : \mathbb{1}) \oplus (\mathbf{F} : \mathbb{1})$, $Gender = (\text{male} : \mathbb{1}) \oplus (\text{female} : \mathbb{1})$ or $(n) = (1 : \mathbb{1}) \oplus \dots \oplus (n : \mathbb{1})$ for any positive integer n, which gives a domain representing $\{1, \dots, n\}$. The map constructor can be used to define arrays such as $Patch = (i : (n), j : (m)) \rightarrow Point$ representing Bézier patches, and vectorfields of different dimensions such as $Vectorfield1 = \{Point\} \rightarrow FLOAT$, which could be used for sensor data such as water levels, and $Vectorfield2 = \{Point\} \rightarrow Point$, which could be used for modelling other measurements such as wind capturing force and direction by a two-dimensional vector. Finally, $TimeSeries = (d : DATE, t : TIME) \rightarrow Vectorfield1$ could be used to model a series of observed data over time.

Complex types are used in connection with nested attributes extending the definitions in [21].

Definition 2. The set $\mathcal{A}$ of *nested attributes* (over universe $\mathcal{U}$) is the smallest set with $\mathcal{U} \subseteq \mathcal{A}$ satisfying $X(A_1, \dots, A_n), X\{A\}, X[A], X\langle A \rangle, X_1(A_1) \oplus \dots \oplus X_n(A_n), X(A_1 \rightarrow A_2) \in \mathcal{A}$ with labels $X, X_1, \dots, X_n$ and $A, A_1, \dots, A_n \in \mathcal{A}$.

The type assignment tp extends naturally from $\mathcal{U}$ to $\mathcal{A}$ as follows:

- $tp(X(A_1, \dots, A_n) = (a_1 : tp(A_1), \dots, a_n : tp(A_n))$ with labels $a_1, \dots, a_n$,
- $tp(X_1(A_1) \oplus \cdots \oplus X_n(A_n)) = (X_1 : tp(A_1)) \oplus \cdots \oplus (X_n : tp(A_n))$,
- $tp(X\{A\}) = \{tp(A)\}$, $tp(X[A]) = [tp(A)]$, $tp(X\langle A\rangle) = \langle tp(A)\rangle$, and
- $tp(X(A_1 \rightarrow A_2)) = tp(A_1) \rightarrow tp(A_2)$.

2.2 Entity and Relationship Types

Following [21] the major difference between entity and relationship types is the presence of components $r : R$ (with a role name r and a name R of an entity or relationship type) for the latter ones. We will therefore unify the definition, and simply talk of database types as opposed to the data types in the previous subsection. We will, however, permit structured components.

Definition 3. The set $\mathcal{C}$ of *component expressions* is the smallest set containing all database type names E, all set and multiset expressions $\{E\}$ and $\langle E\rangle$, respectively, all union expressions $E_1 \oplus \cdots \oplus E_n$ with component expressions E, E_i that are not union expressions, and all list expressions $[E]$ with component expressions E. A *structured component* is a pair $r : E$ with a role name r and a component expression $E \in \mathcal{C}$.

Note that this definition does neither permit record and map constructors in component expressions nor full orthogonality for union, set, list and multiset constructors. The reason for the absence of the record constructor is that it corresponds to aggregation, i.e. whenever a component of a relationship type has the structure of a record, it can be replaced by a separate relationship type. The reason for the absence of the map constructor is that functions on entities and relationships that depend on instances seem to make very little sense and are not needed at all. The reason the restricted combinations of the other constructors are the intrinsic equivalences observed in [16]. If in $\{E\}$ we had a union component expression $E = E_1 \oplus \cdots \oplus E_n$, this would be equivalent to a record expression $(\{E_1\}, \dots, \{E_n\})$, to which the argument regarding records can be applied. The same holds for multiset expressions, while nested union constructors can be flattened. In this way we guarantee to deal only with normalised and thus simplified structured components that do not contain any hidden aggregation.

Definition 4. A *database type* R of level $k \geq 0$ consists of a finite set $comp(R) = \{r_1 : E_1, \dots, r_n : E_n\}$ of structured components with pairwise different role names $r_1, \dots, r_n$, and a finite set $attr(R) = \{A_1, \dots, A_k\} \subseteq \mathcal{A}$ of nested attributes. Each E_i is a database type of level at most $k-1$, and unless $comp(R) = \emptyset$ at least one of the E_i must have exactly the level $k-1$.

Note that this definition enforces $comp(R) = \emptyset$ iff R is a type of level 0. So we call types of level 0 *entity types*, and types of level $k > 0$ relationship types. In the following we use the notation $R = (comp(R), attr(R))$ for a type.

Note that while we discarded full orthogonality for component constructors, we did not do this for the nested attributes, leaving a lot of latitude to modellers. The rationale behind this flexibility is that the attributes should reflect pieces of information that is meaningful within the application context. For instance, using an attribute shape with $tp(shape) = Polygon$ (thus, shape $\in \mathfrak{U}$) indicates that the structure of polygons as lists of pairs of floating point numbers is not relevant for the conceptual model of the application, whereas the alternative having a nested attribute shape([point(x-coord, y-coord)]) with tp(x-coord) = tp(y-coord) = $FLOAT$ would indicate that points and their coordinates are conceptually relevant beyond representing a data type. Nested attributes also give rise to generalised keys, whereas we do not break into the structure of complex types for this.

Furthermore, the way we define structured components permits alternatives and bulk constructions in database types, which can be used to model a farm with a set of paddocks and a time series of measured water levels, but either disjoint unions nor sets, list and multisets can be used to model first-class database types, i.e. a set of paddocks will never appear outside a component. This differs from [21], where disjoint unions *clusters* are used independently from relationship types, and from [7], where this has been extended to sets, lists and multisets. The reason is that such stand-alone constructors are hardly needed in the model, unless they appear within a component of a database type.

2.3 Schemata and Instances

Finally, we put the definitions of the previous subsections together to define schemata and their instances in the usual way.

Definition 5. A *GERM schema* $\mathcal{S}$ is a finite set of database types, such that whenever $r_i : E_i$ is a component of $R \in \mathcal{S}$ and the database type name E appears in E_i, then also $E \in \mathcal{S}$ holds.

The definition of structural schema, which is normally just called schema, covers the syntactic side of our conceptual model. For the semantics we need instances of schemata, which we will define next starting with "entities". For this, if $\mathcal{I}(E)$ is a set of values for a database type name E, then this defines a unique set of values $\mathcal{I}(E_i)$ for each $E_i \in \mathfrak{C}$. This extension is defined in the same way as the extension of *dom* from base types to complex types.

Definition 6. An *entity* e of type R is a mapping defined on $comp(R) \cup attr(R)$ that assigns to each $r_i : E_i \in comp(R)$ a value $e_i \in \mathcal{I}(E_i)$, and to each attribute $A_j \in attr(R)$ a value $v_j \in dom(A_j)$. Here $\mathcal{I}(E_i)$ is built from sets of entities $\mathcal{I}(E)$ for all E appearing in E_i.

We use the notation $e = (r_1 : e_1, \dots, r_n : e_n, A_1 : v_1, \dots, A_k : v_k)$ for an entity e of type $R = (\{r_1 : E_1, \dots, r_n : E_n\}, \{A_1, \dots, A_k\})$. Strictly speaking, if R is of level $k > 0$, e should be called a *relationship*.

Definition 7. An *instance* $\mathcal{I}$ of a GERM schema $\mathcal{S}$ is an $\mathcal{S}$-indexed family $\{\mathcal{I}(R)\}_{R \in \mathcal{S}}$, such that $\mathcal{I}(R)$ is a finite set of entities of type R, and only these sets are used in the definition of entities.

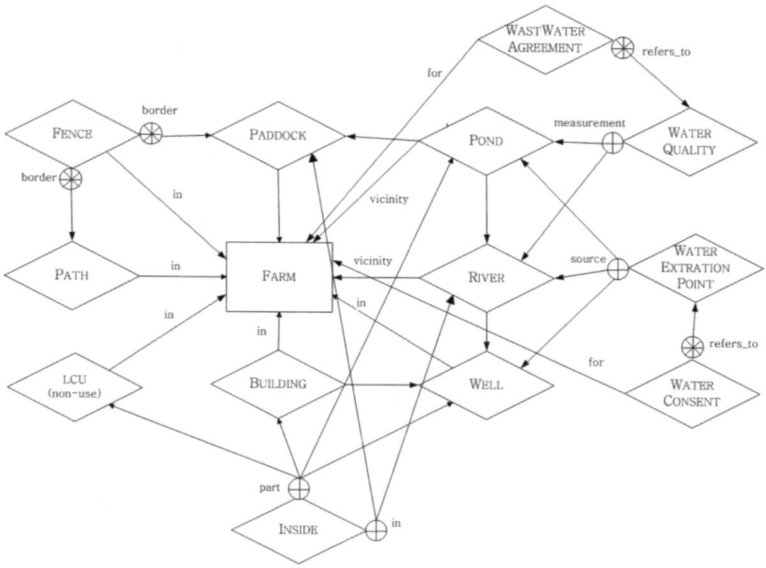

Fig. 1. Sketch of a GERM schema for a WFP (attributes omitted) including types for water consent, quality and waste water agreement

Example 2. Let us look at a sketch of a GERM schema for a WFP as illustrated in Figure 1. At its core we have a schema capturing the geographic information related to a farm. The central entity type FARM will have attributes owner, boundary and address with $tp(\text{boundary}) = \mathit{PolyBezier}$, and $tp(\text{owner}) = tp(\text{address}) = \mathit{STRING}$. The type PADDOCK is used to capture the major (farming) units with attributes boundary and usage of types $tp(\text{boundary}) = \mathit{PolyBezier}$ and $tp(\text{usage}) = (\text{cattle} : \mathbb{1}) \oplus (\text{dairy} : \mathbb{1}) \oplus (\text{hort} : \mathbb{1}) \oplus (\text{sheep} : \mathbb{1}) \oplus \cdots \oplus (\text{other} : \mathbb{1})$, respectively. For BUILDING we have attributes kind and area with another enumeration type associated with kind, and $tp(\text{area}) = \mathit{Polygon}$. Other landcare units with non-agricultural usage are captured by the type LCU with an attribute luc with $tp(\text{luc}) = (\text{bush} : \mathbb{1}) \oplus (\text{rock} : \mathbb{1}) \oplus (\text{slope} : \mathbb{1})$. The relationship type FENCE has a set of PADDOCK components, a set of PATH components referring to the paddocks and paths it borders and and attribute shape with $tp(\text{shape}) = \{\mathit{PolyLine}\}$. The type PATH has attributes location with $tp(\text{location}) = \text{POLYBEZIER}$ indicating the course of the path by a curve, and an attribute width with $tp(\text{width}) = \mathit{FLOAT}$.

The types RIVER, POND and WELL model the water resources of farms. RIVER has attributes left and right, both of type *PolyBezier*, which are used to model the course of the left and right border of a river. For WELL we have attributes depth and boundary of types *FLOAT* and *Circle*, respectively, and POND has a type boundary of type *PolyBezier*. The relationship type INSIDE is needed to model that some units may lie inside others, e.g. a rock LCU may be inside a paddock, a river may have islands, a well may be inside a paddock, a path may cross a paddock, etc. This relationship makes it easier to model "holes" rather than permitting them to be considered as part of the data types.

A water consent for a farm refers to several water extraction points, each referring to a source, which is a river, well or pond. Therefore, WATEREXTRACTIONPOINT has attributes location, minimum, and capacity of types *Point*, *Month* $\rightarrow$ *FLOAT*, and *FLOAT*, respectively. The latter two model the (season-dependent) water level that cannot be fallen below, and the amount of water that could be taken out. WATERCONSENT has an attribute allowance of type *Month* $\rightarrow$ *FLOAT* modelling the total amount of water the farm is permitted to use.

Similarly, WATERQUALITY models measurement of oxygen and nitrate levels and others, and WASTEWATERAGREEMENT models the contracted minmum and maximum values governing water quality. We omit further details.

3 Geometric Types and Algebraic Varieties

Usually, the domain of a type defines the set of values that are used for operations. This is no longer the case with geometric types. For instance, a value of type *Bezier* as defined in the previous section is simply a list of $n+1$ points $\boldsymbol{p}_0, \dots, \boldsymbol{p}_n \in \mathbb{R}^2$. However, it defines a Bézier curve of order n in the two-dimensional Euclidean plane, i.e. a set of points.

Thus, we need a different association *gdom*, which associates with a geometric type t a set of point sets in n-dimensional Euclidean space $\mathbb{R}^n$ together with a mapping $dom(t) \rightarrow gdom(t)$. In the following we will concentrate on the case $n = 2$, i.e. we focus on points, curves and regions in the plane, but most definitions are not bound to this restriction. We will use algebraic varieties and polyhedra to define point sets of interest.

Definition 8. An *(algebraic) variety* V of dimension n is the set of zeroes of a polynomial P in n variables, i.e. $V = \{(x_1, \dots, x_n) \in \mathbb{R}^n \mid P(x_1, \dots, x_n) = 0\}$. A *base polyhedron* H is the intersection of half planes, i.e. $H = \{(x_1, \dots, x_n) \mid P_i(x_1, \dots, x_n) \geq 0 \text{ for } i = 1, \dots, k\}$ with polynomials $P_1, \dots, P_k$. A *polyhedron* H is the finite union of base polyhedra $H_1, \dots, H_\ell$.

Algebraic varieties in the plane cover all classical curves [3]. As $P(x_1, \dots, x_n) = 0 \Leftrightarrow P(x_1, \dots, x_n) \geq 0 \wedge -P(x_1, \dots, x_n) \geq 0$ holds, base polyhedra are simple generalisations.

A representation as in Definition 8 by means of zeroes of polynomials is called an *implicit* representation as opposed to an explicit parametric representation $\gamma(u)$ for reals u [6]. Each parametric representation can always be turned into an implicit one, but the converse is not necessarily true. For most curves of interest, however, we also find rational parametric representations.

Example 3. A Bézier curve of degree n is defined by $n+1$ points $\boldsymbol{p}_0, \dots, \boldsymbol{p}_n$. A parametric representation is $B(u) = \sum_{i=0}^{n} B_{in}(u) \cdot \boldsymbol{p}_i$ $(0 \leq u \leq 1)$ with the

i'th Bernstein polynomial $B_{in}(u)$ of degree n defined as $B_{in}(u) = \binom{n}{i} u^i(1-u)^{n-i}$.

A Bézier curve of order 1 is simply a straight line between the two points defining it. For $n = 2$ and $B(u) = (x, y)$ we obtain quadratic equations $x = au^2 + bu + c$ and $y = du^2 + eu + f$. Dividing these by a and d, respectively, and subtracting them from each other eliminates the quadratic term u^2. This can then be solved to give u, plugged back in to give x and y leading to a polynomial in x and y of degree 2 that defines the implicitisation of the Bézier curve.

Similarly, an $(n \times m)$ array of points $\boldsymbol{p}_{ij}$ defines a Bézier patch with a parametric representation $P(u, v) = \sum_{i=0}^{n} \sum_{j=0}^{m} B_{in}(u) \cdot B_{jm}(v) \cdot \boldsymbol{p}_{ij}$. In this case $u = 0$ and $v = 0$ define Bézier curves $P(0, v)$ and $P(u, 0)$, respectively.

Definition 9. The *geometric domain* $gdom(t)$ of a geometric data type t is a set of point sets. Each element of $gdom(t)$ has an implicit representation by a polyhedron $H = H_1 \cup \cdots \cup H_\ell$ with base polyhedra H_i $(i = 1, \ldots, \ell)$ defined by polynomials $P_{i1}, \ldots, P_{in_i}$. In addition, the variety defined by P_{ij} has an explicit parametric representation $\gamma_{ij}(\boldsymbol{u})$, unless this is impossible.

The definition of polyhedra for polygons or more generally lists of Bézier curves that define a region may require some triangulisation.

Note that in general polyhedra are closed under union and intersection, but not under set difference. Polyhedra are always closed with respect to the standard topology on $\mathbb{R}^n$, but the difference of closed sets is not necessarily closed. We may, however, regain a polyhedron by building the closure. Thus, it may be useful to have the *interior* $\overset{\circ}{X}$, *boundary* ∂X, and the *closure* $\bar{X}$ available for any point set X. These are defined in the usual way by $\overset{\circ}{X} = \{x \in X \mid \exists U(x).U(x) \subseteq X\}$, $\partial X = \{x \mid \forall U(x).U(x) \cap X \neq \emptyset \neq U(x) - X\}$, and $\bar{X} = X \cup \partial X$. Here $U(x)$ denotes an open environment of the point x.

4 Natural Modelling Algebra

The two layers of GERM support the storage and retrieval of geometric objects within a conceptual model. The challenge is, however, the manipulation of such objects by queries and transactions. For this we now present an algebra on geometric objects. As we always have an internal representation by point sets, we first focus on these.

Standard operations on point sets are of course the Boolean ones, i.e. union, intersection and difference (or complement). In combination with interior, closure and boundary these operations are in principle sufficient to express a lot of relationships between the geometric objects as discussed widely in the conceptual GIS literature (see e.g. [2,19]). For instance, $A - B = \emptyset$ is equivalent to $A \subseteq B$, so we only need difference and an emptyness test. Similarly, $\overset{\circ}{A} \cap B = \emptyset \wedge \partial A \cap \partial B \neq \emptyset$ express that A and B touch each other, but do not intersect.

However, relying on the Boolean set operations is insufficient. We have to address at least two problems: 1) The set of point sets of interest must be closed under the operations. We already remarked at the end of the previous section that this is not true for the set difference (and likewise for the complement). 2) The operations must be numerically stable in the sense that they do not produce larger errors than those that are unavoidable due to the rounding that is necessary when dealing with floating-point representations of real numbers.

We may circumvent the closure problem, as we are merely interested in point sets "up to their boundary", i.e. we could deal with an equivalence relation $\sim$ with $A \sim B$ iff $\bar{A} = \bar{B}$. Then each equivalence class has exactly one closed representative, a polyhedron. The problem is then that the Boolean operations do not preserve this equivalence, and we lose some of the properties of a Boolean algebra. However, these properties are lost anyway by the necessary modifications that we propose to deal with the stability problem.

As to the stability problem some conceptual modellers will argue that this concerns only an implementation. We do not share this opinion, as any result obtained by operations of point sets, i.e. the polyhedra on the internal level, must be re-interpreted by a value of some data type on the surface level. For instance, the union and intersection of polygons must again be represented as a polygon with a surface representation by a sequence of points. Similarly, we must take into account that the intersection of two curves may be more than just a discrete set of points, if stability is addressed. Thus, stability considerations have an non-negligible impact on the surface level of GERM.

4.1 Modification of Boolean Operations

It is known that Boolean operations on point sets may be instable. For instance, for two straight lines their intersection point may be only obtainable with an intolerable error. This problem occurs, when the angle between the two lines is very small. Our solution will replace the intersection operation by a modified operation, which in this case will enlarge the result – so we actually obtain a point set instead of a single point. The enlargement will depend on the operands, so that for the uncritical cases we almost preserve the Boolean operations.

In general, we use the following new operations on point sets: $A \uplus B = A \cup B \cup q(A,B)$ and $A \mathbin{\cap\!\!\!\!\!{\scriptstyle +}\,} B = (A \cap B) \cup q(A,B)$ with a *natural modelling function* q that assigns a point set to a pair of point sets. We do not modify the complement X' of a set X. With $A \mathbin{\cup\!\!\!\!\!{\scriptstyle -}\,} B = (A' \mathbin{\cap\!\!\!\!\!{\scriptstyle +}\,} B')'$ and $A \mathbin{\cap\!\!\!\!\!{\scriptstyle -}\,} B = (A' \uplus B')'$ we obtain two more modified operations.

The simple idea behind these operations is to slightly enlarge (or reduce) unions and intersections in order to cope with the stability problem. The enlargement (or reduction) depends on the arguments; critical operands require larger modifications than uncritical ones. The name "natural modelling" is adopted from [8], as it should reflect properties associated with stability and the original union and intersections operations in a natural way.

Definition 10. A function q from pairs of point sets to point sets is called a *natural modelling function* iff it satisfies the following properties for all A, B:

$$q(A, B) = q(B, A) \qquad q(A', B) = q(A, B) \qquad q(A, \emptyset) = \emptyset$$

We require q to be symmetric, as the stability problem for building intersections and unions does not depend on the order. Analogously, the potential instability caused by A and B is the same as the one caused by A' and B.

Definition 11. The *natural modelling algebra* consists of the set of equivalence classes of polyhedra with respect to $\sim$ and the operations $\uplus$, $\Cap$, $\Cap$ and $\Cup$ with a natural modelling function q.

Hartwig has studied the algebraic properties of the *direct* modelling algebra $(\mathcal{P}(E), \uplus, \Cap)$ and the *small* modelling algebra $(\mathcal{P}(E), \uplus, \Cap)$ [8]. In both cases we obtain a *weak Boolean algebra*, i.e. the existence of neutral and inverse elements is preserved, and the de Morgan laws still hold, but other properties of Boolean algebras have been abandoned.

4.2 Computing with Polyhedra and Surface Representations

The key question is of course how to choose a good natural modelling function q. Before addressing this let us first look at the modified operations on polyhedra. As these are defined by algebraic varieties, it will be decisive (and sufficient) to understand the operations on two half-planes $A = \{(x_1, \dots, x_n) \mid P(x_1, \dots, x_n) \geq 0\}$ and $B = \{(x_1, \dots, x_n) \mid Q(x_1, \dots, x_n) \geq 0\}$. If A and B are plane curves, we have to compute their intersection point(s) in order to determine a surface representation of their union and intersection, respectively. Let us discuss this further for polygons and regions defined by a sequence of Bézier curves.

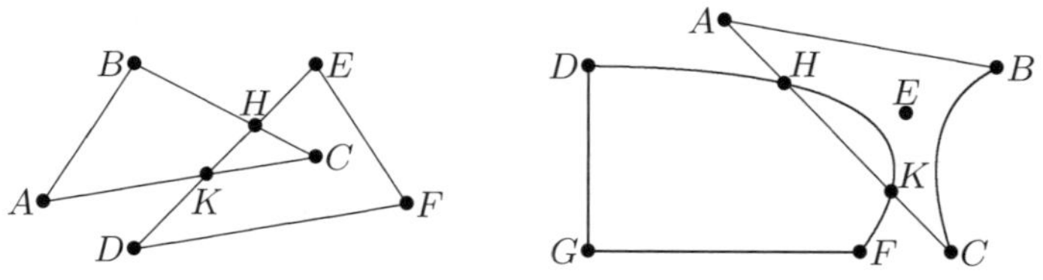

Fig. 2. On the left the intersection of two polygons, on the right the intersection of two regions with a boundary defined by Bézier curves

Example 4. Let us look at the union / intersection of two polygons depicted on the left in Figure 2, one defined by the points A, B, C, the other one by D, E, F. With $A = (1, 1)$, $B = (3, 4)$, $C = (7, 2)$, $D = (3, 0)$, $E = (7, 4)$, and $F = (9, 1)$ the line through D and E is defined by $P(x, y) = x - y - 3 = 0$, and the line through B and C is defined by $Q(x, y) = x + 2y - 11 = 0$. They intersect in the point $H = (5.66, 2.66)$. This intersection divides the plane into four parts depending on whether $P(x, y)$ and $Q(x, y)$ take positive or negative values.

If we can compute the intersection points H and K, then A, B, H, E, F, D, K defines the surface representation of the union, while K, H, C defines the one of the intersection.

However, the angle between the lines DE and AC at the intersection point K is rather small, which may cause a different result defined by the operations $\uplus$ and $\Cap$ instead of $\cup$ and $\cap$, respectively. The resulting polygon for the modified union may become $A, B, H, E, F, D, K_1, K_2$, while the resulting polygon for the modified intersection may become K_1', H, C, K_2' with points K_1, K_2, K_1', K_2' in a small neighbourhood of K.

At H the angle between the two intersecting lines is nearly a right angle, so the modified intersection may coincide with the normal one.

Example 5. Look at the two regions defined on the right in Figure 2, both defined by values of type *PolyBezier*, the first one by $[(A, B), (B, E, C), (C, A)]$, the second one by $[(D, B, F), (F, G), (G, D)]$. As in the previous example the two intersection points H and K of the line (A, C) with the Bézier curve (D, E, F) are decisive for the computation of the union and intersection.

With $A = (16, 5)$, $B = (22, 4)$, $E = (20, 3)$, $C = (21, 0)$, $D = (13, 4)$, $F = (19, 0)$, and $G = (13, 0)$ the parametric representation of the Bézier curve can be easily obtained as $B(u) = (-12u^2+18u+13, -4u^2+4)$, and the straight line gives rise to $x+y-21 = 0$. Substituting $B(u) = (x, y)$ in this gives rise to a quadratic equation with the roots $u_{1/2} = \frac{9 \pm \sqrt{17}}{16}$, i.e. $u_1 = 0.304$ and $u_2 = 0.82$, which define $H = (17.32, 3.64)$ and $K = (19.69, 1.31)$. Then the union can be represented by $[(A, B), (B, E, C), (C, K), (K, F', F), (F, G), (G, D), (D, D', H), (H, A)]$ of type *PolyBezier*, while the intersection is represented by $[(H, H', K), (K, H)]$. Once H and K are known, it is no problem to obtain the necessary points D' and H', as sections of Bézier curves are again Bézier curves.

As in Example 4 the computation of the point K can be expected to be relatively stable, whereas H is not. Using $\uplus$ instead of the usual union, we end up with a modified union represented by $[(A, B), (B, E, C), (C, K), (K, F', F), (F, G), (G, D), (D, D', H_1), (H_1, H_2), (H_2, A)]$ of type *PolyBezier*, where H_1 and H_2 are points in the vicinity of H on the Bézier curve and the straight line (H, A), respectively. Analogously, using $\Cap$ instead of $\cap$, we obtain a representation $[(H_2', H_1')(H_1', H', K), (K, H_2')]$ with points H_1', H_2' in the vicinity of H on the Bézier curve and the straight line (H, K), respectively.

4.3 The Choice of the Natural Modelling Function

In view of the discussion in the previous subsection it is sufficient to consider base polyhedra, i.e. if $H = H_1 \cup \cdots \cup H_n$ and H' are polyhedra, we define $q(H, H') = \bigcup_{i=1}^{n} q(H_i, H')$. Furthermore, for base polyhedra it is sufficient to consider the boundary, i.e. if H and H' are base polyhedra, we define $q(H, H') = q(\partial H, \partial H')$. In the two-dimensional plane $E = \mathbb{R}^2$ we can therefore concentrate on plan curves. If such a curve γ is defined by a union of (sections of) algebraic varieties, say $V_1 \cup \cdots \cup V_n$, then we define again $q(\gamma, \gamma') = \bigcup_{i=1}^{n} q(V_i, \gamma')$. If q is symmetric, the naturalness conditions in Definition 10 are obviously satisfied.

In order to obtain a good choice for the natural modelling function q it is therefore sufficient to look at two curves γ_1 and γ_2 defined by polynomials $P(x, y) = 0$ and $Q(x, y) = 0$, respectively. Let $\boldsymbol{p}_1, \dots, \boldsymbol{p}_n$ be the intersection points of these curves – unless $\gamma_1 = \gamma_2$ we can assume that there are only finitely many. Then we define $q(\gamma_1, \gamma_2) = \bigcup_{i=1}^{n} U_i$ with environments $U_i = U_{\gamma_1,\gamma_2}(\boldsymbol{p}_i)$ as defined next.

Definition 12. For $\varepsilon > 0$ the ε-*band* of a variety $V = \{(x, y) \mid P(x, y) = 0\}$ is the point set $B_\varepsilon(V) = \{(x', y') \mid \exists (x, y) \in V . |x - x'| < \varepsilon \wedge |y - y'| < \varepsilon\}$.

5 Conclusion

In this paper we presented the geometrically enhanced ER model (GERM) as our approach to conceptual geometric modelling. GERM preserves aggregation as the primary abstraction mechanism of the ER model, but loosens the definition of relationship types permitting bulk and choice constructors to be used for components without first-class status of bulk objects. Geometric objects are dealt with within attributes, which can be associated with types for geometric modelling. This defines a syntactic level of GERM that largely remains within the ER framework and thus enables a smooth integration with non-geometric modelling. It also allows users to deal with modelling tasks that involve geometry in a familiar, non-challenging way thereby preserving all the positive experience made with conceptual ER modelling.

The syntactic level is complemented by an internal level that employs algebraic varieties, i.e. sets of zeros of polynomials, to represent geometric objects as point sets. The use of such varieties leads to a significant increase in expressiveness way beyond standard approaches that mostly support points, lines and polygons. In particular, common shapes as defined by circles, ellipses, Bézier curves and patches, etc. are captured in a natural way. However, for polynomials of high degrees we have to face computational problems.

The highly expressive internal level of GERM makes geometric modelling not only very flexible, it is only the basis for an extended algebra that generalises and extends the standard Boolean operators on point sets. By using this algebra, GERM enables a higher degree of accuracy for derived geometric relationships.

Our next short-term goal is to apply GERM to the WFP modelling within SLUI. In order to support the wider SLUI objectives GERM is general enough to capture as well time series data. We are also looking for applications beyond GIS. On the theoretical side we plan to investigate further back and forth translations between the syntactic and the internal level of GERM, and special cases of the natural modelling algebra for specific applications. In this sense this paper is only the start of a larger research programme devoted to geometric conceptual modelling.

References

1. Balley, S., Parent, C., Spaccapietra, S.: Modelling geographic data with multiple representations. IJGIS 18(4), 327–352 (2004)
2. Behr, T., Schneider, M.: Topological relationships of complex points and complex regions. In: Kunii, H.S., Jajodia, S., Sølvberg, A. (eds.) ER 2001. LNCS, vol. 2224, pp. 56–69. Springer, Heidelberg (2001)
3. Brieskorn, E., Knörrer, H.: Plane Algebraic Curves. Birkhäuser-Verlag, Basel (1981)
4. Chen, C.X., Zaniolo, C.: SQL^{ST}: A spatio-temporal data model and query language. In: Laender, A.H.F., Liddle, S.W., Storey, V.C. (eds.) ER 2000. LNCS, vol. 1920, pp. 96–111. Springer, Heidelberg (2000)
5. Frank, A.U.: Map algebra extended with functors for temporal data. In: Akoka, J., Liddle, S.W., Song, I.-Y., Bertolotto, M., Comyn-Wattiau, I., van den Heuvel, W.-J., Kolp, M., Trujillo, J., Kop, C., Mayr, H.C. (eds.) ER Workshops 2005. LNCS, vol. 3770, pp. 194–207. Springer, Heidelberg (2005)
6. Gao, X.S., Chou, S.C.: Implicitization of rational parametric equations. Journal of Symbolic Computation 14, 459–470 (1992)
7. Hartmann, S., Link, S.: Collection type constructors in entity-relationship modeling. In: Parent, C., Schewe, K.-D., Storey, V.C., Thalheim, B. (eds.) ER 2007. LNCS, vol. 4801, pp. 307–322. Springer, Heidelberg (2007)
8. Hartwig, A.: Algebraic 3-D Modeling. A. K. Peters, Wellesley (1996)
9. Hull, R., King, R.: Semantic database modeling: Survey, applications, and research issues. ACM Computing Surveys 19(3), 201–260 (1987)
10. Ishikawa, Y., Kitagawa, H.: Source description-based approach for the modeling of spatial information integration. In: Kunii, H.S., Jajodia, S., Sølvberg, A. (eds.) ER 2001. LNCS, vol. 2224, pp. 41–55. Springer, Heidelberg (2001)
11. Liu, W., Chen, J., Zhao, R., Cheng, T.: A refined line-line spatial relationship model for spatial conflict detection. In: Akoka, J., Liddle, S.W., Song, I.-Y., Bertolotto, M., Comyn-Wattiau, I., van den Heuvel, W.-J., Kolp, M., Trujillo, J., Kop, C., Mayr, H.C. (eds.) ER Workshops 2005. LNCS, vol. 3770, pp. 239–248. Springer, Heidelberg (2005)
12. McKenney, M., Schneider, M.: PLR partitions: A conceptual model of maps. In: Hainaut, J.-L., Rundensteiner, E.A., Kirchberg, M., Bertolotto, M., Brochhausen, M., Chen, Y.-P.P., Cherfi, S.S.-S., Doerr, M., Han, H., Hartmann, S., Parsons, J., Poels, G., Rolland, C., Trujillo, J., Yu, E., Zimányie, E. (eds.) ER Workshops 2007. LNCS, vol. 4802, pp. 368–377. Springer, Heidelberg (2007)
13. Paredaens, J.: Spatial databases, the final frontier. In: Vardi, M.Y., Gottlob, G. (eds.) ICDT 1995. LNCS, vol. 893, pp. 14–32. Springer, Heidelberg (1995)
14. Paredaens, J., Kuijpers, B.: Data models and query languages for spatial databases. Data and Knowledge Engineering 25(1-2), 29–53 (1998)
15. Price, R., Tryfona, N., Jensen, C.S.: Modeling topological constraints in spatial part-whole relationships. In: Kunii, H.S., Jajodia, S., Sølvberg, A. (eds.) ER 2001. LNCS, vol. 2224, pp. 27–40. Springer, Heidelberg (2001)
16. Sali, A., Schewe, K.-D.: A characterisation of coincidence ideals for complex values. Journal of Universal Computer Science 15(1), 304–354 (2009)
17. Salomon, D.: Curves and Surfaces for Computer Graphics. Springer, Heidelberg (2005)

18. Shekhar, S., Vatsavai, R.R., Chawla, S., Burk, T.E.: Spatial pictogram enhanced conceptual data models and their translation to logical data models. In: Agouris, P., Stefanidis, A. (eds.) ISD 1999. LNCS, vol. 1737, pp. 77–104. Springer, Heidelberg (1999)
19. Shekhar, S., Xiong, H. (eds.): Encyclopedia of GIS. Springer, Heidelberg (2008)
20. Stoffel, E.-P., Lorenz, B., Ohlbach, H.J.: Towards a semantic spatial model for pedestrian indoor navigation. In: Hainaut, J.-L., Rundensteiner, E.A., Kirchberg, M., Bertolotto, M., Brochhausen, M., Chen, Y.-P.P., Cherfi, S.S.-S., Doerr, M., Han, H., Hartmann, S., Parsons, J., Poels, G., Rolland, C., Trujillo, J., Yu, E., Zimányie, E. (eds.) ER Workshops 2007. LNCS, vol. 4802, pp. 328–337. Springer, Heidelberg (2007)
21. Thalheim, B.: Entity Relationship Modeling – Foundations of Database Technology. Springer, Heidelberg (2000)

Anchor Modeling

An Agile Modeling Technique Using the Sixth Normal Form for Structurally and Temporally Evolving Data

Olle Regardt[1], Lars Rönnbäck[1], Maria Bergholtz[2], Paul Johannesson[2], and Petia Wohed[2]

[1] Affecto Sweden
[2] DSV, SU/KTH, Stockholm, Sweden
{olle.regardt,lars.ronnback}@affecto.com,
{maria,pajo,petia}@dsv.su.se

Abstract. Maintaining and evolving data warehouses is a complex, error prone, and time consuming activity. The main reason for this state of affairs is that the environment of a data warehouse is in constant change, while the warehouse itself needs to provide a stable and consistent interface to information spanning extended periods of time. In this paper, we propose a modeling technique for data warehousing, called anchor modeling, that offers non-destructive extensibility mechanisms, thereby enabling robust and flexible management of changes in source systems. A key benefit of anchor modeling is that changes in a data warehouse environment only require extensions, not modifications, to the data warehouse. This ensures that existing data warehouse applications will remain unaffected by the evolution of the data warehouse, i.e. existing views and functions will not have to be modified as a result of changes in the warehouse model.

Keywords: anchor modeling, normalization, 6NF, data warehousing, agile development, temporal databases, table elimination.

1 Introduction

Maintaining and evolving data warehouses is a complex, error prone, and time consuming activity. The main reason for this state of affairs is that the environment of a data warehouse is in constant change, while the warehouse itself needs to provide a stable and consistent interface to information spanning extended periods of time. Sources that deliver data to the warehouse change continuously over time and sometimes dramatically. The information retrieval needs, such as analytical and reporting needs also change. In order to address these challenges, data models of warehouses have to be modular, flexible, and track changes in the handled information [16]. However, many existing warehouses suffer from having a model that does not fulfill those requirements. One third of implemented warehouses have at some point, usually within the first four years, changed their architecture, and less than a third quotes their warehouses as being a success [24].

In this paper, we propose a modeling technique, called anchor modeling, that offers non-destructive extensibility mechanisms, thereby enabling robust and flexible representations of changes. A positive consequence of this is that all previous

A.H.F. Laender et al. (Eds.): ER 2009, LNCS 5829, pp. 234–250, 2009.

versions of a schema will be available at any given time as parts of the complete schema [2]. Using anchor modeling results in data models in which only small changes are needed when large changes occur in the surrounding environment, like adding or switching a source system or analytical tool. This reduced need for redesign extends the longevity of a data warehouse, reduces the implementation time, and simplifies maintenance [23].

A key benefit of anchor modeling is that changes in a data warehouse environment only require extensions, not modifications, to the data model. Applications thereby remain unaffected by the evolution of the data model and thus do not have to be immediately modified [21]. Furthermore, evolution through extensions rather than modifications results in modularity, making it possible to decompose data models into small, stable and manageable components. This modularity is also of great value in agile development where short iterations are required. It is possible to construct an initial model with a small number of agreed upon business terms, which later can be seamlessly extended into a final model. Close to half of current data warehouse projects are either behind schedule or over budget [24,4], partly due to having a too large initial project scope.

An anchor model is a relational database schema that displays a high degree of normalization, reuse of data and the ability to store historical data. It uses a small number of model constructs together with a set of guidelines for combining these constructs in designing data models. The high decomposition of the database stems from the fact that attributes become separate tables in the schema. This differs significantly from the currently popular approach of using de-normalized multidimensional models [15] for data warehouses. Even though the origin of anchor modeling were the requirements found in such environments it is a generic modeling approach, also suitable for other types of systems.

This paper is organized as follows. Section 2 defines anchor modeling and a naming convention, Section 3 introduces a running example, Section 4 suggests anchor modeling guidelines, and physical implementation is described in Section 5. In Section 6 advantages of anchor modeling are discussed, Section 7 contrasts the approach versus related research, and Section 8 concludes the paper and gives directions for further research.

2 Basic Notions of Anchor Modeling

In this section, we introduce the basic notions of anchor modeling by first explaining them informally and then giving formal definitions using the relational model. The basic building blocks of an anchor model are *anchors*, *knots*, *attributes*, and *ties*. The highly decomposed relational database schemas that result from anchor models facilitate traceability through metadata, capturing information such as creator, source, and time of creation. Although important, metadata is not discussed further since its use does not differ from that of other modeling techniques.

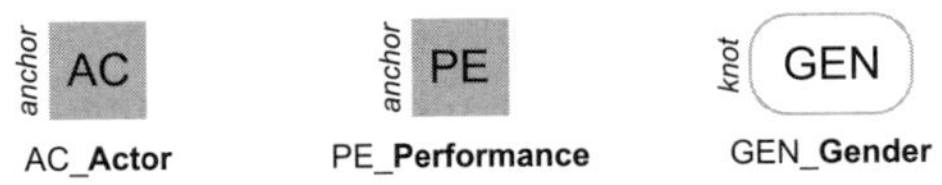

Fig. 1. An anchor is shown as a square and a knot as a rectangle with rounded edges

2.1 Anchors

An anchor represents a set of entities, such as a set of actors or events. See Fig. 1.

Def 1 (Identities). *Let $\mathcal{ID}$ be an infinite set of symbols, which are used as identities.*

In addition to $\mathcal{ID}$, we will also make use of standard data types, such as strings, integers and time types as domains for attributes.

Def 2 (Anchor). *An* anchor *$A(C)$ is a table with one column. The domain of C is $\mathcal{ID}$. The primary key for A is C.*

Example rows of AC_**Actor**(AC_**ID**) are {"4711", "4712"}.

2.2 Knots

A knot is used to represent a fixed set of entities that do not change over time. While anchors are used to represent arbitrary entities, knots are used to manage properties that are shared by many instances of some anchor. A typical example of a knot is GEN_**Gender**, see Fig. 1, which includes two instances, 'Male' and 'Female'. This property, gender, is shared by many instances of the AC_**Actor** anchor, thus using a knot minimizes redundancy. Rather than repeating the strings a single bit per instance is sufficient.

Def 3 (Knot). *A* knot *$K(S, V)$ is a table with two columns. The domain of S is $\mathcal{ID}$, and of V a non-null data type. The primary key for K is S.*

Example rows of GEN_**Gender**(GEN_**ID**, GEN_**Gender**) are {"1, Male", "2, Female"}.

2.3 Attributes

Attributes are used to represent properties of anchors. We distinguish between four kinds of attributes: *static*, *historized*, *knotted static*, and *knotted historized*, see Fig. 2. A static attribute is used to represent arbitrary properties of entities (anchors), where it is not needed to keep the history of changes to the attribute values. A historized attribute is used when changes of the attribute values need to be recorded. A value is considered valid until it is replaced by one with a later time. Valid time [6] is hence represented as an open interval with an explicitly specified beginning. The interval is implicitly closed when an instance with a later valid time is added for the same anchor identity. A knotted static attribute is used to represent relationships between anchors and knots, i.e. to relate an anchor to properties that can take on only a fixed, typically small, number of values. Finally a knotted historized attribute is used when the relation to a value in the knot is not stable and may change over time.

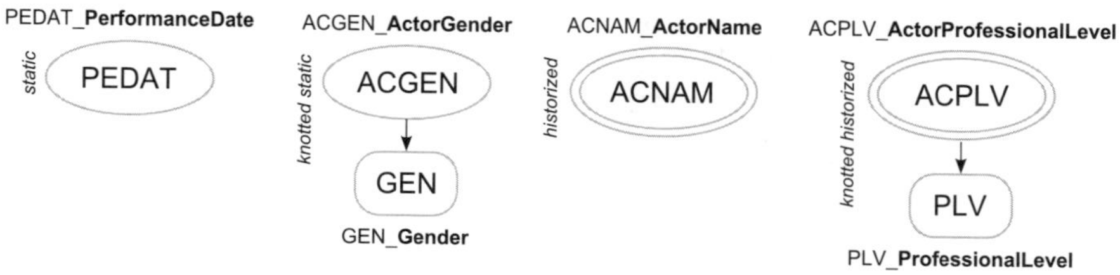

Fig. 2. Attributes are shown as ellipses with a double outline when historized

Def 4 (Static Attribute). *A* static attribute $S_{att}(C, D)$ *for an anchor* $A(C)$ *is a table with two columns. The domain of* C *is* $\mathcal{ID}$, *and of* D *a non-null data type.* $S_{att}.C$ *is a primary key for* S_{att} *and a non-null foreign key with respect to* $A.C$.

Def 5 (Historized Attribute). *A* historized attribute $H_{att}(C, D, T)$ *for an anchor* $A(C)$ *is a table with three columns. The domain of* C *is* $\mathcal{ID}$, *of* D *a non-null data type, and of* T *a non-null time type.* $H_{att}.C$ *is a non-null foreign key with respect to* $A.C$. $(H_{att}.C, H_{att}.T)$ *is a primary key for* S_{att}.

Def 6 (Knotted Static Attribute). *Let* $K(S, V)$ *be a knot. A* knotted static attribute $KS_{att}(C, S)$ *for an anchor* $A(C)$ *is a table with two columns. The domain of* $KS_{att}.C$ *and* $KS_{att}.S$ *is* $\mathcal{ID}$. $KS_{att}.C$ *is a primary key for* KS_{att} *and a non-null foreign key with respect to* $A.C$. $KS_{att}.S$ *is a foreign key with respect to* $K.S$.

Def 7 (Knotted Historized Attribute). *Let* $K(S, V)$ *be a knot. A* knotted historized attribute $KH_{att}(C, S, T)$ *for an anchor* $A(C)$ *is a table with three columns. The domain of* $KH_{att}.C$ *and* $KH_{att}.S$ *is* $\mathcal{ID}$, *and of* T *a non-null time type.* $KH_{att}.C$ *is a non-null foreign key with respect to* $A.C$, *and* $KH_{att}.S$ *is a foreign key with respect to* $K.S$. $(KH_{att}.C, KH_{att}.T)$ *is a primary key for* KH_{att}.

Example rows of ACNAM_**ActorName**(AC_**ID**, ACNAM_**ActorName**, ACNAM_**FromDate**) are {"4711, 'John Doe', 1972-08-20", "4711, 'Jane Doe', 2009-11-09"}.

2.4 Ties

A tie represents associations between two or more entities (anchors). Similarly to attributes, ties come in four variants, *static*, *historized*, *knotted static*, and *knotted historized*. See Fig. 3.

Def 8 (Static Tie). *A* static tie $S_{tie}(C_1, \ldots, C_n)$ *relating a set of anchors* $\{A_1(C_1), \ldots, A_m(C_m)\}$ *is a table with* n *columns satisfying* $n \geq m$ *and* $n \geq 2$, *where for every* i *in* $[1, n]$, $S_{tie}.C_i$ *is a non-null foreign key to some* $A_j.C_j$ *for* j *in* $[1, m]$. *The primary key for* S_{tie} *is a subset of* $(C_1, \ldots, C_n)$.

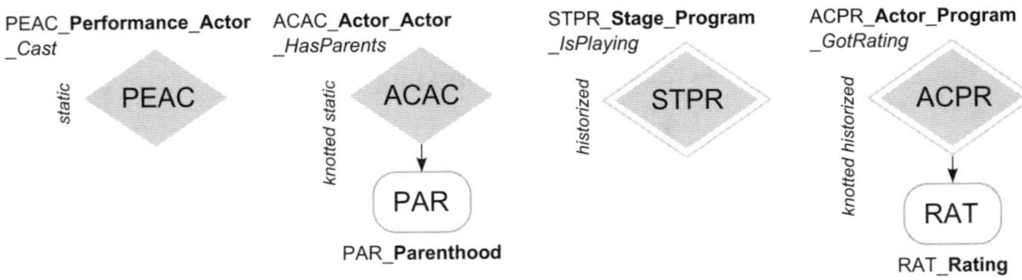

Fig. 3. Ties are shown as diamonds with a double outline when historized

Def 9 (Historized Tie). *A* historized tie $H_{tie}(C_1, \ldots, C_n, T)$ *relating a set of anchors* $\{A_1(C_1), \ldots, A_m(C_m)\}$ *is a table with* $n+1$ *columns satisfying* $n \geq m$ *and* $n \geq 2$*, where for every* i *in* $[1, n]$*,* $H_{tie}.C_i$ *is a non-null foreign key to some* $A_j.C_j$ *for* j *in* $[1, m]$*, and the domain of the last column* T *is a non-null time type. The primary key for* H_{tie} *is a subset of* $(C_1, \ldots, C_n, T)$ *containing* T*.*

Def 10 (Knotted Static Tie). *A* knotted static tie $KS_{tie}(C_1, \ldots, C_n, S_1, \ldots, S_l)$ *relating a set of anchors* $\{A_1(C_1), \ldots, A_m(C_m)\}$ *is a table with* $n+l$ *columns satisfying* $l \geq 1$*,* $n \geq m$ *and* $n \geq 2$*, where for every* i *in* $[1, n]$*,* $KS_{tie}.C_i$ *is a non-null foreign key to some* $A_j.C_j$ *for* j *in* $[1, m]$*, and columns* $S_1, \ldots, S_l$ *are non-null foreign keys to* $K_1, \ldots, K_l$ *where* $K_p(S_p, V_p)$ *is a knot for* p *in* $[1, l]$*. The primary key for* KS_{tie} *is a subset of* $(C_1, \ldots, C_n, S_1, \ldots, S_l)$*.*

Def 11 (Knotted Historized Tie). *A* knotted historized tie $KH_{tie}(C_1, \ldots, C_n, S_1, \ldots, S_l, T)$ *relating a set of anchors* $\{A_1(C_1), \ldots, A_m(C_m)\}$ *is a table with* $n+l+1$ *columns satisfying* $l \geq 1$*,* $n \geq m$ *and* $n \geq 2$*, where for every* i *in* $[1, n]$*,* $KH_{tie}.C_i$ *is a non-null foreign key to some* $A_j.C_j$ *for* j *in* $[1, m]$*, and columns* $S_1, \ldots, S_l$ *are non-null foreign keys to* $K_1, \ldots, K_l$ *where* $K_p(S_p, V_p)$ *is a knot for* p *in* $[1, l]$*, and the domain of the last column* T *is a non-null time type. The primary key for* KH_{tie} *is a subset of* $(C_1, \ldots, C_n, S_1, \ldots, S_l, T)$ *containing* T*.*

Example rows of ACPR_**Actor_Program**_*GotRating*(AC_**ID**, PR_**ID**, RAT_**ID**, ACPR_**FromDate**) are {"4711, 555, 5, 2008-02-13", "4711, 555, 4, 2008-12-24"}.

2.5 Anchor Model

In order to model a universe of discourse an anchor model is used which consists of a set of anchors, knots, attributes and ties.

Def 12 (Anchor Model). *An* anchor model *is a set* $\mathbb{AM} = \{A, K, S_{att}, H_{att}, KS_{att}, KH_{att}, S_{tie}, H_{tie}, KS_{tie}, KH_{tie}\}$*, where* A *is a set of anchors,* K *is a set of knots,* $S_{att}, H_{att}, KS_{att}, KH_{att}$ *are sets of attributes, and* $S_{tie}, H_{tie}, KS_{tie}, KH_{tie}$ *are sets of ties.*

Table 1. The naming conventions, where n is the number of anchor references

Type	Mnemonic length	Example names
Anchor	2	AC_**Actor**, PE_**Performance**
Knot	3	GEN_**Gender**, PAR_**Parenthood**
Attribute	$2+3$	ACGEN_**ActorGender**, ACNAM_**ActorName**
Tie	$2n$, $n \geq 2$	ACAC_**Actor_Actor**_*HasParents*, PEAC_**Performance_Actor**_*Cast*
Content	inherited	AC_**ID**, ACNAM_**FromDate**

2.6 Naming Convention

The names of entities in an anchor model have different parts. The first part of a name is an upper-case mnemonic derived from the actual entity or built up from the adjoining entities. The second part of the name is a human readable descriptive text. See Table 1. Knots on ties do not affect the naming of the tie. Identity columns keep their names, i.e. the column AC_**ID** can be found in the anchor AC_**Actor** as a primary key and in both attributes ACGEN_**Gender** and ACNAM_**ActorName** as a foreign key. All other columns inherit the mnemonic from the containing table.

3 Running Example

The scenario in this example is based on a business arranging stage performances. It is an extension of the example discussed in [14]. An anchor model for this example is shown in Fig. 4.

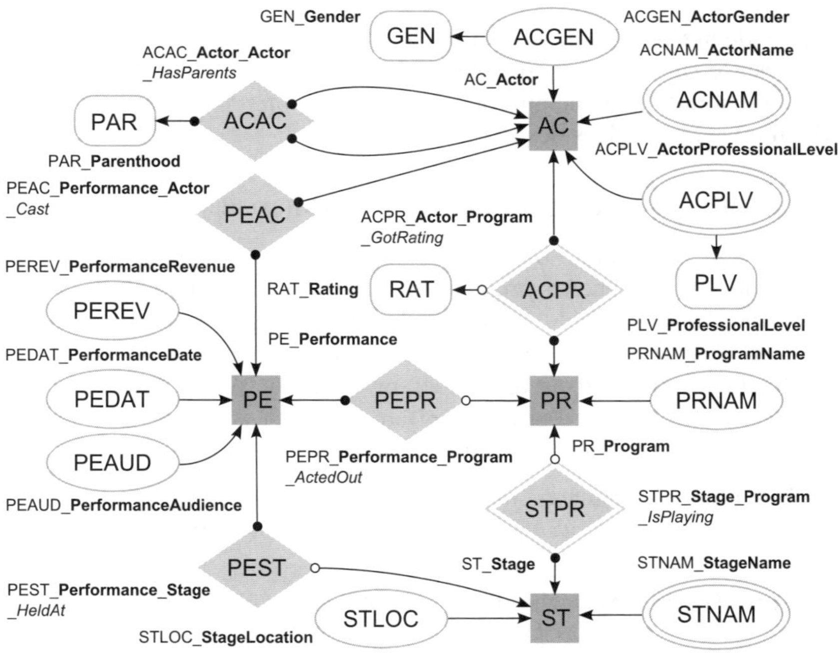

Fig. 4. An example anchor model illustrating different modeling concepts

Four anchors PE_**Performance**, ST_**Stage**, PR_**Program** and AC_**Actor** capture the present entities. Attributes such as PRNAM_**ProgramName** and PEDAT_**PerformanceDate** capture properties of those entities. Some of these attributes, e.g. ACNAM_**ActorName** and STNAM_**StageName** are historized, to capture the fact that they are subject to changes. The fact that an actor has a gender, which is one of two values, is captured through the knot GEN_**Gender** and a knotted attribute called ACGEN_**ActorGender**. Similarly, since the business also keeps tracks of the professional level of actors, the knot PLV_**ProfessionalLevel** and the knotted attribute ACPLV_**ActorProfessionalLevel** are introduced, which in addition is historized to capture attribute value changes.

Furthermore, the relationships between the anchors are captured through ties. In the example the following ties are introduced: PEAC_**Performance_Actor**_*Cast*, PEST_**Performance_Stage**_*HeldAt*, PEPR_**Performance_Program**_*ActedOut*, STPR_**Stage_Program**_*IsPlaying*, ACPR_**Actor_Program**_*GotRating*, and ACAC_**Actor_Actor**_*HasParents* to capture the existing binary relationships.

The historized tie STPR_**Stage_Program**_*isPlaying* is used to capture the fact that stages change programs. The tie ACPR_**Actor_Program**_*GotRating* is knotted to show that actors get ratings on the programs they are playing and historized for capturing the changes in these ratings.

A small black circle on a tie edge in Fig. 4 indicates that the connected anchor is part of the primary key for the tie, while a white circle indicates that it is not.

4 Guidelines for Designing Anchor Models

Anchor modeling has been used in a number of industrial projects. Based on this experience the following guidelines have been formulated. These provide a deeper understanding of the approach as well as support the building of anchor models in a way that gives desired properties.

4.1 Modeling Core Entities and Transactions

Core entities in the domain of interest should be represented as anchors in an anchor model. A well-known problem in conceptual modeling is to determine whether a transaction should be modeled as a relationship or as an entity [11]. In anchor models, the question is formulated as determining whether a transaction should be modeled as an anchor or as a tie. When a transaction has some property, like PEDAT_**PerformanceDate** in Fig. 4, it should be modeled as an anchor. It can be modeled as a tie only if the transaction has no properties.

Guideline (1). *Use anchors for modeling core entities and transactions. A transaction can only be modeled as a tie if it has no properties.*

4.2 Using Static, Historized and Knotted Attributes

Historized attributes are used when versioning of attribute values are of importance. A data warehouse, for instance, is not solely built to integrate data but also to keep a history of changes that have taken place. In anchor models, historized attributes take care of versioning by coupling versioning/history information to a data value in an attribute.

Guideline (2a). *When versioning of attribute values are of importance, use a historized attribute, when not, use a static attribute.*

A knot represents a type with a fixed set of instances that do not change over time. In many respects, knots are similar to the concept of power types [8], which are types with a fixed and small set of instances representing categories of allowed values. In Fig. 2 the anchor AC_**Actor** gets its gender attribute via a knotted static attribute, ACGEN_**ActorGender**, rather than storing the actual gender value (i.e. the string 'Male' or 'Female') of an actor directly in a static attribute. The advantage of using knots is reuse, as attributes can be specified through references to a knot identifier instead of a value. The latter is undesirable because of the redundancy it introduces, i.e. long attribute values have to be repeated resulting in increased storage requirements and update anomalies.

Guideline (2b). *When the instances of an attribute represent categories or can take on only a fixed small set of values, use a knotted attribute.*

Guideline 2a and 2b may be combined, i.e. when both attribute values represent categories and the versioning of these categories are of importance. Further, if attribute values are not stable, i.e. can cease to exist, such that the related anchor instance no longer can be said to have this property, only a knotted historized attribute can capture this fact.

Guideline (2c). *If the instances of an attribute represent categories or a fixed small set of values and either the versioning of these are of importance or if they are not stable, a knotted historized attribute should be used. If versioning is not important and values are stable over time, use a knotted static attribute.*

4.3 Using Static, Historized and Knotted Ties

A static tie is used for relationships that do not change over time. For example, the actors who took part in a certain performance will never change. Typically, anchors modeling transactions or events statically relate to other anchors, i.e. a transaction or event happens at a particular time and does not change afterwards. A historized tie is used for relationships that change over time. For example, the program played at a specific stage will change over time. At any point in time, exactly one relationship will be valid.

Guideline (3a). *When a relationship may change over time, use a historized tie, when it cannot, use a static tie.*

A knotted tie is used for relationships where the instances fall within certain categories. For example, if we have two anchors, AC_**Actor** and PR_**Program**, a relationship between the two may be categorized as 'good', 'bad' or 'medium' indicating how well the actor performed the program. A knot is used to model such categories.

Guideline (3b). *When the instances of a relation belong to certain categories, use a knotted tie.*

Guideline 3a and 3b can also be combined in the case when these categories may change over time. Further, if a relation can cease to exist, only a knotted historized tie can be used to capture this fact. Since a (not knotted) historized tie only models the valid time of a relationship it cannot capture the fact that a relationship is no longer valid.

Guideline (3c). *If the instances of a relation fall within certain categories and these may change over time or if they are not stable, use a knotted historized tie. If categories do not change and instances are stable over time, use a knotted static tie.*

5 Physical Implementation

In this section the physical implementation of an anchor model is discussed.

5.1 Views and Functions

Due to the large number of tables and the added complexity from handling historical data, an abstraction layer in the form of views and functions is added to simplify querying. It de-normalizes the anchor model and retrieves data from a given temporal perspective. There are three different types of views and functions for each anchor corresponding to the most common use cases when querying data: latest view, point-in-time function, and interval function [26,20], all of which are based on an abstract complete view. Views and functions for ties are created in a way analogous with those for anchors.

Complete View. The *complete view* of an anchor is a de-normalization of an anchor-table and its corresponding attribute-tables. It is constructed by left outer joining the anchor with all its attributes.

Latest View. The *latest view* of an anchor is a view based on the complete view, where only the latest values for historized attributes are included. In order to find the latest version a sub-select is added that ensures that the historization date is the latest one for each identity. See Fig. 5.

```
select * from lST_Stage
```

ST_**ID**	STNAM_**StageName**	STNAM_**FromDate**	STLOC_**StageLocation**
1	Shakespeare's Globe	1997-01-01	Maiden Lane
2	Cockpit	1609-01-01	Drury Lane

Fig. 5. The latest view for anchor ST_Stage

Point-in-time Function. The *point-in-time function* is a function for an anchor with a time point as an argument returning a data set. It is based on the complete view where for each attribute only its latest value before or at the given time point is included. A sub-select is added that ensures that the historization time is the latest one earlier than or on the given time point for each identity. See Fig. 6.

```
select * from pST_Stage('1608-01-01')
-------------------------------------------------------------------------------------
ST_ID  STNAM_StageName         STNAM_FromDate       STLOC_StageLocation
-------------------------------------------------------------------------------------
1      The Globe Theatre       1599-01-01           Maiden Lane
```

Fig. 6. The point in time function for anchor ST_Stage at '1608-01-01'

Interval Function. The *interval function* is a function for an anchor taking two time points as arguments and returning a data set. It is based on the complete view where for each attribute only values between the given time points are included. Here the sub-select must ensure that the historization date lies within the two provided dates. See Fig. 7.

```
select * from dST_Stage('1598-01-01', '1998-01-01')
-------------------------------------------------------------------------------------
ST_ID  STNAM_StageName         STNAM_FromDate       STLOC_StageLocation
-------------------------------------------------------------------------------------
1      The Globe Theatre       1599-01-01           Maiden Lane
1      Shakespeare's Globe     1997-01-01           Maiden Lane
2      Cockpit                 1609-01-01           Drury Lane
```

Fig. 7. The interval function for anchor ST_Stage between '1598-01-01' and '1998-01-01'

5.2 Advantages of Table Elimination

Modern query optimizers utilize a technique called table (or join) elimination [18], which in practice implies that tables containing not selected attributes in queries are automatically eliminated. The optimizer will remove table T from the execution plan of a query if the following two conditions are fulfilled: (i) no column from T is explicitly selected, (ii) the number of rows in the returned data set is not affected by the join with T.

The views and functions defined in Section 5.1 are created in order to take advantage of table elimination. The anchor table is used as the left table in the view (or function) with the attributes left outer joined. The left join ensures that the number of rows retrieved is at least as many as in the anchor table. Furthermore, since the join is based on the primary key in the attribute, uniqueness is also ensured, hence the number of resulting rows is equal to the number of the rows in the anchor table. Typical queries only retrieve a small number of attributes, which implies that table elimination is frequently used, yielding reduced access time.

5.3 Effects on Performance

Table elimination has positive effects on performance. The following two scenarios where an anchor model is compared with corresponding 3NF tables illustrate these effects. In both scenarios, a fixed table scanning query in which not all available attributes are selected is used. In the first scenario, an initial model is created with a number of attributes. The size of the model is then increased by adding more attributes, but the number of rows is kept constant. In this situation the execution time for the query will be constant in the anchor model, but growing for the 3NF tables, as they get more columns.

In the second scenario, the same query is used, but now the model keeps its size and the number of rows are increased instead. In this situation the execution time will grow both for the anchor model and the 3NF tables, due to the larger amount of data that has to be scanned. As long as not all of the available attributes are queried for, execution time will grow faster in the 3NF model than in the anchor model. This is because a shorter total row length implies lesser growth rate when new rows are added.

These effects have been validated in Microsoft SQL Server 2005 (scripts and detailed results are available from `http://www.anchormodeling.com`). Table 2 contains aggregated test results from two queries run ten times each for different numbers of rows and attributes in an anchor model and corresponding 3NF tables. The queries group one and two attributes respectively while calculating the average of a third one. This results in table scanning queries, which should behave according to the described scenarios. The results show that the average query times for the anchor model range from twice to half of that in the 3NF model. An anchor model performs better than 3NF when the fraction is below one. Both a larger model size and a larger amount of data gives the anchor model an advantage over 3NF. There is in both cases a threshold after which the anchor model performs better, having extrapolated the number of rows series in some cases. The conclusion is that in many situations anchor modeled databases are less I/O intense under normal querying operations than in other modeling techniques. This makes anchor models suitable in situations where I/O tend to become a bottleneck, such as in data warehousing [17].

Table 2. Average query times in an anchor model as fractions of those in a 3NF model

	Millions of Rows				
Attributes	0.2–0.4	0.6–0.8	1.0–1.2	1.4–1.6	1.8–2.0
10	2.17	1.96	1.84	1.79	1.89
20	1.26	1.22	1.01	0.92	1.10
30	0.94	0.86	0.83	0.91	0.78
40	0.63	0.71	0.64	0.71	0.59
50	0.61	0.55	0.49	0.55	0.56

5.4 Loading Practices

When loading data into an anchor model a zero update strategy is used. This means that only insert statements are allowed and that data is always added, never updated. Delete statements are allowed only when applied to remove erroneous data. A complete history is thereby stored for accurate information [20]. Another reason for not using updates is that they are costly in terms of performance when compared to insert statements.

6 Benefits

The anchor modeling approach offers several benefits. The most important of them are categorized and listed in the following subsections.

6.1 Ease of Modeling

Simple concepts and notation. Anchor models are constructed using a small number of simple concepts (Section 2). This simplicity and the use of modeling guidelines (Section 4) reduce the number of options available when solving a modeling problem, thereby reducing the risk of introducing errors in an anchor model.

Historization by design. Managing different versions of information is simple, as anchor modeling offers native constructs for information versioning in the form of historized attributes and ties (Sections 2.3, 2.4).

Iterative and incremental development. Anchor modeling facilitates iterative and agile development, as it allows independent work on small subsets of the model under consideration, which later can be integrated into a global model. Changing requirements is handled by additions without affecting the existing parts of a model (cf. bus architecture [15]).

Reduced translation logic. The symbols introduced to graphically represent tables in an anchor model (Section 2) can also be used for conceptual and logical modeling. This gives a near 1-1 relationship between all levels of modeling, which simplifies, or even eliminates, the need for translation logic in order to move between them.

6.2 Simplified Maintenance

Ease of temporal querying. In an anchor model, data is historized on attribute level rather than row level. This facilitates tracing attribute changes directly instead of having to analyze an entire row in order to derive which of its attributes have changed. In addition, the predefined views and functions (Section 5.1) also simplify temporal querying.

Absence of null values. There are no null values in an anchor model. This eliminates the need to interpret null values [21] as well as the waste of storage space.

Reusability and automation. The small number of modeling constructs together with the naming convention (Section 2.6) in an anchor model yield a high degree of structure, which can be taken advantage of in the form of reusability and automation. For example, ready-made templates for recurring tasks can be made and automatic code generation is possible, speeding up development.

Asynchronous arrival of data. In an anchor model asynchronous arrival of data can be handled in a simple way. Late arriving data will lead to additions rather than updates, as data for a single attribute is stored in a table of its own (compared to other approaches where a table may include several attributes) [15, pp. 271–274].

6.3 High Performance

High run-time performance. For many types of queries, an anchor model achieves much better performance compared to databases that contain tables with many columns. The combination of fewer columns per table, table elimination (Section 5.2), and minimal redundancy (Section 2.2) restricts the data set scanned during a query, yielding less response time.

Efficient storage. Anchor modeling results in smaller sized databases. The high degree of normalization (Section 7) together with the knot construction (Section 2.2), absence of null values, and the fact that historization never unnecessarily duplicates data means that the total database size will be smaller than that of a corresponding less normalized model.

Parallelized physical media access. When using views and functions (Section 5.1), the high degree of decomposition and table elimination makes it possible to parallelize physical media access by separating the underlying tables onto different media [17]. Tables that are queried more often than others can also reside on speedier media for faster access.

The benefits of the anchor modeling approach are relevant for any database but especially valuable for data warehouses. In particular, the support for iterative and incremental development, the ease of temporal querying, and the management of asynchronous arrival of data help providing a stable and consistent interface to rapidly changing sources of a data warehouse.

7 Related Research

Anchor modeling is compared to other approaches in the following paragraphs.

Data Warehousing Approaches. One well established approach for data warehouse design is the Dimensional Modeling approach proposed by Kimball [15]. In dimensional modeling, a number of star-join schemas (stars for short) are used to capture the modeled domain and each star focuses on a specific process. It is composed of a fact table, for capturing process activites and important messages as well as a number of dimension tables for capturing entities, attributes and descriptions. In contrast to anchor modeling, Kimball advocates a high degree of de-normalization of the dimensions. The rationale for this is to reduce the number of joins needed when accessing the data warehouse and in this way speed up the response time. Furthermore, also Inmon points out that "lots of little tables" leads to performance problems [12, p. 104], however, he does not to the same extent as Kimball advocate complete de-normalization, but leaves this as an issue for the designers. However, though highly normalized, anchor models have proven to offer fast retrieval.

Conceptual Modeling Approaches. Anchor modeling has several similarities to the ORM (Object Role Modeling) approach which was established already during the 1990s [10]. ORM is a modeling notation widely used for conceptual modeling and data base design. In addition [10] also provides a modeling methodology for designing a domain description in an ORM model and translating it into a logical data base design (typically normalized up to the 3NF). An anchor model can be captured in an ORM model by representing the Anchors as Objects types, Attributes as Value types, (Static) Ties as Predicates, Historized Attributes and Ties as Predicates with Time point as one of the predicate's roles, etc. However, there are some essential differences between anchor modeling and ORM. ORM does not have any explicit notation for time, which anchor modeling provides. Furthermore, the methodology provided with ORM [10] for constructing database models, optimizes the models to 3NF which is typical for relational database design.

Anchor modeling is also similar to ER (Entity Relationship) modeling [5] and UML (Unified Modeling Language) [3]. Three constructs have correspondences in ER schemas: anchors correspond to entities, attributes correspond to attributes (anchors and attributes together hence correspond to a class in UML), and a tie maps to a relationship or an association. While the knot-construct has no immediate correspondence to any construct in an ER schema, it is similar to so called power-types [8], i.e. categories of, often intangible, concepts. Power types, and knots, are used to encode properties that are shared by many instances of other, often tangible, concepts. Anchor models offer no general mechanism for generalization/specialization as in EER (Enhanced Entity Relationship) models [7], instead anchor models provide three predefined varieties of attributes and ties in order to represent either temporal properties or relationships to categories.

Less Normalized Databases. A key feature of anchor models is that they display a very high degree of normalization. This stems mainly from the fact that every distinct fact (attribute) in an anchor model is a table of its own, in the form of anchor-key, attribute-value, and optional historical information. In contrast, in an ordinary 3NF schema several attributes are contained within the same table. A table is in sixth normal form iff it satisfies no non-trivial join dependencies, i.e. a 6NF table cannot be decomposed further into relational schemes with fewer attributes [6]. All anchors, knots and attributes will give rise to 6NF tables, and the same applies for ties that result in all-key tables. The only constructs in an anchor model that could give rise to non-6NF tables are those ties in which not all columns are part of the primary key. For an analysis of anchor models and 6NF refer to [19], which is based on the definition of 6NF according to [6].

Temporal Databases. A temporal database is a database with built-in time aspects, e.g. a temporal data model and a temporal version of structured query language [25]. Database-modeling approaches such as the original ER model does not contain language elements that explicitly support temporal concepts. Extensions [9] to ER schemas encompass temporal constructs such as *valid time*, the time (interval) in which a fact is true in the real world, and *transaction time*, the time in which a fact is stored in a database [1,6,13]. Anchor models provide syntax elements for representing the former, i.e. valid time, for both attributes (historized attributes) and ties (historized ties). In addition, if metadata is used transaction time can also be represented. Anchor modeling does not provide a query language with operators dedicated to querying the temporal elements of the model, however it does provide views and functions for simplifying and optimizing temporal queries.

8 Conclusions and Further Research

Anchor modeling is a technique for managing data warehouses that has been proven to work in practice. Several data warehouses have been built (by the consulting company Affecto since 2004) using anchor modeling and are in daily use. The deployment of anchor modeling for very large databases provides a direction for further research.

Anchor modeling is built on a small set of intuitive concepts complemented with a number of guidelines for building anchor models, which supports agile development of data warehouses. A key feature of anchor modeling is that changes only require extensions, not modifications, to an anchor model. This feature is the basis for a number of benefits provided by anchor models, including ease of temporal querying and high run-time performance.

Anchor modeling differs from main stream approaches in data warehousing that typically emphasize de-normalization, which is considered essential for fast retrieval. Anchor modeling, on the other hand, results in highly normalized data models, even in 6NF. Though highly normalized, these data models still offer fast retrieval. This is a consequence of table elimination, where narrow tables with few columns are scanned rather than wide tables with many columns. Validating performance tests have been carried out on Microsoft SQL Server 2005. Full table elimination for views and functions has also been confirmed for recent versions of Oracle, IBM DB2, PostgreSQL, and in part for Teradata (scripts and results can be found on `http://www.anchormodeling.com`). Comparative performance tests as well as physical implementation of views and functions on other DBMS outline a direction for future work.

Another line of research concerns the actual implementation of the anchor model. Most commercial Database Management Systems (DBMS) are mainly row-oriented, i.e. every attribute of one row are stored in a given sequence, followed by the next row and its attributes until the last row of the table. Since anchor models to a large degree consists of binary tables, column stores, i.e. column oriented DBMSs [22] that stores their content by column rather than by row might offer a better solution. Moreover, for OLAP-workloads, which often involve a smaller number of queries involving aggregated columns over *all* data, column stores can be expected to be especially well suited.

Anchor modeling dispenses with the requirement that an entire domain or enterprise has to be modeled in a single step. The possibility of an all-encompassing model is not a realistic option. At some point in time, a change will occur that could not have been foreseen. Anchor modeling is built upon the assumption that perfect predictions never can be made. A model is not built to last, it is built to change.

References

1. Artale, A., Franconi, E.: Reasoning with Enhanced Temporal Entity-Relationship Models. In: Proc. of the 10th Intl. Workshop on Database and Expert Systems Applications (1999)
2. Bebel, B., Eder, J., Koncilia, C., Morzy, T., Wrembel, R.: Creation and Management of Versions in Multiversion Data Warehouses. In: ACM Symposium on Applied Computing (2004)
3. Booch, G., Rumbaugh, J., Jacobson, J.: The Unified Modelling Language User Guide. Addison Wesley, Reading (1999)
4. Carver, A., Halpin, T.: Atomicity and Normalization. In: Thirteenth International Workshop on Exploring Modeling Methods in Systems Analysis and Design, EMMSAD (2008)
5. Chen, P.: The Entity Relationship Model - Toward a Unified View of Data. ACM Transactions on Database Systems 1(1), 9–36 (1976)
6. Date, C.E., Darwen, H., Lorentzos, N.A.: Temporal Data and the Relational Model. Elsevier Science, Amsterdam (2003)
7. Elmasri, R., Navathe, S.B.: Fundamentals of Database Systems, 5th edn. Addison-Wesley, Reading (2006)
8. Fowler, M.: Analysis Patterns: Reusable Object Models. Addison-Wesley, Reading (1997)
9. Gregersen, H., Jensen, J.S.: Temporal Entity-Relationship models a survey. IEEE Transactions on Knowledge and Data Engineering 11, 464–497 (1999)
10. Halpin, T.: Information Modeling and Relational Databases: From conceptual analysis to logical design using ORM with ER and UML. Morgan Kaufmann Publishers, San Francisco (2001)
11. Hay, D.C.: Data Model Patterns: Conventions of Thought. Dorset House Publishing (1996)
12. Inmon, W.H.: Building the Data Warehouse, 3rd edn. John Wiley & Sons, Chichester (2002)
13. Jensen, C.S., Snodgrass, R.T.: Temporal Data Management. IEEE Transactions on Knowledge and Data Engineering 11, 36–44 (1999)
14. Khodorovskii, V.V.: On Normalization of Relations in Relational Databases. Programming and Computer Software 28(1), 41–52 (2002)
15. Kimball, R., Ross, M.: The Data Warehouse Toolkit: The complete guide to Dimensional Modeling, 2nd edn. Wiley Computer Publishing, Chichester (2002)
16. Li, X.: Building an Agile Data Warehouse: A Proactive Approach to Managing Changes. In: Proc. of the 4th IASTED Intl. Conf. (2006)
17. Nicola, M., Rizvi, H.: Storage Layout and I/O Performance in Data Warehouses. In: Proc. of the 5th Intl. Workshop on Design and Management of Data Warehouses (DMDW 2003), pp. 7.1–7.9 (2003)

18. Paulley, G.N.: Exploiting Functional Dependence in Query Optimization, PhD thesis, Dept. of Computer Science, University of Waterloo, Waterloo, Ontario, Canada (September 2000)
19. Regardt, O., Rönnbäck, L., Bergholtz, M., Johannesson, P., Wohed, P.: Analysis of normal forms for anchor models, `http://www.anchormodeling.com/tiedostot/6nf.pdf` valid at May 13th (2009)
20. Rizzi, S., Golfarelli, M.: What time is it in the data warehouse? In: Tjoa, A.M., Trujillo, J. (eds.) DaWaK 2006. LNCS, vol. 4081, pp. 134–144. Springer, Heidelberg (2006)
21. Roddick, J.F.: A Survey of Schema Versioning Issues for Database Systems. Information and Software Technology 37(7), 383–393 (1995)
22. Stonebraker, et al.: C-Store: A column-oriented DBMS. In: Proc. of the 31st VLDB Conference, VLDB Endowment, pp. 553–564 (2005)
23. Theodoratos, D., Sellis, T.K.: Dynamic data warehouse design. In: Mohania, M., Tjoa, A.M. (eds.) DaWaK 1999. LNCS, vol. 1676, p. 802. Springer, Heidelberg (1999)
24. Watson, H.J., Ariyachandra, T.: Data Warehouse Architectures: Factors in the Selection Decision and the Success of the Architectures, Technical Report, Terry College of Business, University of Georgia, Athens, GA (July 2005)
25. Wikipedia, `http://en.wikipedia.org/wiki/Temporal_database` valid at April 11th (2009)
26. Zimanyi, E.: Temporal Aggregates and Temporal Universal Quantification in Standard SQL. ACM SIGMOD Record 35(2), 16–21 (2006)

Evaluating Exceptions on Time Slices

Romans Kasperovics, Michael H. Böhlen, and Johann Gamper

Free University of Bolzano, Dominikanerplatz 3, 39100 Bolzano, Italy

Abstract. Public transport schedules contain temporal data with many regular patterns that can be represented compactly. Exceptions come as modifications of the initial schedule and break the regular patterns increasing the size of the representation. A typical strategy to preserve the compactness of schedules is to keep exceptions separately. This, however, complicates the automated processing of schedules and imposes a more complex model on applications. In this paper we evaluate exceptions by incorporating them into the patterns that define schedules. We employ sets of time slices, termed multislices, as a representation formalism for schedules and exceptions. The difference of multislices corresponds to the evaluation of exceptions and produces an updated schedule in terms of a multislice. We propose a relational model for multislices, provide an algorithm for efficient evaluating the difference of multislices, and show analytically and experimentally that the evaluation of exceptions is a feasible strategy for realistic schedules.

1 Introduction

Public transport schedules describe the arrival and departure times of public transport means for the stations on predefined routes. In this paper we consider an efficient and compact relational database representation of schedules with exceptions. The key aspect is the compact representation of sets of time instants that represent arrival and departure times. The total number of possible time instants is large. For example, in a small city with 15 bus routes the buses are making around 1000 trips a day visiting up to 20 stations per trip. In a period of 2 years such a schedule describes up to 29.2 million departures and arrivals.

Schedule data contain many regular patterns that can be represented compactly using one of existing representation formalisms. Formalism proposed in [1] can capture periodic repetitions using linear functions and constraints. Work in [2] proposes a simple nested (recursive) formalism that is able to capture many simple patterns. Work in [3] describes a formalism, called *time slices*, where nested repetitions occur over the hierarchies of time granularities. Formalisms proposed in [4,5,6,7,8,9,10,11] exploit the same principle, but are more complex and offer higher expressiveness and compactness. Works in [12,13] go beyond and introduce inprecise specifications of repeating events with applications in medical domain.

Schedules are often subject to changes that come as cancellations or additions of public transport services at specific sights and at specific times. These change introduce irregularities that decrease the compactness of the schedule. In this paper we focus on cancellations, because they usually cause more impact on the compactness of the representation. We refer them as *exceptions*.

A.H.F. Laender et al. (Eds.): ER 2009, LNCS 5829, pp. 251–264, 2009.

Line 10A
Piazza Domenicani – Via Cadorna

valid from 2007-01-01 to 2007-06-30

NOTE: The following bus departures are canceled:

- 2007-01-08 at 05:35
- 2007-02-07 at 17:24
- 2007-02-24 at 14:20
- 2007-02-25 at 15:20
- 2007-01-19 at 22:35 and at 22:55
- 2007-06-28 whole day

	Mon-Fri	Sat	Sun
5	15 35	15 35	
6	15 35	15 35	
7	0 12 24 36 48	0 15 30 45	0 15 30 45
8	0 12 24 36 48	0 15 30 45	0 15 30 45
9	0 12 24 36 48	0 15 30 45	0 15 30 45
10	0 12 24 36 48	0 15 30 45	0 15 30 45
11	0 12 24 36 48	0 15 30 45	0 15 30 45
12	0 12 24 36 48	0 15 30 45	0 15 30 45
13	0 12 24 36 48	0 15 30 45	0 15 30 45
14	0 12 24 36 48	0 20 40	0 20 40
15	0 12 24 36 48	0 20 40	0 20 40
16	0 12 24 36 48	0 20 40	0 20 40
17	0 12 24 36 48	0 15 30 45	0 15 30 45
18	0 12 24 36 48	0 15 30 45	0 15 30 45
19	0 12 24 36 48	0 15 30 45	0 15 30 45
20	35 55	35 55	35 55
21	35 55	35 55	35 55
22	35 55	35 55	35 55

Fig. 1. A real-world bus schedule with exceptions

The two main strategies for dealing with exceptions are either evaluating them immediately as they appear or storing separately withoug evaluation. Works in [8,5,7,14,15] store the exceptions separately from the regular schedule. With a small number of exceptions, this strategy allows a compact and understandable representation for the user, but increases the complexity for applications when processing schedules. Figure 1 illustrates the bus schedule for the bus line 10A in Bolzano at the station "Piazza Domenicani" in the direction "Via Cadorna" that we use as a running example. The departure times of a bus are listed for each hour. Validity and exceptions are listed separately.

In this paper we argue for evaluating exceptions immediately as they appear. This strategy facilitates automated processing of large amounts of data at query time. We show that the evaluation of exceptions on realistic schedules is feasible and the actual growth of the representation is small. As a representation formalism for the schedules we use time slices. [3] A time slice combines multiple time granularities and selects certain granules at each granularity level. For example, slice λ_1 = (*wee*{366-391}, *day*{0-5}, *hou*{5-6}, *min*{15,35}) represents minutes 15 and 35 of hours 5 and 6 of the first 6 days of every week from week 366 to week 391. This corresponds to the first two lines of the schedule in Fig. 1 since in our setup week 366 is the first week of January 2007.

A multislice is a set of time slices and can represent general sets of time instants. We use multislices to represent both schedules and exceptions. We define the difference operator on multislices that corresponds to the evaluation of exceptions. We show that for realistic schedules and exceptions the representation size of the resulting schedule increases linearly in the number of exceptions. In the worst case the size of the resulting schedule is bound by the number of represented time instants.

Our technical contributions can be summarized as follows:

- We define the difference of multislices, which is the operation required to evaluate exceptions.
- We present optimization rules that keep the result of the evaluation of exceptions small.

– We propose a relational model for multislices together with algorithms to compute the difference of multislices.
– We implement the difference of multislices in PostgreSQL and report the results of our experiments on real-world data.

The rest of the paper is organized as follows. Section 2 introduces preliminary concepts. Section 3 defines the difference of time slices and multislices. Section 4 explores techniques to minimize the result of the difference of multislices for common cases of input data and provides size estimations for realistic schedules. Sections 5 and 6 describe the implementation and experiments. The paper concludes with related work, conclusions, and future work.

2 Preliminaries

2.1 Time Domain and Granularities

We assume a discrete *time domain*, $\mathcal{A}$, that is a set of time instants equipped with a total order $\leq$. Throughout the paper, we assume that time instants correspond to minutes with the natural chronological order among them. We use timestamps to refer to minutes, e.g., 2007-02-12-07:15.

We adopt some basic notions about time granularities [16,7]. A time *granularity*, G, is a partitioning of $\mathcal{A}$ into non-empty intervals of time instants, termed *granules*. Examples of time granularities are minutes, hours, days, and weeks, abbreviated as '*min*', '*hou*', '*day*', '*wee*', respectively. The granularity of days, for instance, divides the time domain into granules of 1440 minutes, i.e., $day = \{\ldots, [2007\text{-}02\text{-}12\text{-}00{:}00, 2007\text{-}02\text{-}12\text{-}23{:}59], \ldots\}$. We assume a *bottom granularity*, $G_\perp$, where each granule contains exactly one time instant. In this paper minutes are the bottom granularity.

The granules of a granularity G are ordered according to the time domain order. We label the granules of G with a subset of integers, $\mathcal{L}_G$, such that the labeling function $\mathcal{M}_G : \mathcal{L}_G \rightarrow G$ is an isomorphism that preserves the total order $\leq$ [7]. Figure 2 shows a part of the labeling for the running example. For each granularity we assume that the granule with the label 0 is the one that starts at time instant 2000-01-01-00:00. For the labeling function we get then, for instance, $\mathcal{M}_{day}(2599)$ = [2007-02-12-00:00, 2007-02-12-23:59].

We adopt the *bigger-part-inside conversion* [14,11], which is defined as $\downarrow_G^H(i) = \{j \mid |\mathcal{M}_G(j) \cap \mathcal{M}_H(i)| > |\mathcal{M}_G(j) \setminus \mathcal{M}_H(i)| \vee (|\mathcal{M}_G(j) \cap \mathcal{M}_H(i)| = |\mathcal{M}_G(j) \setminus \mathcal{M}_H(i)| \wedge$

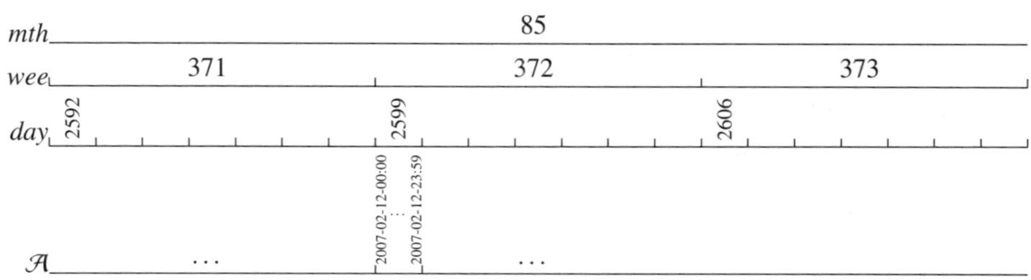

Fig. 2. Labeling granularities *day*, *wee*, and *mth*

$\max(\mathcal{M}_G(j)) \in \mathcal{M}_H(i))\}$. In other words, $\lfloor_G^H(i)$ returns the labels of all granules in G larger part of which is covered by granule i of H. In a case when exactly half of granule j of G is covered by granule i of H, j belongs to $\lfloor_G^H(i)$ if it is the second half. For example, in Fig. 2 we have $\lfloor_{wee}^{mth}(85) = \{370, \ldots, 373\}$.

2.2 Slices

A time *slice* [3] is a finite list of pairs, $\lambda = (G_1X_1, \ldots, G_dX_d)$, where G_i are granularities and X_i are *selectors* that are defined as sets of integers. Each selector X_i specifies a set of granules in G_i with a relative positioning with respect to granularity G_{i-1}. The sequence of granularities $(G_1, \ldots, G_d)$ is the *hierarchy* of the slice [3]. Slice $\lambda_1 = (wee\{366\text{-}391\}, day\{0\text{-}5\}, hou\{5\text{-}6\}, min\{15{,}35\})$ from our running example has hierarchy (*wee*, *day*, *hou*, *min*). The selectors select the corresponding granules at each level of hierarchy, e.g., the first selector {366-391} selects 25 consecutive weeks starting with the first week of January 2007, the selector {0-5} selects the days from Monday to Friday from each of these weeks, etc.

Let $P \subseteq \mathcal{L}_G$ be a set of labels of granularity G and X be a selector. The *selection* of X from P, denoted P/X, is defined as $P/X = P \cap \{\min(P)+i \mid i \in X\}$. Thus, X determines the elements that are selected from P, e.g., $\{2616\text{-}2646\}/\{2, 5, 7, 35\} = \{2618, 2621, 2623\}$.

A slice represents a subset of the time domain $\mathcal{A}$. The semantics of a slice $\lambda = (G_1X_1, \ldots, G_dX_d)$ is defined through the mapping $\mathcal{I}$:

$$\mathcal{I}(\lambda) = \begin{cases} \bigcup_{k \in X_1} \mathcal{M}_{G_1}(k) & |\lambda| = 1 \\ \mathcal{I}\left((G_2 \bigcup_{k \in X_1} (\lfloor_{G_2}^{G_1}(k)/X_2), \ldots, G_dX_d)\right) & |\lambda| > 1 \end{cases} \tag{1}$$

Thus, a slice consisting of a single granularity-selector pair represents all time instants covered by those granules in G_1 selected by X_1. Otherwise, if $|\lambda| = d > 1$, the slice is reduced to a slice of length $d - 1$. This is done by taking in turn each granule in G_1 selected by X_1 and converting it to granularity G_2. Consider again slice $\lambda_1 = (wee\{366\text{-}391\}, day\{0\text{-}5\}, hou\{5\text{-}6\}, min\{15{,}35\})$. First, weeks are mapped to days, yielding $\mathcal{I}((day\{2557\text{-}2562, 2564\text{-}2569, \ldots, 2732\text{-}2737\}, hou\{5\text{-}6\}, min\{15{,}35\}))$. Next, days are mapped to hours and hours into minutes, yielding a total of 624 time instants: {2007-01-01-05:15, 2007-01-01-05:35, ..., 2007-06-30-06:35}.

3 Evaluating Exceptions

3.1 Multislices

Definition 1 (Multislice). *Let $\lambda_1, \ldots, \lambda_p$ be slices with the same hierarchy $(G_1, \ldots, G_d)$. A* multislice *is a finite set of slices, $M = \{\lambda_1, \ldots, \lambda_p\}$, which has hierarchy $(G_1, \ldots, G_d)$ and represents the union of all time instants represented by the individual slices, i.e., $\mathcal{I}(M) = \bigcup_{i=1}^{p} \mathcal{I}(\lambda_i)$.*

With multislices we can represent both schedules as well as exceptions in a uniform way.

Example 1. Consider the schedule in Figure 1. The regular part of it can be represented by a multislice that contains five slices and represents a total of 12720 time instants.

$$
\begin{aligned}
M_{100} = \{\lambda_1 &= (wee\{366\text{-}391\}, day\{0\text{-}5\}, hou\{5\text{-}6\}, && min\{15,35\}),\\
\lambda_2 &= (wee\{366\text{-}391\}, day\{0\text{-}4\}, hou\{7\text{-}19\}, && min\{0,12,24,36,48\}),\\
\lambda_3 &= (wee\{366\text{-}391\}, day\{5\text{-}6\}, hou\{7\text{-}13,17\text{-}19\}, && min\{0,15,30,45\}),\\
\lambda_4 &= (wee\{366\text{-}391\}, day\{5\text{-}6\}, hou\{14\text{-}16\}, && min\{0,20,40\}),\\
\lambda_5 &= (wee\{366\text{-}391\}, day\{0\text{-}6\}, hou\{20\text{-}22\}, && min\{35,55\})\ \}
\end{aligned}
$$

The exceptions to the regular schedule can be represented in a similar way as a multislice with six slices.

$$
\begin{aligned}
M_{101} = \{\lambda_{10} &= (wee\{367\}, day\{0\}, hou\{5\}, && min\{35\}),\\
\lambda_{11} &= (wee\{371\}, day\{2\}, hou\{17\}, && min\{24\}),\\
\lambda_{12} &= (wee\{373\}, day\{5\}, hou\{14\}, && min\{20\}),\\
\lambda_{13} &= (wee\{373\}, day\{6\}, hou\{15\}, && min\{20\}),\\
\lambda_{14} &= (wee\{368\}, day\{4\}, hou\{22\}, && min\{35,55\}),\\
\lambda_{15} &= (wee\{391\}, day\{3\}, hou\{0\text{-}23\}, && min\{0\text{-}59\})\ \}
\end{aligned}
$$

Exceptions introduce irregularities into schedules, i.e., they break one or more regular patterns into several smaller patterns. Technically, when both regular schedules and exceptions are represented as multislices, we have to take the difference of the two to evaluate the exceptions. Below, we first introduce the difference between single slices and then the difference between multislices.

3.2 Difference of Slices

Our definition of the difference of slices is based on Lemma 1, which states that any slice can be split into two slices by splitting a selector. The resulting slices represent disjoint sets of time instants and their union is equal to the set represented by the original slice.

Lemma 1 (Split). *Let* $\lambda_x = (G_1X_1, \ldots, G_dX_d)$, $\lambda_y = (G_1Y_1, \ldots, G_dY_d)$, *and* $\lambda_z = (G_1Z_1, \ldots, G_dZ_d)$ *be slices with the same hierarchy. Furthermore, let* $X_m = Y_m \cup Z_m$ *and* $Y_m \cap Z_m = \emptyset$ *at granularity level* m, $1 \leq m \leq d$, *and* $X_l = Y_l = Z_l$ *for all granularity levels* $l \neq m$. *Then,* λ_y *and* λ_z *represent disjoint subsets of the set represented by* λ_x *and their union is equal to the set represented by* λ_x, *i.e.,* $\mathcal{I}(\lambda_y) \cup \mathcal{I}(\lambda_z) = \mathcal{I}(\lambda_x)$ *and* $\mathcal{I}(\lambda_y) \cap \mathcal{I}(\lambda_z) = \emptyset$.

For example, slice $\lambda_1 = (wee\{366\text{-}391\}, day\{0\text{-}5\}, hou\{5\text{-}6\}, min\{15,35\})$ can be split into the following slices by splitting the selector of weeks:

$$
\begin{aligned}
&(wee\{366,368\text{-}391\}, day\{0\text{-}5\}, hou\{5\text{-}6\}, min\{15,35\})\\
&(wee\{367\}, \qquad\qquad\quad day\{0\text{-}5\}, hou\{5\text{-}6\}, min\{15,35\})
\end{aligned}
$$

Definition 2 (Difference of slices). *Let* $\lambda_x = (G_1X_1, \ldots, G_dX_d)$, $\lambda_y = (G_1Y_1, \ldots, G_dY_d)$ *be two slices. The* difference, $\lambda_x - \lambda_y$, *is a multislice and is defined as follows:*

$$\lambda_x - \lambda_y = \bigcup_{i=1}^{d} \{(G_1X_1 \cap Y_1, \ldots, G_{i-1}X_{i-1} \cap Y_{i-1}, G_iX_i \setminus Y_i, G_{i+1}X_{i+1}, \ldots, G_dX_d)\}$$

Intuitively, the difference of two slices λ_x and λ_y represents all time instants that are represented by λ_x, but not by λ_y. For sets $\mathcal{I}(\lambda_x)$ and $\mathcal{I}(\lambda_y)$ we have $\mathcal{I}(\lambda_x) \setminus \mathcal{I}(\lambda_y) = \mathcal{I}(\lambda_x) \setminus (\mathcal{I}(\lambda_x) \cap \mathcal{I}(\lambda_y))$. Using Lemma 1 we can split slice λ_x into $d + 1$ slices $\lambda_{z,1}, \ldots, \lambda_{z,d}, \lambda_x \cap \lambda_y$ such that $\mathcal{I}(\lambda_x) = \mathcal{I}(\lambda_{z,1}) \cup \cdots \cup \mathcal{I}(\lambda_{z,d}) \cup (\mathcal{I}(\lambda_x) \cap \mathcal{I}(\lambda_y))$. All sets $\mathcal{I}(\lambda_{z,1}), \ldots, \mathcal{I}(\lambda_{z,d}), \mathcal{I}(\lambda_x) \cap \mathcal{I}(\lambda_y)$ are pairwise disjoint, so if we remove $\mathcal{I}(\lambda_x) \cap \mathcal{I}(\lambda_y)$ then we get the result of $\mathcal{I}(\lambda_x) \setminus \mathcal{I}(\lambda_y)$.

The above mentioned splits are performed as follows. For any sets X and Y, the sets resulting from $X \setminus Y$ and $X \cap Y$ are disjoint and their union gives X. Using Lemma 1 we split slice $\lambda_x = (G_1X_1, \ldots, G_dX_d)$ at level 1 with $X_1 \setminus Y_1$ going into one slice and $X_1 \cap Y_1$ going into another slice. As a result we get $\{(G_1X_1 \setminus Y_1, G_2X_2, \ldots, G_dX_d), (G_1X_1 \cap Y_1, G_2X_2, \ldots, G_dX_d)\}$. Then we split the second slice in a similar way at level 2 getting $\{(G_1X_1 \setminus Y_1, G_2X_2, \ldots, G_dX_d), (G_1X_1 \cap Y_1, G_2X_2 \setminus Y_2, G_3X_3, \ldots, G_dX_d), (G_1X_1 \cap Y_1, G_2X_2 \cap Y_2, G_3X_3, \ldots, G_dX_d)\}$. We continue splitting the last slice until we reach level d. At this point the result set contains $d + 1$ slices:

$$
\begin{array}{llll}
\{ (G_1X_1 \setminus Y_1, & G_2X_2, & \ldots, & G_dX_d), \\
\;\;(G_1X_1 \cap Y_1, & G_2X_2 \setminus Y_2, G_3X_3, & \ldots, & G_dX_d), \\
\;\;\vdots & & \ddots & \vdots \\
\;\;(G_1X_1 \cap Y_1, \ldots, & G_{d-2}X_{d-2} \cap Y_{d-2}, & G_{d-1}X_{d-1} \setminus Y_{d-1}, & G_dX_d), \\
\;\;(G_1X_1 \cap Y_1, & \ldots, & G_{d-1}X_{d-1} \cap Y_{d-1}, & G_dX_d \setminus Y_d), \\
\;\;(G_1X_1 \cap Y_1, & & \ldots, & G_dX_d \cap Y_d) \}
\end{array}
$$

Removing the last slice gives the slice difference conforming with Definition 2.

Example 2. Consider $\lambda_1 = (wee\{366\text{-}391\}, day\{0\text{-}5\}, hou\{5\text{-}6\}, min\{15,35\})$, which represents a part of the regular schedule, and $\lambda_{10} = (wee\{367\}, day\{0\}, hou\{5\}, min\{35\})$, which represents one of the canceled buses. The difference of the two slices yields the following multislice:

$$
\begin{array}{rllll}
\lambda_1 - \lambda_{10} = \{ & (wee\{366,368\text{-}391\}, & day\{0\text{-}5\}, & hou\{5\text{-}6\}, & min\{15,35\}), \\
& (wee\{367\}, & day\{4\text{-}5\}, & hou\{5\text{-}6\}, & min\{15,35\}), \\
& (wee\{367\}, & day\{0\}, & hou\{6\}, & min\{15,35\}), \\
& (wee\{367\}, & day\{0\}, & hou\{5\}, & min\{15\}) \}
\end{array}
$$

3.3 Difference of Multislices

Definition 3 (Difference of multislices). *Let $M_x = \{\lambda_{x,1}, \ldots, \lambda_{x,p}\}$ and $M_y = \{\lambda_{y,1}, \ldots, \lambda_{y,q}\}$ be multislices with the same hierarchy $(G_1, \ldots, G_d)$. The difference of M_x and M_y, denoted $M_x - M_y$, is a multislice defined as:*

$$
M_x - M_y = \begin{cases} \bigcup_{\lambda_x \in M_x} (\lambda_x - \lambda_y) & \textit{if } M_y = \{\lambda_y\} \\ (M_x - \{\lambda_{y,1}\}) - \{\lambda_{y,2}, \ldots, \lambda_{y,q}\} & \textit{if } M_y = \{\lambda_{y,1}, \ldots, \lambda_{y,q}\}, q > 1 \end{cases}
$$

Definition 3 reduces the difference of multislices to the difference of individual slices by successively subtracting each slice in M_y from each slice in M_x. The resulting multislice represents all time instants from M_x that are not contained in M_y.

Example 3. Let $M_x = \{\lambda_1, \lambda_4\}$ and $M_y = \{\lambda_{12}, \lambda_{13}\}$ be patterns and exceptions from our running example. Following Definition 3, the difference $M_x - M_y$ is computed by successively subtracting each individual slice in M_y from M_x. This gives a multislice with 32 slices.

In general, when computing the multislice difference for $M_x = \{\lambda_{x,1}, \ldots, \lambda_{x,p}\}$ and $M_y = \{\lambda_{y,1}, \ldots, \lambda_{y,q}\}$ according to Def. 3 we get a multislice with $p \cdot d^q$ slices with a total of $p \cdot d^{q+1}$ selectors. For $M_{100} - M_{101}$ in our running example we have $d = 4$, $p = 5$, and $q = 6$, which gives a multislice with 20480 slices and 81920 selectors. In the next section we show how to minimize multislice difference and Sec. 6 evaluates the performance empirically.

4 Minimizing Multislice Difference

In this section we propose three optimization rules for the computation of the multislice difference followed by a complexity analysis.

4.1 Optimization Rules

The first two rules show how to reduce the number of slices in the resulting multislice by eliminating redundant slices. The third rule shows that many slices share selectors that need to be stored only once.

Rule 1: Disjoint Slices. Two slices, λ_x and λ_y, are *disjoint* if they represent disjoint sets of time instants. The result of the difference of two disjoint slices, $\lambda_x - \lambda_y$, must represent exactly the same set of time instants as λ_x itself. The computation of the difference according to Def. 2 unnecessarily breaks λ_x into smaller slices. Consider the difference $\lambda_1 - \lambda_{11}$ in our running example, which is computed as part of the multislice difference $M_{100} - M_{101}$:

$$\begin{aligned}\lambda_1 - \lambda_{11} = \{\ & (wee\{366\text{-}370{,}372\text{-}391\}, day\{0\text{-}5\}, hou\{5\text{-}6\}, min\{15{,}35\}),\\ & (wee\{371\}, day\{0\text{-}1{,}3\text{-}5\}, hou\{5\text{-}6\}, min\{15{,}35\}),\\ & (wee\{371\}, day\{2\}, hou\{5\text{-}6\}, min\{15{,}35\}),\\ & (wee\{371\}, day\{2\}, hou\{\}, min\{15{,}35\})\ \}\end{aligned}$$

The resulting multislice represents exactly the same set of time instants as λ_1, but uses four slices instead of one. This can be avoided if the two argument slices are first checked for disjointedness. More specifically, let $\lambda_x = (G_1X_1, \ldots, G_dX_d)$ and $\lambda_y = (G_1Y_1, \ldots, G_dY_d)$ be two *disjoint* slices, i.e., $X_l \cap Y_l = \emptyset$ for at least one $l \in 1, \ldots, d$. Then the *difference* between the two slices is $\lambda_x - \lambda_y = \lambda_x$. This rule can be applied during the computation of the difference between two multislices M_x and M_y.

Rule 2: Empty Slices. A slice $\lambda = (G_1X_1, \ldots, G_dX_d)$ is *empty* if at least one of its selectors X_l is the empty set, i.e., $X_l = \emptyset$ for at least one $l \in 1, \ldots, d$. The difference of two non-empty, non-disjoint slices $\lambda_x = (G_1X_1, \ldots, G_dX_d)$ and $\lambda_y = (G_1Y_1, \ldots, G_dY_d)$ produces empty slices when for some levels $l \in 1, \ldots, d$, $X_l \backslash Y_l = \emptyset$. From the semantics of slices it is obvious that an empty slice represents an empty set of time intants and therefore can be removed from the resulting multislice.

Example 4. Consider the difference $\lambda_5 - \lambda_{14}$, which contains four slices, i.e.,

$$\begin{aligned}\lambda_5 - \lambda_{14} = \{ &(wee\{366\text{-}391\}, && day\{0\text{-}6\}, && hou\{20\text{-}22\}, min\{35,55\}),\\ &(wee\{366\text{-}367,369\text{-}391\}, && day\{0\text{-}6\}, && hou\{20\text{-}22\}, min\{35,55\}),\\ &(wee\{368\}, && day\{0\text{-}3,5\text{-}6\}, && hou\{20\text{-}22\}, min\{35,55\}),\\ &(wee\{368\}, && day\{4\}, && hou\{20\text{-}21\}, min\{\}) \}\end{aligned}$$

Since the last slice is empty, it can be removed without any impact on the result.

Rule 3: Identical Selectors. The third optimization rule concerns the reuse of identical selectors. From Def. 2 of the difference of two slices $\lambda_x = (G_1X_1, \ldots, G_dX_d)$ and $\lambda_y = (G_1Y_1, \ldots, G_dY_d)$ it immediately follows that a large number of selectors in the resulting multislice are identical, because they are computed in the same way and thus have the same value (selectors that are computed in different ways but have identical values are considered below). For instance, the selectors $X_1 \cap Y_1$ and X_d appear in $d-1$ slices, the selectors $X_2 \cap Y_2$ and X_{d-1} appear in d–2 slices, etc. Overall, the result of $\lambda_x - \lambda_y$ contains a total of d^2 selectors with only $3d-2$ selectors being different. During the computation of the multislice difference, identical selectors are propagated and produced by each difference operation between slices.

Next, we consider selectors that are computed in different ways but have identical values. More specifically, if $X_l \cap Y_l$ is equal to X_l for some level l, we do not store the result of this intersection again but reuse the selector X_l that is already stored. If $X_l \setminus Y_l = X_l$ then the slices are disjoint and they are eliminated by the first optimization rule. During the calculation of a multislice difference and store identical selectors (i.e., computed in the same way or having the same values) only once, saving in this way both space and computation time.

Example 5. Consider the two multislices M_{100} and M_{101}. After eliminating redundant slices by optimization rule 1 and rule 2, the result of $M_{100} - M_{101}$ contains the 20 slices shown in Fig. 3. By applying rule 3, we only need to store a total of 48 different selectors.

4.2 Complexity Analysis

Often, a regular schedule can be represented as a set of pairwise disjoint slices, and exceptions concern single buses. (Otherwise, an exception can be stored as several slices, each one representing one bus). For such cases we can provide a tighter upper bound for the size of the multislice difference. Since each individual slice $\lambda_y \in M_y$ is disjoint with all but one slice $\lambda_x \in M_x$, only the difference between λ_x and λ_y needs to be computed for the evaluation of $M_x - \{\lambda_y\}$. This step replaces λ_x by d new slices, where d is the size of the hierarchy.

Lemma 2 (Linear Bound). *Let $M_x = \{\lambda_{x,1}, \ldots, \lambda_{x,p}\}$ and $M_y = \{\lambda_{y,1}, \ldots, \lambda_{y,q}\}$ be two multislices with hierarchy $(G_1, \ldots, G_d)$, where all pairs of slices $\lambda_{x,i}, \lambda_{x,j}$, $i \neq j$, are disjoint and each slice in M_y represents exactly one time instant. Then the result size of $M_x - M_y$ has the following* linear bound*:*

$$|M_x - M_y| \leq p + q(d-1)$$

{ (*wee*{366-391}, *day*{5-6}, *hou*{7-13,17-19}, *min*{0,15,30,45}),
(*wee*{366-372,374-391}, *day*{5-6}, *hou*{14-16}, *min*{0,20,40}),
(*wee*{373}, *day*{5}, *hou*{15-16}, *min*{0,20,40}),
(*wee*{373}, *day*{5}, *hou*{14}, *min*{0,40}),
(*wee*{373}, *day*{6}, *hou*{14,16}, *min*{0,20,40}),
(*wee*{373}, *day*{6}, *hou*{15}, *min*{0,40}),
(*wee*{366,368-390}, *day*{0-5}, *hou*{5-6}, *min*{15,35}),
(*wee*{367}, *day*{1-5}, *hou*{5-6}, *min*{15,35}),
(*wee*{367}, *day*{0}, *hou*{6}, *min*{15,35}),
(*wee*{367}, *day*{0}, *hou*{5}, *min*{15}),
(*wee*{391}, *day*{0-2,4-5}, *hou*{5-6}, *min*{15,35}),
(*wee*{366-370,372-390}, *day*{0-4}, *hou*{7-19}, *min*{0,12,24,36,48}),
(*wee*{371}, *day*{0-1,3-4}, *hou*{7-19}, *min*{0,12,24,36,48}),
(*wee*{371}, *day*{2}, *hou*{7-16,18-19}, *min*{0,12,24,36,48}),
(*wee*{371}, *day*{2}, *hou*{17}, *min*{0,12,36,48}),
(*wee*{391}, *day*{0-2,4}, *hou*{7-19}, *min*{0,12,24,36,48}),
(*wee*{366-367,369-390}, *day*{0-6}, *hou*{20-22}, *min*{35,55}),
(*wee*{368}, *day*{0-3,5-6}, *hou*{20-22}, *min*{35,55}),
(*wee*{368}, *day*{4}, *hou*{20-21}, *min*{35,55}),
(*wee*{391}, *day*{0-2,4-6}, *hou*{20-22}, *min*{35,55}) }

Fig. 3. Optimized Result of $M_{100} - M_{101}$

When the set of exceptions becomes very large, the linear bound in Lemma 2 becomes loose and we can provide a better estimation.

Lemma 3 (Instant Bound). *Let* $M_x = \{\lambda_{x,1}, \ldots, \lambda_{x,p}\}$ *and* $M_y = \{\lambda_{y,1}, \ldots, \lambda_{y,q}\}$ *be two multislices with hierarchy* $(G_1, \ldots, G_d)$*, where all slices in* M_x *are pairwise disjoint. Then the size of the multislice difference,* $M_x - M_y$*, is not greater than the number of represented time instants, i.e.,*

$$|M_x - M_y| \leq |\mathcal{I}(M_x) \setminus \mathcal{I}(M_y)|$$

For a schedule with a large regular part and a relatively small number of exceptions, Lemma 2 provides a tighter bound for the size of the multislice difference. When the number of exceptions becomes large, Lemma 3 provides a tighter bound. Combining the results of the two lemmas, we get $\min(p + q(d-1), |\mathcal{I}(M_x) \setminus \mathcal{I}(M_y)|)$ as the upper bound for the multislice difference.

5 Implementation

Below we present a relational representation of multislices and an algorithm that calculates the difference of multislices using this relational representation. Both, the model and the algorithm support the optimizations described in the previous section.

Relational Representation of Multislices. We represent selectors as finite sets of non-empty, non-overlapping, and non-adjacent intervals of integers (also termed *temporal elements* [17]) and store them in a table SEL(xid, st, en). Each tuple in table SEL stores

MSL_x

mid	sid
100	1
100	2
100	3
100	4
100	5

SLI_x

sid	lev	gid	xid
1	1	*wee*	650
1	2	*day*	652
1	3	*hou*	655
1	4	*min*	660
2	1	*wee*	650
2	2	*day*	651
2	3	*hou*	656
2	4	*min*	661
3	1	*wee*	650
3	2	*day*	654
3	3	*hou*	657
3	4	*min*	664
4	1	*wee*	650
4	2	*day*	654
4	3	*hou*	658
4	4	*min*	663
5	1	*wee*	650
5	2	*day*	653
5	3	*hou*	659
5	4	*min*	662

SEL_x

xid	st	en
650	366	391
651	0	4
652	0	5
653	0	6
654	5	6
655	5	6
656	7	19
657	7	13
657	17	19
658	14	16
659	20	22
660	15	15
660	35	35
661	0	0
661	12	12
661	24	24
661	36	36
661	48	48
662	35	35
662	55	55
663	0	0
663	20	20
663	40	40
664	0	0
664	15	15
664	30	30
664	45	45

MSL_y

mid	sid
101	10
101	11
101	12
101	13
101	14
101	15

SLI_y

sid	lev	gid	xid
10	1	*wee*	665
10	2	*day*	671
10	3	*hou*	679
10	4	*min*	684
11	1	*wee*	666
11	2	*day*	670
11	3	*hou*	676
11	4	*min*	685
12	1	*wee*	667
12	2	*day*	674
12	3	*hou*	677
12	4	*min*	683
13	1	*wee*	667
13	2	*day*	675
13	3	*hou*	678
13	4	*min*	683
14	1	*wee*	668
14	2	*day*	673
14	3	*hou*	680
14	4	*min*	686
15	1	*wee*	669
15	2	*day*	672
15	3	*hou*	681
15	4	*min*	682

SEL_y

xid	st	en
665	371	371
666	367	367
667	373	373
668	368	368
669	391	391
670	0	0
671	2	2
672	3	3
673	4	4
674	5	5
675	6	6
676	5	5
677	14	14
678	15	15
679	17	17
680	22	22
681	0	23
682	0	59
683	20	20
684	24	24
685	35	35
686	15	15
686	35	35
686	55	55

Fig. 4. Relational Representation of M_{100} and M_{101}

an interval specified by its start ('st') and end point ('en') and an identifier ('xid') of the set the interval belongs to. For example, the selector {7-13, 17-19} is represented by the two tuples $(657, 7, 13)$ and $(657, 17, 19)$. Slices are stored in a table SLI(sid, lev, gid, xid). A single slice is represented by a set of tuples with a common identifier 'sid'. Each tuple of a slice corresponds to a level 'lev' of the hierarchy and refers to its granularity 'gid' and selector 'xid'. Multislices are stored in a table MSL(mid, sid). A multislice is represented by a set of tuples with a common identifier 'mid'. Each tuple of a multislice contains a reference 'sid' to a slice contained in this multislice. Figure 4 shows the relational representation of the two multislices $M_{100} = \{\lambda_1, \lambda_2, \lambda_3, \lambda_4, \lambda_5\}$ and $M_{101} = \{\lambda_{10}, \lambda_{11}, \lambda_{12}, \lambda_{13}, \lambda_{14}, \lambda_{15}\}$.

MSDiff Algorithm. Algorithm MSDiff takes as an input the identifiers of two multislices M_x and M_y (column 'mid' of table MSL) and returns the identifier of multislice M_z, where $M_z = M_x - M_z$. At the beginning M_z is initialized with the slices from M_x. The outer loop iterates through slices $\lambda_{y,j}$ in M_y. After each iteration j M_z' stores the result of $M_z - \{\lambda_{y,j}\}$, which then makes new M_z for the next iteration. The inner loop calculates $\lambda_z - \lambda_{y,j}$ for each slice λ_z in M_z applying the optimizations from Section 4. Function GetSel implements the third optimization rule by storing a history of calculation of selectors and performing the actual calculation only if the history for both input parameters is empty. For the sake of space, we give the algorithm in pseudo-code. For our experiments we implemented it in PostgreSQL as a stored function written in PL/pgSQL language.

Function `MSDiff`(M_x, M_y)

```
M_z := M_x;
foreach slice λ_y in M_y do
    M'_z := ∅;
    foreach slice λ_z in M_z do
        disjoint:= false;
        for i := 1 to d do // d slices
            empty:= false;
            λ := ∅;
            for l := 1 to d do // d levels
                (X_∩, X_\) := GetSel (Z_l, Y_l);
                if l > i then X := Z_l;
                else if l = i then X := X_\;
                else X := X_∩;
                if X_∩ = ∅ then
                    disjoint:= true;
                    break dslices;
                if X = ∅ then
                    empty:= true;
                    break dlevels;
                λ := λ ∪ {(G_l, X)};
            if not empty then M'_z := M'_z ∪ {λ};
        if disjoint then M'_z := M'_z ∪ {λ_z};
    M_z := M'_z;
return M_z
```

Using the linear bound from Lemma 2 the complexity of MSDiff can be estimated as $O(pq + dq^2)$, where $p = |M_x|$, $q = |M_y|$, and d is the length of the hierarchy of both multislices.

6 Experiments

Testing Bounds. To illustrate the growth of the result of the difference of multislices we took multislice M_{82} with hierarchy (*wee*, *day*, *hou*, *min*) that contains 5 slices and represents 124 time instants. We created multislice M_{200} which contains 124 slices where each slice represents a distinct time instant in $\mathcal{I}(M_{82})$. We shuffled the slices inside M_{200} randomly. We ran MSDiff algorithm on M_{82} and M_{200} and recorded the size of the intermediate results stored in M_z after each iteration of the main loop. Figure 5 displays the results of this experiment. The raged line shows the number of slices in the result for a different number of exceptions. The ascending straight line corresponds to the linear bound according to Lemma 2. The descending straight line corresponds to the instant bound according to Lemma 3.

Having 124 slices ordered randomly we tried to hit the worst case of the difference of multislices staying within realistic assumptions from Section 4. This experiment reveals that the actual growth of the result is more optimistic than the bounds given in Section 4.

Effectiveness of Optimizations. To illustrate the effectiveness of each optimization rule we created two sets of the input data and ran MSDiff algorithm first with all

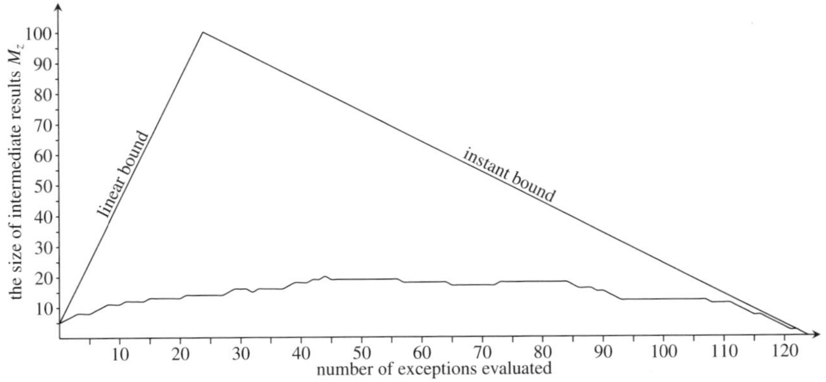

Fig. 5. Testing bounds

Table 1. Effectiveness of optimizations

Input Size				Optimization Rules	Output Size	
$\lvert SLI_x \rvert$	$\lvert SEL_x \rvert$	$\lvert SLI_y \rvert$	$\lvert SEL_y \rvert$		$\lvert SLI_z \rvert$	$\lvert SEL_z \rvert$
20	27	24	24	{}	81920	50927[a]
				{1}	116	176
				{1, 2}	80	130
				{1, 2, 3}	80	76
100	81	2400	2400	{}	≈ 1.7e+361	< 67117442[b]
				{1}	7400	12786
				{1, 2}	5096	9212
				{1, 2, 3}	5096	4568

[a] The result contains many empty selectors which are represented by 0 tuples.

[b] The values are estimated, we did not perform the actual computations.

optimizations switched off, and then more 3 times activating optimizations one-by-one in the order they were described. The first input set is composed of two multislices M_{100} and M_{101} from Example 1. For the second set we took a more complex schedule described by 25 slices representing around 60 thousand time instants in the period of 2 years. We assumed that in this period 1% of all departures gets cancelled or modified. We generated a set of 600 exceptions uniformly distributed over the period of the schedule. Table 1 shows the results of this experiment.

To get an impression of the impact of the optimizations on a full schedule of Bolzano, and not on just a fragment of it, one can multiply the given numbers by 300, assuming 15 bus routes and 20 stops per route.

7 Related Work

The term time slices was coined by Niezette et al., however, the idea of combining multiple time granularities for representing sets of time instants is quite intuitive. Similar constructs appear in [4,6] where it is implemented using *slicing* and *dicing* operators.

In [5] it is implemented through *select* and *foreach* operators. In [8] it is implemented using *Select_Periods* operator. In [7] it is called a *vector label*. In [10] the corresponding construct is called a *granularity sequence*. In [11] it is a combination of a *partitioning access format* and *partitioning access tree*. The industrial software, such as [18,19], use a specific case of time slices with hierarchies (*day*, *min*) or (*day*, *sec*). Time slices are simple and efficient for storage, interpretation and automatic processing of schedule data. We aim to enable the use of the general form of time slices in data-intensive systems, such as public transport systems. Dealing with exceptions is a primary problem for such kind of representation formalisms.

The works we reviewed contain three main strategies to deal with exceptions. In [8,5,7] union and difference operations make a part of the compact notation itself. This approach allows to avoid evaluating exceptions while storing the history of all exceptions as set algebra expressions. The negative aspect of this approach is a higher complexity of query evaluation. In [14,15] exceptions are stored as a plain list. Such a strategy, however, does not save from the need to evaluate exceptions, because of possible exceptions to exceptions. Work in [1] defines a relational representation and the difference operation for the representation formalism *linear repeating points*. The essense of linear repeating points formalism are linear functions and sets of simple constraints attached to each function. We followed the same strategy as in [1], namely, evaluation of exceptions. To our knowledge we are the first to evaluate exceptions on time slices and to analize the growth of the size of the resulting representation.

8 Conclusions and Future Work

In this paper we used sets of slices, termed multislices, as a feasible approach for a compact representation of schedules with exceptions in databases. We defined the difference of multislices which allows the evaluation of exceptions on a regular schedule. Instead of storing exceptions separately from the regular schedule, we proposed to immediately evaluate them. This keeps the representation of a schedule simple and more compact and facilitates the automatic processing of schedules at query time. We showed that for realistic schedules and exceptions the size of the resulting schedule increases linearly in the number of exceptions, while in the worst case it is bound by the number of represented time instants. Experimental analyses with real-world schedules showed even better compression ratios.

Future work includes the following aspects: additional optimization rules, slices with different hierarchies, irregular granularities, and more detailed experimental studies.

References

1. Kabanza, F., Stevenne, J.-M., Wolper, P.: Handling infinite temporal data. In: PODS, pp. 392–403 (1990)
2. Behr, T., de Almeida, V.T., Güting, R.H.: Representation of periodic moving objects in databases. In: Proceedings of the 14th International Workshop on Geographic Information Systems, ACM-GIS (2006)

3. Niezette, M., Stevenne, J.-M.: An efficient symbolic representation of periodic time. In: Proceedings of the First International Conference on Information and Knowledge Management (November 1992)
4. Leban, B., McDonald, D.D., Forster, D.R.: A representation for collections of temporal intervals. In: Proceedings of AAAI 1986, pp. 367–371 (Augest 1986)
5. Chandra, R., Segev, A., Stonebraker, M.: Implementing calendars and temporal rules in next generation databases. In: Proceedings of ICDE 1994, Washington, DC, USA, pp. 264–273. IEEE Computer Society, Los Alamitos (1994)
6. Bettini, C., de Sibi, R.: Symbolic representation of user-defined time granularities. In: TIME, pp. 17–28 (1999)
7. Ning, P., Wang, X.S., Jajodia, S.: An algebraic representation of calendars. Ann. Math. Artif. Intell 36(1-2), 5–38 (2002)
8. Terenziani, P.: Symbolic user-defined periodicity in temporal relational databases. IEEE Trans. Knowl. Data Eng. 15(2), 489–509 (2003)
9. Egidi, L., Terenziani, P.: A mathematical framework for the semantics of symbolic languages representing periodic time. In: TIME, pp. 21–27 (2004)
10. Kasperovičs, R., Böhlen, M.H.: Querying multi-granular compact representations. In: Li Lee, M., Tan, K.-L., Wuwongse, V. (eds.) DASFAA 2006. LNCS, vol. 3882, pp. 111–124. Springer, Heidelberg (2006)
11. Ohlbach, H.J.: Periodic temporal notions as tree partitionings. Forschungsbericht/research report PMS-FB-2006-11, Institute for Informatics, University of Munich (2006)
12. Cukierman, D.R., Delgrande, J.P.: The sol theory: A formalization of structured temporal objects and repetition. In: Proceedings of TIME 2004. IEEE Computer Society Press, Los Alamitos (2004)
13. Anselma, L.: Recursive representation of periodicity and temporal reasoning. In: TIME, pp. 52–59 (2004)
14. Dawson, F., Stenerson, D.: Internet calendaring and scheduling core object specification, icalendar (1998)
15. Skoll, D.K.: Remind tool manual (2000)
16. Lago, U.D., Montanari, A., Puppis, G.: Compact and tractable automaton-based representations of time granularities. Theor. Comput. Sci 373(1-2), 115–141 (2007)
17. Gadia, S.K.: A homogeneous relational model and query languages for temporal databases. ACM Trans. Database Syst. 13(4), 418–448 (1988)
18. Google Inc.: Google Transit Feed Specification (Febuary 2008)
19. Weber, C., Brauer, D., Kolmorgen, V., Hirschel, M., Provezza, S., Hulsch, T.: Fahrplanbearbeitungssystem FBS – Anleitung. iRFP (September 2006)

A Strategy to Revise the Constraints of the Mediated Schema

Marco A. Casanova[1], Tanara Lauschner[1], Luiz André P. Paes Leme[1], Karin K. Breitman[1], Antonio L. Furtado[1], and Vânia M.P. Vidal[2]

[1] Department of Informatics – PUC-Rio – Rio de Janeiro, RJ – Brazil
{casanova,tanara,lleme,karin,furtado}@inf.puc-rio.br
[2] Department of Computing, Federal University of Ceará – Fortaleza, CE – Brazil
vvidal@lia.ufc.br

Abstract. In this paper, we address the problem of changing the constraints of a mediated schema *M* to accommodate the constraints of a new export schema E_0. We first show how to translate the constraints of E_0 to the vocabulary of *M*, creating a set of constraints C_0 in such a way that the schema mapping for E_0 is correct. Then, we show how to compute the new version of the constraints of *M* to accommodate C_0 so that all schema mappings, including that for E_0, are correct. We solve both problems for subset and cardinality constraints and specific families of schema mappings.

Keywords: constraint revision, mediated schema, Description Logics.

1 Introduction

A *mediated environment* consists of a *mediated schema M*, several *export schemas* $E_1,...,E_n$, that describe data sources, and *schema mappings* $\gamma_1,...,\gamma_n$ such that γ_i defines (some of) the concepts of *M* in terms of the concepts of E_i, for each $i \in [1,n]$. To help define the mappings and maintain the constraints of *M*, we also introduce *import schemas* $I_1,...,I_n$ such that I_i is the set of concepts of *M* that γ_i contains definitions for.

The constraints of the mediated schema are relevant for a correct understanding of what the semantics of the external schemas have in common. For example, consider a virtual store mediating access to online booksellers. Then, the class hierarchy of the mediated schema indicates what the booksellers' book classifications have in common; if the mediated schema enforces that all books must have ISBNs, then it means that all booksellers must have the same requirement; if it allows books with no (known) authors, then at least one bookseller must so allow; and so on.

We may break the process of adding a new export schema E_0 to the mediated environment into three steps. The *concept revision step* adjusts the vocabulary of *M* to perhaps include classes and properties originally defined in E_0. The *mapping revision step* creates the local mapping γ_0, and perhaps modifies the other mappings. The import schema I_0 comprises the set of concepts of *M* that γ_0 defines. Finally, the *constraint revision step* applies a minimum set of changes to the set of constraints of *M* to account for the set of constraints of E_0.

A.H.F. Laender et al. (Eds.): ER 2009, LNCS 5829, pp. 265–279, 2009.

One may have to iterate through these three steps since, in particular, revising the constraints of the mediated schema interacts with the definition of the schema mappings. For example, the local mapping γ_0 may have to be readjusted to preserve the class hierarchy of the mediated schema, or the class hierarchy of the mediated schema may have to be changed to reflect the class hierarchy of E_0 as seen through γ_0 [10].

In this paper, we are primarily concerned with the constraint revision step, with a bias to mediated environments in the context of the Web. Maintaining mediated environments in such context becomes a challenge because the number of data sources may be large and, moreover, the mediator does not have much control over the data sources, which may join or leave the mediated environment at will.

We break the constraint revision step in two sub-steps. Recall that the import schema I_0 is the set of concepts of M that γ_0 defines. The *constraint translation step* translates the constraints of E_0 to the concepts of I_0, creating a set of constraints C_0 in such a way that γ_0 is correct with respect to C_0. Intuitively, as a result of this step, we express the semantics of E_0 in terms of the concepts of M, which is the only schema that users have access to. The difficulty here lies in that γ_0 defines concepts of M in terms of the concepts of E_0, whereas we need a mapping in the inverse direction to translate the constraints of E_0 to the concepts of M.

The *least constraint change step* applies a minimum set of changes to the constraints of M to accommodate C_0 in such a way that all schema mappings remain correct. This step intuitively means to harmonize the semantics of E_0 with the semantics of all export schemas previously added to the mediated environment, captured in the constraints of M. The key questions here are to precisely define what it means to apply a minimum set of changes to a set of constraints, and to guarantee that the mappings remain correct.

The contributions of this paper are twofold. First, for a family of conceptual schemas and schema mappings, we show how to perform constraint translation without actually computing the inverse mapping. We prove that, in some precise sense, the translation is the best possible. Second, to define how to change the constraints of the mediated schema, we introduce a lattice of sets of constraints and the notion of least upper bound of two sets of constraints. Again for the same family of conceptual schemas and schema mappings, we show how to compute the least upper bound that generates the revised set of constraints of the mediated schema.

Research in schema matching [2], as well as in ontology matching [8], tends to concentrate on vocabulary matching techniques, ignoring the question of constraint revision. Calvanese et al. [5] introduce a Description Logics framework, similar to that in Section 2, to address schema integration and query answering. Atzeni et al. [1] cover the traditional problem of rewriting a schema from one model to another, but they do not touch on the more complex problem of generating a new set of constraints that generalizes a pair of sets of constraints from different schemas, which we address in Section 4. Curino et al. [7] describe a software tool to support schema evolution that uses mapping invertibility. Fagin et al. [9] study mapping invertibility in the context of source-to-target tuple generating dependencies and formalize the notion of quasi-inverse. By contrast, we show in Section 3 how to generate the best possible set of subset and cardinality constraints without computing the inverse mapping.

This paper is organized as follows. Section 2 introduces an expressive family of conceptual schemas and a family of mappings. Section 3 focuses on constraint translation. Section 4 discusses constraint lattices and shows how to generate the revised set of constraints of the mediated schema. Finally, Section 5 contains the conclusions.

We refer the reader to [6] for proofs for the results stated in Sections 3 and 4, comprehensive examples, and a detailed comparison with related work.

2 Basic Definitions

2.1 A Brief Review of Concepts from Description Logics

We adopt a family of *attributive languages* [4] defined as follows. A *language* $\mathcal{L}$ in the family is characterized by an *alphabet* $\mathcal{A}$, consisting of a set of *atomic concepts*, a set of *atomic roles*, the *universal concept* and the *bottom concept*, denoted by $\top$ and $\bot$, respectively, the *universal role* and the *bottom role*, also denoted by $\top$ and $\bot$, respectively, and a set of *constants*.

The set of *role descriptions* of $\mathcal{L}$ is inductively defined as

- An atomic role and the universal and bottom roles are role descriptions
- If p and q are role descriptions, then the following expression is a role description
  $p \circ q$ (the composition of p and q)

The set of *concept descriptions* of $\mathcal{L}$ is inductively defined as

- An atomic concept and the universal and bottom concepts are concept descriptions
- If $a_1,...,a_n$ are constants, then $\{a_1,...,a_n\}$ is a concept description
- If e and f are concept descriptions and p is a role description, then the following expressions are concept descriptions

$\neg e$	(negation)		
$e \sqcap f$	(intersection)	$e \sqcup f$	(union)
$\exists p.e$	(full existential quantification)	$\forall p.e$	(value restriction)
$(\leq n\ p)$	(at-most restriction)	$(\geq n\ p)$	(at-least restriction)

Given an atomic concept A, a *restriction of* A is an intersection of the form $A \sqcap e$.

An *interpretation* s for $\mathcal{L}$ consists of a nonempty set Δ^s, the *domain* of s, whose elements are called *individuals*, and an *interpretation function*, also denoted s, where:

- $s(\top) = \Delta^s$, when $\top$ denotes the universal concept
- $s(\bot) = \top$, when $\bot$ denotes the bottom concept or the bottom role
- $s(A) \subseteq \Delta^s$, for each atomic concept A of $\mathcal{L}$
- $s(\top) = \Delta^s \times \Delta^s$, when $\top$ denotes the universal role
- $s(P) \subseteq \Delta^s \times \Delta^s$, for each atomic role P of $\mathcal{L}$
- $s(a) \in \Delta^s$, for each constant a of $\mathcal{L}$, such that distinct constants denote distinct individuals (the *uniqueness assumption*)

The function s is extended to role and concept descriptions of $\mathcal{L}$ as follows:

- $s(p \circ q)$ is the composition of $s(p)$ with $s(q)$
- $s(\{a_1,...,a_n\})$ is the set $\{s(a_1),..., s(a_n)\}$
- $s(\neg e)$ is the complement of $s(e)$ with respect to the domain Δ^s
- $s(e \sqcap f)$ is the intersection of $s(e)$ and $s(f)$

- $s(e \sqcup f)$ is the union of $s(e)$ and $s(f)$
- $s(\forall p.e)$ is the set of individuals that $s(p)$ relates only to individuals in $s(e)$, if any
- $s(\exists p.e)$ is the set of individuals that $s(p)$ relates to some individual in $s(e)$
- $s(\geq n\ p)$ is the set of individuals that $s(p)$ relates to at least n distinct individuals
- $s(\leq n\ p)$ is the set of individuals that $s(p)$ relates to at most n distinct individuals

A *formula* of $\mathcal{L}$ is an expression of the form u β v, called an *inclusion*, or of the form $u \equiv v$, called an *equivalence*, where u and v are both concept descriptions or they are both role descriptions of $\mathcal{L}$. A *definition* is an equivalence of the form $T \equiv u$, where T is an atomic concept and u is a concept description, or T is an atomic role and u is a role description. An interpretation s for $\mathcal{L}$ *satisfies* $u \sqsubseteq v$ iff $s(u) \subseteq s(v)$, and s *satisfies* $u \equiv v$ iff $s(u) = s(v)$.

In the rest of the paper, we will use the following notation:

- $s \models \sigma$ indicates that an interpretation s satisfies a formula σ
- $s \models \Sigma$ indicates that an interpretation s satisfies all formulas in a set of formulas Σ
- $\Sigma \models \sigma$ indicates that a set of formulas Σ *logically implies* a formula σ, that is, for any interpretation s, if $s \models \Sigma$, then $s \models \sigma$
- $\Sigma \models \Gamma$ indicates that a set of formulas Σ *logically implies* a set of formulas Γ, that is, for any interpretation s, if $s \models \Sigma$, then $s \models \Gamma$
- $Th(\Sigma)$ denotes the *theory induced* by Σ, which is the smallest set of formulas that contains Σ and is closed under logical implication.

Also, in Section 2.3, we will use concept and role descriptions over an alphabet $\mathcal{A}$ which is the union of disjoint alphabets $\mathcal{A}_1,...,\mathcal{A}_n$. The syntax of concept and role descriptions remains the same. An interpretation s for $\mathcal{A}$ is constructed from interpretations $s_1,...,s_n$ for $\mathcal{A}_1,...,\mathcal{A}_n$ in the obvious way, except that we assume that

- *(Domain Disjointness Assumption)* Any pair of interpretations for $\mathcal{A}_i$ and $\mathcal{A}_j$ have disjoint domains, for each $i,j \in [1,n]$, with $i \neq j$

2.2 Extralite Schemas

We will work with *extralite schemas* [10] that, in OWL terminology [3], support *classes* and *properties*, and that admit *domain* and *range* constraints, *subset constraints*, *minCardinality* and *maxCardinality constraints*, with the usual meaning. Formally, an *extralite schema* is a pair $S=(\mathcal{A},C)$ such that

- $\mathcal{A}$ is an alphabet, called the *vocabulary* of S, whose atomic concepts and atomic roles are called the *classes* and *properties* of S, respectively
- C is a set of formulas, called the *constraints* of S, which must be of one the forms
  - *Domain Constraint:* $\exists P.\top \sqsubseteq D$ (property P has domain D)
  - *Range Constraint:* $\top \sqsubseteq \forall P.R$ (property P has range R)
  - *minCardinality constraint:* $D \sqsubseteq (\geq k\ P)$, where D is the domain of P (property P maps each individual in its domain D to at least k distinct individuals)
  - *maxCardinality constraint:* $D \sqsubseteq (\leq k\ P)$, where D is the domain of P (property P maps each individual in its domain D to at most k distinct individuals)
  - *Subset Constraint:* $C \sqsubseteq D$ (class C is a subclass of class D)
- C must have exactly one domain and one range constraint for each property in $\mathcal{A}$

Note that this formalization does not distinguish between object and datatype properties, in OWL terminology. The distinction will be visible in the examples, where the range of an object property will be a class defined in the schema, whereas the range of a datatype property will be a XML Schema type (i.e, a set of datatype values or *literals*). The formal development does not capture this distinction since the notion of domain does not separate individuals that denote class elements from individuals that correspond to datatype values. However, this formal liberality does not reduce the usefulness of the results in Sections 3 and 4.

We will use the terms *class*, *property*, *vocabulary* and *state* interchangeably with *atomic concept*, *atomic role*, *alphabet* and *interpretation*, respectively.

Example 1: Figures 1(a) and 1(c) show schemas for fragments of the Amazon and the eBay databases, using an informal notation. We use the namespace prefixes "`a:`" and "`e:`" to refer to the vocabularies of the Amazon and the eBay schemas.

In Figure 1(a), for example, `a:title` is defined as a (datatype) property with domain `a:Product` and range `string` (an XML Schema data type), `a:Book` is declared as a subclass of `a:Product`, and `a:pub` is defined as an (object) property with domain `a:Book` and range `a:Publ`. Although not indicated in Figure 1(a), we assume that all properties have maxCardinality equal to 1, except `a:author`, which is unbounded. Just to help illustrate the results in Section 3, we assume that `a:pub` has minCardinality equal to 2 and that `a:name` has minCardinality equal to 3.

Figures 1(b) and 1(d) formalize the constraints: the first column shows the domain and range constraints; the second column, the cardinality constraints; and the third column, the subset constraints. Note that there is no maxCardinality constraint for `a:author`, consistently with the fact that a book may have multiple authors. □

2.3 Mediated Environment

A *mediated environment* contains a *mediated schema* M, a *mediated mapping* γ and, for each $k=1,...,n$, an *export schema* E_k, an *import schema* I_k and a *local mapping* γ_k.

Assume that the classes and properties in M are $C_1,...,C_u$ and $P_1,...,P_v$.

Import schemas help breaking the constraint revision problem into two subproblems, as discussed in Sections 3 and 4. They are also a notational convenience to divide the definition of the mappings into two stages: the definition of the mediated mapping and the definition of the local mappings.

We restrict the import schemas as follows:

- for $k=1,...,n$, the vocabulary of I_k is a subset of the vocabulary of M

We do not adopt namespace prefixes, as in the examples, but a more abstract notation to distinguish the occurrence of a symbol in the vocabulary of M from the occurrence of the same symbol in the vocabulary of I_k. For each class C_i (or property P_j) in the vocabulary of M, we denote the occurrence of C_i (or P_j) in the vocabulary of I_k by C_i^k (or P_j^k); we also say that C_i^k (or P_j^k) *matches* C_i (or P_j).

The mediated mapping γ defines the classes and properties of M as unions of classes and properties from the import schemas so that it becomes a simple task to revise it when an import schema is added or removed. Most of the complexity is

a:Product		a:Publ	
a:title	range string	a:name	range string
a:price	range decimal	a:address	range string
a:currency	range string		
a:Book		a:Book is-a a:Product	
a:isbn	range string	a:Music is-a a:Product	
a:author	range string	a:Video is-a a:Product	
a:pub	range a:Publ	a:PC-HW is-a a:Product	

Fig. 1(a). Informal definition of the Amazon schema

∃a:title.⊤ ⊑ a:Product	a:Product ⊑ (≤ 1 a:title)	a:Book ⊑ a:Product
⊤ ⊑ ∀a:title.string	a:Product ⊑ (≤ 1 a:price)	a:Music ⊑ a:Product
...	a:Product ⊑ (≤ 1 a:currency)	a:Video ⊑ a:Product
∃a:pub .⊤ ⊑ a:Book		a:PC-HW ⊑ a:Product
⊤ ⊑ ∀a:pub.a:Publ	a:Book ⊑ (≤ 1 a:isbn)	
...	a:Book ⊑ (≥ 2 a:pub)	
∃a:name .⊤ ⊑ a:Publ		
⊤ ⊑ ∀a:name.string	a:Publ ⊑ (≥ 3 a:name)	
...	a:Publ ⊑ (≤ 1 a:address)	

Fig. 1(b). Formal definition of (some of) the constraints of the Amazon schema

e:Seller		e:Product	
e:name	range string	e:type	range string
e:Offer		e:ean	range integer
e:qty	range integer	e:title	range string
e:price	range double	e:author	range string
e:currency	range string	e:edition	range integer
e:seller	range e:Seller	e:year	range integer
e:product	range e:Product	e:pub	range string

Fig. 1(c). Informal definition of the eBay schema

∃e:name.⊤ ⊑ e:Seller	e:Seller ⊑ (≤ 1 e:name)	(no subset constraints)
⊤ ⊑ ∀e:name.string	e:Offer ⊑ (≤ 1 e:qty)	
...	e:Offer ⊑ (≤ 1 e:price)	
∃e:seller.⊤ ⊑ e:Offer	...	
⊤ ⊑ ∀e:seller.e:Seller	e:Product ⊑ (≤ 1 e:type)	
∃e:product.⊤ ⊑ e:Offer	e:Product ⊑ (≤ 1 e:ean)	
⊤ ⊑ ∀e:product.e:Product	e:Product ⊑ (≤ 1 e:title)	
...	...	

Fig. 1(d). Formal definition of (some of) the constraints of the eBay schema

therefore isolated in the local mappings. This restriction reflects the idea that, in the context of the Web, data sources are independent.

More precisely, we restrict the mediated mapping as follows:

- for each $i=1,...,u$, the mapping γ contains a definition of the form

$$C_i \equiv e_i^1 \sqcup ... \sqcup e_i^n \qquad (1)$$

where e_i^k is the class C_i^k of I_k that matches C_i, if it exists, or the bottom concept $\bot$, otherwise, for each $k=1,...,n$

- for each $j=1,...,v$, the mapping γ contains a definition of the form

$$P_j \equiv p_j^1 \sqcup ... \sqcup p_j^n \tag{2}$$

where p_j^k is the property P_j^k of I_k that matches P_j, if it exists, or the bottom role $\perp$, for each $k=1,...,n$

We use $\perp$ just as a notational convenience so that Equations (1) and (2) have exactly one concept description (or role description) from each import schema.

For each $k=1,...,n$, the local mapping γ_k defines the classes and properties of I_k in the terms of the vocabulary of the export schema E_k. We restrict γ_k as follows:

- for each class C_i^k of I_k, the local mapping γ_k contains a definition of the form

$$C_i^k \equiv \rho_i^k \tag{3}$$

where ρ_i^k is a concept description over the vocabulary of E_k

- for each property P_j^k of I_k, the local mapping γ_k contains a definition of the form

$$P_j^k \equiv \pi_j^k \tag{4}$$

where π_j^k is a role description over the vocabulary of E_k

We introduce $\bar{\gamma}_k$ as the *function induced by* γ_k, defined as the function from states of E_k into states of I_k such that, for each state s of E_k, $\bar{\gamma}_k(\boldsymbol{s}) = \boldsymbol{r}$ iff

- $\boldsymbol{r}(C_i^k) = \boldsymbol{s}(\rho_i^k)$, if $C_i^k \equiv \rho_i^k$ is the definition for class C_i^k in γ_k
- $\boldsymbol{r}(P_j^k) = \boldsymbol{s}(\pi_j^k)$, if $P_j^k \equiv \pi_j^k$ is the definition for property P_j^k in γ_k

Likewise, we introduce $\bar{\gamma}$ as the *function induced by* the mediated mapping γ and the local mapping $\gamma_1,...,\gamma_n$ as the mapping from states of $E_1,...,E_n$ into states of M such that, for states $\boldsymbol{s}_1,...,\boldsymbol{s}_n$ of $E_1,...,E_n$, $\bar{\gamma}(\boldsymbol{s}_1,...,\boldsymbol{s}_n) = \boldsymbol{r}$ iff, for $i=1,...,u$ and $j=1,...,v$

- $\boldsymbol{r}(C_i) = \boldsymbol{s}_1(e_i^1) \cup ... \cup \boldsymbol{s}_n(e_i^n)$, if $C_i \equiv e_i^1 \sqcup ... \sqcup e_i^n$ is the definition of C_i in γ
- $\boldsymbol{r}(P_j) = \boldsymbol{s}_1(p_j^1) \cup ... \cup \boldsymbol{s}_n(p_j^n)$, if $P_j \equiv p_j^1 \sqcup ... \sqcup p_j^n$ is the definition of P_j in γ

Example 2: Figure 2 describes a mediated environment that contains:

- the mediated schema `Sales`, shown in Figure 2(a), with namespace prefix "`s:`" and the constraints shown in Figure 2(b); in particular, the minCardinality constraint for `s:Book` follows from the remarks in Example 3
- the Amazon and the eBay schemas, shown in Figure 1, as export schemas
- the import schema for the Amazon export schema (not shown in Figure 2), with the same classes and properties as `Sales`, but prefixed with "`ai:`"
- the import schema for the eBay export schema (not shown in Figure 2), with the same classes and properties as `Sales`, but prefixed with "`ei:`"
- the mediated mapping shown in Figure 2(c)
- the local mapping, shown in Figure 2(d), defining the classes and properties of the Amazon import schema in terms of its export schema; in particular, `ai:pub` is defined as the composition of `a:pub` with `a:name`

- the local mapping, shown in Figure 2(e), defining the classes and properties of the the eBay import schema in terms of its export schema; in particular, `ei:Music` and `ei:Book` are defined as restrictions of `e:Product`. □

s:Product
  s:title   range string
s:Book
  s:pub   range string
	s:Book is-a s:Product
	s:Music is-a s:Product

Fig. 2(a). The Sales mediated schema

∃s:title.⊤ ⊑ s:Product ⊤ ⊑ ∀ai:title.string ∃s:pub.⊤ ⊑ s:Book ⊤ ⊑ ∀ai:pub.string	s:Product ⊑ (≤ 1 s:title) s:Book ⊑ (≥ 6 s:pub)	s:Book ⊑ s:Product s:Music ⊑ s:Product

Fig. 2(b). Constraints of the Sales mediated schema

s:Product ≡ ai:Product ⊓ ei:Product s:Music ≡ ai:Music ⊓ ei:Music s:Book ≡ ai:Book ⊓ ei:Book	s:title ≡ ai:title ⊓ ei:title s:pub ≡ ai:pub ⊓ ei:pub

Fig. 2(c). Mediated schema mapping

ai:Product ≡ a:Product ai:Music ≡ a:Music ai:Book ≡ a:Book	ai:title ≡ a:title ai:pub ≡ a:pub)a:name

Fig. 2(d). Local schema mappings from the Amazon export schema to its import schema

ei:Product ≡ e:Product ei:Music ≡ e:Product ⊓ ∃e:type.{'music'} ei:Book ≡ e:Product ⊓ ∃e:type.{'book'}	ei:title ≡ e:title ei:pub ≡ e:pub

Fig. 2(e). Local schema mappings from the eBay export schema to its import schema

3 Constraint Translation

Consider a mediated environment with a mediated schema M, a mediated mapping γ and, for each $k=1,...,n$, an export schema E_k, an import schema I_k and a local mapping γ_k. By *constraint translation* we mean the problem of translating the constraints of E_k to the vocabulary of I_k, creating the set of constraints IC_k in such a way that γ_k induces a mapping from consistent states of E_k into consistent states of I_k.

To motivate the discussion, we start with an example.

Example 3: We first observe that the definitions in a local mapping are adequate to translate queries over the import schema (and hence the mediated schema) into queries over the export schema. They also help translating constraints of the import schema into constraints of the export schema. For example, suppose that

$$\exists \texttt{ai:pub}.\top \sqsubseteq \texttt{ai:Book} \tag{5}$$

is a constraint of the Amazon import schema. Using the definitions in Figure 2(d), we may translate the constraint in (5) to the Amazon export schema by replacing `ai:pub` by `a:pub ) a:name` and `ai:Book` by `a:Book`, obtaining

$$\exists\,(\texttt{a:pub})\texttt{a:name}).\top \sqsubseteq \texttt{a:Book} \tag{6}$$

However, the constraint translation problem is in the opposite direction: how to express the constraints of the Amazon export schema in terms of the vocabulary of its import scheme, thereby eventually exposing the semantics of the Amazon export schema to the users.

Figure 3(a) contains the translation of the constraints of the Amazon export schema, shown in Figure 1(b), to the corresponding import schema, in view of the local mapping defined in Figure 2(d). In particular, recall from Figure 2(d) that `ai:pub` ≡ `a:pub ) a:name` and `ai:Book` ≡ `a:Book`. This has several consequences. First, the domain and range of `ai:pub` are `ai:Book` and `string`. Second, `ai:pub` has minCardinality 6 with respect to `ai:Book` since, observing Figure 1(b), `a:pub` has minCardinality 2 with respect to `a:Book` and `a:name` has minCardinality 3 with respect to `a:Publ`. The other constraints follow directly from those of the Amazon export schema, since each of the other classes and properties of the import schema are defined in terms of a single class or property of the Amazon export schema.

Figure 3(b) contains the translation of the constraints of the eBay export schema, shown in Figure 1(c), to the corresponding import schema, in view of the local mapping defined in Figure 2(e). In particular, recall from Figure 2(e) that `ei:Music` and `ei:Book` are defined as restrictions of `e:Product`. As a consequence, we have the two subset constraints shown on the third column of Figure 3(b). Note that the original eBay schema has no subset constraints (see Figure 1(d)). □

$\exists \texttt{ai:title}.\top \sqsubseteq \texttt{ai:Product}$ $\top \sqsubseteq \forall \texttt{ai:title}.\texttt{string}$ $\exists \texttt{ai:pub}.\top \sqsubseteq \texttt{ai:Book}$ $\top \sqsubseteq \forall \texttt{ai:pub}.\texttt{string}$	$\texttt{ai:Product} \sqsubseteq (\leq 1\ \texttt{ai:title})$ $\texttt{ai:Book} \sqsubseteq (\geq 6\ \texttt{ai:pub})$	$\texttt{ai:Book} \sqsubseteq \texttt{ai:Product}$ $\texttt{ai:Music} \sqsubseteq \texttt{ai:Product}$

Fig. 3(a). Constraints of the import schema for the Amazon (export) schema

$\exists \texttt{ei:title}.\top \sqsubseteq \texttt{ei:Product}$ $\top \sqsubseteq \forall \texttt{ei:title}.\texttt{string}$ $\exists \texttt{ei:pub}.\top \sqsubseteq \texttt{ei:Book}$ $\top \sqsubseteq \forall \texttt{ei:pub}.\texttt{string}$	$\texttt{ei:Product} \sqsubseteq (\leq 1\ \texttt{ei:title})$ $\texttt{ei:Book} \sqsubseteq (\leq 1\ \texttt{ei:pub})$	$\texttt{ei:Book} \sqsubseteq \texttt{ei:Product}$ $\texttt{ei:Music} \sqsubseteq \texttt{ei:Product}$

Fig. 3(b). Constraints of the import schema for the eBay (export) schema

In what follows, we formalize and generalize the arguments outlined in Example 3, indicating how to translate subset constraints and cardinality constraints separately.

Definition 1: Let EC_k be the set of constraints of E_k. The *translation* of the subset constraints in EC_k for γ_k is the set Σ_k of all subset constraints $C \sqsubseteq D$ such that γ_k has definitions for C and D of the form $C \equiv \rho_C$ and $D \equiv \rho_D$ and $EC_k \models \rho_C \sqsubseteq \rho_D$.

The translation of cardinality constraints, in Definition 2, follows from Proposition 1, which captures simple facts about such constraints. For example, if `a:pub` has minCardinality 2 with respect to `a:Book`, then trivially `a:pub` has minCardinality 1 with respect to `a:Book`; likewise, if `a:isbn` has maxCardinality 1 with respect to `a:Book`, then trivially `a:isbn` has maxCardinality 2 with respect to `a:Book`.

To improve readability, we use *min[k,P]* to abbreviate the minCardinality constraint $D \beta (\geq k\ P)$, and *max[k,P]* for the maxCardinality constraint $D \beta (\leq k\ P)$, where D is implicit from the domain constraint for P.

Proposition 1: For any property P of E_k, we have:

(i) $EC_k \models min[h,P]$ iff there is $min[g,P]$ in EC_k such that $h \leq g$.

(ii) $EC_k \models max[h,P]$ iff there is $max[g,P]$ in EC_k such that $h \geq g$.

Definition 2: Let EC_k be the set of constraints of E_k. The *translation* of the cardinality constraints in EC_k for γ_k is the set κ_k defined as follows. For each property P in I_k, if the definition of P in γ_k is $P \equiv P_1 \circ P_2 \circ \ldots \circ P_r$, then

(i) If $min[\, g_i^j, P_i\,]$ are all the minCardinality constraints in EC_k for property P_i, for $i \in [1,r]$ and $j \in [1,s_i]$, then κ_k contains a minCardinality constraint of the form $min[g,\ P]$, with $g = \prod_{i=1}^{r} max(\{\, g_i^j \ / \ j = 1,\ldots,s_i \,\})$. If EC_k has no minCardinality constraints for P_i, then so does κ_k.

(ii) If $max[\, h_i^j, P_i\,]$ are all the maxCardinality constraints in EC_k for property P_i, for $i \in [1,r]$ and $j \in [1,t_i]$, then κ_k contains a maxCardinality constraint of the form $max[h,\ P]$, with $h = \prod_{i=1}^{r} min(\{\, h_i^j \ / \ j = 1,\ldots,t_i \,\})$. If EC_k has no maxCardinality constraints for P_i, then so does κ_k.

We are now ready to combine Definitions 1 and 2 to indicate how to translate the subset and cardinality constraints of E_k into constraints of I_k.

Definition 3: Let EC_k be the set of constraints of E_k. The *translation* of the subset and cardinality constraints in EC_k for γ_k is the set $IC_k = \Sigma_k \cup \kappa_k$.

We establish, in Proposition 2, that IC_k is a correct translation of the subset and cardinality constraints of E_k with respect to γ_k. Then, we state, in Proposition 3, that IC_k is the largest theory of subset and cardinality constraints such that γ_k induces a mapping from consistent states of E_k into states of I_k that satisfy the theory. Thus, Definition 3 indicates the best possible translation for the subset and cardinality constraints of E_k to the vocabulary of I_k.

Proposition 2: γ_k induces a mapping from consistent states of E_k into states of I_k that satisfy IC_k.

Proposition 3: Let Φ be any set of subset and cardinality constraints such that γ_k has definitions for their classes and properties. Suppose that γ_k induces a mapping from consistent states of E_k into states of I_k that satisfy Φ. Then, $\Phi \subseteq IC_k$.

In summary, Definitions 1, 2 and 3 indicate, for the families of conceptual schemas and schema mappings introduced in Section 2, how to translate subset and cardinality constraint without computing inverse mappings. Propositions 2 and 3 assert that the translation is correct and the best possible. We refer the reader to [6] for the translation of domain and range constraints.

4 Constraint Revision

Consider again a mediated environment with a mediated schema M, a mediated mapping γ and, for each $k=1,...,n$, an export schema E_k, an import schema I_k and a local mapping γ_k. Assume that V and MC are the vocabulary and the set of constraints of M.

If we take import schemas into account, we may refine the steps required to add a new export schema E_0 to the mediated environment as follows:

1. *(Concept revision step)* Create the revised vocabulary V_r of the mediated schema, perhaps by including in V classes and properties originally defined in E_0, and define the import schema I_0 for E_0.
2. *(Mapping revision step)* Create the revised mediated mapping γ_r, and define the local mapping γ_0 between I_0 and E_0.
3. *(Constraint revision step)* Create the revised set of constraints MC_r by computing the set IC_0 of constraints of I_0, and applying a minimum set of changes to MC to account for IC_0.

In this section, we assume that the first two steps have already been performed, resulting in the revised vocabulary V_r, the revised mediated mapping γ_r, and the definitions of the import schema I_0 for E_0 and the local mapping γ_0 between I_0 and E_0. In particular, note that γ_r must be a set of definitions as in Equations (1) and (2). We also assume that the set IC_0 of constraints of I_0 have already been computed, as discussed in Section 3. We focus on how to create the revised set of constraints. The reader should bear in mind the notation just introduced, which will be used in what follows.

There are two questions here: (1) what it means to apply a minimum set of changes to a set of constraints; (2) how to maintain the correctness of the schema mappings. To address the first question, we introduce a lattice of sets of constraints. The second question then follows from a property of the lattice.

Recall from Section 2.1, that $Th(\Phi)$ denotes the theory induced by a set of formulas Φ. Let 7 be the set of all sets of constraints. Then, (7, $\models$) is a lattice where, given any two sets of constraints, Φ_1 and Φ_2, their greatest lower bound (g.l.b.) is $\Phi_1 \Delta \Phi_2 = Th(\Phi_1) \cup Th(\Phi_2)$ and their least upper bound (l.u.b.) is $\Phi_1 \Delta \Phi_2 = Th(\Phi_1) \cap Th(\Phi_2)$. Note that $\Phi_i \models \Phi_1 \nabla \Phi_2$ and $\Phi_1 \Delta \Phi_2 \models \Phi_i$, for $i=1,2$.

We argue that MC_r can be taken as the l.u.b. of MC and the translation of IC_0 to V_r.

Definition 4: The *translation* of IC_0 to V_r is the set of constraints C_0 defined as follows: for each β in IC_0, the set C_0 contains β' constructed by replacing in β each class C_i^0, of the vocabulary of I_0, by C_i, the class of V_r that C_i^0 matches, and each property P_j^0, of the vocabulary of I_0, by P_j, the property of V_r that P_j^0 matches.

We now give a simple example that partially illustrates the constraint revision step.

Example 5: Consider the `Sales` mediated schema shown in Figure 2. Let `BN` be a new export schema (say, a fragment of the Barnes&Noble database), shown in Figures 4(a) and (b). To include `BN` in the mediated environment, we perform three steps:

(Concept revision step). Assume that the vocabulary of `Sales` is not changed and that the import schema for `BN` has classes `bi:Book`, `bi:Music` and `bi:Product`, and properties `bi:title` and `bi:pub`.

(Mapping revision step) Figures 4(c) and (d) show the revised mediated mapping and the local schema mapping from the `BN` export schema to its import schema.

(Constraint revision step.) According to the discussion in Section 3, the import schema for `BN` has only two subset constraints, σ_1 and σ_2, where

σ_1 : `bi:Book` $\sqsubseteq$ `bi:Product` σ_2 : `bi:Music` $\sqsubseteq$ `bi:Product`

This follows from Definition 1, using the subset constraints of `BN` (Figure 4(b)) and the local mapping between `BN` and its import schema (Figure 4(d)). Also note that `b:CultProd` is not in the vocabulary of the import schema for `BN`.

Using Definition 4, we translate σ_1 and σ_2 to the vocabulary of `Sales`, replacing `bi:Book` by `s:Book`, `bi:Music` by `s:Music` and `bi:Product` by `s:Product`. This results in τ_1 and τ_2, where

τ_1 : `s:Book` $\sqsubseteq$ `s:Product` τ_2 : `s:Music` $\sqsubseteq$ `s:Product`

Let SC be the set of constraints of `Sales` (Figure 2(b)). Let C be the set of constraints of the import schema of `BN`, after translation to the vocabulary of `Sales`. The revised set of constraints of the mediated schema, $SC_r = SC = C$, is such that: (1) SC_r contains τ_1 and τ_2 (just as SC), since τ_1 and τ_2 are in both SC and C; (2) SC_r has no cardinality constraints (unlike SC), since C has no cardinality constraints (by the middle column of Figure 4(b), `BN` has no cardinality constraints). Thus, adding `BN` to the mediated environment affects the constraints of `Sales`. □

We are now ready to argue that MC_r can be taken as the l.u.b. of MC and C_0.

Proposition 4: Let $MC_r = MC \nabla C_0$. Assume that:

(i) The mediated mapping γ and the local mapping $\gamma_1,...,\gamma_n$ induce a mapping from consistent states of $E_1,...,E_n$ into consistent states of M.

(ii) The local mapping γ_0 induces a mapping from consistent states of E_0 into consistent states of I_0.

Then, the revised mediated mapping γ_r and the local mappings $\gamma_0,\gamma_1,...,\gamma_n$ induce a mapping from consistent states of EC_0, EC_1,..., EC_n into states of the revised mediated schema that satisfy MC_r .

The proof of Proposition 4 depends on assuming that γ_r defines the classes and properties of V_r as unions of classes and properties from the vocabularies of the import schemas. Since $MC_r = MC = C_0$, with respect to $(7, \models)$, we may consider that MC_r is the least way to revise MC and yet retain correctness of the mappings, in view of Proposition 4.

The solution to the least constraint revision problem outlined up to this point gives no indication on how to select a finite set of constraints that generates $MC \nabla C_0$. In the rest of this section, we therefore show how to compute the subset and cardinality constraints in the l.u.b. of two sets of constraints.

b:Product
  b:title range string
b:Book
  b:pub range string
	b:CultProd is-a b:Product
	b:Music is-a b:CultProd
	b:Book is-a b:CultProd

Fig. 4(a) The new export schema BN to be added to the mediated environment

$\exists$b:title.$\top \sqsubseteq$ b:Product $\sqsubseteq \forall$b:title.string $\exists$b:pub.$\top \sqsubseteq$ b:Book $\top \sqsubseteq \forall$b:pub.string	(no cardinality constraints)	b:Book $\sqsubseteq$ b:CultProd b:Music $\sqsubseteq$ b:CultProd b:CultProd $\sqsubseteq$ b:Product

Fig. 4(b). Constraints of the new export schema BN

s:Product ≡ bi:Product ⊔ ai:Product ⊔ ei:Product s:Music ≡ bi:Music ⊔ ai:Music ⊔ ei:Music s:Book ≡ bi:Book ⊔ ai:Book ⊔ ei:Book	s:title ≡ bi:title ⊔ ai:title ⊔ ei:title s:pub ≡ bi:pub ⊔ ai:pub ⊔ ei:pub

Fig. 4(c). Revised Mediated mapping of the mediated environment

bi:Product ≡ b:Product bi:Music ≡ b:Music bi:Book ≡ b:Book	bi:title ≡ b:title bi:pub ≡ b:pub

Fig. 4(d). Local schema mappings from the BN export schema to its import schema

Proposition 5 provides a simple way to compute the subset constraints that are logical consequences of a set of such constraint.

Proposition 5 (Subset Constraint Chaining): Let $\sigma_1,\ldots,\sigma_n$ be a sequence of subset constraints. Suppose that, for each $i \in [1,n]$, σ_i is of the form $A_i \sqsubseteq A_{i+1}$. Then, we have that $\sigma_1,\ldots,\sigma_n \models \sigma$, where σ is the subset constraint $A_1 \sqsubseteq A_{n+1}$.

We say that $\sigma_1,\ldots,\sigma_n$, with the characteristics listed in Proposition 5, is a *chain of subset constraints connecting* A_1 *to* A_{n+1}, and that σ is the result of *chaining* $\sigma_1,\ldots,\sigma_n$.

The final result shows how to compute the subset and cardinality constraints in the l.u.b. of two sets of constraints.

Proposition 6: Let Γ_1 and Γ_2 be two sets of constraints. Construct set Γ as follows:

(i) Let $A \sqsubseteq B$ be the result of chaining a sequence of subset constraints from Γ_1, as well as the result of chaining a sequence of subset constraints from Γ_2. Then, $A \sqsubseteq B$ is in Γ.

(ii) For each property P, let $min[\, g_i^j , P\,]$ be the minCardinality constraints in Γ_i for P, for $i=1,2$ and $j \in [1,s_i]$. Then, $min[g,P]$ is in Γ, where $g=min(\{g_1,g_2\})$ and $g_i = max(\{\, g_i^j \;/\; j=1,\ldots,s_i \,\})$, for $i=1,2$. If either Γ_1 or Γ_2 have no minCardinality constraints for P, then so does Γ.

(iii) For each property P, let $max[\, h_i^j , P\,]$ be the maxCardinality constraints in Γ_i for P, for $i=1,2$ and $j \in [1,t_i]$. Then, $max[h,P]$ is in Γ, where $h=max(\{h_1,h_2\})$

and $h_i = min(\{ h_i^j \ / \ j = 1,...,t_i \})$, for $i=1,2$. If either Γ_1 or Γ_2 have no max-Cardinality constraints for *P*, then so does Γ.

Then, Γ is the set of all subset and cardinality constraints in $\Gamma_1 \nabla \Gamma_2$.

We refer the reader to [6] for a complete account of all families of constraints introduced in Section 2.2, including the domain and range constraints, which were omitted from the discussion for brevity.

In summary, computing the cardinality and subset constraints in the l.u.b. of two sets of constraints can be broken into computing the subset constraints in the l.u.b., which is straightforward by Chaining (Proposition 6 (i)), and computing the cardinality constraints in the l.u.b. (Proposition 6 (ii-iii)). This apparently simple fact is not necessarily true when other families of constraints are considered.

5 Conclusions

For the families of schemas and mappings defined in Section 2, we showed in Section 3 how to translate subset and cardinality constraints of the export schema to the import schema without computing inverse mappings. This problem reoccurs in other situations, such as how to express view constraints. The difficulty of the problem lies in that the definitions are in the inverse direction, as illustrated in Example 3.

To address the least constraint revision problem, we first introduced a lattice of sets of constraints. Then, again for the families of schemas and mappings defined in Section 2, we showed in Section 4 how to generate the subset and cardinality constraints of the revised set of constraints of the mediated schema.

Extending the results of this paper to domain and range constraints is fairly simple, but omitted here for brevity (see [6]). As future work, we are investigating families of constraints that include keys and disjointness constraints, which is a more difficult question, since disjointness and subset constraints may lead to inconsistencies.

References

[1] Atzeni, P., Cappellari, P., Torlone, R., Bernstein, P.A., Gianforme, G.: Model-independent schema translation. The VLDB Journal 17(6), 1347–1370 (2008)

[2] Bernstein, P., Melnik, S.: Model management 2.0: manipulating richer mappings. In: Proc. 27th ACM SIGMOD Int'l. Conf. Management of Data, Beijing, China, pp. 1–12 (2007)

[3] Breitman, K., Casanova, M., Truszkowski, W.: Semantic web: concepts, technologies, and applications. Springer, London (2007)

[4] Calvanese, D., Lenzerini, M., Nardi, D.: Description Logics for Conceptual data modeling. In: Chomicki, J., Saake, G. (eds.) Logics for Databases and Information Systems, Kluwer Academic Publishers, Dordrecht (1998)

[5] Calvanese, D., De Giacomo, G., Lembo, D., Lenzerini, M., Poggi, A., Rosati, R., Ruzzi, M.: Data Integration through DL-Lite-A Ontologies. In: Proc. 3rd Int'l. Workshop on Semantics in Data and Knowledge Bases, pp. 26–47 (2008)

[6] Casanova, M.A., Lauschner, T., Paes Leme, L.A., Breitman, K.K., Furtado, A.L.: A Strategy to Revise the Constraints of the Mediated Schema. Technical Report MCC34/09, Department of Informatics, PUC-Rio (April 2009)

[7] Curino, C.A., Moon, H.J., Zaniolo, C.: Graceful database schema evolution: the PRISM workbench. Proc. VLDB Endowment 1(1), 761–772 (2008)

[8] Euzenat, J., Shvaiko, P.: Ontology matching. Springer, Heidelberg (2007)

[9] Fagin, R., Kolaitis, P.G., Popa, L., Tan, W.-C.: Quasi-inverses of schema mappings. In: Proc. 26th ACM SIGMOD Symp. on Principles of Database Systems, pp. 123–132.

[10] Leme, L.A.P., Casanova, M.A., Breitman, K.K., Furtado, A.L.: Instance-based OWL Schema Matching. In: Proc. 11th Int'l. Conf. on Enterprise Inf. Systems, Milan, Italy (2009)

Schema Normalization for Improving Schema Matching*

Serena Sorrentino[2], Sonia Bergamaschi[1], Maciej Gawinecki[2], and Laura Po[1]

[1] DII - University of Modena and Reggio Emilia, Italy
[2] ICT Doctorate School - University of Modena and Reggio Emilia, Italy
name.surname@unimore.it

Abstract. Schema matching is the problem of finding relationships among concepts across heterogeneous data sources (heterogeneous in format and in structure). Starting from the "hidden meaning" associated to schema labels (i.e. class/attribute names) it is possible to discover relationships among the elements of different schemata. Lexical annotation (i.e. annotation w.r.t. a thesaurus/lexical resource) helps in associating a "meaning" to schema labels. However, accuracy of semi-automatic lexical annotation methods on real-world schemata suffers from the abundance of non-dictionary words such as compound nouns and word abbreviations. In this work, we address this problem by proposing a method to perform schema labels *normalization* which increases the number of comparable labels. Unlike other solutions, the method semi-automatically expands abbreviations and annotates compound terms, without a minimal manual effort. We empirically prove that our normalization method helps in the identification of similarities among schema elements of different data sources, thus improving schema matching accuracy.

1 Introduction

Schema matching is a critical step in many applications such as: data integration, data warehousing, E-business, semantic query processing, peer data management and semantic web applications [14]. In this work, we focus on schema matching in the context of data integration [2], where the goal is the creation of mappings between heterogeneous data sources (heterogeneous in format and in structure). Mappings are obtained by a schema matching system by using a set of semantic matches (e.g. location = area) between different schemata. A powerful mean to discover matches is the understanding of the "meaning" behind the names denoting schemata elements, i.e. labels in the following [17]. In this context, lexical annotation, i.e. the explicit association of the "meaning" (synset/sense in WordNet (WN) terminology [8]) to a label w.r.t. a thesaurus (WN in our case) is a key tool.

* **Acknowledgements:** This work was partially supported by MUR FIRB Network Peer for Business project (http://www.dbgroup.unimo.it/nep4b) and by the IST FP6 STREP project 2006 STASIS (http://www.dbgroup.unimo.it/stasis).

A.H.F. Laender et al. (Eds.): ER 2009, LNCS 5829, pp. 280–293, 2009.

The strength of a thesaurus, like WN, is the presence of a wide network of semantic relationships among words meanings, thus providing a corresponding inferred semantic network of lexical relationships among the labels of different schemata. Its weakness, is that it does not cover, with the same detail, different domains of knowledge and that many domain dependent terms, as *non-dictionary words*, may not be present in it. Non-dictionary words include compound nouns (CNs), abbreviations etc.

The result of automatic lexical annotation techniques is strongly affected by the presence of these non-dictionary words in schemata. For this reason, a method to expand abbreviations and to semantically "interpret" CNs is required. In the following, we will refer to this method as schema labels *normalization*. Schema labels normalization helps in the identification of similarities between labels coming from different data sources, thus improving schema mapping accuracy.

A manual process of label normalization is laborious, time consuming and itself prone to errors. Starting from our previous works on semi-automatic lexical annotation of structured and semi-structured data sources [3], we propose a semi-automatic method for the normalization of schema labels able to expand abbreviations and to annotate CNs w.r.t. WN.

Our method is implemented in the MOMIS (Mediator envirOnment for Multiple Information Sources) system [4,2]. However, it may be applied in general in the context of schema mapping discovery, ontology merging and data integration system. Moreover, it might be effective for reverse engineering tasks, when we need to abstract an entity relationship schema for a legacy database.

The rest of the paper is organized as follows. In Section 2, we define the problem in the context of schema matching; in Sections 3, 4 and 5 we describe our method with reference to classification of labels for normalization, abbreviations expansion and CNs interpretation, respectively. Section 6 describes related works; in Section 7 we demonstrate the effectiveness of the method with extensive experiments on real-world data sets; finally Section 8 is devoted to conclusion and future work.

2 Problem Definition

Elements names represent an important source for assessing similarity between schema elements. This can be done semantically by comparing their meanings.

Definition 1. *Lexical annotation of a schema label is the explicit assignment of its meaning w.r.t. a thesaurus.*

Starting from the lexical annotation of schema labels we can derive lexical relationships among them on the basis of the semantic relationships defined in WN among their meanings.

Definition 2. *A compound noun (CN) is a word composed of more than one word called CN constituents. It is used to denote a concept, and can be interpreted by exploiting the meanings of its constituents.*

Definition 3. *An abbreviation is a shortened form of a word or phrase, that consists of one or more letters taken from the word or phrase.*

Definition 4. *Let S and T be two heterogeneous schemata, and $E_S = \{s_1, ..., s_n\}$ and $E_T = \{t_1, ..., t_k\}$, respectively, the set of labels of S and T. A lexical relationship is defined as the triple $< s_i, t_j, R >$ where $s_i \in E_S$, $t_j \in E_T$ and R specifies a lexical relationship between s_i and t_j. The lexical relationships are:*

- SYN: (Synonym-of), defined between two labels that are synonymous (it corresponds to a WN synonym relationship);
- BT: (Broader Term), defined between two labels where the first is more general then the second (the opposite of BT is NT, Narrower Term) (it corresponds to a WN hypernym/hyponym relationship);
- RT: (Related Term) defined between two labels that are related in a meronymy hierarchy (it corresponds to a WN meronym relationship).

Figure 1 shows two schemata to be integrated, containing many labels with non-dictionary CNs (e.g. "CustomerName"), acronyms (e.g. "PO") and word abbreviations (e.g. "QTY"). These labels cannot be directly annotated, because they do not have an entry in WN. Schema label normalization (also called *linguistic normalization* in [14]) is the reduction of the form of each label to some standardized form that can be easily recognized. In our case, with labels normalization we intend the process of abbreviations expansion, and CNs interpretation.

Definition 5. *The interpretation of a CN is the task of determining the semantic relationships holding among the constituents of a CN.*

Definition 6. *Abbreviation expansion is the task of finding a relevant expansion (long form) for a given abbreviation (short form).*

Schema labels normalization improves the schema matching process by reducing the number of discovered *false positive/false negative relationships.*

Definition 7. *Let $< s_i, t_j, R >$ be a lexical relationship. Then it is a false positive relationship, if the concept denoted by the label s_i is not related by R to the concept denoted by the label t_j.*

For example, let us consider the two schema labels "CustomerName" and "CLIENTADDRESS", respectively in the source "PurchaseOrder" and "PO" (Figure 1). If we annotate separately the terms "Customer" and "Name", and "CLIENT" and "ADDRESS", then we would discover a SYN relationship between them, because the terms "Customer" and "CLIENT" share the same WN meaning. In this way, a false positive relationship is discovered because these two CNs represent "semantically distant" schema elements.

Definition 8. *Let $< s_i, t_j, R >$ be a lexical relationship. R is a false negative relationship if the concept denoted by the label s_i is related by R to the concept denoted by the label t_j, but the schema matching process does not return this relationship.*

Let us consider two corresponding schema labels: "amount" of the "PurchaseOrder" source and "QTY" (abbreviation for "quantity") of the "PO" source (Figure 1). Without abbreviation expansion we cannot discover that there exists a SYN relationship between the elements "amount" and "QTY".

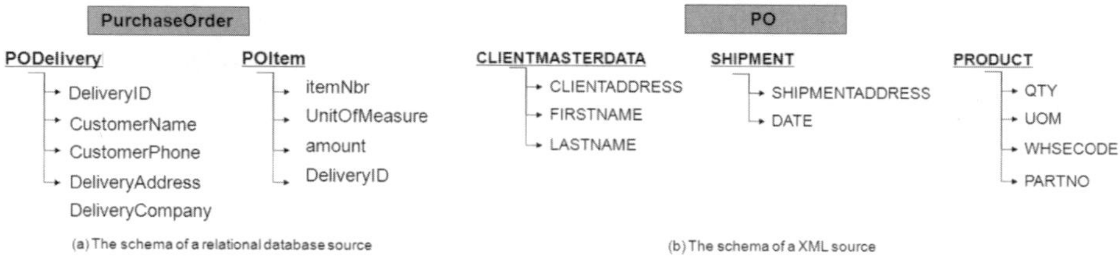

Fig. 1. Graph representation of two schemata with elements containing abbreviations and CNs: (a) relational database schema, (b) XML schema

3 Classifying Schema Labels for Normalization

The schema labels normalization process consists of three phases: (1) classification for normalization, (2) abbreviation expansion and (3) CNs interpretation. In this section we focus on the first phase.

Classification for normalization consists of the following three steps: (1) selecting whole labels that need to be normalized, (2) tokenizing selected labels into separate words, and (3) identifying abbreviations among isolated words. To select labels that need to be normalized, we propose the following classification heuristic:

Definition 9. *A label has to be normalized, if (a) it occurs on the list of standard schema abbreviations or (b) neither it nor its stem has an entry in a dictionary.*

In this way CNs which have an entry in WN (e.g. "company name") will be treated as single words, while for CNs that do not have an entry in WN (non-dictionary CNs) we apply our CNs interpretation method. Additionally, the list of standard schema abbreviations is employed here to reduce the number of false negatives caused by *legitimate* English words, that have been used for abbreviations in the schema context, e.g. "id", the prevalent abbreviation in analyzed schemata, is a dictionary word in WN.

We perform tokenization by using one of the pre-existing approaches [9]: *simple* – based on camel case and punctuation, and *greedy* – handling also multi-word names without clearly defined word boundaries, e.g. 'WHSECODE'. The latter iteratively looks for the biggest prefixing/suffixing dictionary words and user-defined abbreviations in non-dictionary words.

For instance, let us assume we are classifying "PODelivery" label. This is not a dictionary word nor a standard schema abbreviation, thus classified for normalization. The tokenization splits it into into: "PO" and "Delivery" words, where the first is identified as an abbreviation.

4 Automatic Abbreviations Expansion

Automatic abbreviation expansion of already identified abbreviations requires the execution of the following steps: (1) searching for potential long forms for the given short form; and (2) selecting the most appropriate long form from the set of potential long form candidates.

A schema can contain both *standard* and *ad hoc* abbreviations. Standard abbreviations either (a) denote important and repeating domain concepts (*domain standard abbreviations*), e.g. "ISBN" (International Standard Book Number) or (b) are standard suffix/prefix words used to describe how a value of a given schema element is represented (*standard schema abbreviations*), e.g. "Ind" (Indicator). On the contrary, ad hoc abbreviations are mainly created to save space, from phrases that would not be abbreviated in a normal context [22,11].

To observe how different types of abbreviations can be handled automatically we analyzed short forms and their corresponding long forms in several open-source schemata . Based on our manual inspection, we found two sources relevant for finding possible long form candidates for ad hoc abbreviations: (a) *context* (C) of short form occurrence, as it is common practice to an attribute name with a short form of a class name, for instance "recentchanges" table contains "rc_user" and "rc_params"; (b) a *complementary schema* (CS) that we integrate with inspected schema; e.g. a short form "uom" in the XML schema (Figure 1b) can be expanded with long form "unit Of Measure" from the relational database schema (Figure 1a). Moreover, we found online abbreviation dictionary (OD) very useful for expanding domain standard abbreviations. Finally, as the list of standard schema abbreviations is bound we were able to discover a list of possible expansions for all of them and define as a user-defined dictionary (UD).

4.1 Proposed Algorithm for Abbreviation Expansion

To handle different types of abbreviations the algorithm uses four aforementioned sources of long forms. However, the syntax of a short form itself does not provide any mean for distinguishing between ad hoc and standard abbreviations and thus we are not able to choose in advance the relevant source for expansion of a given short form. Nevertheless, we can consider the context and complementary schema as the most relevant sources in general, because they closely reflect the intention of a schema designer.

For each identified abbreviation the algorithm inquires all four sources for long form candidates, scores candidates according to the relevance of the source, combines scores of repeating long forms and chooses the top-scored one. The whole process is shown in Figure 2.

INPUT: sf – short form occurrence, **OUTPUT:** lf – long form for sf
compute the list $L_{UD} := (< lf_{UD}, 1 >)$, where lf_{UD} is a matching long form in UD
compute the list $L_{CS} := (< lf_{CS}, 1 >)$, where lf_{CS} is a matching long form in CS
compute the list $L_C := (< lf_C, 1 >)$, where lf_C is a matching long form in C of sf
compute the list $L_{OD} := (< lf_{OD,i}, sc_{OD}(lf_{OD,i}) >)_i$, where $lf_{OD,i}$ is
  a matching long form in OD
$L = L_{UD} \cup L_{CS} \cup L_C \cup L_{OD}$ // combine long forms scores
$lf := \arg\max_{lf_i \in L} sc(lf_i)$

Fig. 2. Procedure for selecting a long form for the given short form

Combining expansion sources. Technically, for each identified short form sf the algorithm creates a list of long form candidates: $(< lf_i; sc(lf_i) >)_i$ obtained from all the sources where $sc(lf_i) \in [0, 1]$. The algorithm selects the top-scored long form candidate from the list. If the list is empty, then the original short form is preserved. The score of lf_i $(sc(lf_i))$ is computed by combining scores from the single sources:

$$sc(lf_i) = \alpha_{UD} \cdot sc_{UD}(lf_i) + \alpha_{CS} \cdot sc_{CS}(lf_i) + \alpha_{C} \cdot sc_{C}(lf_i) + \alpha_{OD} \cdot sc_{OD}(lf_i)$$

where $\alpha_{UD} + \alpha_{CS} + \alpha_{C} + \alpha_{OD} = 1$ are weights of sources relevance.

Obtaining expansions from sources. For a user-defined dictionary, a context and a complementary schema sources the score of lf_i is 1, if lf_i is found in the given source or 0 – otherwise. To define a *context* let us suppose sf_i be a short form identified in a label l. The label l is either: (a) an attribute of a class c or (b) a class belonging to schemata s. Then the context of sf_i is the class c or schema s. The context is retrieved for possible long form candidates using the four abbreviation patterns (practically, regular expressions created from characters of a short form) proposed in [7]. The *labels* in the schema complementary to the schema in which sf appears are retrieved for matching long form candidates using the same abbreviation patterns as in the context. Only the first matching candidate is considered. For instance, when expanding the "PO" abbreviation in "PODelivery" element the algorithm receives the following expansions from the particular sources: (a) from online dictionary: "Purchase Order", "Parents Of", (b) from context: "Purchase Order", (c) from complementary schema: "Purchase Order". The context of "PODelivery" is in this case the name of its schema, while "PO" is a complementary schema. Next, the algorithm merges lists of proposed candidates into a single one: "Purchase Order", "Parents Of".

Scoring expansions from an online dictionary. The online dictionary may suggest more then one long form for a given short form. For this purpose we propose disambiguation technique based on two factors: (a) the number of domains a given long form shares with both schemata and (b) its popularity in these domains. The intuition is that only those expansions are relevant, that are the most popular in the domains described by both schemata. We assume information about the domain of a long form and its popularity is given by the online dictionary.

Practically, we may define score of a long form candidate — $sc_{OD}(lf_i)$ — as follows:

$$sc_{OD}(lf_i) = \sum_{d \in CD(lf_i, schemata)} \frac{p(lf_i, d)}{P_{schema}},$$

$$P_{schema} = \sum_{j} \sum_{d \in CD(lf_j, schemata)} p(lf_j, d),$$

$$CD(lf_i, schemata) = D(lf_i) \cap D(schemata)$$

where $D(schemata)$ is a list of prevalent WN Domains[1] associated with schemata to integrate [3]. If there is no shared domain for any long form candidate, then score is computed as a general popularity of a long form candidate. Computation of $CD(lf_i, schemata)$ — the intersection of prevalent domains and domains associated with long form lf_i — involves the mapping between the categorization system of an online abbreviation dictionary and WN Domains classification. The mapping has been created by obtaining automatically all corresponding domains for words in names of categories, and then, manually, by analyzing sample abbreviations in questionable mappings.

There can be more than one online dictionary entry describing the same long form lf_i, but in different domains. Therefore, the entry can be modeled as a combination of a long form lf_i and a domain $d_{i,k} \in D(lf_i)$ in which it appears with the associated popularity. Formally, we define the t-th dictionary entry in the following form: $< e_t, p(e_t) >$, where $e_t =< lf_i; d_{i,k}) >$ and $d_{i,k} \in D(lf_i)$ is the k-th domain in the set of domains $(D(lf_i))$, in which the long form lf_i appears. The popularity $p(e_t)$ is not explicitly reported by the considered dictionary but can be easily estimated from the order of descending popularity in respect to which entries are returned by the dictionary. Thus we are able to calculate $p(e_t)$ using the following induction: $p(e_{t+1}) = p(e_t)/\kappa$, $p(e_1) = 1.0$, where $\kappa > 1$ is an experimentally defined factor[2].

For example, commerce, sociology and metrology are the prevalent domains for the schemata in Figure 1. Among three entries (with given categories) returned by the dictionary for "PO" — "Purchase Order" (Accounting), "Parents Of" (Law), "Purchase Order" (Military) — only the first one matters, because its category is mapped to commerce WN Domain — one of the schemata domains.

5 Compound Noun Interpretation

In order to perform semi-automatic CNs annotation, a method for their interpretation need to be devised. In the natural language disambiguation literature different CNs classifications have been proposed [21,19]. In this work we use the classification introduced in [21], where CNs are classified in four distinct categories: *endocentric*, *exocentric*, *copulative* and *appositional* and we consider only endocentric CNs.

Definition 10. *An Endocentric CN consists of a head (i.e. the categorical part that contains the basic meaning of the whole CN) and modifiers, which restrict this meaning. A CN exhibits a modifier-head structure with a sequence of nouns composed of a* head *noun and one or more modifiers where the head noun occurs always after the modifiers.*

The constituents of endocentric compounds are noun-noun or adjective-noun, where the adjective derives from a noun (e.g. "dark room", where the adjective "dark" derives from the noun "darkness"). Our restriction on endocentric CNs is

---

[1] http://wndomains.itc.it/wordnetdomains.html

[2] In experiments we successfully use $\kappa := 1.2$.

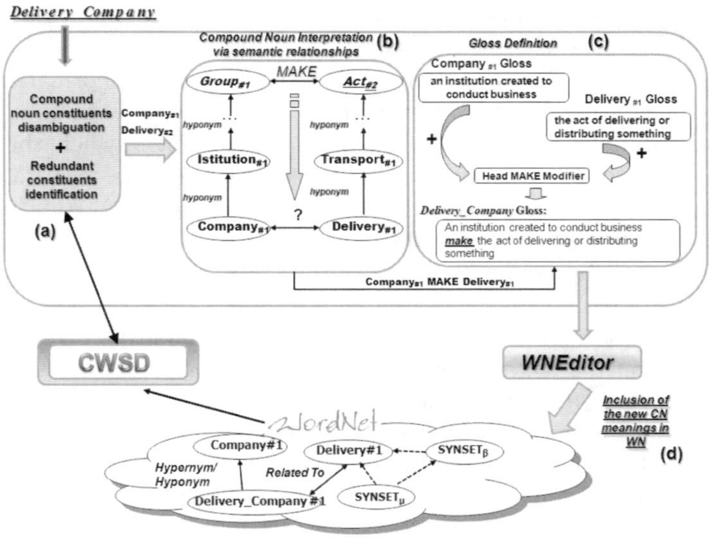

Fig. 3. The CNs interpretation process

motivated by the following observations: (1) the vast majority of CNs of schemata fall in endocentric category; (2) endocentric CNs are the most common type of CNs in English; (3) exocentric and copulative CNs, which are represented by a unique word, are often present in a dictionary; (4) appositional CNs are not very common in English and less likely used as elements of a schema. We consider endocentric CNs composed of only two constituents, because CNs consisting of more than two words need to be constructed recursively by *bracketing* them into pairs of words and then interpreting each pair.

Our method can be summed up into four main phases: (1) CN constituents disambiguation; (2) redundant constituents identification; (3) CN interpretation via semantic relationships; (4) creation of a new WN meaning for a CN.

Phase 1. CN constituents disambiguation

In this phase the correct WN synset of each constituent is chosen in two steps:

1. *Compound Noun syntactic analysis*: this step performs the syntactic analysis of CN constituents, in order to identify the syntactic category of its head and modifier. If the CN does not fall under the endocentric syntactic structure, then it is ignored;
2. *Disambiguating head and modifier*: this step is part of the general lexical disambiguation problem. By applying our CWSD (Combined Word Sense Disambiguation) algorithm [3], each word is automatically mapped onto its corresponding WN 2.0 synsets.

As shown in Figure 3-a, for example, for the schema element "DeliveryCompany" we obtain the two constituents annotated with the correspondent WN meanings (i.e. "$Company_{\#1}$" and "$Delivery_{\#1}$").

Phase 2. Redundant constituents identification and pruning
During this phase we control whether a CN constituent is a *redundant word*. Redundant words are the words that do not contribute new information as their semantic contribution can be derived from the schema or from the lexical resource. For example, the typical situation in a schema is when the name of a class is a part of its attribute name (see for instance the "SHIPMENTADDRESS" attribute of the "SHIPMENT" class in Figure 1-b). As a result, the constituent class name is not considered, because the relationship holding among a class and its attributes can be derived from the schema.

Phase 3. CN interpretation via semantic relationships
This phase concerns selecting from a set of predefined relationships the one that in the best way captures the semantic relation between the meanings of a head and a modifier. The problem of devising a set of semantic relationships to be considered for the CNs interpretation has been widely discussed in the natural language disambiguation literature [12]. In [19] Levi defines a set of nine possible semantic relationships to interpret CNs: CAUSE ("flu virus"), HAVE ("college town"), MAKE ("honey bee"), USE ("water wheel"), BE ("chocolate bar"), IN ("mountain lodge"), FOR ("headache pills"), FROM ("bacon grease") and ABOUT ("adventure story"). On the contrary, Finin in [16] claims an unlimited number of semantic relationships. We choose the Levi semantic relationships set, as it is the best choice in the simplified context of a data integration scenario. According to [15], our method is based on the following assumptio

Definition 11. *The semantic relationship between a head and its modifier of a CN is derived from the one holding between their top level WN nouns in the WN nouns hierarchy.*

The WN nouns hierarchy has been proven to be very useful in the CNs interpretation task [12]. The top level concepts of the WN hierarchy are the 25 *unique beginners* (e.g. act, animal, artifact etc.) for WN English nouns defined by Miller in [8]. These unique beginners were selected after considering all the possible adjective-noun or noun-noun combinations that could be expected to occur and are suitable to interpret noun-noun or adjective-noun CNs as in our case.

For each possible couple of the unique beginners we manually associate the relationship from the Levi's set that best describes the meaning of this couple. For example, for the unique beginner pair "group and act" we choose the Levi's relationship MAKE (e.g. "group MAKE act"), that can be expressed as: a group performs an act. In this way, as shown in Figure 3b, we are able to interpret the label "DeliveryCompany" with the MAKE relationship, because "Company" is an hyponym of "group" and "Delivery" is an hyponym of "act".

Our method requires an initial human intervention to associate to each pair of unique beginners the right relationship. However, it may be considered acceptable, when compared with the much greater effort required for other approaches based on pre-tagged corpus where the number of CNs to be annotated is much higher [12,18]. Moreover, the method is independent from the domain under consideration and can be applied to any thesaurus providing a wide network of hyponym/hypernym relationships between defined meanings.

Phase 4. Creation of a new WN meaning for a CN
During this phase, we create a new WN meaning for the given CN. We distinguish the following two steps:

1. *Gloss definition*: during this step we create the *gloss* to be associated with a CN, starting from the relationship associated to it and exploiting the glosses of the CN constituents. Figure 3-c shows an example of this phase. The glosses of the constituents "Company" and "Delivery" are joined together according to the relationship MAKE.
2. *Inclusion of the new CN meaning in WN*: the insertion of a new CN meaning into the WN hierarchy implies the definition of its relationships with the other WN meanings. As the concept denoted by a CN is a subset of the concept denoted by the head, we assume that a CN inherits most of its semantics from its head [21]. Starting from this consideration, we can infer that the CN is related, in the WN hierarchy, to its head by an hyponym relationship. Moreover, we represent the CN semantics related to its modifier by inserting a generic relationship RT (*Related term*), corresponding to WN relationships as *member meronym*, *part meronym* etc. However, the insertion of these two relationships is not sufficient, it is necessary to discover also the relationships of the new inserted meaning w.r.t. the other WN meanings. For this purpose, we use the WNEditor tool to create/manage the new meaning and to set relationships between it and the WN ones [4]. The WNEditor automatically retrieves a list of candidate WN meanings sharing similarities with the new meaning. Then, the user is asked to explicitly declare the type of relationship (hyponymy, meronymy etc.) to relate the new meaning to another, if any. Figure 3-d shows an example of this step.

6 Related Work

The problem of linguistic normalization has received much attention in different areas such as: machine translation, information extraction, information retrieval.

Many abbreviation expansion techniques are based on the observation that in documents the short forms and their long forms usually occur together in patterns. Selecting the most relevant long form is made w.r.t. different factors such as: *inverted frequency* [13], *document scope* [7] or *syntactic similarity* [11].

Many works in the literature for interpreting CNs involve costly pre-tagged corpus and heavy manual intervention [12,18]. These approaches are based on a statistic co-occurrence of a relationship r between two words on corpus that contain different CNs manually labeled with the right semantic relationship. According to [15], we claim that the cost of acquiring knowledge from manually tagged corpus for different domains may overshadow the benefit of interpreting the CNs.

Table 1. Characteristics of test schemata

Number of	Labels	Non-dictionary words	CNs	Abbreviations
Schema 1	117	66	33	62
Schema 2	51	28	28	24

Surprisingly, current schema integration systems either do not consider the problem of abbreviation expansion at all or solve it in non-scalable way by inclusion of a simple user-defined abbreviation dictionary [20,1]. Lack of scalability comes from the fact that: (a) the vocabulary evolves over the time and it is necessary to maintain the table of abbreviations and (b) the same abbreviations can have different expansions depending on the domain. Moreover, this approach still requires an intervention of a schema/domain expert.

Similarly, in the context of data integration and schema mapping only a few papers address the problem of CNs interpretation. In [23] a preliminary CNs comparison for ontology mapping is proposed. This approach suffers from two main problems: first, it starts from the assumption that the ontology entities are accompanied with comments that contain words expressing the relationship between the constituents of a CN; second, it is based on a set of rules manually created. The well know CUPID algorithm [20], during the schema labels normalization phase, considers abbreviations, punctuation, etc. but not CNs. Generally, schema and ontology matching tools employing *syntactical matching* techniques do not interpret nor normalize CNs but they treat words in CNs separately [6].

7 Experimental Results

We implemented our method for schema labels normalization in the MOMIS system [2]. Schema labels normalization is performed during the lexical annotation phase: during this phase each schema element of a local source is semi-automatically annotated by the CWSD algorithm. We tested the performance of our method over the two relational schemata of the well known Amalgam integration benchmark for bibliographic data [10]. Table 1 summarizes the test schemata features that are particularly suitable for the test.

Our evaluation goals were: (1) measuring the performance of our method, (2) checking whether our method improves the *lexical annotation* process and finally (3) estimating the effect of schema labels normalization on the *lexical relationships discovery* process.

7.1 Evaluating Schema Labels Normalization Method

The normalization process consists of: classification, abbreviations expansion and CNs interpretation. Since the errors of each step can be cumulated in the phases following, we evaluated performance of each step separately (using correct manually prepared input) and then as a whole.

Table 2. Result of evaluation of schema labels normalization method

	Precision	Recall
Total labels normalization (after GT/Ispell)	0.84	0.74

Classification. We consider a label correctly classified for normalization if w.r.t. manual classification the label has been correctly tokenized and all abbreviations and CNs in the label have been identified. We evaluated classification method in two variants depending on the tokenization method used: (1) `ST`: simple and (2) `GT/Ispell`: greedy with Ispell English words list[3] as a dictionary (see Section 3 for details). The `ST` reaches nearly the same correctness (0.92) as `GT/Ispell` (0.93), because the schemata contain relatively few labels with unclearly undefined word boundaries (e.g. "bktitle").

Abbreviations expansions. W.r.t. manually classified and tokenized schemata labels the algorithm *expanded abbreviations* correctly in 90% of identified abbreviations. There are two reasons for errors: (a) lack of correct expansions in the external sources (context, documentation, online dictionary); and (b) partial matching of multi-words abbreviations, e.g. there is no correct matching in any source for "RID", but "ID" can be found in user-defined dictionary, while "R", standing for "record", in the element context.

CNs interpretation. has been evaluated in terms of recall (the number of correct interpretation divided by the total number of CNs) and precision (the number of correct interpretations divided by the total number of interpreted CNs). During the evaluation process, a CN has been considered *correctly interpreted* if the Levi's relationship manually selected was the same as the one returned by our method. The CNs interpretation method obtains good result both for precision (0.86) and recall (0.75). However, the recall value is affected by the presence in the schemata of CNs such as "ManualPublished" or "ArticlePublished" that our method is not able to interpret as these terms are not endocentric CNs.

Table 2 shows the result of the whole schema labels normalization process by using our automatic classification, abbreviation expansion and semi-automatic CNs interpretation together.

7.2 Evaluating the Lexical Annotation Process

The annotation results have been evaluated in terms of recall (the number of correct annotations divided by the total number of schema labels) and precision (the number of correct annotations divided by the total number of annotations). Table 3 shows the result of lexical annotation performed by CWSD without/with our normalization method. Without schema normalization, CWSD obtains a very low recall value, because a lot of CNs and abbreviations are present in the schemata. The application of our method permits to increase the recall while preserving the high precision.

[3] Ispell is a popular tool for spelling errors correction: http://wordlist.sourceforge.net/

Table 3. Comparison of lexical annotation (CWSD) without/with normalization

	Precision	Recall
CWSD	0.81	0.35
CWSD + Labels Normalization	0.83	0.78

Table 4. Comparison of lexical relationships discovered without/with normalization

	Precision	Recall	F-Measure
Lexical rel. discovered	0.58	0.33	0.42
Lexical rel. discovered + Normalization	0.90	0.75	0.82

7.3 Evaluating the Discovered Lexical Relations

To evaluate the quality of the lexical relationship discovered, we use the match quality measure defined in [5]. In particular, we compare the manually determined lexical relationships (MR) with the relationships returned by our semi-automatic method (AR). We determine: the true positives, i.e. correctly identified relationships (B), as well as the false positives (C) and the false negatives (A). Based on the cardinalities of these sets, the following quality measure are computed:

- *Precision*= $\frac{|B|}{|B|+|C|}$ reflects the reliability of the relationships predictions;
- *Recall*= $\frac{|B|}{|A|+|B|}$ specified the share of real relationships that is found;
- *F-Measure*= $2*\frac{Precision*Recall}{Precision+Recall}$ – a combined measure of precision and recall.

Table 4 shows the result of the lexical relationships discovery process without/with normalization. In the first row we show the discovered lexical relationships without abbreviation expansion and considering the constituents of a CNs as single words with an associated meaning. Without schema labels normalization we discover few lexical relationships with low precision due the presence of a lot of false positive relationships. Instead, with our method we are able to improve recall and precision significantly.

8 Conclusion and Future Work

In this paper we presented a method for the semi-automatic normalization of schema elements labeled with abbreviations and CNs in a data integration environment. The experimental results have shown the effectiveness of our method, which significantly improves the result of the automatic lexical annotation process, and as a consequence, improves the quality of the discovered inter-schema lexical relationships. We demonstrated that, due to the frequency and productivity of non-dictionary words, a data integration system, during the lexical annotation phase, cannot ignore CNs and abbreviations without compromising recall. Future work will be devoted to investigate on the role of the set of semantic relationships chosen for the CNs interpretation process.

References

1. Aumueller, D., Do, H.H., Massmann, S., Rahm, E.: Schema and ontology matching with COMA++. In: SIGMOD 2005, pp. 906–908 (2005)
2. Bergamaschi, S., Castano, S., Vincini, M.: Semantic integration of semistructured and structured data sources. SIGMOD Record 28(1), 54–59 (1999)
3. Bergamaschi, S., Po, L., Sorrentino, S.: Automatic annotation for mapping discovery in data integration systems. In: SEBD 2008, pp. 334–341 (2008)
4. Beneventano, D., Bergamaschi, S., Guerra, F., Vincini, M.: Synthesizing an integrated ontology. IEEE Internet Computing 7(5), 42–51 (2003)
5. Do, H.H., Melnik, S., Rahm, E.: Comparison of schema matching evaluations. In: Web, Web-Services, and Database Systems, pp. 221–237 (2002)
6. Le, B.T., et al.: On ontology matching problems - for building a corporate semantic web in a multi-communities organization. ICEIS (4), 236–243 (2004)
7. Hill, E., et al.: AMAP: automatically mining abbreviation expansions in programs to enhance software maintenance tools. In: MSR (2008)
8. Miller, G.A., et al.: Wordnet: An on-line lexical database. International Journal of Lexicography 3, 235–244 (1990)
9. Feild, H., et al.: An Empirical Comparison of Techniques for Extracting Concept Abbreviations from Identifiers. In: SEA 2006 (November 2006)
10. Miller, R.J., et al.: The Amalgam Schema and Data Integration Test Suite (2001), http://www.cs.toronto.edu/miller/amalgam
11. Uthurusamy, R., et al.: Extracting knowledge from diagnostic databases. IEEE Expert: Intelligent Systems and Their Applications 8(6), 27–38 (1993)
12. Nastase, V., et al.: Learning noun-modifier semantic relations with corpus-based and wordnet-based features. In: AAAI (2006)
13. Wong, W., et al.: Integrated scoring for spelling error correction, abbreviation expansion and case restoration in dirty text. In: AusDM 2006, pp. 83–89 (2006)
14. Euzenat, J., Shvaiko, P.: Ontology matching. Springer, Heidelberg (2007)
15. Fan, J., Barker, K., Porter, B.W.: The knowledge required to interpret noun compounds. In: IJCAI, pp. 1483–1485 (2003)
16. Finin, T.W.: The semantic interpretation of nominal compounds. In: AAAI, pp. 310–312 (1980)
17. Giunchiglia, F., Shvaiko, P., Yatskevich, M.: S-match: an algorithm and an implementation of semantic matching. In: Semantic Interoperability and Integration (2005)
18. Lapata, M.: The disambiguation of nominalizations. Computational Linguistics 28(3), 357–388 (2002)
19. Levi, J.N.: The Syntax and Semantics of Complex Nominals. Academic Press, New York (1978)
20. Madhavan, J., Bernstein, P.A., Rahm, E.: Generic schema matching with cupid. In: VLDB, pp. 49–58 (2001)
21. Plag, I.: Word-Formation in English. Cambridge Textbooks in Linguistics. Cambridge University Press, New York (2003)
22. Ratinov, L., Gudes, E.: Abbreviation Expansion in Schema Matching and Web Integration. In: WI 2004, pp. 485–489 (2004)
23. Su, X., Gulla, J.A.: Semantic enrichment for ontology mapping. In: Meziane, F., Métais, E. (eds.) NLDB 2004. LNCS, vol. 3136, pp. 217–228. Springer, Heidelberg (2004)

Extensible User-Based XML Grammar Matching

Joe Tekli, Richard Chbeir, and Kokou Yetongnon

LE2I Laboratory UMR-CNRS, University of Bourgogne - 21078 Dijon France
{joe.tekli,richard.chbeir,kokou.yetongnon}@u-bourgogne.fr

Abstract. XML grammar matching has found considerable interest recently due to the growing number of heterogeneous XML documents on the web and the increasing need to integrate, and consequently search and retrieve XML data originated from different data sources. In this paper, we provide an approach for automatic XML grammar matching and comparison aiming to minimize the amount of user effort required to perform the match task. We propose an open framework based on the concept of tree edit distance, integrating different matching criterions so as to capture XML grammar element semantic and syntactic similarities, cardinality and alternativeness constraints, as well as data-type correspondences and relative ordering. It is flexible, enabling the user to chose mapping cardinality (*1:1*, *1:n*, *n:1*, *n:n*), in comparison with existing static methods (constrained to *1:1*), and considers user feedback to adjust matching results to the user's perception of correct matches. Conducted experiments demonstrate the efficiency of our approach, in comparison with alternative methods.

Keywords: XML and Semi-structured data, XML grammar, schema matching, structural similarity, tree edit distance, vector space model.

1 Introduction

With the growing amount of heterogeneous XML information on the Web, i.e., documents originated from different data-sources, there is an increasing need to perform XML data integration, data warehousing and consequently XML information extraction, search and retrieval. All these applications require, in some way or another, XML document and grammar similarity evaluation. In this area, most work has focused on estimating similarity between XML documents, which is relevant in several scenarios such as change management and data warehousing [6][7], structural querying [28][38], and document clustering [8][25]. Yet, few efforts have been dedicated to comparing XML grammars, useful for data integration purposes, in particular the integration of DTDs/XML schemas that contain nearly or exactly the same information but are constructed using different structures [11][22]. XML grammar comparison is mainly exploited in data warehousing [27] (mapping data sources to warehouse schemas), message translation [27] as well as XML data maintenance and schema evolution [17].

In this study, we address the XML grammar comparison problem, i.e., the comparison of DTDs [4] and/or XML Schemas [26] based on their most common

A.H.F. Laender et al. (Eds.): ER 2009, LNCS 5829, pp. 294–314, 2009.

characteristics. In fact, the effectiveness of grammar matching systems is assessed w.r.t. (with respect to) the amount of manual work required to perform the matching task [10], which depends on: i) the level of simplification in the representation of the grammars, and ii) the combination of various matching techniques [9]. In general, most XML-related grammar matching methods in the literature are developed for generic schemas and are consequently adapted to XML grammars, e.g., [9][11][19][22]. On one hand, they often induce certain simplifications to XML grammars in order to perform the match task. In particular, constraints on the existence, repeatability and alternativeness of XML elements (e.g., '?', '+' and '*' in DTDs, or *minoccurs* and *maxoccurs* in XML Schemas) are disregarded [9][14]. On the other hand, they usually exploit individual matching criterions to identify similarities [22][31] (evaluating for instance the syntactic similarity between element labels, disregarding semantic meaning) and thus do not capture all element resemblances. Methods that do consider several criterions (semantic similarity, data-type similarity…) usually utilize machine learning techniques [11] or basic mathematical formulations (e.g., *max*, *ave*, …) [9] which are usually not adapted to XML-based data in combining the results of different matchers.

Thus, our main goal is to develop an effective XML grammar matching method minimizing the amount of manual work needed to perform the match task. This requires i) considering the characteristics and constraints of the XML grammars being matched (in comparison with existing 'grammar simplifying' approaches, e.g., [9][14]), and ii) providing a flexible and extensible framework for combining different matching criterions (in comparison with existing static methods, e.g., [22][31]) that is adapted to the semi-structured nature of XML grammars (in comparison with relatively generic approaches, e.g., [11][19]).

Hence, the contributions of our paper can be summarized as follows: i) introducing a generic tree representation model, that copes with the expressive power of common XML grammars, without being constrained to a specific grammar language (e.g., DTD[4] or XSD[26]) ii) providing an open framework, founded on the well known concept of tree edit distance, for integrating different matching criterions to evaluate the similarity between XML grammar trees, and iii) developing a prototype to evaluate and validate our approach. Note that to our knowledge, this is the first attempt to exploit tree edit distance in an XML grammar matching context. The remainder of the paper is organized as follows. In Section 2, we depict our XML grammar tree representation model. Section 3 develops our tree edit distance based XML grammar matching framework. Section 4 presents our prototype and experimental results. Section 5 briefly reviews background in XML schema matching. Section 6 concludes the paper.

2 XML Grammar Tree Representation

We first provide definitions describing the basic notions of *ordered labeled tree*, *first level sub-tree*, and *XML grammar constraint operators*, exploited in developing our grammar tree model.

Def. 1 - Ordered Labeled Tree: It is a rooted tree in which the nodes are labeled and ordered. We denote by *T[i]* the ith node of *T* in preorder traversal, and by *R(T)=T[0]* its root •

Def. 2 - First Level Sub-tree: Given a tree T with root p of degree k, the first level sub-trees, $FL\text{-}SbTree_T = \{T_1, \ldots, T_k\}$ of T are the sub-trees rooted at the children of p: $p_1, \ldots, p_k$ •

Def. 3 - XML Grammar Constraint Operators: These are operators utilized to specify constraints on the existence and repeatability of elements/attributes. They consist of two main groups: *cardinality constraints* (*cc*) and *alternativeness constraints* (*ac*).

With cardinality constraint operators, it is possible to specify whether an element is optional ('?' in DTD – equivalent to *minoccurs=0* in XSD) or whether it may occur several times (i.e., '*' in DTD for 0 or more times – equivalent to *minoccurs=0* and *maxoccurs='unbounded'* in XSD – and '+' in DTD for 1 or more times, equivalent to *maxoccurs='unbounded'* in XSD). It is also possible to specify whether an attribute is optional (*Implied*) or mandatory (*Required*). An element/attribute with no constraints is mandatory.

Alternativeness constraint operators specify whether some sub-elements are alternative w.r.t. each other (the *Or* operator, represented by '|' in DTD – *choice* in XSD) or are grouped in a sequence (*And* operator, represented by ',' in DTD – *sequence* in XSD). An additional hybrid operator, *All*, is introduced in XSD [26], which allows its sub-elements to appear in any order, such as all of them appear at once, or not at all. •

With most existing XML grammar matching methods, grammars are represented as simplified XML-like trees or graph structures[1], e.g., [16][19][31]. Here, we provide here a tree model that i) captures the structural properties of XML grammars, ii) and accurately considers their most common characteristics.

First, we define the notions of *composite alternativeness constraint* and *alternativeness constraint vector*, central to preserving the structural levels of XML grammar elements/attributes.

Def. 4 - Composite alternativeness constraint: It is an alternativeness operator, i.e., *And*, *Or* or *All* (cf. Definition 3), to which we associate a cardinality constraint, e.g., ?, *, … (cf. Definition 3), in order to underline the repeatability of groups of elements. Formally, it can be represented as a doublet *cac = (sac, cc)* where *sac* is a simple alternativeness constraint and *cc* the corresponding cardinality constraint. For instance, XSD declaration *<All MinOccurs=0><element name='a'><element name='b'></All>* corresponds to an *(All, MinOcc=0)* composite constraint associated to both elements *a* and *b* •

Def. 5 - Alternativeness constraint vector: It is a vector $\overline{ac}$ of simple and/or composite alternativeness constraints, underlining the disposition of a grammar element w.r.t. its siblings and parent element in the grammar. For instance, in DTD declaration *((a | b)?, c)*, vector *<And, (Or, ?)>* would be associated to elements *a* and *b*, while vector *<And>* is associated to *c* •

Def. 6 – XML Grammar Tree: Formally, we model an XML Grammar as a rooted ordered labeled tree $D = (N_D, E_D, L_D, CC_D, \overline{AC_D}, T_D, g_D)$ where: N_D is the set of nodes

[1] Graphs are considered when recursive definitions come to play, which we do not treat in our current study.

in D, $E_D \subseteq N_D \times N_D$ is the set of edges (element/attribute containment relation), L_D is the set of labels corresponding to the nodes of D ($L_D = El_D \cup A_D$ such as El_D and A_D designate respectively the labels of the elements and attributes of D), CC_D is the set of cardinality constraints associated to the elements and attributes of D (i.e., '?', '*', '+', *MinOccurs*, *MaxOccurs*, *'Required'*, *'Implied'* and *null*, cf. Definition 3), $\overline{AC_D}$ is the set of alternativeness constraint vectors associated to the elements and attributes of D (central to preserving the structural levels of XML grammar nodes, cf. Figures 2 and 3), T_D is the set of data-types ($T_D = ET \cup AT$, includes the basic XML element data-types ET = {'#PCDATA', 'ANY', *'String'*, *'Decimal'*, …, *Composite*} and attribute data-types AT = {'CDATA', 'ID', 'IDREF', …}), and g_D is a function $g_D: N_D \rightarrow L_D, CC_D, \overline{AC_D}, T_D$ that associates a label $l \in L_D$, a cardinality constraint $cc \in CC_D$, an alternative constraint vector $\overline{ac} \in \overline{AC_D}$ and a data-type $t \in T_D$ to each node $v \in V_D$ •

Def. 7 – XML Grammar Tree Node: A node $n \in N_D$ of XML grammar tree $D = (N_D, E_D, L_D, CC_D, \overline{AC_D}, T_D, g_D)$ is represented by a quintuplet $n = (l, cc, \overline{ac}, t, Ord)$ where $l \in L_D$, $cc \in CC_D$, $\overline{ac} \in \overline{AC_D}$ and $t \in T_D$ are respectively its label, cardinality constraint, alternativeness constraint vector and node data-type. The additional *Ord* component underlines the DTD node's order w.r.t. its siblings. It is detailed in the following section •

In XML documents, attributes are usually treated as unordered nodes[2]. In other words, the order, left-to-right, of attribute nodes corresponding to a given element is not relevant (e.g., *<Paper title="…" Genre="…">* is equivalent to *<Paper Genre="…" Title="…">*). Consequently, the same is true for attributes in XML grammars. In addition, grammar element nodes connected via the *Or* and *All* operators are unordered [26] (e.g., DTD declaration *Paper (Author | Publisher)* is equivalent to *Paper (Publisher | Author)*). Thus, the XML grammar tree would encompass ordered parts, i.e., elements connected via the *And* operator, and unordered ones, i.e., elements connected via the *Or*/*All* operators as well as attribute nodes.

However, algorithms for computing the edit distance between unordered trees are generally *NP-complete* whereas those for comparing ordered trees are of polynomial complexity [2]. Thus, transforming the XML grammar tree into a fully ordered tree would help amend the time efficiency of the edit distance based match operation. This can be done by representing attribute nodes as children of their encompassing element nodes appearing before all sub-element node siblings, and consequently sorting all node siblings, left-to-right by node label. This can be achieved using efficient sorting algorithms such as *Quicksort*, *MergeSort*, *Bucketsort* [15]. An ordering score *Ord*, will be associated to each node, underlining the reordering magnitude of the node. The *Ord* score will be exploited in the matching framework so as to increase/decrease the plausibility of a given match: nodes closer to their initial positions, i.e., with lesser *Ord* scores, would constitute better match candidates. For $n \in N_D$:

$$n.Ord = \frac{NbHops(InitPosition(n), FinalPosition(n))}{(Number\ of\ siblings\ under\ parent\ of\ n) - 1} \in [-1,1] \quad (1)$$

[2] The Document Object Model, http://www.w3.org/DOM

Note that the ordering score *Ord* is not modified when sorting attribute nodes and/or element nodes connected via the *Or*/*All* operators since they are initially unordered.

Consider the XML grammars in Figure 1. Corresponding tree representations are depicted in Figures 2 and 3 (note that elements of the same structural level are represented in a stair-like manner to fit in page margins). Now since XML grammars are represented as special ordered labeled trees (cf. Definition 6), the problem of matching two grammars comes down to matching the corresponding trees (similarly to [16][19]).

```
<!ELEMENT Paper ((Publisher | Author+), PaperLength?, url*)>
<!ATTLIST Paper Title CDATA #IMPLIED>
<!ATTLIST Paper  Genre CDATA>
<!ELEMENT Publisher (#PCDATA)>
<!ELEMENT Author (FirstName, MiddleName?, LastName)>
<!ELEMENT PaperLength (#PCDATA)>
<!ELEMENT url (Homepage, Download+)?>
<!ELEMENT Homepage (#PCDATA)>
<!ELEMENT Download (#PCDATA)>
<!ELEMENT FisrtName (#PCDATA)>
<!ELEMENT MiddleName (#PCDATA)>
<!ELEMENT LastName (#PCDATA)>
```

a. Paper.dtd

```
<element name= "Publication">
  <sequence>
    <element name= "Title" type="String"/>
    <element name= "Year" type= "Date"/>
    <choice>
      <element name= "Author" maxoccurs= "unbounded">
        <sequence>
          <element name= "First" type= "String">
          <element name= "Last" type= "String">
        </sequence>
      </element>
      <element name= "Editor" maxoccurs= "unbounded">
        <all>
          <element name= "Name" type= "String">
          <element name= "Country" type= "String">
        </all>
      </element>
    </choice>
    <element name= "Publisher" type= "String" minoccurs= "0" />
    <element name= "Length" type= "Decimal"/>
    <element name="Link" type="String" minoccurs= "0"/>
  </sequence>
</element>
```

b. Publication.xsd

Fig. 1. Sample XML grammars

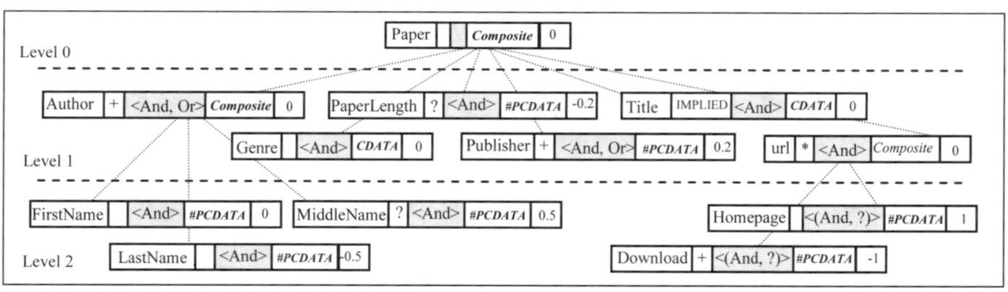

Fig. 2. Tree representation *P* of grammar *Paper.dtd* in Figure 1

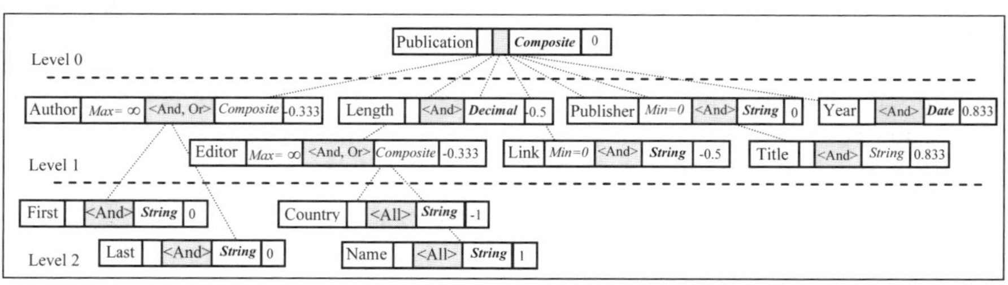

Fig. 3. Tree representation *Q* of grammar *Publication.xsd* in Figure 1

3 XML Grammar Matching Framework

Tree edit distance methods have been widely utilized to compare XML documents, represented as Ordered Labeled Trees, and have been proven optimal w.r.t. less accurate structural comparison methods [5]. A great advantage of edit distance is that along the similarity value, a mapping between the nodes in the compared trees is provided in terms of the edit script (i.e., sequence of edit operations transforming one tree into another). This is crucial for schema matching, and would constitute the output of the match operation. Our matching framework consists of four main components: i) the *Edit Distance* component for computing the distance (similarity) between DTD trees, ii) the extensible *Matchers* component, encompassing several matching algorithms, exploited via *Edit Distance* to capture XML grammar node resemblances, iii) the *Mapping Identification* component, interacting with *Edit Distance* to identify the edit script (*ES_Extraction*), and consequently the edit distance mappings, and iv) the *UserFeed* component to consider user mappings and feedback in producing matching results.

The overall architecture of our grammar matching approach is depicted in Figure 4, and will be detailed in the following sections.

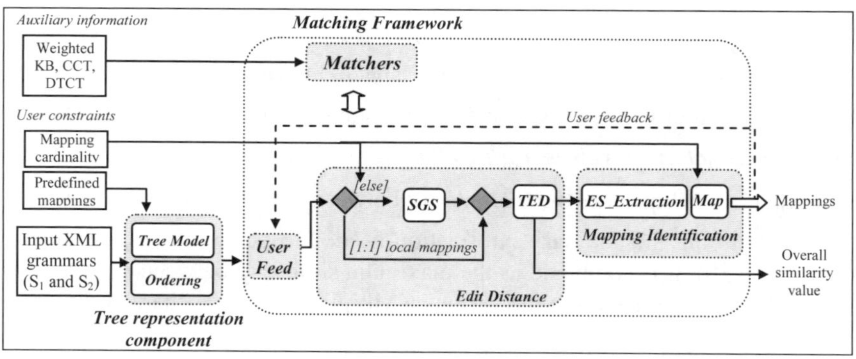

Fig. 4. Simplified activity diagram describing our edit distance matching framework

3.1 Edit Distance Component

Several algorithms have been developed to compute a distance, as the sum of a sequence of basic edit operations that can transform one tree structure into another. In the context of XML, the most recent and efficient proposals, e.g., [25][32], have stressed on the importance of considering XML sub-tree similarities in computing edit distance, as a crucial requirement to obtaining more accurate results. Here, we follow a similar strategy in comparing grammars. We first develop a dedicated method, *SGS*, to compute the *Similarity* between XML *Grammar Sub-trees*, based on the vector space model in information retrieval [21]. XML grammar sub-tree similarities are consequently exploited as tree edit operations' costs in a dynamic programming tree edit distance algorithm (*TED*, cf. system architecture in Figure 4).

Note that our grammar comparison method can be viewed as an extension of [32], one of the most recent tree edit distance based methods for comparing XML document structures.

3.1.1 Similarity between XML Grammar Sub-trees (SGS)

In evaluating XML grammar sub-tree similarity, one should consider all node characteristics (element names, depth and relative order, cardinality constraints, alternativeness constraint vectors, data-types, and ordering scores, cf. Definitions 6 and 7) so as to produce accurate results. To do so, we exploit the vector space model in information retrieval [21].

When comparing two grammar sub-trees SbT_i and SbT_j, each would be represented as a vector $\overline{V}$ ($\overline{V_i}$ and $\overline{V_j}$) with weights underlining the similarities between each of their nodes.

Def. 8 – Sub-tree vector: For two sub-trees SbT_i and SbT_j, vectors V_i and V_j are produced in a space which dimensions represent, each, a distinct indexing unit. An indexing unit stands for a single node $n_r \in SbT_i \cup SbT_j$, such as $1 < r < M$ where M is the number of distinct nodes in both SbT_i and SbT_j. The coordinate of a given sub-tree vector V_i on dimension n_r is noted $w_{Vi}(n_r)$ and stands for the weight of n_r in sub-tree SbT_i •

Def. 9 – Node weight: The weight of a node label n_r in vector $\overline{V_i}$ (representing sub-tree SbT_i) is composed of two factors, a node/vector similarity factor $Sim(n_r, \overline{V_i}, Aux)$ and a depth factor $D\text{-}factor(n_r)$ such as $w_{Vi}(n_r) = Sim(n_r, \overline{V_i}, Aux) \times D\text{-}factor(n_r) \in [0, 1]$.

- $Sim(n_r, \overline{V_i}, Aux)$ quantifies the similarity between node n_r and sub-tree vector $\overline{V_i}$, Aux underlining the auxiliary information needed to perform the comparison (cf. Definition 10). It is computed as the maximum similarity between n_r and all nodes of sub-tree SbT_i considering the various XML grammar node characteristics (Definition 7). Formally, $Sim(n_r, \vec{V}_i, Aux) = \underset{n \in \vec{V_i}}{Max}(Sim(n_r, n, Aux)) \in [0, 1]$.
- $D\text{-}factor(n_r)$ considers the hierarchical depth of node v_r in assessing its weight w.r.t. sub-tree vector $\overline{V_i}$. Note that node depth is not only a structural characteristic in XML, but is also of semantic relevance. It follows the intuition that information placed near the root node of an XML document is more important than information further down in the hierarchy [1][38]. Thus, higher nodes should have a greater semantic influence.

$$D\text{-}factor(n.l) = \frac{1}{1+n.d} \in [0,1] \quad \text{where } n.d \text{ designates the depth of node } n \bullet \qquad (2)$$

Def. 10 – Similarity between XML grammar nodes: It quantities the similarity between two XML grammar nodes, considering their various characteristics. Given two nodes n and m:

$$\begin{aligned}\text{Sim}(n, m, Aux) = {} & w_{\text{Label}} \times \text{Sim}_{\text{Label}}(n.l, m.l, KB) + \\ & w_{\text{CConstraint}} \times \text{Sim}_{\text{CConstraint}}(n.cc, m.cc, CCT) + \\ & w_{\text{AConstraint}} \times \text{Sim}_{\text{AConstraint}}(n, m.\overline{ac}, CCT) + \\ & w_{\text{Data-Type}} \times \text{Sim}_{\text{Data-Type}}(n.t, m.t, DTCT) + \\ & w_{\text{OrdScore}} \times \text{Sim}_{\text{OrdScore}}(n.Ord, m.Ord)\end{aligned} \quad (3)$$

where $w_{Label} + w_{CConstraint} + w_{AConstraint} + w_{Data\text{-}Type}\ w_{OrdScore} = 1$ and $(w_{Label}, w_{Constraint}, w_{AConstraint}, w_{Data\text{-}Type}, w_{OrdScore}) \geq 0$, having Sim_{Label}, $Sim_{CConstraints}$, $Sim_{AConstraints}$, $Sim_{Data\text{-}Types}$ and $Sim_{OrdScore}$ the similarity scores between corresponding node labels, cardinality constraints, alternative constraint vectors, data-types and ordering scores. Each of those similarity scores is to be computed by the corresponding matcher (Section 3.2). *Aux={KB, CCT, DTCT}* designates the auxiliary data sources required by the matchers to compute node similarity: *KB* (knowledge base), *CCT* (constraint compatibility table) and *DTCT* (data-type compatibility table [33]) •

Following *Formula (3)*, different weights are assigned to the different node components, reflecting the impact of each of the element characteristics in identifying the mappings. In fact, several methods for combining matcher results have been investigated in [9], among which the *maximum*, *minimum*, *average* and *weighted sum* functions. Here, we exploit the latter as it provides more flexibility, adapting the process w.r.t. the user's perception of similarity.

Having transformed XML grammar sub-trees into weighted vectors, the similarity between two sub-trees is evaluated using a measure of similarity between vectors such as the *inner product,* the *cosine measure*, the *Jaccard measure*, etc. Here, we adopt the *cosine measure* widely exploited in information retrieval [21].

Algorithm *SGS* for computing XML grammar sub-tree similarity consists in building and comparing sub-tree vectors as described above. *SGS* is consequently exploited to identify the similarities between each and every pair of sub-trees (SbT_i, SbT_j) in the two trees T_1 and T_2 being compared, as well as their similarities with the whole trees T_1 and T_2 respectively. Tree operations costs would hence vary as follows [32]:

$$\text{Cost}_{\text{InsTree/DelTree}}(\text{SbT}_i) = \sum_{\text{All nodes } n \text{ of SbT}_i} \text{Cost}_{\text{Ins/Del}}(n) \times \frac{1}{1 + \text{Max}(SGS(\text{SbT}_i, \text{SbT}_j, \text{Aux}))} \quad (4)$$

3.1.2 Tree Edit Distance (*TED*)

The tree edit distance algorithm *TED*, utilized in our study, is an adaptation of Nierman and Jagadish's main edit distance process [25]. In addition to tree insertion/deletion operations' costs which vary w.r.t. DTD sub-tree similarities (using *SGS*), *TED* (Figure 7) considers XML grammar node similarities in computing update operations costs (cf. Figure 7, line 6). Using the update operation, *TED* compares the roots of sub-trees considered in the recursive process (at startup, these would correspond to the grammar tree roots). The cost of the update operation would vary as:

$$\text{Cost}_{\text{Upd}}(n, m, Aux) = 1 - Sim(n, m, Aux) \quad \in [0, 1] \quad (5)$$

where *Sim(n, m, Aux)* underlines the similarity between tree nodes *n* and *m*, *Aux* standing for the auxiliary information required by the various matchers to assess XML grammar node similarity (knowledge base *KB*, constraint table *CCT* and data-type compatibility table *DTCT*).

Hence, following *Formula (5)*, the more initial and replacing nodes are similar, the lesser should be the update operation cost, which would transitively yield a lesser minimum cost edit script (higher similarity value). In short, the *TED* algorithm goes through all sub-trees of the grammar trees being compared. It exploits sub-tree insertion/deletion costs (via *SGS*) and update operations costs (cf. *Formula (5)*), which reflect the similarities between each sub-tree in the source/destination trees being compared, to produce the overall distance value.

3.2 Element Matchers

As mentioned previously, we make use of dedicated matchers to evaluate the similarities between XML grammar tree node labels, constraints, data-types, and ordering scores, their results being integrated in the tree edit distance framework to produce relevant grammar element mappings. Recall that the use of independent matchers provides flexibility in performing the match operation since it is possible to select or disregard different matchers (i.e., different match criterions) following the task at hand. Table 1 presents the matchers we included in our XML grammar matching approach so far, along with the different kinds of auxiliary information they exploit. More details are provided in the technical report [33].

Table 1. XML grammar element matchers

Matcher			Type	Target	Auxiliary Information
Label			Composite	Labels	Knowledge base
	Syntactic		Composite	Labels	---
		String- ED [34]	Simple	Labels	---
		N-Gram [13]	Simple	Labels	---
	Semantic		Composite	Labels	Knowledge base
		Lin [18]	Simple	Element labels	Knowledge base
		WuPalmer [35]	Simple	Element labels	Knowledge base
Cardinality Constraint [33]			Simple	Cardinality constraints	Constraint compatibility table
Data-Type [33]			Simple	Data-Types	Data-type compatibility table
OrdScore [33]			Simple	Ordering scores	---
Alternativeness Constraint [33]			Hybrid	Alternativeness constraint vectors	Constraint compatibility table

Similarly to computing XML grammar node similarity (cf. *Formula (3)*), we exploit the *weighted sum* function in combining the results of simple matchers, since it enables the user to choose the weight of each matcher in accordance with her notion of similarity. For each of the composite matchers *CM* and its component ones $M_{i=1..n}$, similarity is evaluated as follows:

$$\mathrm{Sim}_{\mathrm{CM}} = \sum_{i=1...n} w_i \times \mathrm{Sim}_{\mathrm{M_i}} \in [0, 1] \qquad (6)$$

where $\sum_{i=1...n} w_i = 1$, $(w_{i=1...n}) \geq 0$ and $(Sim_{M\, i=1...n}) \in [0, 1]$

3.3 Edit Script Extraction and Mapping Identification

Identifying the similarity between two XML grammars is useful in applications such as grammar clustering [16], and can be exploited as a pre-processing schema integration phase [27]. Yet, the grammar matching operation itself requires identifying element correspondences, where edit distance mappings come to play. The *Edit Distance* component returns the edit distance between XML grammar trees, i.e., similarity (*Sim=1/(1+Dist)*). Identifying mappings requires a post-processing of the edit distance result. This amounts to edit script extraction.

3.3.1 Edit Script Extraction

In fact, edit distance computations are generally undertaken in a dynamic manner, combining and comparing the costs of various edit operations to identify the minimum distance (maximum similarity). Nonetheless, to identify the minimum cost edit script itself, one has to process the intermediary edit distance computations, going throw the edit distance matrixes, (which we identify as *{Dist[][]}*) tracing the edit script operations costs. Our algorithm for identifying the minimum cost tree edit script is provided in Figure 6. It considers as input the grammar trees being compared as well as the related edit distance matrixes computed via tree edit distance component. It outputs the corresponding edit script (simplified tree operation syntaxes are shown in Figure 6 for ease of algorithm presentation). As it traverses the edit distance matrixes, the algorithm identifies corresponding tree insertion/deletion and node update operations, gradually building the edit script. Thus, XML grammar tree mappings are deduced from the edit script, graphically depicting which edit operations apply to nodes in the grammar trees.

3.3.2 Mapping Identification

As stated previously, the schema matching problem comes down to identifying mappings between the elements of two schemas S_1 and S_2. Edit distance mappings are deduced from the minimum cost edit script between S_1 and S_2, graphically depicting which edit operations apply to which nodes in the grammar trees. In other words, they depend on the edit distance operations that are allowed and how they are used. In our approach, we make use of five edit operations: *insert node*, *delete node*, *update node*, *insert tree* and *delete tree* [32]. Hence, the mapping between two XML grammar trees S_1 and S_2 is constructed:

- Simple *1:1* mapping edges are introduced to connect:
  - Nodes that initially match. Two nodes of S_1 and S_2 initially match if they are identical (nodes with identical labels, constraints, data-types, order and depth).
  - Nodes related by the update operation.
- Simple *1:1* and complex *1:n*, *n:1* or *n:n* mapping edges connect:
  - Sub-trees of S_1, affected by *tree deletion*, to similar sub-trees in S_2. Such edges are identified when computing the similarity between sub-trees of S_1 and S_2. No edges are introduced if the sub-tree being deleted from S_1 has no similarities in S_2.
  - Sub-trees of S_2 that are affected by the *tree insertion* operation, to similar sub-trees in S_1. No edges are introduced if the inserted sub-tree has no similarities in S_1.

Node insertion/deletion operations are treated as *tree insertion/deletion* ones. Note that *node insertions/deletions* are utilized to compute the costs of *tree insertion/deletion* operations and are not directly employed in the main edit distance algorithm.

Figure 5 shows the mapping results corresponding to the edit distance computations between two XML grammar trees *D* and *T* extracted from those in Figures 2 and 3. Note that in this figure, we only show node labels for the sake of presentation. The edit script transforming tree *D* into *T*, *ES(D, T) = Upd(D[2], T[2]), Upd(D[3], T[3]), DelTree(D[4]), InsTree(T_2)*.

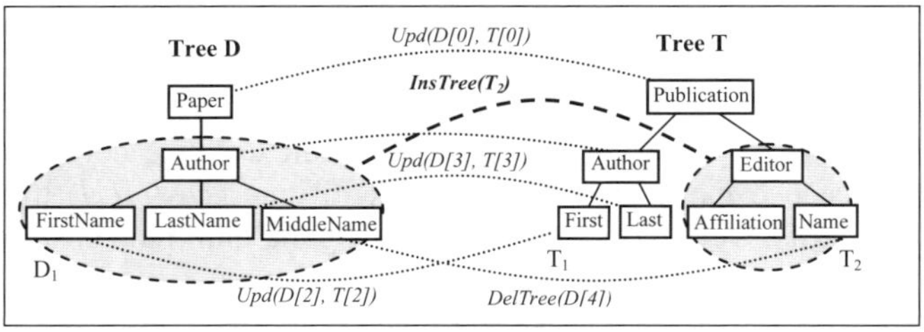

Fig. 5. XML grammar tree mappings

Note that each of the nodes *D[0]*, *D[1]*, *D[2]*, *D[3]* and *T[0]*, *B[1]*, *B[2]*, *B[3]* in grammar trees *D* and *T* participates in an individual *1:1* mapping. In addition, *D[1]*, *D[2]*, *D[3]*, *D[4]*, and *T[5]*, *T[6]*, *T[7]* participate in an *n:n* mapping. In short, our approach produces all kinds of mapping cardinalities, ranging from *1:1* to *n:n*. Nonetheless, the nature of a mapping is often dependent on user requirements or the requirements of the module exploiting the mapping results. In general, existing matching approaches tend to focus on *1:1* mappings [11]. Such mappings are usually easier to comprehend, evaluate and manipulate by users and automated processes alike. Nevertheless, complex *1:n*, *n:1* and *n:n* mappings are required in certain application domains, mainly in automatic document transformation [2]. Thus, we provide the user with a flexible schema matching framework able to produce either:

- *1:1* mappings (easier to assess, and especially useful for query discovery [24]),
- All kinds of mappings (no cardinality restrictions).

Restricting mapping cardinalities to *1:1* cardinality means disregarding all kinds of sub-tree similarities and repetitions when comparing the grammar trees. In other words, we disable algorithm *SGS* and only make use of the main edit distance process *TED* in our edit distance component (cf. Figure 4). In this case, tree insertion/deletion mapping edges (which induce complex *1:n*, *n:1* and *n:n* mappings) are eliminated, and we are left with *1:1* mappings.

Process *Map* (omitted here due to its intuitiveness) coupled with *ES_Extraction* (cf. Figure 4) is dedicated to producing grammar mappings, in the form (M, S_1, S_2) where $M \subseteq N_{S1} \times N_{S2}$. It simply generates mappings following the rules above, and associates related mapping scores.

3.3.3 Mapping Scores

Most schema matching approaches associate scores to the identified mappings. These scores underline values, usually in the *[0, 1]* interval, that reflect the plausibility of the corresponding matches (*0* for strong dissimilarity, *1* for strong similarity, and values in between). With respect to edit distance, mapping scores denote, in a roundabout way, the costs of the edit operations inducing the corresponding mappings:

- Mappings linking identical nodes are assigned a maximum similarity, *MapScore = 1*.
- Mappings underlining the update operation between two nodes are assigned scores as follows: $MapScore = 1 - Cost_{Upd}(n, m, Aux) \in [0, 1]$, *1* being the maximum update operation cost (*Formula (5)*). In other words, the mapping score designates node similarity, $Sim(n, m, Aux) \in [0, 1]$.
- Following the same logic, mappings corresponding to tree insertion/deletion operations are assigned scores as follows:

$$MapScore = \frac{\sum_{\text{All nodes } n \text{ of S}} Cost_{Ins/Del}(n) - Cost_{InsTree/DelTree}(S)}{\sum_{\text{All nodes } n \text{ of S}} Cost_{Ins/Del}(n)} \in [0, 1], \text{ having}$$

$\sum_{\text{All nodes } x \text{ of S}} Cost_{Ins/Del}(x)$ the maximum tree insertion/deletion operation cost for the sub-tree at hand. Hence, the mapping scores will follow the similarities between inserted/delete grammar sub-trees.

Table 2 shows the mappings generated in our running example, as well as corresponding mapping scores (computational details are omitted for simplicity). In addition to the *Edit Distance* and *Mapping Identification* components, our matching framework encompasses a *UserFeed* component, enabling users to manually match a few hard-to-match elements.

Table 2. Matching nodes of grammar trees *D* and *T* (Figure 5)

Match cardinality	Nodes of tree D	Nodes of tree T	Mapping Scores
1:1	D[0] (*l*= '*Paper*')	T[0] (*l* ='*Publication*')	0.1667
	D[1] (*l*= '*Author*')	T[1] (*l* ='*Author*')	1
	D[2] (*l*= '*FirstName*')	T[2] (*l* ='*First*')	0.5556
	D[3] (*l*= '*LastName*')	T[3] (*l* ='*Last*')	0.5714
	D[4] (l = '*MiddleName*')	T[6] (T[6].l = '*Name*')	0.4628
n:n	D[1],D[2],D[3],D[4] (sub-tree D_1)	T[5],T[6],T[7] (sub-tree T_2)	0.4266

3.4 User Input Constraints and User Feedback

Considering user input constraints and feedback in grammar matching could improve matching accuracy. User mappings are particularly useful in matching ambiguous schema elements [11].

Consider for instance elements of labels '*url*' and '*Link*' in grammars *Paper.dtd* and *Publication.xsd* of Figure 1 respectively. These elements have neither syntactically nor semantically similar labels (that is if using a generic WordNet-based taxonomy as a reference knowledge base). In addition, element '*url*' in *Paper.dtd* encompasses two sub-elements, of labels '*Homepage*' and '*Download*', both of them identifying links. In such situations, the system is left with a set of confusing matching possibilities ('*url*'↔'*Link*', '*Homepage*'↔'*Link*' or '*Download*'↔'*Link*', which is where user constraints come to play.

In our approach, we enable the user to explicitly specify matching elements as input to the match operation, i.e., input user constraints. Likewise, after the execution of the match operation, if the user is still not happy with the produced matches, she can provide new ones i.e., user feedback, then run the edit distance process once again to output new mappings. In essence, we consider user input constraints and feedback in our grammar matching framework by updating input grammar trees following the constraints at hand, and consequently comparing the updated trees. Thus, we define the *UserFeed* grammar transformation operation as follows:

```
Algorithm ES_Extraction()

Input: Trees A and B, {Dist[][]} the set of distance matrixes
       computed by eTED among which the starting matrix
       Dist[][]_A,B
Output: Edit script ES transforming A to B

Begin
 i = Degree(A)          // |FL-SbTree_A|
 j = Degree(B)          // |FL-SbTree_B|

 While (i>0 and j>0)
 {
    If (Dist[i][j]_A,B = Dist[i-1][j]_A,B + Cost_DelTree(A_i)
    {
       ES = ES + DelTree(A_i)
       i = i-1
    }
    Else if (Dist[i][j]_A,B=Dist[i][j-1]_A,B + Cost_InsTree(B_j))
    {
       ES = ES + InsTree(B_j)
       j = j-1
    }
    Else
    {
       If (A_i ≠ B_j)       //Recursive formulation
       {
          ES_Extraction_Core(A_i, B_j, Dist[][]_Ai,Bj )
       }
       i=i-1
       j=j-1
       }
  }

  While (i>0)     // identifying remaining deletions
  {
       ES = ES + DelTree(A_i)
       i = i-1
  }

  While (j>0)     // identifying remaining insertions
  {
       ES = ES + InsTree(B_j)
       j = j-1
  }

  If (i = 0 and j = 0 and R(A_i) ≠ R(B_j))
  {
       ES = ES + Upd(R(A_i), R(B_j))
  }

Reorder(ES)      // Reversing edit operations' order
Return ES        // Edit script transforming tree A to B

End
```

Fig. 6. Edit script extraction algoritm

```
Algorithm EditDistance()

Input: Trees A and B, operations costs
       Cost_DelTree/Cost_InsTree for all sub-trees
       in A/B, Aux = {KB, CCT, DCT}
Output: Edit distance between A and B

Begin
M = Degree(A)          // |FL-SbTree_A|
N = Degree(B)          // |FL-SbTree_B|

Dist [][] = new [0...M][0...N]
Dist[0][0] = Cost_Upd(R(A), R(B), Aux)

For (i = 1 ; i ≤ M ; i++)
{ Dist[i][0] = Dist[i-1][0] + Cost_DelTree(A_i) }

For (j = 1 ; j ≤ N ; j++)
{ Dist[0][j] = Dist[0][j-1] + Cost_InsTree(B_j) }

For (i = 1 ; i ≤ M ; i++)
{
For (j = 1 ; j ≤ N ; j++)
 {
  Dist[i][j] = min{
        Dist[i-1][j-1] + EditDistance(A_i, B_j),
        Dist[i-1][j] + Cost_DelTree(A_i),
        Dist[i][j-1] + Cost_InsTree(B_j)   }
 }
}

Return Dist[M][N]
End
```

Fig. 7. Tree edit distance algorithm

```
Algorithm UserFeed()

Input: Grammar tree A, user matches (preM, A,
B)
Output: Transformed grammar tree A'

Begin

A' = A
M = Degree(A')        // |FL-SbTree_A|

For (i = 1 ; i ≤ M ; i++)
{
   If(R(A_i) ∈ (preM, A, B))
   { A' = A' - A_i' }
   Else
   { A_i' = UserFeed(A_i , (preM, A, B)) }
}

End
```

Fig. 8. User feed transformation algorithm

Def. 11 – UserFeed: It is an operation that transforms an XML grammar tree *A* into *A'*, such as in the destination tree *A'*, nodes corresponding to predefined matches are eliminated, along with their corresponding sub-trees.

Formally, *UserFeed(A, (preM, A, B)) = A'* where:

- *A* and *B* are the grammar trees being compared by the system.
- *(preM, A, B)* is the set of predefined user matches from *A* to *B* such as $preM \subseteq V_A - \{R(A)\} \times V_B - \{R(B)\}$, where V_A and V_B designate respectively the sets of nodes of trees *A* and *B*, *R(A)* and *R(B)* underlining the corresponding grammar tree roots.
- *A'* is the transformed tree, $A' = A - \{set\ of\ sub\text{-}trees\ A_i \,/\, R(A_i) \in (preM, A, B)\}$

Thus, w.r.t. user constraints, our *Edit Distance* component will be comparing the transformed grammar trees, where nodes corresponding to predefined matches are eliminated, along with their corresponding sub-trees (structural matching being sibling and ancestor preserving [29]). Note that tree roots (*R(A)* and *R(B)*) are not included in the predefined user matches since their inclusion would indicate that the whole grammar trees actually match, thus eliminating the need to perform the matching task in the first place. Disregarding predefined matches in the edit distance process would i) eliminate the possibility of *automatically* modifying these matches and ii) lessen the risk of attaining confusing matches by reducing the number of match candidates. The *UserFeed* process is shown in Figure 8. User mappings are thus added to those produced by the system: $(M, A, B) = (SystemM, A, B) \cup (preM, A, B)$.

4 Experimental Evaluation

We have implemented our XML grammar matching framework in the experimental XS^3 prototype (*XML Structural and Semantic Similarity*)[3].

4.1 Matching Experiments

To our knowledge, a common benchmark with *gold standard* matchings for evaluating the quality of XML grammar matching methods does not exist to date. Hence, we conducted our experiments using a select collection of real and synthetic XML grammars (including those exploited in our running example). Real DTDs and XML Schemas were acquired from various online sources[4]. Consequently, we ran our matching approach and compared the generated matches to the manually defined ones. *Precision (PR)*, *Recall (R)*, *F-value* and *Overall* results are shown in Figure 9. Note that the *Overall* metric, introduced in [22], quantifies the amount of user effort needed to perform the match task, i.e., effort needed to transform the match result produced by the system to the user intended one:

$$Overall = R \times (2 - \frac{1}{PR}) \text{ having } PR \neq 0 \tag{7}$$

---

[3] Available at http://www.u-bourgogne.fr/Dbconf/XS3

[4] http://www.acm.org/sigmod/xml, http://www.cs.wisc.edu/niagara/, http://www.BizTalk.org, ...

In all tests, all basic matchers were considered with equal weights ($w_{Label} = w_{Cardinality} = w_{Data\text{-}Type} = w_{Alternativeness} = w_{Ord} = 0.2$ whereas $w_{String\text{-}ED} = w_{N\text{-}Gram} = w_{Lin} = w_{WuPalmer} = 0.5$). Note that in this study, we do not address the issue of tuning matcher weights. This would require a thorough analysis of the relative effect of each individual matcher and criterion on matching quality (similarly to [9]), which we report to a dedicated study. Extracts of WordNet were adopted as reference knowledge bases, and default *DTCT* and *CCT* tables were exploited. Details concerning all experiments are provided in the technical report [33].

4.1.1 Evaluation of Our Running Example

When matching grammars *Paper.dtd* and *Publication.xsd* (cf. Figures 3, 4), the system identified *6* correct mappings, disregarded *2*, and generated *2* incorrect ones (Table 3). The mappings which are missed by the system (*'PaperLenght'-'Length'* and *'Download-Link'*) are in fact replaced by others (e.g., *'Genre'-Length'* and *'Paper-Length'-'Link'*) which seem more structurally plausible. Recall that the topological structure of grammar nodes (i.e., sibling ordering and ancestor/descendent relations) is crucial in determining the mappings, following our approach, since we focus on semi-structured and structured data (which is not necessarily verified with user mappings). Despite some inconsistencies in the matching results, *PR, R, F-Value* and particularly *Overall* show that more than half of the mappings generated by the system are correct, which is obviously easier than manually performing the match task.

Table 3. Matching *Paper.dtd* and *Publication.xsd* of Figure 5

Manual Mappings	
paper.dtd	publication.dtd
Paper	Publication
Author	Author
FirstName	First
LastName	Last
PaperLength	Length
Publisher	Publisher
Title	Title
Download	Link

System Mappings		
paper.dtd	publication.dtd	Scores
Paper	Publication	0.8849
Author	Author	0.9667
FirstName	First	0.8378
LastName	Last	0.7886
Publisher	Publisher	0.84
Title	Title	0.8367
PaperLength	Link	0.7841
Genre	Length	0.7414

PR= 0.75 R = 0.75 F-Value=0.75 Overall = 0.5.

4.1.2 Evaluation on Real World and Synthetic Grammars

Hereunder, we present the results of 18 match tasks, each matching two different grammars (including those of our running example). In 12 of the 18 match tasks, the system effectively identified most user mappings, while disregarding some, and generating a few false ones. In task #2, the system achieved *PR=R=Overall=1* due to the high resemblance between the grammars being matched (*bib.dtd* and *bookstore.dtd* [5]). Negative *Overall* was obtained in 6 of the 18 matching operations. This is due to the structural heterogeneity between the grammars being matched, the system generating mappings which are structurally coherent (respecting sibling order and ancestor/descendent relations) but which do not correspond to actual user mappings (user mappings do not necessarily verifying structural integrity). Note that in cases where *Overall* is negative, *PR* is lesser than *0.5*, indicating that it would be easier for the

[5] Available at http://www.cs.wisc.edu/niagara/ and http://www.xmlfiles.com respectively.

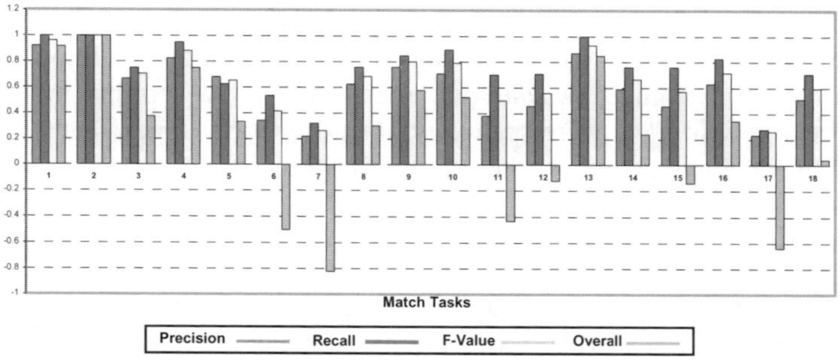

Fig. 9. PR, R and Overall results

user to carry out the matching by hand, instead of correcting the system generated ones. In short, our system seems efficient in identifying XML grammar mappings since it yielded positive *Overall* results for more than ⅔ of the experiments, while maintaining relatively high *PR* and *R* values.

4.1.3 Improvements via User Feedback

In addition to testing the raw capabilities of the system, we conducted experiments to evaluate the effect of user feedback on matching quality. We considered the six matching tasks where negative *Overall* was achieved in the initial matching phase (tasks n# *6*, *7*, *11*, *12*, *15* and *17*). For each task, we carried out three runs, providing an extra user input mapping at each run. Results in Figure 10 show that user feedback amends *Precision*, *Recall*, *F-Value* and *Overall* levels w.r.t. the number of user input mappings: the more input mappings are provided, the lesser the mapping ambiguities, the better the mapping quality. With respect to *Overall* in particular, the system

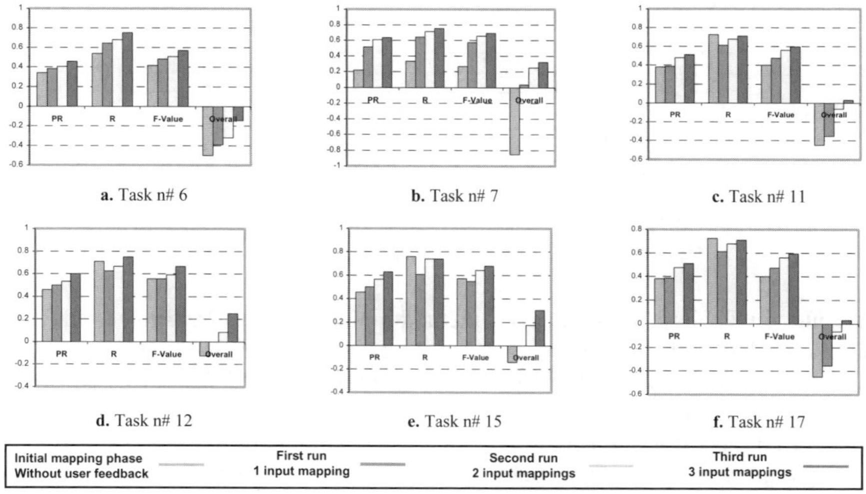

Fig. 10. Comparing *PR*, *R*, *F-value* and *Overall* results for matching tasks n# 6, 7, 11, 12, 15 and 17 to evaluate the effectiveness of our approach in incorporating user feedback

obtained positive values with three out of six tasks (tasks n# *7*, *12* and *15*), right after the first run. In these tasks, manually resolving one mapping has eliminated enough ambiguity for the system to produce more than half of the correct mappings. The *Overall* levels of task n# 6 were gradually amended by feedback, but obviously require more user mappings to cross the zero barrier (i.e., $PR > 0.5$).

4.2 Comparative Study

In order to further evaluate our method, we conducted a comparative study to assess its effectiveness w.r.t. existing XML grammar matching methods. In short, our method is i) dedicated to XML grammars, ii) considers all basic XML grammars characteristics, iii) while being extensible to different matchers (which are crucial to minimizing user effort in undertaking the match task). However, existing methods are either i) too generic (not adapted to the structured nature of XML, e.g., [9][11]), ii) too restrictive (simplifying grammar constraints, e.g., [19][31]) or ii) too specific (not flexible nor extensible to additional matching criterions, [16][36]). Table 4 sums up the differences between our method and its alternatives.

Table 4. Comparing our method to alternative solutions

Approach	Considers cardinality constraints	Considers alternativeness constraints	Considers data-types	Extensible to several Matchers	Flexible w.r.t. mapping cardinalities	Dedicated to XML grammars
Madhavan, 01 [19]	×	×	✓	×	× (1:1, 1:n)	×
Melnik et al. 02 [22]	×	×	✓	×	× (1:1)	×
Doan *et al.*, 01 [11]	×	×	×	✓	× (1:1)	✓ (DTD)
Jeong *et al*, 07 [14]	×	×	×	✓	× (undefined)	✓ (XSD)
Su *et al.* 01 [31]	×	×	✓	×	× (1:1)	✓ (DTD)
Do and Rahm,02 [9]	×	×	✓	✓	× (1:1)	×
Lee *et al.*, 02 [16]	✓	×	×	×	× (1:1)	✓ (DTD)
Yi *et al.*, 04 [36]	×	✓ (restrictive)	✓ (restrictive)	×	× (1:1)	✓ (XSD)
Our Approach	✓	✓	✓	✓	✓	✓

Table 5. Average *PR*, *R*, *F-Value* and *Overall* values

<table>
<tr><th colspan="2"></th><th>PR</th><th>R</th><th>F-Value</th><th>N# of negative Overalls</th></tr>
<tr><td rowspan="4">Our Approach</td><td>Without user feedback</td><td>0.6096</td><td>0.7488</td><td>0.6667</td><td>6</td></tr>
<tr><td>User feedback:
1 input mapping</td><td>0.6517</td><td>0.7703</td><td>0.7027</td><td>2</td></tr>
<tr><td>User feedback:
2 input mappings</td><td>0.6700</td><td>0.7909</td><td>0.7221</td><td>2</td></tr>
<tr><td>User feedback:
3 input mappings</td><td>0.6842</td><td>0.8048</td><td>0.7367</td><td>1</td></tr>
<tr><td colspan="2">COMA</td><td>0.7205</td><td>0.5101</td><td>0.5790</td><td>2</td></tr>
<tr><td colspan="2">XClust</td><td>0.5047</td><td>0.554</td><td>0.5251</td><td>7</td></tr>
<tr><td colspan="2">Relaxation Labelling</td><td>0.4629</td><td>0.3030</td><td>0.3224</td><td>11</td></tr>
</table>

Results, in Table 5, show that our method yields average *Precision* levels higher than those achieved by its predecessors, to the exception of *COMA*. That is due to the generic nature of *COMA* (which was not originally designed for XML) considering mappings which are not necessarily structurally coherent (i.e., they do not verify sibling order nor ancestor/descendent relations), and which happen to correspond to user mappings. Such mappings are replaced by structurally valid ones using our approach, but which might not be correct w.r.t. the user (similarly to the *falsely* detected mappings in Table 3, which our system replaced by structurally correct ones). On the other hand, our method consistently maintains *Recall* levels higher than those of all its alternatives. In cases where higher/lower *Precision/Recall* levels are obtained simultaneously, the *F-Value* measure is used to evaluate overall result quality. With respect to all 18 matching tests, our method yields higher average *F-Values* in comparison with *COMA, XClust* and *Relaxation Labelling.* Note that the *Overall* measure is non-linear in terms of *Precision* and *Recall.* Thus, its averaging is meaningless here. Hence, we exploit *Overall* by assessing the number of matching tasks with negative *Overall* values (i.e., where more than half the produced mappings are incorrect). Results show that our method, in its initial (pre-feedback) matching phase, produces 6 negatives (negative *Overall* with 6 matching tasks), 2 negatives after the first feedback run (with 1 user mapping for each of the 6 tasks), and only 1 negative after the third run. In comparison, *COMA* produced negative *Overall* values with 2 matching tasks, *XClust* produced 7, and *RL* produced 11 negatives respectively.

In addition, we conducted experiments to evaluate the time complexity of our method. Results show that our approach is polynomial (quadratic) in grammar tree size, and grows linearly w.r.t. knowledge base size (i.e., number of concepts in the reference *KB*) when running the *Semantic* label matcher. Timing graphs and detailed results are omitted due to lack of space.

5 Background and Related Works

The effectiveness of schema matching systems is assessed w.r.t. the amount of manual work required to perform the matching task [10], which depends: i) the level of simplification in the representation of the schema, and ii) the combination of various matching techniques [9].

On one hand, most approaches in the literature, [2][16][19][22][30][31][36] require various simplifications in the grammars being matched, thus inducing adapted schema representations upon which the matching processes are executed. In this context, *XClust* [16] and *Relaxation Labeling* [36] seem more sophisticated than previous matching systems in comparing XML grammars. They induce the least simplifications to the grammars being compared. *XClust* only disregarding the *Or* operator, whereas *Relaxation Relabeling* considers most XML Schema-related repeatability and alternativeness constraints but with restrictive declarations (operator concatenations such as in *root(a, b, (c|d))* are not allowed, only single declarations such as *root(a, b, c)* or *root(a | b | c)*).

On the other hand, most methods in the literature are *hybrid*, [16][19][22][31][36], in that various matching criterions (e.g., the linguistic and structural aspects of XML grammars) are simultaneously assessed in a specific manner within a single algorithm. In contrast, few approaches follow the alternative *composite* matching logic, i.e., combining the results of several independently executed matching algorithms, thus providing more flexibility in performing the matching as is it possible to select, add or remove different matching algorithms following the match task at hand. *LSD* [11] and *NNPLS* [14] and based on supervised learning techniques, and encompass each a training phase which could require substantial manual effort prior to launching the matching process. However, *Coma* [9] underlines a more generic framework for schema matching, providing various mathematical formulations (*max*, *min*, *ave, …*) to combine matching results, and thus is not specifically adapted to XML grammars.

6 Conclusion

In this paper, we proposed a framework for XML grammar matching and comparison, based on the concept of tree edit distance. To our knowledge, this is the first attempt to exploit tree edit distance in an XML grammar matching context. Our approach aims at minimizing the amount of manual work needed to perform the match task by i) considering all basic XML grammar characteristics via a dedicated tree model, and ii) combining different matching criterions in a flexible and adapted way to deal with XML. In addition, our method is flexible in producing either *1:1* or all kinds of mapping cardinalities (*1:1*, *1:n*, *n:1* and *n:n*), following user preferences and the application at hand. It also considers user input constraints and user feedback in adjusting mapping results. We have implemented the approach and conducted various tests to validate its efficiency, in comparison with alternative methods, and have evaluated its time complexity.

As continuing work, we are currently investigating the extension of our method to deal with user derived data-types. These are allowed in the XSD language [26] via dedicated data-type restriction and extension operators (which do not exist in DTDs). In this context, dedicated knowledge bases and user defined semantics would have to be considered to assess the relatedness between the various data-types [12]. We also plan to investigate XML grammars with recursive declarations. Here, it would be interesting to extend our XML grammar tree model to a more general graph model (e.g. topic maps), and try to adapt our tree edit distance framework accordingly. We also plan to study the effect of different matchers and criterions on matching quality, proposing (if possible) weighting schemes that could help the user tune her input parameters to obtain optimal results.

Acknowledgements

We are grateful to Phil Bernstein and Sabine Maßmann for providing us with their test schemas in order to conduct our matching experiments.

References

[1] Bertino, E., Guerrini, G., Mesiti, M.: A Matching Algorithm for Measuring the Structural Similarity between an XML Document and a DTD and its Applications. Elsevier Computer Science 29(23-46) (2004)

[2] Bille, P.: A Survey on Tree Edit Distance and Related Problems. Theoretical Computer Science 337(1-3), 217–239 (2005)

[3] Boukottaya, A., Vanoirbeek, C.: Schema Matching for Transforming Structured Documents. In: The Int. ACM Symposium on Document Engineering, pp. 101–110 (2005)

[4] Bray, T., Paoli, J., Sperberg-McQueen, C.M., Mailer, Y., Yergeau, F.: Extensible Markup Language (XML) 1.0 5th edn., W3C recommendation (November 2008), `http://www.w3.org/TR/REC-xml/`

[5] Buttler, D.: A Short Survey of Document Structure Similarity Algorithms. In: Proc. of ICOMP, pp. 3–9 (2004)

[6] Chawathe, S., Rajaraman, A., Garcia-Molina, H., Widom, J.: Change Detection in Hierarchically Structured Information. In: ACM SIGMOD Record, pp. 493–504 (1996)

[7] Cobéna, G., Abiteboul, S., Marian, A.: Detecting Changes in XML Documents. In: ICDE, pp. 41–52 (2002)

[8] Dalamagas, T., Cheng, T., Winkel, K., Sellis, T.: A methodology for clustering XML documents by structure. Inormation Systems 31(3), 187–228 (2006)

[9] Do, H.H., Rahm, E.: COMA: A System for Flexible Combination of Schema Matching Approaches. In: VLDB Conference, pp. 610–621 (2002)

[10] Do, H.H., Melnik, S., Rahm, E.: Comparison of Schema Matching Evaluations In: Proc. of GI-Workshop on the Web and Databases, pp. 221–237 (2002)

[11] Doan, A., Domingos, P., Halevy, A.Y.: Reconciling Schemas of Disparate Data Sources: A Machine Learning Approach. In: Proc. of the SIGMOD Conference (2001)

[12] Formica, A.: Similarity of XML-Schema Elements: A Structural and Information content Approach. The Computer Journal 51(2), 240–254 (2008)

[13] Hall, P., Dowling, G.: Approximate String Matching. Computing Surveys 12(4), 381–402 (1980)

[14] Jeong, B., Lee, D., Cho, H., Lee, J.: A Novel Method for Measuring Semantic Similarity for XML Schema Matching. Expert Systems with Applications: An International Journal 34(3), 1651–1658 (2008)

[15] Knuth, D.: Sorting by Merging. In: The Art of Computer Programming, pp. 158–168. Addison-Wesley, Reading (1998)

[16] Lee, M., Yang, L., Hsu, W., Yang, X.: XClust: Clustering XML Schemas for Effective Integration. In: Proc. of CIKM, pp. 292–299 (2002)

[17] Leonardi, E., et al.: DTD-Diff: A Change Detection Algorithm for DTDs. DKE 61(2), 384–402 (2007)

[18] Lin, D.: An Information-Theoretic Definition of Similarity. In: Proc. of the Int. Conf. on ML, pp. 296–304 (1998)

[19] Madhavan, J., Bernstein, P., Rahm, E.: Generic Schema Matching With Cupid. In: VLDB, pp. 49–58 (2001)

[20] Maguitman, A.G., Menczer, F., Roinestad, H., Vespignani, A.: Algorithmic Detection of Semantic Similarity. In: Proc. of WWW, pp. 107–116 (2005)

[21] McGill, M.J.: Introduction to Modern Information Retrieval. McGraw-Hill, New York (1983)

[22] Melnik, S., Garcia-Molina, H., Rahm, E.: Similarity Flooding: A Versatile Graph Matching Algorithm and its Application to Schema Matching. In: Proceedings of ICDE (2002)

[23] Miller, G.: WordNet: An On-Line Lexical Database. Journal of Lexicography (1990)

[24] Miller, R., Hass, L., Hermandez, M.A.: Schema Mapping as Query Discovery. In: VLDB, pp. 77–88 (2000)

[25] Nierman, A., Jagadish, H.V.: Evaluating structural similarity in XML documents. In: WebDB, pp. 61–66 (2002)

[26] Peterson, D., Gao, S., Malhotra, A., Sperberg-McQueen, C.M., Thompson, H.S.: W3C XML Schema Definition Language (XSD) 1.1 Part 2: Datatypes (January 2009), http://www.w3.org/TR/xmlschema11-2/

[27] Rahm, E., Bernstein, P.A.: A Survey of Approaches to Automatic Schema Matching. The VLDB Journal 10, 334–350 (2001)

[28] Schlieder, T.: Similarity Search in XML Data Using Cost-based Query Transformations. In: Proc. of SIGMOD WebDB, pp. 10–24 (2001)

[29] Shasha, D., Zhang, K.: Approximate Tree Pattern Matching. In: Pattern Matching in Strings, Trees and Arrays. Oxford Press, Oxford (1995)

[30] Su, H., Kuno, H., Rundensteiner, E.A.: Automating the Transformation of XML Documents. In: Proc. of ACM Workshop on Web Information and Data Management, pp. 68–75 (2001)
[31] Su, H., Padmanabhan, S., Lo, M.L.: Identification of Syntactically Similar DTD Elements for Schema Matching. In: Advances in Web-Age Information Management Conf., pp. 145–159 (2001)
[32] Tekli, J., Chbeir, R., Yetongnon, K.: A Fine-Grained XML Structural Comparison Approach. In: Parent, C., Schewe, K.-D., Storey, V.C., Thalheim, B. (eds.) ER 2007. LNCS, vol. 4801, pp. 582–598. Springer, Heidelberg (2007)
[33] Tekli, J., Chbeir, R., Yetongnon, K.: An XML Grammar Comparison Framework – Technical Report (2008), `http://www.u-bourgogne.fr/DbConf/XMG/`
[34] Wagner, J., Fisher, M.: The String-to-String correction problem. Journal of ACM 21(1), 168–173 (1974)
[35] Wu, Z., Palmer, M.: Verb Semantics and Lexical Selection. In: Proc. of the 32nd Annual Meeting of the Associations for Computational Linguistics, pp. 133–138 (1994)
[36] Yi, S., Huang, B., Chan, W.T.: XML Application Schema Matching Using Similarity Measure and Relaxation Labeling. Information Sciences 169(1-2), 27–46 (2005)
[37] Zhang, K., Shasha, D.: Simple Fast Algorithms for the Editing Distance between Trees and Related Problems. SIAM Journal 18(6), 1245–1262 (1989)
[38] Zhang, Z., Li, R., Cao, S., Zhu, Y.: Similarity Metric in XML Documents. In: Knowledge and Experience Management Workshop (2003)

Modeling Associations through Intensional Attributes

Andrea Presa, Yannis Velegrakis, Flavio Rizzolo, and Siarhei Bykau

University of Trento
{apresa,velgias,flavio,bykau}@disi.unitn.eu

Abstract. Attributes, a.k.a. slots or properties, are the main mechanism used to define associations between concepts or individuals modeling real world entities in a knowledge base. Traditionally, an attribute is defined by an explicit statement that specifies the name of the attribute and the entities it associates. This has three main limitations: (i) it is not easy to apply to large amounts of data, even if they share the same characteristics, since explicit definitions are needed for each concept or individual; (ii) it cannot handle future data, i.e., when new concepts or individuals are inserted in the knowledge base their attributes need to be explicitly defined; and (iii) it assumes that the data engineer, or the user that is introducing a new attribute, has access and privileges to modify the respective objects. The above may not be practical in many real ontology application scenarios. We are introducing a new form of attribute in which the domain and range are not specified explicitly but intensionally, through a query that defines the set of concepts or individuals being associated. We provide the formal semantics of this new form of attribute, describe how to overcome syntax constraints that prevent the use of the proposed attribute, study its behavior, show efficient ways of implementation, and experiment with alternative evaluation strategies.

1 Introduction

We are witnessing a tremendous increase in the amount of data that is becoming available online. To effectively access this data, we need to be able to successfully understand its semantics. Schemas have to a large degree contributed towards that direction, but they have not fully fulfilled their role – they are mainly driven by performance or technical motivations and do not always communicate accurately the semantics of the data. For modeling complex data semantics, ontologies, rather than schemas, are typically used. Ontologies are free from the structural restrictions that schemas have. A ten thousand feet view of an ontology is a collection of concepts (or classes) and individuals (or instances) associated through *isA* and *attribute* relationships. In the ontology jargon [1], the latter are referred to as *slots* or *properties* and they are used to describe features of a class or an individual. Each attribute has a type and can be restricted to draw its values from a specific pool of values.

A limitation of the attribute modeling constructs in current ontology formalisms is their static nature. More specifically, the existence of an attribute between two concepts or individuals depends solely on whether the slot has been explicitly defined or not. This prevents the implementation of batch assignment of attributes to groups of concepts/individuals that are currently present in the knowledge base or that may appear in

A.H.F. Laender et al. (Eds.): ER 2009, LNCS 5829, pp. 315–330, 2009.

the future. For instance, in many practical scenarios, attributes are assigned to individuals based on some common characteristics. Currently, this task requires first finding the individuals that have these characteristics, iterate over them, and explicitly assign to them the attribute of interest. Furthermore, if one or more individuals satisfying these characteristics are introduced at some future point in time, they will not be automatically assigned the attribute, unless a special ad-hoc mechanism has been put in place, or the ontology administrator manually assigns it to each such individual.

A different issue related to the current ontology mechanisms has to do with the way additional/super-imposed information can be attached to the structures of a knowledge base. Recall that ontologies is one of the main vehicles of communicating data semantics. To better achieve that goal, designers typically attach to the ontology constructs additional information that is not considered part of the ontology itself, yet assists in better communicating the data meaning. The RDF/RDFS standard [2,3] has provisioned a special single-string text field named *comment* for that purpose. The *comment* mechanism has two main limitations. First, it confines the ontology engineer to provide a single piece of plain text, whereas recording a comment that has some structure is typically more useful. For instance, we may want to insert a comment on an RDF resource along with the date and the name of the person that created the comment. Current practices include all that information in the comment text, but the text needs to be parsed every time the individual parts are to be identified. Second, attaching information to existing concepts or individuals of an ontology means that the user needs to have the privileges to do so. This is not always the case since many different users, other than the ontology owner, may need to add information of different kinds.

In this work, we advocate the need for *intensional attributes*[1], i.e., attributes whose domain and range have been intensionally defined. Individuals are assigned to the intensional attributes' domain and range in a similar fashion in which they are assigned to the extensions of defined concepts in Description Logics (DL) TBoxes [4] (as opposed to the explicit way individuals are assigned to the primitive concepts). To some extent, this kind of definition looks also similar to the way derived elements in UML[2] are defined. However, the notion of intensional attributes is fundamentally different from both derived elements and derived concepts. Derived elements or concepts are used to describe entities, while intenional attributes are used to describe derived relationships between entities. In that sense, intensional attributes do not replace but actually complement DL TBoxes and UML derived elements. In our solution we employ queries in order to specify the domain and range of the intensional attributes. We claim that queries are an excellent tool to implement intensional attributes since they provide the ideal mean to refer to sets of data declaratively. The idea of using queries for intensional definitions has also been proposed in other forms in different fields [5,6,7,8,9]. However, to the best of our knowledge, this is the first effort towards using that idea for attributes in ontologies to tackle the previously presented issues.

Our contributions are the following: (i) we redefine the notion of an attribute to include those for which the associated concepts or individuals are described intensionally; (ii) we describe how we can overcome RDF/RDFS limitations that prevent the use

[1] The term *intensional* should not be confused to the term *intentional*.

[2] http://www.uml.org

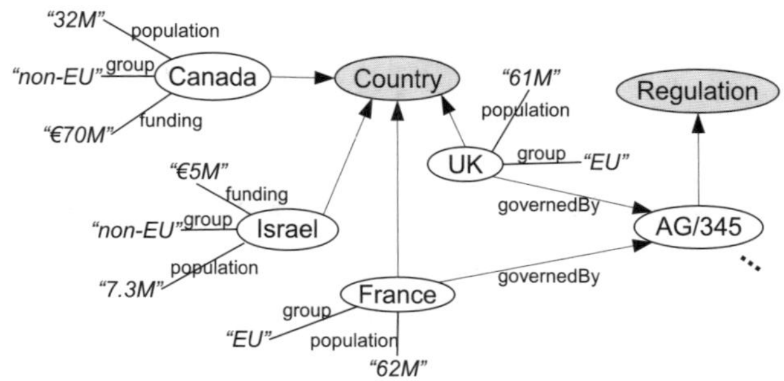

Fig. 1. Ontology example

of the proposed kind of attributes; (iii) we describe how the new form of association can be realized in OWL and RDF ontologies; (iv) we provide techniques to efficiently implement ontology browsing and query answering for this new form of association; (v) we experimentally evaluate alternative techniques and describe our findings.

2 Illustrative Example

To motivate our proposal and illustrate our solution, we describe here an example drawn from a real application with which we have worked. Consider a financial department that handles projects funded by the European Union (EU). The EU not only funds projects in countries that are members of the EU block but also in certain countries outside it. However, the funding is governed by different regulations depending on whether the recipient country is inside or outside the block. Consider an ontology modeling countries as illustrated in Figure 1. Countries (class Country) are distinguished as EU or non-EU through the attribute group. Some readers may (rightfully) claim that the right modeling of this situation is through two sub-classes of the class Country; however, this was modeled in practice by an attribute. Each EU country is associated through the governedBy attribute to the AG/345 regulation (an instance of the Regulation class). Each such attribute has been explicitly introduced to the respective countries by the ontology engineer after checking whether the country belongs or not to the EU block. This is a laborious task; it requires the data administrator to manually visit each country's data, test whether it belongs to the EU block and assign the specific attribute. It also requires continuous monitoring, so that if a new EU country is introduced, the attribute governedBy with value AG/345 will be assigned to it. Furthermore, it may be the case that the specific data engineer does not have full privileges to modify the individual country.

Our proposal is that the administrator could introduce instead an intensional attribute governedBy as illustrated in Figure 2. The attribute has at one end (as a range) the individual AG/345, and on the other (as a domain) the query Q1 that selects all the individual countries belonging to the EU block. For ease of presentation, we use a simplified notation of queries, i.e., $x.a{=}v$ indicates that the attribute a of class/individual x has a value v. In reality, we are using an actual query language, but the details will be described later on. Note how we use the attribute rdf:type=C in order to indicate that the results of

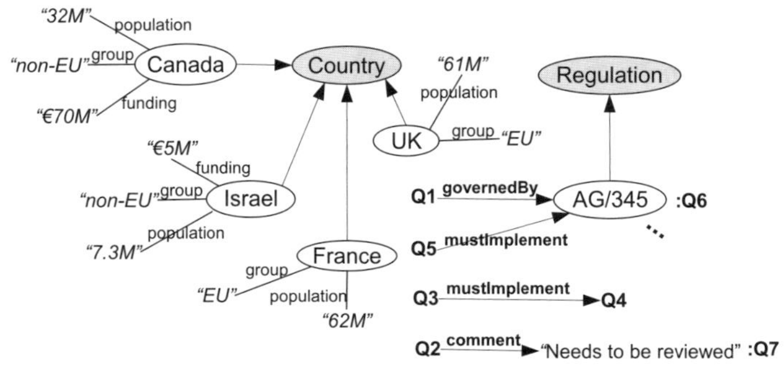

Q1: { x such that x.rdf:type=Country and x.group="EU" }
Q2: { x such that x.rdf:type=Country and x.population $\leq$ 20) }
Q3: { x such that x.rdf:type=Country }
Q4: { x such that x.rdf:type=Regulation and x.code="EMR*" }
Q5: { x such that x.rdf:type=Country and x.funding $>$ 10M and x.funding $<$ 100M }
Q6: { x such that x=AG/345 }
Q7: { x such that x="Needs to be reviewed" }

Fig. 2. Ontology example with intensional attributes

a query are individuals of some specific class C, and that in order to mention a specific individual or class we use a trivial form of a query (e.g., query Q6 in Figure 2).

Apart from the obvious saving in space and human effort for not having to repeat the attribute for every EU country, using the intensional approach has also the additional advantage of covering future data. In particular, if a new country becomes a member of the EU, an ontology administrator following the traditional approach would have to explicitly associate it to the regulation AG/345. In contrast, using our proposed approach, the administrator has to do no action: the moment the country becomes a member of the EU (i.e., by setting the group attribute to the EU value) it automatically satisfies the conditions of query Q1 and becomes part of its answer set, which has the effect of attaching attribute governedBy with value AG/345 to it.

As a different example, assume that a user would like to add some super-imposed information on the countries, indicating that every country with a population smaller than 20 millions will have to be reviewed. To add this kind of "annotation" on the countries, the user will have to explicitly introduce it either by utilizing the *comment* feature provided by the RDF/RDFS model (assuming of course that the ontology is expressed in RDF/RDFS) or by adding a special attribute with the appropriate text to each such country. Allowing the user to add attributes of this kind, as suggested by the latter solution, may not always be feasible or desirable. It may not be feasible because the user may not have permissions to edit the ontology. Even if this is not the case, it may not be desirable since adding attributes to the ontology concepts and individuals without some control mechanism may alter their semantics. In contrast, by using an intensional attribute between a string with the aforementioned statement and the query Q2 shown in Figure 2, the desired result can be achieved even without having permissions to modify the Country individuals.

Note that queries may exist on either or both parts of an intensional attributes. An example demonstrating such a situation is the following. EU has introduced a set of financial regulations, containing the code "EMR", that need to be followed by every country that is to receive EU funding. Without intensional attributes, the ontology needs to have on every country a number of attributes mustImplement one for each regulation that contains the encoding "EMR". However, using the intensional features, just the attribute mustImplement with domain Q3 and range Q4 as illustrated in Figure 2 will be enough. (Query Q3 returns the set of all countries and Q4 returns all regulations whose code attributes contain the string "EMR".)

Intensional attributes may share the same name as long as their domain and range queries are different. For instance, consider now that all countries, EU and non-EU, have to implement regulation AG/345 if the funding they receive is between 10 and 100 million (illustrated by attribute mustImplement with Q5 as domain in Figure 2). Since all answers of Q5 are countries, then Q5 is included in Q3 and thus all members of Q5 have already a mustImplement attribute defined (with values from the regulation individuals in the answer set of query Q4). However, the definition of the new intensional attribute will include AG/345 as an additional regulation that only members of Q5 must have. This result could *not* have been achieved by only one intensional attribute mustImplement with domain Q5∪Q3 and range Q4∪Q6 because this definition would add AG/345 to all countries, even to those whose funding is outside the range specified by Q5 (i.e., outside 10M<funding<100M). Thus, in order to correctly capture the requirement, a new intensional attribute mustImplement from Q5 to Q6 has to be present.

3 Intensional Attributes

As a knowledge base we follow the traditional definition that consists of a set of classes, individuals and attributes. In particular, we define a *knowledge base* S as the set of *classes* $\mathcal{C}$, *individuals* $\mathcal{I}$ that are instances of classes in $\mathcal{C}$, *names* $\mathcal{N}$ and *literals* $\mathcal{L}$ belonging to atomic types in a set $\mathcal{T}$. A knowledge base also contains a set of *attributes* $\mathcal{A}$. An attribute is a named association between a class and a type or another class, or between an individual and an atomic value (i.e., literal) or another individual. In other words, $\mathcal{A} \subseteq (\mathcal{C} \times \mathcal{N} \times (\mathcal{T} \cup \mathcal{C})) \cup (\mathcal{I} \times \mathcal{N} \times (\mathcal{A} \cup \mathcal{I}))$. According to the above definition, an attribute can be represented as a triple $\langle s, p, v \rangle$, where s is a class or an individual, p is a name (typically referred to as the name of the attribute), and v is a class, a type, an individual or a literal value.

We extend the above traditional definition of a knowledge base to include a set of *intensional attributes*. An intensional attribute is defined as a triple $\langle q_d, n, q_r \rangle$, where q_d is a query that returns a set of classes or individuals, and q_r a query that returns a set of classes, individuals, or literals. A knowledge base with intensional attributes will be referred to as an *intensional base*.

Example 1. Figure 2 shows an example of an intensional base. Triples ⟨Q3,mustImplement,Q4⟩ and ⟨Q5,mustImplement,Q6⟩ are examples of intensional attributes. In particular, ⟨Q1,governedBy,Q6⟩ and ⟨Q2,comment,Q7⟩ are attributes in which one of the two queries returns always only one element in its answer set: Q6 returns always the individual AG/345, and Q7 the literal "Needs to be reviewed". ■

Intuitively, an intensional attribute $\langle q_d, n, q_r \rangle$ is a short-hand for a set of attributes (each one with the same name n) between a member in the answer set of query q_d and a member in the answer set of the query q_r.

Example 2. Consider again the example of Figure 2. Attribute mustImplement is equivalent to the addition of an attribute mustImplement from every element in the result set of Q3 (i.e., every country) to every element in the result set of query Q4, i.e., every regulation containing the string "EMR" in its code. Similarly, the semantics of governedBy is to associate to every EU country a governedBy attribute to regulation AG/345. Finally, the semantics of comment is to attach the string literal "Needs to be reviewed" to every country with population smaller than 20 millions. ■

The formal semantics of an intensional base, and consequently of the intensional attributes in it, are realized through the notion of the *canonical base*. Intuitively, a canonical base is an intensional base in which every intensional attribute has been replaced by the set of traditional attributes it represents.

Definition 1. *Let* $S{=}\langle \mathcal{C}, \mathcal{I}, \mathcal{T}, \mathcal{L}, \mathcal{A}, \mathcal{D} \rangle$ *be an intensional base, where* $\mathcal{C}, \mathcal{I}, \mathcal{T}, \mathcal{L}, \mathcal{A}, \mathcal{D}$ *are the classes, individuals, types, literals, attributes and intensional attributes respectively. The canonical base of* S*, denoted as* $Can(S)$*, is a knowledge base* $\langle \mathcal{C}, \mathcal{I}, \mathcal{T}, \mathcal{L}, \mathcal{A}' \rangle$ *for which* $A'{=}A \cup \{\langle r_d, n, r_r \rangle \,|\, \exists \langle q_d, n, q_r \rangle \in D\colon r_d \in eval(q_d) \wedge r_r \in eval(q_r)\}$*. The function* $eval$ *is a function that evaluates the query provided as an argument and returns its results.* ■

The semantics of the knowledge base with intensional attributes are the same as the semantics of its canonical base.

Definition 2. *Let* q *be a query or a reasoning task over an intensional base* S*. The result of* q *over* S *is defined as the result of the evaluation of* q *over* $Can(S)$*.* ■

Note that according to the above definition, no extension, special adjustments or operators need to be added to the query language in order to allow querying intensional bases. Of course, what needs to be adjusted is the actual evaluation mechanism which will be the topic of Section 5. Furthemore, note that when evaluating queries used in intensional attributes we do not consider other intensional previously defined attributes. That way, we avoid having recursive definitions.

To record intensional attributes in RDF, we have extended the RDF/RDFS model by introducing a new class Query. Every query is represented as an instance of that class, that has an attribute expression which is a string representing the query expression. Furthermore, we have created the class Intensional Attribute as a subclass of Property in which we have restricted the attributes domain and range to instances of the class Query. Figure 3 illustrates these extensions. The figure provides the major RDF/RDFS constructs as described by W3C [3] along with our proposed extensions which are indicated in the figure with shadowed nodes.

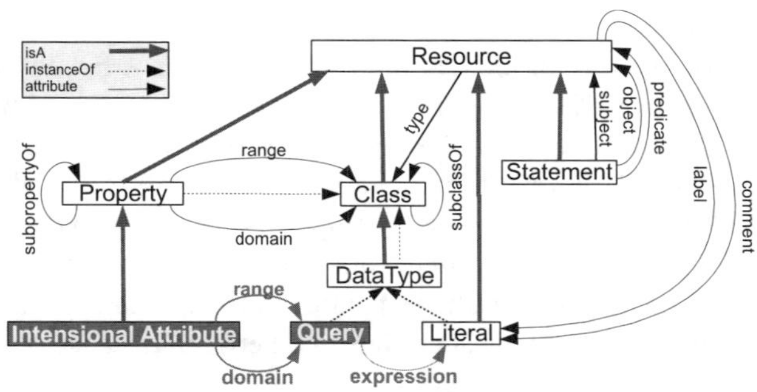

Fig. 3. The RDF/RDFS Schema model, extended to support intensional attributes

The queries used in the intensional attributes are queries supported by the system on which the framework runs. Thus, the complexity of supporting intensional attributes is only restricted by the complexity of the queries supported by the reasoner of the system. No additional reasoning is required (in the worst case scenario) than evaluating the query. However, for the practical class of queries that we consider in the next section and by using the evaluation technique that is described there, it will be shown that the complexity for the reasoner is linear to the size of the conditions in the query expression and the number of the attributes that exist in the knowledge base.

4 Realization of Intensional Attributes

To better understand the intuition behind intensional attributes, one can consider the paradigm of *defined concepts* in Description Logics (or DL) [10]. A DL terminological box (TBox) consists of two kinds of concepts, the *primitive* and the *defined*. Primitive concepts are those whose extensions are specified by explicit statements associating each individual to the respective concept. A defined concept, on the other hand, is a concept whose extension is specified through a logical expression. Every individual that satisfies the expression of a defined concept is considered automatically a member of its extension. Our proposed intensional attributes can be seen as an extension of the idea of defined concepts to attributes.

To realize intensional attributes, a solution that easily comes in mind is to exploit the ability of RDFS on defining domain and range constraints. Unfortunately, we show next that this is not possible. Let $\langle q_d, m, q_r \rangle$ be an intensional attribute. One can introduce two defined concepts C_d and C_r, using the query expressions q_d and q_r, respectively. Then, attribute m can be defined with concept C_d as domain and concept C_r as range. A limitation of this approach is that one needs to introduce two new defined concept for each different intensional attribute. In a relational database, this is similar to create a view for every query that is to be answered in the system. Naturally, this is not practical, first because the number of the queries may be large, and second, because access rights may not permit users to create new views (respectively, concepts). Furthermore, the knowledge base may be based on core DL, as most of the DL systems, which does not support the definition of attributes on defined concepts.

An alternative solution that avoids the introduction of new concepts is the use of the query expression directly in the definition of the property. For instance, the definition of property governedBy in Figure 2, could have been achieved by using in the domain part the OWL abstract syntax expression SubClassOf(intersectionOf(Country restriction(group value("EU"))) restriction(governedBy value(AG/345))) which represents query $Q1$. This idea, no matter how close it appears to be to what we are trying to achieve, is fundamentally different from the one behind intensional properties. According to the OWL specifications [11], the semantics of the domain and range classes of a property is that all its property instances must be between instances of these classes; however, the property definition itself does not specify what specific individuals participate in the property instance. In other words, defining the property hasCar with class Person as a domain and class Car as a range, does not automatically associate any of the individuals in the extension of Person with any of the individuals in the extension of Cars. In contrast, the semantics of the intensional attributes is that every individual in the extension of the domain class is *automatically* associated through the property with every individual in the extension of the range class.

For expressing the queries used in the definitions of the intensional attributes, we decided to use SPARQL [12] since it is one of the popular ontology query languages. We need to note, however, that the selection of the language is a design choice and does not affect the semantics of the intensional attribues. Since the role of intensional attributes is to associate classes or individuals with other classes, individuals or literals, it is natural to assume that each such query returns a set of one of those three kinds. Using SPARQL syntax, we can express queries Q1 through Q7 from Figure 2 as follows:

```
Q1: select ?x where {?x rdf:type Country . ?x group "EU"}
Q2: select ?x where {?x rdf:type Country . ?x population ?p . FILTER (?p <=20)}
Q3: select ?x where {?x rdf:type Country}
Q4: select ?x where {?x rdf:type Regulation . ?x code "EMR"}
Q5: select ?x where {?x rdf:type Country . ?x funding ?f . FILTER (?f > 10M &&
                                                              ?f < 100M)}
Q6: select distinct ?x where {?x rdf:type ?y . FILTER (str(?x) = "AG/345")}
Q7: select distinct ?x where {?z ?y ?x . FILTER (?x = "Needs to be reviewed")}
```

Note that, in contrast to relational query languages, in SPARQL it is not possible to return a constant that does not exist in the knowledge base. For instance, in SQL we can say select "mystring" which will return an answer set containing only the value "mystring". To achieve the same behavior in SPARQL, we need to have somehow the string explicitly stored in the knowledge base. To overcome this limitation, in our implementation we use a special class that stores as instances all the possible strings used in the queries. Thus, any query that needs to return only one value, like Q7 above, will indeed return the expected result. This is not a limitation of our approach, rather a way to overcome an SPARQL restriction.

5 Supporting Intensional Attributes Functionality

To support the intensional attribute functionality in a way that is transparent to the end user, we have investigated three main approaches that we describe next.

5.1 The Materialized Approach

The idea of the *materialized* approach is that all intensional attributes are materialized as regular attributes. When a new intensional attribute $\langle q_d, m, q_r \rangle$ is introduced in the knowledge base, the queries q_d and q_r are evaluated generating the result sets S_D and S_R. Then, for every member d in S_D and for every member r in S_R an attribute $\langle d, m, r \rangle$ is introduced in the knowledge base. Therefore, with the materialized approach, finding the intensional attributes of a class or individual is reduced to finding its regular attributes. When a new class/individual is introduced in the knowledge base, the system needs to find whether it needs to be assigned one or more intensional attributes, (recall the ability of the intensional attributes to be assigned to future data). To do this, the system has to go through all the queries of the intensional attributes and evaluate them in order to determine whether the class or individual is part of the answer set of any of them. One possible optimization for this process is to use an indexing mechanism similar to the one described in Section 5.3.

5.2 The Lazy Approach

The other extreme of the materialized approach is the *lazy* approach. According to it, no materialization takes place and the systems keeps only the definitions of the intensional attributes. This offers great space savings compared to the materialized approach. Furthermore, insertion or deletion of data does not require any action.

The limitation of the lazy approach is its high cost during browsing and query answering. The system can always find whether a class or an individual x has an intensional attribute $\langle q_d, m, q_r \rangle$ by simply evaluating queries q_d and q_r and testing whether x belongs to their answer set. Given a class or an individual x, to find its intensional attributes the system has to evaluate all the queries of all the stored intensional attribute definitions. This is the same process that the materialized approach had to perform when some new data is inserted into the intensional base. However, assuming that updates are not performed very often, we rather pay such a cost during data modification than during browsing or query answering.

5.3 The Indexed Approach

To avoid the two extremes of the lazy and the materialized approach, we looked for a method with a reasonable performance during query answering and a reduced cost in terms of space. As a result, we developed the *indexed* approach. Its basic idea is that, instead of fully materializing the intensional attributes as in the materialized approach, we create special index structures that allow us to find the intensional attributes of a given class/individual with a much lower cost than the one required when evaluating all the queries in the lazy approach.

In this approach, we restrict our attention to the special class of queries consisting of a set of attribute conditions. This class is equivalent to the select-project-join queries in relational database systems which have been found to constitute a large portion of those met in real application scenarios [7]. In what follows, we concentrate on select-project queries for reasons of presentation. The addition of the join does not alter the

DTable

Qd	Name	Qr
Q1	governedBy	Q6
Q2	comment	Q7
Q3	mustImplement	Q4
Q5	mustImplement	Q6
...	...	...

MTable

Q	Max	Cr
Q1	2	0
Q2	1	0
Q3	1	0
Q4	2	0
Q5	1	0
Q6	1	0
...	...	...

ETable

Attr	Value	Q
group	EU	Q2
hasURI	"AG/345"	Q6
hasURI	"EMR"	Q4
rdf:type	Country	Q1
rdf:type	Country	Q2
rdf:type	Country	Q3
rdf:type	Country	Q5
rdf:type	Regulation	Q4
...	...	...

ITable

Cond	Q
population $\leq$ 00020	Q2
___funding $>$ 00010	Q5
___funding $>$ 00020	Q10
___funding $>$ 00100	Q12
___funding $<$ 00010	Q11
___funding $<$ 00050	Q10
___funding $<$ 00100	Q5
...	...

Fig. 4. DTable, MTable, ETable and ITable examples

methodology or the results. Thus, we assume the indexed approach is used for queries of the SPARQL form:

$$\text{select } ?o \text{ where } \{?o \text{ rdf:type } c\ .\ Conds\}$$

where c is a specific class (not a variable) and $Conds$ is a series of conditions combined by the "." operator. Each condition in $Conds$ is of the form: $?o$ attributeName $?v$. FILTER($?v\langle OP\rangle attributeValue$). The operator $\langle OP\rangle$ can be one of the $=$, $<$, $\leq$, $>$ or $\geq$. The meaning of such a condition is that the class or individual o has an attribute $attributeName$ whose value is related to the $attributeValue$ as specified by the $\langle OP\rangle$ operator. For readability purposes, we will write conditions like the above as: $attributeName\langle OP\rangle attributeValue$.

The index consists of four tables: DTable, MTable, ETable, and the ITable. (Figure 4 illustrates the contents of the tables for the knowledge attributes in the intensional base of Figure 2.) Note that their structure permits the implementation in both relational and triple store systems. We explain their structures, roles and uses in the next paragraphs.

The DTable is a 3-column table used to record the list of the defined intensional attributes. The first and last columns record the domain and range queries, respectively, while the second one records the attribute names. More specifically, a tuple $[q_d, m, q_r]$ in DTable indicates the existence of an intensional attribute $\langle q_d, m, q_r\rangle$.

The MTable is also a 3-column table. It contains one entry for each query. The first column of the table specifies the query. The second column is an integer and specifies the number of equality conditions, i.e., conditions of the form $attributeName{=}attributeValue$, that the respective query has. The use of the third attribute will be described shortly. We require every query to have at least one equality condition on the type. We explicitly add condition rdf:type=owl:Thing to any query with no type condition. This guarantees at least one entry in the MTable for every query. Note, for instance, that query Q2 has in the middle column the value 1, since the only equality condition is the one on the type (The condition on the population is not an equality).

The ETable is the placeholder of the equality conditions of the queries in the intensional attributes. It consists of three columns recording the attribute name, the value of the equality condition, and the query name, respectively. (We assume that each query used in the intensional base is assigned a unique-name identifier.) All three values are stored as strings. Figure 4 contains an ETable for the queries in our running example.

Tables MTable and ETable need to be updated when intensional attributes are introduced or removed from the system. When an intensional attribute $\langle q_d, m, q_r\rangle$ is introduced, it is first inserted in table DTable, and then its queries q_d and q_r are analyzed. For every equality condition $cond$ they contain, a tuple $[q, cond]$ is inserted in ETable, where q is q_d or q_r. In addition, the tuples $[q_d, n_d, 0]$ and $[q_r, n_r, 0]$ are inserted in table MTable, where n_d and n_r are integers indicating the number of equality conditions of q_d and q_r, respectively. In the case of a deletion of an intensional attribute $\langle q_d, m, q_r\rangle$, the only action required is the removal from the tables DTable, MTable, and ETable of any tuple referring to query q_d and q_r.

Assume now that the system needs to find the intensional attributes of a class or an individual o. The system has first to find the queries that have o in their answer set. (To simplify the presentation we will ignore for the moment the inequality conditions.) To do so, all the values in the column Cr of MTable are initially set to 0. Then for each non-intensional[3] attribute $attrName$ with value $attrValue$, a lookup is performed on table ETable for tuples containing values *attrName* and *attrValue* in columns Attr and Value, respectively, and the Q column value of those tuples is retrieved. For each query q in the retrieved set, the Cr value of the tuples in table MTable that have q in column Q is increased by one. At the end of the process, the queries for which their MTable has the same value in columns Max and Cr are those for which the non-intensional attributes of o satisfy the query condition, thus o is in their answer set. Let $\mathcal{Q}$ be the set of such queries, and let us call it the *candidate set*. The intensional attributes of o are those in table DTable that have in column Qr or Qd a query that belongs in the candidate set $\mathcal{Q}$.

Example 3. As an example of the described process, consider the index structures illustrated in Figure 4, and the individual Canada of Figure 2. The specific individual has four (attributes, value) pairs: rdf:type=Country, group=non-EU, funding=70M and population=32M. A set of polling requests on ETable, one for each (attribute, value) pair, shows that Q1, Q2, Q3 and Q5 satisfy rdf:type=Country (no other pair is satisfied). Then, we increase by 1 the Cr column of the MTable for the tuples of the four queries mentioned above. The result table MTable will be the one of Figure 4 with the tuples of Q1, Q2, Q3 and Q5 having value 1 in column Cr. Among them only the Q2, Q3 and Q5 agree with the value in their respective column Max, which means that Canada satisfies all equality conditions of Q2, Q3 and Q5, thus, it belongs in their answer set. It does not, however, belong to the answer set of query Q1 since its Cr column value 1 is smaller than its Max column value 2. ∎

In the discussion so far we have considered only equality conditions. We see next how inequality conditions, i.e., conditions involving $>$ and $<$, are handled. Table ITable serves that purpose. It consists of two columns. The first column (Cond) is a column that contains the inequality conditions of every query used in the intensional attributes. The second column specified the query in which this inequality condition exists. If the same condition appears in more than one query, then the table has multiple entries, one for each query in which it appears. The values in the column Cond are strings of a fixed $2N$+1 character length used to record an inequality condition. The first N characters are used for the attribute name, the next character for

[3] The reason why only the non-intensional attributes are considered will be explained later.

the operator, and the last N for the value. If the attribute name is smaller than N in length, it is padded with underscores or zeros, depending on whether it is a string or a number. For instance, if N is 15, the string representation of the condition $population < 20$ is "_____population$<$000000000000020". We will denote by $PD(attrName\langle OP\rangle attrValue)$ the padded string representation of the condition $attrName\langle OP\rangle attrValue$. We will represent by MAX and MIN the two strings of N characters each with the following property: each character of MAX has all its bits to 1, and each character of MIN has all its bits to 0. This means that any comparison of an N-character string s to MAX will find s to be (lexicographically) smaller, and any comparison to MIN will find it larger. When a query q has a condition of the form $attrName\langle OP\rangle attrValue$, then its padded string representation is entered in the ITable along with the query q in the respective column. Given a class/individual o, the ITable is used to provide the list of queries with an inequality condition that is not satisfied by o. If o has an attribute attrName with a value attrValue, then we search on ITable for entries x that have Cond satisfying one of the following four specifications:

$PD(\text{attrName}>\text{attrValue}) < \text{x.Cond} < PD(\text{attrName}>\text{MAX})$
$PD(\text{attrName}\geq\text{attrValue}) < \text{x.Cond} < PD(\text{attrName}\geq\text{MAX})$
$PD(\text{attrName}<\text{MIN}) < \text{x.Cond} < PD(\text{attrName}<\text{attrValue})$
$PD(\text{attrName}\leq\text{MIN}) < \text{x.Cond} < PD(\text{attrName}\leq\text{attrValue})$

The queries found in this step are removed from the list of candidate queries Q that was generated in the process of equality conditions described earlier. What finally remains is the set of queries for which all their conditions are satisfied by the class/individual o that was inserted. Given these queries, one can find from the DTable the intensional attributes of o.

Example 4. Consider again the index structures illustrated in Figure 4, and the individual Canada of Figure 2. The ITable contains the inequality conditions of all queries in our intensional base example. From the equality process described in Example 3, we obtained the list of candidate queries for Canada: Q2, Q3 and Q5. Now, we need to eliminate from the candidate list those queries whose inequality conditions are not satisfied by the attributes of Canada. Therefore, for each (attribute, value) pair in Canada we create four requests to ITable, one for each range condition described above. For instance, for funding=70M, we create the following requests:

"___funding$>$00070" $<$ x.Cond $<$ "___funding$>$99999"
"___funding$\geq$00070" $<$ x.Cond $<$ "___funding$\geq$99999"
"___funding$<$00000" $<$ x.Cond $<$ "___funding$<$00070"
"___funding$\leq$00000" $<$ x.Cond $<$ "___funding$\leq$00070"

where 00000 and 99999 are the MIN and MAX of strings of length 5, respectively. The first request matches condition "___funding$>$00100" in ITable, which corresponds to Q12. The third request matches conditions "___funding$<$00010" and "___funding$<$00050", which correspond to Q11 and Q10, respectively. (Since there are only strict inequality conditions in ITable, the second and fourth requests match no attribute). Thus, Q10, Q11, and Q12 are queries whose inequality conditions are not satisfied and should be

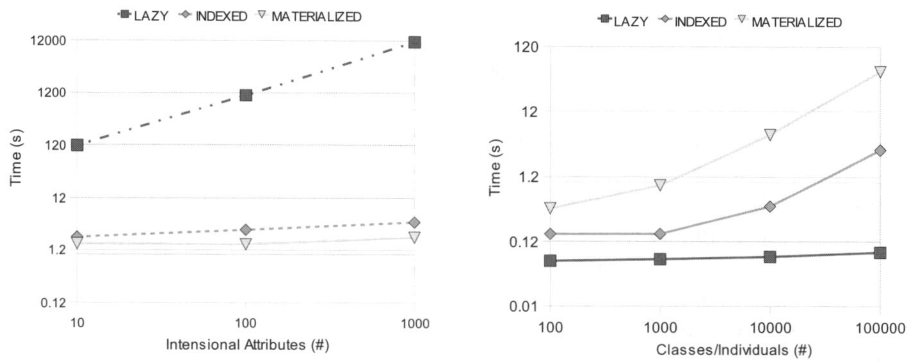

(a) (b)

Fig. 5. Running times for finding (a) and inserting (b) intensional attributes

removed from the candidate list. However, since they are not in the list, no actual action is performed.

We repeat the same process for every attribute-value pair of Canada. When we perform the polling for population=32M, the ("population≤00000" < x.Cond < "population≤00032") matches the condition "population≤00020" in ITable, resulting in Q2 being removed from the candidate list. Since the candidate list at the end of the process is Q3 and Q5, we conclude that the individual Canada is in the domain of the intensional attributes: ⟨Q3,mustImplement,Q4⟩, and ⟨Q5,mustImplement,Q6⟩ ∎

An extreme case is the one involving queries that have absolutely no constraints, and special consideration needs to be taken for them. Although we are taking care of such situations, we expect that this kind of queries will be extremely rare, since they simply assign an intensional attribute to every element that exists in the intensional base.

6 Experimental Evaluation

To evaluate the three implementation strategies, i.e., the lazy, the materialized and the indexed, we have conducted a number of experiments. We have repeated each experiment three times starting each time with a cold Java Virtual Machine (JVM). Our report time is the average of these three independent runs. The experiments were carried on a Windows XP machine powered by a 1.66 GHz CPU with 2 GB of RAM. The implementation utilizes the Protégé 3.3.1 plugin within the Eclipse environment. We used two different backends: the AllegroGraph 3.1 triple store[4] for the classes and individuals, and thus for the materialized implementation, and MySQL Server 5.0[5] for the tables and the intensional definitions in the indexed and lazy implementations, respectively.

One of the basic operations we need to evaluate is the time required to find the intensional attributes of a give class/individual. Figure 5(a) shows the time required for this task for different sizes of the data. For this first set of experiments, we populated

[4] http://agraph.franz.com/allegrograph

[5] http://www.mysql.com

the knowledge base with 100000 classes/individuals and we tested the performance of our three approaches with three sets of intensional attributes: 10, 100 and 1000. The conclusion of the experiments were that the lazy approach does not scale well since it has to run the queries of all intensional attribute definitions, so the performance of this approach heavily depends on the number of intensional attributes stored in the system. In contrast, both materialized and indexed implementations have good performance regardless of the number of intensional attributes. There are different reasons for this in each optimized implementation. In the materialized approach, intensional attributes are translated to regular attributes, so the time in the graph corresponds to just finding the actual class/individual in the ontology storage. In the indexed approach, the time corresponds to evaluating simple queries in tables DTable, MTable, ETable and ITable, which are much smaller than the entire knowledge base. Note that the illustrated graphs here are in logarithmic scale.

In contrast to finding the intensional attributes, the task of inserting a new class/individual in the knowledge base has the opposite results, as shown in Figure 5(b). For this set of experiments, we used a fix number of 1000 intensional attributes and varied the number of classes/individuals in the knowledge base from 100 to 100000, as shown on the x axis. Note that any class/individual may have any number of intensional attribute definitions, hence the number of intensional definitions could be larger than the number of classes/individuals in the system (which is the case for the knowledge base of size 100 in the graph).

For an insertion using the materialized implementation, the times reported corresponds to evaluating all queries of the intensional attributes in order to find which ones to materialize in the new class/individual. This is essentially the same process the lazy approach performs for finding the intensional attributes of a given class/individual. The times reported for the insertion using the indexed implementation, on the other hand, corresponds to updating the information of the DTable, MTable, ETable and ITable, with the data of the queries in the new intensional attribute. Finally, the reported times for the lazy approach correspond to storing the queries of the new intensional attribute in the knowledge base, which requires just to store the intensional definition in the system.

7 Related Work

The idea of using queries for intensional definitions is not new. Derived concepts in Description Logics [4] are defined through logical expressions, i.e., queries. Derived elements in UML are also defined with some sort of logical expressions, although much simpler than those used in Description Logics. Virtual and materialized views in database management systems also use queries to describe their contents [7]. Queries as data values have been implemented in a number of commercial database systems such as INGRESS [5] and Oracle [13]. They have also been studied in the context of relational algebra [6] and Meta-SQL [8]. There have been numerous proposals for metadata management that include some kind of association between metadata and data, either by relating individuals values [14], subsets of the attributes in a tuple [15], or XML data with a complex structure [16]. The use of queries as data values for associating data and metadata has been studied in [9], where the authors propose a unified mechanism for modeling and querying across both data and metadata.

An ontology is a formal explicit description of concepts, or classes, in a domain of discourse [1]. An ontology, along with a set of individual instances, constitutes a knowledge base. In the context of the Semantic Web [17], ontologies are represented through formalisms like RDF [2] and OWL [11], and queried with ontology query languages such as SPARQL [12]. To the best of our knowledge, this is the first effort towards using queries to introduce intensional attributes in ontologies in order to tackle the issues described in this work.

8 Conclusion

We proposed an extension of the RDF and OWL formalisms with intensional attributes, i.e., attributes that have no explicit specification for the classes or individuals they associate (the domain and range of the attributes are specified through intensional expressions represented by queries). This work can be seen as an extension to attributes of the notion of derived concepts in Description Logics. Intensional attributes offer flexibility, great space and time savings, and can also be applied to future data. We investigated possible implementations and proposed one that provides good performance and space tradeoffs.

Acknowledgments. The current work has been partially supported by the EU grant GA-215032 and ICT-215874.

References

1. Noy, N.F., McGuinness, D.L.: Ontology development 101: A guide to creating your first ontology. Technical report, Stanford Knowledge Systems Laboratory KSL-01-05 (2001)
2. W3C: Resource description framework, RDF (2004), http://www.w3.org/TR/rdf-concepts/
3. W3C: RDF vocabulary description language 1.0: RDF Schema (2004), http://www.w3.org/TR/rdf-schema/
4. Baader, F., Nutt, W.: Basic Description Logics. In: Description Logic Handbook, pp. 43–95 (2003)
5. Stonebraker, M., Anton, J., Hanson, E.N.: Extending a Database System with Procedures.. TODS 12(3), 350–376 (1987)
6. Neven, F., Bussche, J.V., Gucht, D.V., Vossen, G.: Typed Query Languages for Databases Containing Queries. In: PODS, pp. 189–196 (1998)
7. Lenzerini, M.: Data Integration: A Theoretical Perspective. In: PODS, pp. 233–246 (2002)
8. van den Bussche, J., Vansummeren, S., Vossen, G.: Towards practical meta-querying. Inf. Syst. 30(4), 317–332 (2005)
9. Srivastava, D., Velegrakis, Y.: Intensional Associations between Data and Metadata. In: SIGMOD, pp. 401–412 (2007)
10. Borgida, A., Brachman, R.J.: Modeling with Description Logics. In: Description Logic Handbook, pp. 349–372 (2003)
11. W3C: OWL web ontology language reference (2004), http://www.w3.org/TR/owl-ref/

12. W3C: SPARQL query language for RDF (2008), http://www.w3.org/TR/rdf-sparql-query/
13. Gawlick, D., Lenkov, D., Yalamanchi, A., Chernobrod, L.: Applications for Expression Data in Relational Database System.. In: ICDE, pp. 609–620 (2004)
14. Buneman, P., Khanna, S., Tan, W.C.: On propagation of deletions and annotations through views. In: PODS, pp. 150–158. ACM, New York (2002)
15. Geerts, F., Kementsietsidis, A., Milano, D.: MONDRIAN: Annotating and querying databases through colors and blocks. In: ICDE, p. 82 (2006)
16. Bertino, E., Castano, S., Ferrari, E.: On specifying security policies for web documents with an XML-based language. In: SACMAT, pp. 57–65 (2001)
17. W3C: Semantic web (2008), http://www.w3.org/2001/sw/

Modeling Concept Evolution: A Historical Perspective

Flavio Rizzolo, Yannis Velegrakis, John Mylopoulos, and Siarhei Bykau

University of Trento, Trento, 38100, Italy
{flavio,velgias,jm,bykau}@disi.unitn.eu

Abstract. The world is changing, and so must the data that describes its history. Not surprisingly, considerable research effort has been spent in Databases along this direction, covering topics such as temporal models and schema evolution. A topic that has not received much attention, however, is that of concept evolution. For example, Germany (instance-level concept) has evolved several times in the last century as it went through different governance structures, then split into two national entities that eventually joined again. Likewise, a caterpillar is transformed into a butterfly, while a mother becomes two (maternally-related) entities. As well, the concept of Whale (a class-level concept) changed over the past two centuries thanks to scientific discoveries that led to a better understanding of what the concept entails. In this work, we present a formal framework for modeling, querying and managing such evolution. In particular, we describe how to model the evolution of a concept, and how this modeling can be used to answer historical queries of the form "How has concept X evolved over period Y". Our proposal extends an RDF-like model with temporal features and evolution operators. Then we provide a query language that exploits these extensions and supports historical queries.

1 Introduction

Conceptual modeling languages – including the ER Model, UML class diagrams and Description Logics – are all founded on a notion of "entity" that represents a "thing" in the application domain. Although the state of an entity can change over its lifetime, entities themselves are atomic and immutable. Unfortunately, this feature prevents existing modeling languages from capturing phenomena that involve the evolution of an entity into something else, such as a caterpillar becoming a butterfly, or Germany splitting off into two Germanies right after WWII. In these cases, there is general agreement that an entity evolves into one or more different entities. Moreover, there is a strong relationship between the two, which is not captured by merely deleting one entity and then creating another. For example, the concept of Whale evolved over the past two centuries in the sense that whales were considered some sort of fish, but are now recognized as mammals. We are interested in modeling this kind of evolution relationship, not only at the instance and class levels but also across levels: instances may evolve into classes and viceversa. This notion of evolution is independent from the way the relationship between instances and classes is modeled [1].

In Databases, considerable amount of research effort has been spent on the development of models, techniques and tools for modeling and managing data changes. These range from data manipulation languages, and maintenance of views under changes [2],

A.H.F. Laender et al. (Eds.): ER 2009, LNCS 5829, pp. 331–345, 2009.

to schema evolution [3] and mapping adaptation [4]. To cope with the history of data changes, temporal models have been proposed for the relational [5] and ER [6] models, for semi-structured data [7], XML [8] and for RDF [9]. Almost in its entirety, existing work on data changes is based on a data-oriented point of view. It aims at recording and managing changes that are taking place at the values of the data. What has been completely overlooked are other types of changes, such as an entity evolving/mutating into another, or an entity "splitting off" into several others.

In this work, we present a framework for modeling the evolution of concepts over time and the evolving relationships among them. The framework allows posing new kinds of queries that previously could not have been expressed. For instance, we aim at supporting queries of the form: How has a concept evolved over time? From what other concepts has it evolved and into what others has it resulted? What other concepts have affected its evolution over time? What concepts are indirectly related to it and how? These kinds of queries are of major importance for many interesting areas:

Historical Studies. Modern historians are interested in studying the history of human achievements, events and important persons. In addition, they want to understand how systems, tools, concepts, and techniques have evolved throughout the history. For them it is not enough to query a data source for a specific moment in history. They need to ask questions on how concepts and the relationships that exist between them have changed over time. Historians may be interested in the evolution of countries like Germany, with respect to territory, political division, etc. Alternatively, they may want to study the evolution of scientific topics, e.g., how the concept of biotechnology has evolved from its beginnings as an agricultural technology to the current notion that is coupled to genetics and molecular biology.

Entity Management. Web application and integration systems are progressively moving from tuple and value-based towards entity-based solutions, i.e., systems in which the basic data unit is an entity, independently of its logical modeling [10]. Furthermore, web integration systems, in order to achieve interoperability, may need to provide unique identification for the entities in the data they exchange [11]. Entities do not remain static over time: they evolve, merge, split, get created and disappear. Knowing the history of each entity, i.e., how it has been formed and from what, paves the ground for successful entity management solutions and affective information exchange.

Life Sciences One of the Biology fields is the study of the evolution of the species since life started on earth. To better understand the secrets of nature, it is important to model how the different species have evolved, from what, if and how they have disappeared, and when.

Our contributions are the following: (i) we consider a conceptual model enhanced with the notion of a lifetime of a class, individual and relationship, (ii) we further extend the temporal model [9] with consistency conditions and additional constructs to model merges, splits, and other forms of evolution among class-level and instance-level concepts; (iii) we introduce a query language that allows the answering of queries regarding the lifetime of concepts as well as the way they have evolved over time, along with other associated (via evolution) concepts; and finally, (iv) we present a case study in which we have applied our framework.

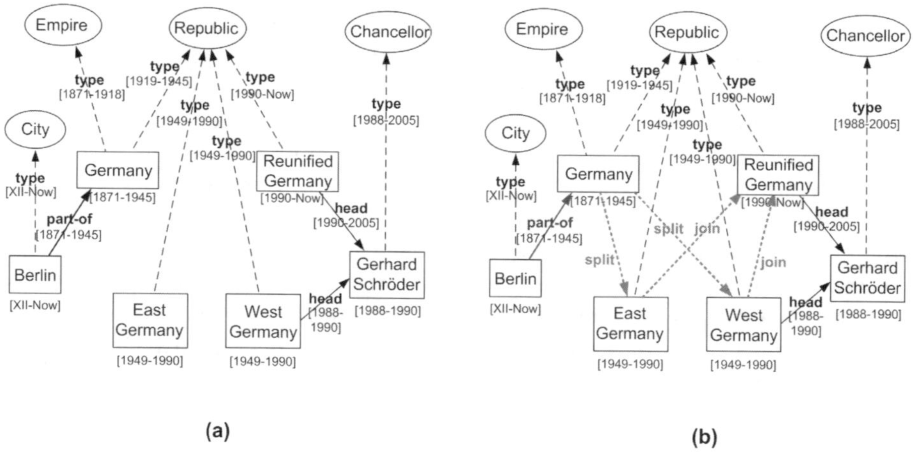

Fig. 1. The concepts of Germany, in a temporal model **(a)** and in our evolutionary model **(b)**

2 A Motivating Example

Consider the knowledge base of a historian that records information about countries and their political governance. A fraction of that information modeling a part of the history of Germany is illustrated in Figure 1 (a). In it, the status of Germany at different times in history has been been modeled through different individuals or through different instantiations. In particular, since 1871 and until 1945, Germany has been an empire and later a republic. This change is modeled by the multiple instantiation of Germany to Empire and Republic respectively. Shortly after the end of the World War II, Germany was split in four zones[1] that in 1949 formed the East and West Germany. These two parts lasted until 1990, when they were merged to form the republic of Germany as we know it today, which is modeled through the individual Reunified Germany.

To model the validity of each state of Germany at the different periods, a temporal model similar to temporal RDF [9] can be used. The model associates to each concept or individual a specific time frame. The time frames assigned to the individuals that model Germany are illustrated in Figure 1 through the intervals next to each individual. The same applies to every property, instance and subclass relationship. Note, for example, how the instantiation relationship of Germany to Empire has a temporal interval from 1871 to 1918, while the one to Republic has a temporal interval from 1918 to 1945. It is important for such a knowledge base to contain no inconsistencies, i.e., situations like having an instantiation relationship with a temporal interval bigger than the interval of the class it instantiates. Although temporal RDF lacks this kind of axiomatization, a mechanism for consistency checking needs to be in place for the accurate representation of concepts and individuals in history. Our solution provides an axiomatization of the temporal RDF that guarantees the consistency of the historical information recorded in a knowledge base.

Consider now the case of a historian that is interested in studying the history of Germany. Typical historian queries are those asking for all the leaders and constituents of a

[1] The information of the four zones is not illustrated in the Figure 1.

country from all its phases through time. Using traditional query mechanisms, the historian will only be able to retrieve the individual Germany. Using keyword based techniques, she may be able to also retrieve the remaining individuals modeling Germany at different times, but this under the assumption that each such individual contains the keyword "Germany". Applying terminology evolution [12], it is possible to infer that the four terms for Germany, i.e., Germany, East Germany, West Germany, and Reunified Germany refer to related concepts regardless of the keywords that appear in the terms. Yet, in neither case the historian will be able to reconstruct how the constituents of Germany have changed over time. She will not be able to find that the East and West Germany were made by splitting the pre-war Germany and its parts, neither that East and West Germany were the same two that merged to form the Reunified Germany. We propose the use of explicit constructs to allow the modeling of the sequential conceptual evolution in knowledge bases, as exemplified in Figure 1(b) by split, join and part-of.

3 Temporal Knowledge Bases

We consider an RDF-like data model. The model is expressive enough to represent ER models and the majority of ontologies and schemas that are met in practice [13]. It does not include certain OWL Lite features such as *sameAs* or *equivalentClass*, since these features have been considered to be out of the main scope of this work and their omission does not restrict the functionality of the model.

We assume the existence of an infinite set of *resources* $\mathcal{U}$, each with a *unique resource identifier* (URIs), and a set of *literals* $\mathcal{L}$. A *property* is a relationship between two resources. Properties are considered resources. We consider the existence of the special properties: rdfs:type, rdfs:domain, rdfs:range, rdfs:subClassOf and rdfs:subPropertyOf, which we denote for simplicity as type, dom, rng, subc, and subp, respectively. The set $\mathcal{U}$ contains three special resources: rdfs:Property, rdfs:Class and rdf:Thing, which we denote for simplicity as Prop, Class and Thing, respectively. The semantics of these resources as well as the semantics of the special properties are those defined in RDFS [14]. Resources are described by a set of triples that form a knowledge base.

Definition 1. *A* knowledge base Σ *is a tuple* $\langle U, L, T\rangle$*, where* $U \subseteq \mathcal{U}$*,* $L \subseteq \mathcal{L}$*,* $T \subseteq \mathcal{U}\times \mathcal{U}\times \{\mathcal{U}\cup\mathcal{L}\}$*, and* U *contains the resources* rdfs:Property, rdfs:Class, *and* rdf:Thing. *The set of* classes *of the knowledge base* Σ *is the set* $C{=}\{x \mid \exists\langle x, \text{type}, \text{rdfs:Class}\rangle \in T\}$. *Similarly, the set of* properties *is the set* $P{=}\{x \mid \exists\langle x, \text{type}, \text{rdfs:Property}\rangle \in T\}$. *The set* P *must contain the RDFS properties* type, dom, rng, subc, *and* subp. *A resource* i *is said to be an* instance *of a class* $c \in C$ *(or of type* c*) if* $\exists\langle i, \text{type}, c\rangle \in T$. *The set of* instances *is the set* $I{=}\{i \mid \exists\langle i, \text{type}, y\rangle \in T\}$.

A knowledge base can be represented as a hypergraph called an *RDF graph*. In the rest of the paper, we will use the terms knowledge base and RDF graph equivalently.

Definition 2. *An* RDF graph *of a knowledge base* Σ *is an hypergraph in which nodes represent resources and literals and the edges represent triples.*

Example 1. Figure 1(a) is an ilustration of an RDF Graph. The nodes Berlin and Germany represent resources. The edge labeled part-of between them represents the triple ⟨Berlin,part-of,Germany⟩. The label of the edge, i.e., part-of, represents a property.

To support the temporal dimension in our model, we adopt the approach of Temporal RDF [9] which extends RDF by associating to each triple a time frame. Unfortunately, this extension is not enough for our goals. We need to add time semantics not only to relationships between resources (what the triples represent), but also to resources themselves by providing temporal-varying classes and individuals. This addition and the consistency conditions we introduce below are our temporal extensions to the temporal RDF data model.

We consider time as a discrete, total order domain $\mathbb{T}$ in which we define different granularities. Following [15], a *granularity* is a mapping from integers to *granules* (i.e., subsets of the time domain $\mathbb{T}$) such that contiguous integers are mapped to non-empty granules and granules within one granularity are totally ordered and do not overlap. Days and months are examples of two different granularities, in which each granule is a specific day in the former and a month in the latter. Granularities define a lattice in which granules in some granularities can be aggregated in larger granules in *coarser* granularities. For instance, months are a coarser granularity than days because every granule in the former (a month) is composed of an integer number of granules in the latter (days). In contrast, months are not coarser (nor finer) than weeks.

Even though we model time as a point-based temporal domain, we use intervals as abbreviations of sets of instants whenever possible. An ordered pair $[a, b]$ of time points, with a, b granules in a granularity, and $a \leq b$, denotes the closed interval from a to b. As in most temporal models, the current time point will be represented with the distinguished word *Now*. We will use the symbol $\mathcal{T}$ to represent the infinite set of all the possible temporal intervals over the temporal domain $\mathbb{T}$, and the expressions $i.start$ and $i.end$ to refer to the starting and ending time points of an interval i. Given two intervals i_1 and i_2, we will denote by $i_1 \sqsubseteq i_2$ the containment relationship between the intervals in which $i_2.start \leq i_1.start$ and $i_1.end \leq i_2.end$.

Two types of temporal dimensions are normally considered: *valid* time and *transaction* time. Valid time is the time when data is valid in the modeled world whereas transaction time is the time when data is actually stored in the database. Concept evolution is based on valid time.

Definition 3. *A* temporal knowledge base Σ_T *is a tuple* $\langle U, L, T, \tau \rangle$, *where* $\langle U, L, T \rangle$ *is a knowledge base and* τ *is function that maps every resource* $r \in U$ *to a temporal interval in* $\mathcal{T}$. *The temporal interval is also referred to as the* lifespan *of the resource. The expressions* $r.start$ *and* $r.end$ *denote the start and end points of the interval of* r, *respectively. The* temporal graph *of* Σ_T *is the RDF graph of* $\langle U, L, T \rangle$ *enhanced with the temporal intervals on the edges and nodes.*

For a temporal knowledge base to be semantically meaningful, the lifespan of the resources need to satisfy certain conditions. For instance, it is not logical to have an individual with a lifespan that does not contain any common time points with the lifespan of the class it belongs to. Temporal RDF does not provide such a mechanism, thus, we are introducing the notion of a consistent temporal knowledge base.

Definition 4. *A* consistent temporal knowledge base *is a temporal knowledge base* $\Sigma_\tau = \langle U, L, T, \tau \rangle$ *that satisfies the following conditions:*

1. $\forall r \in L \cup \{\textsf{Prop}, \textsf{Class}, \textsf{Thing}, \textsf{type}, \textsf{dom}, \textsf{rng}, \textsf{subc}, \textsf{subp}\}$: $\tau(r) = [0, Now]$;

2. $\forall\langle d,p,r\rangle \in T : \tau(\langle d,p,r\rangle)\sqsubseteq\tau(d)$ *and* $\tau(\langle d,p,r\rangle)\sqsubseteq\tau(r)$;
3. $\forall\langle d,p,r\rangle \in T$ *with* $p \in \{\mathsf{type},\mathsf{subc},\mathsf{subp}\}$: $\tau(d)\sqsubseteq\tau(r)$.

Intuitively, literals and the special resources and properties defined in RDFS need to be valid during the entire lifespan of the temporal knowledge base, which is $[0, Now]$ (Condition 1). In addition, the lifespan of a triple needs to be within the lifespan of the resources that the triple associates (Condition 2). Finally, the lifespan of a resource has to be within the lifespan of the class the resource instantiates, and any class or property needs to be within the lifespan of its superclasses or superproperties (Condition 3).

4 Modeling Evolution

Apart from the temporal dimension that was previously described, two new dimensions need to be taken into consideration to successfully model evolution: the mereological and the causal.

Mereology [16] is a sub-discipline in philosophy that deals with the ontological investigation of the part-whole relationships. It is used in our model to capture the parthood relationship between concepts in a way that is carried forward as concepts evolve. Such a relationship is modeled through the introduction of the special property part-of, which is reflexive, antisymmetric and transitive. A property part-of is defined from a resource x to a resource y if the concept modeled by resource x is part of the concept modeled by resource y. Note that the above definition implies that every concept is also a part of itself. When x is a part of y and $x \neq y$ we say that x is a *proper part* of y. Apart from this special semantics, part-of behaves as any other property in a temporal knowledge base. For readability and presentation reasons, we may use the notation $x \overset{\text{part-of}}{\longrightarrow} y$ to represent the existence of a triple $<x$,part-of,$y>$ in the set T of a temporal knowledge base $\Sigma_{\mathcal{T}}$.

To capture the causal relationships, i.e., the interdependency between two resources, we additionally introduce the notion of becomes, which is an antisymmetric and transitive relation. For similar reasons as before, we may use the notation $x \overset{\text{becomes}}{\longrightarrow} y$ to represent the fact that $(x, y) \in$ becomes. Intuitively, $x \overset{\text{becomes}}{\longrightarrow} y$ means that the concept modeled by resource y originates from the concept modeled by resource x. We require that $\tau(x).end < \tau(y).start$.

To effectively model evolution, we introduce the notion of a *liaison*. A liaison between two concepts is another concept that keeps the former two linked together in time by means of part-of and becomes. In other words, a liaison is part of at least one of the concepts it relates and has some causal relationship to a part of the other.

Definition 5 (Liaison). *Let* A, B *be two concepts of a temporal knowledge base with* $\tau(A).start < \tau(B).start$, *and* x, y *concepts for which* $x \overset{\text{part-of}}{\longrightarrow} A$ *and* $y \overset{\text{part-of}}{\longrightarrow} B$. *A concept* x *(or* y*) is said to be a* liaison between A and B *if either* $x \overset{\text{becomes}}{\longrightarrow} y$ *or* $x = y$.

The most general case of a liaison is graphically depicted in Figure 2 (a). The boxes A and B represent the two main concepts whereas the x and y represent two of their respective parts. Figure 2 (b) illustrates the second case of the definition in which x and

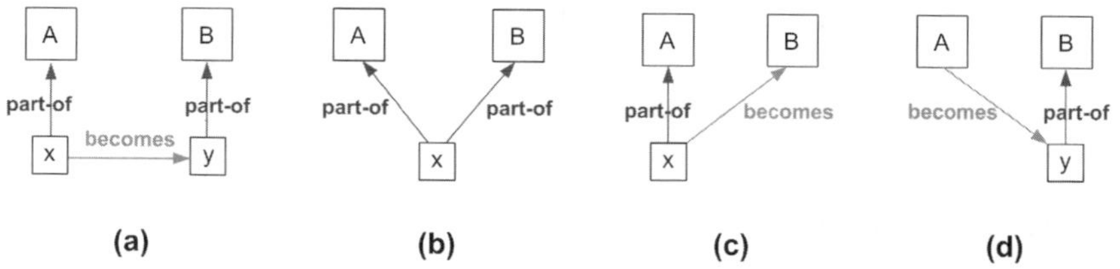

Fig. 2. Liaison examples

y are actually the same concept. Figure 2 (c) (respectively, (d)) shows the special case in which y (respectively, x) is exactly the whole of B (respectively, A) rather than a proper part of it.

To model the different kinds of evolution events that may exist, we introduce four evolution terms: join, split, merge, and detach.

[join]. The join term, denoted as join$(c_1 \ldots c_n, c, t)$, models the fact that every part of a concept c born at time t comes from a part of some concept in $\{c_1, \ldots, c_n\}$. In particular:

- $\tau(c).start{=}t$;
- $\forall x$ s.t. $x \overset{\text{part-of}}{\longrightarrow} c$: $\exists c_i$ s.t. x is a liaison between c_i and c, or $x = c_i$, with $1{\leq}i{\leq}n$.

[split]. The split term, denoted as split$(c, c_1 \ldots c_n, t)$, models the fact that every part of a concept c ending at time t becomes the part of some concept in $\{c_1, \ldots, c_n\}$. In particular:

- $\tau(c).end{=}t$;
- $\forall x$ s.t. $x \overset{\text{part-of}}{\longrightarrow} c$: $\exists c_i$ s.t. x is a liaison between c and c_i, or $x = c_i$, with $1{\leq}i{\leq}n$.

[merge]. The merge term, denoted as merge(c, c', t), models the fact that at least a part of a concept c ending at a time t becomes part of an existing concept c'. In particular:

- $\tau(c).end{=}t$;
- $\exists x$ s.t. $x \overset{\text{part-of}}{\longrightarrow} c'$ and x is a liaison between c and c'.

[detach]. The detach term, denoted as detach(c, c', t), models the fact that the new concept c' is formed at a time t with at least one part from c. In particular:

- $\tau(c').start{=}t$;
- $\exists x$ s.t. $x \overset{\text{part-of}}{\longrightarrow} c$ and x is a liaison between c and c'.

Note that in each evolution term there is only one concept whose lifespan has necessarily to start or end at the time of the event. For instance, we could use a join to represent the fact that different countries joined the European Union (EU) at different times. The information of the period in which each country participated in the EU is given by the interval of each respective part-of property.

We record the becomes relation and the evolution terms in the temporal knowledge base as *evolution triples* $\langle c, term, c' \rangle$, where $term$ is one of the special *evolution properties* becomes, join, split, merge, and detach. Evolution properties are *meta-temporal*, i.e., they describe how the temporal model changes, and thus their triples do not need to satisfy the consistency conditions in Definition 4. A temporal knowledge base with a set of evolution properties and triples defines an *evolution base*.

Definition 6. *An* evolution base Σ_T^E *is a tuple* $\langle U, L, T, E, \tau\rangle$*, where* $\langle U, L, T, \tau\rangle$ *is a temporal knowledge base,* U *contains a set of evolution properties, and* E *is a set of evolution triples. The* evolution graph *of* Σ_T^E *is the temporal graph of* $\langle U, L, T, \tau\rangle$ *enhanced with edges representing the evolutions triples.*

The time in which the evolution event took place does not need to be recorded explicitly in the triple since it can be retrieved from the lifespan of the involved concepts. For instance, detach(Kingdom of the Netherlands, Belgium, 1831) is modeled as the triple: ⟨Kingdom of the Netherlands, detach, Belgium⟩ with $\tau(\text{Belgium}).start = 1831$.

For recording evolution terms that involve more than two concepts, e.g. the join, multiple triples are needed. We assume that the terms are indexed by their time, thus, the set of (independent) triples that belong to the same terms can be easily detected since they will all share the same start or end time in the lifespan of the respective concept. For instance, split(Germany, East Germany, West Germany, 1949) is represented in our model through the triples ⟨Germany, split, East Germany⟩ and ⟨Germany, split, West Germany⟩ with $\tau(\text{East Germany}).start = \tau(\text{West Germany}).start = 1949$.

Note that the evolution terms may entail facts that are not explicitly represented in the knowledge base. For instance, the split of Germany into West and East implies the fact that Berlin, which is explicitly defined as part of Germany, becomes part of either East or West. This kind of reasoning is beyond the scope of the current work.

5 Query Language

We define a navigational query language to traverse temporal and evolution edges in an evolution graph. This language is analogous to nSPARQL [17], a language that extends SPARQL with navigational capabilities based on nested regular expressions. nSPARQL uses four different axes, namely **self**, **next**, **edge**, and **node**, for navigation on an RDF graph and node label testing. We have extended the nested regular expressions constructs of nSPARQL with temporal semantics and a set of five *evolution axes*, namely **join**, **split**, **merge**, **detach**, and **becomes** that extend the traversing capabilities of nSPARQL to the evolution edges. The language is defined according to the following grammar:

$$exp := \textbf{axis} \mid \textbf{t-axis} :: a \mid \textbf{t-axis} :: [exp] \mid exp[I] \mid exp/exp \mid exp|exp \mid exp^*$$

where a is a node in the graph, I is a time interval, and **axis** can be either **forward**, **backward**, **e-edge**, **e-node**, a **t-axis** or an **e-axis**, with **t-axis** $\in$ {**self**, **next**, **edge**, **node**} and **e-axis** $\in$ {**join**, **split**, **merge**, **detach**, **becomes**}.

The evaluation of an evolution expression exp is given by the semantic function $\mathcal{E}$ defined in Figure 3. $\mathcal{E}[\![exp]\!]$ returns a set of tuples of the form $\langle x, y, I\rangle$ such that there is a path from x to y satisfying exp during interval I. For instance, in the evolution base of Figure 1, $\mathcal{E}[\![\textbf{self} :: \text{Germany}/\textbf{next} :: \text{head}/\textbf{next} :: \text{type}]\!]$ returns the tuple

$$
\begin{aligned}
\mathcal{E}[\![\textbf{self}]\!] &:= \{\langle x, x, \tau(x)\rangle \mid x \in U \cup L\}\\
\mathcal{E}[\![\textbf{self}::r]\!] &:= \{\langle r, r, \tau(r)\rangle\}\\
\mathcal{E}[\![\textbf{next}]\!] &:= \{\langle x, y, \tau(t)\rangle \mid t = \langle x, z, y\rangle \in T\}\\
\mathcal{E}[\![\textbf{next}::r]\!] &:= \{\langle x, y, \tau(t)\rangle \mid t = \langle x, r, y\rangle \in T\}\\
\mathcal{E}[\![\textbf{edge}]\!] &:= \{\langle x, y, \tau(t)\rangle \mid t = \langle x, y, z\rangle \in T\}\\
\mathcal{E}[\![\textbf{edge}::r]\!] &:= \{\langle x, y, \tau(t)\rangle \mid t = \langle x, y, r\rangle \in T\}\\
\mathcal{E}[\![\textbf{node}]\!] &:= \{\langle x, y, \tau(t)\rangle \mid t = \langle z, x, y\rangle \in T\}\\
\mathcal{E}[\![\textbf{node}::r]\!] &:= \{\langle x, y, \tau(t)\rangle \mid t = \langle r, x, y\rangle \in T\}\\
\mathcal{E}[\![\textbf{e-edge}]\!] &:= \{\langle x, \textbf{e-axis}, [0, Now]\rangle \mid t = \langle x, \textbf{e-axis}, z\rangle \in E\}\\
\mathcal{E}[\![\textbf{e-node}]\!] &:= \{\langle \textbf{e-axis}, y, \tau(t)\rangle \mid t = \langle z, \textbf{e-axis}, y\rangle \in E\}\\
\mathcal{E}[\![\textbf{e-axis}]\!] &:= \{\langle x, y, [0, Now]\rangle \mid \exists\, t = \langle x, \textbf{e-axis}, y\rangle \in E\}\\
\mathcal{E}[\![\textbf{forward}]\!] &:= \textstyle\bigcup_{\textbf{e-axis}} \mathcal{E}[\![\textbf{e-axis}]\!]\\
\mathcal{E}[\![\textbf{backward}]\!] &:= \textstyle\bigcup_{\textbf{e-axis}} \mathcal{E}[\![\textbf{e-axis}^{-1}]\!]\\
\mathcal{E}[\![\textbf{self}::[exp]]\!] &:= \{\langle x, x, \tau(x) \cap I\rangle \mid x \in U \cup L, \exists \langle x, z, I\rangle \in \mathcal{P}[\![exp]\!], \tau(x) \cap I \neq \emptyset\}\\
\mathcal{E}[\![\textbf{next}::[exp]]\!] &:= \{\langle x, y, \tau(t) \cap I\rangle \mid t = \langle x, z, y\rangle \in T, \exists \langle z, w, I\rangle \in \mathcal{P}[\![exp]\!], \tau(t) \cap I \neq \emptyset\}\\
\mathcal{E}[\![\textbf{edge}::[exp]]\!] &:= \{\langle x, y, \tau(t) \cap I\rangle \mid t = \langle x, y, z\rangle \in T, \exists \langle z, w, I\rangle \in \mathcal{P}[\![exp]\!], \tau(t) \cap I \neq \emptyset\}\\
\mathcal{E}[\![\textbf{node}::[exp]]\!] &:= \{\langle x, y, \tau(t) \cap I\rangle \mid t = \langle z, x, y\rangle \in T, \exists \langle z, w, I\rangle \in \mathcal{P}[\![exp]\!], \tau(t) \cap I \neq \emptyset\}\\
\mathcal{E}[\![\textbf{axis}^{-1}]\!] &:= \{\langle x, y, \tau(t)\rangle \mid \langle y, x, \tau(t)\rangle \in \mathcal{E}[\![\textbf{axis}]\!]\}\\
\mathcal{E}[\![\textbf{t-axis}^{-1}::r]\!] &:= \{\langle x, y, \tau(t)\rangle \mid \langle y, x, \tau(t)\rangle \in \mathcal{E}[\![\textbf{t-axis}::r]\!]\}\\
\mathcal{E}[\![\textbf{t-axis}^{-1}::[exp]]\!] &:= \{\langle x, y, \tau(t)\rangle \mid \langle y, x, \tau(t)\rangle \in \mathcal{E}[\![\textbf{t-axis}::[exp]]\!]\}\\
\mathcal{E}[\![exp[I]]\!] &:= \{\langle x, y, I \cap I'\rangle \mid \langle x, y, I'\rangle \in \mathcal{E}[\![exp]\!] \text{ and } I \cap I' \neq \emptyset\}\\
\mathcal{E}[\![exp/e\text{-}exp]\!] &:= \{\langle x, y, I_2\rangle \mid \exists \langle x, z, I_1\rangle \in \mathcal{E}[\![exp]\!], \exists \langle z, y, I_2\rangle \in \mathcal{E}[\![e\text{-}exp]\!]\}\\
\mathcal{E}[\![exp/t\text{-}exp]\!] &:= \{\langle x, y, I_1 \cap I_2\rangle \mid \exists \langle x, z, I_1\rangle \in \mathcal{E}[\![exp]\!], \exists \langle z, y, I_2\rangle \in \mathcal{E}[\![t\text{-}exp]\!] \text{ and}\\
&\qquad I_1 \cap I_2 \neq \emptyset\}\\
\mathcal{E}[\![exp_1|exp_2]\!] &:= \mathcal{E}[\![exp_1]\!]\ cup \mathcal{E}[\![exp_2]\!]\\
\mathcal{E}[\![exp^*]\!] &:= \mathcal{E}[\![\textbf{self}]\!] \cup \mathcal{E}[\![exp]\!] \cup \mathcal{E}[\![exp/exp]\!] \cup \mathcal{E}[\![exp/exp/exp]\!] \cup \ldots
\end{aligned}
$$

$$
\begin{aligned}
\mathcal{P}[\![e\text{-}exp]\!] &:= \mathcal{E}[\![e\text{-}exp]\!]\\
\mathcal{P}[\![t\text{-}exp]\!] &:= \mathcal{E}[\![t\text{-}exp]\!]\\
\mathcal{P}[\![t\text{-}exp/exp]\!] &:= \{\langle x, y, I_1 \cap I_2\rangle \mid \exists \langle x, z, I_1\rangle \in \mathcal{E}[\![t\text{-}exp]\!], \exists \langle z, y, I_2\rangle \in \mathcal{E}[\![exp]\!] \text{ and}\\
&\qquad I_1 \cap I_2 \neq \emptyset\}\\
\mathcal{P}[\![e\text{-}exp/exp]\!] &:= \{\langle x, y, I_1\rangle \mid \exists \langle x, z, I_1\rangle \in \mathcal{E}[\![e\text{-}exp]\!], \exists \langle z, y, I_2\rangle \in \mathcal{E}[\![exp]\!]\}\\
\mathcal{P}[\![exp_1|exp_2]\!] &:= \mathcal{E}[\![exp_1|exp_2]\!]\\
\mathcal{P}[\![exp^*]\!] &:= \mathcal{E}[\![exp^*]\!]
\end{aligned}
$$

$$
\begin{aligned}
t\text{-}exp &\in \{\textbf{t-axis}, \textbf{t-axis}::r, \textbf{t-axis}::[exp], \textbf{t-axis}[I]\}\\
e\text{-}exp &\in \{\textbf{e-axis}, \textbf{e-axis}::[exp], \textbf{e-axis}[I], \textbf{forward}, \textbf{backward}\}
\end{aligned}
$$

Fig. 3. Formal semantics of nested evolution expressions

$\langle$Germany, Chancellor, $[1988, 2005]\rangle$. It is also possible to navigate an edge from a node using the **edge** axis and to have a nested expression $[exp]$ that functions as a predicate which the preceding expression must satisfy. For example, $\mathcal{E}[\![\textbf{self}[\textbf{next}::\text{head}/\textbf{self}::\text{Gerhard Schröder}]]\!]$ returns $\langle$Reunified Germany, Reunified Germany, $[1990, 2005]\rangle$ and $\langle$West Germany, West Germany, $[1988, 1990]\rangle$.

In order to support evolution expressions, we need to extend nSPARQL triple patterns with temporal and evolution semantics. In particular, we redefine the evaluation of an nSPARQL triple pattern $(?X, exp, ?Y)$ to be the set of triples $\langle x, y, I\rangle$ that result

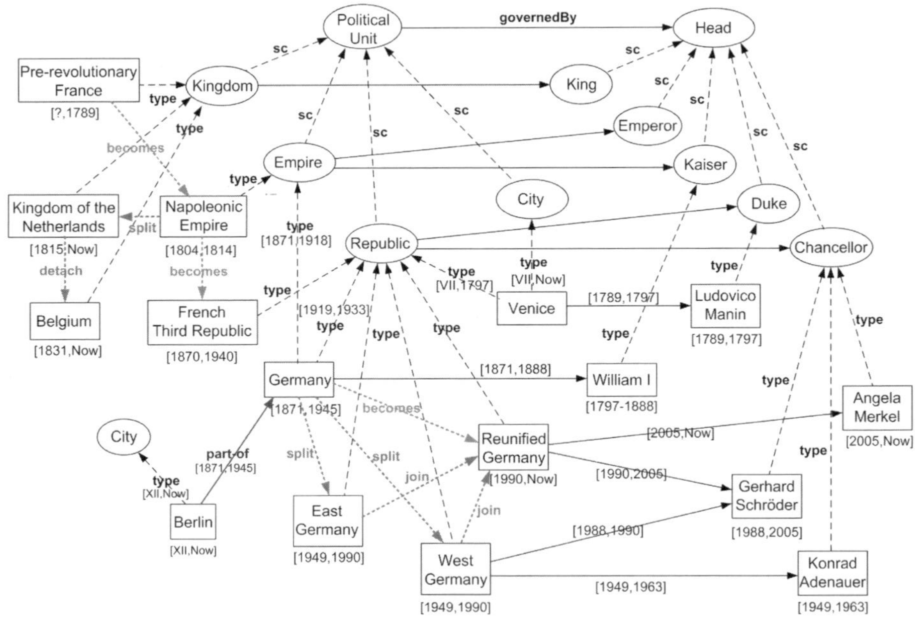

Fig. 4. The evolution of the concepts of Germany and France and their governments (full black lines represent governedBy properties)

from the evaluation of the evolution expression exp, with the variables X and Y bound to x and y, respectively. In particular:

$$\mathcal{E}[\![(?X, exp, ?Y)]\!] := \{(\theta(?X), \theta(?Y)) \mid \theta(?X) = x \text{ and } \theta(?Y) = y \text{ and } \langle x, y, I\rangle \in \mathcal{E}[\![exp]\!]\}$$

Our language includes all nSPARQL operators such as AND, OPT, UNION and FILTER with the same semantics as in nSPARQL. For instance:

$$\mathcal{E}[\![(P_1 \text{ AND } P_2)]\!] := \mathcal{E}[\![(P_1)]\!] \bowtie \mathcal{E}[\![(P_2)]\!]$$

where P_1 and P_2 are triple patterns and $\bowtie$ is the join on the variables P_1 and P_2 have in common. A complete list of all the nSPARQL operators and their semantics can be found in [17].

6 Application Scenarios

Consider an evolution base that models how countries have changed over time in terms of territory, political division, type of government, etc. Classes are represented by ovals and instances by boxes. A small fragment of that evolution base is illustrated as a graph in Figure 4.

Germany is a concept that has changed several times along history. The country was unified as a nation-state in 1871 and the concept of Germany first appears in our historical knowledge base as Germany at instant 1871. After WWII, Germany was divided into four military zones (not shown in the figure) that were merged into West and East

Germany in 1949. This is represented with two split edges from the concept of Germany to the concepts of West Germany and East Germany. The country was finally reunified in 1990, which is represented by the coalescence of the West Germany and East Germany concepts into Unified Germany via two merge edges. These merge and split constructs are also defined in terms of the parts of the concepts they relate. For instance, a part-of property indicates that Berlin was part of Germany during $[1871, 1945]$. Since that concept of Germany existed until 1945 whereas Berlin exists until today, the part-of relation is carried forward by the semantics of split and merge into the concept of Reunified Germany. Consider now a historian who is interested in finding answers to a number of evolution-related queries.

[Example Query 1]: How has the notion of Germany changed over the last two centuries in terms of its constituents, government, etc.? The query can be expressed in our extended query language as follows:

$$\begin{array}{l}\mathbf{Select}\ ?Y, ?Z, ?W\\ (?X, \mathbf{self}::\text{Reunified Germany}/\mathbf{backward}^*[1800, 2000]/, ?Y)\ \text{AND}\\ (?Y, \mathbf{edge}, ?Z)\ \text{AND}\ (?Z, \mathbf{edge}, ?W)\end{array}$$

The query first binds $?X$ to Reunified Germany and then follows all possible evolution axes backwards in the period $[1800, 2000]$. All concepts bound to $?Y$ are in an evolution path to Reunified Germany, namely Germany, West Germany, and East Germany. Note that, since the semantics of an * expression includes **self** (see Figure 3), then Reunified Germany will also bind $?Y$. The second triple returns in $?Z$ the name of the properties of which $?Y$ is the subject, and finally the last triple returns in $?W$ the objects of those properties. By selecting $?Y, ?Z, ?W$ in the head of the query, we get all evolutions of Germany together with their properties.

[Example Query 2]: Who was the head of the German government before and after the unification of 1990? The query can be expressed as follows:

$$\begin{array}{l}\mathbf{Select}\ ?Y\\ (?X, \mathbf{self}::\text{Reunified Germany}/\mathbf{join}^{-1}[1990]/\mathbf{next}::\text{head}[1990], ?Y)\ \text{AND}\\ (?Z, \mathbf{self}::\text{Reunified Germany}/\mathbf{next}::\text{head}[1990], ?Y)\end{array}$$

The first triple finds all the heads of state of the Reunified Germany before the unification by following $\mathbf{join}^{-1}[1990]$ and then following $\mathbf{next}::\text{head}[1990]$. The second triple finds the heads of state of the Reunified Germany. Finally, the join on $?Y$ will bind the variable only to those heads of state that are the same in both triples, hence returning the one before and after the mentioned unification.

Consider now the evolution of the concept of biotechnology from a historical point of view. According to historians, biotechnology got its current meaning (related to molecular biology) only after the 70s. Before that, the term biotechnology was used in areas as diverse as agriculture, microbiology, and enzyme-based fermentation. Even though the term "biotechnology" was coined in 1919 by Karl Ereky, a Hungarian engineer, the earliest mentions of biotechnology in the news and specialized media refer to a set of ancient techniques like selective breeding, fermentation and hybridization. From the 70s the dominant meaning of biotechnology has been closely related to genetics.

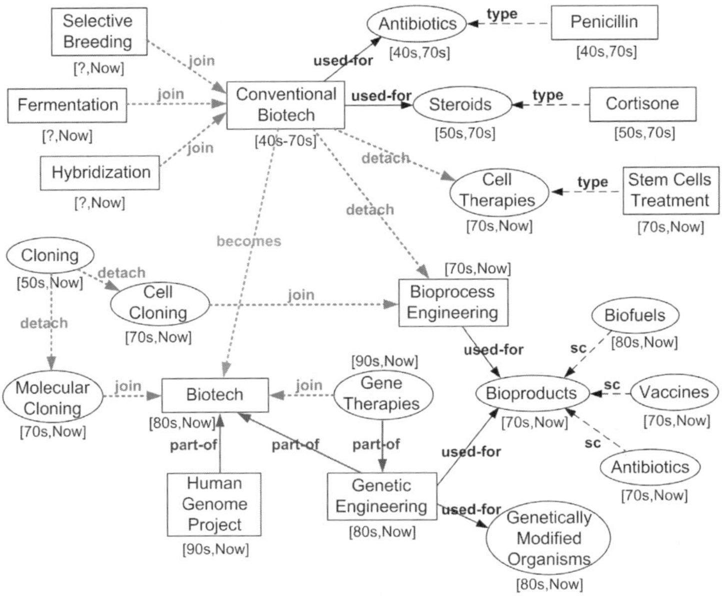

Fig. 5. The evolution of the concept of Biotechnology

However, it is possible to find news and other media articles from the 60s to the 80s that use the term biotechnology to refer to an environmentally friendly technological orientation unrelated to genetics but closely related to bioprocess engineering. Not only the use of the term changed from the 60s to the 90s, but also the two different meanings coexisted in the media for almost two decades.

Figure 5 illustrates the evolution of the notion of biotechnology since the 40s. As in the previous example, classes in the evolution base are represented by ovals and instances by boxes. The used-for property is a normal property that simply links a technological concept to its products. The notions of Selective breeding, Fermentation and Hybridization existed from an indeterminate time until now and in the 40s joined the new topic of Conventional Biotech, which groups ancient techniques like the ones mentioned above. Over the next decades, Conventional Biotech started to include more modern therapies and products such as Cell Therapies, Penicillin and Cortisone. At some point in the 70s, the notions of Cell Therapies and Bioprocess Engineering matured and detached from Conventional Biotech becoming independent concepts. Note that Cell Therapies is a class-level concept that detached from the an instance-level concept. The three concepts coexisted in time during part of the 70s, the latter two coexist even now. During the 70s, the notion of Conventional Biotech stopped being used and all its related concepts became independent topics. In parallel to this, the new topic of Biotech started to take shape. We could see Biotech as an evolution of the former Conventional Biotech but using Genetic Engineering instead of conventional techniques. Concepts and terms related to the Biotech and Genetic Engineering topics are modeled with a part-of property. In parallel to this, the concept of Cloning techniques started to appear in the 50s, from which the specialized notions of Cell Cloning and Molecular Cloning techniques detached in the 70s and joined the notions of Bioprocess Engineering and Biotech, respectively. This latter is an example of class-level concepts joining instance-level concepts.

[Example Query 3]: Is the academic discipline of biotechnology a wholly new technology branch or has it derived from the combination of other disciplines? Which ones and how? The query requires to follow evolution paths and return the traversed triples in addition to the nodes in order to answer the question of "how". The query is expressed in our language as follows:

$$\begin{array}{l}\textbf{Select } ?Y, ?Z, ?W \\ (?X, \textbf{self}::\text{Biotechnology}/\textbf{backward}^*, ?Y) \text{ AND} \\ (?Y, \textbf{e-edge}/\textbf{self}, ?Z) \text{ AND } (?Z, \textbf{e-node}, ?W)\end{array}$$

The first triple binds $?Y$ to every node reachable from Biotechnology following evolution edges backwards. Then, for each of those nodes, including Biotechnology, the second triple gets all the evolution axes of which the bindings of $?Y$ are subjects whereas the third triple get the objects of the evolution axes. This query returns, (Biotech, $\mathbf{becomes}^{-1}$, Conventional Biotech), (Conventional Biotech, $\mathbf{join}^{-1}$, Hybridization), (Conventional Biotech, $\mathbf{join}^{-1}$, Fermentation), and (Conventional Biotech, $\mathbf{join}^{-1}$, Selective Breeding).

[Example Query 4]: Which scientific and engineering concepts and disciplines are related to the emergence of cell cloning? We interpret "related" in our model as being immediate predecessors/successors and "siblings" in the evolution process. That is, from a concept we first find its immediate predecessors by following all evolution edges backwards one step. We then follow from the result all evolution edges forward on step and we get the original concept and some of its "siblings". Finally, we repeat the same process in the opposite direction following evolution edges one step, first forward and then backwards. Based on this notion, we can express the query as follows:

$$\begin{array}{l}\textbf{Select } ?Y, ?Z, ?W \\ (?X, \textbf{self}::\text{Cell Cloning}, ?Y) \text{ AND } ?(Y, \textbf{backward} \mid \textbf{backward}/\textbf{forward}, ?Z) \\ \text{AND } (?Y, \textbf{forward} \mid \textbf{forward}/\textbf{backward}, ?W)\end{array}$$

The first triple will just bind Cell Cloning to $?Y$. The second triple follows the **detach** edge back to Cloning, and then the **detach** edge forward to Molecular Cloning. The third triple starts again from Cell Cloning and follows the **join** edge forward to Bioprocess Engineering and then the detach edge backwards to Conventional Biotech. All these concepts will be returned by the query.

7 Related Work

Managing Time in Databases: Temporal data management has been extensively studied in the relational paradigm [5]. For semi-structured data, one of the first models for managing historical information as an extension of the Object Exchange Model (OEM) was introduced in [7]. A versioning scheme for XML was first proposed in [18].

Versioning approaches store the information of the entire document at some point in time and then use edit scripts and change logs to reconstruct versions of the entire document. In contrast, [19] and [8] maintain a single temporal document from which versions of any document fragment (even single elements) can be extracted directly when needed. A survey on temporal extensions to the Entity-Relationship (ER) model is presented in [6].

Change Management in Ontologies: There is a fundamental distinction between an actual update and a revision in knowledge bases [20]. An update brings the knowledge base up to date when the world it models has changed. Our evolution framework models updates since it describes how real-world concepts have changed over time. In contrast, a revision incorporates new knowledge from a world that has not changed. An approach to model revision in RDF ontologies has been presented in [21]. The survey in [22] provides a thorough classification of the types of changes that occur in ontologies. However, there is no entry in their taxonomy that corresponds to the kind of concept evolution we developed in this work; in fact, they view evolution as a special case of versioning. Similarly to versioning in databases, ontology versioning study the problem of maintaining changes in ontologies by creating and managing different variants of it [23]. Highly related, yet different, to concept evolution is the problem of terminology evolution that studies how terms describing the same notion in a domain of discourse are changing over time [12]. Closer to our work is the proposal in [24] for modeling changes in geographical information systems (GIS). They use the notion of a change bridge to model how the area of geographical entities (countries, provinces, etc.) evolve. A change bridge is associated with a change point and indicates what concepts become obsolete, what new concepts are created, and how the new concepts overlap with older ones. Since they focus on the GIS domain, they are not able to model causality and types of evolution involving abstract concepts beyond geographical entities.

8 Conclusion

In this work we studied the novel problem of concept evolution, i.e., how the semantics of an entity changes over time. In contrast to temporal models and schema evolution, concept evolution deals with mereological and causal relationships between concepts. Recording concept evolution also allows users to pose queries on the history of a concept. We presented a framework for modeling evolution as an extension of temporal RDF with mereology and causal properties expressed with a set of evolution terms. Furthermore, we presented an extension of nSPARQL that allows navigation over the history of the concepts. Finally, we applied our framework in two real world scenarios, the history of Germany and the evolution of biotechnology, and we showed how queries of interest can be answered using our proposed language.

Acknowledgments. The current work has been partially supported by the EU grants GA-215032 and ICT-215874.

References

1. Parsons, J., Wand, Y.: Emancipating instances from the tyranny of classes in information modeling. ACM Trans. Database Syst. 25(2), 228–268 (2000)
2. Blakeley, J., Larson, P.A., Tompa, F.W.: Efficiently Updating Materialized Views. In: SIGMOD, pp. 61–71 (1986)
3. Lerner, B.S.: A Model for Compound Type Changes Encountered in Schema Evolution. ACM Trans. Database Syst. 25(1), 83–127 (2000)
4. Velegrakis, Y., Miller, R.J., Popa, L.: Preserving mapping consistency under schema changes. VLDB J. 13(3), 274–293 (2004)
5. Soo, M.D.: Bibliography on Temporal Databases. sigmodrec 20(1), 14–23 (1991)
6. Gregersen, H., Jensen, C.S.: Temporal Entity-Relationship models - a survey. IEEE Trans. Knowl. Data Eng. 11(3), 464–497 (1999)
7. Chawathe, S., Abiteboul, S., Widom, J.: Managing historical semistructured data. Theory and Practice of Object 5(3), 143–162 (1999)
8. Rizzolo, F., Vaisman, A.A.: Temporal XML: modeling, indexing, and query processing. vldbj 17(5), 1179–1212 (2008)
9. Gutiérrez, C., Hurtado, C.A., Vaisman, A.A.: Temporal RDF. In: ESWC, pp. 93–107 (2005)
10. Dong, X., Halevy, A.Y., Madhavan, J.: Reference Reconciliation in Complex Information Spaces. In: SIGMOD, pp. 85–96 (2005)
11. Palpanas, T., Chaudhry, J., Andritsos, P., Velegrakis, Y.: Entity Data Management in OKKAM. In: SWAP, pp. 729–733 (2008)
12. Tahmasebi, N., Iofciu, T., Risse, T., Niederee, C., Siberski, W.: Terminology evolution in web archiving: Open issues. In: International Web Archiving Workshop (2008)
13. Lenzerini, M.: Data Integration: A Theoretical Perspective. In: PODS, pp. 233–246 (2002)
14. W3C: RDF vocabulary description language 1.0: RDF Schema (2004), `http://www.w3.org/TR/rdf-schema/`
15. Dyreson, C.E., Evans, W.S., Lin, H., Snodgrass, R.T.: Efficiently supported temporal granularities. IEEE Trans. Knowl. Data Eng. 12(4), 568–587 (2000)
16. Keet, C.M., Artale, A.: Representing and reasoning over a taxonomy of part-whole relations. Applied Ontology 3(1-2), 91–110 (2008)
17. Pérez, J., Arenas, M., Gutierrez, C.: nSPARQL: A navigational language for RDF. In: ISWC, pp. 66–81 (2008)
18. Chien, S., Tsotras, V., Zaniolo, C.: Efficient management of multiversion documents by object referencing. In: VLDB, pp. 291–300 (2001)
19. Buneman, P., Khanna, S., Tajima, K., Tan, W.: Archiving scientific data. In: SIGMOD, pp. 1–12 (2002)
20. Katsuno, H., Mendelzon, A.O.: On the difference between updating a knowledge base and revising it. In: KR, pp. 387–394 (1991)
21. Konstantinidis, G., Flouris, G., Antoniou, G., Christophides, V.: On RDF/S ontology evolution. In: SWDB-ODBIS, pp. 21–42 (2007)
22. Flouris, G., Manakanatas, D., Kondylakis, H., Plexousakis, D., Antoniou, G.: Ontology change: classification and survey. Knowledge Eng. Review 23(2), 117–152 (2008)
23. Klein, M.C.A., Fensel, D.: Ontology versioning on the semantic web. In: SWWS, pp. 75–91 (2001)
24. Kauppinen, T., Hyvönen, E.: Modeling and reasoning about changes in ontology time series. In: Ontologies: A Handbook of Principles, Concepts and Applications in Information Systems, pp. 319–338 (2007)

FOCIH: Form-Based Ontology Creation and Information Harvesting

Cui Tao[1,⋆], David W. Embley[1,⋆], and Stephen W. Liddle[2]

[1] Department of Computer Science
[2] Information Systems Department
Brigham Young University, Provo, Utah 84602, U.S.A.

Abstract. Creating an ontology and populating it with data are both labor-intensive tasks requiring a high degree of expertise. Thus, scaling ontology creation and population to the size of the web in an effort to create a web of data—which some see as Web 3.0—is prohibitive. Can we find ways to streamline these tasks and lower the barrier enough to enable Web 3.0? Toward this end we offer a form-based approach to ontology creation that provides a way to create Web 3.0 ontologies without the need for specialized training. And we offer a way to semi-automatically harvest data from the current web of pages for a Web 3.0 ontology. In addition to harvesting information with respect to an ontology, the approach also annotates web pages and links facts in web pages to ontological concepts, resulting in a web of data superimposed over the web of pages. Experience with our prototype system shows that mappings between conceptual-model-based ontologies and forms are sufficient for creating the kind of ontologies needed for Web 3.0, and experiments with our prototype system show that automatic harvesting, automatic annotation, and automatic superimposition of a web of data over a web of pages work well.

Keywords: ontology generation from forms, information harvesting from the web, automatic annotation of web pages, web of data, Web 3.0.

1 Introduction

Many see the next generation web (Web 3.0) as a web of data in which users query for facts directly rather than use search engines to find pages that contain facts. A major impediment to this Web 3.0 vision is content creation. Creating the required ontologies and populating them with data yields a web of data, but both ontology creation and ontology population are human-intensive tasks requiring a high degree of expertise.

To alleviate this problem, researchers are developing ways to make Web 3.0 creation "human scalable." Typifying this desire, the *Journal of Web Semantics* recently called for papers on "human-scalable and user-friendly tools that open the Web of Data to the current Web user." Efforts to create user-friendly,

⋆ Supported in part by the National Science Foundation under Grant #0414644.

A.H.F. Laender et al. (Eds.): ER 2009, LNCS 5829, pp. 346–359, 2009.

web-scalable tools are on the agenda of many research labs around the world. Researchers are interested both in easing the burden of ontology creation and in automatic semantic annotation:

- With regard to easing the burden of manual ontology creation (e.g., via Protege [17] or OntoWeb [21]), researchers are developing semi-automatic ontology generation tools. Tools such as OntoLT [5], Text2Onto [7], OntoLearn [16], and KASO [26] use machine learning methods to generate an ontology from natural-language text. These tools usually require a large training corpus, and, so far, the results are not very satisfactory [18]. Tools such as OntoBuilder [9], TANGO [24], and the ones developed by Pivk et al. [18] and Benslimane et al. [4] use structured information (HTML tables and forms) as a source for learning ontologies. Structured information makes it easier to interpret new items and relations. These approaches, however, derive concepts and relationships among concepts from source data, not from users, and thus do not provide the control some users need to express the ontological world-views they desire.
- With regard to enabling automatic annotation, typical approaches (e.g., [2,11,15,25]) base their work on information extraction [19]. Post-extraction alignment with ontologies, however, is their main drawback [11]. A way to overcome this drawback is through "extraction ontologies"—ontologies with data recognizers that are able to directly and automatically extract and thus annotate data with respect to specified ontologies (e.g., [8,12,13]). Extraction ontologies, however, rely on human expertise to manually create, assemble, and tune reference sets and data recognizers, thus creating a significant human-scalability problem. In another direction that tends to overcome both the alignment drawback and the manual-creation drawback, researchers propose structuring unstructured data for query purposes [6] or doing "best-effort" information extraction [20]. These approaches, however, yield less precise results both for the ontological structure of the data and for the annotation of the data with respect to the ontological structure.

We created FOCIH (Form-based Ontology Creation and Information Harvesting, pronounced *foh*·sī) to (1) ease the burden of manual ontology creation while still giving users control over ontological views; and (2) enable automatic annotation that aligns with user-specified ontologies, does not require manual creation of extraction ontologies, and is precise. The aim is to facilitate semi-automatic construction of a web of data. The form-based part of the FOCIH name emphasizes the means by which a user creates an ontology—namely by creating a form. By "form" we do not mean an HTML form in particular, but rather the concept of a form like the kind people use every day, with labels and spaces for information to be written. The information-harvesting part of the name emphasizes FOCIH's ability to harvest information by automatically filling in the form for each page in a web site containing machine-generated display pages (usually hidden-web-site pages). FOCIH provides for semi-automatically annotating information according to any view users want—thus opening a pathway to the envisioned Web 3.0.

We present the details of these contributions as follows. Section 2 describes how users create forms and annotate a sample page by filling in the form. Section 3 explains how FOCIH generates ontologies based on user-created forms. Section 4 discusses path and instance recognition which allows FOCIH to automatically harvest and annotate information with respect to the created form and thus semantically annotate web pages with respect to the ontology generated from the form. Section 5 describes our experiences with our prototype, including experimental performance measurements. Section 6 presents current and future work: reverse-engineering tables and ontologies for FOCIH form initialization; initial population of FOCIH forms using information-extraction ontologies; and synergistic creation of information-extraction ontologies—all in an effort to further reduce, and in some cases entirely eliminate, the work required of the knowledge worker. In Section 7, we make concluding remarks about FOCIH and tie in the work presented here with a vision of how to create Web 3.0—a vision of how to automatically superimposition of a web of data over a web of pages.

2 Form Creation and Annotation

The FOCIH GUI has two modes of operation: form creation and form annotation. Form creation allows users to create forms in accord with how they wish to organize their information. Form annotation allows users to annotate pages with respect to created forms. We use the form about countries and the web page for the Czech Republic in Figure 1 as a running example. The screen shot in Figure 1 shows the running example at the end of the form-annotation mode.

FOCIH has five basic form elements from which users can choose: *single-label/single-value element* ( ), *single-label/multiple-value element* ( ), *multiple-label/multiple-value element* ( ), *mutually-exclusive choice element* ( ),

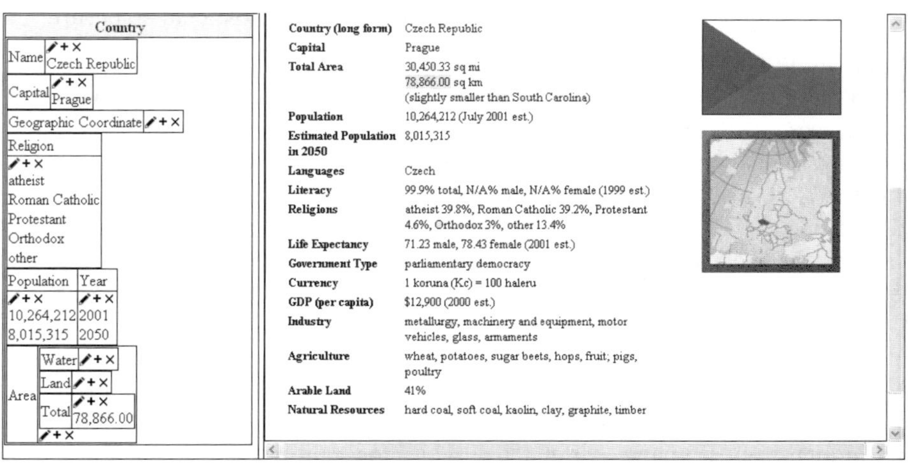

Fig. 1. A Filled-in Form with a Source Data Page

and *non-exclusive choice element* ( ). A user begins with an empty base form with only a place for a form title and icons ( ) for each of the form elements. The user can edit the title; Figure 1 shows that the user has chosen *Country* as the title for the form. Clicking on a form-element icon causes the element to appear. The user then has control to edit form labels.

Thus, for the single-label/single-value elements in Figure 1, the user has clicked on the single-label/single-value icon ( ) and has then labeled the form element *Name*, and has again clicked on the icon and labeled the form element *Capital*, and again for *Geographic Coordinate*. (At this point in form creation, the form fields in the elements would still be empty as is *Geographic Coordinate* field in Figure 1.)

For the single-label/multiple-value element in Figure 1, the user has clicked on the single-label/multiple-value icon ( ) and has labeled the element *Religion*. Multiple-label/multiple-value elements are similar except that they have multiple columns. The user can expand/contract the number of columns as desired. In Figure 1, the user has created a multiple-label/multiple-value element with two columns, *Population* and *Year*.

Area in Figure 1 illustrates the possibility of nesting form elements inside one another. *Area* is a single-label/single-value form element. Nested within it, the user has nested a form with three single-label/single-value form elements: *Water*, *Land*, and *Total*. In general, users can nest an entire form inside any other form element. The nesting can continue to any depth.

Choice elements, which we do not illustrate in this example, let users specify decompositions of concepts. Informally, we can think of choice elements like check boxes or radio buttons in typical user interfaces. A radio button indicates mutually-exclusive values in the decomposition, whereas check boxes admit multiple overlapping values.

Users annotate a page from a web site with respect to a created form by filling in the form. For example, to annotate the string "Prague" as the *Capital* of the Czech Republic, a user drags the mouse cursor over "Prague" to highlight it in the source and then clicks on the pencil icon ( ) in the single-entry *Capital* field. FOCIH adds 'Prague" to the form field under *Capital* as Figure 1 shows.

The user can add multiple values in a multiple-value element by highlighting and adding each, one by one. The user must be careful to put related values in the same row for multiple-column form elements. For example, the user must put *Population* 10,264,212 and *Year* 2001 in the same row as Figure 1 shows.

The user can also concatenate two or more highlighted values to form a single value in the form. After placing the first value in a form field, the user highlights the second (third, ...) and clicks on the plus icon ( ) rather than the pencil icon. For example, suppose a web site displays *Geographic Coordinate* information by listing longitude and latitude separately, but the user wants them combined into a single compound value. The user would first enter the longitude value in the *Geographic Coordinate* field in the usual way and then highlight the latitude value and click on the plus icon (rather than on the pencil icon) in the *Geographic Coordinate* field.

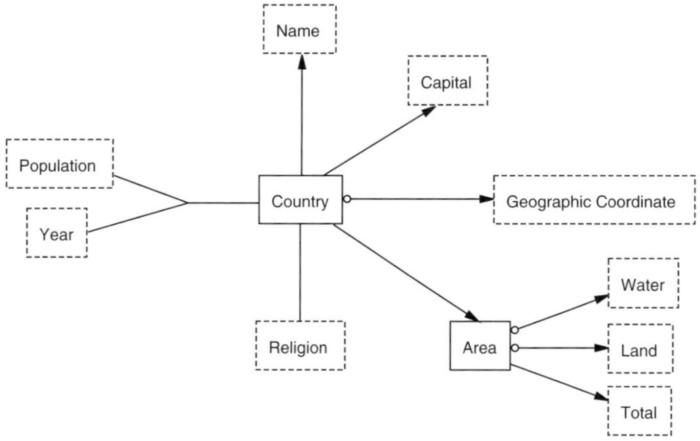

Fig. 2. Graphical View of a Sample Ontology

3 Ontology Generation

From a created form, FOCIH can infer and generate an ontology. Figure 2 shows a generated ontology for the form in Figure 1. We use OSM [8] as the conceptual-model basis for an extraction ontology. The advantage of OSM is that it has a high-level graphical representation that directly translates to predicate calculus. Thus, when appropriately limited, it translates in a straightforward way to OWL and to various description logics [3]. Even more important, however, is OSM's ability to support data extraction from source documents [8].

Based on the form title, FOCIH generates a non-lexical concept with this title as the name. Thus, for the form in Figure 1, FOCIH generates the concept *Country* with a solid box as Figure 2 shows. Every label in the form also represents a concept in the corresponding ontology; the label is the name for the concept. Form concepts with nested components become non-lexical object sets. Thus, *Area* is non-lexical. Form concepts without nested components become lexical object sets. Thus, the remaining concepts are all lexical, represented by dashed boxes.

FOCIH generates relationship sets[1] among the concepts as follows.

Single-label/single-value form elements. Between the form-title concept T and each top-level single-label/single-value form element S, FOCIH generates a functional binary relationship set from T to S. Thus, FOCIH generates functional relationship sets from *Country* to *Name*, *Capital*, *Geographic Coordinate*, and *Area* respectively as Figure 2 shows. Similarly, between each form element E and a single-label/single-value form element S nested inside E, FOCIH also generates a functional binary relationship set from E to S. Thus, FOCIH generates functional relationships from *Area* to *Water*, *Land*, and *Total* respectively.

[1] Lines connecting concepts denote relationship sets. Arrowheads on lines denote functional relationship sets from tail-side concepts to head-side concepts.

Single-label/multiple-value form elements. Between each form-title concept T and each single-label/multiple-value concept M, FOCIH generates a non-functional binary relationship set between T and M. Thus FOCIH accommodates the possibly many *Religions* for each *Country* as Figure 2 shows. Although our running example has no nested single-value/multiple-value form elements, FOCIH also creates non-functional binary relationship sets between a parent form element and each nested child single-label/multiple-value form element.

Multiple-label/multiple-value form elements. Between the form-title concept and each multiple-label form element as well as between each form element and a multiple-label concept nested within it, FOCIH generates either an n-ary relationship set or a set of binary relationship sets. If the multiple-label element is the only element in the form or the only element nested under another form element, FOCIH generates a set of binary relationship sets between the form-title concept and each of the concepts in the multiple-label element; otherwise FOCIH generates an n-ary relationship set. Thus, FOCIH generates an n-ary relationship set among *Country*, *Population*, and *Year* since the *Population-Year* element does not stand by itself as the only form element in the *Country* form.

Choice form elements. FOCIH generates a non-functional binary relationship set between the form-title concept and a top-level choice form element. For both mutually-exclusive and non-exclusive choice elements, FOCIH generates a generalization/specialization (an is-a relationship among concepts) with the header label as the generalization concept and each of the labels on the choice list as specialization concepts. Nesting choice form elements within choice elements extends the generalization/specialization hierarchy.

Although FOCIH is able to generate all concepts, relationship sets, and generalization/specialization hierarchies, it can generate only some of the constraints that may be desirable. FOCIH knows that relationship-set constraints from parent content to child concept should be functional when the child concept is a single-label/single-value element. From a form specification alone, however, FOCIH is not able to determine whether the inverse direction of a binary relationship set is functional. Names of countries, for example, might be unique and therefore functionally determine countries. In these cases, FOCIH initially imposes no constraints. Thus, in Figure 2, the *Name-Country* relationship set is not bijective. FOCIH, however, can later modify constraints based on observations as it harvests information from source documents. The non-mandatory constraints on the three relationship sets in Figure 2 appear because FOCIH observes that the first page from which it harvests information (i.e., the page in Figure 1) has no *Geographic Coordinate*, no *Water* area, and no *Land* area.

4 Automatic Semantic Annotation

Although users fill in a form manually, they only need to do this once for a single page from a site like the web site for the page in Figure 1 in which each of the many pages is machine-generated. To harvest and annotate information from the remaining pages, FOCIH determines the layout pattern for instance values in the first page and uses these patterns to extract instance values from remaining pages. To succeed FOCIH must (1) identify paths in HTML DOM trees leading to nodes that contain instance values and (2) identify the substrings in DOM-tree nodes that represent the instance values.

Machine-generated web pages are *sibling pages*–pages with the same regular structure. Thus, we can usually locate corresponding DOM-tree nodes by following the same XPath from root to node. While harvesting information, FOCIH may encounter minor variations in the XPaths. If so, it adjusts by recording the variations and then searching for DOM-tree nodes in the remaining pages with any of the node's XPath variants.

A user-highlighted value can be the entire DOM-tree node (e.g, "Prague" in Figure 1) or a proper subpart of the string that constitutes the DOM-tree node (e.g., just the populated value in Figure 1). For proper substrings within a node, FOCIH needs to know how to find the correct subpart within a DOM-tree node. Moreover, since a value can be composed of one or more highlighted values from one or more DOM-tree nodes (e.g., when longitude and latitude are in separate DOM-tree nodes), FOCIH needs to know how to compose values from different substrings of different nodes from the source page.

Considering these possibilities, we observe that there are two kinds of patterns: (1) individual patterns for entire strings, proper substrings, and string components, and (2) list patterns. Particularly for list patterns, but also as context for individual patterns, FOCIH has a default list of delimiters: ",", ";", ":", "|", " /", "\", "(", ")", "[", "]", "{", "}", *sos* (start of string) and *eos* (end of string). FOCIH also has a library of regular-expression recognizers for values in common formats, such as numbers, numbers with commas, decimal numbers, positive/negative integers, percentages, dates, times, and currencies [8].

- An *individual pattern* has left and right contexts and a regular-expression instance recognizer. For example, for the highlighted area value "78,866.00", the left context can be "\bsq\s*mi\s*" (word boundary with "sq" and "mi" surrounded by zero or more whitespace characters), the right context can be "\s*sq\s*km$" ("sq" and "km" surrounded by whitespace characters and then end of string), and the instance recognizer can be decimal number.
- A *list pattern* has a left context, a right context, a regular-expression instance recognizer, and a delimiter. The list of agriculture products in Figure 1 could have as its left context *sos*, as its right context *eos*, as its instance recognizer "\b([a-z]\s*)+\b" (any lower-case word or words), and as its delimiter "(,\s*)|(;\s*)" (either a comma-space or a semicolon-space).

We now explain how FOCIH detects and establishes patterns. FOCIH first determines whether a pattern is an individual pattern or a list pattern. Given a DOM-tree node and all its highlighted values, FOCIH groups the highlighted values that go to the same form entry together. If only one highlighted value from a node goes to a form entry, FOCIH establishes an individual pattern; and if several go to a form entry, FOCIH establishes a list pattern.

Secondly, for both individual and list patterns, FOCIH determines the context information. To determine the left or the right context of a highlighted value in a DOM-tree node, FOCIH initially takes the substring that is on the left or on the right of the highlighted substring until it reaches other highlighted values or the beginning or the end of the whole node string. FOCIH can further generalize the context in two ways. (1) If some of the context is recognizable as an instance of one of the regular-expression recognizers, FOCIH substitutes the recognized substring in the context by the recognizer. (2) FOCIH can generalize the context information when it sees more sibling-node contents during its harvesting phase of operation. Sometimes FOCIH cannot locate the context information in a newly encountered sibling page. This usually means that the initial context from the original sample page is too specific. FOCIH then tries to generalize the context by comparing context strings with the pattern and allowing non-delimiter characters that differ to be replaced by an expression that permits any characters.

Thirdly, for both individual and list patterns, FOCIH determines the regular expression pattern of the substrings of interest. If a highlighted substring can be recognized by a regular-expression recognizer in our library, FOCIH uses it as the instance recognizer for the pattern. If not, then the instance recognizer is an expression that recognizes any string. In this case, proper recognition depends on the left and right context, and for lists also the delimiter.

Finally, for list patterns, FOCIH compares the substrings between highlighted values to find delimiters. Looking particularly for delimiters in our list of delimiters, FOCIH attempts to identify a simple delimiter-separated list. It then constructs a regular expression for the delimiter. The agriculture list in Figure 1 is an example. For this list FOCIH creates the delimiter expression "[,;]\s*". For more complex cases such as the religions list in Figure 1, the list separator can include commentary or other values. In the religions list a percentage plus a comma and space separate the names of the religions, and the delimiter expression should be "\s*\d+(.\d+)?%,\s*". FOCIH generates this delimiter expression by (1) discovering that the percentage recognizer in the library recognizes part of every substring between highlighted values, (2) observing that a comma follows every percentage, and (3) noticing that the combination of the percentage and the comma covers the intervening substrings. In general, FOCIH checks library instance recognizers and standard delimiters to see if they cover intervening substrings; and when this is insufficient, FOCIH adds general character recognizers to cover the intervening substrings.

With path recognition and instance recognition in place, FOCIH can locate the information of interest from all the sibling pages in a site and appropriately associate each item of information with the generated ontology. FOCIH can thus semantically annotate each page in the site. In our implementation, FOCIH annotates each page and saves the annotated information in an RDF file. The information saved not only identifies each item of information and links it to a concept in the ontology, but also records its location on the page. Thus, we are able to superimpose a web of data (the RDF files) over a web of pages and produce—at least as a research prototype—the envisioned Web 3.0.[2]

[2] For a full explanation of how we store the RDF files, link them to web pages, and query them either with SPARQL or our free-form query processor, see [23].

5 Experimental Results

Correctly generating ontologies for user-created forms is not difficult. How well FOCIH can automatically harvest and annotate information from sibling pages with respect to generated ontologies depends on how uniform the pages are. As an indication of what might be expected, we tested FOCIHs ability to do instance recognition by considering a number of different web pages.

We examined FOCIH's performance harvesting information from a collection of web pages about countries. For our experiment, we restricted our attention to 40 European country pages like the Czech Republic page in Figure 1. Starting with a human-created annotation for Germany, we ran FOCIH over the 40 pages, with the following results. For fields where the entire target node was the desired value (such as the country's official name or its capital), precision and recall were 100%. Several fields, such as the country's area or its population in a given year (the second of the population/year pairs in our test sample), required extraction from a proper subpart of the text of the target node. For the country's area, which was bounded on the left by the string "sq mi" and on the right by the string "sq km", precision and recall were 100%. For population as of a given year, precision was 100% for all values and recall ranged between 95% and 100%. But with a few additional annotation examples, recall rose to 100%.[3] Precision and recall were also 100% for lists of agricultural products. These 100% results are due to the regularity of the set of country pages.

As expected, the FOCIH prototype is less accurate on less regular elements. For example, the religions list exhibited significant variety from one page to the next. From our seed annotation of the Germany country page, the inferred list pattern was able to extract only about two thirds of the religion data correctly. When we added alternate annotation patterns, which FOCIH derived from other seed pages, precision rose to 95% while recall rose to 96%. A more sophisticated generalizing recognizer, which we are developing, should achieve even better precision and recall.

In principle, FOCIH is always able to achieve 100% precision and recall, since the user can always fix every partial or incorrect annotation. However we want to avoid human dependency as much as possible in order to achive greater scalability. Thus, FOCIH has three modes of operation: (1) fully automatic, (2) verify each annotation, and (3) verify only when FOCIH suspects it may be in error. When the tool operates interactively (Modes 2 and 3), users may adjust the automatically extracted annotations to further train the harvester. Currently, our prototype implements only the first mode, but even now users can choose different initial pages and re-run the remaining pages to achieve effects similar to Modes 2 and 3.

In addition to the country pages sample, we applied FOCIH to web pages from the Gene Expression Omnibus site [10] and several e-commerce sites. The

[3] In our current implementation, we have to restart FOCIH when giving additional annotation examples. We have not yet coded our prototype to generalize and make adjustments on the fly as it harvests.

results in these cases were similar to results for country pages. FOCIH works well on pages that exhibit a high degree of regularity, and achieves less accuracy on pages or items within pages that are less regular.

An interesting avenue for future work that we discovered while annotating and harvesting e-commerce site pages is the interaction between HTML mark-up and the underlying text. Sometimes there is information we wish to extract in the mark-up itself (e.g., text in the "alt" attribute of image elements on the NewEgg.com site indicate the number user rating of a particular item). It would also be useful in several cases to take advantage of mark-up tags to delimit items in a list or to separate fields where one field is nested in the DOM tree within another field's node. For example, BarnesAndNoble.com embeds authors in an "em" element nested within an "h1" element representing the book title. Also, it is common to hyperlink items in a list, and thus the "a" tag structure could help parse list items. We are considering ways to generalize our annotation tool to allow annotation of mark-up text, and we are also working on a more robust implementation of FOCIH that will take advantage of these opportunities.

6 Further Reduction of Labor-Intensive Tasks

FOCIH helps users who do not know conceptual modeling to create ontologies and harvest and annotate information with respect to these ontologies. We want this process to be convenient with as much of the burden as possible shifted to the system. We see two major opportunities to further reduce labor-intensive tasks: (1) automatic initial form creation and (2) automatic initial form fill-in.

Often tables are "mirror images" of forms. When they are and when they only use FOCIH-equivalent layout structures, we can immediately generate FOCIH forms for them. As an example, consider the table in Figure 3. The nesting is the same as the nesting allowed in FOCIH forms. For example, the nesting

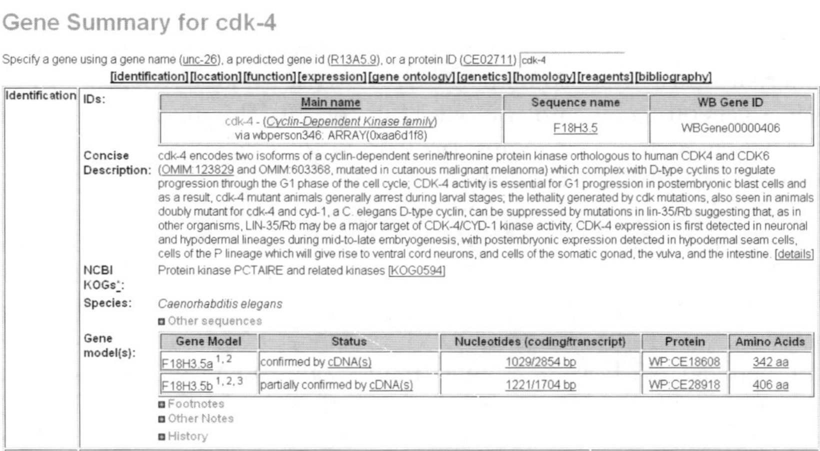

Gene Summary for cdk-4

Specify a gene using a gene name (unc-26), a predicted gene id (R13A5.9), or a protein ID (CE02711) cdk-4

[identification] [location] [function] [expression] [gene ontology] [genetics] [homology] [reagents] [bibliography]

Identification

IDs:

Main name	Sequence name	WB Gene ID
cdk-4 - (Cyclin-Dependent Kinase family) via wbperson346: ARRAY(0xaa6d1f8)	F18H3.5	WBGene00000406

Concise Description: cdk-4 encodes two isoforms of a cyclin-dependent serine/threonine protein kinase orthologous to human CDK4 and CDK6 (OMIM:123829 and OMIM:603368, mutated in cutanous malignant melanoma) which complex with D-type cyclins to regulate progression through the G1 phase of the cell cycle; CDK-4 activity is essential for G1 progression in postembryonic blast cells and as a result, cdk-4 mutant animals generally arrest during larval stages; the lethality generated by cdk mutations, also seen in animals doubly mutant for cdk-4 and cyd-1, a C. elegans D-type cyclin, can be suppressed by mutations in lin-35/Rb suggesting that, as in other organisms, LIN-35/Rb may be a major target of CDK-4/CYD-1 kinase activity; CDK-4 expression is first detected in neuronal and hypodermal lineages during mid-to-late embryogenesis, with postembryonic expression detected in hypodermal seam cells, cells of the P lineage which will give rise to ventral cord neurons, and cells of the somatic gonad, the vulva, and the intestine. [details]

NCBI KOGs*: Protein kinase PCTAIRE and related kinases [KOG0594]

Species: *Caenorhabditis elegans*

Other sequences

Gene model(s):

Gene Model	Status	Nucleotides (coding/transcript)	Protein	Amino Acids
F18H3.5a [1,2]	confirmed by cDNA(s)	1029/2854 bp	WP:CE18608	342 aa
F18H3.5b [1,2,3]	partially confirmed by cDNA(s)	1221/1704 bp	WP:CE28918	406 aa

Footnotes

Other Notes

History

Fig. 3. A Sample Table from WormBase (www.wormbase.org)

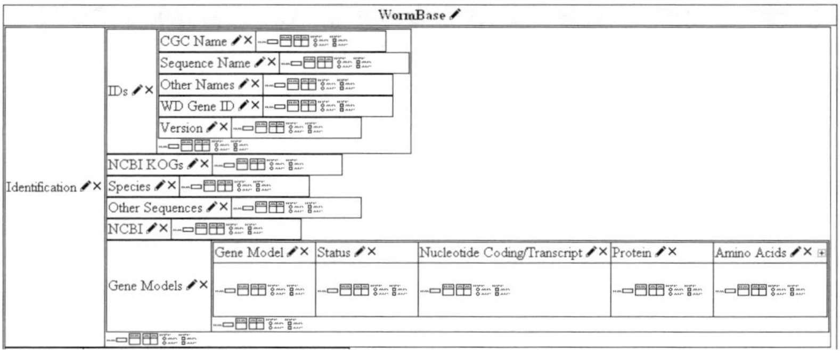

Fig. 4. Generated Form for Table in Figure 3 (Partial)

of the single-label/single-value elements *Genetic Position*, *Genomic Position*, and *Genomic Environs* under *Location* in Figure 3 is identical to the nesting of *Water*, *Land*, and *Total* under *Area* in Figure 1. Isomorphic variations are acceptable, such as the nested table under *IDs* that has only one row, which we can consider as a simple layout variation of a group of single-label/single-value elements rather than a multiple-label/multiple-value element. With allowance for this variation, an analysis of the table in Figure 3 yields the form in Figure 4. A user can then modify the form, if desired, and use it to harvest information.

We have implemented this reverse-engineering of tables into FOCIH forms based on a system called TISP (Table Interpretation for Sibling Pages) [22]. TISP converts tables from sites like hidden-web sites that have machine-generated sibling pages into FOCIH forms and thus into FOCIH-generated ontologies. (Indeed, we generated the FOCIH form in Figure 4 with this implemented system.) Moreover, tables are not the only front-end structures from which we can derive forms. We have implemented a transformation algorithm to convert OWL ontologies to OSM ontologies and another algorithm to convert XML-Schema specifications to OSM ontologies. We have yet to implement an algorithm to convert OSM ontologies to FOCIH forms, but the process is reasonably straightforward given our algorithm that translates OSM ontologies to nested scheme trees [1,14].

Besides generating an ontology, our TISP-to-FOCIH implementation also automatically harvests and annotates the data in the original table—indeed in all the sibling tables from a site (e.g., in the table in Figure 3 and all the sibling tables of the WormBase site). Thus, the system can also fill in the forms, and there is nothing for a user to do assuming the user is satisfied with the ontology automatically constructed by the TISP-to-FOCIH implementation. However, to facilitate the initial form-filling process for a form obtained in another way—perhaps by reverse-engineering an OWL ontology to a form—we need an extraction ontology [8]. If we have an extraction ontology for the application, the system may be able to entirely, or at least partially, fill-in the form for the first page. If we do not have an extraction ontology for the application, after FOCIH harvests information from one web site for the application, we have many sample values for each concept in the ontology. These sample values are enough to enable FOCIH to begin to construct an extraction ontology. Thus, for a subsequent site in the same domain, FOCIH would likely be able to automatically initialize a form with some of its values extracted from a page. A user may need to add additional values and perhaps correct some values that may have been erroneously extracted. For each new site, FOCIH adds to the knowledge of the extraction ontology, and thus "learns" as it harvests and annotates, making the extraction ontology increasingly better over time and thus also shifting the burden for annotating increasingly more from the user to the system.

7 Concluding Remarks

We have implemented FOCIH, a form-specification and information-harvesting tool. FOCIH lets users who are not experts in conceptual modeling or in ontology languages create an ontology and semantically annotate web pages with respect to the created ontology. We are able to guarantee that any user who can specify an ordinary form and can cut-and-paste values from web pages can successfully create an ontology and annotate web pages. Our implementation philosophy, however, is to shift as much of the the burden of ontology creation and semantic annotation to FOCIH as we can. Thus, we provide for: (1) automatic harvesting of information from the sibling pages of an initial annotated page; (2) automatic creation of FOCIH forms and corresponding ontologies by reverse engineering structured documents such as tables, database schemas, OWL ontologies, or XML-schema specifications; (3) automatic initial form fill-in via extraction ontologies; and (4) semi-automatic creation of extraction ontologies.

Experience using FOCIH and experimental results are encouraging. Running the FOCIH prototype over dozens of pages on multiple sites shows that automatic harvesting performs well. The prototype often achieves near-perfect information harvesting for well-structured elements, which appear to be fairly common. More work needs to be done in processing sites with less regular structure, but the results achieved so far indicate that we can generalize our prototype implementation to cover less-regular pages. As for automatic creation of FOCIH forms, our implementation via TISP works well. And, as for our use of extraction ontologies with FOCIH, we still need to integrate our implementations and make them work synergistically. In the past, we have experimented extensively with extraction ontologies and have been able to achieve high precision and recall results for the domains we have studied (e.g., see [8]), so we are hopeful that the integration will bring about the expected synergy resulting in an even greater shift of the workload to the machine.

As FOCIH harvests information of interest, it semantically annotates the pages from which it extracts information and generates RDF data files. Hence, in the larger system in which FOCIH is embedded, the data of interest from a web site becomes accessible through a standard query interface. Queries yield not only direct answers, but for each retrieved data value also yield links back to the page from which the data was extracted. All of this points toward enabling the Web 3.0 vision—the superimposition of a web of data over a web of pages.

References

1. Al-Kamha, R.: Conceptual XML for Systems Analysis. PhD dissertation, Brigham Young University, Department of Computer Science (June 2007)
2. Arlotta, L., Crescenzi, V., Mecca, G., Merialdo, P.: Automatic annotation of data extracted from large web sites. In: Proceedings of the Sixth International Workshop on the Web and Databases (WebDB 2003), San Diego, California, pp. 7–12 (June 2003)
3. Baader, F., Nutt, W.: Basic description logics. In: Baader, F., Calvanese, D., McGuinness, D., Nardi, D., Patel-Schneider, P. (eds.) The Description Logic Handbook, ch. 2, pp. 43–95. Cambridge University Press, Cambridge (2003)
4. Benslimane, S.M., Malki, M., Rahmouni, M.K., Benslimane, D.: Extracting personalised ontology from data-intensive web application: an HTML forms-based reverse engineering approach. Informatica 18(4), 11–534 (2007)
5. Buitelaar, P., Olejnik, D., Sintek, M.: A protégé plug-in for ontology extraction from text based on linguistic analysis. In: Bussler, C.J., Davies, J., Fensel, D., Studer, R. (eds.) ESWS 2004. LNCS, vol. 3053, pp. 31–44. Springer, Heidelberg (2004)
6. Chu, E., Baid, A., Chen, T., Doan, A., Naughton, J.F.: A relational approach to incrementally extracting and querying structure in unstructured data. In: Proceedings of the 33rd International Conference on Very Large Data Bases (VLDB 2007), Vienna, Austria, pp. 1045–1056 (September 2007)
7. Cimiano, P., Völker, J.: Text2Onto–a framework for ontology learning and data-driven change discovery. In: Montoyo, A., Muńoz, R., Métais, E. (eds.) NLDB 2005. LNCS, vol. 3513, pp. 227–238. Springer, Heidelberg (2005)
8. Embley, D.W., Campbell, D.M., Jiang, Y.S., Liddle, S.W., Lonsdale, D.W., Ng, Y.-K., Smith, R.D.: Conceptual-model-based data extraction from multiple-record web pages. Data & Knowledge Engineering 31(3), 227–251 (1999)
9. Gal, A., Anaby-Tavor, A., Trombetta, A., Montesi, D.: A framework for modeling and evaluating automatic semantic reconciliation. The VLDB Journal 14(1), 50–67 (2005)
10. Gene expression omnibus (2009), http://www.ncbi.nlm.nih.gov/geo/
11. Kiryakov, A., Popov, B., Terziev, I., Manov, D., Ognyanoff, D.: Semantic annotation, indexing, and retrieval. Journal of Web Sematics 2(1), 49–79 (2004)
12. Laclavík, M., Šeleng, M., Gatial, E., Balogh, Z., Hluchý, L.: Ontology based text annotation – OnTeA. In: Duzi, M., Jaakkola, H., Kiyoki, Y., Kangassalo, H. (eds.) Proceedings of Information Modelling and Knowledge Bases XVIII, Frontiers in Artificial Intelligence and Applications, vol. 154, pp. 311–315. IOS Press, Amsterdam (2007)
13. Michelson, M., Knoblock, C.A.: Unsupervised information extraction from unstructured, ungrammatical data sources on the world wide web. International Journal of Document Analysis and Recognition 10(3–4), 211–226 (2007)
14. Mok, W.Y., Embley, D.W.: Generating compact redundancy-free XML documents from concptual-model hypergraphs. IEEE Transactions on Knowledge and Data Engineering 18(8), 1082–1096 (2006)
15. Mukherjee, S., Yang, G., Ramakrishnan, I.V.: Automatic annotation of content-rich HTML documents: Structural and semantic analysis. In: Fensel, D., Sycara, K., Mylopoulos, J. (eds.) ISWC 2003. LNCS, vol. 2870, pp. 533–549. Springer, Heidelberg (2003)

16. Navigli, R., Velardi, P., Cucchiarelli, A., Neri, F.: Quantitative and qualitative evaluation of the OntoLearn ontology learning system. In: Proceedings of the 20th International Conference on Computational Linguistics, Geneva, Switzerland, pp. 1043–1050 (August 2004)
17. Noy, N.F., Sintek, M., Decker, S., Crubezy, M., Fergerson, R.W., Musen, M.: Creating semantic web contents with Protègè-2000. IEEE Intelligent Systems 16(2), 60–71 (2001)
18. Pivk, A.: Automatic ontology generation from web tabular structures. AI Communications 19(1), 83–85 (2006)
19. Sarawagi, S.: Information extraction. Foundations and Trends in Databases 1(3), 261–377 (2008)
20. Shen, W., DeRose, P., McCann, R., Doan, A., Ramakrishnan, R.: Toward best-effort information extraction. In: Proceedings of the ACM SIGMOD International Conference on Management of Data, Vancouver, British Columbia, Canada, pp. 1031–1042 (June 2008)
21. Spyns, P., Oberle, D., Volz, R., Zheng, J., Jarrar, M., Sure, Y., Studer, R., Meersman, R.: OntoWeb - A semantic web community portal. In: Karagiannis, D., Reimer, U. (eds.) PAKM 2002. LNCS (LNAI), vol. 2569, pp. 189–200. Springer, Heidelberg (2002)
22. Tao, C., Embley, D.W.: Automatic hidden-web table interpretation, conceptualization, and semantic annotation. Data & Knowledge Engineering (in press, 2009)
23. Tao, C., Embley, D.W., Liddle, S.W.: Enabling a web of knowledge. Technical report, Brigham Young University (submitted for publication—draft manuscript available at deg.byu.edu) (2009)
24. Tijerino, Y.A., Al-Muhammed, M., Embley, D.W.: Toward a flexible human-agent collaboration framework with mediating domain ontologies for the semantic web. In: Proceedings of the ISWC 2004 Workshop on Meaning Coordination and Negotiation, Hiroshima, Japan, pp. 131–142 (November2004)
25. Vargas-Vera, M., Motta, E., Domingue, J., Lanzoni, M., Stutt, A., Ciravegna, F.: MnM: Ontology driven tool for semantic markup. In: Proceedings of the Workshop Semantic Authoring, Annotation & Knowledge Markup (SAAKM 2002), Lyon, France (July 2002)
26. Wang, Y., Völker, J., Haase, P.: Towards semi-automatic ontology building supported by large-scale knowledge acquisition. In: AAAI Fall Symposium On Semantic Web for Collaborative Knowledge Acquisition, Arlington, Virginia, vol. FS-06-06, pp. 70–77 (October 2006)

Specifying Valid Compound Terms in Interrelated Faceted Taxonomies

Anastasia Analyti[1], Yannis Tzitzikas[1,2], and Nicolas Spyratos[3]

[1] Institute of Computer Science, FORTH-ICS, Greece
[2] Department of Computer Science, University of Crete, Greece
[3] Laboratoire de Recherche en Informatique, Universite de Paris-Sud, France
{analyti,tzitzik}@ics.forth.gr, spyratos@lri.fr

Abstract. In previous work, we proposed an algebra whose operators allow to specify the valid compound terms of a faceted taxonomy, in a flexible manner (by combining positive and negative statements). In this paper, we treat the same problem but in a more general setting, where the facet taxonomies are not independent but are (possibly) interrelated through narrower/broader relationships between their terms. The proposed algebra, called *Interrelated Facet Composition Algebra* (*IFCA*), is more powerful, as the valid compound terms of a faceted taxonomy can be derived through a smaller set of declared valid and/or invalid compound terms. An optimized (w.r.t. the naive approach) algorithm that checks compound term validity, according to a well-formed IFCA expression, and its worst-time complexity are provided.

Keywords: interrelated faceted taxonomies, valid compound terms, algebra, dynamic taxonomies, web search.

1 Introduction

The provision of effective and efficient general-purpose access services for end-users is a challenging task. In general, we could say that query services are either too simplistic (e.g., free text queries in IR systems or Web search engines), or too sophisticated (e.g., SQL queries or Semantic Web Queries). On the other hand browsing is either too simplistic (e.g., plain Web links) or very application specific (dynamic pages derived by specific application programs). Information exploration services could bridge this gap and provide effective and efficient general purpose access services. Indeed, dynamic taxonomies [8,10] and faceted search [15,17,4] is a successful example [11] that is currently very common in E-commerce applications in the Web (e.g., eBay Express[1]).

Roughly, a *faceted taxonomy* is a set of taxonomies, each one describing the domain of interest from a different (preferably orthogonal) point of view [4]. Having a faceted taxonomy, each domain object (e.g., a book or a Web page)

[1] http://www.express.ebay.com/

A.H.F. Laender et al. (Eds.): ER 2009, LNCS 5829, pp. 360–373, 2009.

can be indexed using a *compound term*, i.e., a set of terms from the different facets.

For example, assume that the domain of interest is a set of hotel Web pages in Greece, and suppose that we want to provide access to these pages according to three facets: the *Location* of the hotels, the *Sports* facilities they offer, and the *Season* they are open, as shown in Figure 1. Each object can be described using a compound term. For example, a hotel in Crete which provides sea ski and wind-surfing facilities, and is open during the summer will be described by the compound term $\{Crete, SeaSki, Windsurfing, Summer\}$.

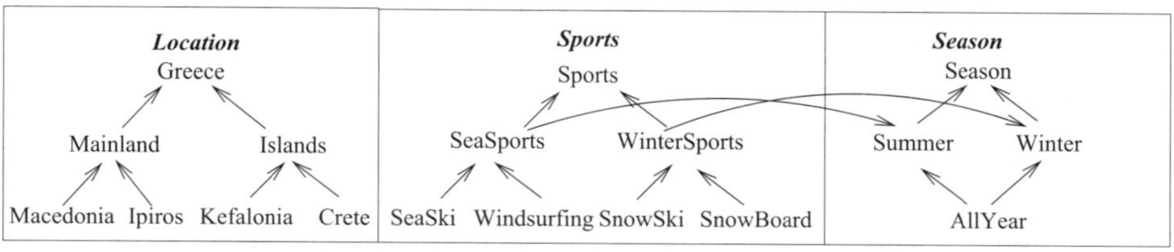

Fig. 1. Three interrelated facets

Faceted taxonomies carry a number of well known advantages over single taxonomies (clarity, compactness, scalability), but they also have a severe drawback: the high cost of avoiding invalid compound terms, i.e. compound terms that do not apply to any object in the domain. For example, the compound term $\{Crete, SnowBoard\}$ is an invalid compound term, as there are no hotels in Crete offering snow-board facilities. The interaction paradigm of faceted search and dynamic taxonomies can enable users to browse only nodes that correspond to valid compound terms [15,17,8] (e.g. see demos[2,3]). However, if the computation of such compound terms is based *only* on the objects that have already been indexed (as in [17]) then this interaction paradigm cannot be exploited, in the case where there are no indexed objects.

The availability of algebraic expressions describing the valid compound terms of a faceted taxonomy enables the *dynamic* generation of *navigation trees*, whose nodes correspond to valid compound terms, only [15]. These navigational trees can be used for indexing (for avoiding errors) and browsing. Additionally, if we have a *materialized faceted taxonomy* $\mathcal{M}$ (i.e., a corpus of objects indexed through a faceted taxomony) then specific mining algorithms (such as, these in [13]) can be used for expressing the extensionally valid compound terms of $\mathcal{M}$ in the form of an algebraic expression. Obviously, such mined algebraic expressions enable the user to take advantage of the aforementioned interaction scheme, without having to resort to the (possibly, numerous) instances of $\mathcal{M}$. Furthermore, algebraic expressions describing the valid compound terms of a faceted taxonomy can be exploited in other tasks, such as retrieval optimization [15], configuration management [1], consistency control [14], and compression [12].

[2] `http://flamenco.berkeley.edu/demos.html`

[3] `http://simile.mit.edu/wiki/Longwell_Demos`

This algebraic approach was first proposed in [15], where the *Compound Term Composition Algebra* (*CTCA*) was defined. CTCA has *four operators* (two positive and two negative), based on which one can built an *algebraic expression* to specify the valid compound terms of a faceted taxonomy, in a flexible and easy manner. In each algebraic operation, the designer has to declare either a small set of compound terms known to be valid (from which other valid compound terms are inferred), or a small set of compound terms known to be invalid (from which other invalid compound terms are inferred).

For example, if a user declares (in a positive operation) that the compound term $\{Crete, SeaSki\}$ is valid then it is inferred that the compound term $\{Crete, SeaSports\}$ is also valid. On the other hand, if a user declares (in a negative operation) that the compound term $\{Crete, WinterSports\}$ is invalid then it is inferred that the compound term $\{Crete, SnowBoard\}$ is also invalid. In our example, this means that the designer can specify all valid compound terms of the faceted taxonomy by providing a relatively small number of (valid or invalid) compound terms. This is an important feature as it minimizes the effort needed by the designer. Moreover, only the expression defining the set of valid compound terms needs to be stored (and not the set itself), as an inference mechanism can check whether a compound term belongs to the set of defined compound terms, in polynomial time [15]. Based on this inference mechanism, an algorithm for deriving navigation trees, *on the fly*, is provided in [15] and is implemented in the FASTAXON system [16].

In this paper, we also treat the problem of specifying the valid compound terms of a faceted taxonomy but, in contrast to CTCA, we assume that facets can be interrelated through narrower/broader relationships (denoted by $<_{\mathrm{F}}$) between their terms. The proposed algebra, called *Interrelated Facet Composition Algebra* (*IFCA*), includes *three operators* (one positive and two negative). Compared to CTCA, the present approach is more powerful, as the valid compound terms can be derived through a smaller set of declared valid and/or invalid compound terms. Thus, the effort needed to build the desired algebraic expression is reduced. For example, in Figure 1, assume that the facets *Sports* and *Season* are related by adding the following relationships: $SeaSports <_{\mathrm{F}} Summer$ and $WinterSports <_{\mathrm{F}} Winter$, meaning that all hotels offering sea sports are open in summer, and that all hotels offering winter sports are open in winter. Assume now that the designer declares the compound term $\{Crete, SeaSports\}$ as valid. Then, we can infer that $\{Crete, Summer\}$ is also valid. Additionally, if the designer declares that the compound term $\{Hersonissos, Winter\}$ is invalid then we can infer that $\{Hersonissos, WinterSports\}$ is also invalid.

Apart from defining IFCA, in this paper, we present an algorithm for checking compound term validity, according to a well-formed IFCA expression. The algorithm is optimized w.r.t. the naive approach and its worst-time complexity is provided. We could say that CTCA and IFCA, are fully *intensional* algebras, in contrast to dynamic taxonomies [8], or Formal Concept Analysis [3], which are both *intensional* (due to the existence of hierarchies and their semantics) and *extensional* (as they discard compound terms with empty extension).

Further, as we have shown in [14,1], *Description Logics* (DLs) [2] and *definite logic programs* [7] cannot represent the "mode interchange" from positive to negative operations (and vice-versa)[4] that occur in a general CTCA, and thus also IFCA, expression.

The remaining of this paper is organized as follows: Section 2 describes formally compound taxonomies and interrelated faceted taxonomies. Section 3 describes the Interrelated Facet Composition Algebra. Section 4 presents an algorithm that checks compound term validity, according to a well-formed IFCA expression, along with its worst-time complexity. Finally, Section 5 concludes the paper and identifies issues for further research.

2 Interrelated Faceted Taxonomies

In this section, we define compound taxonomies and interrelated faceted taxonomies.

A *terminology* is a finite set of names, called *terms*. A *taxonomy* is a pair $(\mathcal{T}, \leq)$, where $\mathcal{T}$ is a *terminology* and $\leq$ is a partial order over $\mathcal{T}$, called *subsumption*. A *compound term* over $\mathcal{T}$ is any subset of $\mathcal{T}$. For example, the following sets of terms are compound terms over the taxonomy *Sports* of Figure 1: $s_1 = \{SeaSki, Windsurfing\}$, $s_2 = \{SeaSports\}$, and $s_3 = \emptyset$.

A *compound terminology* S over $\mathcal{T}$ is any set of compound terms that contains the compound term $\emptyset$. The set of all compound terms over $\mathcal{T}$ can be ordered using the *compound ordering* over $\mathcal{T}$, defined as: $s \preceq s'$ iff $\forall t' \in s'$, $\exists t \in s$ such that $t \leq t'$. That is, $s \preceq s'$ iff s contains a narrower term for every term of s'. In addition, s may contain terms not present in s'. Roughly, $s \preceq s'$ means that s carries more specific information than s'. For example, $\{SeaSki, Windsurfing\} \preceq \{SeaSports\} \preceq \emptyset$. We say that two compound terms s, s' are *equivalent* $s \sim s'$ iff $s \preceq s'$ and $s' \preceq s$. For example, $\{SeaSki, SeaSports\}$ and $\{SeaSki\}$ are equivalent. Intuitively, equivalent compound terms carry the same information. Note that if $s \sim s'$ then $minimal_{\leq}(s) = minimal_{\leq}(s')$.

A *compound taxonomy* over $\mathcal{T}$ is a pair $(S, \preceq)$, where S is a compound terminology over $\mathcal{T}$, and $\preceq$ is the compound ordering over $\mathcal{T}$ restricted to S. Let $P(\mathcal{T})$ be the set of all compound terms over $\mathcal{T}$ (i.e., the powerset of $\mathcal{T}$). Clearly, $(P(\mathcal{T}), \preceq)$ is a compound taxonomy over $\mathcal{T}$.

Let s be a compound term. The broader and the narrower compound terms of s are defined as follows: $\texttt{Br}(s) = \{s' \in P(\mathcal{T}) \mid s \preceq s'\}$ and $\texttt{Nr}(s) = \{s' \in P(\mathcal{T}) \mid s' \preceq s\}$.

Let S be a compound terminology over $\mathcal{T}$. The broader and the narrower compound terms of S are defined as follows: $Br(S) = \cup\{\texttt{Br}(s) \mid s \in S\}$ and $Nr(S) = \cup\{\texttt{Nr}(s) \mid s \in S\}$.

We say that a compound term s is *valid* (resp. *invalid*), if, in the current state of affairs, there is at least one (resp. no) object of the underlying domain

[4] Though, as shown in [1], this mode "interchange" can be represented through logic programs with lists and weak negation under Clark's semantics [7], with no computational advantage.

indexed by all terms in s. We assume that every term of $\mathcal{T}$ is valid. However, a compound term over $\mathcal{T}$ may be invalid. Obviously, if s is a valid compound term, all compound terms in $\mathtt{Br}(s)$ are valid. Additionally, if s is an invalid compound term, all compound terms in $\mathtt{Nr}(s)$ are invalid.

One way of designing a taxonomy is by identifying a number k of different aspects of the domain of interest and then designing one taxonomy per aspect. As a result, we obtain a set of taxonomies $F_i = (\mathcal{T}_i, \leq_i)$, for $i = 1, ..., k$, called *facets*. In our framework, facets may be related through a narrower/broader relation $<_{\mathtt{F}}$ between their terms. We require that the transitive closure[5] of the union of $<_{\mathtt{F}}$ with the facet subsumption relations $\leq_i$, for $i = 1, ..., k$, that is $\leq = ((\bigcup_{i=1}^{k} \leq_i) \bigcup <_{\mathtt{F}})^*$, is a partial order over $\mathcal{T} = \bigcup_{i=1}^{k} \mathcal{T}_i$. Thus, $\leq$ includes *only trivial* cycles.

Specifically, given a set of facets and a relation $<_{\mathtt{F}}$, we define an *interrelated faceted taxonomy* as follows:

Definition 1 (Interrelated faceted taxonomy). Let $\{F_1, ..., F_k\}$ be a set of taxonomies, where $F_i = (\mathcal{T}_i, \leq_i)$, for $i = 1, ..., k$, and $\mathcal{T}_i \cap \mathcal{T}_j = \emptyset$, if $i \neq j$. Additionally, let $<_{\mathtt{F}} \subseteq \bigcup_{i \neq j} \mathcal{T}_i \times \mathcal{T}_j$ and let $\leq = ((\bigcup_{i=1}^{k} \leq_i) \bigcup <_{\mathtt{F}})^*$ such that $\leq$ is a partial order. Then, the pair $\mathcal{F} = (\mathcal{T}, \leq)$, where $\mathcal{T} = \bigcup_{i=1}^{k} \mathcal{T}_i$, is a taxonomy that we call the *interrelated faceted taxonomy generated* by $\{F_1, ..., F_k\}$ and $<_{\mathtt{F}}$. We call the taxonomies $F_1, ..., F_k$ the *facets* of $\mathcal{F}$. Additionally, if $<_{\mathtt{F}} = \emptyset$ then $\mathcal{F}$ is also called *simple faceted taxonomy.*

Clearly, all definitions introduced so far apply also to an interrelated faceted taxonomy $\mathcal{F} = (\mathcal{T}, \leq)$. For example, the set $S = \{\{Islands\}, \{SeaSports\}, \{Greece, SeaSports\}, \emptyset\}$ is a compound terminology over the terminology $\mathcal{T}$ of the interrelated faceted taxonomy, shown in Figure 1. Additionally, the pair $(S, \preceq)$ is a compound taxonomy over $\mathcal{T}$. For reasons of brevity, we omit the term $\emptyset$ from the example compound terminologies.

3 The Interrelated Facet Composition Algebra

Let $\mathcal{F} = (\mathcal{T}, \leq)$ be the interrelated faceted taxonomy, generated by a set of facets $\{F_1, ..., F_k\}$ and a relation $<_{\mathtt{F}}$. To begin with, we associate each facet $F_i = (\mathcal{T}_i, \leq_i)$ with a compound terminology T_i that we call the *basic compound terminology* of F_i. The basic compound terminologies are the "building blocks" of our algebra. Specifically, $T_i = Br\{\{t\} \mid t \in \mathcal{T}_i\} \cap \mathcal{P}(\mathcal{T}_i)$, for $i = 1, ..., k$.

For example, in Figure 1, the basic compound taxonomy of *Season* is: $\{\{Season\}, \{Summer\}, \{Winter\}, \{AllYear\}, \{Summer, Winter\}\}$. As every term t of a facet is considered valid, all compound terms in T_i are valid compound terms over $\mathcal{T}_i$.

Let $\mathcal{S}$ denote the set of all compound terminologies over $\mathcal{T}$. The *Interrelated Facet Composition Algebra* (*IFCA*) is an algebra over $\mathcal{S}$, which includes three operations, namely the *plus-product*, the *minus-product*, and the *minus-self-product*

[5] Given a binary relation R, we shall use R^* to denote its reflexive and transitive closure.

operations. For defining the desired compound taxonomy, the designer has to formulate an algebraic expression e, using these three operations and initial operands the basic compound terminologies. The plus-product, minus-product, and minus-self-product operations of IFCA operate over a set of compound terminologies $S_1, ..., S_n$ and generalize the corresponding operations of CTCA [15].

Let $S_1, ..., S_n$ be compound terminologies over $\mathcal{T}$. The *domain* of $S_1, ..., S_n$, denoted by $\mathcal{D}_{S_1,...,S_n}$, is the powerset of all terms in $\mathcal{T}$ that appear in $S_1, ..., S_n$. For example, let $S_1 = \{\{Greece, Sports\}, \{Season\}\}$ and let $S_2 = \{\{Season\}, \{Summer\}\}$ then[6] $\mathcal{D}_{S_1,S_2} = \mathcal{P}(\{Greece, Sports, Summer\})$. Intuitively, the set of compound terms $\mathcal{D}_{S_1,...,S_n}$ is used to delimit the range of the IFCA plus-product and minus-product operations over $S_1, ..., S_n$.

Additionally, we provide the auxiliary operation $\oplus$ over $\mathcal{S}$, called *product*. This operation results in a compound terminology, whose compound terms are all possible combinations (unions) of compound terms from its arguments. Specifically, let $S_1, ..., S_n \in \mathcal{S}$. The *product* of $S_1, ..., S_n$ is defined as: $S_1 \oplus ... \oplus S_n = \{ s_1 \cup ... \cup s_n \mid s_i \in S_i\}$. Examples of the product operation are provided in [15]. It is easy to see that: $\emptyset \in S_1 \oplus ... \oplus S_n \subseteq \mathcal{D}_{S_1,...,S_n}$.

Let $S_1, ..., S_n$ be compound terminologies over $\mathcal{T}$. Intuitively, the *plus-product* operation $\oplus_P(S_1, ...S_n)$ specifies valid compound terms in $\mathcal{D}_{S_1,...,S_n}$, through a declared set of valid compound terms $P \subseteq \mathcal{D}_{S_1,...,S_n}$.

Definition 2 (Plus-product operation). Let $S_1, ..., S_n \in \mathcal{S}$ and $P \subseteq \mathcal{D}_{S_1,...,S_n}$. The *plus-product* of $S_1, ..., S_n$ with respect to P is defined as follows:

$$\oplus_P(S_1, ..., S_n) = Br(S_1 \cup ... \cup S_n \cup P) \cap \mathcal{D}_{S_1,...,S_n}. \qquad \square$$

This operation results in a compound terminology consisting of the compound terms in $\mathcal{D}_{S_1,...,S_n}$ which are broader than an element of the initial compound terminologies union P. This is because, assuming that all compound terms of S_i, for $i = 1, ..., n$, and P are valid then all compound terms in $Br(S_1 \cup ... \cup S_n \cup P)$ are also valid. We delimit this set to $\mathcal{D}_{S_1,...,S_n}$, as we are interested only in the compound terms, formed by terms appearing in $S_1, ..., S_n$.

It is easy to see that: (i) the operation plus-product is commutative, (ii) the smaller the parameter P, the smaller the resulting compound terminology, and (iii) for any parameter P, we need to consider only its minimal (with respect to $\leq$) elements. The last property can be used for optimization, i.e., for minimizing the space needed for storing the parameter P.

The following proposition shows that the application of a $\oplus_P$ operation[7] on other $\oplus_P$ operations results in a single $\oplus_P$ operation, allowing the simplification of an IFCA expression.

Proposition 1. Let the compound terminologies $S_i \in \mathcal{S}$, for $i = 1, ..., n$. It holds: $(\oplus_{P_1}(S_1, ..., S_l)) \oplus_{P_2} (\oplus_{P_3}(S_{l+1}, ..., S_n)) = \oplus_{minimal_{\leq}(P_1 \cup P_2 \cup P_3)}(S_1, ..., S_n)$.

Let $S_1, ..., S_n$, where $n \geq 2$, be compound terminologies over $\mathcal{T}$. Intuitively, the *minus-product* operation $\ominus_N(S_1, ...S_n)$ specifies which compound terms in

[6] For $S \subseteq \mathcal{T}$, $\mathcal{P}(S)$ denotes the powerset of S.

[7] For binary operations, we also use the infix notation.

$S_1 \oplus ... \oplus S_n$ are invalid, through a declared set of invalid compound terms $N \subseteq \mathcal{D}_{S_1,...,S_n}$.

Definition 3 (Minus-product operation). Let $S_1, ..., S_n \in \mathcal{S}$, where $n \geq 2$, and let $N \subseteq \mathcal{D}_{S_1,...,S_n}$. The *minus-product* of $S_1, ..., S_n$ with respect to N is defined as follows:

$$\ominus_N(S_1, ..., S_n) = Br(S_1 \oplus ... \oplus S_n - Nr(N)) \cap \mathcal{D}_{S_1,...,S_n}. \qquad \square$$

This operation results in a compound terminology consisting of all compound terms in $\mathcal{D}_{S_1,...,S_n}$, which are broader than a compound term in $S_1 \oplus ... \oplus S_n - Nr(N)$. This is because, all compound terms in $Nr(N)$ are invalid. Assuming a closed-world assumption over $S_1 \oplus ... \oplus S_n$, all compound terms in $S_1 \oplus ... \oplus S_n - Nr(N)$ are considered valid. Therefore, all compound terms in $Br(S_1 \oplus ... \oplus S_n - Nr(N))$ are also valid. We delimit this set to $\mathcal{D}_{S_1,...,S_n}$, as we are interested only in the compound terms, formed by terms appearing in $S_1, ..., S_n$.

It is easy to see that: (i) the operation minus-product is commutative, (ii) the larger the parameter N, the smaller the resulting compound terminology, and (iii) for any parameter N, we need to consider only its maximal (with respect to $\leq$) elements. The last property can be used for optimization, i.e., for minimizing the space needed for storing the parameter N.

Let T_i be a basic compound terminology. Intuitively, the *minus-self-product* operation $\overset{*}{\ominus}_N (T_i)$ specifies which compound terms in $\mathcal{P}(\mathcal{T}_i)$ are invalid, through a declared set of invalid compound terms $N \subseteq \mathcal{P}(\mathcal{T}_i)$.

Definition 4. Let T_i be a basic compound terminology and $N \subseteq \mathcal{P}(\mathcal{T}_i)$. The *minus-self-product* of T_i with respect to N is defined as follows: $\overset{*}{\ominus}_N (T_i) = \mathcal{P}(\mathcal{T}_i) - Nr(N)$. $\square$

The minus-self-product operation of IFCA coincides with the minus-self-product operation of CTCA.

For defining the desired compound taxonomy, the designer has to formulate an IFCA expression e, defined as follows:

Definition 5 (IFCA expression). An IFCA expression over an interrelated faceted taxonomy $\mathcal{F} = (\mathcal{T}, \leq)$, generated by a set of facets $\{F_1, ..., F_k\}$ and a relation $<_F$, is defined according to the following grammar:

$$e ::= \oplus_P(e, ..., e) \mid \ominus_N (e, ..., e) \mid \overset{*}{\ominus}_N (T_i) \mid T_i. \qquad \square$$

The outcome of the evaluation of an expression e is denoted by S_e and is called the *compound terminology* of e. In addition, $(S_e, \preceq)$ is called the *compound taxonomy* of e. If e is the final expression that characterizes an interrelated faceted taxonomy $\mathcal{F} = (\mathcal{T}, \leq)$, the compound terms in S_e are considered *valid*[8] and the compound terms in $\mathcal{P}(\mathcal{T}) - S_e$ are considered *invalid*. We are especially interested in *well-formed* IFCA expressions, defined as follows:

[8] Obviously, in this case $Br(S_e) = S_e$.

Definition 6 (Well-formed expression). An IFCA expression e over an interrelated faceted taxonomy $\mathcal{F}$ is *well-formed* iff:

1. each basic compound terminology T_i appears at most once in e,
2. for every subexpression $\ominus_N(e_1, ..., e_n)$ of e, it holds: (i) $Nr(N) \cap S_{e_i} = \emptyset$, for all $i = 1, ..., n$, and (ii) $Nr(N) \cap S_e = \emptyset$, and
3. for every subexpression $\overset{*}{\ominus}_N (T_i)$ of e, it holds: (i) $Nr(N) \cap T_i = \emptyset$ and (ii) $Nr(N) \cap S_e = \emptyset$. □

Constraint (1) above is applied for simplifying IFCA expressions and improving the performance of our algorithms. This constraint is also imposed to well-formed CTCA expressions. Constraints (2.i) and (3.i) ensure that the valid compound terms of an expression e increase as e expands (see Proposition 2). For example, if we omit constraint (2.i) then a valid compound term according to an expression $T_1 \oplus_P T_2$ could be invalid according to a larger expression $(T_1 \oplus_P T_2) \ominus_N T_1$. Let N be the parameter of a minus-product or minus-self-product subexpression of e. Constraints (2.ii) and (3.ii) ensure that every compound term in $Nr(N)$ will not be found to be valid from another operation in e.

Proposition 2 (Monotonicity). Let $\mathcal{F}$ be an interrelated faceted taxonomy. If e is a well-formed IFCA expression and e' is a subexpression of e then $S_{e'} \subseteq S_e$.

The monotonicity property of well-formed IFCA expressions enables the specification of the valid compound terms of an interrelated faceted taxonomy, in a systematic and gradual manner. Additionally, from the monotonicity property, it follows that if an IFCA expression is well-formed then all subexpressions of e are also well-formed.

The following proposition expresses that IFCA is also more size-efficient than CTCA. We define the *parameter size* of an expression e as: $size(e) = |\mathcal{P}_e \cup \mathcal{N}_e|$, where $\mathcal{P}_e$ denotes the union of all P parameters of e, and $\mathcal{N}_e$ denotes the union of all N parameters of e.

Proposition 3 (Size-efficiency). Let $\mathcal{F}$ be an interrelated faceted taxonomy, generated by a set of facets $\{F_1, ..., F_k\}$ and a relation $<_{\mathsf{F}}$. Additionally, let $\mathcal{F}'$ be the simple faceted taxonomy, generated by the facets $\{F_1, ..., F_k\}$ (with the relation $<_{\mathsf{F}}$ ignored). Then, for every well-formed CTCA expression e' over $\mathcal{F}'$, there is a well-formed IFCA expression e over $\mathcal{F}$ that (i) has smaller or equal parameter size with e' and (ii) $S_e = S_{e'}$.

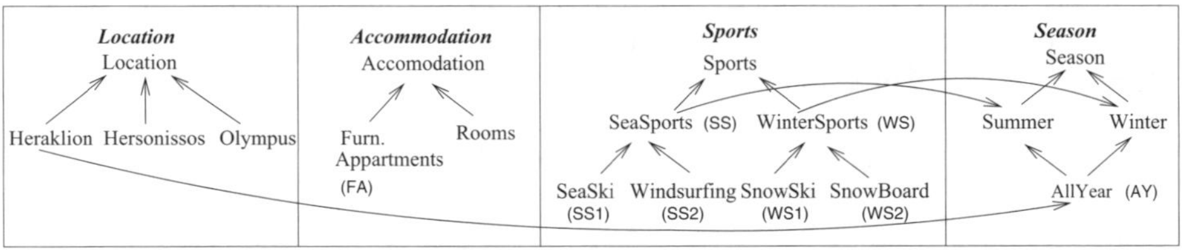

Fig. 2. An interrelated faceted taxonomy

The following proposition shows that a property, similar to that of Proposition 1 for plus-products, also holds for the minus-products of well-formed IFCA expressions.

Proposition 4. Let $\mathcal{F}$ be an interrelated faceted taxonomy. Additionally, let $e' = (\ominus_{N_1}(e_1, ..., e_l)) \ominus_{N_2} (\ominus_{N_3}(e_{l+1}, ..., e_n))$ be a subexpression of a well-formed IFCA expression e over $\mathcal{F}$. It holds: $S_{e'} = \ominus_{maximal_{\leq}(N_1 \cup N_2 \cup N_3)}(S_{e_1}, ..., S_{e_n})$.

As an example of IFCA, suppose that we want to index a set of hotel Web pages, according the *location* of the hotels, the kind of *accommodation*, the *facilities* they offer, and the *season* they are open. Assume now that the designer employs the interrelated faceted taxonomy $\mathcal{F}$, shown in Figure 2. From all possible compound terms, available domain knowledge suggests that only certain compound terms are valid. Omitting the compound terms which are singletons or contain top terms of the facets, and considering from the equivalent compound terms only one, 52 valid compound terms remain.

Rather than being explicitly enumerated, these compound terms can be algebraically specified. For example, the following plus-product operation can be used:

$\oplus_P(Location, Accommodation, Sports, Season)$, where:

$$\begin{aligned} P = \; & \{\{Heraklion, FA\}, \{Heraklion, Rooms\}, \{Hersonissos, FA, SS1\}, \\ & \{Hersonissos, FA, SS2\}, \{Hersonissos, Rooms, SS1\}, \{Hersonissos, Rooms, SS2\}, \\ & \{Olympus, FA, WS1\}, \{Olympus, FA, WS2\}, \{Olympus, Rooms, WS1\}, \\ & \{Olympus, Rooms, WS2\}, \{Olympus, Rooms, AllYear\}\} \end{aligned}$$

Note that the compound terms in P are 11. Alternatively, the same result can be obtained by the shorter minus-product operation:

$\ominus_N(Location, Accommodation, Sports, Season)$, where:

$$\begin{aligned} N = \; & \{\{Heraklion, Sports\}, \{Hersonissos, Winter\}, \{Olympus, SS\}, \\ & \{Olympus, FA, Summer\}, \{SS, Winter\}, \{WS, Summer\}\} \end{aligned}$$

The following, even shorter, IFCA expression e achieves the same result by combining the operations *plus-product* and *minus-product*:

$e = \ominus_N(Location, Accommodation, Sports) \oplus_P (Season)$, where:

$$\begin{aligned} N = \; & \{\{Heraklion, Sports\}, \{Hersonissos, WS\}, \{Olympus, SS\}\} \\ P = \; & \{\{Olympus, Rooms, AllYear\}\} \end{aligned}$$

This algebraic expression e will be our running example (well-formed) IFCA expression. We want to note that if $<_{\mathrm{F}}$ is ignored, the parameter size of the shortest CTCA expression e' such that $S_{e'} = S_e$ is 8 (see Proposition 3).

4 Checking Compound Term Validity

Below, we present an algorithm $IsValid_{\mathrm{I}}(e, s)$ which takes as input a well-formed IFCA expression e over an interrelated faceted taxonomy $\mathcal{F}$=($\mathcal{T}$, $\leq$) and a compound term $s \subseteq \mathcal{T}$, and returns TRUE, if $s \in S_e$, or FALSE, otherwise (i.e., if $s \notin S_e$). As it is shown in the explanations of the algorithm, $IsValid_{\mathtt{I}}(e, s)$ is optimized w.r.t. the naive approach.

Before we present the algorithm, we provide a few notations and definitions. Let $\mathcal{F}{=}(\mathcal{T}, \leq)$ be an interrelated faceted taxonomy, generated by a set of facets $\{F_1, ..., F_k\}$ and $<_{\mathtt{F}}$. Additionally, let e be an IFCA expression over $\mathcal{F}$. The *facets* of e are defined as: $F(e) = \{F_i \mid F_i \text{ appears in } e\}$. Clearly, $F(e) \subseteq \{F_1, ..., F_k\}$. We shall denote by $F(t)$ the facet to which a term $t \in \mathcal{T}$ belongs, e.g., in Figure 2, we have $F(SeaSki) = Sports$. Moreover, if $s \subseteq \mathcal{T}$, we define $F(s) = \bigcup\{F(t) \mid t \in s\}$.

Let $t, t' \in \mathcal{T}$ and let e be an IFCA expression over $\mathcal{F}$. We define: $t' <^{e}_{\mathtt{F}} t$ iff t' is a *maximal* (w.r.t. $\leq$) term such that: $t' \leq t$, $F(t') \in F(e)$, and $F(t') \neq F(t)$. For example, let e' be the first subexpression of our running example IFCA expression e. Then, $WinterSports <^{e'}_{\mathtt{F}} Winter$, while $SnowSki \not<^{e'}_{\mathtt{F}} Winter$ (note that $SnowSki \leq WinterSports$).

Algorithm 41. $IsValid_{\mathtt{I}}(e, s)$
Input: A well-formed IFCA expression e and a compound term $s = \{t_1, ..., t_m\} \subseteq \mathcal{T}$
Output: TRUE, if s belongs to S_e, or FALSE, otherwise

(1) If $s = \emptyset$ then *return*(TRUE);
(2) If $F(s) \not\subseteq F(e)$ then *return*(FALSE);
(3) If s is singleton then *return*(TRUE);
(4) Case(e) { `/* Check the parse tree of` e `*/`
(5) $\oplus_P(e_1, ..., e_n)$:
(6) If $\exists\, p \in P$ such that $p \preceq s$ then *return*(TRUE);
(7) For $i = 1, ..., n$ do {
(8) Let $S' = \{\{t'_1, ..., t'_m\} \mid (t'_j = t_j$ and $F(t_j) \in F(e_i))$ or $(t'_j <^{e_i}_{\mathtt{F}} t_j$ and $F(t_j) \notin F(e_i))$, for $j = 1, ..., m\}$;
(9) For all $s' \in S'$ do { `/* Note that` $s' \in$ `Nr(`s`) */`
(10) If $IsValid_{\mathtt{I}}(e_i, s')$=TRUE then *return*(TRUE);
`/* Note that` $s' \in S_{e_i}$. `Thus,` $s \in S_e$ `*/`
} `/* End For */`
} `/* End For */`
(11) $\ominus_N(e_1, ..., e_n)$:
(12) If $\exists\, n \in N$ such that $s \preceq n$ then *return*(FALSE);
(13) Let $S' = \{\{t'_1, ..., t'_m\} \mid t'_j = t_j$ or $\exists i \in \{1, ..., n\}$ s.t. $(t'_j <^{e_i}_{\mathtt{F}} t_j$ and $F(t_j) \notin F(e_i))$, for $j = 1, ..., m\}$;
(14) For all $s' \in S'$ do { `/* Note that` $s' \in$ `Nr(`s`) */`
(15) Let $\langle s'_1, ..., s'_n \rangle$ be the partition of s' s.t. $F(s'_i) \subseteq F(e_i)$, for $i = 1, ..., n$;
(16) $i = 1$;
(17) $flag$ =TRUE;
(18) While $flag$=TRUE and $i \leq n$ do {
(19) If $IsValid_{\mathtt{I}}(e_i, s'_i)$=FALSE then $flag$ =FALSE;
(20) $i = i + 1$;
} `/* End While */`
(21) If $flag$ =TRUE then *return*(TRUE); `/*` $s' \in S_e$. `Thus,` $s \in S_e$ `*/`
} `/* End For */`
(22) $\overset{*}{\ominus}_N (T_i)$: If $\exists\, n \in N$ such that $s \preceq n$ then *return*(FALSE) else *return*(TRUE);

```
(23)     Tᵢ: If ∃ t ∈ 𝒯ᵢ such that {t} ⪯ s then return(TRUE);    /* s ∈ Tᵢ ⊆ Sₑ */
    }  /* End Case */
(24) return(FALSE);
```

The algorithm $IsValid_{\mathtt{I}}(e,s)$ for a well-formed IFCA expression e and $s=\{t_1,...,t_m\}\subseteq\mathcal{T}$ is based on the parse tree of the expression e.

- If $e=\oplus_P(e_1,...,e_n)$ and $F(s)\subseteq F(e)$ then it is checked if it exists $p\in P$ such that $p\preceq s$ (Step 6). If this is the case then $IsValid_{\mathtt{I}}(e,s)$ returns TRUE. Obviously, in this case, $s\in Br(P)\subseteq\oplus_P(e_1,...,e_n)$. Otherwise, $IsValid_{\mathtt{I}}(e_i,s')$ is called (Step 10), for all $i=1,...,n$, and $s'\in S'$, where $S'=\{\{t'_1,....,t'_m\}\mid(t'_j=t_j$ and $F(t_j)\in F(e_i))$ or $(t'_j<^{e_i}_{\mathtt{F}}t_j$ and $F(t_j)\notin F(e_i))\}$ (Steps 7-8). It holds that $\forall s\in S'$, $s'\preceq s$. Note that Step 8 has been optimized, as in a naive approach all compound terms $s'\preceq s$ would had been considered for computing S'. If any of the $IsValid_{\mathtt{I}}(e_i,s')$ calls, for $i=1,...,n$, returns TRUE then $IsValid_{\mathtt{I}}(e,s)$ returns TRUE (Step 10). Obviously, in this case, $s\in Br(S_{e_1}\cup...\cup S_{e_n})\cap\mathcal{D}_{S_{e_1},...,S_{e_n}}\subseteq\oplus_P(e_1,...,e_n)$.
- If $e=\ominus_N(e_1,...,e_n)$ and $F(s)\subseteq F(e)$ then it is checked if it exists $n\in N$ such that $s\preceq n$ (Step 12). If this is the case then $IsValid_{\mathtt{I}}(e,s)$ returns FALSE. Obviously, in this case, $s\in Nr(N)$. Thus, $s\notin S_{e_1}\oplus...\oplus S_{e_n}-Nr(N)$, and as e is well-formed, $s\notin\ominus_N(e_1,...,e_n)$. Otherwise, the set $S'=\{\{t'_1,....,t'_m\}\mid t'_j=t_j$ or $\exists i\in\{1,...,n\}$ s.t. $(t'_j<^{e_i}_{\mathtt{F}}t_j$ and $F(t_j)\notin F(e_i))$, for $j=1,...,m\}$ is computed (Step 13). It holds that $\forall s\in S'$, $s'\preceq s$. Note that Step 13 has been optimized, as in a naive approach all compound terms $s'\preceq s$ would had been considered for computing S'. Then, for all $s'\in S'$, the partition[9] $\langle s'_1,...,s'_n\rangle$ of s' such that $F(s'_i)\subseteq F(e_i)$, for $i=1,...,n$, is computed (Step 15). Then, $IsValid_{\mathtt{I}}(e_i,s'_i)$ is called (Step 19), for all $i=1,...,n$. If $IsValid_{\mathtt{I}}(e_i,s'_i)$ returns TRUE, for all $i=1,...,n$, then $IsValid_{\mathtt{I}}(e,s)$ returns TRUE. Obviously, in this case, $s\in Br(S_{e_1}\oplus...\oplus S_{e_n})\cap\mathcal{D}_{S_{e_1},...,S_{e_n}}-Nr(N)$. As e is well-formed, $s\in\ominus_N(e_1,...,e_n)$.
- If $e=\overset{*}{\ominus}_N(T_i)$ and $F(s)=\{F_i\}$ then it is checked if it exists $n\in N$ such that $s\preceq n$ (Step 22). If this is the case then $IsValid_{\mathtt{I}}(e,s)$ returns FALSE. Obviously, in this case, $s\in Nr(N)$. Otherwise, $IsValid_{\mathtt{I}}(e,s)$ returns TRUE. Obviously, in this case $s\in\mathcal{P}(\mathcal{T}_i)-Nr(N)$.
- If $e=T_i$ and $F(s)=\{F_i\}$ then it is examined if it exists $t\in\mathcal{T}_i$ such that $\{t\}\preceq s$ (Step 23). Obviously, in this case, $s\in T_i=Br\{\{t\}\mid t\in\mathcal{T}_i\}\cap\mathcal{P}(\mathcal{T}_i)$.

Note that since the $\leq$ relation is a partial order, algorithm $IsValid_{\mathtt{I}}(e,s)$ always terminates.

Continuing our running example, note that it holds:
$IsValid_{\mathtt{I}}(e,\{Olympus, FA, Winter\})$ =TRUE.
The trace of this call is as follows:

[9] Since e is a well-formed IFCA expression, there is only one such partition. This is due to condition (1) of Def. 6 (Well-formed expression).

```
Call IsValid_I(⊖_N(Location, Accommodation, Sports) ⊕_P (Season),
                {Olympus, FA, Winter});
  It holds that ∄p ∈ P s.t. p ⪯ {Olympus, FA, Winter};
  Compute S' = {{Olympus, FA, WS}};
  Call IsValid_I(⊖_N(Location, Accommodation, Sports), {Olympus, FA, WS});
    It holds that ∄n ∈ N s.t. {Olympus, FA, WS} ⪯ n;
    Compute S' = {{Olympus, FA, WS}};
    Compute partition ⟨{Olympus}, {FA}, {WS}⟩ of s' ∈ S';
    Call IsValid_I(Location, {Olympus});
      Return(TRUE);
    Call IsValid_I(Accommodation, {FA});
      Return(TRUE);
    Call IsValid_I(Sports, {WS});
      Return(TRUE);
    Return(TRUE);
  Return(TRUE);
```

Additionally, it holds: $IsValid_{\mathtt{I}}(e, \{Hersonissos, Winter\})$ =FALSE.
The trace of this call is as follows:

```
Call IsValid_I(⊖_N(Location, Accommodation, Sports) ⊕_P (Season),
                {Hersonissos, Winter});
  It holds that ∄p ∈ P s.t. p ⪯ {Hersonissos, Winter};
  Compute S' = {{Hersonissos, WS}};
    /* Note that F({Hersonissos, WS}) = {Location, Sports} */
  Call IsValid_I(⊖_N(Location, Accommodation, Sports), {Hersonissos, WS});
    It holds that ∃n ∈ N s.t. {Hersonissos, WS} ⪯ n;
    Return(FALSE);
  Compute S' = {};     /* Note that ∄t' ∈T_Season s.t. t' ≤ Hersonissos */
    Return(FALSE);
  Return(FALSE);
```

To provide the worst-time complexity of $IsValid_{\mathtt{I}}(e, s)$, a few auxiliary definitions are needed.

Let e be a well-formed IFCA expression over an interrelated faceted taxonomy $\mathcal{F} = (\mathcal{T}, \leq)$ and let $s \subseteq \mathcal{T}$. We define: $d_s^e = max_{t \in s}(|\{t'' \in \mathcal{T} \mid t'' <_{\mathtt{F}}^{e} t', t' \leq t\}|)$. For our running example IFCA expression e and $s = \{Hersonissos, Winter\}$, it holds that $d_s^e = 1$, while $d_s^{Season} = 0$.

Finally, let $|s_e^{\mathtt{max}}|$ be the size of the largest compound term, appearing in a P or N parameter of e. For our running example IFCA expression e, $|s_e^{\mathtt{max}}| = 3$.

Proposition 5. Let e be a well-formed IFCA expression over an interrelated faceted taxonomy $\mathcal{F} = (\mathcal{T}, \leq)$ and let $s \subseteq \mathcal{T}$. The worst-time complexity of $IsValid_{\mathtt{I}}(e, s)$ is in: $O(|s|^{d_s^e+1} * |s_e^{\mathtt{max}}| * |\mathcal{T}|^2 * |\mathcal{P}_e \cup \mathcal{N}_e|)$.

In computing the worst-time complexity of $IsValid_{\mathtt{I}}(e, s)$, the component $|s| * |s_e^{\mathtt{max}}| * |\mathcal{T}|^2$ corresponds to the maximun-time needed to check $p \preceq s'$, for all $p \in \mathcal{P}_e$ and $s' \preceq n$, for all $n \in \mathcal{N}_e$, in lines (6), (12), and (22) of Algorithm 41, respectively. Note that $|s'| \leq |s|$. Additionally, the factor $|s|^{d_s^e}$ corresponds to the maximum number of times that $IsValid_{\mathtt{I}}(.)$ is called in lines (10) and

(19) of Algorithm 41. Specifically, the factor $|s|^{d_s^e}$ is due to lines (8) and (13) of Algorithm 41.

Note that: (i) the call $IsValid_{\mathtt{I}}(e,s)$ can replaced, for optimization reasons, by $IsValid_{\mathtt{I}}(e, minimal_{\leq}(s))$[10], (ii) if s contains only one term of each facet then $|s| \leq |F(e)|$, and (iii) if $<_{\mathtt{F}}= \emptyset$ then $d_s^e = 0$.

Let $\mathcal{F}$ be an interrelated faceted taxonomy with $<_{\mathtt{F}}= \emptyset$ and let e is a well-formed CTCA expression e over $\mathcal{F}$. Then, e can be mapped directly to a well-formed IFCA expression e' such that (i) $S_{e'} = S_e$ and (ii) the computational complexity of $IsValid_{\mathtt{I}}(e', s)$ coincides with the computational complexity of $IsValid(e,s)$ (this algorithm is provided in [15], for checking compound term validity, according to a well-formed CTCA expression e).

5 Concluding Remarks

Faceted taxonomies are used in marketplaces [11], e-government portals [9], publishing museum collections on the Semantic Web [5], browsing large data sets from mobile phones [6], and several other application domains. Interest in faceted taxonomies is also indicated by several projects, like SemWeb[11], SWED[12], and SIMILE[13].

In this paper, we generalized previous work and provided an algebra, called *Interrelated Facet Composition Algebra* (IFCA), for specifying the valid terms over a faceted taxonomy $\mathcal{F}$, whose facets may be interrelated (through narrower/broader relationships between their terms). An optimized (w.r.t. the naive approach) algorithm that checks compound term validity, according to a well-formed IFCA expression, and its complexity were also provided. In contrast to *Compound Term Composition Algebra* (CTCA) [15], IFCA supports narrower/broader relationships between the terms of the different facets, thus reducing the size of the desired algebraic expressions and the effort needed by the designer to build the desired algebraic expression. Additionally, considering $<_{\mathtt{F}}$ during the formulation of a well-formed IFCA expression, we avoid conceptual errors (i.e., that a compound term is incorrectly specified as valid/invalid) that may be introduced during the formulation of a (well-formed) CTCA expression. The complexity of the compound term validity algorithms of CTCA and IFCA coincide, in the case that $\mathcal{F}$ is a simple faceted taxonomy (i.e., an interrelated faceted taxonomy with $<_{\mathtt{F}}= \emptyset$).

Issues for further research include: (i) generalizing the supported framework such that the relation $\leq$ between the terms of $\mathcal{F}$ is allowed to include non-trivial cycles, (ii) devising an algorithm for deciding whether an IFCA expression e is well-formed, (iii) devising *mining* algorithms (similar to these for CTCA [13]) that, given a materialized interrelated faceted taxonomy $\mathcal{M}$, derive well-formed IFCA expressions, defining the extensionally valid compound terms of $\mathcal{M}$. Finally, we plan to implement our proposed IFCA framework.

[10] Obviously, $s \in S_e$ iff $minimal_{\leq}(s) \in S_e$.

[11] `http://www.seco.tkk.fi/projects/semweb/`

[12] `http://www.swed.org.uk/`

[13] `http://simile.mit.edu/`

References

1. Analyti, A., Pachoulakis, I.: Logic Programming Representation of the Compound Term Composition Algebra. Fundamenta Informaticae 73(3), 321–360 (2006)
2. Baader, F., Calvanese, D., McGuinness, D.L., Nardi, D., Patel-Schneider, P.F. (eds.): The Description Logic Handbook: Theory, Implementation, and Applications. Cambridge University Press, Cambridge (2003)
3. Ganter, B., Wille, R.: Formal Concept Analysis: Mathematical Foundations. Springer, Heidelberg (1999)
4. Hearst, M.: Design Recommendations for Hierarchical Faceted Search Interfaces. In: ACM SIGIR 2006 Workshop on Faceted Search, pp. 26–30 (2006)
5. Hyvönen, E., Mäkelä, E., Salminen, M., Valo, A., Viljanen, K., Saarela, S., Junnila, M., Kettula, S.: MUSEUMFINLAND - Finnish Museums on the Semantic Web. Journal of Web Semantics 3(2-3), 224–241 (2005)
6. Karlson, A.K., Robertson, G.G., Robbins, D.C., Czerwinski, M.P., Smith, G.R.: FaThumb: a Facet-Based Interface for Mobile Search. In: Procs. of the SIGCHI conference on Human Factors in Computing Systems (CHI 2006), pp. 711–720 (2006)
7. Lloyd, J.W.: Foundations of Logic Programming. Springer, Heidelberg (1987)
8. Sacco, G.M.: Dynamic Taxonomies: A Model for Large Information Bases. IEEE Transactions on Knowledge and Data Engineering 12(3), 468–479 (2000)
9. Sacco, G.M.: Guided Interactive Information Access for E-Citizens. In: Wimmer, M.A., Traunmüller, R., Grönlund, Å., Andersen, K.V. (eds.) EGOV 2005. LNCS, vol. 3591, pp. 261–268. Springer, Heidelberg (2005)
10. Sacco, G.M.: Research Results in Dynamic Taxonomy and Faceted Search Systems. In: Procs. of the 1st International Workshop on Dynamic Taxonomies and Faceted Search (in conjunction with DEXA 2007), pp. 201–206. IEEE Computer Society, Los Alamitos (2007)
11. Tofte, I., Sæth, K.J., Jansson, K.: A case study of Vinmonopolet.no: faceted search and navigation for e-commerce. In: Procs. of the 4th Nordic Conference on Human-Computer Interaction (NordiCHI 2006), pp. 489–490 (2006)
12. Tzitzikas, Y.: An Algebraic Method for Compressing Symbolic Data Tables. Journal of Intelligent Data Analysis (IDA) 10(4), 243–359 (2006)
13. Tzitzikas, Y., Analyti, A.: Mining the Meaningful Term Conjunctions from Materialised Faceted Taxonomies: Algorithms and Complexity. Knowledge and Information Systems (KAIS) 9(4), 430–467 (2006)
14. Tzitzikas, Y., Analyti, A., Spyratos, N.: Compound Term Composition Algebra: The Semantics. LNCS Journal on Data Semantics 2, 58–84 (2005)
15. Tzitzikas, Y., Analyti, A., Spyratos, N., Constantopoulos, P.: An Algebra for Specifying Valid Compound Terms in Faceted Taxonomies. Data and Knowledge Engineering (DKE) 62(1), 1–40 (2007)
16. Tzitzikas, Y., Launonen, R., Hakkarainen, M., Korhonen, P., Leppänen, T., Simpanen, E., Törnroos, H., Uusitalo, P., Vänskä, P.: FASTAXON: A system for FAST (and faceted) tAXONomy design. In: Atzeni, P., Chu, W., Lu, H., Zhou, S., Ling, T.-W. (eds.) ER 2004. LNCS, vol. 3288, pp. 841–843. Springer, Heidelberg (2004), `http://fastaxon.erve.vtt.fi/`
17. Yee, K., Swearingen, K., Li, K., Hearst, M.: Faceted Metadata for Image Search and Browsing. In: Proceedings of the Conf. on Human Factors in Computing Systems (CHI 2003), pp. 401–408 (April 2003)

Conceptual Modeling in Disaster Planning Using Agent Constructs

Kafui Monu and Carson Woo

University of British Columbia, Sauder School of Business, 2053 Main Mall, Vancouver BC, Canada
kafui.monu@sauder.ubc.ca, carson.woo@ubc.ca

Abstract. A disaster plan contains rules to be used by responders to deal with a disaster and save lives. Usually, the plan is not enacted by those who created it. This results in difficulty for responders in utilizating the plan.

Conceptual models have been used to gain a better understanding of disaster plans. Unfortunately, the conceptual modeling grammars used to create these conceptual models focus only on the external view of the responders and how they interact with one another; they do not represent the internal view (e.g., assumptions and reasoning) used in their decision making. Without representing the internal view, responders will not know, for example, whether the objective assumed by planners is appropriate for their specific situation.

In this paper, we propose to overcome this problem by utilizing constructs from the intelligent agent literature since they can represent roles, interactions, assumptions, and decision-making. To understand the practicality and usefulness of conceptually representing both external and internal views of different roles in a disaster plan, we performed a case study on the role in the disaster plan of a local Emergency Operations Centre (EOC). The results of the case study show that conceptual modeling using agent constructs has great potential for aiding disaster responders in understanding disaster plans. Because of the model, the assumptions that were hidden in the plan can now be extracted and shown to disaster responders and the efficacy of a plan can be evaluated before it needs to be enacted.

Keywords: Modeling Grammar, Intelligent Agent, Disaster Management.

1 Introduction

To prepare for disasters, organizations perform disaster management techniques such as disaster planning, which creates response plans that are used to mitigate the effects of a disaster and coordinate a response. Unfortunately, there is usually a gap between disaster plans and the actual response. This is because different groups of responders focus on their own small set of responsibilities and ignore parts of the plan that they do not think are important. The ignored part, however, may aid interaction with other organizations [9]. If responders had a better understanding of the rationale behind the plan, then it may lead to better utilization.

For easier understanding of a disaster plan, one tool is needed to do the following; 1) present the interactions between the responders, 2) identify the hidden assumptions

A.H.F. Laender et al. (Eds.): ER 2009, LNCS 5829, pp. 374–386, 2009.

of the plan, and 3) communicate this information to responders. With this knowledge, responders will know which actions may affect other responders and the reason for the actions responders are supposed to make according to the plan. To achieve these goals, conceptual modeling grammars have been developed to represent disaster plans [6, 8]. A conceptual modeling grammar contains concepts that can be used to represent the business domain and rules for how those concepts relate to one another [17]. Existing grammars can represent actions and interactions but they do not explicitly capture responders' reasoning process or the rationale for performing actions in the plan. To overcome this weakness, we turn to the "agent" concept.

The "agent" concept represents active entities that decide how to change their environment. Due to its ability to represent interactions as well as the reasoning process of decision making, it may prove useful in representing roles in disaster plans. In this paper, we used the Conceptual Agent Model (CAM) [14] because it is an agent conceptual modelling grammar. Our objective is not to learn about the applicability of CAM in disaster planning. Rather, by applying CAM in a case study, we are interested in understanding the usefulness and challenges of using the agent concept in analyzing and communicating the assumptions in a disaster plan.

In Section 2, we will discuss disaster management and attempts to use conceptual modeling to analyse disaster plans. In Section 3, we will discuss agent conceptual modeling grammars and why we chose CAM. In Section 4, we will outline our studies, and in Section 5 we will conclude our work with some future research directions.

2 Disaster Management and Planning

Disasters are any events that may cause major disruptions to structures and systems that support populations. This can include natural hazards as well as man-made disasters [2]. Disaster management is the discipline of reacting to disasters. One problem that plagues disaster management is the creation and application of disaster plans [2]. Disaster plans are assumed to prepare an effective and timely response to disasters and mitigate problems that occur because of the event, but it has been found that plans are often not enough.

> "...the fact that a plan assigns specific responsibilities does not necessarily imply that those who have been assigned the responsibilities are aware of their role, accept the role assigned to them, understand how to perform that role, or even have the capability to perform it" [9, p. 495].

Therefore, those who enact the plan may not be aware, accept or understand the plan due to their own narrow interests [9]. To alleviate this problem, disaster responders usually perform extensive disaster simulation exercises for "... training purpose, and for evaluating plans" [4, p. 78]. Conducting these exercises, responders gain an understanding of interconnected actions and can evaluate whether the actions in a plan are appropriate for their situation. However, it may take several exercises to fully "debug" the plan, which is a problem since these exercises are "costly, in terms of money, time, and political capital" [4, p. 78].

Another possible way of gaining information about disaster plans is by understanding the context of a situation during a disaster. The 5W1H model which models a situation by asking who, what, when, where, why, and how for each situation, has been used to develop these systems [15]. Unfortunately, to analyze disaster plans, this information would have to be gathered through interviews and it would not provide an accurate picture of the disaster plan since most people are unaware of even their own part of the plan [9]. Also, to generate the entire context, most of the information (who, what, when, where, why, and how) needs to be available to make an inference about decision making [15] and the correct kind of 5W1H questions need to be asked to understand the situation. Therefore, the 5W1H model may be very useful for creating context aware systems for disaster response, but its lack of specificity, need for almost total information, and dependence on user created data, makes it problematic for analyzing complex multi-layered disaster plans.

2.1 Conceptual Modeling in Disaster Management

The overall task of understanding a disaster plan is challenging since disaster management is complex, involving many complicated interrelationships between people, organizations, and infrastructure [10]. Due to this complexity, some researchers have suggested the use of conceptual models to aid in this understanding [6, 8]. Note that these conceptual models are different from those used in implementing information systems (e.g., [11]) because their focus is on understanding the information systems rather than disaster plans.

Hoogendorn et. al. provide concepts such as role, input, and output to model the organizations involved in disaster planning [8]. They also keep track of the events in the disaster plan with constructs that represent organizational change. Fahland and Woith base their modeling grammar on petri nets, which use concepts called places and transitions [6]. Very much like a workflow model, this model shows how responders transition between different actions during a disaster. These two modeling grammars represent the actions and interactions that may occur during a disaster and provide an overview of how the roles act according to the plan. This means that responders can understand how actions influence each other. However, the grammars do not represent ***how*** responders make decisions; only ***what*** decisions are made. Without representing the rationale for action, responders cannot identify and evaluate the assumptions behind the plan without performing expensive exercises.

Krutchen et. al. mention that the agent concept is useful in representing disaster responders [10]. The agent concept is based on the "intelligent agent" software concept and is used to represent entities that can actively affect the environment [14]. An intelligent agent is adaptive, reactive, communicative, and autonomous [18]. That is, an agent reads the environment, "thinks" about how to achieve a goal, and can interact with the environment. This means the agent concept can represent both the internal (learning, reasoning, etc.) and external (actions and interactions) views of actors in a domain. For this reason, we propose to use conceptual models based on the agent concept to understand disaster plans.

3 Using the Agent Concept in Conceptual Modeling

Currently there are several conceptual agent modeling grammars that may be able to represent the disaster management domain: i*, MibML, and CAM. The i* grammar was developed to represent the underlying motivations behind business processes and aid the gathering of early phase requirements [19]. It does this by focusing on a concept called the intentional actor, which is represented in i*'s two models: the Strategic Dependency Model and Strategic Rationale Model. The Strategic Dependency Model represents a specific relationship between the actors in the system, the one between the depender, who needs something, and the dependee, the person who provides a good or service [19]. Once the dependencies have been modelled, the analyst can use the Strategic Rationale Model to show more details of the relationship between the actors' tasks, and goals.

The Multiagent Based Integrative Business Modelling Language (MibML) is another grammar used to represent agents [20]. The grammar can also be used to create conceptual models for agent systems in business. In MibML, agents take on roles within the domain. The MibML grammar represents interactions between the roles and some internal aspects of an agent.

Both i* and MibML do not explicitly represent a crucial aspect of agents, the decision making process that connects the agent's goals to its actions [13]. The i* grammar has mean-ends links, which show which tasks fulfill which goals, but the rationale for the links is not represented. The MibML grammar has a "knowledge" construct, but it does not show how the agent decides what to do in the environment, only what it knows. Therefore, these modeling grammars are not suitable for our purpose of modeling the decision making process.

Lastly, the Conceptual Agent Model (CAM) defines an agent as an entity that is aware of the world and can affect its world by deciding to take actions [14]. It has constructs which are specifically created to represent agent decision making (i.e., reasoning, procedures, and goals). For this reason, we use CAM in our case study to analyze a disaster plan.

3.1 The Conceptual Agent Model

CAM utilizes system theory [1, 5, 12], a model of feedback systems [3], and Bunge's ontology as adapted by Wand and Weber [16] (BWW ontology) to derive a minimal set of constructs needed to describe agents [14], which are ***perceptions, actions, resources, capabilities, goals, reasoning, beliefs, learning, and procedures***.

More specifically, in CAM, an agent is an entity that is aware of the world through its ***perceptions*** and can affect its world by taking ***actions*** using ***resources***. However, the agent has to have the ***capability*** to use these resources properly. The agent performs actions to achieve a specific ***goal*** and must decide, using ***reasoning***, which actions it wants to take to achieve its goal. The agent observes its world and may form ***beliefs***, or assumptions, about the world based on its perceptions. By ***learning*** about the world in this way, the agent can then reason as to what it is going to do. When thinking about its goal, the agent develops options of what it wants to do. These wants are grouped together as a ***procedure*** and tell us how the agent achieves its goals. When a procedure is decided upon, it directs the actions of the agent.

Along with presenting the constructs, Monu et. al. split the agent into two components, the simulator and the effector [14]. The ***simulator*** can be considered the "mind" of the agent, since it decides what actions to take to achieve its goal, while the ***effector*** is the part of the agent that can change the environment.

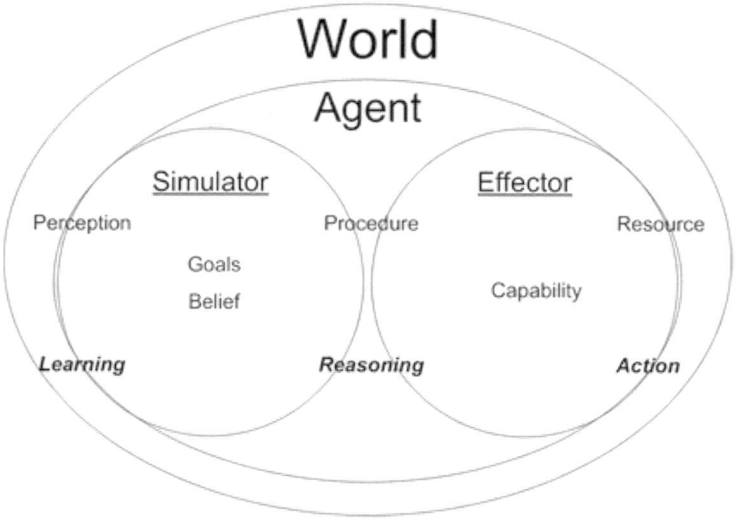

Fig. 1. Intelligent Agent Concepts [14]

Figure 1 shows graphically how the different agent constructs relate to the world, simulator, and effector. If a construct is inside a circle then it belongs to that component, however if it lies between circles then it is part of both components. For instance, the resource construct belongs to the agent's effector and the world. The italicized constructs are dynamic constructs and are directly related to the construct above it; perception is tied to learning, reasoning is tied to procedures, and actions are tied to resources. We also show the internal properties and states of the simulator (goals and beliefs) and the effector (capabilities). The simulator is a representation of the internal view, while the effector represents the external view.

Since the paper focuses on identifying the hidden assumptions behind decision making in a disaster plan, we focus on the Reasoning and Procedure concepts. It is stated in [13] that Reasoning selects Procedure and Procedure directs Action.

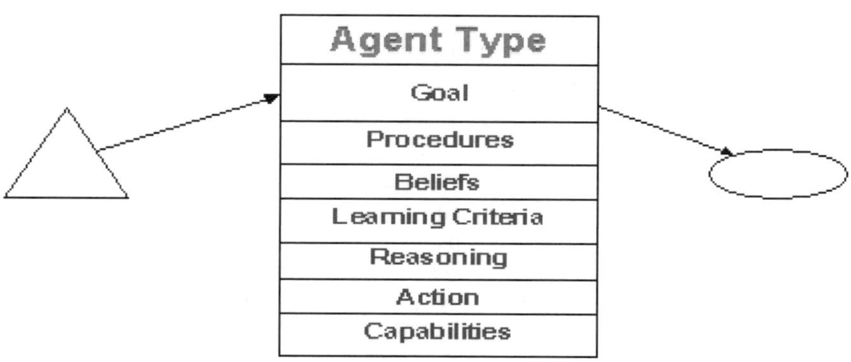

Fig. 2. Symbols to Represent Conceptual Agents

The authors also present a set of symbols to be used to represent the constructs. This is shown in Figure 2. Perceptions and resources in Figure 2 are displayed as either agent or system variables. System variables are properties that make up the state of the world and are shown as ovals, while agent variables refer to agent properties that are not part of its effector or simulator and are shown as triangles. In the representation, the difference between resources and perceptions is shown by the agent's relation to the variables. If an interaction arrow goes from the variable to the agent, then it is a perception. However, if the interaction arrow goes from an agent to a variable, then the variable is a resource.

4 Agent Conceptual Modeling in Disaster Planning

As mentioned in Section 1, we are interested in understanding the usefulness and challenges of using agent conceptual modeling in analyzing and communicating the assumptions in a disaster plan. Since agent concepts have not been used to represent disaster plans, we first must determine how an agent conceptual model can represent information explicitly in the disaster plan, which is presented in Section 4.1. Then, we develop steps to aid individuals in deriving and analyzing agent concepts from disaster plans, which we show in Section 4.2. Then, in Section 4.3, we present an example of using agent concepts in disaster planning through a case study.

Our proposition is that a conceptual model that represents decision making, which is not explicitly documented in the disaster plan, will be useful for responders in their live exercise. However, since it is difficult to get access to a live exercise and even ask a responder to use an unproven conceptual model, we will present the conceptual model to a programmer interested in simulating decision-making in disaster response as an evaluation of the model. If he finds it useful to accomplish his programming task, then we have demonstrated the conceptual model's ability in communicating the details of the roles in the disaster plan.

4.1 Representing the Disaster Plan Using Agent Constructs

To ensure that agent constructs can represent disaster plans, we model an existing plan. Since most plans outline the tasks that need to be performed by certain roles in an organization during a disaster, we should be able to represent the external view (actions, resources, and interactions) of the roles in the model. However, if the internal view of the roles is not explicitly mentioned in the disaster plan, we cannot know the rationale behind the actions assigned to responders in the plan. Gathering the internal view is difficult because planners are not responders and may have retired or moved on since the plan was created. We hypothesize that it is possible to reverse-engineer the internal view if we can determine the relationship between the agent constructs.

4.2 Using Agent Constructs to Derive Decision Making

To determine the relationship between the agent constructs, we use the following agent literature. Miller provides an early set of constructs to describe decision-making by artificial intelligence [12], Bratman has the basis for an effective framework for

Table 1. Investigation of Reasoning using Agent Literature

Agent Literature	Relationship	Notes
"Our desires… give us reasons for actions", "our interest is in determining what sort of action is recommended by the agent's relevant desire-belief reasons" [4, pp. 24 and 47]	Goals used by Reasoning.	By incorporating the goal we can select the correct action.
"…a function which maps sequences of percepts to actions" [18, p. 39]	Perceptions/ Input used by Reasoning.	The perception must be used to understand the world and choose an action accordingly.
"The background framework against which practical reasoning and planning typically includes not only prior intentions and plans but also flat-out beliefs" [4, p. 36]	Reasoning uses Beliefs.	Reasoning uses assumptions (i.e. beliefs) about the outcome of actions to choose how to act.
"an overall program which determines what alternatives to select in each single choice of the sequence. For instance in working on a mathematical problem, an algorithm which is a rule for solving all problems of a certain kind" [12, p. 433]	Reasoning selects Procedure.	These rules are conditional statements of what the agent wants to do based on beliefs and perceptions.
"Plans as I shall understand them are mental states involving an appropriate sort of commitment to action" [4, p. 29]	Procedures can direct Action.	"Plans" can be called procedures.

building software agents called the Belief-Desire-Intention model or BDI [4], and Wooldridge provides an excellent overview of software agents [18]. In Table 1, we show how reasoning is viewed by this set of literature in relating reasoning to other agent concepts.

We can see from Table 1 that reasoning is made up of three elements: some knowledge of the world be it through observation (perception) or assumption (belief), a specific instance of that knowledge which is in accordance with its goal, and a procedure. Therefore, a generic format for reasoning can be written as: *if [knowledge] = [value] then [procedure]*. Goals are used by reasoning to determine the "correct" value for the belief and/or perception that triggers a procedure. In fact, the term "[*knowledge*] = [*value*]" can be considered as the rationale for the agent's actions. However, in most disaster plans the specific goal of the role is implied or assumed to be known by the actor and is not explicitly stated. Therefore, we will need to identify the agent's goal before we can determine its reasoning.

4.2.1 Identifying Goals

To determine the goal of an agent, we can use the statements in Table 1. Since procedure directs how the agent changes its environment, the consequences of the procedure are how the agent affects the environment. Since reasoning is used to achieve the agent's goal by selecting procedures, we deduce that the consequences of the procedure must contribute to the goal of the agent. Therefore, the steps for identifying goals with only procedures are:

1) Identify the procedures,
2) Determine how the world is changed when procedures are enacted (consequences),
3) Determine similarities between the consequences and,
4) Combine the classifications of consequences.

The assumption is that all actions taken by the agent are part of its goal and can be used to infer its objective. We also must use domain knowledge to be able to determine how procedures affect the world. For example, if an agent had the procedure "Buy a cake", the consequence of the procedure would be "Agent has a cake". If another procedure was "Buy birthday gift for friend" then the consequence would be "Friend gets birthday gift". We can classify both consequences as "Birthday party prepared for friend" and therefore identify part, or all, of the agent's goal.

4.2.2 Identifying Reasoning Using the External View

To determine the reasoning rules, we use the goal and perception/belief of the agent (as mentioned in second paragraph in Section 4.2). Once we know the perceptions and beliefs (and the correct value) that trigger the procedures, then we have determined the conditions under which the procedures will occur, which is part of the reasoning process of the agent. However, since disaster plans focus on the external view, we will only focus on perceptions, which represent part of an agent's interaction with the environment. This results in the following steps for identifying reasoning:

1) Identify perceptions of the agent,
2) Identify the procedures of the agent,
3) Identify the goal of the agent,
4) Divide the goal into partial goals that have distinctly different effects on the environment,
5) Determine which perceptions are important for performing the procedure,
6) Determine which procedures are used to fulfill a partial goal,
7) Determine the perception(s) that are related to changes in the environment that are a result of the procedure,
8) Determine the value of the perception(s) that reflects a state of the world opposite to that of the partial goal attached to the procedure, and
9) Combine the perception(s)' values to determine the condition under which the procedure would be enacted.

Using the same example from Section 4.2.1, if the perceptions of the agent are messages from other people about what they will bring to the party, and the agent's supply of money, we can use these to determine its reasoning. If we want to know when the agent will enact the "Buy a cake" procedure, we begin by identifying that the agent is interested in preparing a party for the friend. We can also determine that its perception about who will bring what to the party is tied to the procedure. Using domain knowledge, we know that if no one volunteers to bring the cake, then that is the opposite of the agent's goal. Therefore, only if the agent perceives that no one will bring the cake will it enact the procedure "Buy a cake".

4.3 Case Study

For the case study, we analyzed a disaster plan developed by a local Emergency Operation Centre (EOC). This is an ideal plan since the EOC helps "a multitude of agency officials coordinate their disaster response" [7, p. 75] and the EOC roles make many decisions. The role we chose to analyze was the Emergency Planning Coordinator (EPC), who is the head of the planning section of the EOC. The EPC ensures that situation reports in the EOC are accurate so that the information can be incorporated into disaster plans, and reports directly to the EOC director. In this section we use the steps described in Section 4.1 and 4.2 to: 1) model the disaster plan, 2) determine a role's partial goals, and 3) derive reasoning for a role.

4.3.1 Conceptual Model of the Emergency Operations Centre Disaster Plan

The EOC plan details the tasks that roles perform before, during, and after a disaster. For each role, the plan states its inputs, outputs, and concerns. For instance, an input for the EOC director role is media releases of the disaster, its output is a log that keeps track of all the decisions it has made during the disaster, and a concern is to give support to authorities and ensure all needed disaster response actions are accomplished. We mapped the input, outputs, and concerns to the *perception*, *resource*, and *procedure* concepts, respectively. This provided us the external view of the roles.

To ensure that the conceptual model facilitates responders in performing their tasks, we asked an observer to use the model to compare the plan during a live exercise. The observer noted that the conceptual model gave her a quick overview of the plan so that she could compare the interactions that were supposed to happen with what was happening in the exercise. This gave us the confidence that these three agent concepts can be used to represent and communicate interactions found in the plan.

4.3.2 Deriving Partial Goals of the Emergency Planning Coordinator

We then used the perceptions, procedures, and resources from the conceptual model to analyze the EPC role (Figure 3). There are many procedures in this role, however, due to space limitations, we will show the analyses of a few rather than all procedures. In Table 2, we show the consequence of some of the procedures and then classify the results.

Table 2. Consequences of Emergency Planning Coordinator's Procedures

Procedures	Consequence of Procedures	Classification of Consequences
Ensure that Planning position logs and other necessary files are maintained	Planning records are kept.	Information on EOC activities are recorded
.	.	.
.	.	.
.	.	.
Chair the EOC Action Planning meetings approximately two hours before the end of each operational period	EOC knows what actions need to be taken	Information on EOC activities are recorded
Provide technical services, such as environmental advisors and other technical specialists to all EOC sections as required	EOC sections have technical services.	EOC objectives are being met
Ensure Risk Management Officer is involved in Action Planning process	Action plan incorporates risk.	Concerns outside of planning will be included in the emergency response effort

From Table 2, we establish that the EPC's goal is to ensure that information on EOC activities are available during and after the disaster, the EOC objectives are being met, and concerns outside of planning are brought into the emergency response effort. Now we can use the goal, perceptions, and procedures to uncover its reasoning.

4.3.3 Deriving the Reasoning of the Emergency Planning Coordinator

Using the information in Table 2 and the steps outlined in Section 4.2.2, we determined the reasoning rules of the EPC. Again, due to space limitations, in Table 3 we show only certain reasoning rules by specifying some procedures, and their relevant perceptions, partial goals, and conditions.

Table 3. Reasoning rules for the Emergency Response Coordinator

Procedures	Perception	Partial Goal	Condition
Ensure that Planning position logs and other necessary files are maintained	Status report, situation reports, situation unit message	Information on EOC activities are recorded	Reports are not the same as situation unit message
Chair the EOC Action Planning meetings approximately two hours before the end of each operational period	EOC knows what actions need to be taken	Information on EOC activities are recorded	
. . .	. . .	. . .	. . .
Provide technical services, such as environmental advisors and other technical specialists to all EOC sections as required	Request for technical assistance	EOC objectives are being met	There is a request for assistance
Ensure Risk Management Officer is involved in Action Planning process	Action Planning Meeting.	Concerns outside of planning will be included in the emergency response effort	Risk officer is not at the Action Planning Meeting or is not contributing

4.3.4 Evaluation

We evaluated the information gained from the study by speaking with a programmer interested in developing a disaster response simulation program based on the plan. A step needed for this simulation is the development of disaster scenarios. These scenarios would provide a time-line of how different roles interacted with each other in a specific instance of a disaster. This scenario could then be inputted into the simulation and the response could be "played out".

The programmer found the conceptual model useful because it aided him in visualizing interactions among roles. The reasoning developed in Table 3 was useful because it helped him determine what the roles would do in the scenario, and the goal was useful because it provided a guideline for the agent's actions in the plan. This is important because the plan does not provide detailed enough actions for the scenario,

Fig. 3. CAM model of the Emergency Planning Coordinator and Interacting Roles

and more detailed actions will need to be created to fill out the scenario. However, these actions should be congruent with the disaster plan so that the goal can act as a guideline for the programmer in creating compatible actions.

Moreover, in developing the conceptual model, we also discovered some missing assumptions of the Emergency Planning Coordinator. They were detected by identifying procedures in Table 3 that do not have corresponding perceptions. For example, there is no perception that informs the agent about the end of an operational period, and therefore it has no way to know when to chair an action planning meeting.

5 Conclusion

A disaster response plan helps responders react to disasters. However, since a plan only acts as a guide, and those who enact the plan are usually not those who created it, the rationale for actions in the plan may not be understood when it is used in a disaster. This could lead to responders incorrectly understanding the priorities of or ignoring certain vital actions detailed in the plan. Although conceptual modeling has been proposed to support the understanding of disaster plans, they do not represent the rationale of actions and knowledge used in the responder's reasoning. In this paper, we proposed to overcome this weakness by utilizing concepts from the intelligent agent literature to represent the disaster plan in a conceptual model.

In order to understand the potential effectiveness of using agent conceptual modeling in disaster planning, we needed to first determine what agent constructs were explicitly documented in disaster plans, and whether conceptual models represented using those constructs were useful to responders. We were able to represent the plan by using the perception, procedure, and resource constructs. An observer of a live exercise confirmed that such a conceptual model is useful as an overview of interactions in the plan. Second, we needed to determine how to acquire the role's rationale and decision making process since they were unavailable in the plan and the responders did not develop the original plan. To determine the reasoning of a role, we found, through agent literature, that it could be defined as a combination of procedures, beliefs and/or perceptions, and goals. Since most plans do not specify the goals of the role, we developed steps to determine the goal. We then used these steps in a case study to determine a role's goal and reasoning.

We evaluated the information gathered from the study by showing it to a programmer interested in simulating disaster response, based on the plan. He found the information useful since it clearly shows the interaction between the roles, provides information of when actions will be performed in a disaster, and provides guidelines for developing actions for the role that are still consistent with the plan.

We also found that assumptions of the plan can be identified using the model. In some instances, we could not determine which perception in the plan informed the role about how to choose a procedure. The missing knowledge identified two important limitations to the study. First, as mentioned, reasoning can contain beliefs, perceptions, or both. The disaster plan did not show the beliefs of the agent, so we could only determine the perceptions used in reasoning. Procedures that were only enacted using internal knowledge of the agent could not be identified. Secondly, tying the perceptions to procedures cannot be done without domain knowledge. Therefore, creating the model requires some knowledge of the disaster management domain to be useful.

For future research, we are interested in testing the conceptual model by representing responders in a live disaster simulation exercise. In this case, we may be able to discover additional rationale beyond what the agent constructs can produce. We are also interested in working with the programmer to gather more information needed to develop his scenarios (e.g., the sequence of events and the timing of the response) and determine if they can be useful to responders.

The results of the study illustrate the potential of agent conceptual modeling in disaster planning. We hope that the application of these conceptual models will lead to better disaster plans, increase the efficacy of disaster response, and save lives.

Acknowledgements

This research is sponsored by the Joint Infrastructure Interdependencies Research Project (JIIRP) from NSERC and PSEPC (Government of Canada), now Safety Canada. We thank the members of the JIIRP projects for their assistance in our work.

References

1. Ackoff, R.L.: Towards a System of Systems Concepts. Management Science 17, 661–671 (1971)
2. Ahmed, N.: Managing Disasters. Kilaso Books, New Delhi (2003)
3. Bertalanffy, L.: General Systems Theory: Foundations, Development, Applications. George Braziller, New York (1968)
4. Bratman, M.E.: Intentions, Plans and Practical Reasoning. Harvard University Press, Cambridge (1987)
5. Churchman, C.W.: The Systems Approach. Dell Publishing, New York (1979)
6. Fahland, D., Woith, H.: Towards Process Models for Disaster Response. In: Proceedings of PM4HDPS 2008, Milan, Italy (2008)
7. Hightower, H.C., Coutu, M.: Coordinating Emergency Management: A Canadian Example. In: Sylves, R.T., Waugh Jr, W.L. (eds.) Disaster Management in the U.S. and Canada, pp. 69–98. Charles C. Thomas Publisher, Ltd., Springfield (1996)
8. Hoogendorn, M., Jonker, C.M., Popova, V., Sharpanskyh, A., Xu, L.: Formal modeling and comparing of disaster plans. In: Van de Walle, B., Carlé, B. (eds.) Proceedings of ISCRAM, Brussels, Belgium (2005)
9. Kartez, J.D., Lindell, M.K.: Planning for Uncertainty: The case for local disaster planning. Journal of the American Planning Association 53, 482–498 (1987)
10. Krutchen, P., Woo, C.C., Monu, K., Sootedeh, M.: A conceptual model of disasters encompassing multiple stakeholder domains. International Journal of Emergency Management 5, 25–56 (2008)
11. Mansourian, A., Rajabifard, A., Valadan Zoej, MJ., Williamson, IP.: Using SDI and web-based system to facilitate disaster management. Computers & Geosciences 32, 303–315 (2006)
12. Miller, J.G.: Living Systems. McGraw-Hill, New York (1978)
13. Monu, K.A.: Conceptual Modeling Method to Use Agents in Systems Analysis. In: McBrien, P.J. (ed.) Online Proceedings of CAiSE 2008 Doctoral Consortium, Montpellier, France (2008), http://www.doc.ic.ac.uk/~pjm/caisedc2008/monu.pdf
14. Monu, K., Wand, Y., Woo, C.C.: Intelligent Agents as a Modeling Paradigm. In: Avison, D.E., Galletta, D.F. (eds.) Proceedings of ICIS, Las Vegas, NV, USA, pp. 167–179 (2005)
15. Oh, Y., Schmidt, A., Woo, W.: Designing, Developing, and Evaluating Context-Aware Systems. In: Proceedings of MUE 2007, Seoul, Korea, pp. 1158–1163 (2007)
16. Wand, Y., Weber, R.: On the deep structure of information systems. Information Systems Journal 5, 203–223 (1995)
17. Wand, Y., Weber, R.: Research Commentary: Information Systems and Conceptual Modeling - A Research Agenda. Information Systems Research 13, 363–376 (2002)
18. Wooldridge, M.: Intelligent Agents. In: Weiss, G. (ed.) Multiagent Systems: A Modern Approach to Distributed Artificial Intelligence, pp. 27–77. MIT Press, Cambridge (1999)
19. Yu, E.: Modelling Organizations for Information Systems Requirements Engineering. In: Proceeding of the First IEEE Symposium on Requirements Engineering, San Diego, CA., USA, pp. 34–41 (1993)
20. Zhang, H., Kishore, R., Ramesh, R.: Semantics of the MibML Conceptual Modeling Grammar: An Ontological Analysis Using the Bunge-Wand-Weber Framework. Journal of Database Management 18, 1–19 (2007)

Modelling Safe Interface Interactions in Web Applications

Marco Brambilla[1], Jordi Cabot[2], and Michael Grossniklaus[1]

[1] Dipartimento di Elettronica e Informazione, Politecnico di Milano
Piazza Leonardo da Vinci 32, I-20133 Milano, Italy
{mbrambil,grossniklaus}@elet.polimi.it

[2] Department of Computer Science, University of Toronto
St. George Street 140, M5S 3G4 Toronto, Canada
jcabot@cs.toronto.edu

Abstract. Current Web applications embed sophisticated user interfaces and business logic. The original interaction paradigm of the Web based on static content pages that are browsed by hyperlinks is, therefore, not valid anymore. In this paper, we advocate a paradigm shift for browsers and Web applications, that improves the management of user interaction and browsing history. *Pages* are replaced by *States* as basic navigation nodes, and *Back/Forward* navigation along the browsing history is replaced by a full-fledged interactive application paradigm, supporting transactions at the interface level and featuring *Undo/Redo* capabilities. This new paradigm offers a safer and more precise interaction model, protecting the user from unexpected behaviours of the applications and the browser.

1 Introduction

The Web has evolved from a platform for navigating hypertext documents to a platform for implementing complex business applications. Pages nowadays contain *complex business logics* both at the client and at the server side. User interaction is able to deal with *several kinds of events*, generated both by users and systems. In this context, the original interaction paradigm of the Web is not valid anymore.

Browsers themselves, that still provide the traditional features of *Back* and *Forward* page navigation along the browsing history, are inadequate for dealing with the complexity of current applications [1]. Several user events are missed by this paradigm, and the Web application behaviour is indeterministic with respect to the actions allowed by the different browsers. Results for the same application vary depending on the browser and on the settings defined for it. These buttons are also problematic when navigating links that trigger side effects.

With RIA applications, this problem is even more pronounced as the user is often sent back to the initial state of the whole Web application when using the Back button instead of just moving back one interaction step in the current page. For example, the initial release of GMail suffered from this problem as the

A.H.F. Laender et al. (Eds.): ER 2009, LNCS 5829, pp. 387–400, 2009.

whole application was made available using one single URL[1]. In the meantime, the problem has been recognised by both Web application providers as well as by browser developers. More recent releases of GMail, for instance, append unique message identifiers to the URL to improve the user experience, while browsers such as Microsoft Internet Explorer 8 provide embedded functionality to handle AJAX navigation[2]. These efforts document that the problem of navigating complex Web applications is relevant, but there is not yet a generic and systematic way to address this problem based on standard Web engineering methods. Thus, several major applications do not address this issue at all and suffer from all the above-mentioned problems.

Therefore, we propose to evolve the interaction paradigm by moving the Web (and the supporting browsers) from the browsing paradigm based on *Pages*, with related *Back* and *Forward* actions, to a full-fledged interactive application paradigm, based on the concept of *State*, that features *Undo* and *Redo* capabilities, and transactional properties. This results in a safer interaction environment where users can navigate freely through Web applications and undo/redo their actions without experiencing unexpected application behaviour, including the side effects generated by the user interactions. Safety of the interfaces is therefore increased with respect to possible wrong or unexpected behaviours of the user, that is granted to always navigate among correct application states.

This paper is organised as follows. In Sect. 2, we continue to motivate the relevance of our work. Section 3 presents our modeling approach based on state machines and Sect. 4 presents the application programming interface designed to support the interface models and ensure its consistent behaviour. Section 5 discusses some methodological guidelines for adopting the approach and Sect. 6 describes our implementation experiences. Finally, we compare our approach to related works in Sect. 7 and conclude in Section 8.

2 Motivation

As the Web matures into an application platform, the concept of Web pages becomes less important, while the state of these applications gains in relevance.

In the page-base approach of traditional Web applications parameters are passed from one page to another using HTTP requests. Naturally, this can lead to problems when pages are visited in a different order or out of context. The state-based approach, on the other hand, represents the Web application as a finite state machine. The state of the page is then read from a global state repository when a page is accessed and stored back when the state is left (either to go to a different page or to move to a different state within the same page).

Currently, browsers are still designed to deal with page-based Web sites which causes the problems mentioned in the introduction. To illustrate these problems and motivate our approach we will use the GMail Web application as a running

---

[1] `http://mail.google.com/mail/?ui=1`

[2] `http://msdn.microsoft.com/en-us/library/cc288472.aspx`

example. GMail, as well as many other known Web sites, suffers from several interaction problems, due to the widespread adoption of AJAX.

For instance, GMail "fold" and "unfold" functionality in the message view to hide or expand conversations does not work together with the Back and Forward buttons, being implemented purely using JavaScript and CSS. Another chain of interactions that sometimes demonstrates the unexpected behaviour of the Back button is related to the login action: after logging in, users are presented with an overview of their inbox and can then select a message, which is then displayed. The expected outcome of using the Back button on this page would be to bring the user back to the inbox page. However, the use of the back button redirects the user back to the login page.

Additionally, some parts of the GMail interface should exhibit transactional properties in the sense that there is an "all or nothing" semantics over all states involved in the interaction. In particular, it should not be possible to step backwards through the states of a transaction once it has been completed. For instance, currently, if users display and then delete messages, they are redirected to the inbox and notified that the message has been moved to the trash. If, then, however, the user clicks the Back button, the deleted message reappears again, but the effect of deleting the message is not undone, i.e. the message remains deleted which confuses the user. We believe that in a state-based Web application, clicking the back button should rollback the whole delete transaction, redirecting the user to the state of the inbox previous to deleting the message and undoing the removal operation.

Many other famous Web sites suffer from the same problems: iGoogle.com, linkedin.com, maps.google.com, www.surveymonkey.com, www.hostelworld.com, www.lastminute.com, www.amazon.co.uk, www.gap.com, among many others, even including the official examples of AJAX and FLEX[3]. In general, almost no site (including the ones developed with pure server-side technology) is able to preserve the complete history of the navigation, that includes the input submitted by the user in the forms, which should be retrieved once the Back button is clicked. Other critical issues are not addressed at all by Web applications, including: rollback (or compensation) of side effects in correspondence to backward navigation and fine grained back and forward managements, e.g., at the level of fields in a form.

Existing Web design methods such as WebML [2], Hera [3], OOHDM [4], etc. already provide models intended for the specification of hypertext navigation. Even though some of them have been extended to support basic RIA features, they lack of mechanisms for exactly specifying fine-grained user interactions, since they operate at the granularity of pages and components. In this paper, we propose a modelling approach and run-time support system designed to allow the specification and implementation of safe user interactions in Web applications. The methodology is complementary and orthogonal to existing approaches in the sense that is can be used in addition to an existing language. Our approach is based on the shift of paradigm from page-based navigation to

[3] e.g., `http://examples.adobe.com/flex3/devnet/dashboard/main.html`

state-based interaction. We apply the principle of separation of concerns, thus defining a specific model for interface navigation behaviour.

3 Modeling Safe Interfaces

This section introduces our modelling approach for the definition of the interface interaction aspects of Web applications. Our proposal is based on the the state machines sublanguage of the UML [5] which we have adapted to the Web applications domain by adding concepts like *Page*, *GraphicalElement*, *Transaction* and so forth.

The abstract syntax of the language is partly described by the MOF-compliant metamodel depicted in Fig. 1. The language permits to define Web pages (*Page* metaclass) and decompose them in a set of interaction substates (*State* metaclass), where exceptional states (*ExceptionState* subclass) are useful to specify the default application behaviour in case of unexpected errors. State transitions (*Transition* metaclass) are triggered by events (class *TriggerEvent*) on the graphical elements of the interface (*GraphicalElement* metaclass). The possible triggering events are predefined in the enumeration *EventType* to facilitate their definition and a more homogeneous treatment. Transitions may involve the execution of a sequence of action instances (*Action* metaclass). Actions may alter the state of the graphical elements in the page or change the population/value of the Web application data. Links between pages can be inferred by detecting transitions between states in different pages.

As an example, Fig. 2(a) shows a subset of the GMail Web application interface definition, as commented before. The first page (shown using a *package* symbol) is the *Login page* and the second page is the *Mail page* that provides all functionality of the GMail client. The Login page has only one state, *Show Login* (drawn using a circle shape; a bold border denotes that this is the initial state for the page), that displays the input fields for user name and password (not shown in the figure). After the user submits this form, the Web application progresses to the *Show Inbox* state on the Mail page that displays a list of all mails. On the same page, selecting a message moves the application to the *Show Message* state where the selected message is displayed. In this state, the *next* and *previous* transitions allow the user to step through all messages currently in the inbox. This model makes it clear that clicking the Back button when in the state *ShowMessage*, users have to be moved back one state (to the *Show Inbox* or the same *ShowMessage* state, depending if they arrived to the current state via the *next*, the *previous* or the *show* transition) but never back to the previous page (as it happens when the modeling language does not allow designers to specify state-based interfaces).

Transitions may be part of a transaction. As usual, rolling back a transaction implies undoing all changes done since its beginning. That is why each action needs to provide not only the definition of the changes performed when executing the action (the *do* behaviour specification) but also the *undo* specification (if possible) that will be used if the transaction must be rolled back. For predefined actions (e.g.,

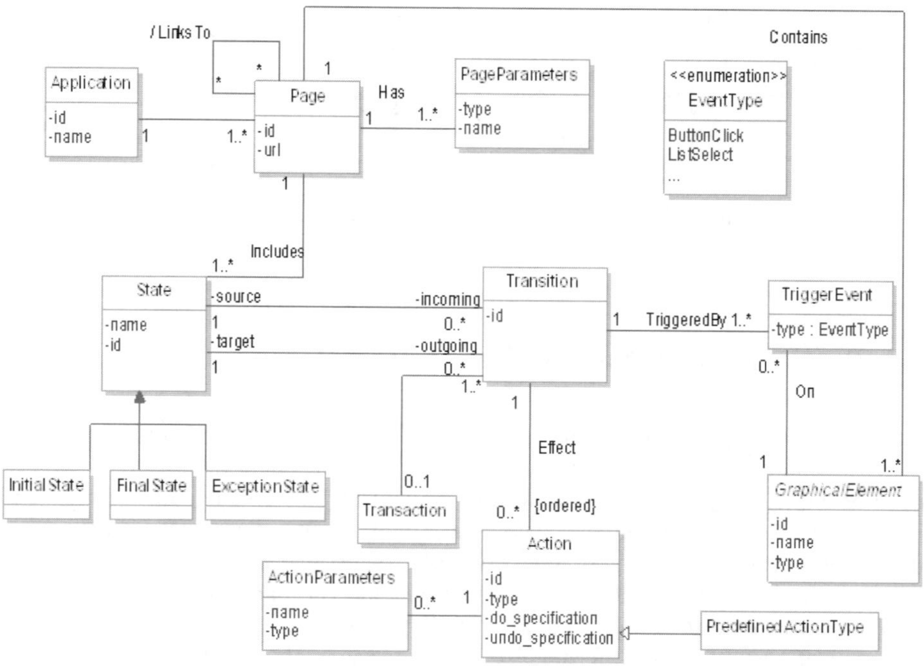

Fig. 1. Interaction metamodel

create new object, update an attribute, enable a button, ...), the behavior of the *do* and *undo* operations may be skipped and a default behaviour depending on the action type can be predefined and used instead. For other actions this behaviour must be provided by the designer as part of the interface modelling process. Transactions can span over different pages and sets of side effects. An example for this notion of a transaction is the chain of states shown in Fig. 2(b) that deletes the currently displayed message. The transaction is denoted by the dashed box enclosing states *Show Message* and *Delete Message*. Defining this transaction avoids the unexpected behaviour described in the previous section.

GraphicalElement is an abstract class that could be decomposed into a set of *Button*, *ComboBox*, *EditField*, ... subclasses (not shown in the figure). Depending on how we plan to use this interaction model (see Sect. 5) these classes can be directly taken from the metamodel of the Web modeling language we integrate our approach with.

Additionally, we have defined several well-formedness rules (WFRs) that enforce a consistent relationship between the different components of the interface when specified using our metamodel. Examples of well-formedness rules are: all pages must have at least one initial state, the type of trigger event must be compatible with the kind of graphical element associated to the event or that transitions in a transaction must represent a consecutive sequence of steps in the interaction. These WFRs can be formally expressed using a textual language like OCL.

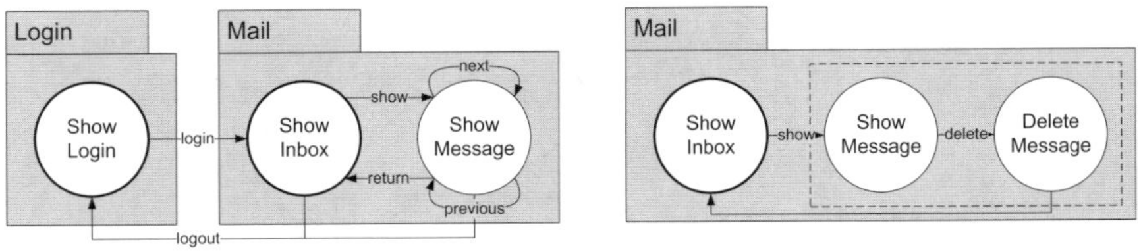

(a) Login and mail page (b) Transaction for deleting a message

Fig. 2. State models for GMail

4 Tracking User Interaction at Run-Time

Once the interface has been modeled, we need to ensure that its implementation provides the expected behaviour at run-time. To achieve this, we need two types of knowledge: (1) the static information defined by the designer in the previous interface model; and (2) the execution trace of all events, state visits, page access and actions executed so far (e.g., to be able to retrieve the correct state of the interface and application data state when clicking the back button).

The data structures required for the latter aspect are shown in the class diagram of Fig. 3. Each different execution of the Web application is recorded in the *ApplicationExecution* class. In each execution, we record all visits to the states defined in the interface model. For each visit, we record the transitions that lead/exited to/from the visit and the event that triggered those transitions. Even more important, we record all actions executed during the process including all the arguments used when executing those actions and the current values of all graphical elements at that point (e.g. items selected in each combobox, state of the checkboxes, ...). Every time we visit a state in a different page, we also record the page access plus the parameters used when loading the page.

By recording all these pieces of information, we are able to recreate the complete state of the application at any previous point of time, and thus, ensure a safe interaction behaviour. This information is managed through an API we have predefined to ease the development of Web applications following our proposal. A subset of the API is described in Tab. 1. For each method we describe the class where the method is attached[4], its input and output parameters and a short description of its semantics. Methods `getNext` and `getPrevious` can be used by the application developer to query the next or previous visit in the history, respectively. Instead, the `do` and `undo` method are then used to actually perform a move to the next or previous visit and, thus, they manipulate the history records during the process. The method *redo* re-visits a state that has already been visited. As the event and parameters to move to the new state have already been recorded by our framework in this case, they do not have to be provided once more. Notice that the navigation trace recording is not expected to reduce significantly the application performances, since other application parts (e.g.,

[4] We could also add all methods to a single class, following the *Facade* pattern.

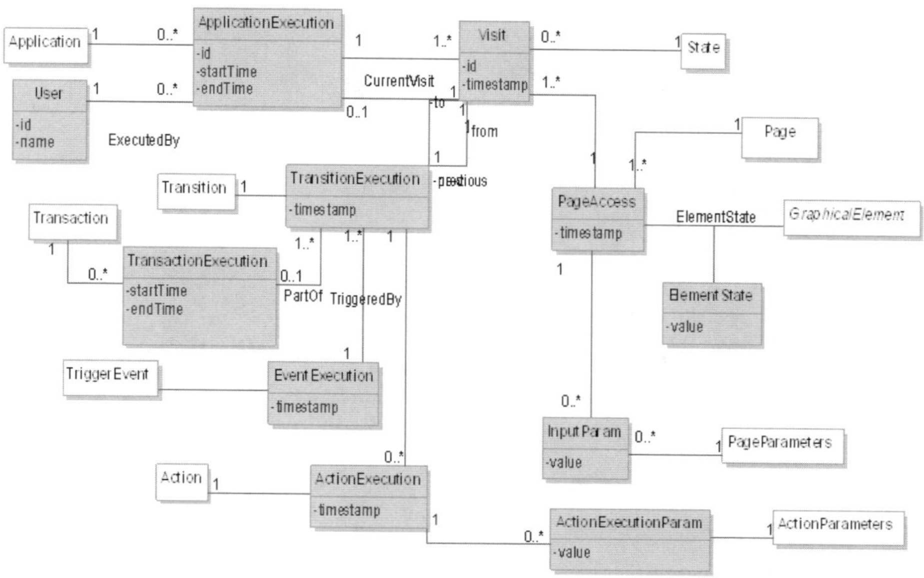

Fig. 3. Class diagram to track the user interaction

Table 1. API Methods (Excerpt)

Method	Remarks
`State::getNextState(Event e): State`	informs about the next state to go based on the current one and the given event
`Visit::getNext(): Visit`	queries next visit
`Visit::getPrevious(): Visit`	queries previous visit
`ApplicationExecution::do (EventExec e, Parameter[] p): Visit`	moves to next visit
`ApplicationExecution::redo():Visit`	moves to the (previously visited) next visit
`ApplicationExecution::undo():Visit`	moves to previous visit reversing all executed actions
`Visit::clone():Visit`	creates a clone of the visit
`ActionExecution::do (ActionExecutionParam[] params)`	executes the action
`ActionExecution::undo (ActionExecutionParam[] params)`	undoes the effect of the action
`TransitionExecution::undo()`	undoes all actions associated to the transition
`TransactionExecution::rollback()`	rollbacks the transaction

AJAX interfaces) are more likely to become bottlenecks. The complexity of the stored data is in line with the standard logging information of Web applications.

To show how the API can be used to enforce safe interaction semantics, we show a sequence diagram that sketches the operation sequence executed in response to a user click on the Back button in Fig. 4. Once the *ApplicationExecution* instance receives this event (intercepted by means of JavaScript code in the client browser),

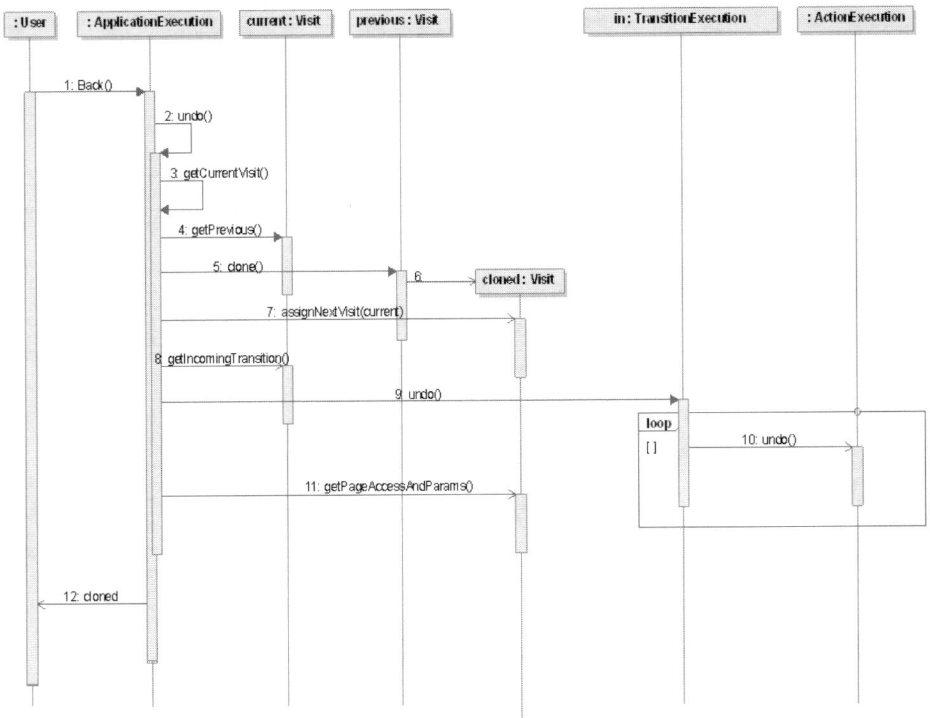

Fig. 4. Sequence diagram for the *Back* operation

it accesses the visit previous to the current one, which is where the user must be redirected. The redirection is performed by cloning the previous visit (i.e., creating a new one, with identical properties) instead of just pointing directly to it. This allows the correct behaviour of the undo/redo mechanism also in the case of partially rolled back history, where the user goes back and forth several times over the same interaction sequence. This clone visit is inserted in the history of the navigation, for tracking purposes, with the following values: (1) its next visit is the current visit at the beginning of the execution of the back operation and (2) the previous visit is the same as the one of the visit we have cloned. That is, a redo operation would move the user back to the initial visit state. An additional Back operation would move another step back in the sequence of visits. At the end of the operation, this cloned visit is returned as the new current one and can be used by the Web server to retrieve all the needed information (including the related page access and parameters) to compute the Web page.

The procedure for rolling back a transaction would be similar, with an initial iteration to undo all visits until the last visit before starting the transaction.

5 Methodology

This section proposes methodology guidelines for adopting our approach, possibly combined with other design methods. Indeed, our method can be used both

(1) together with an existing Web engineering method and (2) as a stand-alone approach that directly exploits the API just focusing on the design of the state behaviour of the application. In the following, we provide an indication of how to use our method in the two aforementioned scenarios.

5.1 Integration with WebML

Due to the orthogonality of the issues addressed by our approach with respect to existing Web engineering methods, it is straightforward to blend it within an existing design methodology for Web applications.

The joint use of our method with existing approaches requires to identify:

- the set of primitives that overlap with the existing modelling language (and therefore that can be directly mapped one onto the other);
- the set of primitives that are not defined nor covered in the existing modelling language (and therefore need to be introduced);
- and the set of primitives that conflict or partially intersect the semantics of some existing primitives (and therefore require to resolve the conflict).

To demonstrate the feasibility and neutrality of the approach with respect to the modelling methodology of choice, we show how the approach can be used together with WebML (Web Modeling Language) [2], a methodology for designing Web applications. The choice of WebML is due to its widespread adoption, the availability of a MDE tool-suite (WebRatio[5]), and our knowledge of its basic usage and semantics.

The combination of our approach with WebML and WebRatio has two main advantages: the possibility of extending a well established code generation framework for covering the new features (i.e., through invocations to our API); and the availability of a huge set of real industrial application models that can be exploited for validating our approach.

Given a multi-model design approach such as WebML, two ways can be followed for merging the two methods: (1) defining a new modeling view of the application, that orthogonally describes the state modeling as a separate aspect of the application; (2) blending the state modeling concepts within one of the existing types of models provided by the methodology. The latter is convenient when there is an overlap some modelling primitives of the methodology already include concepts that overlap with our method.

WebML is a good example of integration according to the approach (2), since the hypertext model includes examples for all the three categories of primitives mentioned above:

- the *page* concept already exists in WebML and perfectly maps to the new *page* concept;

[5] http://www.webratio.com

- the *state* and *transaction* concepts do not exist in WebML[6], and therefore need to be explicitly introduced in the notation;
- finally, some concepts actually create some conflict with the existing models. Such conflicts could be due to the semantics of the concept or to its granularity. For instance, the *transition* concept partially overlaps with the WebML link concept, and therefore needs to be reconciled. On the other side, some granularity conflicts arise because some WebML features are more coarse-grained than we expect in our model: e.g., primitives such as *Entry units* encapsulate the whole behaviour of a form; primitives such as *Landmarks* represent sets of links coming into a page.

To clarify how these issues are solved in concrete cases, we exemplify in Fig. 5 a simple visual integration of a WebML hypertext model with the concepts of our proposal. The picture shows in black thin lines the native WebML concepts (pages, units, operations, and links) of a hypertext model describing a simplified email management interface: a *Home page* contains a form for the *Login*, which triggers the login server-side action and then redirects to the *Email page*. There, the user is shown a hierarchy of email *Folders*, that can be browsed. Once a folder is selected, the list of contained *Emails* is shown, and a specific *Message* can be chosen for looking at its details. Then the user can either delete the current message or reply to it. For replying, they can click on a link that leads to the *Send Message* page, which includes the *New Msg* form. Once the message is submitted, its data is recorded and the message is sent.

This basic WebML model, however, does not cover safe state management at all. Therefore, we extend it with our approach, by adding State, Transition, and Transaction primitives on top the hypertext model. States (represented by gray rounded boxes) are added as an orthogonal dimension over sets of WebML units. Notice that the distribution of units within the states is arbitrary, according to the logic that the designer wants to convey. Transitions (represented as thick arrows) basically map to WebML links, when they connect one state to another. Transactions (shown as dot-dashed boxes) surround set of states. WebML server-side operations are regarded as *Actions* in our approach, and thus are associated to the related transitions.

In the example, state *S1* is associated to the completion of the login form and to the click on the submit button. The exiting transition *T1* leads to state *S2* and comprises the action *Login*. Analogous definitions are assumed for the other states. Notice that states can be defined over set of units (e.g., *S2*), but also on sub-units (e.g., groups of fields in a form, such as *S5* and *S6*). This allows undo and redo actions to be performed at different granularity levels. Due to transactions (e.g., *TRANS1*), safe interaction is granted also upon deletion or updates of contents.

[6] A transaction concept actually exist, but it represents an atomic set of server-side actions to be performed altogether within a single server request; therefore, it does not collide with our concept. For clarity, we will refer to that concept as "server-side transaction".

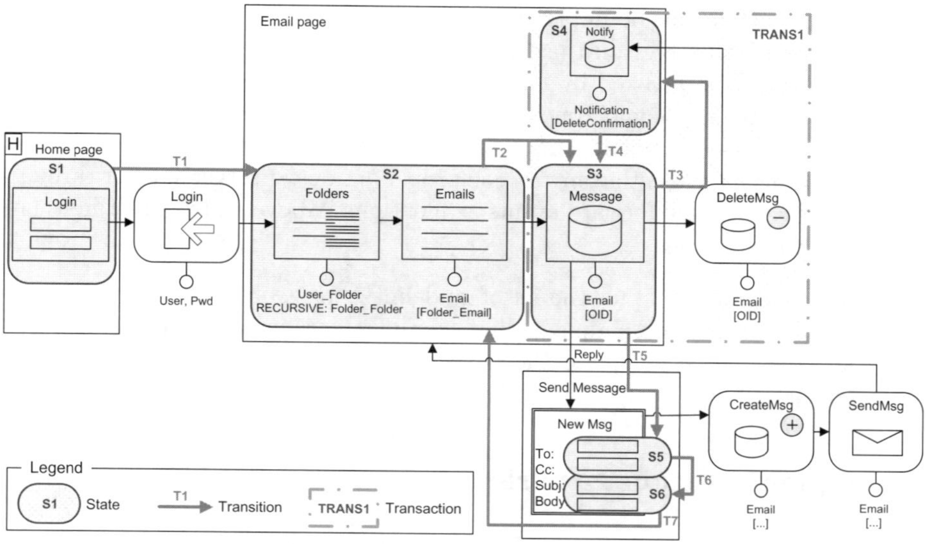

Fig. 5. Example of WebML hypertext model integrated with state awareness

Notice that one aspect that cannot be graphically addressed in this representation is the definition of the reverse actions for allowing rollbacks. This must be defined separately for non-predefined actions. For predefined ones, the reverse procedure is already implicit in the semantics of the action definition and thus does not need to be explicitly defined by the designer again.

5.2 Standalone Approach

Another possible usage of our approach consists of directly exploiting our API for the design and implementation of Web applications. This approach is suitable for traditional developers that are not familiar with model-driven design. Therefore, they are familiar with using existing APIs for getting immediate benefits within the developed application. The most they are willing to do is adopting a very simple visual notation to summarize the general application structure, which can be achieved through the simple notation we have proposed so far for modeling pages, states, transitions, and transactions.

Through that notation, it is possible to describe the aspects covered by the approach and to use it to guide the implementation phase. This can be done through a set of implementation guidelines that rely on the adoption of the API described in Tab. 1, as roughly summarized here.

- *basic events* (i.e., user clicks) can be captured by the default behaviour of the browser when managing hypertext links.
- *advanced events* (e.g., clicks on the back-forward button, right clicks, drag and drop, and so on) can be captured by JavaScript embedded within the pages, e.g., by adopting an AJAX library.

- *change of state* can be implemented by embedding the appropriate calls to the methods that register the change of state, in the server-side actions. Such actions must be invoked by *any* state-relevant hyperlink (in case of simple events) or by any asynchronous invocation (in case of AJAX events).
- *undo and redo* actions can be implemented through appropriate links/ buttons on the page, that invoke the proper actions at server side; or through capturing the back-forward events as mentioned above and redirecting them to the same actions.

Therefore, once the API plus the set of guidelines—possibly more precisely specified and illustrated with simple coding examples—are provided to the developers, they are able to complete the development by quickly implementing the state-specific aspects of the application.

6 Implementation Experience

This section aims at briefly reporting our experience in implementing the proposed approach. The setting where our approach has been tested is within the J2EE framework. The (partially) presented API in Sect. 4 has been implemented as a set of Java classes and respective methods. The API has been tested in the context of a few Web applications, that have been implemented through a set of JSP pages and Servlets that coherently invoke the API. Management of special events has been delegated to the AJAX Prototype (and Scriptaculous)[7] libraries. The server-side architecture is based on Struts. However, thanks to the independence from the technology, our approach can obviously be implemented in any other environment.

7 Related Work

Most traditional methods for user interface design use state machines (in different flavours) as the underlying formalism. An early approach proposing state-based definition of general user interfaces is Jacob [6]. Later, similar techniques were adopted by the Hypermedia community to specify navigation [7] and by the Web Engineering community to express the structure and behaviour of Web sites. For example, Leung et al. [8] were among the first to propose the use of statecharts to address the growing complexity of dynamic Web sites. Later, StateWebCharts [9] were proposed, a refinement of previous approaches that extend statecharts with more concepts targeted towards the modelling of Web applications. Finally, Draheim and Weber [10] propose the use of bipartite state machines to model both the pages and the server actions on them.

In the domain of model-driven Web engineering, the necessity to support the specification of RIAs was recognised early on [11]. Proposals in this direction include an extension to WebML [12] and the RUX-Model [13], ADV-Charts [14],

[7] `http://www.prototypejs.org/`, `http://script.aculo.us/`

and and orchestration model for widgets [15]. Nevertheless, most existing Web design methodologies such as WebML [2], Hera [3], OOHDM [4], etc. do not provide concepts to precisely specify complex application states. While these approaches support the specification of the desired interface behaviour, they do not consider the problems caused by the user-interaction with the Web browser (such as the *Amazon bug*) nor do they provide any kind of transactional support for interface interactions.

Currently, the only possibility that designers have is to identify the potential interaction problems using, for example, an existing verification/validation technique [16] and, then, correct these issues during the implementation phase. The particular issues arising from using the browser's Back button in modern Web applications, however, have been addressed by a number of approaches. For example, Milic et al. [1] study the different problems that can occur in the context of back navigation and have proposed a specific solution called Smartback. Alternative approaches have been proposed [17,18,19]. To address the problems identified by these authors in a generic and model-based design method is precisely the goal of our method.

8 Conclusions

This paper presented a new method for modelling and implementing safe interface interactions in Web applications that includes transactional properties and full-fledged undo and redo capabilities. The method is based on decomposing pages in a set of states linked by transitions executed in response to user events. An API allows to record the complete trace of the interactions, thus allowing consistent back and forward navigation, including the possibility of rolling back a sequence of interaction steps defined as a transaction at the model-level. Our approach improves the browsing user experience within complex business applications and makes the behaviour deterministic regardless of the browser and the implementation technologies.

As future work we plan to extend the code generator of WebML/WebRatio for supporting the new features of our approach (i.e., the API invocations) and validate the scalability and completeness of such generator and of our new primitives upon several existing WebML models of real industrial applications. Finally, we aim at developing a simple code generation prototype that transforms our standalone models to skeletons of Java and JSP code that invoke our API.

Acknowledgements. Work supported by the project TIN2008-00444 from the Spanish Ministry of Education and Science, by the 2007 BP-A 00128 grant from the Catalan Government, and by grant PBEZ2-121230 from the Swiss Science Foundation (SNF).

References

1. Milic-Frayling, N., Jones, R., Rodden, K., Smyth, G., Blackwell, A., Sommerer, R.: Smartback: Supporting Users in Back Navigation. In: Proc. WWW 2004, pp. 63–71 (2004)

2. Ceri, S., Fraternali, P., Bongio, A., Brambilla, M., Comai, S., Matera, M.: Designing Data-Intensive Web Applications. The Morgan Kaufmann Series in Data Management Systems. Morgan Kaufmann Publishers Inc., San Francisco (2002)
3. Vdovják, R., Frăsincar, F., Houben, G.-J., Barna, P.: Engineering Semantic Web Information Systems in Hera. Journal of Web Engineering 1(1-2), 3–26 (2003)
4. Schwabe, D., Rossi, G., Barbosa, S.D.J.: Systematic Hypermedia Application Design with OOHDM. In: Proc. Hypertext 1996, pp. 116–128 (1996)
5. Object Management Group: UML 2.0 Superstructure Specification (2004)
6. Jacob, R.J.K.: A Specification Language for Direct-Manipulation User Interfaces. ACM Trans. Graph. 5(4), 283–317 (1986)
7. de Oliveira, M.C.F., Turine, M.A.S., Masiero, P.C.: A Statechart-based Model for Hypermedia Applications. ACM Trans. Inf. Syst. 19(1), 28–52 (2001)
8. Leung, K.R.P.H., Hui, L.C.K., Hui, S.M., Tang, R.W.M.: Modeling Navigation by Statechart. In: Proc. COMPSAC 2000, pp. 41–47 (2000)
9. Winckler, M., Palanque, P.: StateWebCharts: A Formal Description Technique Dedicated to Navigation Modelling of Web Applications. In: Proc. Intl. Workshop on Design, Specification and Verification of Interactive Systems, pp. 279–288 (2003)
10. Draheim, D., Weber, G.: Modelling Form-based Interfaces with Bipartite State Machines. Interacting with Computers 17(2), 207–228 (2005)
11. Preciado, J.C., Linaje, M., Sánchez, F., Comai, S.: Necessity of Methodologies to Model Rich Internet Applications. In: Proceedings of International Symposium on Web Site Evolution, Budapest, Hungary (September 26, 2005), pp. 7–13 (2005)
12. Bozzon, A., Comai, S., Fraternali, P., Toffetti Carughi, G.: Conceptual Modeling and Code Generation for Rich Internet Applications. In: Proceedings of International Conference on Web Engineering, Menlo Park, CA, USA (July 10-14, 2006), pp. 353–360 (2006)
13. Linaje, M., Preciado, J.C., Sánchez-Figueroa, F.: A Method for Model Based Design of Rich Internet Application Interactive User Interfaces. In: Proceedings of International Conference on Web Engineering, Como, Italy (July 16-20, 2007), pp. 226–241 (2007)
14. Urbieta, M., Rossi, G., Ginzburg, J., Schwabe, D.: Designing the Interface of Rich Internet Applications. In: Proc. LA-WEB 2007, pp. 144–153 (2007)
15. Pérez, S., Díaz, O., Meliá, S., Gómez, J.: Facing Interaction-Rich RIAs: The Orchestration Model. In: Proc. ICWE 2008, pp. 24–37 (2008)
16. Alalfi, M.H., Cordy, J.R., Dean, T.R.: A Survey of Analysis Models and Methods in Website Verification and Testing. In: Baresi, L., Fraternali, P., Houben, G.-J. (eds.) ICWE 2007. LNCS, vol. 4607, pp. 306–311. Springer, Heidelberg (2007)
17. Biel, B., Book, M., Gruhn, V., Peters, D., Schäfer, C.: Handling Backtracking in Web Applications. In: Proc. EUROMICRO 2004, pp. 388–395 (2004)
18. Ceri, S., Daniel, F., Matera, M., Rizzo, F.: Extended Memory (xMem) of Web Interactions. In: Proc. ICWE 2006, pp. 177–184 (2006)
19. Baresi, L., Denaro, G., Mainetti, L., Paolini, P.: Assertions to Better Specify the Amazon Bug. In: Proc. SEKE 2002, pp. 585–592 (2002)

A Conceptual Modeling Approach for OLAP Personalization

Irene Garrigós, Jesús Pardillo, Jose-Norberto Mazón, and Juan Trujillo

Lucentia Research Group,
Department of Software and Computing Systems – DLSI,
University of Alicante, Spain
{igarrigos,jesuspv,jnmazon,jtrujillo}@dlsi.ua.es

Abstract. Data warehouses rely on multidimensional models in order to provide decision makers with appropriate structures to intuitively analyze data with OLAP technologies. However, data warehouses may be potentially large and multidimensional structures become increasingly complex to be understood at a glance. Even if a departmental data warehouse (also known as data mart) is used, these structures would be also too complex. As a consequence, acquiring the required information is more costly than expected and decision makers using OLAP tools may get frustrated. In this context, current approaches for data warehouse design are focused on deriving a unique OLAP schema for all analysts from their previously stated information requirements, which is not enough to lighten the complexity of the decision making process. To overcome this drawback, we argue for personalizing multidimensional models for OLAP technologies according to the continuously changing user characteristics, context, requirements and behaviour. In this paper, we present a novel approach to personalizing OLAP systems at the conceptual level based on the underlying multidimensional model of the data warehouse, a user model and a set of personalization rules. The great advantage of our approach is that a personalized OLAP schema is provided for each decision maker contributing to better satisfy their specific analysis needs. Finally, we show the applicability of our approach through a sample scenario based on our CASE tool for data warehouse development.

Keywords: OLAP, personalization, data warehouse, conceptual model.

1 Introduction

Data warehouses have been traditionally conceived as databases structured to support decision making processes. It is widely accepted that the development of data warehouses is based on multidimensional modeling which structures information into facts and dimensions [1]. A fact contains useful measures of a business process (sales, deliveries, etc.), whereas a dimension represents the context (product, customer, time, etc.) for analyzing a fact [2].

OLAP (*On-Line Analytical Processing*) technologies have been devised to facilitate querying the large amount of data stored in data warehouses by navigating through multidimensional structures [3]. Therefore, current approaches

A.H.F. Laender et al. (Eds.): ER 2009, LNCS 5829, pp. 401–414, 2009.

for OLAP start by defining a multidimensional model [4] in order to obtain a unified OLAP schema over which all decision makers intuitively fulfil their information needs. However, this unique OLAP schema may be quite large as it may deliver information to many kinds of decision makers who may have different needs [5], *e.g.*, an international manager expects to analyze sales by country, while a national manager needs to analyze sales by city. Therefore, decision makers are often forced to understand and navigate along the whole complex OLAP schema to find and acquire adequate data which is a costly and frustrating task. Even if a departmental data warehouse (also known as data mart) is developed to ameliorate this situation, data mart structures would be still too complex.

To overcome these drawbacks, we argue that the OLAP schema should be personalized in order to provide customized views over the original data warehouse for every particular user, thus better satisfying decision makers. Interestingly, the research agenda proposed in [6] identifies OLAP personalization as one of the main topics to be addressed by both academics and practitioners.

Several OLAP approaches provide personalized views to the decision makers focusing on different aspects (see Sect. 2 for details). However, none of them personalize schemas at the conceptual level. This may cause several problems like difficult maintenance, no independence of the target platform, evolution of the information requirements, etc. Furthermore, none of these approaches allows to apply personalization at runtime taking into account the user behaviour, but only preferences over data stated at design time. Also, current commercial OLAP tools (*e.g.*, Oracle Discoverer or Pentaho Mondrian) take the whole multidimensional schema of the underlying data warehouse as an input and allow designers to customize it by specifying which elements of a sort are preferred over their peers. The main drawback of this way of proceeding is that designers have to customize the schema manually, being prone to mistakes and time consuming.

To tackle the aforementioned problems, this paper presents a modeling approach for OLAP personalization at the conceptual level (see Fig. 1) by providing two new designers artifacts together with the multidimensional model: (i) a *user model* that captures all the user-related information needed to personalization, and (ii) a set of *personalization rules* that specify the required personalization actions. These new artifacts allow to personalize the multidimensional model obtaining OLAP schemas tailored to each decision maker (see Fig. 1). The resulting personalized OLAP schemas help simplify the analysis since they only contain the required multidimensional structures and the number of required OLAP operations is therefore lower than using the non-personalized schema. Another contribution of the paper is providing the first novel classification of the OLAP personalization dimensions, to the best of our knowledge (see Sect. 4 for a detailed view).

The remainder of the paper is structured as follows. Related work is reviewed next. Sect. 3 presents a modeling example to motivate our approach. Sect. 4 presents the proposed modeling approach for OLAP personalization. A sample application of this approach is described in Sect. 5. Finally, conclusions are given in Sect. 6, together with a summary of our expected future work.

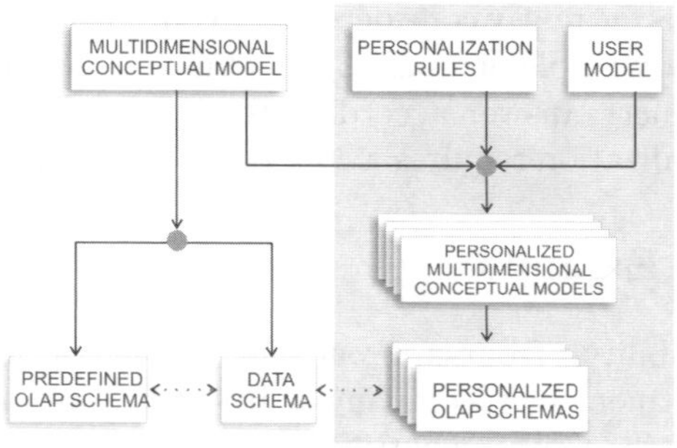

Fig. 1. Our approach to personalizing OLAP models

2 Related Work

Current approaches for personalization in multidimensional databases and OLAP focus on defining preferences of users on specific data in the same way that traditional databases do. For example, the work presented in [7] applies the characterization of preferences as order relations given in [8] into multidimensional data. In [9] OLAP preferences are considered together with visualization constraints for overcoming the limitations imposed by different users' devices. Unfortunately, these approaches consider OLAP preferences on data instances rather than on multidimensional structures. However, these structures, such as dimension hierarchies, have a strong impact in OLAP analysis and they should be considered in OLAP personalization, *e.g.*, by stating that monthly data are preferred to yearly and daily data. This issue is considered a main open problem in OLAP personalization in [6].

Remarkably, personalization approaches should not be only based on capturing preferences but also a more general user modeling including interests and skills of users [10]. In this sense, several approaches [5,11] state that preferences of the users should be defined depending on their context. However, to consider a wider spectrum of personalization issues, more complex mechanisms are required.

This work overcomes the aforementioned drawbacks since our personalization rules refer (i) to elements of the multidimensional model in order to consider both personalization in data instances and structures, and (ii) to a user model in order to consider every important user needs apart from preferences or context. Other features of our approach improve current work about OLAP personalization:

- Unlike relational databases where personalization is mostly expressed directly in a SQL query, an OLAP personalization requires more interactive approaches since the data warehouses needs to be queried in a friendly and visual way by means of sophisticated graphical interfaces [6]. A promising solution consists of modeling events to express personalization through an OLAP front-end, *e.g.*, personalization rules for OLAP can be defined as ECA (Event-Condition-Action) [12], as is done in our approach.

– Personalization is currently considered in an ad-hoc manner, when the OLAP schema is already implemented, *e.g.*, defining algorithms to order tuples returned as a query answer according to user preferences. However, more complex personalization requires a conceptual approach as addressed herein.

3 Motivating Example

To show the advisability of our approach we define the following sample scenario: a sales department of a company is interested in analyzing who bought (*Customer*) and where (*Store*), what (*Product*), when (*Time*), and under which conditions (*Promotion Media*). Assume the multidimensional model of Fig. 2 defined in a class diagram by means of the UML profile for multidimensional modeling presented in [13].

Sales are represented as a *Fact* class ( ) and the contexts of analysis are represented as *Dimension* classes ( ). Measures for *Fact* classes (*i.e.*, *UnitSales*, *StoreCost*, and so on) are represented as *FactAttributes* (FA). With respect to dimensions, each level of a dimension hierarchy is specified by a *Base* class. Every *Base* class (B) contains a number of descriptive attributes (D). Associations between pairs of *Base* classes ( ) represent aggregation paths: role r represents the direction in which the hierarchy rolls-up (*i.e.*, aggregating data in a coarser level of detail), whereas role d represents the direction in which the hierarchy drills-down (*i.e.*, disaggregating data in a finer level of detail). In this example we only focus on two of the dimensions: *Store* and *Product*.

Even focusing on these two dimensions, the multidimensional model gets rather complex, so does the decision maker navigation. For example, a national manager who is interested in analyzing sales to launch a new promotion for foreign customers is interested in analyzing only units sold by region made in his/her own country, taking into account customers from abroad. However, s/he must be aware of all the model, which is complex because a lot of operations are required before obtaining the right information.

4 Our Approach to Modeling Personalization in OLAP

To better position our approach, we provide a novel classification to characterize the design space of OLAP personalization by three orthogonal dimensions, comprising the *factors* to base the personalization on, the types of *personalization actions* and *nature* of the personalization.

– Personalization can be influenced by several factors. We can consider user-specific characteristics (independent of the domain) and the user requirements when analyzing the data. By considering the user behaviour we can derive the preferences or interest on different elements of the system. Moreover, it is important to consider the changing user-context in order to define personalization strategies. Our proposal considers all the defined factors, so we can base the personalization on the *user characteristics*, *requirements*, *behaviour* and *context*.

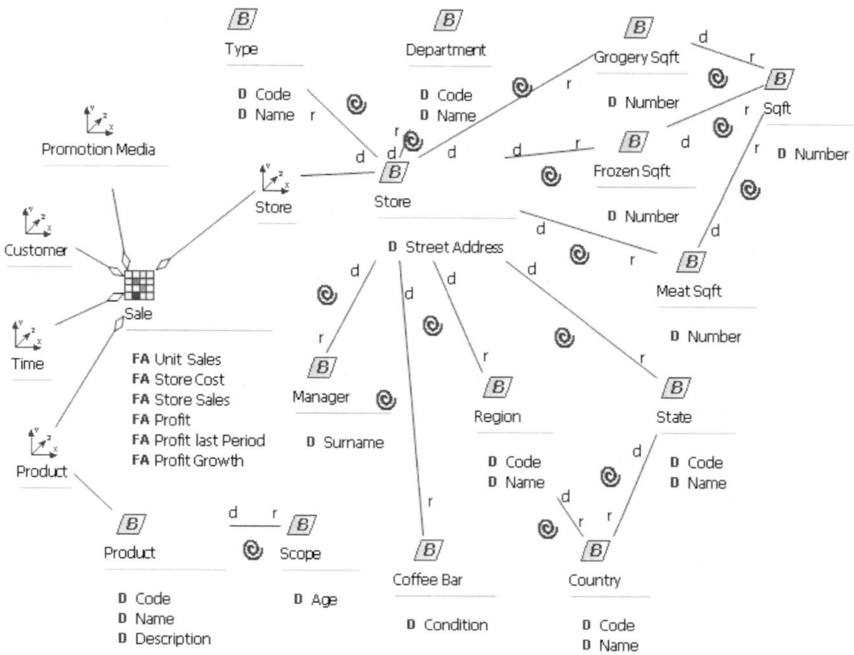

Fig. 2. OLAP model for sales analysis

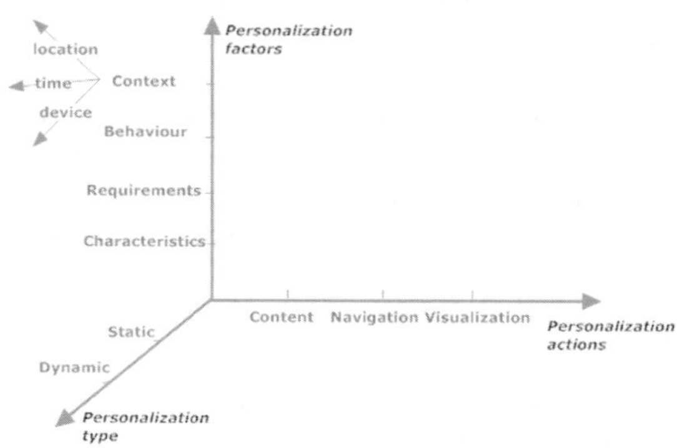

Fig. 3. OLAP Personalization Dimensions

– The second dimension considered is the type of personalization actions. Personalization can be applied over the *content* of the OLAP system (*e.g.*, selecting certain fact instances according to a condition), it can also be applied over the OLAP *navigation* (*e.g.*, selecting the aggregation paths to be shown). Personalization actions can also be applied over the *visualization* of the OLAP cube (*e.g.*, marking the most visited aggregation paths in bold). The action types considered in this approach are *content* and *navigation*. Defining personalization actions over the *visualization* implies modeling the

visualization issues at the conceptual level, which is out of the scope of this paper. Our aim is to complete the presented approach studying personalization over the *visualization*.
- Finally, personalization can be either *static* or *dynamic* depending on how and when the user-specific OLAP cube is built. We talk about *static personalization* when different versions of the OLAP cube are generated at design time for different user types. Personalization is *dynamic* when the personalized OLAP cube is being built at runtime, *e.g.*, depending on the user behaviour or context. Our proposal considers both *static* and *dynamic* personalization. However, this work only focuses on the *dynamic* part (*i.e.*, we define at design time the personalization to be performed at runtime), since it is the most challenging personalization type for OLAP due to its interactive nature.

We define personalization like the process of adapting the system to certain user-related information (*e.g.*, user's goals, needs, characteristics, behaviour and context). The structure of the user-related information needed to personalize is specified in a so-called *user model*. To define personalization strategies based on these data, we define personalization ECA (Event-Condition-Action) rules. Personalization has been intensively studied in other areas [14] such as Web Engineering. Actually, OLAP personalization resembles personalization of Web applications, since both allow heterogeneous audience to navigate through complex data spaces with growing complexity and increasing amount of information. Due to these similarities, we have decided to use PRML *(Personalization Rules Modeling Language)* [15] to specify the personalization rules. This is a rule-based high level language originally created to specify personalization upon Web applications. PRML has been successfully applied to several Web systems and an engine to perform these rules has been implemented [15,16]. We have adapted this language to peculiarities of OLAP systems (such as complex operations required to analyze data), as it will be explained throughout the next sections.

4.1 User Model

Personalization is a user-centered process, therefore, user modeling is the basis for personalization support [10]. OLAP users are decision makers who use OLAP front-end tools to navigate, select and filter multidimensional data structures to obtain the right information [6]. In order to provide a personalized OLAP model, relevant knowledge about the decision maker should be captured. The structure of the data required for personalization is specified in the user model. This model should be defined based on the personalization requirements we want to support in a concrete system. The information specified in the user model builds the *user profile* and will be updated during the lifetime of the system. The information stored in the user model typically contains data related to the user (*e.g.*, user characteristics like age or language, user browsing device, etc) and may also contain information related to the domain (*e.g.*, preferences over data). OLAP personalization can be defined on the basis of the following criteria (this is not a closed classification though, it can be extended with new types of personalization-relevant data depending on particular scenarios):

User Characteristics: It refers to information that is directly related to the description of the decision maker. Typical characteristics are the *language*, the *user role*, or the *department*. For example, we can translate multidimensional structures to the language of the user.

User Context: These information characterize the surrounding environment on which an OLAP session is performed. Several relevant types of context for OLAP personalization are described as follows:

location, it refers to information relative to the geographical location of the decision maker: *e.g.*, Spain `country` or Alicante `city`.
time, it refers to information relative to the temporal frame when the OLAP session is performed: *e.g.*, 13/03/2009 `calendar date` or 10:00 `hour`.
device, the system can be personalized depending on the user browsing device information: *e.g.*, we can personalize by taking into consideration the `screen size` or the `device type`.

User Requirements: Decision makers require information that has some specific features when it is provided (security, performance tuning, user configurations, etc.) [17]. These features are constraints that the OLAP system must fulfil to satisfy expectations of each particular user.

User Behaviour: We can track the user browsing behaviour in the OLAP system and infer the interest or preferences he has on certain elements. For this purpose we store information about OLAP operations performed by the decision maker. For example, we can offer shortcuts for the most visited aggregation paths, sort certain measures taking into account the user preferences, etc.

The user model is represented by means of a UML profile in a class diagram. Several stereotypes have been defined in this UML profile as shown in Fig. 4.

The different criteria considered (characteristics, requirements, context) in the user model are defined as an extension of the UML class concept which has attributes and operations (also extensions of the UML concepts). There have been defined different stereotypes for representing the different types of criteria (*i.e.*, `<<Characteristic>>`, `<<Requirement>>`, `<<DeviceContext>>`, `<<TimeContext>>`, `<<LocationContext>>`) in the final model. The user and the session are also defined extending the UML class concept with the stereotypes `<<User>>` and `<<Session>>` respectively. Finally, the events representing the OLAP operations performed by users are also defined as new stereotypes.

An sample user model defined for the motivating example (see Sect. 3) is shown in Fig. 5. As aforementioned, in this model we store different information needed to fulfil the personalization requirements initially specified for the OLAP system. The specified requirements for this example are the following:

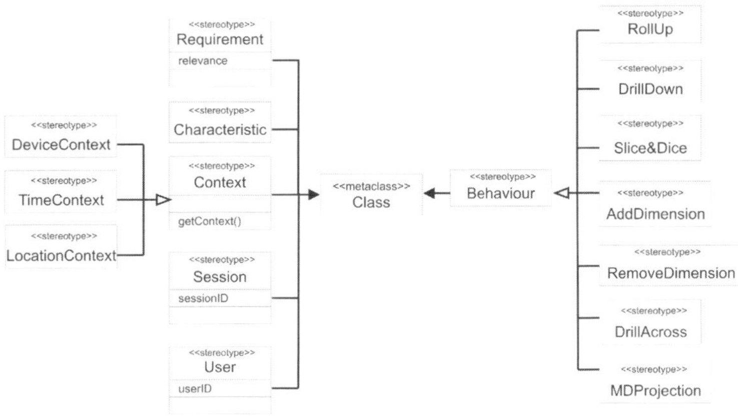

Fig. 4. UML profile for the OLAP User Model

- *The regional sales manager will be able to analyze sales by region.* To fulfill this requirement we have to store the decision maker role in the user model as we can see in Fig. 5.
- *If the decision maker is not interested enough in the aggregation path from store to department, then it is hidden.* To cope with this requirement we need to acquire the decision maker interest on this path. For this purpose we have the *DepPath* class in the user model. This class represents a rollup event triggered by the user behaviour and stores the number of times it is performed. In this example, this value is stored as long-term data (*i.e.*, independent of the session), because the designer wants to personalize on basis of the total number of rollups done to the *department* base.
- *Depending on the decision maker location the storeCost fact attribute is shown in a different currency.* To cope with this requirement the data we need to store is the decision maker location during the current session.
- *The decision maker from the old people department will only see products which scope is people whose age is greater than 65.* In this case we need again to store the department of the decision maker, which will be stored in the *Department* class.

All the required information is stored in the user model. When the information has to be gathered at runtime (*e.g.*, user location, user interest) a PRML rule to update the user model is defined. Moreover personalization rules are needed to specify the actions needed to fulfill the personalization requirements. Some of these rules are defined in Sect. 4.2.

4.2 Personalization Model

After specifying the structure of the data needed for personalization, the designer should define the personalization actions to apply to the OLAP system. As

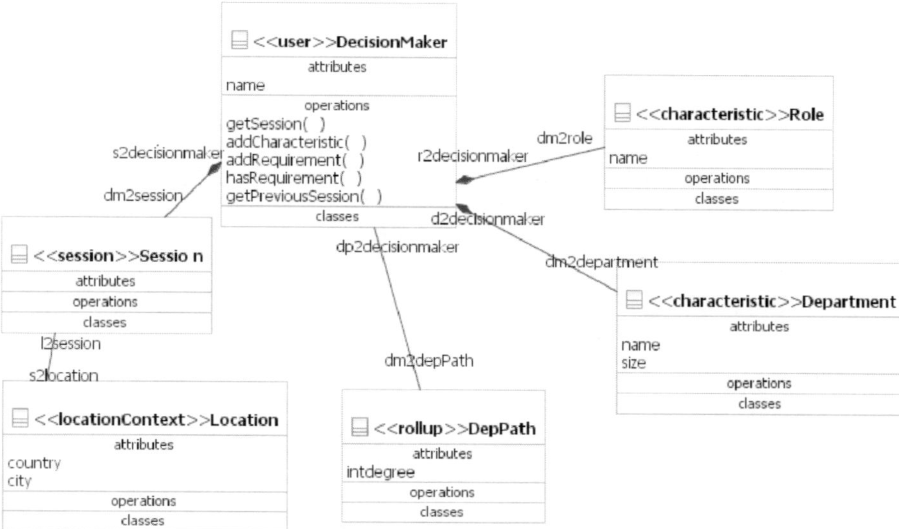

Fig. 5. User model for the motivating example

aforementioned, we define the personalization model by a set of Event-Condition-Action rules. The rules express the following: *when an event is triggered if a condition is fulfilled an action is performed*.

Fig. 6 shows (an excerpt of) the metamodel for the PRML language extended for OLAP systems. It defines the set of constructs of the language such as the different parts that form a PRML rule and the different events and the actions supported. It is worth noting that the PRML metamodel can be extended if a new kind of event or action is detected. The main element of the metamodel is the *Rule* metaclass which represents the concept of rule containing the elements that define it. The elements defining a rule are the ones that represent its main structure and are explained along the following sections.

Tracking Events. OLAP tools provide an interactive analysis of data based on operations that manipulate multidimensional structures [3]. This interactive analysis generates events when the decision maker performs OLAP operations. The events we consider are based on the OLAP operations defined in [18]:

- *AddDimension(Dimension d)*: this event is triggered when the user adds a new *Dimension* class *d* during the OLAP analysis.
- *RemoveDimension(Dimension d)*: this event is triggered when the user deletes an existing *Dimension* class *d* during the OLAP analysis.
- *Rollup(Base sourcebase, Base targetbase)*: this event is triggered when data is aggregated from one level of detail (*sourcebase*) to a coarser one (*targetbase*).
- *DrillDown(Base sourcebase, Base targetbase)*: this event is triggered when data is disaggregated from one level of detail (*sourcebase*) to a finer one (*targetbase*).

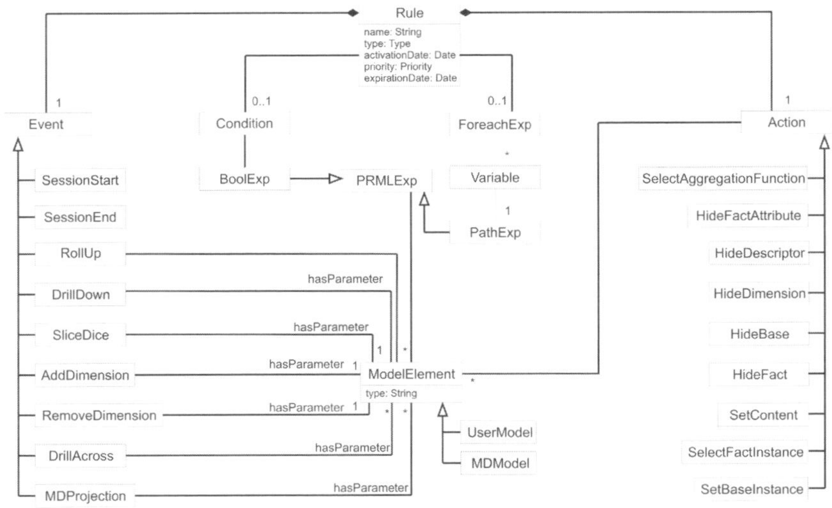

Fig. 6. An excerpt of our PRML metamodel for OLAP

- *DrillAcross(Fact sourcefact, Fact targetfact, Dimension d)*: this event is triggered when data of one *Fact* class (*targetfact*) is obtained from other *Fact* class (*sourcefact*) through a common *Dimension* class *d*.
- *MultidimensionalProjection(FactAttribute measure)*: this event is triggered when a *FactAttribute measure* is selected from those available in the related fact.
- *SliceDice(PRMLExp condition)*: this event is triggered when a *PRMLExp* is applied as a *condition* in order to obtain a filtered set of data.

Besides the previously described events, events related to the OLAP session should be considered. On the one hand, the *start session* event is triggered when the OLAP session is initiated by the user, whereas the *end session* event indicates the end of the OLAP session.

Rule Conditions. When specifying conditions, PRML rules can refer to different elements of the conceptual models in order to define boolean expressions. As already explained, personalization is mainly based on the user model information. A mechanism to access the user model structures is needed. To access a certain element of a model, PRML navigates over the model using path expressions (PE). These expressions are based on the path expressions defined in OCL [19]. The PE to access information defined in the user model, always contain the prefix "UM" and the source concept is always the user class, to identify the user that is actually analyzing the data. As an example for a PE over the user model defined in Fig. 5, consider that we want to access the role of the decision maker. The PE expression would be `UM.DecisionMaker.dm2role.name`. Analogous to OCL, we navigate through the model concepts by the target roles of the relationships between model elements.

Furthermore, a PRML rule can also refer to information from the multidimensional model for specifying some needed conditions to define personalization actions. In the same way, in the personalization actions we may need to refer to an element of the multidimensional model to be modified. In this case PE contain the "MD" prefix and the source concept of the PE is always the *Fact* class we want to access. In this case to navigate through the model elements we go over the *Base* classes and *Descriptor* attributes of the multidimensional model, for instance, to refer to the *name* on the *State* we use `Sale.Store.State.Name`.

Personalization Actions over OLAP models. Personalization rules can contain two kinds of actions. On one hand, as aforementioned, satisfying a personalization requirement may imply acquiring knowledge about the user at the runtime. For this purpose, an acquisition action has been defined to update the user model. On the other hand, other actions have been defined to personalize the multidimensional model. These actions are described as follows:

- *setContent(Property name, ValueSpecification value)*: this action allows to update the value of an property of the user model or the value of a *FactAttribute* or *Descriptor* property of the multidimensional model. The new value can be a literal or a formula.
- *hideFactAttribute(FactAttribute name)*: this action allows to filter which *FactAttributes* properties will be shown.
- *hideDescriptor(Descriptor name)*: this action allows to filter which *Descriptor* properties will be shown.
- *hideFact(Fact name)*: this action allows to filter which *Fact* classes will be shown.
- *hideBase(Base name)*: this action allows to filter which *Base* classes will be shown.
- *hideDimension(Dimension name)*: this action allows to filter which *Dimension* classes will be shown.
- *hideAggregationFunction(FactAttribute fa, Set(AggregationFunction) af)*: this action filters the set of aggregation functions applied over a *FactAttribute* propety.

The next section shows the applicability of our approach by means of a sample scenario based on the multidimensional model described in Sect. 3.

5 Sample Application

In order to show the applicability of our approach, this section defines a couple of sample situations in which personalization rules are applied over the multidimensional model described in Sect. 3. We put the focus on exemplifying how to provide personalized aggregation paths to decision makers. This is a key problem to be faced when personalizing an OLAP system because the inappropriate setting of the aggregation paths very likely derives in useless information [6].

Example 1 (Filtering aggregation paths). Different users may need to aggregate data at different levels of detail according to their specific information requirements. For example, a regional sales manager needs to analyze sales by region instead of by state. Therefore, a personalization rule is required to hide the state *Base* class, thus allowing the manager to better focus on regional sales. It is worth noting that the user role has been previously gathered from user requirements and stored in the user model. This rule is triggered when users log in. If the user role is "RegionalSalesManager" then the *Base* class state from the multidimensional model is hidden.

```
Rule:hideStateBase
When SessionStart do
If (UM.DecisionMaker.dm2Role.name=‘‘RegionalSalesManager’’) then
hideBase(MD.Sale.Store.State)
endIf endWhen
```

Example 2 (Filtering aggregation paths by user interest). Interest of the users in different multidimensional elements can be inferred by their data analysis behaviour. For instance, we can hide an aggregation path that the user is not interested enough in. We define the following requirement: *if the decision maker has not enough interest in aggregating the sales by department we hide this path.* To cope with this requirement, the first step is to gather the user interest in that aggregation path. For this purpose we define the interest of the user as the times s/he does rollup from store to department, and we store this information in the user model by means of the following rule:

```
Rule:updateDepInterest
When Rollup(‘Store’,‘Department’) do
setContent(UM.DecisionMaker.dm2depPath.intdegree,
UM.DecisionMaker.dm2depPath.intdegree+1)
endWhen
```

This rule updates the user interest degree in the aggregation path to department when a rollup action is performed from store to this *Base* class. The personalization rule has to be defined to hide the Department *Base* class if the interest degree is less than certain threshold previously defined by the designer.

```
Rule:hideDepartmentBase
When SessionStart do
If (UM.DecisionMaker.dm2depPath.intdegree<threshold) then
hideBase(MD.Sale.Store.Department)
endIf endWhen
```

The proposed approach is implemented on the basis of the prototype tool presented in [20] which allows to define multidimensional models at the conceptual level and derive a unified OLAP schema. This prototype is developed inside the *Eclipse Modeling Framework.* The extensions done to this prototype allow to conceptually define the user model and the set of personalization rules in order to generate user-specific OLAP schemas at runtime.

6 Conclusions

Current approaches for data warehouse development focus on deriving a unique OLAP schema from the multidimensional model for all decision makers. However, due to the overwhelming volume of information that OLAP schemas contain, personalization is highly convenient in order to provide personalized schema tailored to specific users, improving their satisfaction [5]. Therefore, modeling OLAP personalization is a cornerstone in the development of data warehouses [6].

Few proposals consider OLAP personalization, but to the best of our knowledge, they lack several important issues: (i) none of the existing approaches consider personalization at runtime, (ii) they mainly focus on data instances without considering personalization of data structures, (iii) they mainly focus on defining user preferences and do not take into consideration other important factors (*e.g.*, user behaviour), (iv) none of these approaches provide a conceptual modeling solution for defining personalization. To overcome these drawbacks, this paper presents a modeling approach for OLAP personalization at the conceptual level by providing two new design artifacts together with the multidimensional model: (i) a *user model* which captures all the user-related information needed to personalization, and (ii) a set of *personalization rules* which specify the required personalization actions. These models allow to personalize the multidimensional model obtaining a set of user-specific OLAP schemas. Finally, the applicability of our approach is shown by a sample scenario.

As a short-term future work we plan to complete the approach with the definition of complex events (*i.e.*, sequence of OLAP operations) that allow to define more complex personalization strategies. Moreover, we plan to extend this approach considering visualization aspects of the OLAP system. It is also interesting to study the satisfaction of the decision makers by means of usability tests and experiments.

Acknowledgements. This work has been supported by the ESPIA (TIN2007-67078) project from the Spanish Ministry of Education and Science, and by the QUASIMODO (PAC08-0157-0668) project from the Castilla-La Mancha Ministry of Education and Science (Spain). Jesús Pardillo and Jose-Norberto Mazón are funded by the Spanish Ministry of Education and Science under FPU grants AP2006-00332 and AP2005-1360, respectively.

References

1. Kimball, R., Ross, M.: The Data Warehouse Toolkit. Wiley & Sons, Chichester (2002)
2. Jarke, M., Lenzerini, M., Vassiliou, Y., Vassiliadis, P.: Fundamentals of Data Warehouses. Springer, Heidelberg (2000)

3. Choong, Y.W., Laurent, D., Marcel, P.: Computing appropriate representations for multidimensional data. Data Knowl. Eng. 45(2), 181–203 (2003)
4. Rizzi, S., Abelló, A., Lechtenbörger, J., Trujillo, J.: Research in data warehouse modeling and design: dead or alive? In: Song, I.Y., Vassiliadis, P. (eds.) DOLAP, pp. 3–10. ACM, New York (2006)
5. Stefanidis, K., Pitoura, E., Vassiliadis, P.: Modeling and Storing Context-Aware Preferences. In: ADBIS, pp. 124–140 (2006)
6. Rizzi, S.: OLAP preferences: a research agenda. In: DOLAP, pp. 99–100 (2007)
7. Mouloudi, H., Bellatreche, L., Giacometti, A., Marcel, P.: Personalization of mdx queries. In: BDA (2006)
8. Kießling, W.: Foundations of Preferences in Database Systems. In: VLDB, pp. 311–322 (2002)
9. Bellatreche, L., Giacometti, A., Marcel, P., Mouloudi, H., Laurent, D.: A personalization framework for OLAP queries. In: Song, I.Y., Trujillo, J. (eds.) DOLAP, pp. 9–18. ACM, New York (2005)
10. Ioannidis, Y.E., Koutrika, G.: Personalized systems: Models and methods from an ir and db perspective. In: VLDB, p. 1365 (2005)
11. Jerbi, H., Ravat, F., Teste, O., Zurfluh, G.: Management of context-aware preferences in multidimensional databases. In: ICDIM, pp. 669–675 (2008)
12. Ravat, F., Teste, O.: Personalization and OLAP databases. In: Volume New Trends in Data Warehousing and Data Analysis of Annals of Information Systems, pp. 71–92. Springer, Heidelberg (2009)
13. Luján-Mora, S., Trujillo, J., Song, I.-Y.: A UML profile for multidimensional modeling in data warehouses.. Data Knowl. Eng. 59(3), 725–769 (2006)
14. Kappel, G., Pröll, B., Retschitzegger, W., Schwinger, W.: Modelling Ubiquitous Web Applications - The WUML Approach. In: ER (Workshops), pp. 183–197 (2001)
15. Garrigós, I.: A-OOH: Extending Web Application Design with Dynamic Personalization. PhD thesis, University of Alicante, Spain (2008)
16. Garrigós, I., Cruz, C., Gómez, J.: A prototype tool for the automatic generation of adaptive websites. In: Casteleyn, S., Daniel, F., Dolog, P., Matera, M., Houben, G.J., Troyer, O.D. (eds.) AEWSE. CEUR Workshop Proceedings, CEUR-WS.org., vol. 267 (2007)
17. Soler, E., Stefanov, V., Mazón, J.-N., Trujillo, J., Fernández-Medina, E., Piattini, M.: Towards comprehensive requirement analysis for data warehouses: Considering security requirements. In: ARES, pp. 104–111. IEEE Computer Society, Los Alamitos (2008)
18. Pardillo, J., Mazón, J.-N., Trujillo, J.: Bridging the semantic gap in OLAP models: platform-independent queries. In: DOLAP, pp. 89–96 (2008)
19. Object Management Group: Unified Modeling Language (UML), version 2.1.1. (February 2007), `http://www.omg.org/technology/documents/formal/uml.htm`
20. Pardillo, J., Mazón, J.-N., Trujillo, J.: Model-driven metadata for OLAP cubes from the conceptual modelling of data warehouses. In: Song, I.-Y., Eder, J., Nguyen, T.M. (eds.) DaWaK 2008. LNCS, vol. 5182, pp. 13–22. Springer, Heidelberg (2008)

Creating User Profiles Using Wikipedia

Krishnan Ramanathan and Komal Kapoor

HP Labs, 24, Salarpuria arena, Hosur Road, Adugodi, Bangalore – 560 030
krishnan.ramanathan@hp.com, komal.bitsgoa@gmail.com

Abstract. Creating user profiles is an important step in personalization. Many methods for user profile creation have been developed to date using different representations such as term vectors and concepts from an ontology like DMOZ. In this paper, we propose and evaluate different methods for creating user profiles using Wikipedia as the representation. The key idea in our approach is to map documents to Wikipedia concepts at different levels of resolution: words, key phrases, sentences, paragraphs, the document summary and the entire document itself. We suggest a method for evaluating profile recall by pooling the relevant results from the different methods and evaluate our results for both precision and recall. We also suggest a novel method for profile evaluation by assessing the recall over a known ontological profile drawn from DMOZ.

Keywords: User profiles, User modeling, Hierarchy, Personalization, DMOZ, Wikipedia, Evaluation.

1 Introduction

Personalized information services promise to reduce information overload and provide targeted, relevant content and ads to users. Companies such as Google, Yahoo, Microsoft and Amazon are trying to provide personalized home pages, search and recommendations. An important aspect of personalization is the creation of a high quality user profile that provides an accurate representation of the user interests. Although many websites create user profiles, the profiles they create have significant limitations, namely 1) most users are reluctant to allow online sites to store their search keywords and other data for privacy reasons 2) websites get to see only that fraction of user activity that is on their sites and cannot construct a complete user profile 3) profiles created on different websites are not portable, mainly because the website doesn't expose the profile to the users themselves.

Creating user profiles on a client device overcomes the problem of privacy by allowing users to share only parts of the profile and being in control of the profile at all times. The client device sees all the user actions and hence the profile is likely to be more comprehensive than the one a website constructs by logging user actions on the specific site. Since the user owns the profile, the user can share it with the site of the user's choice as also with competing service providers. The user may upload the profile to a trusted site and cloud services may access the profile by suitably compensating the user. Studies have shown that people are unwilling to explicitly specify their

A.H.F. Laender et al. (Eds.): ER 2009, LNCS 5829, pp. 415–427, 2009.

profile interests [Kobsa, 2007]. Hence, most prior research has focused on creating implicit user profiles. There are broadly three approaches to creating implicit user profiles: using term vectors, using machine learning and using ontology such as the Open Directory project (DMOZ).

In the term vector approach (also called the Bag of words (BOW) approach), the user interests are maintained as a vector of weighted terms. One could use a single term vector for representing all the user interests or could have multiple term vectors, one for each topic or interest. The term weighting reflects the frequency of the word in the document (the term frequency TF) and within the entire corpus (the inverse document frequency IDF). Although the term vector approach is popular, it has some serious drawbacks. Multi-word phrases are broken into separate features (e.g .the phrase economic governance is separated into the words economic and governance). Synonymous words (e.g. happiness and joy) are mapped into different components and polysemous words (e.g. Apple could be a fruit or computer) are considered the same. Finally, words unrelated to web page content occur frequently on web pages (e.g. "home page").

In the machine learning approach [Pazzani and Billsus, 1997], the user model is based on positive and negative examples of his interests. This approach is not used frequently because of the difficulty in getting labeled samples (there have been some attempts at this, for example [Matchmine]). Also, the learning needs to be incremental and has to tackle the problem of concept drift because of changing user interests.

In the ontological approach, a preexisting ontology like DMOZ has been used to represent the profile [Chirita *et al.*, 2005]. The profile is built by mapping or classifying user documents to an existing ontology. The ontology defines (and restricts) the vocabulary of the profile. Once the profile is built, tree distance measures are used to measure the relatedness of two nodes in the profile. DMOZ is a large ontology; most users will have only a fraction of interests represented in DMOZ. Also, using DMOZ requires building classifiers for each node in DMOZ, constructing and maintaining multiple classifiers on a client device would be very challenging. Hence a profile representation that has less ambiguity than words and does not require building many classifiers is preferable.

In this paper, we propose a method for creating user profiles using Wikipedia as the reference vocabulary. Our method maps documents to Wikipedia concepts and generates a hierarchical tree of concepts using the method of [Xu *et al.*, 2007]. The resultant profiles are highly readable; this overcomes some of the problems in earlier methods of evaluating the precision of the user profile. One critical question is: what is the right resolution of the document to extract concepts? One possibility is to extract high frequency words from the document and map them to Wikipedia concepts, however might miss the context of the surrounding words and sentences. To answer this question we used our method to derive profiles using document words, sentences, paragraphs, key phrases, the document summary and the entire document. We also evaluated the resultant profiles for precision and recall. Our main contributions in this paper are

1. We propose a method for creating hierarchical user profiles using Wikipedia concepts. We propose a method for distinguishing informational and recreational

interests in the profile from the commercial interests. We found that highly readable profiles are obtained in this manner.

2. We develop different ways of mapping documents (web pages in our study) to Wikipedia concepts for the purpose of profile generation. We found that generating key phrases from the document and using it to create the profile results in coherent profiles as well as good precision,
3. We propose a method for evaluating recall by pooling profiles generated by different methods. We also propose a new method to evaluate the user profiles by constructing them from web pages that are drawn out of a known hierarchy. We found that our method is able to maintain a high fidelity with a known profile.

The organization of the rest of the paper is as follows. In section 2, we explain the related work in creating user profiles. In section 3, we discuss the proposed method of generating user profiles using Wikipedia concepts as the profile representation. Section 4 discusses the different ways to map documents to Wikipedia concepts. Section 5 presents an evaluation of the user profiles and section 6 concludes the paper.

2 Related Work

One of the key challenges in personalization is to construct accurate user models containing demographic interests, preferences, intent and behavior information [Gauch *et al.*, 2007]. Studies have shown that the information a server misses out on can really hurt personalization [Padmanaban and Zheng, 2001] and it is preferable to use all available information on the client side for personalization [Teevan *et al.*,2005].

Many works have addressed the development of an efficient representation for the user profile. Traditionally, term vectors have been used to represent user interests. However, these suffer from the well known polysemy and synonymy problems. In order to address the polysemy problem inherent with term-based profiles, a weighted semantic network in which each node represents a concept has been proposed. [Minio and Tasso, 1996] have constructed semantic networks where each node contains a particular word found in the corpus and arcs between the nodes represent their co-occurrence information. "Synonym sets," or synsets obtained using WordNet have been used to incorporate more semantic information in each node [SiteIF project, 1998].

Researchers have attempted to utilize ontologies for generating semantically enriched ontology-based user profiles. [Trajkova and Gauch, 2004] have weighted concepts in a reference ontology based on the similarity between the Web pages visited by a user and the concepts in a domain ontology. Concepts with a non-zero weight have been used to create the user profile. The ontological approach to user profiling has also proven to be successful in addressing the cold-start problem in recommender systems [Middleton *et al.*, 2003].

Wordnet [Wordnet] has been used as reference ontology; but Wordnet is manually built and has a restricted coverage. The DMOZ taxonomy is used as the basis for various research projects in the area of Web personalization. In the framework [Seig *et al.*, 2007], the user context is represented using an ontological user profile, which is an annotated instance of DMOZ. To get around the need to build classifiers to map web pages to nodes in DMOZ, [Chirita *et al.*, 2005] require the user to input nodes in DMOZ that are of interest to them. However, users do not like to give these kinds of inputs. Moreover, the DMOZ hierarchy also represents the collective belief of a number of people and may not have enough detail to capture specific interests of a user.

The alternative is to build a hierarchy from scratch. [Godoy and Amandi, 2005] present an algorithm that uses both implicit and explicit indicators of user interest to construct a hierarchical profile. Nodes in the profile are term vectors and leaves are words representing user interests. The algorithm uses cohesiveness with respect to the cluster centroid to assign new words to clusters. User Interest Hierarchy (UIH) which captures a continuum of general to specific interests of the user have certain advantages on a flat set of words [Kim and Chan, 2007]. Phrases have been used in addition to words to enrich features in UIH.

Recently, the Wikipedia corpus has been used for semantically rich feature generation in text processing problems [Gabrilovich and Markovich, 2006]. Wikipedia has been used to overcome the shortages of the BOW approach in document classification by embedding background knowledge constructed from Wikipedia into a semantic kernel, which is used to enrich the representation of documents [Wang and Domeniconi, 2008]. Such a semantic kernel has been shown to be able to keep multi-word concepts unbroken, captures the semantic closeness of synonyms, and performs word sense disambiguation for polysemous terms.

3 The Proposed Method

In this section, we propose the novel approach of constructing hierarchical user profiles using Wikipedia as the vocabulary for describing user interests. In a hierarchical profile the most general concepts are located near the root of the hierarchy and more specific concepts are located near the leaves. The user profile obtained by mapping documents viewed by the user to Wikipedia concepts is more compact and readable as compared to profiles that use words. In our proposed method, creating a user profile using Wikipedia is a three step process. First the documents (web pages in our case) are mapped to a set of Wikipedia concepts. Then a hierarchical profile is constructed from these concepts. Finally, these concepts are annotated with information that may be helpful in information filtering or advertising.

3.1 Generating Wikipedia Concepts

Input text is mapped to Wikipedia concepts according to the algorithm described by [Gabrilovich and Markovich, 2007].First all the Wikipedia topics and the content of the topics are indexed using Apache Lucene [ApacheLucene]. The Wikipedia dump of November 26, 2006 has been used in our experiments. To map input text to a concept, we query the Wikipedia index with the text. The titles of the documents that are returned (the “hits” in Lucene terminology) as the query results constitute the mapping of the input text to the Wikipedia concepts. We select the top twenty results for further processing. The process is illustrated in Figure 1.

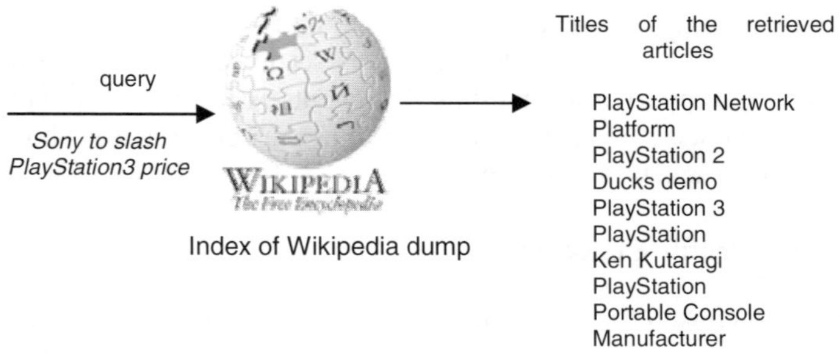

Fig. 1. Mapping sentences to Wikipedia concepts

3.2 User Profile Generation

We use all the documents in the web cache of the user to generate his profile. Each document in the web cache is first mapped to twenty Wikipedia concepts. The detailed procedure of mapping a document to Wikipedia concepts is covered in section 4. The actual profile generation from the Wikipedia concepts collected over all the documents in the user cache was done by adapting the algorithm in [Xu *et al.*, 2007] which in turn was based on the hierarchical profile creation algorithm of [Kim and Chan, 2003]. This algorithm builds a hierarchical tree in top-down fashion using two heuristic rules. The first rule identifies similar terms by co-occurrence within the document. These terms are merged into a single concept if the Jaccard overlap is above a threshold defined by the delta parameter. The second rule identifies more general terms, again using co-occurrence. Specific terms are made the children of general terms. Subsumption is not implied in the parent-child relationship, specifically the child need not have an "is-a" relation with the parent.

Terms are chosen for inclusion in the profile if they appear across different documents (this is called the support of the terms, we use the same terminology in our evaluation). The minsup parameter is the minimum support for a term to be considered for inclusion in the profile. First all the Wikipedia concepts are retrieved from the concepts index. Each concept is either merged with a similar concept, made a child of another concept or remains as an independent concept.

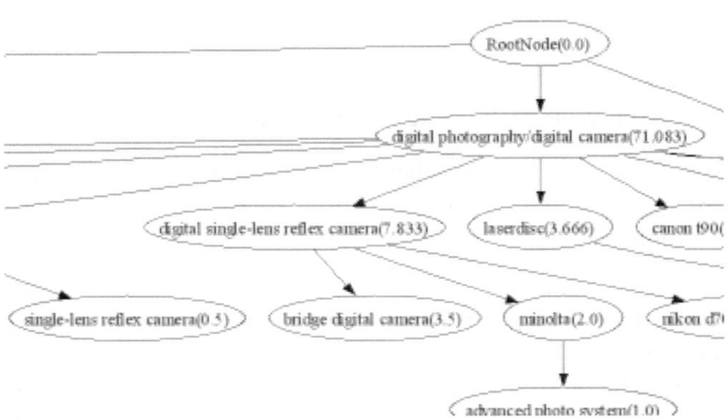

Fig. 2. Hierarchical user profile from Wikipedia concepts

We set the minsup parameter in the algorithm of [Xu *et al.*, 2007] to 2 and the delta parameter to 0.6. The minsup parameter was set lower because the probability of a concept getting support from multiple documents is lower than a word occurring in multiple documents. A snapshot from a profile thus generated is shown in Figure 2, the numbers in brackets are the support (strength of user interest) for each concept.

3.3 Tagging Profile Concepts

After the hierarchical profile is generated, the concepts in the profile are tagged in two ways

- as being of transactional interest or recreational interest.
- with the recency of the user interest in a concept

Some concepts may be of both transactional and recreational interest. For instance, a user having photography as a hobby and has searched for cameras with purchase intent would have photography tagged as both a transactional and recreational interest.

For tagging concepts as being of transactional interest, we first crawled pages from shopping sites that allowed crawling. We then mapped the contents of each page to Wikipedia concepts and labeled those concepts as having transactional value. This gave a list of a shopping concepts, some of which we filtered manually as they did not pertain to shopping. After the filtering, we had about 7000 topics of transactional interest. For tagging recreational and hobby content, we just picked the topics under the recreational and hobby categories in Wikipedia. This yielded about 300 topics.

The recency of the user interest in a particular concept is based on the age of the pages in the users' web cache supporting the concept

$$\text{Recency} = \sum_{\text{supporting pages}} 1/e^{(\text{todays\_date - date\_page\_was\_accessed\_by\_user})}$$

The exponential decay ensures that recency of interest is significant only if a page mapped to the concept in the last week or so. This would allow a potential advertiser to target concepts of current interest to the consumer and to stop advertising after the interest wanes (this could happen if the user bought the item he was looking for). Due to limitations of space, we will omit an evaluation of the efficacy of tagging in this paper. The algorithm for generating the hierarchical user profile and annotating the concepts is as below.

Input: Web pages from users web cache or documents from file system

Output: A hierarchical user profile where nodes are Wikipedia concepts. Nodes are annotated with strength and recency of user interest and whether the node is potentially of shopping interest

Algorithm:

1. Map each of the user web pages (or documents) to Wikipedia concepts. Store the concepts in an index.
2. Construct a hierarchical profile from the index. The concepts may be retrieved from the index in a user specified order (e.g. date of browsing the page). The nodes are labeled with the strength of the user interest

3. After the profile is constructed, the nodes are annotated with recency of user interest. If the node is deemed to be as shopping interest, the node is labeled as being of shopping interest

---

Algorithm 1. User profile generation algorithm

4 Wikipedia Concept Selection

Our profile creation technique is heavily dependent on the mapping of documents to concepts in Wikipedia. In this section we discuss the different techniques used to map a document to Wikipedia concepts. In all these cases, the text is fed as a conjunctive query to the Lucene index (as explained in section 3.1) for mapping text to Wikipedia concepts.

4.1 Wikipedia Concept Selection Using Document Words

In the method proposed by [Gabrilovich and Markovich, 2007], bi-grams are extracted from the document and mapped to Wikipedia concepts. However this would be very expensive to do on a client device. In order to reduce the computational expense, we chose a subset of words from the document to map to a Wikipedia concept as follows. We first compute the average word frequency of each word in the document. We then chose only those words that had length of at least four characters and frequency equal or greater than the average word frequency.

4.2 Wikipedia Concept Selection Using Document Key Phrases

Given an input document, we first identify important keywords using the method in [Zhang and Cheng, 2007]. We then construct a graph where the nodes of the graph are the high frequency words in the document and associate the following weights with each word. If the word occurs in the document title, document abstract or paragraph title, it is assigned a higher weight; if it occurs anywhere else in the document it is assigned a lower weight (weights were 5 and 1 in our study). The objective is to give more importance to those words that occur in document title, the abstract or paragraph titles. Next, we create edges between those nodes of the graph if words associated with the nodes co-occur in same sentence. The link weight is the minimum of the word weights assigned to words in the previous step. We then find the maximally connected components in the graph, this is called a concept.

We then extract key phrases from this concept graph as follows. We first find all the n-grams (n=2 or 3) in the document. One constraint we imposed was that the n-grams should not have intervening stop words. We then test if these n-grams are part of a concept (as extracted above), if it is we choose the n-gram as a key phrase. We use at least 2% of the total number of key phrases generated and at most 30 key phrases (because of the query length restrictions imposed by search engines).

4.3 Wikipedia Concept Selection Using Document Sentences and Paragraphs

We first extract the individual sentences in the document. Document sentences are mapped to semantic concepts in Wikipedia by virtue of query "hits" using the Lucene engine as described previously. This mapping can be captured as a bipartite graph, with one set of nodes (or vertices) denoting the document sentences and the other set of nodes denoting the Wikipedia concepts. An edge between a sentence node and a concept node indicates a mapping between the corresponding document sentence and Wikipedia concept, while the absence of an edge indicates that there is no mapping. Figure 3 illustrates this sentence-concept bipartite graph for a small document of three sentences.

After the entire document has been processed in this manner, we identify the Wikipedia concepts that got "hit" multiple times by different sentences in the document. The larger the number of hits, the more that particular concept represents the document. Twenty Wikipedia concepts having the largest number of hits are selected as the concepts for the document.

Figure 4 shows the matrix representation of the bipartite sentence-concept graph corresponding to the sentence-concepts graph in Figure 3. In the above figure, concept C3 will be chosen as representative of the document since both sentence 1 and sentence 2 map to it.

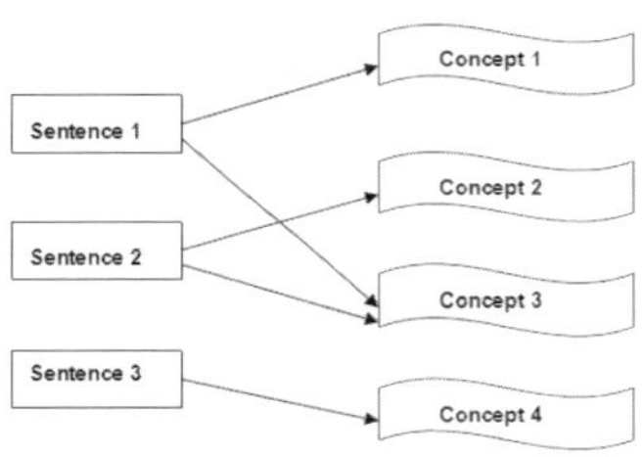

Fig. 3. Bipartite sentence-concepts graph

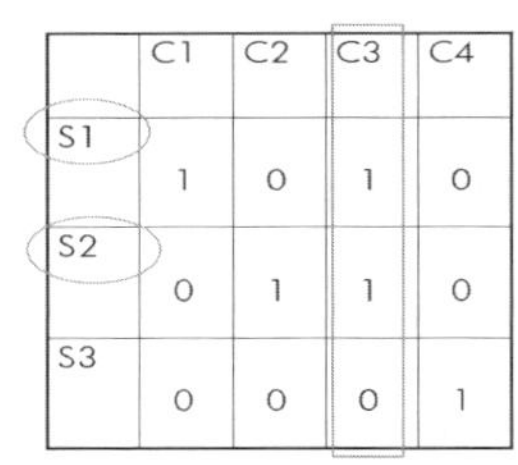

Fig. 4. Matrix representation of bipartite graph

The mapping using document paragraphs is similar to the sentence mapping method. The difference is that paragraphs in the document are identified and queried to the Lucene index instead of sentences.

4.4 Wikipedia Concept Selection Based on the Document Summary

For constructing a document summary, a bipartite graph is constructed as explained in section 4.3. The concepts with the column sum in the matrix representation of the bipartite graph above a certain threshold vote for the sentences to be selected in the summary. In the example of the previous section 4.3 (Figure 4), Wiki concept 3 is hit by both sentence 1 and 2. Assuming both the threshold was set at 2 hits, sentence 1 and 2 are chosen as the two sentence summary of this three sentence document. The summary of the document therefore includes only those sentences from the document that map to the important concepts identified for the document. Irrelevant sentences or sentences expressing ideas not related to main theme of the document are eliminated.

Querying the Lucene index with the document summary obtained in the above manner is expected to yield better concepts.

4.5 Wikipedia Concept Selections Using the Entire Document

The entire document is input as one long query to the Lucene index and the top twenty concepts are selected. The advantage is that the context of the entire document is used in the query; the disadvantage is that the performance of the system could get degraded by the use of long queries.

5 Evaluation

Evaluation of user profile algorithms presents several challenges. Firstly, there is the absence of a standard corpus of documents and web pages against which a user profile algorithm can be evaluated. This could be overcome by collecting individual users browsing history, building a user profile and performing a user evaluation on the profile. This still does not overcome the subjectivity of individual users; in fact, the same user may identify different profile items/concepts as being most relevant at different points in time. Despite these limitations, we still use this method as one of our evaluation methods. We also suggest a novel evaluation method for hierarchical profiles, namely to evaluate their fidelity for documents drawn from a known hierarchy. For this evaluation, we pick sub-hierarchies from DMOZ and evaluate how many of the DMOZ concepts were captured in the Wikipedia profile.

5.1 Profile Precision and Recall

We evaluated the profile on a collection of 1500 web pages from the browsing history of the first author. We generated concepts at different levels of support (less than 3, between 3 and 5, greater than 5) using all the six concept mapping methods. Different number of concepts is generated at different levels of support. There are fewer concepts with high support (support greater than 5) and many concepts with low support (support less than 3).

Precision and recall are the commonly used evaluation measures in information retrieval and are defined in the context of our user profile evaluation as follows.

$$\text{Precision} = \frac{\text{Number of relevant concepts}}{\text{Number of concepts in the profile}}$$

$$\text{Recall} = \frac{\text{Number of relevant concepts detected by profiler}}{\text{Total number of relevant concepts}}$$

For evaluating precision, concepts were considered relevant if the user was willing to assign a rank of 5 on a 1-5 scale. The filter we used in rating relevance was whether the user would be willing to receive daily news on the topic. This is admittedly extreme but we used such a strict criterion because we found a lot of concepts that are relevant but not very interesting. Also, we were interested in comparing the precision of the six methods we proposed, not the absolute precision. The graph for the precision with the different approaches is shown in Figure 5.

From the figure, it can be observed that there is no consistent behavior across the different methods. The document level mapping performed better for concepts with low support (less than 3) and high support (greater than 5) while the paragraph level mapping performed better for medium support (between 3 and 5). Mapping key phrases to Wikipedia concepts yielded the best average precision across support levels, also the profile concepts generated with this method were more coherent and readable.

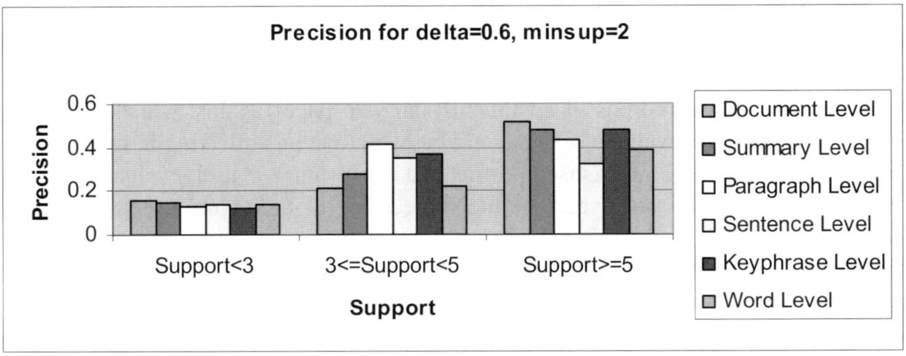

Fig. 5. Precision of the profiles generated by the six methods

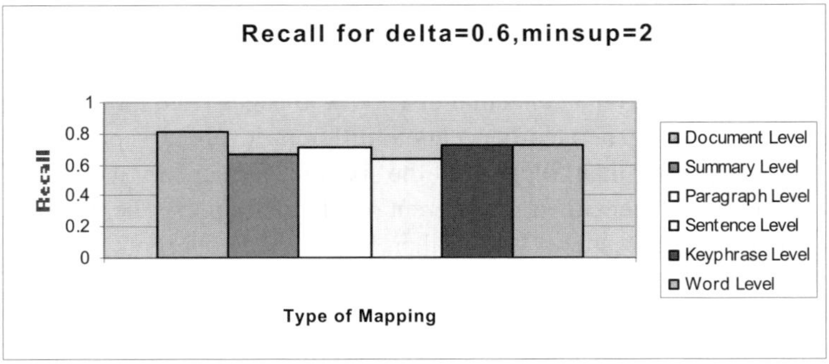

Fig. 6. Recall of the concepts in profile for the six methods

While it is possible to evaluate concepts for precision, recall is trickier since all the concepts of interest to the user are not known (which is the point in constructing the user profile). Yet we would like to know which concepts a particular approach missed. We evaluate recall by pooling in all the relevant concepts identified for evaluating precision and considering this as the total number of relevant concepts. The comparison of the recall of the six methods is shown in Figure 6.

The recall is highest when the mapping to Wikipedia concepts is at the document level. The word level and key phrase level mapping also yielded acceptable levels of recall. This suggests that these methods could suffice for most practical purposes. The document level mapping requires a significantly higher time compared to the word level or key phrase level mapping for generating the profile, the word level mapping may be more suitable for devices with low computing power (such as mobile phones or netbooks).

5.2 Profile Fidelity

We define profile fidelity as the ability of the profiler to pick concepts drawn from a known ontology. To evaluate the profile fidelity, we collected web pages from sub-trees in DMOZ. Figure 7 shows one such DMOZ sub-tree which we used. Here the concepts were three authors, two places and two companies. All the web pages under the DMOZ nodes formed the collection used for creating the user profile. Our goal is to see if the concepts in the DMOZ sub-trees are reflected in the hierarchical profile generated by our profiler. Thus recall and not precision is used as a measure profile fidelity.

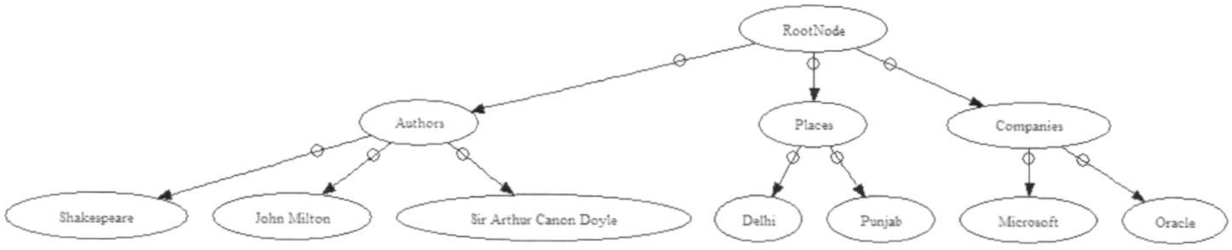

Fig. 7. DMOZ sub-trees for evaluating profile fidelity

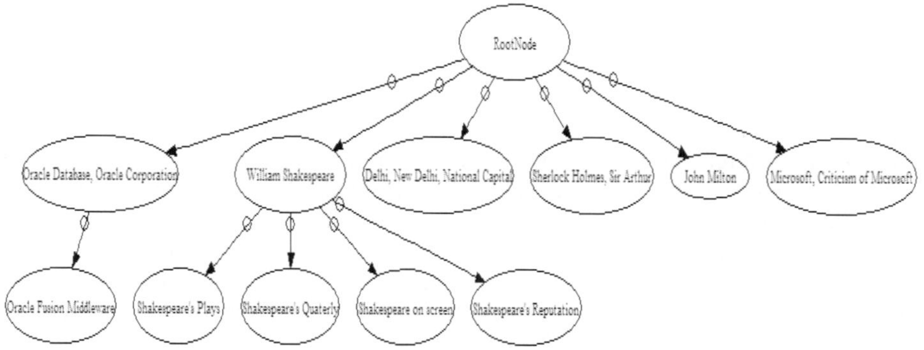

Fig. 8. Profile for pages drawn from DMOZ sub-trees in figure 7

The user profile for the DMOZ sub-tree was generated by mapping the key phrases to Wikipedia concepts. Figure 8 shows the Wikipedia profile obtained by running our profiler on the web pages collected from the DMOZ sub-trees in Figure 7. We consider the recall to be perfect if the concept represented by the DMOZ node also appears in the hierarchical profile generated by our algorithm. Concepts in the DMOZ sub-tree and the user profile obtained from the pages drawn from the DMOZ sub-tree are compared manually and human judgment is used to access whether they are equivalent. In this specific case, six DMOZ concepts out of seven (all concepts except Punjab) were reflected in the profile; hence the recall would be 6/7.

We repeated the experiment for ten sub-trees drawn from different parts of DMOZ. Table 1 shows the recall for the different DMOZ sub-trees. The average recall was 0.86.

This indicates that our profiler was able to capture most of the concepts from the underlying DMOZ ontology. In our experiments we did not evaluate the structure of the user profile against that of the DMOZ sub-tree as the hierarchical profile generation algorithm used in building the profile cannot club concepts into the categories in which DMOZ pages are organized. We thus aim to only evaluate the ability of the profiler to pick concepts equivalent to the DMOZ node from all the pages under the DMOZ node.

Table 1. Recall for the Profile concepts

DMOZ experiment	Profile concepts	DMOZ concepts	Recall
1	6	8	0.75
2	6	7	0.857
3	5	5	1
4	6	7	0.857
5	4	5	0.8
6	6	6	1
7	6	6	1
8	5	7	0.71
9	6	8	0.875
10	7	8	0.75

6 Conclusions

In this paper, we have proposed and evaluated the creation of user profiles using Wikipedia as the representation. We generated the document to Wikipedia concepts mapping at different resolutions. We suggested a novel way of evaluating recall by pooling the relevant results generated by all the methods. The results indicate that key phrase level mapping is preferable. We also proposed a new way of evaluating hierarchical profiles by drawing web pages from a known ontology like DMOZ.

In future work, we plan to use more reliable methods of annotating documents with Wikipedia concepts such as those in [Milne and Witten, 2008] and [Wang and Domeniconi, 2008]. We also plan to evaluate the utility of the profile in applications such as video sourcing, news filtering and search re-ranking. We are also planning to conduct a study with advertisers to understand the value of the profile based on Wikipedia-concepts from an advertising perspective.

Acknowledgements

We would like to thank Somnath Banerjee, Julien Giraudi and Vidhya Govindaraju for their assistance in implementation of the profiler.

References

[ApacheLucene] `http://lucene.apache.org`

[Chirita et al.,2005] Chirita, P.A., Nejdl, W., Paiu, R., Kohlschutter, C.: Using ODP data to personalize search. In: SIGIR (2005)

[Gabrilovich and Markovich, 2006] Gabrilovich, E., Markovich, S.: Overcoming the brittleness bottleneck with Wikipedia: Enhancing Text Categorization with Encyclopedic Knowledge. In: Proc. of the AAAI conference (2006)

[Gauch et al., 2007] Gauch, S., Speretta, M., Chandramouli, A., Micarelli, A.: User profiles for personalized information access. In: Brusilovsky, P., Kobsa, A., Nejdl, W. (eds.) Adaptive Web 2007. LNCS, vol. 4321, pp. 54–89. Springer, Heidelberg (2007)

[Godoy and Amandi, 2005] Godoy, D., Amandi, A.: User profiling for web page filtering. IEEE Internet computing (July-August 2005)

[Kim and Chan, 2003] Kim, H., Chan, P.: Learning implicit user interest hierarchy for context in personalization. In: Proceedings of IUI 2003 (2003)

[Kobsa, 2007] Kobsa, A.: Privacy enhanced personalization. CACM 50(8) (August 2007)

[Matchmine] http://www.matchmine.com

[Middleton et al.,2003] Middleton, S., Shadbolt, N., Roure, D.D.: Capturing interest through inference and visualization: Ontological user profiling in recommender systems. In: Proceedings of the International Conference on Knowledge Capture, K-CAP 2003, Sanibel Island, Florida, October 2003, pp. 62–69 (2003)

[Milne and Witten, 2008] Milne, D., Witten, I.H.: Learning to link with Wikipedia. In: Proc. of CIKM (2008)

[Minio and Tasso, 1996] Minio, M., Tasso, C.: User Modeling for Information Filtering on Internet Services: Exploiting an Extended Version of the UMT Shell. In: UM 1996 Workshop on User Modeling for Information Filtering on the WWW, Kailua-Kona, Hawaii, January 2-5 (1996), http://ten.dimi.uniud.it/~tasso/UM-96UMT.html

[Padmanabhan and Zheng, 2001] Padmanabhan, B., Zheng, Z., Kimbrough, S.O.: Personalization from incomplete data: What you don't know can hurt. In: Proceedings of ACM SIGKDD (2001)

[Pazzani and Billsus, 1997] Pazzani, M., Billsus, D.: Learning and revising user profiles: The identification of interesting websites. Machine Learning journal 27, 313–331 (1997)

[Sieg et al.,2007] Sieg, A., Mobasher, B., Burke, R.: Web search personalization with ontological user profiles. In: Proceedings of the CIKM conference (2007)

[SiteIF project, 1998] Stefani, A.: Strappavara, Personalizing Access to Web Sites: The SiteIF Project. In: Proceedings of the 2nd Workshop on Adaptive Hypertext and Hypermedia HYPERTEXT 1998 Pittsburgh, June 20-24 (1998), http://www.contrib.andrew.cmu.edu/~plb/HT98_workshop/Stefani/Stefani.html

[Teevan et al., 2005] Teevan, J., Dumais, S., Horvitz, E.: Personalizing search via automated analysis of interests and activities. In: Proceedings of SIGIR 2005 (2005)

[Trajkova and Gauch, 2004] Trajkova, J., Gauch, S.: Improving Ontology based user profiles. In: Proceedings of RIAO 2004. University of Avignon, France (2004)

[Wang and Domeniconi, 2008] Wang, P., Domeniconi, C.: Building semantic kernels for text classification using Wikipedia. KDD 2008 (2008)

[Wordnet] http://wordnet.princeton.edu/

[Xu et al., 2007] Xu, Y., Zhang, B., Chen, Z., Wang, K.: Privacy enhancing personalized web search. In: Proceedings of the WWW conference (2007)

[Zhang and Cheng, 2007] Zhang, Z., Cheng, H.: Keyword extracting as text chance discovery. IEEE Fuzzy systems and knowledge discovery conference, FSKD (2007)

Hosted Universal Composition: Models, Languages and Infrastructure in mashArt

Florian Daniel[1], Fabio Casati[1], Boualem Benatallah[2], and Ming-Chien Shan[3]

[1] University of Trento - Via Sommarive 14, 38050 Trento - Italy
{daniel,casati}@disi.unitn.it

[2] University of New South Wales- Sydney NSW 2052, Australia
boualem@cse.unsw.edu.au

[3] SAP Labs- 3410 Hillview Avenue, Palo Alto, CA 94304, USA
ming-chien.shan@sap.com

Abstract. Information integration, application integration and component-based software development have been among the most important research areas for decades. The last years have been characterized by a particular focus on web services, the very recent years by the advent of web mashups, a new and user-centric form of integration on the Web. However, while service composition approaches lack support for user interfaces, web mashups still lack well engineered development approaches and mature technological foundations.

In this paper, we aim to overcome both these shortcomings and propose what we call a *universal* composition approach that naturally brings together data and application services with user interfaces. We propose a unified component model and a universal, event-based composition model, both able to abstract from low-level implementation details and technology specifics. Via the *mashArt* platform, we then provide *universal composition as a service* in form of an easy-to-use graphical development tool equipped with an execution environment for fast deployment and execution of composite Web applications.

1 Introduction

The advent of Web 2.0 led to the participation of the user into the content creation and application development processes, also thanks to the wealth of social web applications (e.g., wikis, blogs, photo sharing applications, etc.) that allow users to become an active contributor of content rather than just a passive consumer, and thanks to *web mashups* [1]. Indeed, especially mashup tools enable fairly sophisticated development tasks, mostly inside the browser. They allow users to develop their own applications starting from existing content and functionality. Some applications focus on integrating RSS or Atom feeds, others on integrating RESTful services, others on simple UI widgets, etc. Many mashup approaches are innovative in that they tackle integration at the user interface level (most mashups integrate presentation content, not "just" data) and aim at simplicity more than robustness or completeness of features (up to the point that advanced web users, not only professional programmers, can develop mashups).

A.H.F. Laender et al. (Eds.): ER 2009, LNCS 5829, pp. 428–443, 2009.

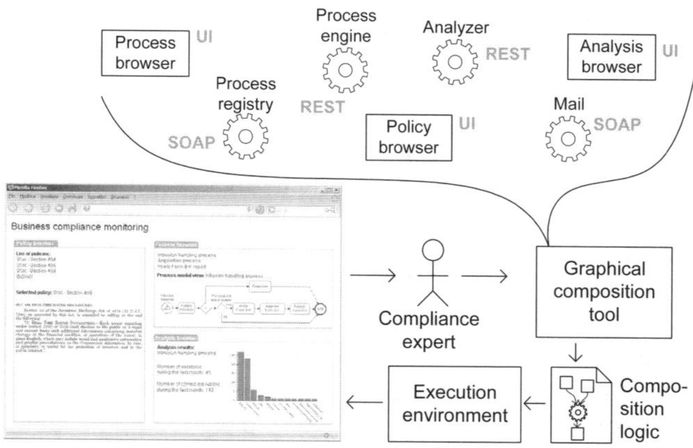

Fig. 1. Reference scenario: development of a business compliance monitoring application

Inspired by and building upon research in SOA and capturing the trends of Web 2.0 and mashups, this paper introduces the concept of *universal integration*, that is, the creation of composite web applications that integrate data, application, and user interface (UI) components. Our aim is to do what service composition has done for integrating services, but to do so at all layers, not just at the application layer, and remove some of the limitations that constrained a wider adoption of workflow/service composition technologies. Universal integration can be done (and is being done) today by joining the capabilities of multiple programming languages and techniques, but it requires significant efforts and professional programmers. In this paper we provide abstractions, models and tools so that the development and deployment of universal compositions is greatly simplified, up to the extent that even non-professional programmers can do it in their web browser.

Scenario. To exemplify the needs for universal integration, in Figure 1 we present the scenario that will accompany us throughout this paper, i.e., the development of a business compliance monitoring (BCM) web application starting from existing services and components.

A company's compliance expert wants to develop a web application that allows her to correlate company policies (representing the regulations the company is subject to) with process execution data and compliance analysis data and, in case a compliance violation by a process execution is detected, send a notification email. For this purpose, she wants to integrate a variety of different components already existing inside the company: components with own UI (*Policy browser*, *Process browser*, and *Analysis browser*), SOAP web services (*Process registry*, *Process engine*), and RESTful web services (*Analyzer* and *Mail* services). In addition to the "traditional" concerns of service composition (mainly revolving around the sequential or conditional invocation of components), UI components need to be *synchronized*: user interaction with the policy browser (e.g., to select a policy) must cause the process browser UI to change (showing processes affected by the policy). In general, in composed UIs, all components may have to change at the same time as they need to display consistent information. This also means that UI components must somehow be able to react to user input (that's what they have been designed for), but also to programmatic input: in the example above, the process component should be notified of the selection in the policy browser and change its UI accordingly. Additional challenges are related to the fact that the components are heterogeneous in nature, that developers need to master multiple communication protocols, client- and server-side programming techniques, different service and application architectures and programming languages, and must be able to integrate the event-driven philosophy of UIs with the control-flow-based philosophy of service orchestrations. These are only a few of the difficulties they encounter in their task; many others still lie in the details (e.g., how to deploy and maintain such complex integration logic).

Ideally, as shown in Figure 1, there would be a composition tool that hides the described implementation details and allows developers to graphically specify the desired composition logic, to execute it, and to obtain straight away the web application in the lower left corner of the figure. Currently, there are no integration instruments available that can cope with the described heterogeneity of components and that rely on one single integration paradigm only. Service composition approaches cannot handle UIs, and UI technologies are not designed with service integration in mind. Our compliance expert therefore falls back to various programming languages and tools or complex frameworks like J2EE and .NET along with AJAX scripting for UI, which makes applications harder to develop and maintain, and certainly beyond the reach of non-programmers. Yet, as more and more web applications offer their UI as components, open APIs toward them, or both (a la Google Maps), the importance of universal integration is likely to grow even faster in future.

Approach and contributions. In the following we describe a universal composition model and tool, called *mashArt*. MashArt aims at *empowering users with easy-to-use and flexible abstractions and techniques to create and manage composite web applications.* In particular, in this paper we make the following contributions:

- A *universal component model*, allowing the modeling of UI components, application components (e.g., services with an API) and data components (representing feeds or access to XML/relational data) using a unified model.
- A *universal composition model*, to combine the building blocks and expose the composition as a MashArt component, possibly accessible via rest/soap, and/or providing feeds, and/or having its own (composed) UI.
- The *mashArt platform* which is a service providing a number facilities for facilitating the rapid development and management of composite web applications. MashArt is entirely hosted and web-based, with zero client-side code.

In this paper we focus on the conceptual and architectural aspects of mashArt, which constitute the most innovative contributions of this work, namely the *component* and *composition models* as well as the *development* and *runtime* part of the infrastructure. The reader is referred to the mashArt web site (*http://mashart.org/ER09*) for more technical details.

We next introduce the principles that guide our work (Section 2), and then discuss the state of the art (Section 3). In Section 4 and Section 5we introduce the mashArt unified component and composition models. Section 6 describes the platform and hosted execution environment. Section 7 provides concluding remarks.

2 Guiding Principles

We aim at universal integration, and this has fundamental differences with respect to traditional composition. In particular, the fact that we aim at also integrating UI implies (i) that *synchronization*, and not (only) orchestration a la BPEL, should be adopted as interaction paradigm, (ii) that components must be able to react to both human user input and programmatic interaction, and (iii) that we must be able to design the UI of the *composite* application, not just the behavior and interaction among the components. This shows the need for a model based on state, events and synchronization more than on method calls and orchestration. We recognize in particular that *events*, *operations*, a notion of *state* and *configuration properties* are all we need to model a universal component. With respect to the design of the composite UI, we assume developers will use their favorite Web development tool (we do not aim at competing with these tools, although we do offer a simple templating mechanism for rapid development of prototype applications that run in the browser). Rather, we make it easy to embed mashArt components inside a Web application.

On the data side, we realize that *data* integration on the Web may also require different models: for example RSS feeds are naturally managed via a pipe-oriented data flow/streaming model (a-la Yahoo Pipes) rather than a variable-based approach as done in conventional service composition.

Another dimension of universality lies in the interaction protocols. MashArt aims at hiding the complexity of the specific protocol or data model supported by each component (REST, SOAP, RSS, Atom, JSON, etc) so a design goal is that from the perspective of the composer all these specificities are hidden – with the exceptions of the aspects that have a bearing on the composition (e.g., if a component is a feed, then we are aware that it operates, conceptually, by pushing content periodically or on the occurrence of certain events).

Generality and universality are often at odds with the other key design goal we have: *simplicity*. We want to enable advanced web users to create applications (an old dream of service composition languages which is still somewhat a far reaching objective). This means that mashArt must be fundamentally simpler than programming languages and current composition languages. We target the complexity of creating web pages with a web page editor, or the complexity of building a pipe with Yahoo Pipes (something that can be learned in a matter of hours rather than weeks).

To achieve simplicity we make two design decisions: first, we keep the composition model lightweight: for example, there are no complex exception or transaction mechanisms, no BPEL-style structured activities or complex dead-path elimination semantics. This still allows a model that makes it simple to define fairly sophisticated applications. Complex requirements can still be implemented but this needs to be done in an "ad hoc" manner (e.g., through proper combinations of event listeners and component logic) but there are no specialized constructs for this. Such constructs may be added over time if we realize that the majority of applications need them.

The second decision is to focus on simplicity only *from the perspective of the user* of the components, that is, the designer of the composite applications. In complex applications, complexity must reside somewhere, and we believe that as much as possible it needs to be inside the components. Components usually provide core functionalities and are reused over and over (that's one of the main goals of components).Thus, it makes sense to have professional programmers develop and maintain components. We believe this is necessary for the mashup paradigm to really take off. For example, issues such as interaction protocols (e.g., SOAP vs. REST or others) or initialization of interactions with components (e.g., message exchanges for client authentication) must be embedded in the components.

3 State of the Art

Service composition approaches. A representative of service orchestration approaches is BPEL [6], a standard composition language by OASIS. BPEL is based on WSDL-SOAP web services, and BPEL processes are themselves exposed as web services. Control flows are expressed by means of structured activities and may include rather complex exception and transaction support. Data is passed among services via variables (Java style). So far, BPEL is the most widely accepted service composition language. Although BPEL has produced promising results that are certainly useful, it is primarily targeted at professional programmers like business process developers. Its complexity (reference [6] counts 264 pages) makes it hardly applicable for web mashups.

Many variations of BPEL have been developed, e.g., aiming at invocation of REST services [7]and at exposing BPEL processes as REST services [8]. In [9] the authors describe Bite, a BPEL-like lightweight composition language specifically developed for RESTful environments. IBM's Sharable Code platform [10] follows a different strategy for the composition of REST or SOAP services: a domain-specific programming language from which Ruby on Rails application code is generated, also comprising user interfaces for the Web. In [11], the authors combine techniques from declarative query languages and services composition to support multi-domain queries over multiple (search) services. All these approaches focus on the application and data layer; UIs can then be programmed on top of the service integration logic. mashArt features instead universal integration as a paradigm for the simple and seamless composition of UI, data, and application components. We argue that universal integration will provide benefits that are similar to those that SOA and process centric integration provided for simplifying the development of enterprise processes.

UI composition approaches. In [12] we discussed the problem of integration at the presentation layer and concluded that there are no real UI composition approaches readily available: Desktop UI component technologies such as .NET CAB [13] or Eclipse RCP [14] are highly technology-dependent and not ready for the Web. Browser plug-ins such as Java applets, Microsoft Silverlight, or Macromedia Flash can easily be embedded into HTML pages; communications among different technologies remain however cumbersome (e.g., via custom JavaScript). Java portlets [15] or WSRP [2] represent a mature and Web-friendly solution for the development of portal applications; portlets are however typically executed in an isolated fashion and communication or synchronization with other portlets or web services remains hard. In addition, portals do not provide support for service orchestration logic. The Web mashup paradigm aims at addressing the above shortcomings. Mashup development is still an ad-hoc and time-consuming process, requiring advanced programming skills (e.g., wrapping web services, extracting contents from web sites, interpreting third-party JavaScript code, etc).

Computer-aided web engineering tools. In order to aid the development of web applications, the web engineering community has so far typically focused on model-driven design approaches. Among the most notable and advanced model-driven web engineering tools we find, for instance, WebRatio [16] and VisualWade [17]. The former is based on a web-specific visual modeling language (WebML), the latter on an object-oriented modeling notation (OO-H). Similar, but less advanced, modeling tools are also available for web modeling languages/methods like Hera, OOHDM, and UWE. All these tools provide expert web programmers with modeling abstractions and automated code generation capabilities, which are however far beyond the capabilities of our target audience, i.e., advanced web users and not web programmers.

Mashup tools. These tools typically provide easy-to-use graphical user interfaces and extensible sets of components for mashup development also by non-professional programmers. For instance, Yahoo Pipes (http://pipes.yahoo.com) focuses on data integration via RSS or Atom feeds via a data-flow composition language. UI integration is not supported. Microsoft Popfly (http://www.popfly.ms) provides a graphical user interface for the composition of both data access applications and UI components. Services orchestration is not supported. JackBe Presto (http://www.jackbe.com) adopts a Pipes-like approach for data mashups and allows a portal-like aggregation of UI widgets (mashlets) visualizing the output of such mashups.IBM QEDWiki (http://services.alphaworks.ibm.com/qedwiki) provides a wiki-based (collaborative) mechanism to glue together JavaScript or PHP-based widgets. Intel Mash Maker (http://mashmaker.intel.com) features a browser plug-in which interprets annotations inside web pages allowing the personalization of web pages with UI widgets.

Although existing mashup approaches have produced promising results, techniques that cater for simple and universal integration of web components are needed. These techniques are necessary to transition Web 2.0 programming from elite types of computing environments to environments where users leverage simple abstractions to create composite web applications over potentially rich web components developed and maintained by professional programmers. With this aim in mind, in the following we describe the mashArt models and system.

4 The mashArt Component Model

The first step toward the universal composition model is the definition of a component model. *MashArt* components wrap UI, application, and data services and expose their features/functionalities according to the mashArt component model. The model described here extends our initial UI-only component model presented in [3] to cater for universal components.

The model is based on four abstractions: state, events, operations, and properties. The *state* is represented as a set of name-value pairs. What the state exactly contains and its level of abstraction is decided by the component developer, but in general it should be such that its change represents something relevant and significant for the other components to know. For example, for our *Process browser* component, we can change the color in which the process is displayed or rearrange the process graph.

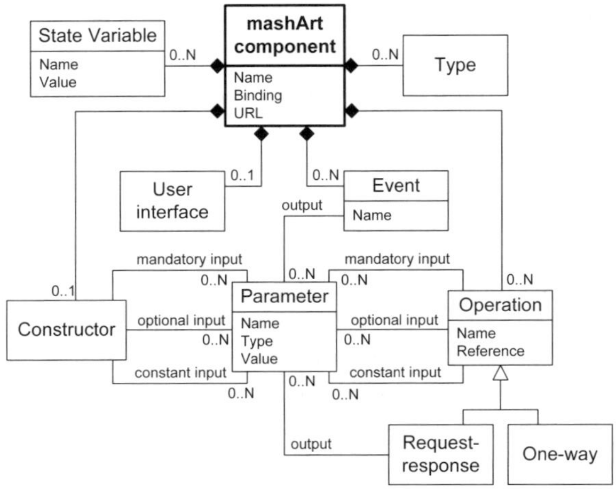

Fig. 2. The mashArt component model

This is irrelevant for the other components that need not be notified of these changes. Instead, clicking on a specific process or drilling down on a specific step may lead other components to show related information or application services to perform actions (e.g., compute compliance indicators). This is a state change we want to capture. In our case study, the state for the *Process browser* component is the process or process step that is being displayed. Modeling state for application components is something debatable as services are normally used in a stateless fashion. This is also why WSDL does not have a notion of state. However, while implementations can be stateless, from a modeling perspective it can be useful to model the state, and we believe that its omission from WSDL and WS-* standards was a mistake (with many partial attempts to correct it by introducing state machines that can be attached to service models). For example, an application component may provide relations between compliance policies and processes that need to observe the policies, and can raise a state change event each time processes need to be compliant with newly defined policies, so that other components can be informed and for example change the displayed information or compute compliance indicators for the new policy. Although not discussed here, the state is a natural bridge between application services and data-oriented services (services that essentially manipulate a data object).

Events communicate state changes and other information to the composition environment, also as name-value pairs. External notifications by SOAP services, callbacks from RESTful services, and events from UI components can be mapped to events. When events represent state changes, initiated either by the user by clicking on the component's UI or by programmatic requests (through operations, discussed below), the event data includes the new state. Other components subscribe to these events so that they can change their state appropriately (i.e., they synchronize). For instance, when selecting a process in the *Process browser* component, an event is generated that carries details about the performed selection.

Operations are the dual of events. They are the methods invoked as a result of events, and often represent state change requests. For example, the *Process browser* component will have a state change operation that can request that the component displays a specific process. In this case, the operation parameters include the state to which the component must evolve. In general, operations consume arbitrary parameters, which, as for events, are expressed as name-value pairs to keep the model simple. *Request-response* operations also return a set of name-value pairs – the same format as the call – and allow the mapping of request-response operations of SOAP services, Get and Post requests of RESTful services, and Get requests of feeds. *One-way* operations allow the mapping of one-way operations of SOAP services, Put and Delete requests of RESTful services, and operations of UI components. The linkage between events and operations, as we will see, is done in the composition model. We found the combination of (application-specific) states, events, and operations to be a very convenient and easy to understand programming paradigm for modeling all situations that require synchronization among UI, application, or data components.

Finally, *configuration properties* include arbitrary component setup information. For example, UI components may include layout parameters, while service components may need configuration parameters, such as the username and password for login. The semantics of these properties is entirely component-specific: no "standard" is prescribed by the component model. Again, they are name-value pairs.

In addition to the characteristics described above, components have aspects that are *internal*, meaning that they are not of concern to the composition designer, but only to the programmer who creates the component. In particular, a component might need to handle the invocation of a service, both in terms of mapping between the (possibly complex) data structure that the service supports and the flat data structure of mashArt (name-value pairs), and also in terms of invocation protocol (e.g., SOAP over http). There are two options for this: The first is to develop ad hoc logic in form of a wrapper. The wrapper takes the mashArt component invocation parameters, and with arbitrary logic and using arbitrary libraries, builds the message and invokes the service as appropriate. The second is to use the built-in mashArt bindings. In this case, the component description includes component bindings such as *component/http*, *component/SOAP*, *component/RSS*, or *component/Atom*. Given a component binding, the runtime environment is able to mediate protocols and formats by means of default mapping semantics; mappings can also be customized (more details are provided in the implementation section).In summary, the mashArt model intuitively accommodates multiple component models, such as UI components, SOAP and RESTful services, RSS and Atom feeds. Figure 2 combines the previous considerations in a meta-model for mashArt components.

In Figure 3 we introduce our graphical modeling notation for mashArt components that captures the previously discussed characteristics of components, i.e., state, events, operations, and UI. *Stateless* components are represented by circles, *stateful* components by rectangular boxes. Components with *UI* are explicitly labeled as such. We use arrows to model *data flows*, which in turn allow us to express events and operations: arrows going out from a component are *events*; arrows coming in to a component are *operations*. There might be multiple events and operations associated with one component. Depending on the particular type of operation or event of a stateless service, there might be only one incoming data flow (for one-way operations), an incoming and an outgoing data flow (for request-response operations), or only an outgoing data flow (for events). Operations and events are bound to their component by means of a simple dot-notation: *component.(operation|event)*.

The actual model of a specific component is specified by means of an abstract component *descriptor*, formulated in the *mashArt Description Language* (MDL) available on the mashArt web site *http://mashart.org/ER09*). MDL is for mashArt components what WSDL is for web services, though considerably simpler and aiming at universal components.

5 Universal Composition Model

Since we target universal composition with both stateful and stateless components, as well as UI composition, which requires synchronization, and service composition, which is more orchestrational in nature, the resulting model combines features from *event-based* composition with *flow-based* composition. As we will see, these can naturally coexist without making the model overly complex.

In essence, composition is defined by linking events (or operation replies) that one component emits with operation invocations of another component. In terms of flow control, the model offers conditions on operations and split/join constructs, defined by tagging operations as optional or mandatory. Data is transferred between components following a pipe/data flow approach, rather than the variables-based approach typical of BPEL or of programming languages. The choice of the data flow model is motivated by the fact that while variables work very well for programs and are well understood by programmers, data flows appear to be easier to understand for non-programmers as they can focus on the communication between a pair of components. This is also why frameworks such as Yahoo Pipes can be used by non-programmers.

To keep the solution simple as per our requirements (yet, as complete and flexible as necessary) we had to make some compromises. For example, the model comes without any structured or complex system activities (e.g., scopes, nested scopes, subprocesses, timers) and does not include transaction management or exception handling. If more complex modeling constructs are necessary (e.g., a join construct with a special data merging function, a complex data transformation service, or a death-path elimination BPEL-style), they can be (i) implemented using the language constructs (although they could require many components and events and render the graph complex), (ii) integrated in the form of dedicated services (implemented as components), or (iii) by creating a BPEL subflow invoked by mashArt (this is supported by the tool but not described here, as it is implementation and not an original contribution). The model and the language described here provide for the necessary basic composition logic, while more complex logics are integrated without requiring any extension at the language level. As we go along and we realize that certain features are crucial, they will be added to the model.

The universal composition model is defined in the Universal Composition Language (UCL), which operates on MDL descriptors only. UCL is for universal compositions what BPEL is for web service compositions (but again, simpler and for universal compositions). A universal composition is characterized by:

- *Component declarations*: Here we declare the components used in the composition and provide references to the MDL descriptor of each component. This allows access to all component details (e.g., the binding). Optionally, declarations may also contain the setting of constructor parameters.

- *Listeners*: Listeners are the core concept of the universal composition approach. They associate events with operations, effectively implementing simple publish-subscribe logics. Events produce parameters; operations consume them (static parameter values may be specified in the composition). Inside a listener, inputs and outputs can be arbitrarily connected (by referring to the respective IDs and parameter names) resulting into the definition of *data flows* among components. An optional condition may restrict the execution of operations; conditional statements are XPath statements expressed over the operation's input parameters. Only if the condition holds, the operation is executed.
- *Type definitions*: As for mashArt components, the structures of complex parameter values can be specified via dedicated data types.

We are now ready to compose our reference BCM application. Composing an application means connecting events and operations via data flows, and, if necessary, specifying conditions constraining the execution of operations. The graphical model in Figure 3represents for instance the "implementation" of the BCM scenario described earlier. We can see the three UI components *Policy*, *Process* and *Analysis* and the four stateless service components *Repository*, *Engine*, *Analyzer* and *Mail* (*Repository* is invoked two times). The composition has four listeners:

1. If a user selects a policy from the list of policies (*PolicySelected* event), we retrieve the list of processes associated with that policy from the repository (*Repository.GetProcsByPolicy* operation). Then we ask the process engine which of those processes are actually deployed in the system (*Engine.GetProcs*) and display the processes (*ShowProcesses* operation) in the *Process* component. In parallel, we also forward the retrieved processes to the *Analyzer* service, which retrieves possible analysis results for the first process (*Analyzer.GetResults*) and causes the *Analysis* component to render them.
2. By selecting another process (*ProcessSelected*) from the list rendered by the *Process* component, the user can view the respective compliance analyses (if any) by synchronizing the *Analysis* UI component (*ShowAnalysis*).
3. If a user selects a process, we retrieve the whole list of policies associated with that particular process (*Repository.GetPolicyByProc*) and show it in the *Policy* UI component (*ShowPolicy*).
4. Finally, if by looking at the analysis data the user detects a compliance violation (*ViolationDetected*), she can send an email to a responsible person (*Mail.SendMail*).

The graphical model represents the information that is necessary to understand the composition from the composer's point of view. Of particular interest for the structure of the composition is the distinction between stateful and stateless components: Stateful components handle multiple invocations during their lifetime; stateless components always represent only one invocation. This explains why the *Repository* service is placed twice in the model for its two invocations, while the *Analysis* UI component is placed only once, even though it too is invoked twice.

Regarding the semantics of the two data flows leaving the *Engine* service, it is worth noting that we allow the association of a *condition* to each operation. A *condition* is a Boolean expression over the operation's input (e.g., simple expressions over

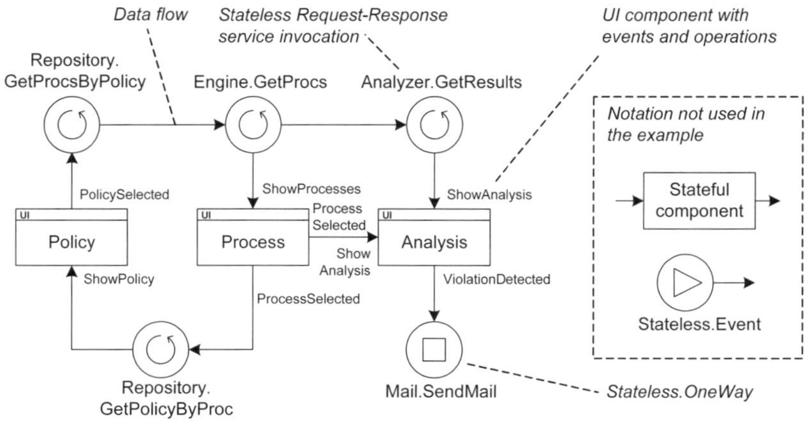

Fig. 3. Composition model for the BCM application

name-value pairs like in *SQL where* clauses) and constrains the execution of the operation. The two data flows in Figure 3 leaving the *Engine* service represent a *parallel branch* (conjunctive semantics); if conditions where associated with either *ShowProcesses* or *Analyzer.GetResults* the flows would represent a *conditional branch* (disjunctive semantics). A similar logic applies to operations with multiple incoming flows that can be used to model *join* constructs. Inputs may be *optional*, meaning that they are not mandatory for the execution of the operation. If only mandatory inputs are used, the semantics is conjunctive; otherwise, the semantics is disjunctive.

A branch/join inside a listener corresponds to a *synchronous* branch/join. We speak instead of an *asynchronous* branch/join, when branching and joining a flow requires defining two listeners, one with the branch and one with the join. The listener with the branch terminates with multiple operations; the listener with the join reacts to multiple events or operation results. Again, events may be optional or mandatory. If only mandatory events are used, the semantics is conjunctive; if optional events are used, the semantics is disjunctive. There is no BPEL-style dead path elimination, and in case of conjunctive joins a FIFO semantic is used for pairing events. The combination of events/operations with a graph and with optional/mandatory inputs naturally combine a pub/sub approach with an orchestration approach.

Notice that although the model in the example shows a connected graph, this is not true in general for universal compositions. Indeed, if a composition contains components that need not be synchronized, the respective listeners will be disconnected, resulting in a disconnected directed graph.

Finally, data passing does not require any variables to store intermediate results. Parameter names and data types only refer to the data and the data structures exchanged via data flows. Data transformations are defined by connecting the event or feed parameters with the parameters of the operations invoked as a result of the event triggering. More complex mappings require knowledge about the exact data type of each of the involved parameters. In general, our approach supports a variety of data transformations: (i) simple parameter mappings as described above; (ii) inline scripting, e.g., for the computation of aggregated or combined values; (iii) runtime XSLT transformations; and (iv) dedicated data transformation services that take a data flow

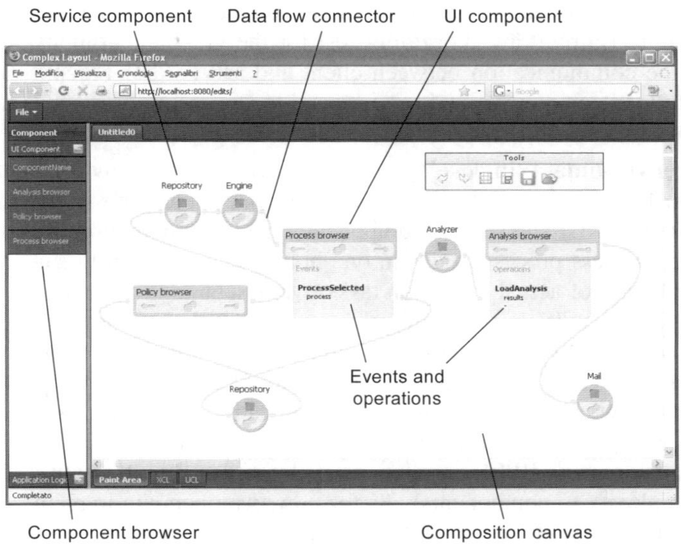

Fig. 4. The mashArt editor

in input, transform it, and produce a new data flow in output. The use of the dedicated data transformation services is enabled by UCL's extensibility mechanism.

6 Implementing and Provisioning Universal Compositions

Development environment. In line with the idea of the Web as integration platform, the mashArt editor runs inside the client browser; no installation of software is required. The screenshot in Figure 4 shows how the universal composition of Figure 3 can be modeled in the editor. The modeling formalism of the editor slightly differs from the one introduced earlier, as in the editor we can also leverage interactive program features to enhance user experience (e.g., users can interactively choose events and operations from respective drop-down panels). But the expressive power of the editor is the same as discussed above.

The *list of available components* on the left hand side of the screenshot shows the components and services the user has access to in the online registry (e.g., the *Policy Browser* or the *Registry* service). The *modeling canvas* at the right hand side hosts the composition logic represented by *UI components* (the boxes), *service components*(the circles), and *listeners* (the connectors). A click on a listener allows the user to map outputs to inputs and to specify optional input parameters.

In the lower part of the screenshot, tabs allow users to switch between different views on the same composition: visual model vs. textual UCL, interactive layout vs. textual HTML, and application preview. The layout of an application is based on standard HTML templates; we provide some default layouts, own templates can easily by uploaded. Laying out an application simply means placing all UI components of the composition into placeholders of the template (again, by dragging and dropping components). The preview panel allows the user to run the composition and test its correctness. Compositions can be stored on the mashArt server.

The implementation of the editor is based on JavaScript and the Open-jACOB Draw2D library (http://draw2d.org/draw2d/) for the graphical composition logic and AJAX for the communication between client and server. The registry on the server side, used to load components and services and to store compositions, is implemented as a RESTful web service in Java. The platform runs on Apache Tomcat.

Execution environment. In developing a mashArt execution environment, the issues that need to be solved include (i) the seamless integration of stateful and stateless components and of UI and service components, (ii) the conciliation of short-lived and long-lasting business process logics in one homogeneous environment, (iii) the consistent distribution of actual execution tasks over client and server, and (iv) the transparent handling of multiple communication protocols. We now detail these issues.

Stateful components may internally maintain state variables as well as the state in their UI, raising events upon state changes. Stateful application components may be implemented as wrappers that manage communications with an external service, the state itself, and possible correlation logic (that is, stateful wrappers may internally embed the analogous of BPEL correlation sets logic, consistently with the approach of pushing complexity to components). As for now, wrappers are implemented by component developers, even though we are implementing mechanisms for embedding state management and correlation management in MDL and UCL extensions.

Short-lived process logics are represented by listeners that involve stateful components or synchronous service invocations only. Such logics can easily be executed at the client side. Stateful components are instantiated inside the client browser or the server-side framework and run there locally. The lifetime of client-side components strictly depends on the user's browsing behavior, e.g., the user might leave the composite application by navigating to another page or by closing the browser. *Long-lasting* process logics are represented by listeners that involve asynchronous service invocations and external notifications or callbacks. Such logics typically require the availability of a web server and a constantly available runtime environment, which can only be guaranteed on the server side. The optimal *distribution* of components and tasks over client and server is another problem that needs to be addressed. For instance, UI components typically run on the client side, while we wait for notifications by an external web service on the server side. Depending on the kind of process logics and the nature of the involved components, the association of components to either the client or the server side may be computed at startup of the composite application. For now, we can handle client-side components and external notifications.

Finally, the handling of *multiple communication protocols* (e.g., SOAP and plain http) requires either the implementation of wrappers or of message adapters that mediate between the native protocols of remote services and the internal message format of the execution environment. Depending on the binding, a suitable protocol adapter is selected. For instance, the *component/http* binding allows issuing arbitrary Get, Post, Put, or Delete http calls to a specified URI. Adapters can be customized for individual components: the content that is sent is specified by a text document (e.g., a SOAP-compliant XML document) that can include references to operation parameters (surrounded by $ signs) that are replaced by the mashArt framework with the actual values at runtime. In this way, we can implement many kinds of message exchanges (e.g., SOAP- or REST-based). Reply values can be similarly mapped using XPath expressions inside the component definition.

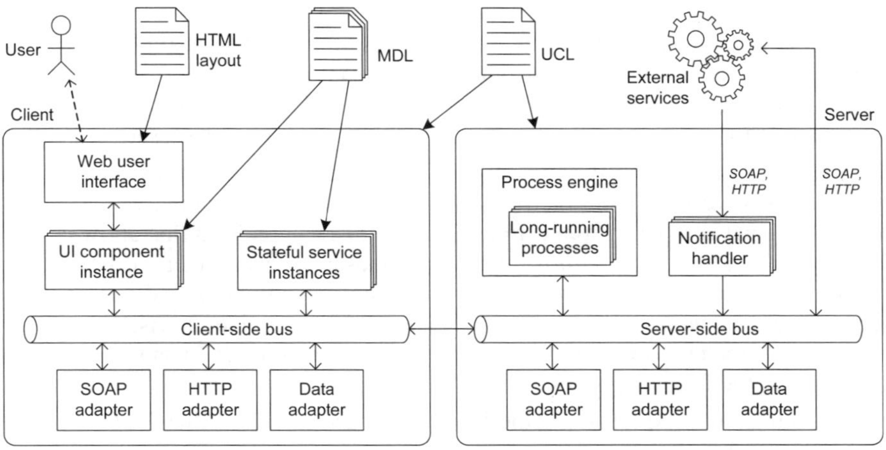

Fig. 5. Universal execution framework

Figure 5 contextualizes the previous considerations in the functional architecture of our execution environment. The environment is divided into a client- and a server-side part, which exchange events via a synchronization channel. On the client side, the user interacts with the application via its UI, i.e., its UI components, and thereby generates events that are intercepted by the client-side event bus. The bus implements the listeners that are executed on the client side and manage the data and SOAP-HTTP adapters. The data adapter performs data transformations, the SOAP-HTTP adapters allow the environment to communicate with external services. Stateful service instances might also use the SOAP-HTTP adapters for communication purposes. The server-side part is structured similarly, with the difference that the handling of external notifications is done via dedicated notification handlers, and long-lasting process logics that can be isolated from the client-side listeners and executed independently can be delegated to a conventional process engine (e.g., a BPEL engine).

The whole framework, i.e., UI components, listeners, data adapters, SOAP-HTTP adapters, and notification handlers are instantiated when parsing the UCL composition at application startup. The internal configuration of how to handle the individual components is achieved by parsing each component's MDL descriptor (e.g., to understand whether a component is a UI or a service component). The composite layout of the application is instantiated from the HTML template filled with the rendering of the application's UI components.

The client-side environment is an evolution of the already successfully implemented and tested UI integration framework of the Mixup project [3], that was however limited to UI components only. The environment comes with an AJAX implementation of the UCL and MDL parsers and is integrated with the mentioned online registry storing components and compositions. The server-side environment has successfully passed a prototype implementation (the effort of several Master theses) based on Java and the Tomcat web server. The integration with the external process engine (e.g., Active-BPEL) and of the client- and server-side parts is ongoing.

A first conclusion that can be drawn from our experiences is that performance does not play a major role on the client side. This is because in a given composition, only a limited number of components run on the client, and the client needs to handle only one instance of the application. On the server-side, performance becomes an issue if multiple composite applications with a high number of long-lasting processes are running in the same web server. Although we did not run scalability experiments yet, the re-use of existing and affirmed technologies, simple servlets for notification handlers, and BPEL engines for process logics will provide for the necessary scalability.

MashArt at work in the BCM example. Once components are in place and we have searched what we need from the registry (via the *registry browser*), we are ready to define universal composite applications. The mashArt ingredients that allow composition are the *graphical UCL editor* for the drag-and-drop development of UCL compositions and the *execution environment* for the hosted execution of ready compositions. Furthermore, an *online monitoring and analysis* tool provides a visual analysis of active and completed executions. The development of our BCM application would thus occur in the following steps:

1. The compliance expert starts the UCL editor and composes the *UCL logic* of the application by putting together the required components, found in the registry.
2. Still in the graphical editor, she can define the applications appearance by applying a simple *layout* template (e.g., an HTML template with <*div*>placeholders; some templates are readily available, own ones can easily be uploaded) and placing the composition's UI components.
3. After checking a preview of the application in the editor, she stores the UCL composition in the *online registry*, and the application appears in the registry browser.

Once the new composite application has been defined, it can be executed either through the registry browser or via a dedicated URI. As the application is started, the *runtime environment* parses the UCL file, loads the layout, and instantiates UI components using the constructor parameters specified in the UCL file. During the execution of the application, the runtime environment logs the occurrence of events and operation calls. Authorized users can then monitor and analyze executions of compositions through an interface that allows the graphical exploration of the events. We discuss neither the monitoring interface nor the authorization model as they do not correspond to significant innovations or contributions of the paper. The authorization model is essentially role-based, while the monitoring and analysis is (in the present version) limited to a graphical process-oriented GUI for monitoring each instance and a reporting infrastructure to view statistics on executions (e.g., average lifetime, statistics on the duration on each operation, detection of outliers).

7 Conclusion

In this paper, we have considered a novel approach to UI and service composition on the Web, i.e., *universal composition*. This composition approach is the foundation of the mashArt project, which aims at enabling even non-professional programmers (or Web users) to perform complex UI, application, and data integration tasks online and in a hosted fashion (integration as a service). Accessibility and ease of use of the composition instruments is facilitated by the simple composition logic and implemented by the intuitive graphical editor and the hosted execution environment. The platform comes with an online registry for components and compositions and will provide tools for monitoring and analysis of hosted compositions.

The key findings of our work are: (i) state and events/operations are the main abstractions we need for universal integration; (ii) it is possible to provide a simple yet universal composition model by combining synchronization constructs with flow-based ones; (iii) essential to simplicity is the separation of what is simple and exposed to the composer from what is complex and exposed to professional programmers (creating reusable components); (iv) universal composition requires a division of client-side and server-side composition logic for scalability and usability purposes.

Acknowledgments. We thank Maristella Matera, Jin Yu and Regis Saint-Paul for their contribution to the Mixup framework.

References

[1] Yu, J., et al.: Understanding Mashup Development and its Differences with Traditional Integration. Internet Computing 12(5), 44–52 (2008)

[2] OASIS. Web Services for Remote Portlets (August 2003), `http://www.oasis-open.org/committees/wsrp`

[3] Yu, J., et al.: A Framework for Rapid Integration of Presentation Components. In: WWW 2007, pp. 923–932 (2007)

[4] Alonso, G., Casati, F., Kuno, H., Machiraju, V.: Web Services: Concepts, Architectures and Applications. Springer, Heidelberg (2003)

[5] Dustdar, S., Schreiner, W.: A survey on web services composition, *Int. J. Web Grid Services 1(1), 1–30 (2005)*

[6] OASIS. Web Services Business Process Execution Language Version 2.0 (April 2007), `http://docs.oasis-open.org/wsbpel/2.0/OS/wsbpel-v2.0-OS.html`

[7] Pautasso, C.: BPEL for REST. In: Dumas, M., Reichert, M., Shan, M.-C. (eds.) BPM 2008. LNCS, vol. 5240, pp. 278–293. Springer, Heidelberg (2008)

[8] van Lessen, T., et al.: A Management Framework for WS-BPEL. In: ECoWS 2008, Dublin (2008)

[9] Curbera, F., Duftler, M., Khalaf, R., Lovell, D.: Bite: Workflow composition for the web. In: Krämer, B.J., Lin, K.-J., Narasimhan, P., et al. (eds.) ICSOC 2007. LNCS, vol. 4749, pp. 94–106. Springer, Heidelberg (2007)

[10] Maximilien, E.M., et al.: An Online Platform for Web APIs and Service Mashups. Internet Computing 12(5), 32–43 (2008)

[11] Braga, D., et al.: Optimization of Multi-Domain Queries on the Web. In: VLDB 2008, Auckland, pp. 562–573 (2008)

[12] Daniel, F., et al.: Understanding UI Integration - A Survey of Problems, Technologies, and Opportunities. In: IEEE Internet Computing, pp. 59-66 (May 2007)

[13] Microsoft Corporation. Smart Client - Composite UI Application Block (December 2005), `http://msdn.microsoft.com/en-us/library/aa480450.aspx`

[14] The Eclipse Foundation. Rich Client Platform (October 2008), `http://wiki.eclipse.org/index.php/RCP`

[15] Sun Microsystems. JSR-000168 Portlet Specification (October 2003), `http://jcp.org/aboutJava/communityprocess/final/jsr168/`

[16] Acerbis, R., et al.: Web Applications Design and Development with WebML and WebRatio 5.0. TOOLS (46), pp. 392-411 (2008)

[17] Gómez, J., Bia, A., Parraga, A.: Tool support for model-driven development of web applications. In: Ngu, A.H.H., Kitsuregawa, M., Neuhold, E.J., Chung, J.-Y., Sheng, Q.Z. (eds.) WISE 2005. LNCS, vol. 3806, pp. 721–730. Springer, Heidelberg (2005)

From Static Methods to Role-Driven Service Invocation – A Metamodel for Active Content in Object Databases

Stefania Leone[1], Moira C. Norrie[1],
Beat Signer[2], and Alexandre de Spindler[1]

[1] Institute for Information Systems, ETH Zurich
CH-8092 Zurich, Switzerland
{leone,norrie,despindler}@inf.ethz.ch
[2] Vrije Universiteit Brussel
Pleinlaan 2, 1050 Brussels, Belgium
bsigner@vub.ac.be

Abstract. Existing object databases define the behaviour of an object in terms of methods declared by types. Usually, the type of an object is fixed and therefore changes to its behaviour involves schema evolution. Consequently, dynamic configurations of object behaviour are generally not supported. We define the notion of role-based object behaviour and show how we integrated it into an existing object database extended with a notion of collections to support object classification and role modelling. We present a metamodel that enables specific services to be associated with objects based on collection membership and show how such a model supports flexible runtime configuration of loosely coupled services.

1 Introduction

Object databases typically adopt the type model of object-oriented programming languages such as Java as the data model. Behaviour is usually tightly coupled to an object by defining methods in the object class and every instance of that class will have the same behaviour. The only way of adapting that behaviour is to introduce a subclass with overriding methods.

However, we have seen recent trends in programming and also system design that aim for a looser and more flexible coupling of objects and behaviour. For example, both aspect-oriented programming (AOP) and service-oriented architectures (SOAs) have been used as the basis for supporting context-aware applications by providing context-dependent behaviour [1,2]. AOP deals with the coupling of objects and behaviour at the programming level and requires recompilation to cope with changes. SOAs offer much more flexibility as the binding of services can be done at runtime. Our aim is to have that same flexibility *within* a database to allow services to be bound to objects in a role-dependent way and further to be able to change these bindings dynamically.

We present a model that allows active content to be bound to database objects dynamically to support a notion of role-dependent services. The behaviour of an

A.H.F. Laender et al. (Eds.): ER 2009, LNCS 5829, pp. 444–457, 2009.

object is defined through a combination of *intrinsic* and *extrinsic* behaviour with methods in the object class defining the former and services associated with object roles defining the latter. We describe how this concept has been integrated into a system based on the db4o object database[1] extended with a notion of collections to support object classification and role modelling.

We begin in Sect. 2 with a discussion of related work and then provide an overview of our approach along with the associated three levels of application models and the metamodel in Sect. 3. Details of the architecture required to realise the model are presented in Sect. 4 and a description of our implementation is given in Sect. 5. We provide a discussion of the approach in Sect. 6 and concluding remarks are given in Sect. 7.

2 Background

Most object databases, including db4o, provide transparent persistence of programming language object instances. Application developers therefore typically use programming languages such as Java as the data modelling language and there is a one-to-one mapping between application entities and object instances. Essentially, the database schema corresponds to the classes that define the attributes and methods available on object instances. It is well-known that this can lead to certain tensions when it comes to dealing with issues of role modelling due to the fact that the type models of object-oriented programming languages like Java do not support concepts such as multiple instantiation and object evolution. It is therefore difficult to model the fact that application entities may have multiple roles simultaneously and that these roles may change over time. Support for role modelling in object databases was an active area of research in the 1990s and a variety of approaches have been proposed (e.g. [3,4,5,6]). For example, the programming language Smalltalk [7] was extended to support role modelling by having coexisting class and role hierarchies [6]. Each class that is situated somewhere within the class hierarchy can be the root of a role hierarchy which solves the problem of copying data and creating a new data object every time an object has to take a new role. Furthermore, an object can have multiple roles at the same time which is something that is not offered by object-oriented programming languages but is sometimes "enforced" in languages with multiple inheritance by introducing some kind of artificial class hierarchies.

More recently, the notion of adaptive behaviour in databases has received a lot of attention. Traditionally, object behaviour is represented by methods defined within a class and tightly bound to an object through its class definition. Every object instance of a specific class therefore shows the same behaviour defined by its class methods and any behaviour inherited from its superclasses. However, there are cases where a developer may want the behaviour of an instance to vary according to context or for that behaviour to evolve over time. It is therefore desirable to have a distinction between fixed class-based behaviour and some role-driven runtime behaviour that can be flexibly adapted over time.

[1] http://www.db4o.com

The adaptation of behaviour in object-oriented programming languages is normally achieved through inheritance and the overriding of methods in a subclass. Sometimes the inheritance mechanism is misused just to get access to some service functionality provided by another class. However, inheritance should only be used if there is a proper is-a relationship between a class and its superclass and not simply for the sake of code reuse. The problem of these artificial class hierarchies is more serious if we consider programming languages that offer multiple inheritance where it becomes tempting to have one true is-a relationship with multiple other inheritance relationships that are only used for behaviour reuse. Even if the overriding of methods provides a mechanism for behaviour adaptation, this form of adaptivity is only available at compile time since the class definition can generally no longer be changed at runtime. In most object-oriented programming languages, it is not possible for an object to evolve and gain or lose certain behaviour over time. Only a few dynamic object-oriented languages such as Smalltalk offer the possibility to alter class definitions at runtime so that objects may evolve. Other dynamically typed approaches for runtime behaviour adaptation include prototype-based programming languages such as Self [8] where the concept of classes does not exist at all and a cloning mechanism is used for object instantiation.

Methods that do not directly describe any object behaviour are often implemented as library functionality. These library services are generally represented as static methods that access object instances only by passing these objects as arguments within method calls. Also, there is no binding between classes of objects and their associated services. It is up to the programmer to make an explicit connection from an object instance to its services as part of the application implementation process.

Another solution for adding behaviour to a class is offered by AOP [9]. Extra behaviour is defined by so-called *advices* which are executed at well-specified locations (*pointcuts*) within class methods defining the default behaviour. Functionality or services shared by various classes of a software system (e.g. some logging functionality) can be managed in a modular way by this separation of cross-cutting concerns offered by AOP. The modelling of different types of cross-cutting concerns at various levels of concerns is addressed in aspect-oriented modelling (AOM). Note that the introduction of new behaviour in an aspect-oriented program requires the recompilation and reloading of classes.

Web Services [10] and SOAs [11] enable the composition of services and components in distributed computing. While these solutions offer a language independent reuse of business services, their use often requires significant effort from a developer. A service-oriented DBMS (SDBMS) architecture based on the layered architecture presented in [12] is introduced in [13]. The SOA offer some advantages over monolithic architectures in terms of flexibility. However, in this case, it is important to note that the SOA is used for building and adapting a DBMS by coupling different services rather than for developing an application.

Our aim was to get the same flexibility of service-orientation in terms of dynamically coupling services to objects *within* the database in order to be able to support the variable and dynamic aspects of object behaviour as well as maximising the *reuse* of behaviour. Our approach allows domain data objects to be associated with flexible role-driven services.

3 Approach

Our approach extends existing object databases with role modelling functionality to enable role-driven service invocation. We have implemented this in db4o, but note that the approach is general and could be used in other object databases.

A simple object model with standard object-oriented concepts such as classes and objects has been extended with a new classification model based on collections and multiple instantiation inspired by the semantic, object data model OM [14]. The collections semantically group a set of objects and the role of an object is defined by its collection membership. Specific services can be associated with a collection to dynamically extend the behaviour of its member objects. These services can either be executed manually by some user interaction or triggered automatically by specific system events (e.g. the insertion of an object into a collection). The classification of objects is orthogonal to the class hierarchy offered by the object model and, through multiple classification, an object can participate in multiple roles at the same time. The flexible runtime reclassification of objects provides a powerful mechanism to dynamically assign new services to an object without affecting its class definition.

Our solution for providing role-driven service invocation is based on a three-layered modelling approach including *type*, *classification* and *service* models as shown in Fig. 1. The type model deals with type specification in terms of attributes and methods. The classification model is used for defining semantic groupings of objects based on collections and relationships between objects. The service model specifies the bindings between services and collections. As part of our new application development process, each of these three models has to be defined. Note that by introducing a type model and a classification model, we clearly separate typing and classification as proposed in [5]. The three models are orthogonal to each other resulting in a clear separation of concerns. We describe each of these models in turn.

3.1 Type Model

The type model defines the types of the objects for a given application domain. As known from object-oriented models, a type declares a set of attributes and methods. In the example shown in Fig. 1, we have three different types `document`, `latexDocument` and `author`. The `document` type defines a set of attributes such as `creationTime` and `encoding` as well as a method `getSource()` which returns a document's content. The type `latexDocument` is a specialisation of the `document` type as represented by the subtype relationship. For example, the `latexDocument` type provides some special handling of LaTeX packages and further offers a method `compile()` which compiles a LaTeX source document

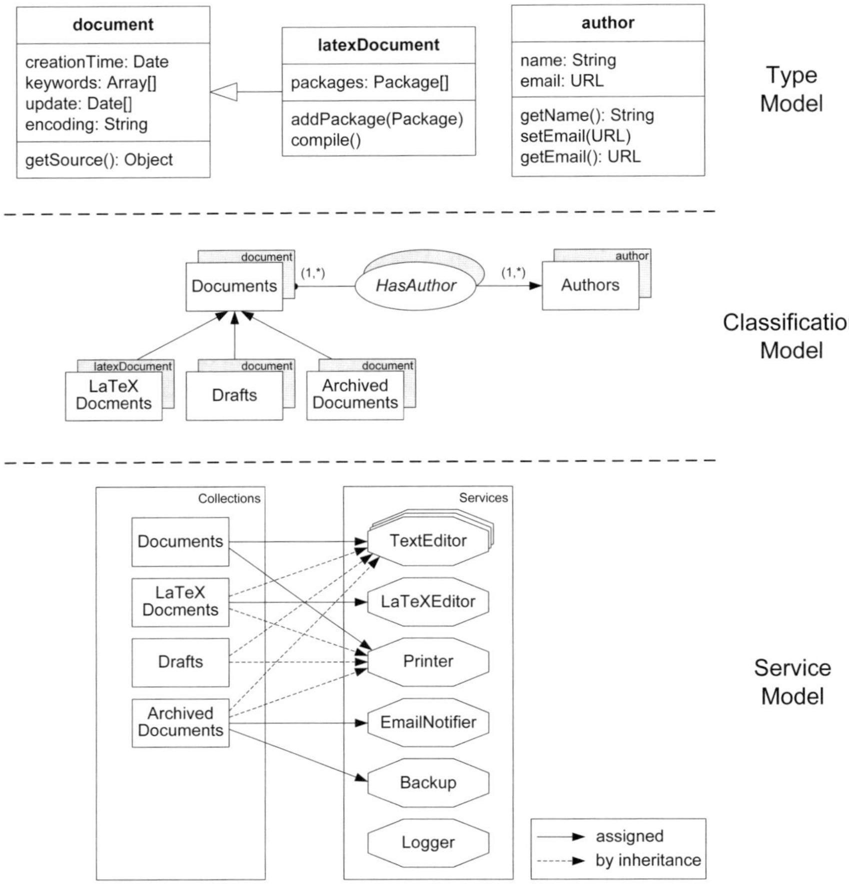

Fig. 1. Type, classification and service model

into an arbitrary output format (e.g. a PDF document). The `author` type defines typical author properties as well as a set of methods to manipulate them. Note that our extended object model supports objects that have multiple of these types through multiple instantiation. An object can gain or lose types at runtime based on specific operators for object evolution.

3.2 Classification Model

For object classification, we introduce the concept of *collections* that have a name and a membertype. In Fig. 1, we use the graphical notation introduced by the OM model [14] where collections are represented by shaded rectangles with the name in the unshaded part and the membertype in the shaded part. An object can be a member of multiple collections at the same time (multiple classification) and be dynamically added to or removed from collections. Furthermore, collections support the notion of a super- and subcollection relationship.

An object in a subcollection will also be in all supercollections and the object is automatically assigned to the corresponding roles.

We also introduce the concept of a *binary collection* with a tuple membertype to represent an *association* from one collection to another. Figure 1 shows a simple example where documents are associated with authors. The `Documents` collection contains objects of type `document` and has the three subcollections `LaTeXDocuments`, `Drafts` and `ArchivedDocuments`. Documents can be associated to authors via the `HasAuthor` association, with each author having authored at least one document and every document having at least one author as indicated by the `(1,*)` cardinality constraints.

The role modelling through classification is represented by the fact that documents can be in the collections `LaTeXDocuments`, `Drafts` and `ArchivedDocuments` simultaneously. Note that there are some collections which do not put further restrictions on the membertype. For example, the `Documents`, `Drafts` and `ArchivedDocuments` collections all have the same `document` membertype. The role of a particular document object can be manipulated by simply adding or removing it from these collections. The fact that a draft of a document may also be archived simply means that the object has to be added to both the `Drafts` and `ArchivedDocuments` collections. However, in some cases, roles may imply additional properties and methods by a more specific subcollection membertype. Through multiple instantiation, objects can therefore gain or lose types and be classified independently of the type hierarchy.

3.3 Service Model

The service model associates services with collections at design- or run-time. On the left-hand side of Fig. 1, we show the set of collections defined in the classification model whereas the right-hand side gives a set of services provided by the system. A service defines arbitrary functionality that can be bound to an object. Services further specify to which type of objects they can be assigned. A service exposes the `Service` interface which contains an `invoke()` method. The binding happens on a collection level where an arbitrary number of services can be assigned to one or multiple collections. These bindings can further be constrained by a given context. Note that the collection membertype must be compatible with the type declared by the service. As a result, a collection defines a context to its members which specifies the set of available services. Furthermore, since all members of a given subcollection are also members of their supercollections, they inherit the service assignments via their supercollections memberships.

We distinguish two types of service invocation. A service can be invoked either automatically based on system events (e.g. if an object is updated, added to or removed from a collection) or explicitly by some user interaction. Our example shows both automatic and manual services. The `Backup` service is an automatically invoked service assigned to the `ArchivedDocuments` collection. It reacts to events generated when a document is inserted into the `ArchivedDocuments` collection. It has a parameter `periodicity` with the value `daily` which means that the service is invoked once a day for a daily backup of all collection members.

There are multiple collections with membertype `document` but only the ones in the `ArchivedDocuments` will be backed up. This shows that it is the collection membership (role) that defines which services are available for a given object rather than its type.

A second automatically invoked service assigned to the `ArchivedDocuments` collection is the `EmailNotifier` service. This service has been configured to react to the removal of an object from the `ArchivedDocuments` collection to automatically send an email to the authors to inform them that the document is no longer archived. Note that to get access to the corresponding authors and their email addresses, the `EmailNotifier` makes use of the `HasAuthor` association in the classification model. Of course, a service can also be bound to multiple collections and therefore the `EmailNotifier` service could be used for various kinds of notifications.

The `TextEditor`, `LaTeXEditor` and `Printer` services are invoked explicitly by some form of user interaction. For an explicit service invocation, the user is normally presented with a dynamically generated graphical user interface from where they can select one of the available services to be executed. In our example, `Documents` are assigned the `TextEditor` and `Print` services. Due to the fact that `LatexDocuments` is a subcollection of `Documents`, the `TextEditor` and `Printer` services are also available to the members of that collection by means of the collection hierarchy. The `Logger` service that is currently not bound to a collection automatically logs information when objects are accessed. Note that there can also be different implementations of a single service which can be exchanged at runtime as indicated for the `TextEditor` service.

It is also possible to compose new services based on existing ones in order to define more complex functionality out of modular service components. For example, the `Backup` service is a composition of a compression service followed by a copy service. For this purpose, each service may have an arbitrary number of services associated in a specific order defining the sequence of execution.

The service layer is extensible in that new services can be added easily. As described later, a service defines the expected type of object to which it can be applied. For example, the `Printer` service is compatible with the `document` type. This means that objects of type `document` or any subtype can be used with that service. The functionality of a service is implemented in its `invoke()` method. The method implementation may contain calls to external applications as in our example where a `Printer` service is used to initiate the print job. A metamodel of our system with all the necessary concepts for the three models described in this section is shown in Fig. 2. As discussed earlier, a collection contains objects of a specific type which is represented by the `HasMembertype` association between `Collections` and `Types`. In our metamodel, collections and types are also objects which means that the `Collections` and `Types` collections are subcollections of the `Objects` collection. `Collections` can be associated with `Services` over the `HasServices` association which can be further constrained by contextual conditions (`Contexts`) defined via the `InContext` association.

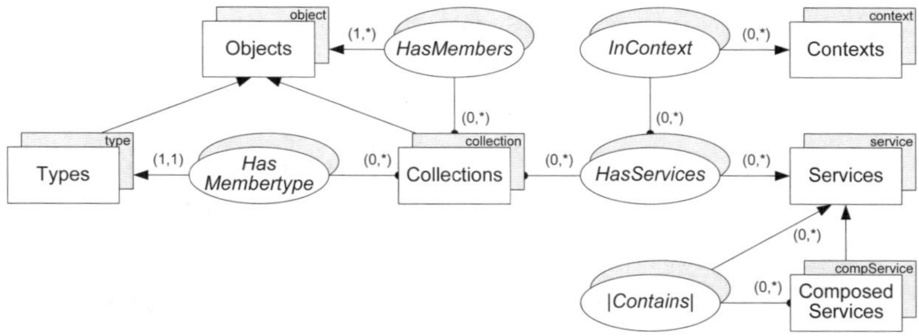

Fig. 2. Role-based service metamodel

A context instance defines a condition that can be evaluated based on information available in the metamodel as well as any external contextual information and returns true if the condition is satisfied. The service is only executed if all associated contextual conditions are satisfied. New services can be composed from existing services based on the `Contains` association and are handled by the `ComposedServices` collection. Note that the `Contains` association is a ranking which means that there is an order defined on the subservice relationship defining the order of precedence when executing multiple cascaded services.

4 Architecture

Our system architecture shown in Fig. 3 combines standard data management components, depicted on the left-hand side of the DBMS, with service components on the right-hand side. The system offers a uniform API that allows an application developer to make use of the functionality presented in the previous section through the database and service API. The data management component implements the typing and classification models and makes them available through the database API, while the service management allows services to be registered and service bindings to be managed based on the service API.

The service manager handles everything that has to do with services including the service library where all available services are registered. Services can be registered and unregistered at design time as well as at runtime. The service manager also manages the service bindings. When assigning a service to a collection, an entry is created in the binding registry which maintains all bindings of services to collections. Note that a service can be assigned to multiple collections and a collection can have multiple services assigned. In summary, the service manager implements the service API offered to the application developer and basically exposes the service model functionality.

As already mentioned, services can either implement functionality themselves, or act as a bridge to third-party functionality and applications. The fact that they can access external functionality is illustrated by the three clouds in the system architecture representing a printer, LaTeX editor and text editor. The

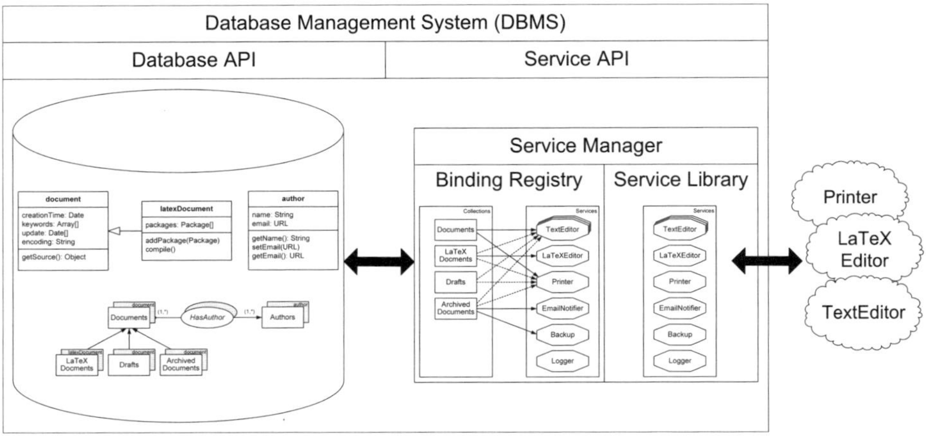

Fig. 3. System architecture

Printer service, for example, accesses printing functionality provided outside the database. In contrast, a Logger service would implement the logging functionality within the database.

The service manager is a runtime component that handles service invocation. An object can invoke a service only in the context of a collection which defines the role of that object. Based on the collection, the service manager determines which services can be invoked by performing a lookup in the binding registry. In the case of manual service invocation, the service manager returns the set of available services. Note that since there is no fixed set of services and the number of assigned services may change at runtime, the interface for selecting a service has to be created dynamically. For example, for an object in LaTeXDocuments, the service manager returns the TextEditor, LaTeXEditor and Printer services and the user then has to explicitly select the service to be invoked.

Automatic service invocation is handled in two different ways. In the case of periodic invocation, the service manager invokes the service based on the defined periodicity. In the case of event-based invocation, the service manager is notified upon an event such as the insertion of an object into a collection. The notification contains the event type, the object that triggered the event and its role and the service manager then invokes the corresponding service.

5 Implementation

The extended object database has been implemented in Java using the db4o object database for persistent object storage and retrieval. db4o offers the same object model as the programming platform it is embedded in, which in our case is the Java object model. We therefore implemented an additional software layer to run on top of db4o that enriches the Java object model with our additional

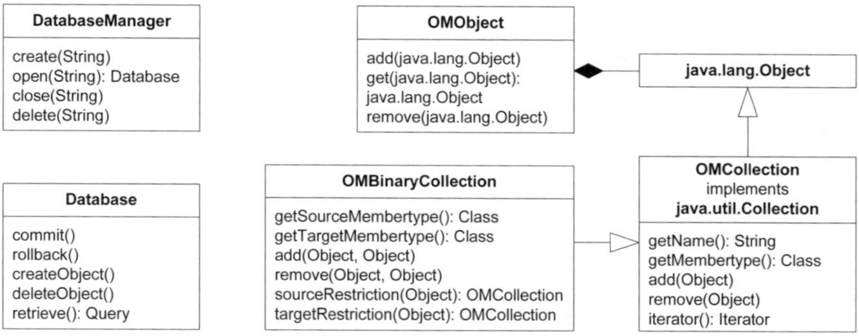

Fig. 4. Database API

concepts for role-based service invocation. We first describe the implementation of the collection and association concepts before presenting our new object implementation for multiple instantiation. The complete set of classes forming the database API is shown in Fig. 4. We will not discuss the `DatabaseManager` and `Database` classes since they offer the same functionality already provided by the underlying db4o object database.

The `OMCollection` class implements the Java collection interface and therefore can be used in the same way as regular Java collections. The main difference lies in the intrinsic behaviour of automatically storing and deleting all members to and from the database as soon as they are added and removed from a collection. Associations are implemented as a binary collection class (`OMBinaryCollection`), a subclass of the `OMCollection` class with a tuple membertype containing the types of the two associated objects.

Since members of a collection have to conform to the collection membertype, objects must be able to evolve and dynamically gain and lose types. For this purpose, we need a mechanism to add multiple types to an object at runtime independently of the inheritance hierarchy. In contrast to the Java object model where each object is an instance of its class, we introduce our own extended object model implementation. We distinguish between an *object* representing an identifiable entity and the concept of an *instance* serving as a container for attribute values defined by its type. Multiple instantiation can then be achieved by adding multiple instances to a single object. We use regular Java objects to represent instances whereas an additional `OMObject` class is introduced to deal with our new notion of objects. As shown in Fig. 4, the `OMObject` class manages a set of instances and provides methods for adding, removing and retrieving any of its instances at runtime. The `OMObject` class also offers transparent persistency for storing and updating objects automatically along with all their instances. Note that collections and binary collections are also represented as objects with the `OMCollection` or `OMBinaryCollection` Java classes as assigned instances.

Fig. 5. Service API

We now explain how the service definition and binding mechanisms have been realised. After a new service has been developed, it has to be deployed to the `ServiceLibrary` class shown in Fig. 5. The implementation of any service must conform to the `Service` interface definition which also forms part of the service API. The `ServiceManager` class provides methods to add and remove services from the service library. It also offers the `bind()` and `unbind()` methods for assigning services to the corresponding collections. In addition to the collection and service to be assigned, the bind method has further optional arguments to specify the event triggering the service and any context classes it depends on. A context is specified by implementing an interface declaring an `evaluate()` method returning a boolean value which indicates whether the service should be invoked or not. The evaluate method has access to any database content as well as the object on which the service has to be invoked. The service manager also contains the `ServiceLibrary` and `BindingRegistry` classes.

To illustrate the usage of our software layer for role-driven service invocation, we show part of the implementation for the application modelled in Sect. 3. Any type represented in the type model is implemented as a regular Java class. For example, the `document` type is defined as follows:

```
class Document {
  Date creation;
  String[] keywords;
  ...
  public Document() {
    this.creation = new Date(System.currentTimeMillis());
  }
  public void addKeyword(String keyword) {
    ...
  }
  ...
}
```

In order to implement the classification domain model, collections and associations have to be created. As stated earlier, collections and binary collections are regular Java classes and can be assigned to `OMObjects` via multiple instantiation. After an object has been created using the database, it is assigned to the collection or binary collection type as shown in the following code excerpt:

```
/* handle to the database 'db' has been assigned previously */
OMObject documents = db.createObject();
documents.add(new OMCollection("Documents", Document.class))
```

Since collections are part of our system's metamodel, they can also be created in a more direct way using the `createCollection()` and `createBinCollection()`

database methods. In the following example, the collections Documents and Authors are created as well as a binary collection for associating documents and authors. Finally, the LaTeXDocuments, Drafts and ArchivedDocuments collections are defined as subcollections of the Documents collection. Note that the membertype of the collection is sent to the creation method in terms of a Java class and, in the case of binary collections, the two membertypes of the tuples have to be provided as shown below:

```
OMObject documents = db.createCollection("Documents", Document.class);
OMObject authors = db.createCollection("Authors", Author.class);
OMObject hasAuthor = db.createBinCollection("HasAuthor", Document.class, Author.class);
OMObject latexDocuments = db.createCollection("LaTeXDocuments", Latex.class);
OMObject drafts = db.createCollection("Drafts", Document.class);
OMObject archivedDocuments = db.createCollection("ArchivedDocuments", Document.class);
latexDocuments.get(OMCollection.class).addSuperCollection(documents);
drafts.get(OMCollection.class).addSuperCollection(documents);
archivedDocuments.get(OMCollection.class).addSuperCollection(documents);
```

Finally we show how the services can be created and assigned to specific collections. In the following example, a service is created as an anonymous class, registered as a service and bound to the Documents collection. Note that, in the invoke method, basic query functionality offered by the Database and BinaryCollection classes has been used to first retrieve the HasAuthor association and then access all author objects for the document that has been removed from the ArchivedDocuments collection. An email notification is sent to each author of the no longer archived document as indicated in the code fragment:

```
Service emailNotifier = new Service() {
  public Class[] getParameterTypes() {
    /* there are no parameters to this service */
    return new Class[] {};
  }
  public Class getExpectedSourceType() {
    return Document.class;
  }
  public void invoke(Object source, Object[] args) {
    OMBinaryCollection hasAuthor = db.retrieveBinCollection("HasAuthor");
    OMCollection authors = hasAuthor.sourceRestriction((OMObject) source);
    for (OMObject current : authors) {
     URL address = current.get(Author.class).getEmail();
     /* send email to address using Java API */
    }
  }
};
```

The newly created service is finally deployed to the service manager. A context object is created which allows the service only to be invoked if permitted by the general notification policy. The service is bound to the ArchivedDocuments collection for invocation on removal events depending on the context evaluation:

```
/* handle to the service manager sm has been assigned previously */
sm.add(emailNotifier);
Context context = new Context() {
 public boolean evaluate() {
  /* return true if notification permitted by general notification policy */
 }
};
sm.bind(emailNotifier, document, archivedDocuments, REMOVAL_EVENT, context);
```

6 Discussion

We have introduced a three-layered modelling approach for dynamic role-based object behaviour in object databases. The implementation of our metamodel covering the concepts of each of these three models resulted in a compact software layer on top of the db4o object database. Standard Java classes are used to represent instances of the type model whereas the classification model is covered by a collection and association framework reflected in an extended database API. Any services specified in the service model are implemented based on a well defined service interface and are bound to objects in a role-dependent manner through the collection interfaces.

The loose coupling and runtime binding of services is addressed by SOAs. While the publishing, registration and configuration of services in SOAs still requires a major effort from a developer, we offer the same flexibility within a database. Most SOAs deal with service invocation on a rather technical level, whereas we offer high-level conceptual constructs for role-based service binding and invocation. In addition to the explicit service invocation offered by SOAs, our approach supports an implicit invocation of services based on the handling of events in combination with an object's role.

In contrast to SOAs where service calls are explicitly reflected in the programming code, our role-based approach enables the configuration of services as extrinsic object behaviour. Instead of dealing with alternative service invocations by cumbersome if-then-else statements, our collection-based object classification enables a highly flexible and dynamic runtime behaviour adaptation by simple reclassification. Note that our active content approach has also been used for the database-driven development of highly interactive systems [15].

The *separation of intrinsic and extrinsic object behaviour* is not addressed in most object-oriented programming languages. While the intrinsic object behaviour is tightly coupled to an object's type, there is often no mechanism for object evolution and the flexible modelling of extrinsic object behaviour. Any form of additional functionality that is non-type-specific is normally implemented via static method calls to external software libraries. However, this implies that a programmer has to deal with if-then-else statements to make use of these library methods in a context-dependent manner. Furthermore, there is no explicitly modelled relationship between this additional functionality and the types of objects to which it should be applied. With our three-layered application development approach, this library service functionality can be bound to objects in a context-sensitive way without affecting an object's type definition and the reusability of object types across different applications.

Just as there is a trend to treat relationships and associations as first-class constructs in modern programming languages in order to enhance the reusability of components [16], we think that our solution leads to a clear separation of concerns in dynamic service binding. This finally results in cleaner component interfaces which are defined by object types and enhances the reusability of types as well as services across different application domains.

7 Conclusion

While the concept of methods in object models is a rather static way of binding behaviour to an object, we have presented an approach that enables a role-based definition of object behaviour. Our three-layered conceptual model provides a clear separation of concerns between the object type specification, the classification and association of objects and the dynamic role-based service invocation on individual objects. By means of a simple example application, we have highlighted how the role-driven service invocation mechanism leads to a cleaner development process by associating objects with role-based behaviour which would otherwise be spread across different static library method calls.

References

1. Dantas, F., Batista, T., Cacho, N.: Towards Aspect-Oriented Programming for Context-Aware Systems: A Comparative Study. In: Proc. of SEPCASE 2007, Minneapolis, USA (May 2007)
2. Gua, T., Punga, H.K., Zhang, D.Q.: A Service-Oriented Middleware for Building Context-Aware Services. Journal of Network and Computer Applications 28 (2005)
3. Pernici, B.: Objects with Roles. In: Proc. of OIS 1990, Cambridge, USA (1990)
4. Albano, A., Bergamini, R., Ghelli, G., Renzo, O.: An Object Data Model with Roles. In: Proc. of VLDB 1993, Dublin, Ireland (August 1993)
5. Norrie, M.C.: Distinguishing Typing and Classification in Object Data Models. In: Information Modelling and Knowledge Bases, vol. VI (1995)
6. Gottlob, G., Schrefl, M., Röck, B.: Extending Object-Oriented Systems with Roles. ACM Transactions on Information Systems 14(3) (1996)
7. Goldberg, A., Robson, D.: Smalltalk-80: The Language and its Implementation. Addison-Wesley, Reading (1983)
8. Ungar, D., Smith, R.B.: SELF: The Power of Simplicity. Lisp and Symbolic Computation 4(3) (1991)
9. Kiczales, G., Lamping, J., Mendhekar, A., Maeda, C., Lopes, C.V., Loingtier, J.-M., Irwin, J.: Aspect-Oriented Programming. In: Aksit, M., Matsuoka, S. (eds.) ECOOP 1997. LNCS, vol. 1241, pp. 220–242. Springer, Heidelberg (1997)
10. Papazoglou, M.: Web Services: Principles and Technology. Prentice-Hall, Englewood Cliffs (2007)
11. Krafzig, D., Banke, K., Slama, D.: Enterprise SOA: Service-Oriented Architecture Best Practices. Prentice-Hall, Englewood Cliffs (2004)
12. Härder, T.: DBMS Architecture – New Challenges Ahead. Datenbank-Spektrum 14 (2005)
13. Subasu, I.E., Ziegler, P., Dittrich, K.R.: Towards Service-Based Database Management Systems. In: Proc. of BTW 2007, Aachen, Germany (March 2007)
14. Norrie, M.C.: An Extended Entity-Relationship Approach to Data Management in Object-Oriented Systems. In: Elmasri, R.A., Kouramajian, V., Thalheim, B. (eds.) ER 1993. LNCS, vol. 823, Springer, Heidelberg (1994)
15. Signer, B., Norrie, M.C.: Active Components as a Method for Coupling Data and Services – A Database-Driven Application Development Process. In: Proc. of ICOODB 2009, Zurich, Switzerland (July 2009)
16. Balzer, S., Gross, T.R., Eugster, P.: A Relational Model of Object Collaborations and its Use in Reasoning about Relationships. In: Ernst, E. (ed.) ECOOP 2007. LNCS, vol. 4609, Springer, Heidelberg (2007)

Business Process Modeling: Perceived Benefits

Marta Indulska[1], Peter Green[1], Jan Recker[2], and Michael Rosemann[2]

[1] UQ Business School, The University of Queensland,
St Lucia, QLD 4072, Australia
{m.indulska,p.green}@business.uq.edu.au
[2] Information Systems Program, Queensland University of Technology,
Brisbane, QLD 4000, Australia
{j.recker,m.rosemann}@qut.edu.au

Abstract. The process-centered design of organizations and information systems is globally seen as an appropriate response to the increased economic pressure on organizations. At the methodological core of process-centered management is process modeling. However, business process modeling in large initiatives can be a time-consuming and costly exercise, making it potentially difficult to convince executive management of its benefits. To date, and despite substantial interest and research in the area of process modeling, the understanding of the actual benefits of process modeling in academia and practice is limited. To address this gap, this paper explores the perception of benefits derived from process modeling initiatives, as reported through a global Delphi study. The study incorporates the views of three groups of stakeholders – academics, practitioners and vendors. Our findings lead to the first identification and ranking of 19 unique benefits associated with process modeling. The study in particular found that process modeling benefits vary significantly between practitioners and academics. We argue that the variations may point to a disconnect between research projects and practical demands.

Keywords: Business process modeling, benefits, modeling advantages, Delphi study.

1 Introduction

Business process modeling – an approach to depict the way organizations conduct current or future business processes – is a fundamental pre-requisite for organizations wishing to engage in business process improvement or Business Process Management (BPM) initiatives. In their most basic form, process models describe, typically in a graphical way, the activities, events and control flow logic that constitutes a business process [1]. Additional information, such as goals, risks and performance metrics for example, can also be included. Accordingly, process models are considered a key instrument for the analysis and design of process-aware Information Systems [2], organizational documentation and re-engineering [3], and the design of service-oriented architectures [4].

A.H.F. Laender et al. (Eds.): ER 2009, LNCS 5829, pp. 458–471, 2009.

Globalization, recent economic turbulence, and regulatory body mandates for process compliance have further contributed to an increased interest in BPM [5] and, hence, business process modeling. A recent study showed that process modeling is behind four of the top six purposes of conceptual modeling [6]. The increased interest is in part manifested by an increase in enquiries and requests for process modeling executive training in the Australian market (e.g., www.bpm-training.com). Anecdotal evidence further suggests that this phenomenon is also present in the USA and the European market. Other indications include, for example, the rapidly growing popularity of the Business Process Modeling Notation (BPMN) [7].

Process modeling on a large, company-wide scale, however, can require substantial efforts in terms of investments in tools, methodologies, training and the actual conduct of process modeling. This scale of modeling demands sound business cases. Studies indicate that individuals (for example, business analysts, managers) have difficulty in obtaining executive management support for process modeling initiatives in organizations [e.g., 8]. Typically, they are unable to communicate and quantify the benefits that can be expected from process modeling activities. In return, executive management often does not see enough evidence to support investments in process modeling initiatives. While substantial research over the last decade contributed to a significantly matured process modeling capability, a wider uptake of process modeling is often limited by such economic assessments. In fact, demonstrating the value of process modeling (and not specific methodological or grammar related issues) is seen as the major challenge by process modeling professionals [9], yet little guidance or related study exists in this area. This finding is a significant problem for initiating process modeling initiatives since rational decision makers make decisions on the basis of their net benefits as perceived by them for their circumstances - that is, benefits outweighing costs. Decision making theory tells us that this has to be evaluated from individual stakeholder perspectives [10]. Therefore, as a first step in this process, we were motivated to explore the perceptions of benefits of process modeling though a large Delphi study.

The main goal of this study is to identify and explore the most compelling benefits that can be derived from process modeling. In reaching such a goal, we are able to provide guidance to organizations on the main process modeling expectations, as well as identify implications for consultancy and tool development and future process modeling research. Accordingly, our study is based on the following research question: *What are the main perceived benefits of process modeling?* We explore this question in a Delphi study setting with three main stakeholder groups of the process modeling ecosystem, *viz.*, *academics* in the business process modeling domain, business process modeling *practitioners*, and *vendors* of business process modeling software tools and consultancy offerings. Our objective is to identify the most compelling benefits believed to be associated with process modeling initiatives, reach consensus on these benefits, and identify how the perception of benefits differs across the three stakeholder groups.

2 Research Approach

2.1 Delphi Study Design

The technique chosen to facilitate the collection of, and consensus on, the benefits of process modeling was the Delphi technique [11] – a multiple-round approach to data collection. Delphi studies are useful when seeking consensus among experts, particularly in situations where there is a lack of empirical evidence [12]. The anonymous nature of a Delphi study can lead to creative results [13], reduces common problems found in studies that involve large groups [12] and allows for a wider participant scope due to the reduction of geographic boundaries [14].

One of the main determinants of success of a Delphi study is the selection of the expert panel, i.e., the study participants [15]. Instead of utilizing a statistical, representative sample of the target population, a Delphi study requires the selection and consideration of qualified experts who have deep understanding of the domain or phenomenon of interest [14].

2.2 Participant Selection

To obtain a comprehensive understanding of the core process modeling benefits, it is important to acknowledge different key stakeholders. The perception of benefits, and/or the perception of their centrality, may vary depending on the perspective taken by respondents. We identify three groups of stakeholders: first, the *practitioners* of business process modeling, that is, the business analysts, system designers, managers and other staff that actively conduct business process modeling projects or have an vested interest in process modeling in their organizations. These participants are chosen because they have first-hand experience with process modeling or its outcomes, and an overall awareness of process modeling advantages and pitfalls. The second group identified is that of the *vendors* of business process modeling software and consulting solutions providing support to the end users. These participants are chosen because they are in close contact with the user community, typically provide first-hand support or active engagement in process modeling initiatives, and have valuable user feedback as well as insights and observations from their consulting activities. The competitive environment within this stakeholder group enforces ongoing innovation, which overall positions vendors as boundary spanners [16] between the academic and the end user community. The last group identified is that of the *academics* in the business process modeling domain, who provide educational services and create new approaches and new knowledge in the business process modeling domain. These participants were chosen because they drive the development of the process modeling research domain, assist the development of methodologies and tools, and also train new generations of process modelers. We took care to ensure a representative sample of the academic community, including academics from the domains of computer science, information systems, and business.

Using these three groups, we designed a Delphi study that was conducted between August and October 2008 in three rounds separately for each group. The risk of being unable to obtain consensus between heterogeneous panelists [17], particularly in the exploration of a potentially broad topic, was further motivation to divide the study into the three related groups of stakeholders to narrow down the possible perspectives of each group. Invitations were based on the expertise of the potential participants. For academics, we screened the program committee of the Business Process Management conference series (www.bpm-conference.org), the most reputable conference in this area. A key selection criterion was the related research track record of a PC member. For vendors, we contacted key management staff from leading software and methodology providers, as reported in current market studies [e.g., 18, 19]. For practitioners, we contacted process managers, and similar roles, of large corporations, who the research team knew through previous collaborations. For each of the three stakeholder groups we aimed for a balanced international representation.

Typically, Delphi study involvement rates of 10 participants are recommended [20] to overcome personal bias in consensus seeking. Seeking to surpass this recommendation, invitations to the study were sent to 134 carefully screened experts (40 practitioners, 34 software vendors, 60 academics), including 11 invitations based on referrals from invited participants. Of these experts, 73 agreed to participate - representing a 55 percent response rate. By the 3rd round of the study, 62 experts were involved – an outstanding ongoing participation rate of 85 percent. At the end of the third round of the Delphi study, the group sizes were *at least* 80 percent greater than the recommended minimum for Delphi studies [20].

3 Study Conduct

3.1 Delphi Study Rounds

In the first round, each participant was asked to list five benefits of business process modeling, together with a brief description of each benefit. Overall, we received 70 (participants) x 5 (benefit items) = 350 individual response items. To overcome challenges related to the number of responses, differences in terminology, term connotation and writing styles, we then codified each response item into a higher level category – e.g. a response of "process models can be used for performance evaluation (mainly using simulation)" was coded as "process simulation", as was "ability to validate a proposed capability ahead of implementation".

In ensuring reliability and validity of this coding, we performed the exercise in multiple rounds. First, three researchers independently coded each of the 350 response items into a higher level category. In a second round, two researchers were independently exposed to the three codifications from the 1st coding round, and created individual, revised 2nd round coding drafts. In a third round, the fourth research group member consolidated the revised codifications and resolved any classification conflicts. Through this multi-round approach we ensured inter-coder reliability as well as validity of the codification exercise.

The second round of the study was designed to obtain consensus from the participants on the codified benefits, as well as on the definitions of the new higher-order categories. The communication for this round provided each participant with a personalized email containing his or her original responses, the agreed classifications per response item, and descriptions of the classifications. The participants were asked to indicate their level of satisfaction with the classification of their responses and the definitions of the classifications, and to provide additional information or suggestions if they were not satisfied with the classification. We received mostly positive responses on our codification (e.g., *"Your categorization is close to the mark."*) as well as a small number of coding and/or definition improvement suggestions (e.g., *"Row 2, 4 and 5 are rightly codified. For row 1 and row 3, I feel the codification is little abstract."*), which were carried out where appropriate.

While it has been recognized that there are times when consensus between study participants may not be possible [17], there is a lack of indication in the literature as to possible measures for determining consensus. A recent Delphi study [22] utilized a satisfaction rating of 7.5 (out of 10) as an indication of consensus. In our study, we also asked the participants to rate their satisfaction with our codification on a scale of 1 to 10 (10 being highest). For the identification of process modeling benefits, being a potentially broad topic, we followed the previous study and assumed consensus at an average satisfaction level of 8 and a standard deviation below 2.0. The average satisfaction scores ranged from 8.569 (Academics), 8.771 (Vendors) to 9.230 (Practitioners) with standard deviations ranging from 1.609 (Academics) to 1.176 (Practitioners).

While our initial study plan allowed for multiple rounds of consensus building, the results obtained indicate that the participants achieved the required consensus levels at the first iteration of the second round. This allowed us to stop the consensus-building process. At the end of round two, and after making required changes to categories/definitions, all response items were ranked in descending order of frequency of occurrence, with items such as *understanding* (17 times), *model-driven process execution* (14 times), *process improvement* (12 times), *documentation* (10 times) and *communication* (10 times) being most frequently mentioned.

Frequency of occurrence is not an accurate measure with which to identify core process modeling benefits. Accordingly, in the third round of the Delphi study, the experts were asked to assign to the benefit items a weighting that reflected the respondent's relative importance of the particular item. In this round, data collection was carried out via an online web form, with separate logins for the different expert panels. The participants were provided with the list of frequently mentioned process modeling benefits (we defined 'frequently mentioned' as each item that was mentioned more than once in the first two rounds). The lists for each Delphi study group also included the consensus definitions of the process modeling benefits and were ranked by frequency of occurrence in descending order. Overall, there were 19 process modeling benefits that were mentioned more than once in the previous Delphi rounds across all groups. Per group, coincidentally, a list of 14 benefits was mentioned in that group's earlier study rounds more than once. Each participant was given 100 points to assign across any of the 14 benefits. The participants were free to assign the 100 points in any distribution, with the only condition being that exactly one hundred points were assigned across the list.

The collected data was analyzed, and the average weightings of each process modeling benefit were derived. From these calculations, we were able to derive top 10 lists of business process modeling benefits, based on the average weightings, for each of the three Delphi study groups. The results are listed in the Appendix and form the basis of the classification of results described in the next section.

3.2 Classification of Results

To better understand the nature of the core process modeling benefits, and their potential impact on organizations and their investments, we sought to classify the benefits into categories based on a benefit typology. A review of literature on the classification and realization of benefits in Information Systems as well as Management domains uncovered several classification schemes [e.g., 23, 24, 25]. We selected Shang and Seddon's [23] benefits classification framework, which is a widely cited and established framework for classifying the benefits of enterprise resource planning (ERP) systems, and its five main dimensions, *viz.* strategic, organizational, managerial, operational, and IT infrastructure. A review of the framework, and its twenty-one sub-dimensions, revealed a close fit to process modeling and process improvement initiatives (for example, sub-dimensions of *cost reduction, cycle time reduction, quality improvement* are directly relevant to processes). Other benefit classification schemes, for example Murphy and Simon's tangible versus quantitative and temporal benefit classification schemes [24], would have been less prescriptive in light of the data available, and would have hence resulted in a biased classification.

We adopted the five dimensions of the framework for our purposes and use the dimension definitions, as listed below, and the sub-dimensions in [23] to guide the mapping process (scope modifications highlighted in *italic*):

- **Strategic benefits:** Benefits *from process modeling* for strategic activities such as long-range planning, mergers & acquisitions, product planning, customer retention.
- **Organizational benefits:** Benefits *from process modeling* to the organization in terms of strategy execution, learning, cohesion, and increased focus.
- **Managerial benefits:** Benefits *from process modeling* provided to management in terms of improved decision making and planning.
- **Operational benefits:** Benefits *from process modeling* related to the reduction of *process* costs, increase of *process* productivity, increase of *process* quality, improved customer service and/or *reduced process execution time.*
- **IT Infrastructure benefits:** Benefits *from process modeling* relating to the IT support of business agility, reduction of IT costs, reduced implementation time.

The adoption of the framework allowed us to map benefits from each of the three top ten lists to one of the five dimensions. In turn, this mapping provides a clear representation of the types, and potential impacts, of process modeling benefits perceived by the three Delphi study participant groups. Similar to the coding exercise discussed earlier, the mapping of the top 10 lists of benefits used a multi-coder approach in order to reduce bias in the classification. Four members of the research group separately classified each benefit on the process modeling benefit list for each of the three study groups. The classifications were then consolidated and agreement statistics were calculated. We estimated inter-rater agreement using Cohen's Kappa [26]. In the first round, we achieved a Kappa of 0.369, which is considered somewhat moderate [27]. In a second round, we then consolidated the individual mappings. In particular, the consolidation involved a review of situations where the four coders had mapped a benefit to a combination of organizational and managerial benefits. Due to some subjectivity in separating organizational and managerial benefits, and due to the overlap in their definitions, situations in which majority rule was exhibited (i.e., three coders mapped a benefit as managerial and one as organizational, or vice versa) were deemed to be classified according to the majority-rule benefit type. We calculated the second round inter-rater agreement using Brennan and Prediger's variation of Cohen's Kappa [26], which was modified to allow calculation of agreement in instances with more than two coders present, and achieved a free-marginal Kappa of 0.639. The obtained Kappa result is classified as one of "substantial agreement" and is the second highest possible Kappa outcome that indicates inter-coder agreement [27]. After these two rounds, the four research team members discussed and amended the mappings until 100% agreement was reached.

4 Findings and Analysis

The design of the study allowed us to derive lists of top 10 process modeling benefits as perceived by three groups of process modeling stakeholders. The full details of each list, including rankings of the benefits based on their centrality, are presented in the Appendix. Inspection of these lists shows that the three groups of stakeholders differ markedly in their perceptions of benefits. While practitioners and vendors share the most commonalities, the academics in general have more dissimilar perceptions of benefits.

Most notably, both the practitioner and vendor groups agree that *process improvement* (the greater ability to improve business processes) is the top process modeling benefit. Similarities also exist in the perception of *understanding* (the improved and consistent understanding of business processes) as a core benefit, being ranked as #2 and #3 respectively by vendors and practitioners. Academics, however, perceive *model-driven process execution* (the ability to derive process execution code from process models), which is not identified by practitioners at all, as the number 1 benefit derived from process modeling activities. The relative mean rating (13.44[1]) indicates that this perception by academics is a particularly strong one. Indeed, it is the strongest weighted item across each of the three lists. Notably, vendors rank this benefit fifth in their top 10 list, with a mean rating of 8.17. The Academics group also identifies *process simulation* and *process verification* as some of the top-5 process modeling benefits – benefits that are not identified by practitioners or vendors, indicating a gap in perception and priorities between academia and industry.

Focusing specifically on the practitioner top 10 process modeling benefits list, we obtain some insights into the drivers of process modeling in organizations. The list of benefits indicates that practitioners make use of process modeling not only to improve processes and measure their performance, but also to elicit, determine and specify system requirements. Moreover, practitioners see advantages in the use of process models to support the identification, capture and management of organizational knowledge, as well as to support business change management practices. Uniquely to the other stakeholder groups, practitioners also realize the value of process modeling in assisting the alignment of organizational practices with organizational goals or other strategic perspectives.

1 Recall that participants were asked to distribute 100 points to the list of identified benefits based on the perceived importance.

In respect of the main *types* of benefits that can be obtained from process modeling, Table 1 shows the results of the mapping of process modeling benefits to Shang and Seddon's benefit framework [23].

Table 1. Top 10 business process modeling benefits for each Delphi study group

	Strategic	Organisational	Managerial	Operational	IT Infrastructure
1				P, V: Process Improvement	A: Model-driven Process Execution
2		V, A: Understanding	P: Process Performance Management		
3		P: Understanding V: Communication		A: Process Improvement	
4			P: Change Management V: Process Performance Management A: Process Simulation		
5				P: Requirements Specification A: Process Verification	V: Model-driven Process Execution
6		A: Communication	P, V: Process Analysis		
7		P: Communication V: Knowledge Management		A: Re-use	
8	P: Alignment	A: Documentation	V: Transparency		
9		P: Knowledge Management	V: Visualisation		A: Ease of Use
10		A: View Integration	V: Governance	P: Re-use	

P: Practitioners, V: Vendors, A: Academics

The clearest indication from the benefit framework mapping is that process modeling in itself does not have significant strategic benefits beyond the improved ability to align business processes with strategic goals or other perspectives. One would expect that the core strategic benefits would derive from Business Process Management initiatives, rather than the initial stages of process modeling. IT infrastructure benefits are also not well represented in process modeling initiatives, with mostly Academics considering some benefits of this type. Because process modeling can be performed without IT support, it is not surprising to see a lack of benefits of this type, particularly from the practitioner perspective. The majority of benefits lie in the organizational and managerial dimensions, with the operational dimension also being well represented. Operational benefits in particular were to be expected given the close link between process modeling and process improvement initiatives. Further investigation of the organizational and managerial benefits indicates that many benefits are intangible in nature – consider, for instance, benefits such as improved transparency, or visualization – indicating why some benefits are hard to demonstrate to executive management in early stages of modeling projects.

Regarding similarities in perceived process modeling benefits across the three groups, we note that of the overall thirty top benefits, the three lists contain 19 unique items, with three process modeling benefits, *viz. process improvement, communication,* and *understanding,* appearing in all three lists, and 5 further benefits appearing in two of the three lists. In Table 2 we present a consolidated ordered list of perceived process modeling benefits across the three stakeholder groups, ranked by the combined average rating and equal weighting of each group independent of the number of participants. We also include in Table 2 the consensually agreed definitions of the overall top ten perceived benefits.

Not surprisingly, support for *process improvement* is identified as the core benefit of process modeling initiatives, followed closely by improved and consistent *understanding* of organizational processes. The third identified main benefit of process modeling is the improved *communication* between process stakeholders and various departments through the use of process models. Interestingly, *model-driven process execution* (a hotly debated topic in academia [e.g., 28]) is the overall fourth ranked process modeling benefit despite the lack of ranking by practitioners. Its high standard deviation – the highest of all benefits in the overall top 10 list – confirms a significant difference of opinion between the three stakeholder groups.

Table 2. Overall (across all 3 stakeholder groups) top 10 business process modeling benefits

Rank	Issue	Description	Mean Rating	Std. Dev.
1	Process improvement	Greater ability to improve business processes	11.452	1.452
2	Understanding	Improved and consistent understanding of business processes	10.787	1.861
3	Communication	Improved communication of business processes across different stakeholder groups	7.539	0.909
4	Model-driven process execution	Ability to facilitate or support process automation, execution or enactment on the basis of the models	7.202	6.771
5	Process performance measurement	Issues related to the definition, identification or modeling of adequate levels of process abstraction.	6.207	5.464
6	Process analysis	Greater ability to model processes to analyze them for possible problems, and/or time/cost reductions	5.266	4.619
7	Knowledge management	Support for identification, capture and management of organizational knowledge	4.276	3.721
8	Re-use	Greater ability to re-use previously designed and validated processes	4.006	3.496
9	Process simulation	Greater ability to see how a current or re-designed process might operate, and its implications	3.093	5.357
10	Change management	Support for business change management practices, results or impacts	3.035	5.256

5 Discussion

The three lists of top 10 benefits derived from different stakeholder groups (refer to the Appendix), and the differences between the lists, allow us to comment on the presence of realized and unrealized benefits of process modeling. We consider practitioners to have the most accurate perception of process modeling benefits in light of actual demands, constraints, modeling capabilities and economic realities. This presumption is because practitioners have first-hand experiences and observations of process modeling initiatives on a daily basis. By contrast, we consider the benefits perceived by academics to be benefits that are mostly yet to be realized in practice, due to the academics' insights into leading research and future developments in the process modeling domain. We expect that vendors, being boundary spanners between academia and industry, perceive the benefits they observe through their clients as well as through provision of new tool or methodology solutions, and changes in the overall business environment.

In other words, we consider the benefits ranked in the practitioners' list to be a representation of benefits that organizations considering process modeling realistically want and expect to achieve. This includes benefits such as *process improvement, process analysis, performance measurement, requirements specification,* and *knowledge*.

The practitioners' and academics' perceptions of process modeling benefits share only four common items, *viz. understanding, process improvement, communication* and *re-use*. Beyond these items, the benefits mentioned by the academic study group appear to be benefits that are yet to be realized in practice. In particular, benefits such as *model-driven process execution* – the ability to facilitate process automation on the basis of conceptual process models – or *process verification* – the ability to verify the syntactical and behavioral correctness of processes on the basis of the models – are benefits that have a stronger link to leading research and prototypes, rather than existing practice. Accordingly, we see the benefits perceived by academics as the future benefits that may be realized once leading research is incorporated into software tools and consultancy offerings by vendors.

Vendors of tool and consultancy offerings, therefore, represent a cohort that is able to observe and influence current process modeling practice whilst at the same time identify novel features or practices from leading research that will be incorporated into future tools or consulting practices. As such, they are positioned as the ideal boundary spanners between these two communities. Given the lack of continuous interaction between practitioners and academics, we see vendors as the 'bridge' that will assist the transition of unrealized benefits to realized benefits. The vendors' list of benefits has in common five benefits with the practitioners' perception, and it also includes benefits that appear to be linked to the current business environment. In particular, benefits such as *transparency, visualization* and *governance* appear to be related to the increasing expectations of compliance to legal and regulatory mandates. We would expect that such benefits will be on the radar of organizations in the near future, especially as the cost of compliance management in organizations increases.

However, it could also be argued that perceived benefits are an explication of the drivers that motivate dealing with an issue, i.e., here process modeling. The significant disconnect that can be observed in the comparison of the two lists of academics and practitioners potentially also points to a misalignment of allocated research resources to practical demands. Process execution, verification and simulation offer without any doubt countless intellectual challenges. However, there is a serious danger that these topics keep a large research community entertained without a sufficient validation that these topics sufficiently matter in practice.

Overall, we see the lists of top 10 benefits as indicative of several situations. The list of practitioners' process modeling benefits suggests currently realized benefits of process modeling. Nevertheless, our own experiences indicate that many organizations still struggle to justify investments in process modeling initiatives. Many of the benefits agreed on by practitioners are indeed benefits that are intangible in nature, difficult to quantify, and for which it is difficult to make a business case. Accordingly, we see a need for the exploration and publication of success and failure case studies relating to these benefits, and in general for further research that explores how such benefits might be measured or estimated. The list of vendors' top 10 process modeling benefits indicates some adoption of leading research and indicates moves towards better visualization of processes as well as support for automation of processes based on conceptual models. The list of top 10 benefits as perceived by academics is indicative of some lack of awareness of the state of current practice in industry, combined with a focus on research developments in the process modeling domain. In particular, benefits such as process verification and view integration are topics that are at current principally discussed in academic literature [e.g., 29]. While process verification, for example, is already available in some prototype tools, it is clearly not yet seen as beneficial to industry practice as the academic community perceives it to be. Accordingly, we see a need for increased communication between academia and practice to better align academic research. Thoroughly identified lists of perceived benefits, as presented in this paper, have without any doubt the potential to re-shape current research agendas. At the same time, they can assist the adoption of research innovations in the process modeling domain to practitioners, and provide further arguments for the wider uptake of process modeling.

6 Conclusions

This study addresses a gap in research on the benefits that can be expected from process modeling initiatives. Through a global Delphi study, we explore the benefits of process modeling, as perceived by three stakeholder groups, *viz.* practitioners, vendors and academics. The study shows that the top 3 expected process modeling benefits are those of *process improvement, understanding* and *communication.* The study also indicates that practitioners also see the benefits of process modeling beyond its link to process improvement. For example, practitioners indicate that requirements specification and knowledge management are also some of the top 10 benefits obtained from process modeling initiatives. Our analysis further shows that the three stakeholder groups have varied perceptions of process modeling benefits, indicating the difference between *realized* benefits in organizations and *unrealized (i.e.,* potential) benefits. The study also highlights the intermediary effect of vendors in helping to transition some of the *unrealized* benefits (as perceived by academics) to realized benefits in actual process modeling practice.

We identify the Delphi study approach as a potential limitation in our work. Delphi studies are said to be susceptible to a number of weaknesses including (1) the flexible nature of study design [13], (2) the discussion course being determined by the researchers [11], and (3) accuracy and validity of outcomes [30]. In our study, measures were taken to minimize their potential impact. Such measures included: (1) establishing assessment criteria for measuring inter-rater agreements; (2) use of multiple coders; (3) using multiple coding rounds and (4) following established methodological guidelines for the conduct of Delphi studies [e.g., 14, 15, 21].

In our future work we seek to provide a detailed analysis of additional qualitative responses gathered in a later fourth round of the study, which exposed the top 10 lists to all participant groups and elicited the comments of the participants. We plan to synthesize the results with those on process modeling issues and future challenges, collected as part of a larger study [9].

References

1. Recker, J., Rosemann, M., Indulska, M., Green, P.: Business Process Modeling: A Comparative Analysis. Journal of the Association for Information Systems 10, 333–363 (2009)
2. Dumas, M., van der Aalst, W.M.P., ter Hofstede, A.H.M. (eds.): Process Aware Information Systems: Bridging People and Software Through Process Technology. John Wiley & Sons, New Jersey (2005)
3. Davenport, T.H., Short, J.E.: The New Industrial Engineering: Information Technology and Business Process Redesign. Sloan Management Review 31, 11–27 (1990)
4. Rabhi, F.A., Yu, H., Dabous, F.T., Wu, S.Y.: A Service-oriented Architecture for Financial Business Processes: A Case Study in Trading Strategy Simulation. Information Systems and E-Business Management 5, 185–200 (2007)
5. Gartner Group: Meeting the Challenge: The 2009 CIO Agenda. EXP Premier Report January2009. Gartner, Inc, Stamford, Connecticut (2009)
6. Davies, I., Green, P., Rosemann, M., Indulska, M., Gallo, S.: How do Practitioners Use Conceptual Modeling in Practice? Data & Knowledge Engineering 58, 358–380 (2006)
7. Recker, J.: Opportunities and Constraints: The Current Struggle with BPMN. Business Process Management Journal 16 (in press, 2010)
8. Indulska, M., Chong, S., Bandara, W., Sadiq, S., Rosemann, M.: Major Issues in Business Process Management: An Australian Perspective. In: Spencer, S., Jenkins, A. (eds.) Proceedings of the 17th Australasian Conference on Information Systems, Australasian Association for Information Systems, Adelaide, Australia (2006)
9. Indulska, M., Recker, J., Rosemann, M., Green, P.: Process Modeling: Current Issues and Future Challenges. In: van Eck, P., Gordijn, J., Wieringa, R. (eds.) Advanced Information Systems Engineering - CAiSE. LNCS, vol. 5565, pp. 501–514. Springer, Amsterdam (2009)
10. Friedman, M.: The Methodology of Positive Economics. In: Friedman, M. (ed.) Essays in Positive Economics, pp. 3–43. University of Chicago Press, Chicago (1953)
11. Dalkey, N., Helmer, O.: An Experimental Application of the Delphi Method to the Use of Experts. Management Science 9, 458–467 (1963)
12. Murphy, M.K., Black, N.A., Lamping, D.L., McKee, C.M., Sanderson, C.F.B., Askham, J., Marteau, T.: Consensus Development Methods, and their Use in Clinical Guideline Development. Health Technology Assessment 2, 1–88 (1998)
13. van de Ven, A.H., Delbecq, A.L.: The Effectiveness of Nominal, Delphi, and Interacting Group Decision Making Processes. Academy of Management Journal 17, 605–621 (1974)
14. Okoli, C., Pawlowski, S.D.: The Delphi Method as a Research Tool: an Example, Design Considerations and Applications. Information & Management 42, 15–29 (2004)

15. Powell, C.: The Delphi Technique: Myths and Realities. Journal of Advanced Nursing 41, 376–382 (2003)
16. Hoe, S.L.: The Boundary Spanner's Role in Organizational Learning: Unleashing Untapped Potential. Development and Learning in Organizations 20, 9–11 (2006)
17. Richards, J.I., Curran, C.M.: Oracles on "Advertising": Searching for a Definition. Journal of Advertising 31, 63–76 (2002)
18. Hall, C., Harmon, P.: The, Enterprise Architecture, Process Modeling, and Simulation Tools Report. BPTrends.com (2007)
19. Blechar, M.J.: Magic Quadrant for Business Process Analysis Tools. Gartner Research Note G00148777. Gartner, Inc, Stamford, Connecticut (2007)
20. Cochran, S.W.: The Delphi Method: Formulation and Refining Group Judgments. Journal of Human Sciences 2, 111–117 (1983)
21. Linstone, H.A., Turoff, M. (eds.): The Delphi Method: Techniques and Applications [Online Reproduction from 1975]. Addison-Wesley, London (2002)
22. de Bruin, T., Rosemann, M.: Using the Delphi Technique to Identify BPM Capability Areas. In: Toleman, M., Cater-Steel, A., Roberts, D. (eds.) Proceedings of the 18th Australasian Conference on Information Systems, The University of Southern Queensland, Toowoomba, Australia, pp. 643–653 (2007)
23. Shang, S., Seddon, P.B.: Assessing and Managing the Benefits of Enterprise Systems: The Business Managers Perspective. Information Systems Journal 12, 271–299 (2002)
24. Murphy, K.E., Simon, S.J.: Intangible Benefits Valuation in ERP Projects. Information Systems Journal 12, 301–320 (2002)
25. Ward, J., Taylor, P., Bond, P.: Evaluation and Realization of IS/IT Benefits: An Empirical Study of Current Practice. European Journal of Information Systems 4, 214–225 (1996)
26. Brennan, R.L., Prediger, D.J.: Coefficient Kappa: Some Uses, Misuses, and Alternatives. Educational and Psychological Measurement 41, 687–699 (1981)
27. Landis, J.R., Koch, G.G.: The Measurement of Observer Agreement for Categorical Data. Biometrics 33, 159–174 (1977)
28. Ouyang, C., van der Aalst, W.M.P., Dumas, M., ter Hofstede, A.H.M., Mendling, J.: From Business Process Models to Process-Oriented Software Systems. ACM Transactions on Software Engineering Methodology 19 (in press, 2009)
29. Wynn, M.T., Verbeek, H.M.V., Van der Aalst, W.M.P., ter Hofstede, A.H.M., Edmond, D.: Business Process Verification – Finally a Reality! Business Process Management Journal 15, 74–92 (2009)
30. Ono, R., Wedemeyer, D.J.: Assessing the Validity of the Delphi Technique. Futures 26, 289–304 (1994)

Appendix

Rank	Practitioners		Vendors		Academics	
	Benefit	Mean Rating	Benefit	Mean Rating	Benefit	Mean Rating
1	Process improvement	11.24	Process improvement	13.00	Model-driven process execution	13.44
2	Process performance measurement	10.29	Understanding	10.17	Understanding	12.88
3	Understanding	9.32	Communication	8.56	Process improvement	10.12
4	Change management	9.11	Process performance measurement	8.33	Process simulation	9.28
5	Requirements specification	8.84	Model-driven process execution	8.17	Process verification	7.84
6	Process analysis	8.63	Process analysis	7.17	Communication	6.80
7	Communication	7.26	Knowledge management	6.78	Re-use	6.44
8	Alignment	6.74	Transparency	6.44	Documentation	5.88
9	Knowledge management	6.05	Visualization	5.78	Ease of use	4.92
10	Re-use	5.63	Governance	5.44	View integration	4.64

Designing Law-Compliant Software Requirements

Alberto Siena[1], John Mylopoulos[2], Anna Perini[1], and Angelo Susi[1]

[1] FBK - Irst, via Sommarive 18 - Trento, Italy
{siena,perini,susi}@fbk.eu
[2] University of Trento, via Sommarive 14 - Trento, Italy
jm@cs.toronto.edu

Abstract. New laws, such as HIPAA and SOX, are increasingly impacting the design of software systems, as business organisations strive to comply. This paper studies the problem of generating a set of requirements for a new system which comply with a given law. Specifically, the paper proposes a systematic process for generating law-compliant requirements by using a taxonomy of legal concepts and a set of primitives to describe stakeholders and their strategic goals. Given a model of law and a model of stakeholders goals, legal alternatives are identified and explored. Strategic goals that can realise legal prescriptions are systematically analysed, and alternative ways of fulfilling a law are evaluated. The approach is demonstrated by means of a case study. This work is part of the Nomos framework, intended to support the design of law-compliant requirements models.

1 Introduction

In an ever-more complex and fluid world, there has been a steady increase in government laws and regulations, industrial standards, and company policies that need to be taken into account during the design of new organisational systems. These laws, regulations and policies need to be analysed and accommodated, somehow, during the definition of requirements for the new system. The problem of compliance to regulations is even more difficult for an existing organisation who has to restructure and reengineer its operation to achieve compliance. The problem is compounded for multi-national organisations whose systems operate in international jurisdictions where multiple, often contradictory laws apply.

The engineering/reengineering of law-compliant organisational information systems has become a major factor in IT-related projects. It has been estimated that in the Healthcare domain, organisations have spent $17.6 billion over a number of years to align their systems and procedures with a single law, the U.S. Health Insurance Portability and Accountability Act (HIPAA), introduced in 1996 [1]. In the Business domain, it was estimated that organisations would spend $5.8 billion in one year alone (2005) to ensure compliance of their reporting and risk management procedures with the Sarbanes-Oxley Act (SOX) [2].

We view the problem of compliance as a modelling problem. Laws are expressed in terms of a set of legal concepts, such as those of "right", "obligation" and "privilege".

A.H.F. Laender et al. (Eds.): ER 2009, LNCS 5829, pp. 472–486, 2009.

Requirements, on the other hand, are expressed in terms of stakeholder goals. The definition of law-compliant requirements is then a problem of transforming, through a systematic process, models of rights, obligations, privileges etc. into models of actors, goals and actor inter-dependencies. This paper proposes such a systematic process for generating law-compliant requirements, given a model of the law and a model of initial stakeholder goals. Our approach is illustrated with an example scenario of a (U.S.) hospital that needs to be compliant with HIPAA while setting up a new information system to manage service reservations. The work reported here is part of the Nomos framework presented in [16]. In earlier work, [16], we introduced a conceptual model for laws and defined the notion of compliance between a model of law and a model of system requirements. In this work, we focus on the process of generating law-compliant requirements.

The rest of the paper is structured as follows: Section 2 recalls the Nomos framework concepts and its modelling language, which is shortly illustrated on the example scenario; Section 3 describes how to build a model of law-compliant requirements starting from a model of law and a set of initial requirements; Section 4 discusses the properties of the generated requirements model; Section 5 reviews the related works; finally, Section 6 concludes.

2 Research Baseline

Nomos[1] is a modelling framework that aims at supporting requirements analysts in dealing with the problem of requirements compliance. It offers a conceptual solution that combines elements of goal orientation with elements of legal theory to argument about compliance of a certain requirements set and to *derive* models of compliant requirements, starting from a model of law.

For its nature, formal proof of run-time compliance can't be given at requirements time: there are properties of law that makes that the compliance condition can only be stated *ex-post* by the judge - e.g., the subsequent design could be wrong, people could behave differently from what is assigned to them according to their roles, software programs could be bugged and also behave differently from what expected, and finally law can be intentionally ambiguous, as pointed out in [3]. For this reason, we have introduced the concept of *Intentional Compliance* [15] as the assignment of actors responsibilities such that if every actor fulfils its goals, then law is respected. We derive a general rule to define the notion of requirements compliance. Given a set of requirements represented as actors goals, R, and a set of domain assumptions D, we say that the requirements are compliant with a law L, and write $R, D \models L$, if, for every possible state of the world, if R holds, then L holds.

Intentionality. In the above formula, R represents the sets of possible alternatives, expressed in terms of stakeholders goals. The Nomos framework adopts a security-oriented extension of the $i*$ modelling framework [19], namely *SecureTropos* [9], to represent stakeholders and their goals. Worth mentioning that this choice is arbitrary - other frameworks could be used or adapted to be used as well, as long as they provide primitives for modelling actors, goals, and security relationships between actors. The

[1] From Greek $N\acute{o}\mu o\varsigma$, which means "norm".

*i** framework [19] models a domain along the two following perspectives: the **strategic rationale** of the actors - i.e., a description of the intentional behaviour of domain stakeholders in terms of their goals, tasks, preferences and quality aspects (represented as softgoals); and the **strategic dependencies** among actors - i.e., the system-wide strategic model based on the relationship between the depender, which is the actor who "wants" something and the dependee, that is the actor who has the *ability* to do something that contributes to the achievement of the depender's original goals. Strategic dependencies can then be secured [9] by adding information on the trust that actors have in each other. Depending on their trust, actors can delegate the execution of plans or achievement of goals, or they can delegate the permission to use resources.

Elements of Legal Theory. The Hohfeld's taxonomy [10] is a milestone of juridical literature that proposes a widely accepted classification of legal concepts. It is grounded on the notion of ***right***, which can be defined as "entitlement (not) to perform certain actions or be in certain states, or entitlement that others (not) perform certain actions or be in certain states"[2]. Rights are classified by Hohfeld in the 8 elementary concepts of *privilege*, *claim*, *power*, *immunity*, *no-claim*, *duty*, *liability*, *disability*, and organised in opposites and correlatives. **Claim** is the entitlement for a person to have something done from another person, who has therefore a **Duty** of doing it; e.g., if John has the claim to exclusively use of his land, others have a corresponding duty of non-interference. **Privilege** (or liberty) is the entitlement for a person to discretionally perform an action, regardless of the will of others who may not claim him to perform that action, and have therefore a **No-claim**; e.g., giving a tip at the restaurant is a liberty, and the waiter can't claim it. **Power** is the (legal) capability to produce changes in the legal system towards another subject, who has the corresponding **Liability**; examples of legal powers include the power to contract and the power to marry. **Immunity** is the right of being kept untouched from other performing an action, who has therefore a **Disability**; e.g., one may be immune from prosecution as a result of signing a contract. Two rights are **correlatives** [10] if the right of a person implies that there exists another person (it's counter-party), who has the correlative right. For example, if someone has the claim to access some data, then somebody else will have the duty of providing that data, so duty and claim are correlatives; similarly, privilege-noclaim, power-liability, immunity-disability are correlatives. The concept of *correlativeness* implies that rights have a **relational nature**. In fact, they involve two subjects: the owner of the right and the one, against whom the right is held - the *counter-party*. Vice versa, the concept of *opposition* means that the existence of a right excludes its opposite.

The Nomos modelling language. The Nomos modelling language, whose meta-model is depicted in Fig. 1, conceives law as a partially ordered set of *Normative Propositions* (NP). Basically, NPs are the most atomic element in which a legal prescription can be subdivided. The core element of a NP is the hohfeldian concept of right (class `Right`). Since rights have a dual nature, the relation of "correlative" or "equivalent" means that the two rights that it connects describe the same reality, but from two different points of view. This results in 4 classes of rights, namely `PrivilegeNoclaim`, `ClaimDuty`, `PowerLiability` and `ImmunityDisability`, which subsume the 8 hohfeldian concepts. The object of rights are *actions*, (as defined in [13]), which consist in the

[2] From `http://plato.stanford.edu/entries/rights/`

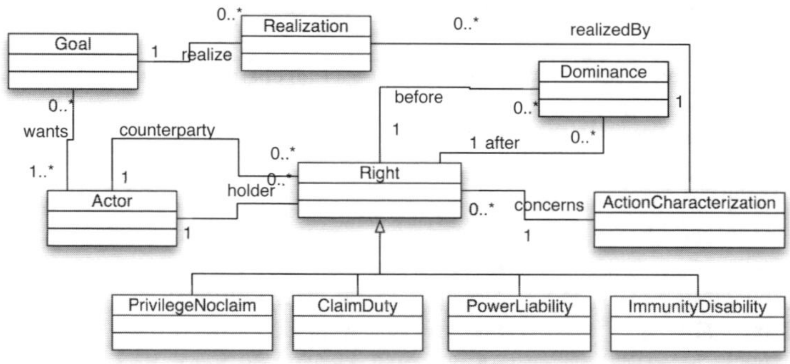

Fig. 1. The Nomos modelling language and its meta-model

description of either something to be done (*behavioural action*) or something to be achieved (*productive action*). In the meta-model we refer to it as `ActionCharact-erization`. Finally, rights address two domain actors (class `Actor`): the right's `holder`, and its `counter-party`. For conditional elements such as exceptions, time conditions and so on we give a uniform representation by establishing an order between normative propositions. Given a set of normative propositions $\{NP_1...NP_n\}$, $NP_k > NP_{k+1}$ - read: NP_k overcomes NP_{k+1} - means that if NP_k is satisfied, then the fulfilment of NP_{k+1} is not relevant. This is captured in the meta-model via the definition of the concept of the class `Dominance`, connected to the class `Right`.

As said, the Nomos meta-model combines elements of legal theory with elements of goal orientation. In Fig. 1, a part of the $i*$ meta-model (taken from [17]) is also depicted. The `Actor` class is at the same time part of NPs (rights concern domain actors) and of the $i*$ meta-model (an actor wants goals). This way, Nomos models are able to inform whether a goal fits the characterisation given by law. In Fig. 1, this is expressed with the concept of **realisation** (class `Realization`), which puts in relation something that belongs to the law with something that belongs to the intentions of actors.

Normative propositions are represented in the Nomos frameworks by means of a visual notation, depicted in Fig. 2, that has been defined as an extension of the $i*$ visual notation. The actors linked by a right (holder and counter-party) are modelled as circles (i.e., $i*$ actors). The specified action is represented as a triangle and linked with both the actors. The kind of right (privilege/noclaim, claim/duty, power/liability, immunity/disability) is distinguished via labels on both the edges of the right relationships. Optionally, it's also possible to annotate with the same labels on the left side the triangle representing the action. The language also introduces a *dominance* relationship between specified actions, represented as a link between two prescribed actions and labelled with a ">" symbol that goes from the dominant action to the dominated one. Finally, a *realisation* relation is used in the language to establish a relation between one element of the intentional model and one element of the legal model.

Running Example. Title 2 of HIPAA addresses the privacy and security of health data. Article §164.502 of HIPAA says that: *(a) A CE may not use or disclose PHI, except as permitted or required by this subpart [...] (1) A covered entity is permitted to use or disclose PHI [...] (i) To the individual; (2) A CE is required to disclose PHI: (i) To an*

Table 1. Some Normative Propositions identified in §164.314 and §164.502

Src §164.	Id	Right	Holder	Counterparty	Action characterisation	Dominances
§502a	NP1	CD	Patient	CE	not DisclosePHI	-
§502a1i	NP2	PN	CE	Patient	DisclosePHI	NP1
§502a2i	NP3	CD	Patient	CE	DisclosePHI	NP1,NP2
§502a2ii	NP4	PL	Secretary	CE	DisclosePHI	NP1
§314a1ii	NP5	CD	CE	BA	no KnownViolations	NP6,NP7,NP8
§314a1ii	NP6	ID	CE	Authority	EndViolation	NP7,NP8
§314a1iiA	NP7	ID	CE	Authority	TerminateContract	NP8
§314a1iiB	NP8	ID	CE	Secretary	ReportTheProblem	-
§314a2iiC	NP9	CD	CE	BA	ReportSecurityLacks	-

Legenda: CD = Claim/Duty; PN = Privilege/Noclaim; PL = Power/Liability; ID = Immunity/Disability

individual, when requested [...]; and (ii) When required by the Secretary. Out of this law fragment, it is possible to identify the normative propositions that compose the law fragment. The identified normative propositions are summarised in Table 1. The first row of the table contains a reference to the source text (more information can be stored here, but it is not shown in the table due to lack of space). "Id" is a unique identifier of the NP. Holder and counterparty are the involved actors. "Action characterisation" is the description of the action specified in the NP. To identify the NPs, prescribing words have been mapped in the right specifiers; e.g., "is permitted" has been mapped into a *privilege*, "is required" has been mapped into a *duty*, and so on. The name of the subjects are extracted by either using an explicit mention made by the law (e.g., "a CE is not in compliance if..."); or, when no subject has been clearly detected, by identifying who carries the interest that the law is furthering. Finally, the priority column establishes the dominance relationships between NPs. For example, an exception like the one in the first sentence ("A CE may not [...] except [...]") has been mapped into a dominance of every other proposition of §164.502 over NP1. Fig. 2 depicts a diagram of §164.314 and §164.502. The diagram is a graphical representation of the NPs listed in Table 1.

3 A Process for Generating Law-Compliant Requirements

Reasoning about goals allows to produce requirements that match the needs of the stakeholders [18,20]. However, goals are the expression of the actors intentionality, so their alignment with legal prescriptions has to be argued. The meta-model of Fig. 1 provides a bridge between intentional concepts, such as goal, and legal concept, such as right. Here we show how to generate law-compliant requirements by means of conceptual modelling. Specifically, we assume to have an initial model of the stakeholders goals and a model of the law.

For example, we depict a scenario in which a US hospital has its own internal reservation system, consisting in the employee personnel answering phone calls and scheduling doctors appointments on an agenda. The hospital wants now to set up a new information system - to manage the reservations, quickly retrieve the availability of rooms and devices in the hospitals, and ultimately optimise the reservation according to the needs of the patients and doctors - and to reduce expenses the hospital wants to outsource the

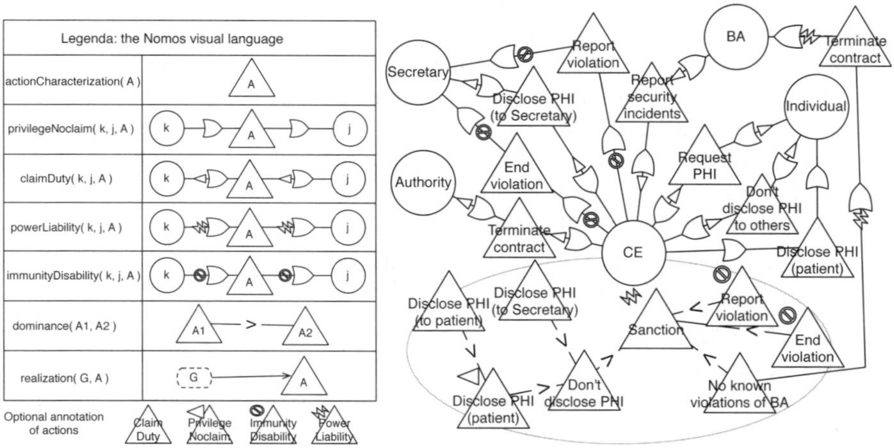

Fig. 2. The Nomos modelling languages: visual representation of §164.314 and §164.502

call center activity to a specialised company. Since the reservation system is intended to deal also with the patients PHI, system requirements have to be carefully analysed to be made compliant with the HIPAA law described in previous section.

In this context, to generate law-compliant requirements the analyst has to answer to four types of questions:

- Which are the actors addressed by laws? And by which laws? Reconciling the stakeholders identified in the domain with the subjects addressed by law is necessary to acquire knowledge on what normative propositions actually address stakeholders.

- What does the law actually prescribes? Are there alternative possibilities to comply with a given prescription?

- How is it possible to allow actors to achieve their own goals while ensuring compliance with the law?

- How is it possible to maintain the compliance condition through the responsibility delegations that generally occur in an organisational structure?

We answer to these questions in a series of steps that form a modelling process. Starting from an initial requirements model (R) and a model of law (L) (and the proper domain assumptions, D), the process allows to generate a new requirements set, such that $R, D \models L$. The output of the process for our running example is depicted in Fig. 3. In the following, we will detail the modelling process that produces that output, describing the *why* and *how* of each step of the process, and its results.

Step 1. Bind domain stakeholders with subjects addressed by law

Why. In the Nomos meta-model of Fig. 1, actors represent the binding element between laws and goals, but during modelling this binding can't be automatically deduced. Actors wanting goals are extracted from the domain analysis, while actors addressed by laws are extracted from legal documents. The different sources of information, as well as the different scope and interests covered, raises the need to know who is actually addressed by which law.

How. The binding is operated by the analyst, possibly comparing how actors are named in the law, with respect to how they are named in the domain analysis - or, if law identifies the addressee by recalling the most notable (intentional) elements of its behaviour, then those elements are compared with the elements of the stakeholders actors behaviour. When a domain actor is recognised to be a law subject, the corresponding rights are assigned to the actor. Actors that are not part of the domain, but that interact with other domain actors have to be added to the requirements model. Otherwise, law subjects can be excluded from the requirements model.

Result. The result of this step is a model of rights as in Fig. 2, in which actual domain stakeholders replace law subjects.

Example. The Hospital under analysis in our domain is an entity covered by the law (CE). The Patient is the actor referred to as the Individual in the law. And the Call Center in this scenario is a business associate (BA) of the covered entity. Some actors, such as the Secretary and what has been called the Authority were not introduced in the domain characterisation, but have legal relations with other actors. Finally, some actors, such as the Doctor and the Data Monitor are not mentioned in the legal documents taken into consideration.

Step 2. Identify legal alternatives

Why. Dominance relations establish a partial order between NPs such that not every NP has actually to be fulfilled. For example, a law $L = \{NP_a, NP_b, NP_c\}$, with $NP_b > NP_a$. This means that NP_b *dominates* NP_a: as long as NP_b holds, NP_a does not, and it is quite common in law. Let suppose that NP_a says that it is mandatory to pay taxes, and NP_b says that it is possible to use the same amount of money, due for taxes, to make investments. $NP_b > NP_a$ means that, if a company makes an investment, then it does not have to pay taxes for the same amount. Now, with the given NPs and dominance relations, companies have two alternatives: $L_1 = \{NP_a, NP_c\}$, and $L_2 = \{NP_b, NP_c\}$. We call these alternative prescriptions *legal alternatives*. As long as many alternative prescriptions exist, the need arises for selecting the most appropriate one. Legal alternatives can be different for a large number of NPs, which can change, appear or disappear in a given legal alternative, together with their dominance relationships, so that the overall topology of the prescription also changes. This causes the risk that the space of alternatives grows too much to be tractable, so the ultimate problem is how to cut it.

How. To solve this problem, we introduce a decision making function that determines pre-emptively whether a certain legal alternative is acceptable in terms of domain assumptions, or if it has to be discarded. The decision making function is applied by the analyst whenever a legal alternative is detected, to accept or discard it. We define four basic decision making function (but hybrid or custom functions can be defined as well):

a) Precaution-oriented decision maker. It wants to avoid every sanction, and therefore tries to realise every duty. Immunities are also realised to avoid sanctions to occur.

b) Opportunistic decision maker. Every alternative is acceptable - including those that involve law violation - if it is convenient in a cost-benefit analysis with respect to the decision maker's goals. In a well-known example of this function, a company has decided to distribute its web browser application, regardless of governmental fines that have been applied, because the cost of changing distribution policy has been evaluated higher than the payment of the fine.

c) Risk prone decision maker. Sanctions are avoided by realising the necessary duties, but ad-hoc assumptions are made that the realised duties are effective and no immunities are needed. This is mostly the case in small companies that do not have enough resources to achieve high levels of compliance.

d) Highly conform decision maker. This is the case in which legal prescriptions are taken into consideration also if not necessary. For example, car makers may want to adhere to pollution-emission laws that will only be mandatory years in the future.

Result. The result of this step is a set of NPs, subset of L, together with their dominance relationships, which represent a model of the legal prescription that the addressed subject actually wants to comply with.

Example. Dominance relations of Table 1 define the possible legal alternatives. NP1 (Don't disclose PHI) is mandatory to avoid the sanction. NP5, No known violations, is also mandatory; however, law recognises that the CE has no control over the BA's behaviour and admits that the CE can be not able to respect this NP. To avoid being sanctioned, in case of violation the CE can perform some actions, End the violation (NP6) or Terminate the contract (NP7). So ultimately, NP6 and NP7 are alternative to NP5. In Fig. 3, the hospital adopts a risk-prone strategy. According to the law model, if a BA of the hospital is violating the law and the hospital is aware of this fact, the hospital itself becomes not compliant. It is however immune from legal prosecution if it takes some actions, such as reporting the violation to the secretary (NP Report violation). However, in the diagram the hospital does not develop any mechanism to face this possibility. Rather, it prefers to believe that the BA will never violate the law (or that the violation will never be known).

Step 3. Select the normative proposition to realise

Why. Another source of variability in law compliance consists in the *applicability conditions* that often exist in legal texts. The *applicability* of a certain NP could depend on many factors, both objective and subjective - such as time, happening of certain events, the decision of a certain actor and so on. For example, an actor may have a duty but only within a fixed period of time or only when a certain event occurs. So the problem arises, of which NP has actually to be realised.

How. Trying to exhaustively capture all the applicability conditions is hard and possibly useless for purposes of requirements elicitation. So, instead of trying to describe applicability in an absolute way (i.e., specify exactly when a NP is applicable), we describe it in *relative* terms: i.e., we describe that *if* an existing NP is actually applicable, then another NP is not applicable. More specifically, we use dominance relation between two NPs, $NP1$ and $NP2$, and write $NP1 > NP2$ to say that, whenever $NP1$ holds (is applicable), then $NP2$ does not hold.

Result. This step returns the bottom-most NP that has to be realised. I.e., if $NP1$ is still not realised, and $NP2$ is already realised, then $NP1 > NP2$ and $NP1$ is returned. If no other NP exist, it returns nothing.

Example. $NP1$ says that *"the CE may not disclose patient's PHI"*, and $NP3$ states that *"A covered entity is required to disclose patient's PHI when required by the*

Secretary" - in this case, $NP1$ and $NP3$ are somehow contraddicting each other, since $NP1$ imposes the non-disclosure, while $NP3$ imposes a disclosure of the PHI. But the dominance relation between $NP3$ and $NP1$ states that, whenever both $NP3$ and $NP1$ - i.e., when the Secretary has required the disclosure, then the dominant NP prevails on the dominated one.

Step 4. Identify potential realisations of normative propositions

Why. Normative propositions specify to addressed subjects actions to be done (*behavioural actions*, according to the terminology used in [13]), or results to be achieved (*productive actions*). As they are specified in legal texts, actions recall goals (or tasks, or other intentional concepts); however, actions and goals differ as (i) goals are *wanted by* actors, whereas actions are *specified to* actors and can be in contrast with their goals; and (ii) goals are *local* to a certain actor - i.e., they exist only if the actor has the *ability* to fulfil them - while actions are *global*, referring to a whole class of actors; for example, law may address health care organisations, regardless whether they are commercial or no-profit, but when compliance is established, the actual nature of the complying actor gains importance; for the same reason, actions are an *abstract* characterisation of a whole set of potential actions as conceived by the legislator. It becomes so necessary to switch form the point of view of the legislator to the point to view of the actor.

How. Given a normative proposition NP that specifies an action A_{NP}, a goal G is searched for the addressed actor, such that: (i) it is *acceptable* by the actor, with respect to its other goals and preferences; (ii) the actor is known to have, or expected to have, the ability to fulfil the goal; and (iii) there is at least one behaviour that the actor can perform to achieve the goal, which makes NP fulfilled. In the ideal case, every behaviour that achieves G also fulfils NP; we write in this case $G \subseteq NP$. Otherwise, G is decomposed to further restrict the range of behaviours, until the above condition is ensured. If it is not possible to exclude that $G \nsubseteq NP$, then G is considered *risky* and the next step (Identify legal risks) is performed.

Result. If found, G (also if it is risky) is put in realisation relation with NP and becomes the top *compliance goal* for NP.

Example. One of the assumptions made for building the diagram of Fig. 3 is that the requirements analysis concerns only the treatment of electronic data. As such, from the point of view of the hospital the non-disclosure duty (NP Don't disclose PHI) is fulfilled if the PHI is not disclosed *electronically*. In the diagram, for the hospital a well-designed set of policies for accessing electronic data (goal policy-based data access) is enough to have the duty realised. This may be true, or may be too simple-minded, or may need further refinement of the goal. This is part of the modelling activity.

Step 5. Identify legal risks

Why. At organisational level, risks have a negative impact on the capability of the organisation to achieve its goals. Using *i** , risks can be treated with risk management techniques that allow to minimise them [4]. For organisations, law is also a source of a particular type of risk, or *legal risk*, which "includes, but is not limited to, exposure to fines, penalties, or punitive damages resulting from supervisory actions, as well as private settlements"[3] Legal risk comes from the fact that compliance decisions may be wrong, incomplete or inaccurate. In our framework, the "realisation" relation that establishes the link between a NP and a goal can't prevent legal risks to arise: for example, a wrong interpretation of a law fragment may lead to a bad definition of the compliance goal. Legal risk can't be completely eliminated. However, the corresponding risk can be made explicit for further treatment.

How. Specifically, when a goal is defined as the realisation of a certain NP, a search is made in the abilities of the actor, with the purpose of finding other intentional elements of its behaviour that can generate a risk. Given a certain risk threshold ϵ, if the subjective evaluation of the generated risk is greater than ϵ, then the risky element has to be modelled.

Result. If some of the requirements may interfere with the compliance goals, then the requirements set is changed accordingly and the new set is returned. If no risky goals have been identified, the requirements set is not changed.

Example. In Fig. 3, we have depicted the need for the hospital to have a hard copy of certain data: it's the goal Print data (assigned to the hospital for sake of compactness). If doctors achieve this goal to print patients PHI, this may prevent the use of a policy-based data access to succeed in the non-disclosure of PHI. This is represented as a negative contribution between Print data and Policy-based data access. To solve this problem, a new goal is added: Prevent PHI data printing, which can limit the danger of data printing. (Notice that here we don't further investigate how PHI printing prevention can actually be achieved.)

Step 6. Identify proof artefacts

Why. During the requirements analysis we aim at providing evidence of *intentional compliance*, which is the assignment of responsibilities to actor such that, if the actor fulfil their goal, then compliance is achieved. *Actual* compliance will be achieved only by the running system. However, in a stronger meaning, compliance can be established only *ex-post* by the judge, and at run-time this will be possible only by providing those documents that will prove the compliance.

How. After a compliance goal is identified, it can be refined into sub-goals. The criterion for deciding the decomposition consists in the capability to identify a proof resource. If a resource can be identified, then such a resource is added to the model; otherwise, the goal is decomposed. The refinement process ends when a proof resource can be identified for every leaf goal of the decomposition tree.

Result. The result of this step is a set of resources that, at run-time, will be able to prove the achievement of certain goals or the execution of certain tasks.

Example. In Fig. 3, the NP Don't disclose PHI is realised by the goal Policy-based data access, which can be proved to keep the PHI not disclosed by means of two resources: the Users DB and the Transactions report.

Step 7. Constrain delegation of goals to other actors

Why. To achieve goals that are otherwise not in their capabilities, or to achieve them in a better way, actors typically delegate to each other goals and tasks. When an actor

[3] Basel Committee on Banking Supervision 2006, footnote 97.

delegates a strategic goal, a weakness arises, which consists in the possibility that the delegatee does not fulfil the delegated goal. If the delegated goal is intended to realise a legal prescription, this weakness becomes critical, because it can generate a non-compliance situation. As such, law is often the source of the security requisites that a certain requirements model has to meet.

How. Specifically, three cases exist for delegation:

1. Compliance goals. Goals that are the realisation of a NP, or belong to the decomposition tree of another goal that in turn is the realisation of a NP, can be delegated to other actors only under specific authorisation.
2. Proof resources. We have highlighted how the identification of proof resources is important for compliance purposes. The usage of proof resources by other actors must then be permitted by the resource owner.
3. Strategic-only goals. Goals that have no impact on the realisation of NPs, can be safely delegated to other actors without need to authorise it.

Result. The result of this activity is a network of delegations and permissions that maintain the legal prescriptions across the dependencies chains.

Example. In Fig. 3, the hospital delegates to the doctors the PHI disclosure to the patients. However, the hospital is the subject responsible towards the patient to disclose its PHI. This means that a vulnerability exists, because if the doctor does not fulfil its goal then the hospital is not compliant. For this reason, using the security-enhanced $i*$ primitives offered by SecureTropos, in the model we have to reinforce the delegation by specifying the trust conditions between the hospital and the doctor (refer to [9] for a deeper analysis on trust, delegation and permission).

4 Results and Discussion

The described process results in a new requirements set, R', represented in Fig. 3 as an extended $i*$ model (i.e., the $i*$ primitives are interleaved with the Nomos and SecureTropos ones), which presents some properties described in the following.

Intentional compliance. The realisation relations show the goals that the actors have developed to be compliant with the law. As said in Section 2, these goals express the *intentional compliance* of the actor, which ultimately refers to the *choices* that are made during the requirements analysis phase. In our example, the hospital under analysis has developed 3 goals due to the legal prescriptions: Delegate doctors to disclose PHI to patients, Policy-based data access and Electronic clinical chart. Notice that the last one is optional and the hospital may choose a different alternative. Notice also that the compliance through the mentioned goals is a *belief* of the hospital, and we don't aim at providing formal evidence of the semantic correctness of this belief.

Strategic consistence. For arguing about compliance, we moved form an initial set of requirements, R. The compliance modelling algorithm basically performs a reconciliation of these requirements with legal prescriptions. The process steps described above implicitly state that, in case of conflicts between NPs and actors goals, compliance with NPs should prevail. However, if a compliance alternative is strategically not acceptable it is discarded. Therefore, if R' is found, then it is consistent with the initial requirements R.

Documentable compliance. If L' is a legal alternative for the law L chosen applying the decision making function, for all NP (addressing actor j) and for every leaf goal, there exists a set of resources, called proof resources, with cardinality ≥ 1. In the example, the intentional compliance achieved by the hospital is partially documentable through the resources Access log, Users DB and Transactions report. However, the prevention of data printing can't be documented according to the goal model, which should therefore be further refined.

Traceability. Speaking of law compliance it is important to maintain traceability between law's source and the choice made to be compliant. In case of a change in the law, in the requirements, or just for documentation purposes, it is necessary to preserve the information of where does a certain requirement come from. Having an *explicit* model of law, and having an *explicit* representation of the link between goals and NPs (the "realisation" relationship), full traceability is preserved when modelling requirements, also through refinement trees and delegation chains. For example, the delegation to the data monitor to Monitor data usage can be traced back to the decision of the hospital to Monitor electronic transactions, which in turn comes from the decision to maintain a Policy-based data access, which is the answer of the hospital to the law prescribing to keep patients PHI not disclosed.

Delegations trustworthiness. Delegations of compliance goals to other actors are secured by means of trust information plus the actual delegation to achieve goals. If this information is missing, then a security hole exists. In our example, the decision to delegate to the data monitor to Monitor data usage depends on a compliance decision (the goal Policy-based data access); if the data monitor fails in achieving its goal, then the compliance of the hospital can be compromised. So, delegating the monitoring to it causes a weakness in the compliance intentions of the hospital.

Legal risk safety. Having made explicit every goal that is intended to achieve compliance The requirements set R' contains a treatment for legal risks that arise from compliance decisions. In Fig. 3, the delegation to doctors to Disclose PHI to patients needs to be secured, since doctors are not addressed by a specific responsibility prevent the PHI disclosure, as the hospital is. Notice that delegations' trustworthiness is not addressed by our framework, and we rely on other approaches for this.

Altogether, these properties as well as the capability to *argue* about them, represents a prominent **advantage** of the framework. However, worth mentioning that our approach is not without **limitations**. Not every kind of normative prescriptions can be successfully elaborated with the Nomos framework. The more norms are technically detailed - such as standards or policies - the less our framework is useful, since technical regulations leave small margin to alternatives and discretion. Furthermore, it's important to stress the fact that the modelling framework and the process we propose is not fully automated; it needs the intervention of the analyst to perform some steps, under the assumption that performing those steps results a support for the analyst itself. More experience with its usage may possibly be converted in further refinement of the approach. Finally, complex aspects of legal sentences, such as time or exceptions, are not addressed by our framework, which ultimately focuses on alternatives exploration and selection through goals - notice that this lack could be a limitation, or an advantage, depending on the needs of the analyst.

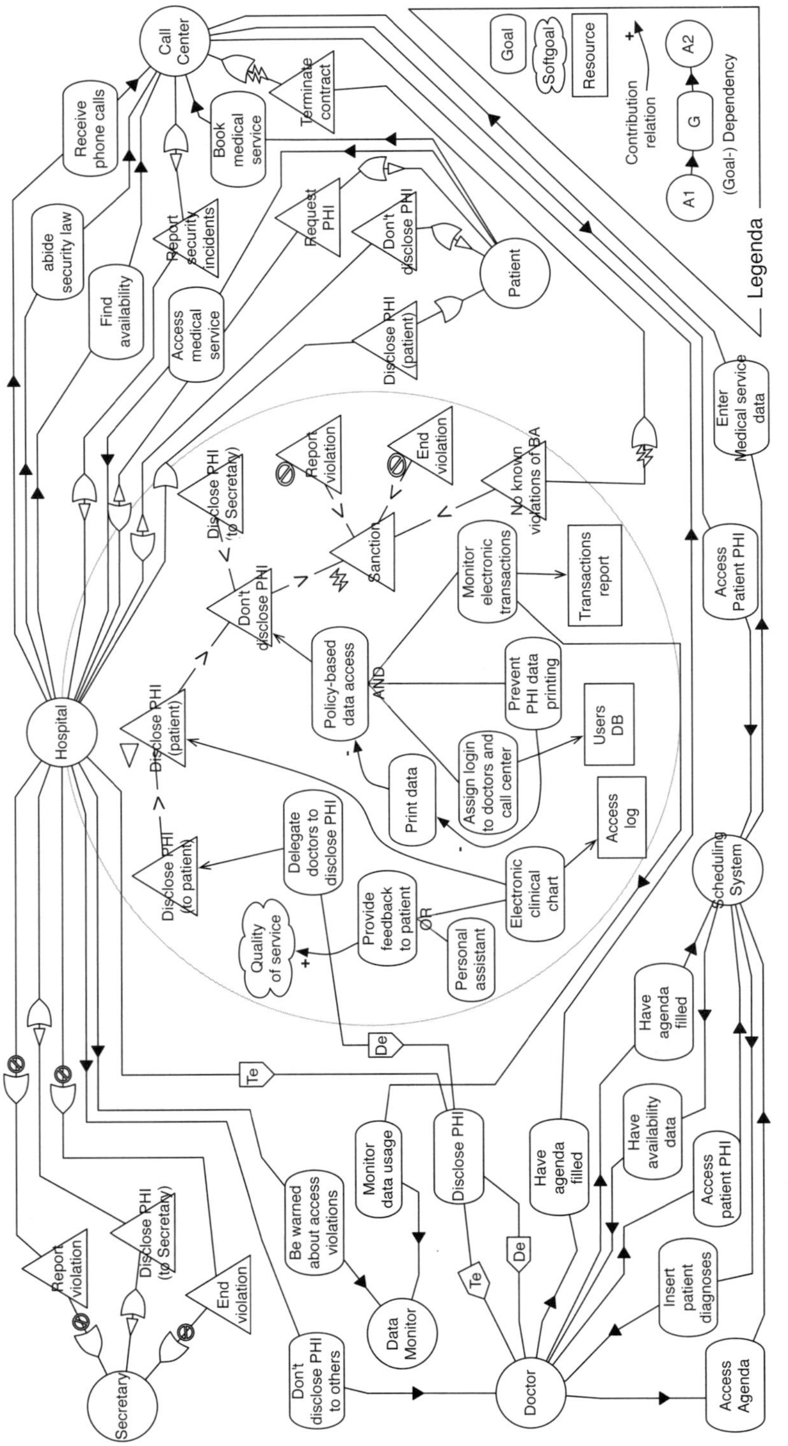

Fig. 3. A goal-oriented model of law-compliant requirements

5 Related Works

Anton and Breaux have developed a systematic process, called semantic parameterisation, which consists of identifying in legal text restricted natural language statements (RNLSs) and then expressing them as semantic models of rights and obligations [5] (along with auxiliary concepts such as actors and constraints). In [12], a somehow similar approach is presented, which however takes into consideration the separation between law and requirements sentences, with the purpose of comparing their semantics to check for compliance.

Secure Tropos [8] is a framework for security-related goal-oriented requirements modelling that, in order to ensure access control, uses strategic dependencies refined with concepts such as trust, delegation and permission, to fulfil a goal, execute a task or access a resource, as well as ownership of goals or other intentional elements. We use that framework to ensure that compliance decisions, once made, are not compromised through the delegation chains in an organisational setting. The main point of departure of our work is that we use a richer ontology for modelling legal concepts, adopted from the literature on law. Models based on the law ontology allow to reason about where and how do compliance properties of requirements are generated. Along similar lines, Darimont and Lemoine have used KAOS as a modelling language for representing objectives extracted from regulation texts [6]. Such an approach is based on the analogy between regulation documents and requirements documents. Ghanavati et al. [7] use GRL to model goals and actions prescribed by laws. This work is founded on the premise that the same modelling framework can be used for both regulations and requirements. Likewise, Rifaut and Dubois use *i** to produce a goal model of the Basel II regulation [11]. Worth mentioning that the authors have also experimented this goal-only approach in the Normative *i** framework [14]. That experience focussed on the emergence of implicit knowledge, but the ability to argue about compliance was completely missing, as well as the ability to explore alternative ways to be compliant.

6 Conclusion

In this paper we addressed the problem of generating a set of law-compliant requirements for a new system, starting from a model of the laws under consideration and a model of stakeholders' original goals. A systematic process has been defined, which consists of specific analysis steps that may be performed iteratively. Each step has been illustrated along a running example. Moreover, relevant properties of the resulting requirements model have been discussed. This research is part of the Nomos framework, whose conceptualisation has been previously introduced in [16]. Further work is ongoing including a formalisation of the compliance condition and evaluation of the Nomos framework on larger case studies.

References

1. Medical privacy - national standards to protect the privacy of personal health information. Office for Civil Rights, US Department of Health and Human Services (2000)

2. Online news published in dmreview.com, November 15 (2004)
3. Anton, A.I., Otto, P.N.: Addressing legal requirements in requirements engineering. In: IEEE Requirements Engineering Conference, RE 2007 (2007)
4. Asnar, Y., Giorgini, P.: Modelling risk and identifying countermeasure in organizations. In: López, J. (ed.) CRITIS 2006. LNCS, vol. 4347, pp. 55–66. Springer, Heidelberg (2006)
5. Travis, D., Breaux, M.W.: Vail, and Annie I. Anton. Towards regulatory compliance: Extracting rights and obligations to align requirements with regulations. In: 14th IEEE Requirements Engineering Conference (RE 2006), Washington, DC, USA, September 2006, pp. 49–58. IEEE Computer Society Press, Los Alamitos (2006)
6. Robert Darimont and Michel Lemoine. Goal-oriented analysis of regulations. In Régine Laleau and Michel Lemoine, editors, *ReMo2V, held at CAiSE'06*, volume 241 of *CEUR Workshop Proceedings*. CEUR-WS.org, 2006.
7. Ghanavati, S., Amyot, D., Peyton, L.: Towards a framework for tracking legal compliance in healthcare. In: Krogstie, J., Opdahl, A.L., Sindre, G. (eds.) CAiSE 2007 and WES 2007. LNCS, vol. 4495, pp. 218–232. Springer, Heidelberg (2007)
8. Giorgini, P., Massacci, F., Mylopoulos, J., Zannone, N.: Requirements engineering meets trust management. In: Jensen, C., Poslad, S., Dimitrakos, T. (eds.) iTrust 2004, vol. 2995, pp. 176–190. Springer, Heidelberg (2004)
9. Giorgini, P., Massacci, F., Mylopoulos, J., Zannone, N.: Modeling security requirements through ownership, permission and delegation. In: IEEE Requirements Engineering Conference (RE 2005), pp. 167–176. IEEE Computer Society, Los Alamitos (2005)
10. Hohfeld, W.N.: Fundamental Legal Conceptions as Applied in Judicial Reasoning. Yale Law Journal 23(1) (1913)
11. Rifaut, A., Dubois, E.: Using goal-oriented requirements engineering for improving the quality of iso/iec 15504 based compliance assessment frameworks. In: RE '08: Proceedings of the 2008 16th IEEE International Requirements Engineering Conference, pp. 33–42. IEEE Computer Society Press, Los Alamitos (2008)
12. Saeki, M., Kaiya, H.: Supporting the elicitation of requirements compliant with regulations. In: Bellahsène, Z., Léonard, M. (eds.) CAiSE 2008. LNCS, vol. 5074, pp. 228–242. Springer, Heidelberg (2008)
13. Sartor, G.: Giovanni Sartor. Fundamental legal concepts: A formal and teleological characterisation. Artificial Intelligence and Law 14(1-2), 101–142 (2006)
14. Siena, A., Maiden, N.A.M., Lockerbie, J., Karlsen, K., Perini, A., Susi, A.: Exploring the effectiveness of normative *i** modelling: Results from a case study on food chain traceability. In: Bellahsène, Z., Léonard, M. (eds.) CAiSE 2008. LNCS, vol. 5074, pp. 182–196. Springer, Heidelberg (2008)
15. Siena, A., Mylopoulos, J., Perini, A., Susi, A.: From laws to requirements. In: 1st International Workshop on Requirements Engineering and Law Relaw (2008)
16. Siena, A., Mylopoulos, J., Perini, A., Susi, A.: The Nomos framework: Modelling requirements compliant with laws. Technical Report TR-0209-SMSP, FBK - Irst (2009), `http://disi.unitn.it/asiena/files/TR-0209-SMSP.pdf`
17. Susi, A., Perini, A., Mylopoulos, J., Giorgini, P.: The Tropos metamodel and its use. Informatica (Slovenia) 29(4), 401–408 (2005)
18. van Lamsweerde, A., Letier, E.: Handling obstacles in goal-oriented requirements engineering. IEEE Transactions on Software Engineering 26(10), 978–1005 (2000)
19. Yu, E.S.-K.: Modelling strategic relationships for process reengineering. PhD thesis, University of Toronto, Toronto, Ontario, Canada (1996)
20. Zave, P., Jackson, M.: Four dark corners of requirements engineering. ACM Transactions on Software Engineering and Methodology (TOSEM) 6(1), 1–30 (1997)

A Knowledge-Based and Model-Driven Requirements Engineering Approach to Conceptual Satellite Design

Walter A. Dos Santos, Bruno B.F. Leonor, and Stephan Stephany

INPE - National Space Research Institute, São José dos Campos, Brazil
walter@dss.inpe.br, brunobfl@yahoo.com.br, stephan@lac.inpe.br

Abstract. Satellite systems are becoming even more complex, making technical issues a significant cost driver. The increasing complexity of these systems makes requirements engineering activities both more important and difficult. Additionally, today's competitive pressures and other market forces drive manufacturing companies to improve the efficiency with which they design and manufacture space products and systems. This imposes a heavy burden on systems-of-systems engineering skills and particularly on requirements engineering which is an important phase in a system's life cycle. When this is poorly performed, various problems may occur, such as failures, cost overruns and delays. One solution is to underpin the preliminary conceptual satellite design with computer-based information reuse and integration to deal with the interdisciplinary nature of this problem domain. This can be attained by taking a model-driven engineering approach (MDE), in which models are the main artifacts during system development. MDE is an emergent approach that tries to address system complexity by the intense use of models. This work outlines the use of SysML (Systems Modeling Language) and a novel knowledge-based software tool, named SatBudgets, to deal with these and other challenges confronted during the conceptual phase of a university satellite system, called ITASAT, currently being developed by INPE and some Brazilian universities.

1 Introduction

Space systems are complex systems designed to perform specific functions for a specified design life. Satellite projects, for instance, demand lots of resources, from human to financial, as well accounting for the impact they play on society. This requires good planning in order to minimize errors and not jeopardize the whole mission.

Therefore satellite conceptual design plays a key role in the space project lifecycle as it caters for specification, analysis, design and verification of systems without actually having a single satellite built. Conceptual design maps client needs to product use functions and is where functional architecture (and sometimes the physical architecture) is decided upon.

A.H.F. Laender et al. (Eds.): ER 2009, LNCS 5829, pp. 487–500, 2009.

Moreover, the lack of a clear vision of the satellite architecture hinders team understanding and communication, which in turn often increases the risk of integration issues. Hence, the conceptual satellite design phase demands efficient support.

Some past approaches to model-driven requirements engineering and related issues have been reported in the literature [10] [3] [14] [15] [16] [1].

This work innovates by employing SysML as a satellite architecture description language, enabling information reuse between different satellite projects as well as it facilitates knowledge integration and management over systems engineering activities. One of them is requirements engineering, more specifically requirements management and tracebility. This is an important phase in the life cycle of satellite systems. This work shows the main advantages of having user requirements being graphically modeled, their relationships explicitly mapped, and system decomposition considered in the early system development activities. In addition, requirements traceability is enhanced by using the SysML Requirements tables. The approach is illustrated by a list of user requirements for the ITASAT satellite.

Furthermore, in order to mitigate risks, this work also proposes a software tool, named SatBudgets that supports XML Metadata Interchange (XMI) information exchange between a satellite SysML model and its initial requirements budgetings via a rule-based knowledge database captured from satellite subsystems experts.

This work is organized as follows. Section 2 presents a short introduction to satellites, the ITASAT project and to SysML. Section 3 shows the SysML satellite modeling. Section 4 covers the SysML satellite requirements engineering. Section 5 introduces the SatBudgets software tool to illustrate information reuse and integration in this domain as well as describes further future work. Finally, Section 6 summarizes this research report.

2 Background

This section presents an overview of the ITASAT satellite and SysML which will be important for the paper context.

2.1 The ITASAT Satellite Project and Its Systems Rationale

A satellite has generally two main parts: (1) The bus or platform where the main supporting subsystems reside; and (2) The payload, the part that justifies the mission. A typical satellite bus has a series of supporting subsystems as depicted in Figure 1. The satellite system is built around a system bus also called the On-Board Data Handling (OBDH) bus.

The bus, or platform, is the basic frame of the satellite and the components which allow it to function in space, regardless of the satellite's mission. The control segment on the ground monitors and controls these components. The platform consists of the following components: (1) Structure of the satellite;

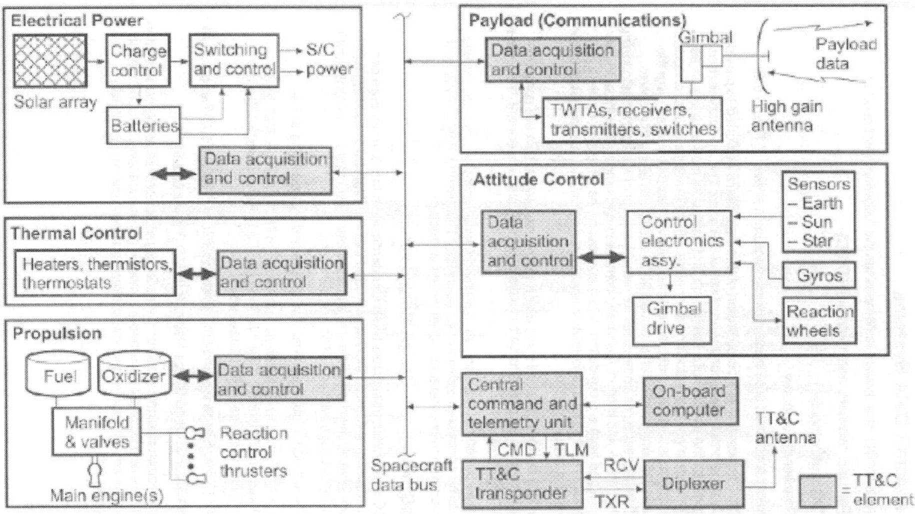

Fig. 1. Block diagram of a typical satellite [16]

(2) Power; (3) Propulsion; (4) Stabilization and Attitude Control; (5) Thermal Control; (6) Environmental Control; and (7) Telemetry, Tracking and Command.

The ITASAT satellite is part of the Small Technological Satellite Development Program funded by Brazilian Space Agency (AEB) with technical coordination of INPE and academic coordination of the Aeronautics Institute of Technology (ITA).

The ITASAT Mission entails the development, the launch and the operation of a small university satellite for use in a low Earth and low inclination orbit, capable of providing operational data collection services to the Brazilian Environmental Data Collection System (DCS), besides testing in orbit experimental payloads.

The general architecture of the ITASAT System is shown in the Figure 2 which includes: (a) The ITASAT satellite with the Data Collection System (DCS) and experimental payloads (space segment); (b) The existing Tracking, Telemetry and Command (TT&C) ground segment with Cuiabá and Alcântara tracking stations and (c) The existing Data Collection ground segment, including the Data Collection Platforms (DCP) networks.

The ITASAT satellite requires all bus functions mentioned earlier to its payloads but propulsion as no orbit maneuvers are foreseen. The Systems rationale for its detailed design follows a N-Tiered development and organization of requirements: (a) Level 0 (Mission Objective) - from which the requirements elicitation process is motivated; (b) Levels 1 and 2, are respectively focused on the definition of "science" and "high-level engineering" requirements; (c) Level 3 (Sub-system Requirements) - where engineering requirements are organized into groups (e.g., ground segment; communications segment; satellite segment)

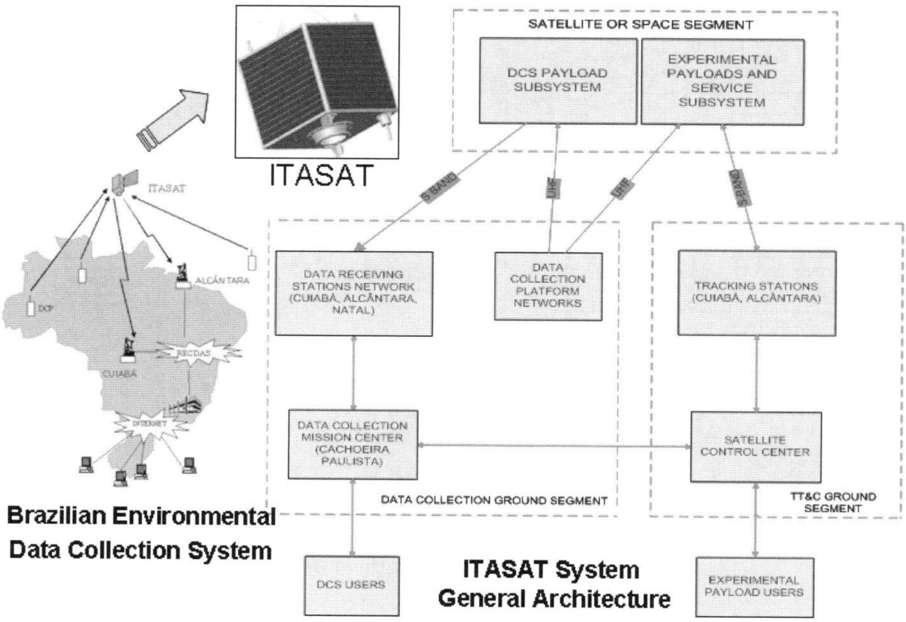

Fig. 2. ITASAT System general architecture [4]

suitable for team development; (d) Levels 4 and 5 requirements are targeted to a specific subsystem (e.g., its payloads on-board) or component (e.g., a printed circuit board) and so on.

This process generates the ITASAT Specification and Documentation Tree and also implicitly generates a highly coupled requirements tree, as depicted in Figure 3, which complicates somewhat systems engineering trade studies so far being manually performed.

For instance, on previous INPE satellite projects, the required electrical capacity for batteries is derived primarily from the power budgeting and orbital parameters of mission statement since batteries are used during eclipse times to provide power. Nevertheless, this is also coupled to others budgetings like mass, structure, etc. The lessons learned from these chained updates, due to coupling issues, justify *per se* an MDE approach to the conceptual design.

2.2 SysML as an Architecture Description Language

System modeling based on an architecture description language is a way to keep the engineering information within one information structure. Using an architecture description language is a good approach for the satellite systems engineering domain.

Architectures represent the elements implementing the functional aspect of their underlying products. The physical aspect is sometimes also represented,

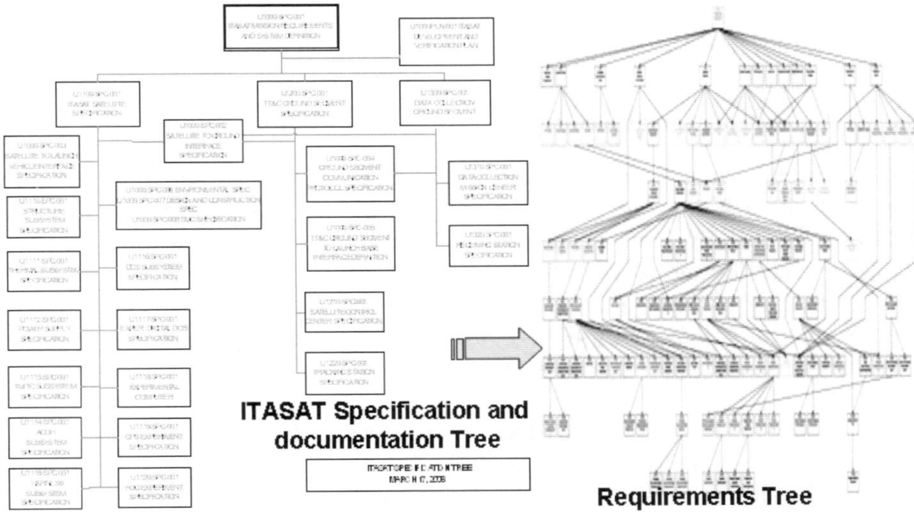

Fig. 3. Tree structure of ITASAT documents [4] and requirements coupling [1]

for instance when the architecture represents how the software is deployed on a set of computing resources, like a satellite.

SysML is a domain-specific modeling language for systems engineering and it supports the specification, analysis, design, verification and validation of various systems and systems-of-systems [17]. It was developed by the Object Management Group (OMG) [11] in cooperation with the International Council on Systems Engineering (INCOSE) [8] as a response to the request for proposal (RFP) issued by the OMG in March 2003. The language was developed as an extension to the actual standard for software engineering, the Unified Modeling Language (UML) [18] also developed within the OMG consortium.

Basically, SysML is used for representing system architectures and linking them with their behavioral components and functionalities. By using concepts like Requirements, Blocks, Flow Ports, Parametric Diagrams and Allocations, it is simple to achieve a profitable way to model systems [17].

This work explores some of the SysML capabilities through an example, the ITASAT student satellite system [4]. The application of SysML presented in this work covers only some the diagrams available in SysML due to paper scope and page restrictions.

3 Conceptual Satellite Design via SysML

Systems Engineering attacks the problem of design complexity of engineering products as it grows larger, more complex and are required to operate as part of a system.

The approach taken is formal and systematic since the great complexity requires this rigor. Another feature of systems engineering is its holistic view and it involves a top-down synthesis, development, and operation. This suggests the decomposition of the system into subsystems and further into components [5].

3.1 Motivation for the Satellite SysML Modeling

Space Systems Engineering is a subclass of the previous mentioned in the sense that it is primarily concerned with space systems, e.g. satellite systems. Therefore it deals with the development of systems, including hardware, software, man-in-the-loop, facilities and services for space applications.

The satellite conceptual stage follows the transformation of customer needs into product functions and use cases, and precedes the design of these functions across the space engineering disciplines (for example, mechanical, electrical, software, etc.).

Model-Driven Engineering (MDE) is the systematic use of models as primary engineering artifacts throughout the engineering lifecycle [14]. MDE can be applied to software, system, and data engineering. MDE technologies, with a greater focus on architecture and corresponding automation, yield higher levels of abstraction product development. This abstraction promotes simpler models with a greater focus on the problem space. Combined with executable semantics this elevates the total level of automation possible.

3.2 The SysML Modeling Approach

SysML allows incrementally detailed description of conceptual satellite design and product architecture. This helps systems engineers which are concerned with the overall performance of a system for multiple objectives (e.g. mass, cost, and power). The systems engineering process methodically balances the needs and capabilities of the various subsystems in order to improve the systems performance, deliver on schedule and on expected cost.

SysML elements in the design represent abstractions of artifacts in the various engineering disciplines involved in the development of the system. The design represents how these artifacts collaborate to provide the product functionalities. The size, volume, and mass constraints often encountered in satellite development programs, combined with increasing demands from customers to get more capability into a given size, make systems engineering methods particularly important for this domain.

This paper explores some of the diagrams available in SysML through the example of the ITASAT satellite system by basically, exploring the block diagram and top-level requirement diagram, both shown in short detail.

SysML diagrams allow information reuse since they can be employed in other similar satellite projects by adapting and dealing with project variabilities. An exploration of these features for the on-board software design of satellites is shown in [6].

SysML allows the utilization of use case diagrams which were inherited from the UML without changes [3]. The use case diagram has been widely applied to specify system requirements. The interaction between ITASAT actors and some

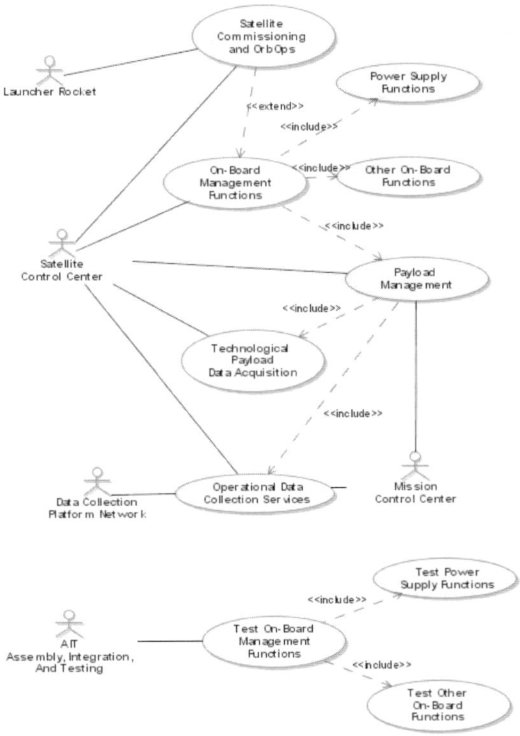

Fig. 4. ITASAT high-level use cases to specify system requirements

key use cases is shown in Figure 4. This diagram depicts five actors and how they relate to the use cases that they trigger in the high-level system view. The figure still describes schematically the composition of a series of low-level use cases hierarchically modeled by employing an ≪include≫ dependency relationship between them. SysML also allows the representation of test use cases which will be further explored in the validation, verification and testing project phases. Figure 4 depicts, as an example, the *Test On-Board Management Functions* use case and how its ≪include≫ dependencies are related to other two test use cases, *Test Other On-Board Functions* and, *Test Power Supply Functions.*

The SysML block diagram is used to show features and high-level relationships. It is used to allow systems engineer to separate basically the responsibilities of the hardware team from the software team. Figure 5 shows the various ITASAT blocks and their interdependencies.

The requirements diagram plays a key role into the SysML model as requirements present in this diagram can also appear in other SysML diagrams linking the problem and solution spaces. Furthermore, the requirements diagram notation provides a means to show the relationships among requirements including constraints. This topic is of high importance to this work hence it is further developed in the next section.

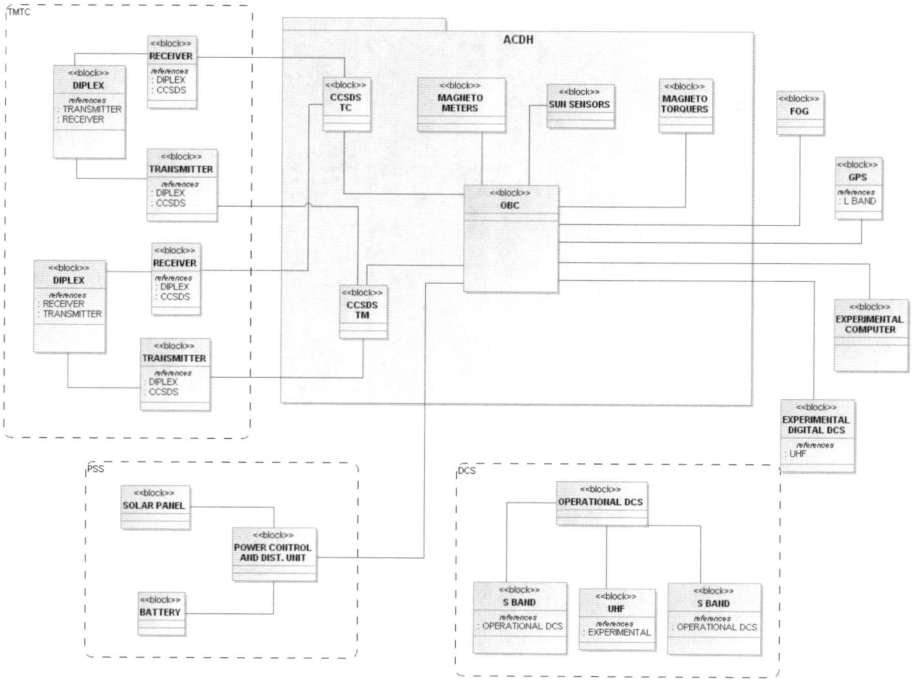

Fig. 5. The ITASAT satellite SysML block diagram

4 The Model-Driven Requirements Engineering Approach

The process of requirements engineering involves various key activities, such as elicitation, specification, prioritization and management of requirements. By using SysML, this section applies this to the satellite conceptual design.

The SysML standard identifies relationships that enable the modeler to relate requirements to other requirements as well as to other model elements [17]. Figure 6 shows a simplified view of the ITASAT requirement tree structure [4]. It also shows how a constraint is attached to a low-level requirement and how traceability may be established.

After top-level requirements are elicited, then starts the decomposition of every system requirement into progressively lower levels of design. This is done by defining the lower-level functions which determine how each function must be performed. Allocation assigns the functions and its associated performance requirements to a lower level design element. Decomposition and allocation starts at the system level, where requirements derive directly from the mission needs, and then proceeds through each segment, subsystem, and component design levels [9]. This process must also warrant closure at the next higher level meaning that satisfying lower-level requirements warrants performance at the next level. Additionally, it roundtrips all requirements tracing back to satisfying mission needs.

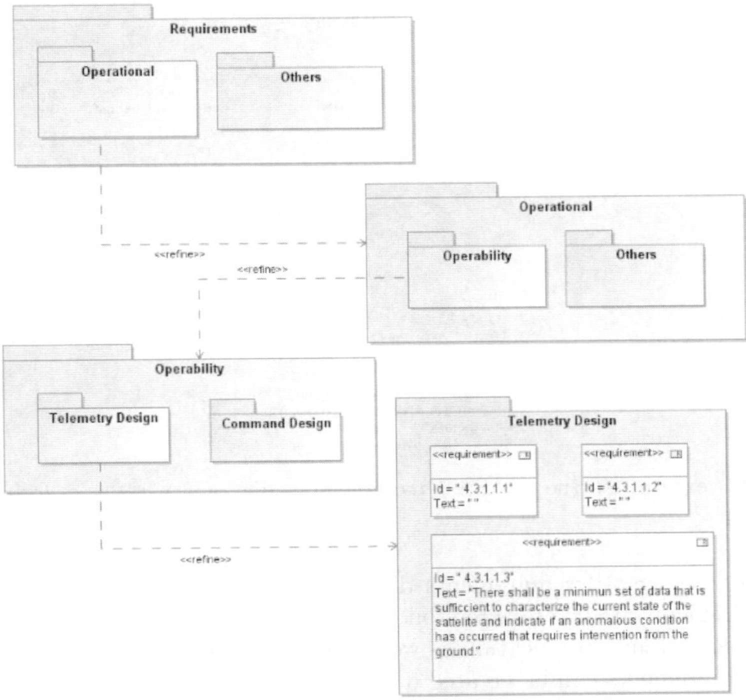

Fig. 6. Requirements tree structure for the ITASAT satellite

Managing requirements is the capability of tracing all system components to output artifacts that have been resulted from their requirement specifications (forward tracing) as well as the capability of identifying which requirement has generated a specific artifact or product (backward tracing) [13].

The great difficulty on tracing requirements is responding the following questions: *What to track?* and *How to track?*. One can say that a requirement is traceable when it is possible to identify *who has originated it, why it exists, which are the requirements related to it? how is it related to other project information.* These information is used to identify all requirement\elements affected by project changes. The specification of requirements can facilitate the communication between the various project stakeholder groups.

There are several published works on requirement engineering and the most common way they employ to requirement tracking is by posing basic questions about the underlying domain [2]. Unfortunately, such questionnaire does not offer generally any classification on the sufficient elements in order to identify all model elements.

By using a SysML requirements diagram, system requirements can be grouped, which contributes to enhance project organization showing explicitly the various relationship types between them [15]. These include relationships for defining requirements hierarchy or containment, deriving requirements, satisfying requirements, verifying requirements and refining requirements [12].

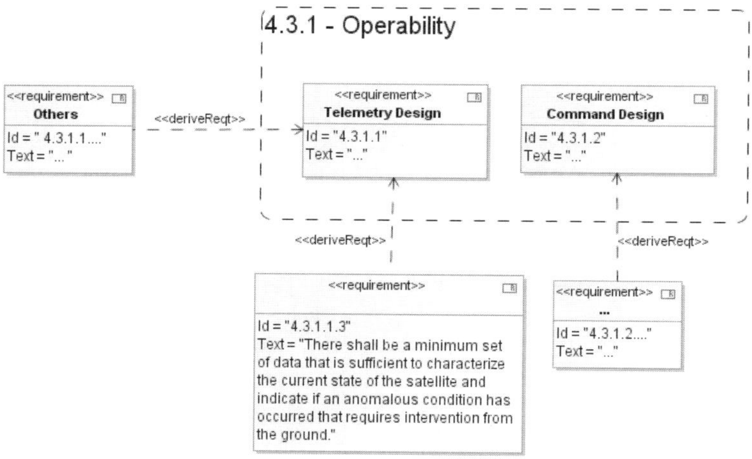

Fig. 7. An excerpt of the ITASAT requirements diagram with a ≪*deriveReqt*≫ relationship

Moreover, the SysML requirements diagram can be employed to standardize how requirements are documented following all their possible relationships. This can provide systems specification as well as be used for requirements modeling.

New requirements can be created during the requirement analysis phase and can be related to the existing requirements or complement the model. Figure 7 presents an excerpt from the ITASAT requirements diagram which utilizes the ≪deriveReqt≫ relationship type showing the derived *Satellite State* requirement from the source *Telemetry Design* requirement inside the Operability requirement SysML package. This allows, for example, a link between high-level (user oriented) and low-level (system oriented) requirements which contributes to explicitly relates the dependency of user requirements mapped into systems requirements.

Similarly, Figure 8 presents another excerpt from the ITASAT power subsystem requirements diagram which utilizes three relationships. Requirements are abstract classes with no operations neither attributes. Subrequirements are related to their "father" requirement by utilizing the ≪containment≫ relationship type. This is shown in Figure 8 as many subrequirements from the *Power Supply Requirements* requirement are connected employing ≪containment≫ relationships. The "father" requirement can be considered a package of embedded requirements.

Additionally, Figure 8 presents the ≪satisfy≫ relationship type which shows how a model satisfies one or more requirements. It represents a dependency relationship between a requirement and a model element, in this case the *Power Supply Functions* use case is satisfied by the *Power Supply Requirements*. Finally, it is shown the ≪verify≫ relationship type where the *Test Power Supply Functions* test use case is verified by the functionalities provided by the *Power Supply Requirements*. This may include standard verification methods for inspection, analysis, demonstration or test.

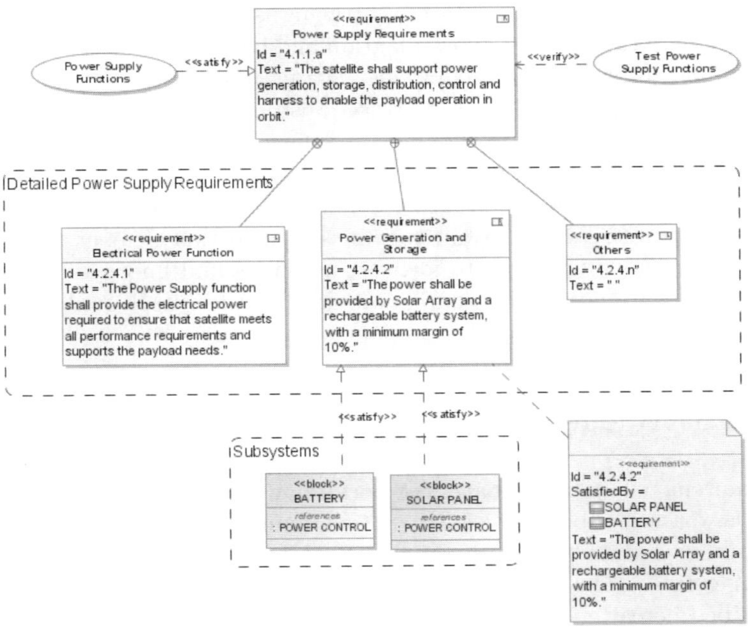

Fig. 8. An excerpt of the ITASAT power subsystem requirements diagram with containment, ≪*satisfy*≫ and, ≪*verify*≫ relationships

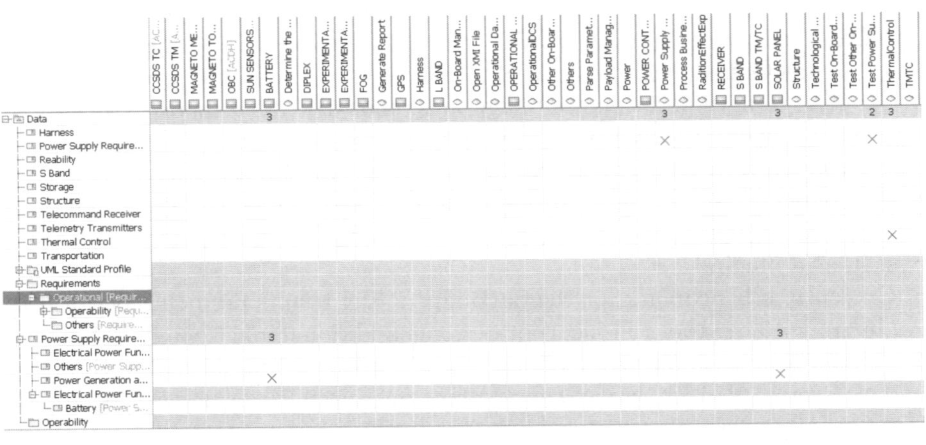

Fig. 9. The tabular matrix notation used to display power-related requirements and their relationships to other model elements

Lastly, SysML allows requirements traceability by using tabular notations. This allows model elements to be traced in SysML via requirements tables which may contain fields like: identifier (ID), name, which requirement is related to it, what type of relationship is held among them.

One such SysML tabular notation for requirements traceability is shown in Figure 9 which is suitable for cross-relating model elements. The figure shows a requirement matrix table where cross-tracing is done between requirements, blocks defined in the ITASAT block diagram and high-level use cases. This table is quite important as it allows requirements traceability.

Additionally, requirements can be traced also by navigating through SysML requirement diagrams on the anchors points shown in Figure 8 by means of stand-out notes. The anchors contain information like the relationship type and with which model element the requirement is related and vice-versa, given a model element it may reference all requirements related to this element. Doing so, it allows a quick and simple way to identify, prioritize and improve requirements traceability. Nevertheless, the resources provided by the SysML are by far beyond the capabilities here presented due to paper page constraint.

5 The SatBudgets Software Tool and Future Work

After requirements analysis, starts the performance budgeting phase. As a case study, this work describes how a software tool, named SatBudgets, supports XMI information exchange between a satellite SysML model and its initial requirements budgetings. The software engineering activities for the SatBudgets tool are described hereafter and employs some MDE concepts enabling information reuse and integration.

The workflow of information from the satellite SysML model to the SatBudgets tool is depicted in Figure 10 and its final report spreadsheet which is employed by systems engineers for iterative designs. The sequence of events is: (a) An XMI file exported from the SysML modeling is read; (b) Parsing of key modeling parameters is performed; (c) Satellite Systems Engineering business rules are applied to infer performance budgetings; and (d) A final report is generated for systems engineers via a free Java report generator framework.

The SatBudgets tool links a SysML satellite model to activities for performance budgetings. The tool currently runs as a stand-alone Java application but it will be aggregated as a Eclipe IDE plugin [7] which already supports SysML as a plugin.

Currently a benchmark for the SatBudgets tool results are being performed. An upgrade to the tool will incorporate some additional functionalities, namely: (1) Model Roundtripping - changes to the spreadsheet will affect SysML model and vice-versa; (2) Web Service support for some specialized rule-processings; (3) Provide Database and web client support; (4) Enhance the database repertoire for Satellite Systems Engineering business rules; (5) Provide an interface to SatBudgets for Eclipse IDE aggregation and (6) Provide an interface to SatBudgets for docking to an in-house Satellite Simulator.

A more complete ITASAT SysML modeling is also expected which may include: (1) Enhancing Block Diagram representation to model detailed subsystems and components, and ports describing their interfaces; (2) Checking dependencies (e.g. analytical) between structural properties expressed using constraints and represented using the parametric diagram; (3) Exploring features behavior modeling, namely interactions, state machine and activities and;

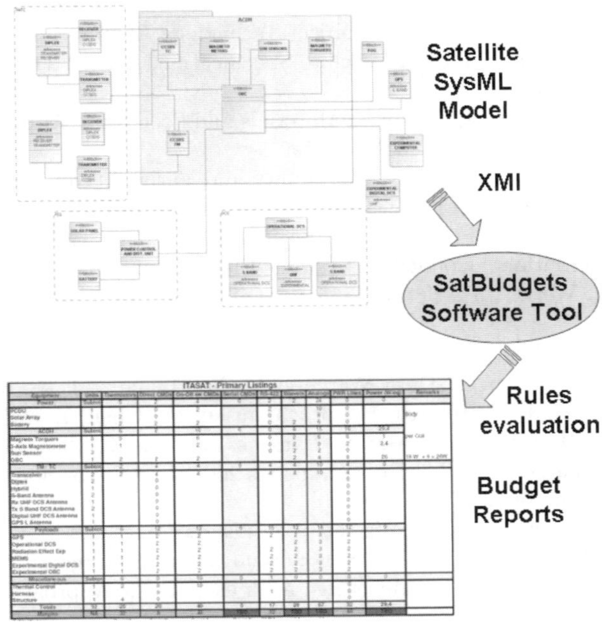

Fig. 10. Workflow for performance budgetings using the SatBudgets Tool

(4) Employing SysML for providing a mechanism to relate different aspects of the model and to enforce traceability across it.

6 Conclusions

Space systems requires strong systems engineering to deal with systems-of-systems complex issues, manufacturing demands and mitigate risks. A case study was presented in this work introducing the use of SysML satellite modeling for requirements engineering and a novel knowledge-based software tool, named SatBudgets to support preliminary conceptual satellite design which demands interdisciplinary skills. By employing SysML as a satellite architecture description language, it enables information reuse between different satellite projects as well as it facilitates knowledge integration and management on systems engineering activities. This work will be further extended to implement MDE automation concepts into the ordinary workflow of satellite systems engineering.

References

1. Austin, M.A., et al.: PaladinRM: Graph-Based Visualization of Requirements Organized for Team-Based Design. The Journal of the International Council on Systems Engineering 9(2), 129–145 (2006)
2. Aurum, A.W.: Engineering and Managing Software Requirements. Springer, Heidelberg (2005)

3. Balmelli, L.: An Overview of the Systems Modeling Language for Products and Systems Development. Journal of Object Technology (2007)
4. Carvalho, T.R., et al.: ITASAT Satellite Specification. INPE U1100-SPC-01 Internal Report (2008)
5. Dieter, G.E.: Engineering Design - a Materials and Processing Approach. McGraw-Hill International Edition, New York (1991)
6. Dos Santos, W.A.: Adaptability, Reusability and Variability on Software Systems for Space On-Board Computing. ITA Ph.D. Thesis (2008)
7. Eclipse, I.D.E.: Eclipse Foundation, `http://www.eclipse.org/`
8. INCOSE: International Council on Systems Engineering, `http://www.incose.org`
9. Larson, W.J., Wertz, J.R.: Space Mission Analysis and Design. McGraw-Hill, New York (2004)
10. Mazon, J.N., Pardillo, J., Trujillo, J.: A Model-Driven Goal-Oriented Requirement Engineering Approach for Data Warehouses. In: Hainaut, J.-L., Rundensteiner, E.A., Kirchberg, M., Bertolotto, M., Brochhausen, M., Chen, Y.-P.P., Cherfi, S.S.-S., Doerr, M., Han, H., Hartmann, S., Parsons, J., Poels, G., Rolland, C., Trujillo, J., Yu, E., Zimányie, E. (eds.) ER Workshops 2007. LNCS, vol. 4802, pp. 255–264. Springer, Heidelberg (2007)
11. OMG: Object Management Group, `http://www.omg.org`
12. SysML, O.M.G.: 1.0 Specification, `http://www.omgsysml.org/`
13. Pressman, R.S.: Software Engineering- a Practitioner's Approach McGraw-Hill (2007)
14. Schmidt, D.C.: Model-Driven Engineering. IEEE Computer (2006)
15. Soares, M., dos, S., Vrancken, J.: Model-Driven User Requirements Specification using SysML. Journal of Software (2008)
16. Souza, P.N.: CITS Lecture Notes. Slides - INPE (2002)
17. SysML: System Modeling Language, `http://www.sysml.org`
18. UML: Unified Modeling Language, `http://www.uml.org`

Virtual Business Operating Environment in the Cloud: Conceptual Architecture and Challenges

Hamid R. Motahari Nezhad, Bryan Stephenson, Sharad Singhal, and Malu Castellanos

Hewlett Packard Labs,
Palo Alto, CA, USA
{hamid.motahari,bryan.stephenson,sharad.singhal, malu.castellanos}@hp.com

Abstract. Advances in service oriented architecture (SOA) have brought us close to the once imaginary vision of establishing and running a virtual business, a business in which most or all of its business functions are outsourced to online services. Cloud computing offers a realization of SOA in which IT resources are offered as services that are more affordable, flexible and attractive to businesses. In this paper, we briefly study advances in cloud computing, and discuss the benefits of using cloud services for businesses and trade-offs that they have to consider. We then present 1) a layered architecture for the virtual business, and 2) a conceptual architecture for a virtual business operating environment. We discuss the opportunities and research challenges that are ahead of us in realizing the technical components of this conceptual architecture. We conclude by giving the outlook and impact of cloud services on both large and small businesses.

Keywords: Cloud Computing, Service Oriented Computing, Virtual Business.

1 Introduction

The idea of creating and running a business over the Internet is not new. Banks and large manufacturers are among the first in exploiting the electronic network capabilities to conduct business-to-business (B2B) interactions through technologies such as EDI [1]. With the introduction of the Web and the rapid increase of internet users in the early 1990s, companies such as Amazon and eBay were among the early entrants to the business-to-consumer (B2C) model of e-commerce. As the Internet is a fast, easy-to-use and cheap medium which attracts millions of users online at any time, today there are very few businesses that do not have a Web presence, and there are many small and medium businesses (SMBs) such as retail shops that solely offer their services and products online.

Looking at the enabling technologies, B2B and B2C e-commerce have benefited from many innovations in the Internet and Web. Moving from static content delivery to dynamic update of page content and the introduction of XML created the first evolution in the path to more efficient and interoperable running of electronic businesses.

A.H.F. Laender et al. (Eds.): ER 2009, LNCS 5829, pp. 501–514, 2009.

A main characteristic of using technologies of the Web 1.0 era is that almost all the backend IT systems are created, operated and maintained by the business owners. Motivated by business agility, operational efficiency, cost reduction and improved competitiveness, during the last decade, businesses have taken advantage of business process outsourcing (BPO) [2]. In BPO, businesses delegate some of the company's non-core business functionality such as IT operations to third-party external entities that specialize in those functions. It is estimated that by 2011 the world-wide market for BPO will reach $677 billion [3].

Up until recently, outsourced services were not necessarily fulfilled online. BPO has become attractive to both large and small businesses with the advent of service oriented computing [15] and specifically Web services and Web 2.0 [5] technologies. This has enabled offering of business process functions as online Web services and actively engaging customers via the Web [4]. It is estimated that BPO represents around 25% of the overall services market [3].

The next evolutionary wave in this space is cloud computing. Cloud computing refers to the offering of hardware and software resources as services across (distributed) IT resources [6]. As a relatively new concept, cloud computing and related technologies have rapidly gained momentum in the IT world. In this article, we study how advances in cloud computing impact the processes of creating and running businesses over the Internet. In particular, we investigate the question of whether the technology is ready to allow business owners to create and run a business using services over the Internet. We refer to this as a "virtual business" in which most or all of its functions are outsourced to online services. It should be contrasted to the concept of "virtual enterprise" [7] which often refers to creating a temporary alliance or consortium of companies to address certain needs with an emphasis on integration technologies, knowledge sharing, and distribution of responsibilities and capabilities.

In the following, in Section 2, we give a short survey of advances in cloud computing, and through an example scenario (Section 3), highlight trade-offs that businesses have to consider in moving to cloud services. Then, in Section 4 we discuss the requirements of an environment for creating and running virtual businesses, and present a conceptual architecture for such an environment. We study to what extent it can be realized and present challenges that are ahead of us in offering such an environment. We discuss the impact of cloud services on large and small businesses and present future outlook in Section 5.

2 Cloud Computing

Cloud computing has emerged as the natural evolution and integration of advances in several fields including utility computing, distributed computing, grid computing, web services, and service oriented architecture [6]. The value of cloud computing comes from packaging and offering resources in an economical, scalable and flexible manner that is affordable and attractive to IT customers. We introduce a framework to study advances in cloud computing. It consists of four dimensions: cloud services, public vs private clouds, cloud service customers, and multi-tenancy as an enabler.

2.1 Cloud Services

As promoted by the vision of "everything as a service" [8] many products are now offered as services under the umbrella of cloud computing. We summarize the main categories in the following.

Infrastructure as a service (IaaS): Hardware resources (such as storage) and computing power (CPU and memory) are offered as services to customers. This enables businesses to rent these resources rather than spending money to buy dedicated servers and networking equipment. Often customers are billed for their usage following a utility computing model, where usage of resources is metered. Examples are Amazon S3 for storage, EC2 for computing power, and SQS for network communication for small businesses and individuals. HP FCS (Flexible Computing Services) offers IaaS for enterprises.

IaaS providers can allocate more computing power and hardware resources to applications on an as-needed basis, and allow applications to scale in a horizontal fashion (several machines running the same application with load balancers distributing the workload). This enables flexibly scaling up or down the amount of required resources on-demand. Statistics show that 80% of computing power and 65% of storage capacity is not efficiently utilized, where a single company privately owns dedicated machines [9]. This is a valuable feature for companies with occasional large computation needs or sudden peaks in demand such as flash crowds.

Database as a service (DaaS): A more specialized type of storage is offering database as a service. Examples of such services are Amazon SimpleDB, Google BigTable, Force.com database platform and Microsoft SSDS. DaaS on the cloud often adopts a multi-tenant architecture, where the data of many users is kept in the same physical table. In most cases, the database structure is not relational. For instance, Microsoft SSDS adopts a hierarchical data model, and data items are stored as property-values or binary objects (Blobs). Google BigTable, Apache HBase and Apache Pig enable saving data in a key-value pair fashion. Each DaaS provider also supplies a query language to retrieve and manipulate data. However, not all support operations such as joins on tables (such as Apache HBase and Amazon SimpleDB).

Software as a service (SaaS): In this model, software applications are offered as services on the Internet rather than as software packages to be purchased by individual customers. There is no official software release cycle, and the customer is free from applying patches or updates as this is handled by the service provider. Customer data is kept in the cloud, potentially based on DaaS. An example is Salesforce.com offering its CRM application as a service. Other examples include Google web-based office applications (word processors, spreadsheets, etc.), Microsoft online CRM and SharePoint, or Adobe Photoshop and Adobe Premiere on the Web. Commercial applications in this category may need a monthly subscription per user (salesforce.com) or can be billed per use, both of which are considerably cheaper than owning and maintaining the software as an in-house solution.

Platform as a service (PaaS): This refers to providing facilities to support the entire application development lifecycle including design, implementation, debugging, testing, deployment, operation and support of rich Web applications and services on the Internet. Most often Internet browsers are used as the development environment. Examples of platforms in this category are Microsoft Azure Services platform,

Google App Engine, Salesforce.com Internet Application Development platform and Bungee Connect platform. PaaS enables SaaS users to develop add-ons, and also develop standalone Web-based applications, reuse other services and develop collaboratively in a team. However, vendor lock-in, limited platform interoperability and limitations of programming platforms in supporting some language features or capabilities are major concerns of using current platforms.

Integration as a service (IaaS2[1]): This is a special case of PaaS which provides facilities for software and service integration. It aims at enabling businesses of all sizes to integrate any combination of SaaS, cloud and on-premise applications without writing any code. Typically, providers offer a library of connectors, mappings and templates for many popular applications (ERP, SaaS, major databases, etc) and a drag and drop interface to configure mediator components and deploy them in the cloud or on-premise. The typical pricing model is subscription-based. Some well-known IaaS2 solutions are Boomi AtomSphere, Bungee Connect and Cast Iron Cloud. These solutions also allow users to develop new adapters or connectors.

There are other types of capabilities that are offered as services in the cloud. Management and monitoring as services are examples. In monitoring as a service, a third-party provider (e.g., Red Hat Command Center) observes SaaS applications or the IT network of an enterprise on behalf of a customer with respect to SLAs and reports performance metrics to the customer. Management as a service includes monitoring but adds responding to events rather than just reporting them.

Another important type of service that is offered on the cloud is people as services. Offering of services by people, e.g., their programming skills per hour on the net, is possibly as old as the Web itself. However, what is new in the cloud is there are people specializing in SaaS or PaaS platforms and offering consultation for businesses that need to use or customize SaaS solutions or integrate solutions from multiple SaaS providers. For example, Salesforce.com AppExchange opens up an opportunity for such people to offer their services.

2.2 Public vs. Private Clouds

It can be argued that the cloud is the result of natural transformation of the IT infrastructure of enterprises over the last decade. The traditional IT architecture was based on having dedicated resources for each business unit in an enterprise. This model leads to under-utilization and waste of IT resources due to resource fragmentation and unequal distribution of workload. To overcome this, enterprises have implemented adaptive infrastructure techniques [10]. These include employing virtualization to address the under-utilization problem complemented with automation techniques to reduce the significant labor costs of IT operations. This type of cloud is called a "private" cloud as it is privately owned by enterprises. Examples of this category are clouds maintained by manufacturers such as Boeing or GM.

On the other hand, there are other cloud offerings (e.g., those provided by Amazon, Google, Microsoft and Salesforce.com) for public use. Some of these clouds e.g., those offered by Amazon and Google, are indeed extensions of their private clouds

---

[1] We refer to it as IaaS2 to differentiate it from IaaS as of Infrastructure as a Service.

that are offered to the public. There are also cloud providers such as Salesforce.com that have created and offered cloud services solely for public use. It is interesting to notice that enterprises and large businesses are mainly the owners and users of private clouds, while public clouds are used by smaller businesses and millions of individual consumers.

In addition to cloud vendors, who own and operate cloud services, there are other providers called out-clouders (re-sellers). Out-clouders acquire and re-sell unused computing resources of enterprises with private clouds [11]. Out-clouding is also a source of income for enterprises who rent out part of their IT resources which they are not utilizing efficiently.

2.3 Cloud Service Customers

In addition to the coarse-grained categorization of cloud users as enterprises, SMBs and individual consumers, it is useful to identify and study various types of customers of cloud services. Understanding the target customers of cloud services and their requirements allows determining what type of services can be used by which customers. We categorize cloud customers as follows: IT administrators, software developers, managers and business owners, and finally individual (business) users. Table 1 shows the distribution of various cloud customers for various cloud services.

Table 1. Cloud Customers vs. Cloud Services

	IaaS	DaaS	SaaS	PaaS	Others
IT administrators	Use to deploy images of existing software	Configure store data	Usage Configuration	N/A	Monitoring as a Service (to setup and monitor SLAs)
Software developers	May use to deploy software	Store data	Mainly to browse and find existing services to reuse and extend	Main users of PaaS	Integration as a Service (IaaS2)
Managers and business owners	N/A	N/A	Occasional users to manage their business	N/A	Monitoring as a service (dashboards), May employ people as services
Business users	N/A	N/A	Main users of SaaS, may perform simple configuration tasks and use add-ons	N/A	

2.4 Multi-tenancy as an Enabler

Multi-tenancy refers to sharing resources among users and/or applications. It is preferred over single-tenancy in cloud services due to higher utilization leading to cost reduction. Enterprises often have thousands of users but typically operate a variety of software environments and applications. Thus in private clouds multi-tenancy is often about having multiple applications and environments deployed on shared resources. In contrast, public clouds have millions of users so service providers try to minimize the number of software applications and environments. Therefore, multi-tenancy is about sharing resources among users (e.g. keeping various users' data in the same table and secured). If public cloud providers offer PaaS, then a variety of application environments are also supported. In this case, multi-tenancy techniques need to enable sharing resources among volumes of applications and users.

3 CloudRetail as a Virtual Business

Exemplary scenario. As an example scenario, let us consider a small fictional company called CloudRetail, from the category of SMBs with a few hundred employees across the country. CloudRetail designs and sells fashionable and eco-friendly clothing and accessories. They use contract manufacturers but sell directly to their customers via their catalog and Website. Their core competency is eco-friendly product design quickly capitalizing on trends in the marketplace. CloudRetail runs software in-house for some functions, such as human resources, customer relationship management (CRM), and their customer-facing web site. They have an IT department which maintains the IT infrastructure inside the company. This IT infrastructure has grown more complex and expensive to maintain as it has grown with the company. It now includes dozens of servers, specialized storage and network equipment, and an ever-growing list of software, much of it to ensure smooth and secure operation of the company. CloudRetail observed they needed to invest heavily last year in website hardware and network bandwidth to be prepared for the rush of orders during the holiday shopping season. CloudRetail is considering options to reduce operational costs, enhance focus on their core competencies, and transfer all non-core business operations, e.g. support functions, to external companies.

Evolving CloudRetail into a virtual business using cloud services. CloudRetail can take advantage of many existing cloud services including CRM, HR, IT infrastructure and the hosting and operation of their website. Using cloud services provides the following benefits: (1) avoiding huge initial investments in hardware resources and software, (2) reducing ongoing operational, upgrade and maintenance costs, (3) scaling up and down hardware, network capacity and cost based on demand, (4) higher availability compared to in-house solutions for small businesses and individual-consumer maintained resources, and (5) access to a variety of software applications and features offered as SaaS that otherwise CloudRetail would have to purchase separately.

However, the potential risks of using cloud services include: (1) while CloudRetail feels relieved from not managing the resources, it will lose direct control of software and data, which was previously internally managed by CloudRetail's staff, (2) increased liability risk due to security breaches and data leaks as a result of using shared external resources, (3) decreased reliability since the service providers may go out of business, causing business continuity and data recovery issues, and (4) SaaS solutions are mainly built as one-size-fits-all customers, although there are sometimes complementary add-ons. CloudRetail is limited to the functionality offered by the SaaS providers and it may be hard to customize solutions based on its needs.

Besides the above trade-offs, some questions to answer by CloudRetail in outsourcing functions to external services are (1) which functions to move to the cloud in what order, (2) how to ensure a smooth migration process given legacy applications in their environment, (3) how to find and select service offerings that meet their requirements and (4) how to establish seamless interoperation between services. For instance, assume they would like to move their website operation, CRM, accounting, and HR systems to cloud services. Customer behavior information from the Web site has to be sent to CRM systems and the accounting function needs information from the Web site on sales and taxes. There is a data integration issue to migrate data from CloudRetail's legacy applications to cloud services.

Currently there is no environment to help CloudRetail address the last three concerns above, i.e., locating services, facilitating the process of using them and managing the whole lifecycle of engagement with cloud services. We discuss issues related to offering of such an environment in the next section.

4 Virtual Business Operating Environment

A large and increasing number of services are available most of which target small businesses and individual consumers (the long tail of service customers). The wide variety and low cost of cloud services provides an unprecedented opportunity and financial motivation for businesses to move their IT infrastructure to services in the cloud. There is a pressing need for an environment that allows SMBs and individual consumers to create and run a virtual business using cloud services. We call this a *virtual business operating environment* (VBOE). Unlike the goal and business models of existing B2B solution providers such as Ariba and CommerceOne, which themselves create a specific software solution (for e-procurement), we envision that a virtual business operating environment enables usage and integration of existing cloud-based solutions. In other words, it may not be a solution provider itself but rather acts as a broker between service customers and cloud solution providers, and not only for the procurement process but also for all aspects of running a business.

4.1 Requirements of a Virtual Business Operating Environment

A virtual business operating environment provides facilities that allow business owners to build their business in a holistic way: define their business, express their requirements, find and engage cloud services that match their needs, compose services if needed, and monitor their business operations over outsourced services. In particular, it should provide the following sub-environments:

Business definition environment: There should be an environment to allow the business owners in CloudRetail to define the business goals and metrics, its structure (e.g., organization chart) and strategies in some form that can be tracked down to the service execution level and managed.

Business services management environment: An enabling feature for CloudRetail is the identification of business functions (such as customer management or Website) that it plans to outsource (we refer to these as *business services*). This environment enables defining the main business functions, and associating the goals, metrics and strategies defined in the business environment to each business service. Moreover, this environment provides facilities to monitor and manage the business interactions with actual services and report to business owners through business dashboards.

IT services marketplace: VBOE should provide an environment where IT solution providers (e.g., CRM solution providers, website hosting, etc.) are listed, advertised and found. The IT solutions should be matched against the requirements of users expressed as part of business functions definition. The services marketplace may support various business models of offering services, e.g., bidding for business functions, pay-per-use or subscription-based payments.

Business services design environment by integration and composition of IT services: A business service, e.g., customer management, may not be fulfilled by a single service but through composition of a set of services (e.g., CRM and marketing). This environment allows services from the marketplace to be configured, integrated and composed to fulfill business services.

In the following, we present a conceptual architecture for a virtual business operating environment, and discuss how it can be realized.

4.2 Virtual Business Operating Environment: Conceptual Architecture

Business architectures have been extensively studied during the last thirty years. Frameworks such as Zachman [12] and industry standards such as TOGAF [13] describe enterprise architecture. In particular, the Zachman framework identifies a number of orthogonal (horizontal and vertical) aspects. The horizontal layers include contextual (goals and strategies of business), conceptual (high-level design), logical (system-level design) and physical (technology model) definitions for an enterprise. The vertical dimensions identify different aspects such as data, function, people and time that characterize the realization of each horizontal dimension. Other recent work shows how a service oriented design and implementation of systems can fit in the Zachman framework [14]. This approach is mainly focused on developing in-house SOA solutions for enterprises. While both cloud services and enterprise services follow SOA principles, they have different requirements (Section 4.3) and therefore different architectural layers. Below, we show what the Zachman framework means in the context of a virtual business based on cloud services by presenting our proposed business architecture depicted in Fig. 1.

The business architecture in an outsourced services environment consists of four layers: *business context, business services, business processes and IT services*. Business context layer provides for the definition of business goals, strategies, structure, policies and performance metrics and indicators. The facilities at this level are targeted for business owners and executives who are rarely IT experts. In the business services layer, the functions (supporting or core) of a business such as human resources, payroll, accounting, etc. are defined as coarse-grained services. Users (e.g.

business/IT architects) at this level identify business services and define their requirements. To simplify the job of users, VBOE may provide an out-of-box business services template and parametric list of requirements for each service. Configuring the parameters enables capturing business requirements in terms of functional and non-functional properties and later matching with the profiles of actual services that may fulfill requirements. The IT services layer represents the solutions (potentially offered in the cloud) that are advertised in VBOE by solution providers. Services may be added to the marketplace via registration but not by finding services in the open Internet. This is because the marketplace requires agreements with IT solution providers to guarantee certain QoS, price and other non-functional aspects offered to customers in the marketplace. Finally, the business processes layer is the representation of selection, design, integration and composition of IT services in the form of workflows that fulfill the requirements of outlined business services. Experts from the marketplace may be involved in helping with the design, development and integration of solutions to fulfill business services. Fig. 1 shows the correspondence of sub-environments of a VBOE with the virtual business architecture, and also the users of various layers/sub-environments.

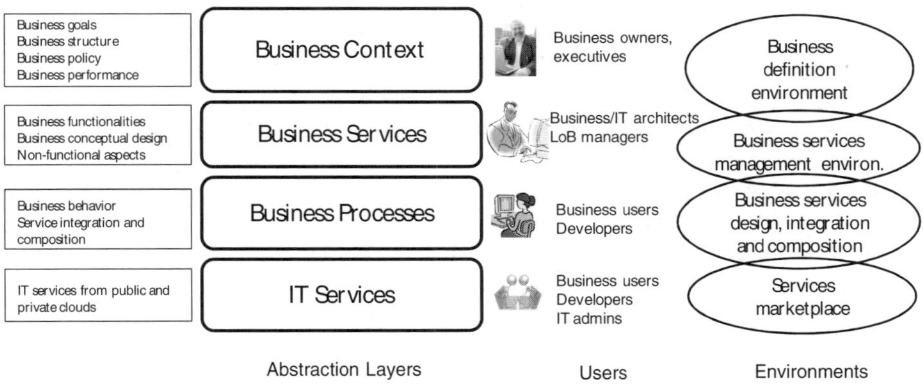

Fig. 1. Business architecture in an outsourced services environment

For example, IT services may include CRM, marketing, Web hosting, Web application system, tax and accounting services. At the business context layer, CloudRetail defines its business goals, budget, revenue targets, metrics, structure (departments) and people. The business services for CloudRetail include functions such as customer management. To fulfill "marketing campaign" business process of this business service, composition of CRM, marketing and Website application services is needed. In this process, Web application, CRM and marketing services has to be integrated so that customer details after registration are sent from the Web application to CRM, and the list and contact details of customers from CRM is sent to the marketing service. The VBOE needs to provide a holistic view of the business across various levels for different users. In the following, we identify the opportunities and challenges of realizing a VBOE.

4.3 Realizing the Virtual Business Operating Environment: Opportunities and Challenges

Let us review how the current advances in SOA, cloud computing and existing standards and methodologies help in realizing a virtual business operating environment, and identify the limitations and challenges. Note that besides the new and unique challenges posed by offering and using services in the cloud, some of which we review in the following, many challenges of realizing a virtual business operating environment are related to locating, composing, integrating and managing services. Most of these are the same as those identified for general services in SOA [15]. In the following, we highlight why fresh solutions for tackling these problems are needed in the cloud services environment.

Business context layer: The Object Management Group (OMG, www.omg.org) has proposed a set of complementary business modeling specifications. In particular, the model of business outlined in the business motivation modeling (BMM) specification v1.0 (www.omg.org/spec/BMM/1.0) can be considered as a baseline for the business context layer. It models a business having elements including "end" (vision, goals, and objectives of the business), "means" to realize the end (mission, strategy, tactics, and directives including business policies and business rules) and assessment elements to define and evaluate the performance of the business. Note that for an SMB not all these components may be necessary, however, these provide guidelines that can be customized to define a business in a virtual business scenario.

Business services layer: Business services can be divided into three categories: common (found in most businesses such as HR or CRM), industry-specific (found in vertical industries of the same type of business) and company-specific (unique to the given business). The environment has to provide blueprints of business functions for business customers, and also allow customers to define company-specific business functions such as insurance management in case of CloudRetail. These high-level descriptions can be used to find IT services from the marketplace that may fulfill the requirements. A more thorough study is needed on how to represent business services and include both functional and non-functional aspects (business-level properties, policies, etc) into this definition [16].

IT services layer: While there is a large body of work in SOA on IT service description, search and management based on both functional and non-functional aspects [15], the following challenges remain:

Service description and search: A first challenge is that not all services that are available on the Internet are described using Web services interfaces (e.g. WSDL) nor are they actually offered online. Some of these services only have textual descriptions with some form-based data entry for service request. Existing service search techniques are mainly focused on the interfaces (functional aspects) of services and only support Web services, e.g., UDDI (www.uddi.org/pubs/uddi_v3.htm) and Woogle [17], or are merely catalogues with keyword search, e.g., seekda.com. Innovative approaches in service search technology are required to combine techniques to consider Web services, REST services as well as services with non-structured and non-standard descriptions. These approaches need to be highly scalable to index millions of services that will be available in the cloud and allow service seekers to pose potentially diverse constraints on service functionality as well as cost, qualities (e.g., availability and reliability), performance, ratings, usage controls, regulatory requirements, and policies for data retention, transfer and protection.

Data modeling, migration, and management challenges: In outsourcing business functions to cloud services, the data should be a first class citizen. An explicit semantically rich representation is needed for business data that is stored in services environments. A related challenge is provenance, that is, the need to track business data over several IT services and their partners (in case it has been shared with third party partners). This requires representing data at a conceptual level (models), as well as metadata about instances of data that are shared/maintained by various service providers. A potential risk of outsourcing business to services is data lock-in. There is a need for data migration mechanisms in scenarios where a business needs to change its service provider (e.g., when service is no longer available or the provider is changed due to business reasons). Explicit data representation plays a key role in data migration scenarios by allowing users to understand which data is kept for them, and how to offload it from the current service.

SLA, data privacy and security concerns: A consequence of using services in the cloud is that the location where data is kept may be out of the customer's control. Currently, there is no support for mandating specific data protection policies to service providers, e.g., where, how long and how data is kept. Another more serious issue is that there is no way to specify the policies on how sensitive data should be shared among cloud service providers. Information is routinely leaked from subcontractors with poor data management practices [18]. Indeed, there is a need for approaches to tag directly the data with security and privacy policies that travel with sensitive data from one provider to another so that the proper technical controls can be enforced by the various providers to protect the data. In addition, there is a need for obfuscating sensitive data and keeping it in this form as it travels and is processed through the cloud. A very recent encryption method [24] makes it possible to apply certain kinds of processing or analytics on the encrypted data and obtain the same results as if they were applied to the original data.

Business processes and integration layer: Although there are significant advances in service and data integration [19,20] and service composition [21,22] in SOA, hard challenges yet to be addressed include how to automatically discover various Web services (including services with text-based interfaces, people services, etc.) that collectively fulfill a business service, how to automatically compose services, and how to integrate data and services [15]. The issue with many existing solutions for Web services composition is that they have been developed assuming WSDL-based interfaces of services and often also availability of behavioral description of services. However, as mentioned before, such rich description may not be found for services. In addition, Web services are not well suited for the efficient handling of massive data sets which makes them inadequate for data-intensive applications [27]. On the other hand, while the RESTful approach to service provisioning is very simple, it does not allow for any automated composition of services [22,23] because the RESTful approach does not advocate explicit representation of exchanged data which is crucial in business settings and automated composition of services.

An observation that may be exploited to develop alternative approaches to simplify the hard problem of automated service composition is that there are many fewer meaningful business cases in which services need to be composed to fulfill certain business functionalities compared to the possible (random) combinations of IT services. Such business functionalities are often needed by many businesses in a VBOE. We anticipate that the integration and composition of IT services will become recurring problems and their solutions will be packaged as services that can be reused. Therefore, a VBOE may not only have service providers offering their own services but also solution providers offering composition of other services that fulfill a popular business function. Indeed, this enables tackling this problem by exploiting the power of the crowd (business users) and enabling reuse of solutions that are ready-to-use by new customers possibly with minor configuration or customization [25].

Data integration as a challenge for service composition: One challenge that is currently underexplored in existing service composition work is data compatibility and integration requirements. Most existing approaches unrealistically assume complete data (message) compatibility between services. However, this is a serious issue hindering development of industrial approaches for service search and composition. It is not possible to consider the functionality composition problem independent of the data compatibility and mapping problem. Data integration is said to be the Achilles heel of cloud computing and it has become a major issue for SaaS companies. The process of integrating data created "in here" with data created "out there" is made increasingly difficult by cloud computing. The trend is to provide IaaS2 (integration as a service) to simplify the very complex integration task to a simple configuration one. Vendors of ETL (Extract-Transform-Load) products like Informatica are moving in this direction where providers of on-demand integration solutions like Boomi already have solutions. All these providers offer adapters/connectors to the most popular enterprise applications and a simple way to define the mapping flows. However, none of them provides an automated way to define these mappings: the user needs to have knowledge of the semantics of the source and target data to be able to map the former to the latter. This is the same old semantic problem investigated since the late 80's in the context of database interoperability and still open after more than 20 years. This problem gets exacerbated in the cloud.

Another trend in data integration is the integration of unstructured or semi-structured data sources which constitute around 70% of the data assets of an organization. The need to integrate these unstructured sources becomes even bigger in the cloud where organizations want to make them available to SaaS applications. This is not trivial, first structured information has to be extracted from the unstructured sources and then it has to be transformed and integrated with the rest of the data (typically in a structured form). For the first task, SaaS offerings have started to appear, for example, Open Calais. For the second task, IaaS2 offerings may help but still the user needs to know the semantics to be able to establish the mappings.

Finally, in the cloud more than in any other environment, there will be a wide variety of quality requirements for the integration process, whether it is with regards to real-time, fault tolerance, performance, etc. None of the existing solutions offers any mechanism to express these requirements, not to mention to assist in the optimization of the integration design to meet such requirements while considering their tradeoffs (e.g., performance versus recoverability) [28].

An all-time debate in another environment may turn more helpful in cloud settings: developing and adopting standardized data models by various service providers working in the same business domains. Indeed, if the vision of service parks is realized

[26] in which communities of services are offered and used together, this idea may seem compelling. It will be an interesting study to weigh-up the efforts of having completely heterogeneous models needing full integration, versus that of developing, making agreements, customizing and adopting standardized models for cloud service providers working in the same business sector.

5 Discussion and Outlook

Small businesses such as CloudRetail have already seen the benefits of using services in the cloud for most non-core functionality. Customers benefit from the economies of scale and the highly optimized IT operations of cloud service providers. The opportunity to avoid capital costs and incur predictable expenses which scale up and down with the current needs of the business is very attractive. Customers with occasional or bursty usage see tremendous benefits, as they only pay for resources when they are using them. Customers with stable usage patterns also benefit due to the lower cost of purchasing services than building them in-house. Unless IT is a core competency of the business, most customers will not be able to attain the same capabilities cheaper by doing it themselves. As one example, Google's corporate email solution is, on average, ten times less expensive than in-house email solutions.

We envision that the low cost of using cloud computing is a key driver of its wide acceptance by individual consumers, SMBs as well as large enterprises. However, large enterprises will employ a hybrid cloud model in which both private and public clouds are present. Many enterprises will run mission-critical applications and store business-sensitive data in the private clouds, while outsourcing their supporting services to the public cloud. In terms of usage of services in the cloud, small SMBs and individual consumers will be the main users of IaaS, DaaS, SaaS and PaaS. Enterprises may demand customization of services as the APIs provided by service providers may not offer the flexibility and features they require. In addition, they may demand instances of services to be deployed in their private clouds for the sake of keeping data onsite and retaining control. This can be seen as a transformation of how enterprises use commercial software as services in the cloud.

The virtual business operating environment for creating and conducting virtual businesses using cloud-based services is a missing piece and the current article lays the foundation of architecture for an environment that addresses this pressing need for businesses that intend to use cloud services.

References

1. Leyland, V.A.: Electronic Data Interchange. Prentice-Hall, Englewood Cliffs (1993)
2. Halvey, J.K., Melby, B.M.: Business Process Outsourcing: Process, Strategies, and Contracts. John Wiley & Sons, Inc, Chichester (2007)
3. Anderson, C., et al.: Worldwide and US Business Process Outsourcing 2007-2011 Forecast: Market Opportunities by Horizontal Business Process, IDC Market Analysis 208290 (2007)
4. The, H.P.: benefits of combining business-process outsourcing and service-oriented architecture, http://h20195.www2.hp.com/PDF/4AA0-4316ENW.pdf

5. Murugesan, S.: Understanding Web 2.0. IEEE IT Professional 9(4), 34–41 (2007)
6. Weiss, A.: Computing in the clouds. ACM netWorker 11(4), 16–25 (2007)
7. Petrie, C., Bussler, C.: Service Agents and Virtual Enterprises: A Survey. IEEE Internet Computing 7(4), 68–78 (2003)
8. Robison, S.: The next wave: Everything as a service, Executive Viewpoint (2007), http://www.hp.com/hpinfo/execteam/articles/robison/08eaas.html
9. Nicholas Carr. The Big Switch: Rewiring the World, from Edison to Google W. W. Norton publishing (2008)
10. HP. HP Adaptive Infrastructure, http://h20195.www2.hp.com/PDF/4AA1-0799ENW.pdf
11. Yarmis, J., et al.: Outclouding: New Ways of Capitalizing on the Economics of Cloud Computing and Outsourcing, AMR Research (2008)
12. Zachman, J.A.: A framework for information systems architecture. IBM Syst. J. 26(3), 276–292 (1987)
13. TOGAF, The Open Group Architecture Framework Version 8.1.1, http://www.togaf.org
14. Ibrahim, M., Long, G.: Service-Oriented Architecture and Enterprise Architecture, http://www.ibm.com/developerworks/webservices/library/ws-soa-enterprise1/?S_TACT=105AGX04&S_CMP=ART
15. Papazoglou, M.P., Traverso, P., Dustdar, S., Leymann, F.: Service-Oriented Computing: State of the Art and Research Challenges. IEEE Computer 40(11) (2007)
16. Scheithauer, G., et al.: Describing Services for Service Ecosystems. International Workshop on Enabling Service Business Ecosystems ESBE (2008)
17. Dong, X., et al.: Similarity search for web services. In: Proceedings of VLDB, pp. 372–383 (2004)
18. The Breach Blog, BNY Mellon Shareowner Services loses backup tape, http://breachblog.com/2008/03/27/bny.aspx
19. Motahari-Nezhad, H.R., et al.: Web Services Interoperability Specifications. IEEE Computer 5(39), 24–32 (2006)
20. Halevy, A., et al.: Data integration: the teenage years. In: Proceedings of VLDB, pp. 9–16 (2006)
21. Dustdar, S., Schreiner, W.: A survey on web services composition. Int. J. Web and. Grid Services 1(1), 1–30 (2005)
22. Brogi, A., Corfini, S., Popescu, R.: Semantics-based composition-oriented discovery of Web services. ACM Trans. Internet Technol 8(4), 1–39 (2008)
23. Benslimane, D., Dustdar, S., Sheth, A.: Services Mashups: The New Generation of Web Applications. IEEE Internet Computing 12(5), 13–15 (2008)
24. Gentry, C.: Fully homomorphic encryption using ideal lattices. In: Proceedings of the 41st Annual ACM Symposium on theory of Computing (2009)
25. Nezhad, M., Li, H.R., Stephenson, J., Graupner Sven, B.: Singhal Sharad: Solution Reuse for Service Composition and Integration. In: 3rd International Workshop on Web Service Composition and Adaptation, WSCA 2009 (2009)
26. Petrie, C., Bussler, C.: The Myth of Open Web Services: The Rise of the Service Parks. IEEE Internet Computing 12(3), 95–96 (2008)
27. Habich, D., et al.: BPELDT – Data-Aware Extension of BPEL to Support Data-Intensive Service Applications. In: Proceedings of the 2nd ECOWS07 Workshop on Emerging Web Services Technology, WEWST 2007 (2007)
28. Dayal, U., Castellanos, M., Simitsis, A., Wilkinson, K.: Data Integration Flows for Business Intelligence. In: Proceedings of EDBT (2009)

Author Index

Printing: Mercedes-Druck, Berlin
Binding: Stein+Lehmann, Berlin